Descent into HELL

into

Civilian Memories of the Battle of Okinawa

Descent
into
HELL

Civilian Memories of the Battle of Okinawa

Ryukyu Shimpo

Foreword by Higa Tatsuro
Introduction by Ota Masahide

Translated with extensive commentary
by Mark Ealey & Alastair McLauchlan

MERWIN

ASIA

Distributed by the University of Hawai'i Press

Library of Congress Control Number: 2014931912

ISBN 978-1-937385-26-2 (Paperback)

ISBN 978-1-937385-27-9 (Hardcover)

Printed in the United States of America

The paper used in this publication meets the minimum requirements of the American National Standard for Information Services—Permanence of Paper for Printed Library Materials, ANSI/NISO Z39/48-1992

CONTENTS

Contents

FOREWORD

Higa Tatsuro
Former President of the *Ryukyu Shimpo*

In the late 1970s, following the reversion of the prefecture to Japanese sovereignty, the perception of the people of Okinawa toward the battle began to fade as we became increasingly absorbed by what we referred to as the "shift in the tide of history" and the "drive for development." In the face of this inexorable reality, and imbued with a sense of mission to convey the truth about a battle that was without precedent in the Pacific War, in 1983 writers of the *Ryukyu Shimpo* commenced work on a series of articles that would go on to be published under the title of *Senka o Horu*.

When I look back on that project carried out almost thirty years ago, I feel proud that a newspaper in Okinawa fulfilled its responsibility to shed light on the terrible experiences of the civilians caught up in the fighting raging around them.

That our interviews encouraged so many Okinawans who had previously been reluctant to discuss their wartime experiences to finally talk about them was a major achievement in itself. In addition, that a project initiated by a newspaper could create opportunities for so many displaced victims of the war to find each other again was particularly pleasing.

This project, carried out mainly by young reporters with no memory of the war, was undertaken with an absolute commitment to fieldwork. I believe that the fact that they went out and talked to so many survivors who were prepared to use their own names and who described their experiences in the very places that they spoke about makes this a civilian history of battle that will stand any amount of historical scrutiny.

In the Battle of Okinawa—if we include local Okinawan residents, combatants on both sides, and people from Japan's colonies who were not necessarily there of their own accord—the lives of more than 200,000 people were lost. Victims of war are not determined according to which side they are on. War is a manifestation of evil that challenges all the accepted parameters of sanity. In that respect, the publication in English of the fruits of that project carried out thirty years ago must help move us toward a better appreciation of the value of peace.

I sincerely hope that the surviving members of the Allied forces who experienced the Battle of Okinawa, and as many other people as possible from other countries, will take the opportunity to read this book.

Higa Tatsuro

ACKNOWLEDGMENTS

Alastair and I are extremely grateful to all the people who offered support to us on this project, a mission that took roughly three years from finding the material to publication. Former president of the *Ryukyu Shimpo*, Takamine Tomokazu, was integral in getting things moving forward. Current staff Imoto Kiyoshi and Uehara Yasushi were very cooperative in early negotiations and in helping us to access information. Shirado Hitoshi guided me around *gama* and old sites throughout southern and central Okinawa and Yoneda Hideaki on Tokashiki-jima. Onaha Yasutake kindly provided useful comments on several key background areas. Former *Ryukyu Shimpo* president Higa Tatsuhiro generously wrote the Foreword to this work from his standpoint of having been in the *Ryukyu Shimpo* executive when the *Senka o Horu* project was undertaken. It was an honor to meet former governor of Okinawa Ota Masahide on several occasions to discuss aspects of the project, and we are very grateful for the materials he provided and of course for his writing the Introduction. Haga Hitomi and Kyan Yukihiro of the Ota Peace Research Institute went out of their way to be helpful. Shirado Hitoshi of the *Ryukyu Shimpo* kindly introduced me first to Gushiken Takamatsu, head of the *Gama-fuya* or Cave-Diggers, which led to my being allowed to assist for one day in a dig near Untamamui near Nishihara, and then to Urasaki Shigeko, noted researcher on the comfort woman issue in Okinawa. Renowned scholar on East Asian affairs Mark Selden of *Japan Focus* and Cornell University provided very useful comments on the introductory pieces.

I acknowledge the Japan Foundation for kindly granting me a research fellowship in late 2011 to be based in Naha for three months as I worked on the translation and visited battle sites around Okinawa. A project of this size and complexity could not have been completed alone, and Alastair McLauchlan has been a marvelous partner-in-translation. Not only did Alastair offer his formidable translation skills, but his wife Jan helped in the final stage of editing and his son Cameron (a translator and writer based in Tokyo) helped us to track down translations of ordinances and guidelines from the years before the Battle of Okinawa. Thomas M. Huber kindly gave advice on military terminology. Former marines Joe A. Drago (I Company 3rd Bn 22nd Marines Sixth Marine Division) and Bill Pierce (Weapons Company 29th Marines 6th Marine Division) were very helpful in relating their experiences and introducing me to battlefield guide Chris Majewski, who runs the Battle of Okinawa Museum in Camp Kinser. Dr. Aritsuka Ryoji, doctor of psychosomatic medicine at the Okinawa Kyodo Hospital and head of the Society for Research on Mental Health in the Battle of Okinawa, kindly explained and provided material on late-onset post-traumatic stress disorder (PTSD) triggered by an experience in the Battle of Okinawa.

My wife Miyuki worked with me to arrange the data to pass on to the cartographers in order to put the series of maps in place and, needless to say, fielded many tricky questions during the translation process.

Hentona Tadatomo, of Nago High School, went out of his way to arrange a guide for me on Ie-jima through Nago High School rugby connections, and my base for operations for eleven weeks from October to December 2012 was kindly provided by Koza High School rugby coach Toma Yutaka and wife Sachiyo. I am also indebted to Arasaki Morito, Morito Satoshi, Uezato Atsushi, Kuwae Takeshi and wife Junko, Hiyane Tadashi and wife Yukari, Aguni Rieko and all the other parents of the rugby players at Koza High School in Okinawa City, as well as Moromizato Makiko in Nago, Yamamoto Daishi and wife Motoko and Kuninaka Takashi in Miyako-jima for various kindnesses during my stays in Okinawa.

Translators' Note

The basis of this work was originally published in the early 1980s in the *Ryukyu Shimpo* newspaper in Okinawa in article form, most of which went on to appear in a book entitled *Senka o Horu* (Digging through the vestiges of war). Three separate series of articles were run in the *Ryukyu Shimpo*, all looking at aspects of the civilian experience of the battle from slightly different angles. So while the majority of the articles that we chose focus on survivors relating their experiences in the context of revisiting a certain cave or shelter, some are from the other two series. We have attempted to group the articles together in chronological order under common themes, but as some are long and cover a range of matters from landings to surrender this was never going to be an easy task.

As a translation project, this work was a challenge for two reasons. First, the original was written for local Okinawan readers, so the content often included unnecessary detail, or needed to be supplemented to allow foreign readers to better understand the flow of events. We attempted to edit out the parts that worked in a series of newspaper articles in 1983 but have lost their relevance when lined up to be translated for a book published in English thirty years later. What appears as *Descent into Hell* is a collection of edited articles mainly from the *Senka o Horu* series, plus our commentary on specific topics added in an attempt to provide a deeper level of context. To the greatest extent possible we want to let the translated articles tell the story, so our commentary focuses on highlighting key themes and giving further detail when relevant.

Second, the original articles were written three decades ago by a team of writers at the *Ryukyu Shimpo* who have long since moved on from their jobs, so asking them for clarification was not possible. We managed to sort out most issues and, while Okinawan place names can be difficult to read, it was only some of the personal names that saw us scratch our heads. We have done our best on that front and are comforted by the fact that during the war most Japanese men accepted their first names being read either in the *kun-yomi* or the *on-yomi*.

The underlying theme that came out in the course of the project was the lack of closure for so many people who were never able to locate the remains of loved ones killed during the battle. This is testimony to the ferocity of the conflict, particularly in the middle two weeks of June 1945 when civilians were caught up in the horrendous slaughter that occurred after the Imperial Japanese Army (IJA) withdrew from Shuri toward Mabuni. It will not take the reader long to understand why we chose the title *Descent into Hell*.

My previous book-length translation was of an historical novel by Akira Yoshimura entitled *Typhoon of Steel* (Junkoku–Rikugun nitouhei Higa Shin'ichi). Yoshimura obviously wrote this novel after reading the series of articles that make up *Senka o Horu*, so there was a clear feeling of déjà vu in the early stages of reading the manuscripts which Alastair and I went on to translate. It was indeed sad timing that Alastair passed away weeks before the publication of this book and a just few short months before we planned to visit the former battlefields on Okinawa in October 2014.

Mark Ealey & Alastair McLauchlan

Introduction

The Battle of Okinawa
Ota Masahide

The last engagement between the armies of Japan and the United States, the Battle of Okinawa was fought in the final stages of the Pacific War, predominantly on the main island of Okinawa, but also on other small islands in its vicinity.

The battle is generally defined as beginning on 1 April 1945 and ending just less than three months later on 23 June. While most American sources and textbooks used at schools in Japan frame the period of the battle this way, this is incorrect for two reasons. The first is that while 1 April is the date on which the main body of U.S. forces landed on the main island of Okinawa, on 26 March U.S. troops landed on the Kerama Islands just off Okinawa but still within the prefecture. The awful tragedy that occurred there in which more than 700 local residents were either directly or indirectly driven by the Japanese military to take their own lives is a compelling reason why we should neither exclude nor place less emphasis on the landings in the Keramas. Not only did the events that occurred there serve as a prelude to the devastation that the people of Okinawa would experience in the next three to four months of 1945, but they undeniably marked the first military action of the Okinawa campaign.

Another good reason is that on that same day, as soon as the U.S. forces landed on Akashima in the Keramas, Adm. Chester W. Nimitz, the commander in chief, U.S. Pacific Fleet and Pacific Ocean Areas, issued U.S. Naval Military Government Directive No. 1, by which the United States suspended Japanese sovereignty and assumed administrative control as an occupying power of all Japanese territory located on or south of latitude 30 degrees north.

Likewise, 23 June cannot be seen as the date when the Battle of Okinawa ended because this is the date when the commander in chief of the 32nd Army, Lt. Gen. Ushijima Mitsuru, and Chief of Staff Cho Isamu committed suicide (in actual fact that occurred on 22 June rather than the date on which organized hostilities came to an end.) As it happens, when General Joseph Stilwell, the commander of the U.S. 10th Army, the main force to land on Okinawa, was instructed by Field Marshal Douglas McArthur, the supreme commander of the

Allied Powers, to receive the surrender of the Japanese forces in the Nansei Islands, among the Japanese representatives who presented themselves at Gen. Stilwell's U.S. 10th Army headquarters in Kadena on 7 September 1945 to sign the six documents that made up the instrument of surrender were Lt. Gen. Noumi Toshiro, the commander of the 28th Division stationed on Miyako-jima, Maj. Gen. Takada Toshisada and Vice-Adm. Kato Tadao from Amami Oshima. The date of the signing was 7 September 1945, so it is only logical to see that as the date when the Battle of Okinawa formally ended. By judging 23 June to represent the end of the battle, the terrible occurrences that became known as the Kume-jima Incident, in which the Japanese military massacred local residents, therefore fall outside of the official historical parameters of the battle. It is also worth noting that American forces landed on Kume-jima on 26 June. In the Kume-jima Incident, after U.S. forces landed, the Japanese garrison killed twenty local residents who had supposedly engaged in "spying" for the enemy. This hideous occurrence represents one of the ugliest aspects of the Battle of Okinawa, and as such inclusion of this massacre is essential for the battle to be considered in its historical entirety. Therefore, we should date the end of the battle as 7 September rather than 23 June.

The Battle of Okinawa was distinct from all other battles in the Pacific War in that it was fought in one of the forty-seven prefectures of Japan, with the majority of the resident civilian population still present. While Iwo Jima, the island that served as a stepping-stone to Okinawa, was also Japanese homeland territory, it was under the administrative control of the Tokyo municipal authorities. Also, its residents had been forcibly evacuated months before, so the only people on the island when the American forces landed in February 1945 were the Imperial Japanese Army. The fighting in the Battle of Saipan in the middle of the previous year saw many Japanese settlers (mostly Okinawans) caught in the crossfire, but the Marianas Islands were not inherently Japanese territory. They had been controlled by Germany until World War 1 and in 1922 were entrusted by the League of Nations to Japan as mandate territories. Similarly, on the continent, Japanese settlers suffered in the hectic retreats in Manchuria and Sakhalin in August 1945, but neither of these locations were inherently Japanese territories. While the people living in urban centers on the main islands of Japan were of course the victims of merciless incendiary bombing in the latter stages of the war, Okinawa was the only prefecture to experience combat on the ground.

The scale of Operation Iceberg and the disparity in the size of the respective forces is noteworthy. The United States mobilized approximately 1,500 naval vessels carrying 548,000 men to launch the invasion of the small islands of Okinawa. In 1945 the total population of the prefecture of Okinawa was less than 450,000 people so the U.S. forces actually outnumbered the residents of Okinawa. In contrast to the huge numbers of American troops available, if we include the locally recruited and poorly trained Home Guard and Student Corps child soldiers, the Japanese forces deployed on Okinawa numbered 110,000, just one-fifth of the American strength.

The horrifying extent of civilian casualties is a key feature of the battle. Over 140,000 people, or about one third of the population, died in the course of the battle and its immediate aftermath. As is covered in the series of articles that make up this book, hundreds of families were completed wiped out. Needless to say, most families in the prefecture will have the name of at least one deceased relative engraved on the Cornerstone of Peace, the marble tablets in Mabuni that bear the names of the more than 240,000 combatants and non-combatants of all nationalities who died in the battle. Among the civilian casualties were members of the Home Guard, as well as teenage soldiers recruited without any basis in law into the Blood and Iron Student Corps and young girls co-opted into nurse's aide units. Within the civilian deaths also was the significant loss of life of Korean young men and women press-ganged into serving as laborers or comfort women.

Another characteristic of the Battle of Okinawa was the incidence of group suicide and parricide among civilians terrified at the prospect of being captured by an enemy portrayed by Japanese soldiers as monsters. This had also occurred in Saipan the previous year, and the Japanese media extolling those who took their lives in this way helped to set the scene for it to occur in Okinawa. While the extent to which Japanese soldiers were involved in encouraging or even compelling locals to take their own lives or kill loved ones has been the subject of heated debate in recent years, including court cases initiated by relatives of Imperial Japanese Army commanders, there is no doubt that the stories told by soldiers who had fought in China about what they had done to the locals made capture sound like a fate worse than death. This work covers some of these tragedies.

The use of "special-attack units" [kamikaze] is also a well-known aspect of the battle. Over 3,050 young men lost their lives carrying out suicide attacks on ships of the U.S fleet sitting off the coast of Okinawa, and 4,900 American sailors were killed as a result. In an era when suicide bombers are painted as religious fanatics, it is important to understand that by and large the pilots who flew on the one-way missions to the seas off Okinawa were relatively well-educated young men driven to contribute to saving their country from what they believed would be obliteration. After all, in the months before the Battle of Okinawa, Japan's urban centers, and tens of thousands of their residents, were being incinerated at a pace that seemed to give credence to the call that only a Divine Wind [kamikaze] could save the nation from destruction. Japanese military leaders, and the emperor, believed that one last furious roll of the dice would see the United States and its allies accept peace terms that allowed Japan's national polity (its national essence with the emperor at the head) to remain in place. As it happens, of course, rather than helping to bring the war to an end on acceptable terms, the ferocity of these kamikaze attacks resulted in pressure being brought to bear by the U.S. Navy on the commander of the ground forces on Okinawa, Lt. Gen. Buckner, to bring the land campaign to an end as quickly as possible. This, it is argued, may have seen him opt for a costly, blunt-instrument approach rather than a slower but less costly second landing.

If we look at losses suffered by both sides in the Battle of Okinawa, while the U.S. forces lost more than 14,000 men killed (with a total of 72,000 either wounded or victims of combat fatigue), the Japanese military lost over 70,000 men with more than 140,000 Okinawans being killed. In addition 10,000 Japanese soldiers were taken prisoner. When describing the battle, Hanson W. Baldwin of the New York Times wrote: "Never before had there been, probably never again will there be, such a vicious sprawling struggle." In every sense of the word, the battle was vicious in the extreme. That the commanders of both sides died in the battle is testimony to the all-encompassing reach of the casualties.

The horrific death toll and the fanatical resistance by the Japanese soldiers affected the thinking of the American leaders and was a significant factor leading to the decision to drop atomic bombs on mainland Japan.

Another feature was that Okinawa was what has been termed a "sute-ishi" (sacrificial stone in the Japanese board game of go) cast away in a desperate attempt to save the main islands of Japan. The Japanese Imperial Army's objective was not to protect the local Okinawans, but instead to engage the Americans in combat for the longest time possible in order to earn time for further defensive preparations on the home islands. Rather than putting efforts into evacuation or the creation of a safe zone for civilians, the Okinawan people were used as a source of labor to build shelters, tunnels and other emplacements, to supplement combat units and to tend to wounded soldiers in circumstances aptly described by the title of this book. With the Imperial Japanese Army supplying itself in the field, having civilians close at hand suited them until the U.S. forces landed, when the common view among the commanders of the 32nd Army changed to civilians being potential spies or merely bodies taking up space in caves and shelters.

The Japanese Army's heartless approach to ejecting local civilians from caves was matched by their killing hundreds, maybe even thousands, of their own soldiers who were too badly wounded to retreat southward from hospital shelters.

Through the Battle of Okinawa the people of the prefecture learned a valuable lesson. They came to understand that the military was motivated solely by its own organizational imperatives, existing to protect abstract concepts of national polity and the imperial system, and that in no sense of the expression did it serve the function of protecting the lives of non-combatants. The fact that that lesson was learned at the expense of well over 140,000 Okinawan lives means that even now, sixty-seven years after Japan was defeated in WW II, the people of Okinawa still value that lesson and sincerely strive to create a peaceful world.

It is important for English speaking readers who read *Descent into Hell* to understand that the origin of all current affairs is to be found in past history. Those who look at the situation that prevails in Okinawa now and sense a growing antagonism among the prefecture's residents toward the presence of American military bases need to be reminded that it was not always like this. Today's situation can be traced back first to the Battle of Okinawa and then to subsequent agreements between the governments of Japan and the United States.

We should remember that from even before the end of the battle, while the residual elements of the Japanese 32nd Army were forcing Okinawans out from caves into the relentless bombardment in southern Okinawa, specially organized units of the United States military were already providing food, clothing, and shelter to displaced residents in areas that it had already secured. The U.S. forces had planned ahead and prepared for this contingency and their kindness in this respect no doubt saved tens of thousands of Okinawans from death by starvation. The years immediately following the surrender of the Japan were marked by strong of feelings of gratitude among Okinawans towards the United States for its efforts to avoid a humanitarian disaster. These feelings continued until the governments of Japan and the United States colluded to concentrate an unfair proportion of the U.S. military presence in Okinawa, including nuclear weapons and highly toxic defoliants for use in the Vietnam War. The current situation in Okinawa may give the impression that ill feeling has prevailed for much longer than is actually the case. I encourage anyone who has an interest in Okinawan affairs to equip themselves with a knowledge of the civilian experience in the battle for these islands fought almost seven decades ago.

Ota Masahide, Govenor of Okinawa 1994-98
7 January 2013

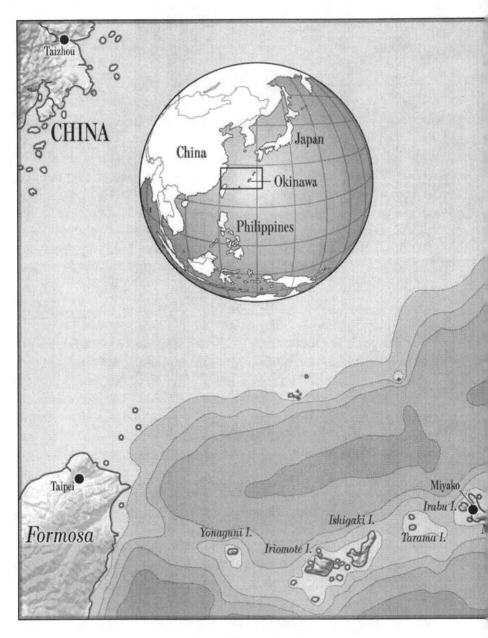

Overview of Okinawa Region

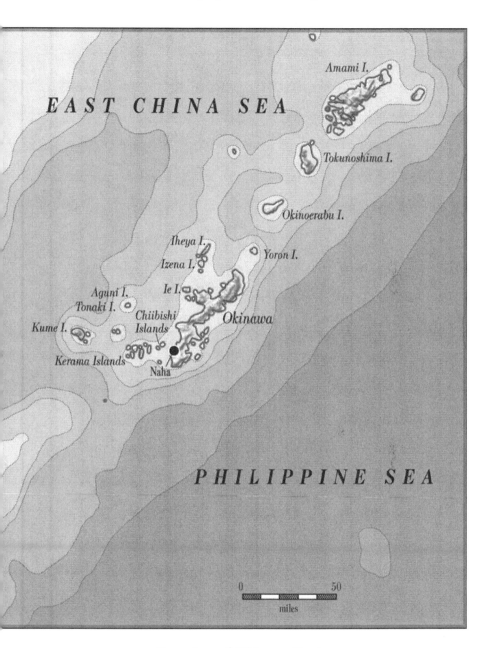

Overview of Okinawa Region

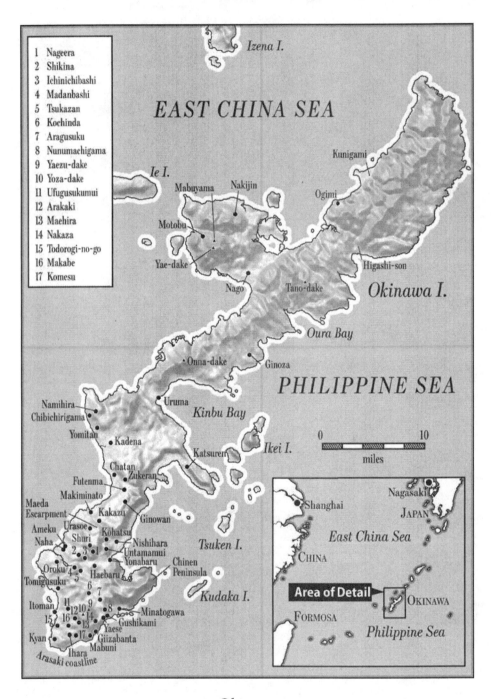

1	Nageera
2	Shikina
3	Ichinichibashi
4	Madanbashi
5	Tsukazan
6	Kochinda
7	Aragusuku
8	Nunumachigama
9	Yaezu-dake
10	Yoza-dake
11	Ufugusukumui
12	Arakaki
13	Maehira
14	Nakaza
15	Todorogi-no-go
16	Makabe
17	Komesu

EAST CHINA SEA

Izena I.

Ie I.

Kunigami

Mabuyama Nakijin

Ogimi

Motobu

Yae-dake

Higashi-son

Nago

Tano-dake

Okinawa I.

Oura Bay

Onna-dake Ginoza

PHILIPPINE SEA

Namihira
Chibichirigama

Uruma

Kinbu Bay

Yomitan Kadena

Katsuren

Ikei I.

0   10
miles

Chatan
Futenma Zukeran
Makiminato

Maeda
Escarpment Kakazu
Ameku Urasoe Ginowan
Naha Shuri Kohatsu
2 3 1 Nishihara
Oroku 4 Untamamui
5 Yonabaru
Tomigusuku Haebaru
6 7
Itoman 11 9
15 16 14 8
17 13 Yaese
Kyan Giizabanta
Ihara Mabuni
Arasaki coastline

Tsuken I.

Chinen
Peninsula

Kudaka I.

Minatogawa
Gushikami

Nagasaki
Shanghai JAPAN
East China Sea
CHINA

Area of Detail OKINAWA

FORMOSA Philippine Sea

Okinawa

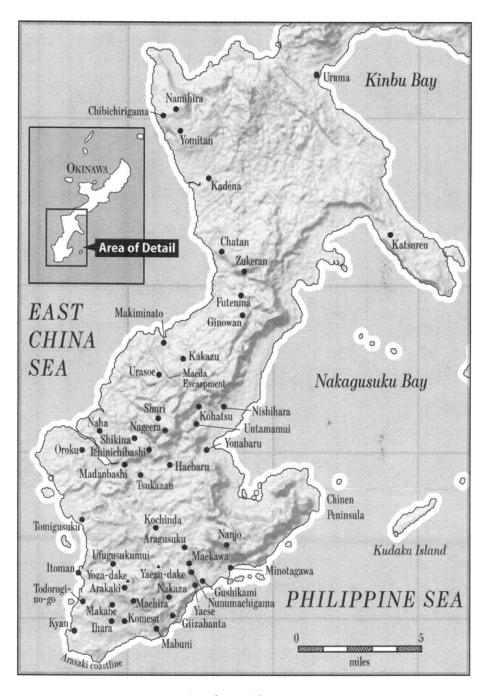

Southern Okinawa

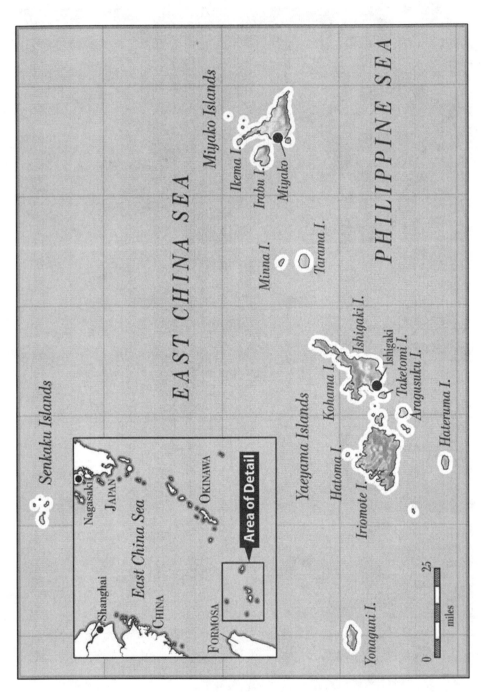

Southern Islands

EAST CHINA SEA

Ie I.

Sesoko I.

Onna-dake

Namihira
Yomitan
Kadena
Kakazu
Naha
Oroku
Itoman
Kyan
Yaese
Mabuni
Yonabaru
Chinen Pen.

Chibishi
Islands
Okinawa I.

Maejima I.

Tokashiki I.

Zamani I.

Kerama Islands

Aka I.

Ojima I.

Tonaki I.

Aguni I.

Kume I.

Ojima I.

Kerama Islands

Shanghai
CHINA
FORMOSA
Nagasaki
JAPAN
East China Sea
OKINAWA
Area of Detail

0   10
miles

Descent

into

Civilian Memories of the Battle of Okinawa

CHAPTER I

THE SOUND OF ARMY BOOTS RINGS OUT
ON THE COBBLESTONES OF SHURI

When the 32nd Army arrived in the town of Shuri, the old prefectural capital's quiet ambience was assailed by the incongruous sight of men in uniform. The sound of army boots rang out on the town's cobblestone streets, and the old castle town of Shuri took on the look of a military base.

Horikawa Yasuo, then a first year pupil at the No. 2 Shuri Kokumin School watched the soldiers with feelings of interest, suspicion, and admiration.

On 10 January 1945, before the 32nd Army moved into its Command Post shelter, it set up at the Kokumin School and the Okinawa Normal School. The U.S. forces landed on Okinawa approximately three months later. Horikawa recalls, "When the soldiers were cleaning their weapons, if I went over to their armory they would let me touch the rifles," proof that the tenseness that came with impending battle was yet to set in.

The Horikawa home was close to the school grounds, so soldiers often appeared, asking if they could buy *zenzai*, the Okinawan form of *o-shiruko*, or sweet, *azuki* bean soup. "They would turn up early in the morning, asking, 'Have you got any *zenzai*?' or 'Do you have any sugar?' They seemed to have a craving for sweet things. I remember an officer yelling at one of the soldiers and punching him, then eating what the soldier hadn't finished. I was only a little kid then, but I remember thinking, 'Why did you do that?' There were also officers who just turned a blind eye though . . ."

Boy soldiers often washed rice containers or their superiors' underwear over by the well in the schoolyard. "I still remember that sometimes they were washing bloodstained undershirts," said Horikawa. Even for a young boy, the brutality that was so ingrained in the Imperial Japanese Army was there for all to see.

Horikawa remembers feeling nervous one day when Lt. Gen. Ushijima approached. Accompanied by several of his adjutants, the commander was on horseback, casually dressed and without his sword. "When four or five of us lined up and bowed to him respectfully, he patted us on the head and said 'Keep up the good work boys.' We were thrilled that he spoke to us." Clearly the young boys revered army commander Ushijima.

After the American forces landed and the bombardment intensified, the civilians still in Shuri took refuge in tombs or natural caves near the Command Post. Yamashiro Jiro, who was sheltering in a tomb near the Command Post's No. 5 tunnel, still remembers a soldier by the name of Minami. "He became friends with my father and often came to our house for dinner. I remember him saying, 'I've got five children too.' We never saw him again after the day he said, 'We're going on an infiltration raid to Urasoe tomorrow.'"

CHAPTER 2

EDUCATION

In describing how education was used as part of Japan's war propaganda, Rubringer suggests that ". . . no modern nation has used schools . . . for the purpose of indoctrination into the political, military and ideological purposes of the state as did Japan in the early twentieth century."[1] During the 1920s, 1930s and early 1940s, reforms to the structure and content of Japan's education system were clearly aimed at helping prepare Japan to go on a war footing. In 1925, an Imperial Ordinance dictated that regular army officers would lead compulsory military training in middle school, while the Education Reform Council of 1935 decreed that national polity and the "Japanese spirit" should be the key foci of compulsory education.[2] From 1937, the war in China resulted directly in academic and media censorship, many newspapers having no option but to close down.[3] An increasingly militarist theme to education was promoted, and in 1938, Army General Araki Sadao was appointed Minister of Education to oversee this process. In 1941, the People's Education Order required pupils to commit to Japan's national polity and dedicate themselves to the Imperial cause. Moreover, three specific textbook revisions during 1940, 1941 and 1943 outwardly glorified war and affirmed acts of military heroism.

As U.S. forces advanced across the Pacific, educational directives increasingly gave way to military rulings. In 1941, all elementary schools were renamed Kokumin Schools (National Schools). The aim of this move was to teach all children from an early age the five ideals of the so-called Imperial Way, namely, (a) to maintain a strong faith in national polity, (b) to contribute intellectually to the Imperial fortune, (c) to remain physically and mentally fit and ready to serve the nation, (d) to enrich national life and (e) to ". . . devote oneself to the cause of the emperor."[4] Thereafter, all children in the third grade and above were made members of the Dai Nippon Seishonen Dan (The Great Japan Youth Organization), issued with special membership badges, and undertook military marching

---

1.   Rubringer, R. 1992: 61.
2.   Rubringer, R. 1992: 60.
3.   Rubringer, R. 1992: 60.
4.   Rubringer, R. 1992: 64.

as a school activity.[5]

Once Okinawa was identified as the American's next target after Saipan, education in the prefecture changed even more dramatically and rapidly. Only those teachers who were prepared to undertake special education in military values received promotion to principal status, while teachers who held alternative beliefs, especially political ideologies such as Marxism, were immediately removed. Each morning, children had to bow to a photograph of the emperor upon arrival at school and bow to the rising sun flag each time they left or entered the classroom. They were also instructed to stop and bow their heads whenever someone shouted out "Three cheers for the Emperor!" Along with such pro-Japanese propaganda, however, schools just as relentlessly pushed the anti-foreigner and anti-American stances as well. Even to school children, the appalling fate awaiting any Japanese soldier or civilian captured by the Americans was clearly spelled out, while the honor of dying for the emperor was rigorously promoted in preference to being captured. When Lt. Omasu Matsuichi of Yonaguni was killed at Guadalcanal in January 1943, his death was lauded as a heroic sacrifice which all Japanese should be willing to copy. In October of that year, the War Ministry launched a "Be like Omasu" campaign in every newspaper in Okinawa.[6] At Omasu's former school, pupils even had to place a photograph of the deceased soldier on their desks before lessons commenced for the day.[7]

As schools took on an increasingly nationalist flavor and classroom teaching adopted a similar military focus, such as math problems being created around calculating numbers of tanks, ships, and bullets. In physical education sessions, boys trained at throwing hand grenades and thrusting bayonets and bamboo spears into straw effigies of Churchill and Roosevelt. Girls practiced fire drills, and even the youngest school children were organized into groups to run around holding Japan's national flag.[8] School songs were replaced by army marches, and English was banned as the "enemy language." Baseball terms such as "safe" and "out" were replaced with Japanese expressions, jazz and other forms of Western entertainment were banned, and children were required to memorize expressions such as "Japan is Number One!" "Hurrah for our flag!" and "Long live the Emperor!" Military officers attached to schools stressed that joining the army was the only honorable pathway for boys to choose and were so successful in

---

5.   *Okinawasen Shimbun*: 2005.
6.   *Ryukyu Shimpo*, 4 December 2011: 95-96.
7.   Okinawa Heiwa Network, 2008: 8-9.
8.   Okinawa Heiwa Network: 2008: 8.

their endeavors that many pupils reported being more in awe of achieving that goal than of doing well academically. In order to find enough recruits for the Blood and Iron Corps and the girls' aides units, many children received their graduation certificates a year early, without having graduated at all.[9]

In June 1944, when the 32nd Army arrived on Okinawa, they unilaterally commandeered school buildings. Schools were officially closed and classes were canceled in favor of children being sent out to help construct military facilities, prepare runways, dig shelters and grow vegetables. Even the girls were required to work during the day and study basic nursing at night. The Okinawan language was also targeted at school as un-Japanese, and children heard speaking it could be made to wear a special tag around their necks for the day as punishment.[10] Adults were initially warned that speaking the local dialect would be regarded as unpatriotic, but during the battle many civilians caught speaking Okinawan were accused of being spies and shot on the spot by Imperial Japanese Army [IJA] soldiers. In a further attempt to subjugate the residents of Okinawa, the local pronunciations for family names were often unilaterally changed to more standard mainland Japanese readings.[11]

Since the Meiji Restoration in 1868, Japan's education system had been widely used as a means of thought control, especially in generating a self-sacrificial loyalty to the emperor and an acceptance of national polity. During the 1940s, this process became increasingly rigorous and, once the Battle of Okinawa was inevitable, all semblance of education on Okinawa gave way to mentally, psychologically, and physically preparing the island and its inhabitants to fight.

Department of Internal Affairs Education Section

"By that stage, the principal's meetings were little more than a mechanism for him to hand out instructions. When the Head of the Internal Affairs Education Section entered the room, everybody stood up and bowed. Bureaucratic control was complete." That was how Maeda Yoshimi, who was posted from the Second Prefectural Middle School in April 1944 to supervise clerical staff in the prefectural Internal Affairs Department's Education Section, recalls how education circles operated back then. The Academic Section, which was overseeing prefectural middle schools, was formerly two separate groups, the Education Administration Section and the Social Education Section, both under the auspices of

---

9. *Okinawasen Shimbun*, 2005.20.
10. Okinawa Heiwa Network, 2008: 7.
11. *Ryukyu Shimpo*, 4 December 2011: 95-96.

the Department of Educational Administration. However, as the situation in the war deteriorated further, management of the organization became increasingly difficult and the Academic Section became part of the Department of Internal Affairs. This was designed to centralize administrative procedures and reduce staff numbers in order to save money that could then be spent on the war effort. Because the Academic Section embraced the twin objectives of "revere your ancestors" and "unification of religion and the state," a considerable number of financial advisors were assigned to work there. Maeda explained, "School inspectors in every department and section held terrific authority. They even sent any teaching staff who objected off to the Sakishima Islands, so even a principal visiting the education unit on ordinary education business would be very nervous when one of these inspectors arrived." The prevailing atmosphere was such that nobody dared disagree with a prefectural instruction at a principal's meeting. The understanding that *even schools have to do their bit when the nation is in trouble* was the norm.

When Maeda was teaching at the Second Prefectural Middle School, he and the students in his charge were mobilized to do a week's work at Yomitan Airfield. "All I can remember is that the work was hard, made even worse because of the awful food," Maeda said. The work involved leveling barren land and clearing away rocks, but the tools they had to work with such as hoes were woefully inadequate. "The only good thing about it was that I bunked with the students in a local classroom and a great spirit developed between the students and myself." Six years earlier, in the fall of 1939, Maeda had worked as a volunteer on a land reclamation project at Nakagawa in Kin-cho. That project was designed to increase food production, but as yet there wasn't the tense foreboding that went with imminent war. Prefectural schools were mobilized one after the other to cultivate tracts of land, which was then allocated to new residents, each new arrival being allocated a dwelling on 660 square meters of land plus 1.5 hectares for cultivation.

The squad of ninety-six volunteer laborers from the Second Prefectural Middle School took the train as far as Kadena and from there walked the approximately 28 kilometers to Nakagawa. The journey lasted the entire day so they arrived around dusk. Maeda remembers that he was delighted when the vice-principal of the primary school where they were to be billeted welcomed them with fish he had just caught and some *awamori* (distilled rice liquor distinctive to Okinawa). However, what he would never forget was the exhilaration of actually standing on the newly reclaimed land.

Two or three months after the newspaper featured an article entitled *Voluntary Labor Project*, Maeda was ordered to attend a six month training course at the Research Center for Spiritual Culture of Japan in the Ministry of Education's Bureau of Education, an organ for teaching nationalistic ideology. "I reckon that Fuchigami, the prefectural governor, saw that article in the paper and I got selected," explained Maeda. As time progressed, education about Japan's war preparations became increasingly intense.

It was toward the end of 1939 when Maeda was sent to the Research Center for Spiritual Culture of Japan in Tokyo. Under the direct control of the Ministry of Education, the center's main purpose was "To create an appropriate ideology for affirming the principles of Japanese national polity and nationalist philosophy, boosting our national culture, opposing foreign ideas and decrying Marxism." Maeda explained, "In other words, its purpose was to embrace nationalism. Engendering a spirit of national cooperation for Japan's move to a war footing was at the very core." During the six months of the course, every morning began with Zen meditation, after which the "basic tenets of national polity" were taught as a process of turning the finest citizens in the country into instructors. The program brought together top instructors and teachers chosen from all over Japan. "We also had lectures to further our understanding of things such as the tea ceremony and the essence of Japanese culture." The research center had responsibility for Japan's ideological focus of the day, so the teachers taking part were also very committed. The things they learned were to be disseminated in their own areas. In the summer of that same year when Maeda finished his training, he started work instructing at seminars where he had brought together teachers and middle school pupils from Okinawa's elementary schools. Taking advantage of the summer vacation, he ran what was known as an *Extended Symposium for National Spirit and Culture*, a month-long residential training seminar in the Normal School gymnasium. "It was the same stuff I'd learned at the research center," he explained. "I taught them pedagogy and literature from a nationalistic perspective. They also had lectures on battlefield tactics." Within a year or two, almost all of the deputy principals who completed the course had been promoted to full principal positions.

In June 1945, an article about the research center appeared in the *Ryukyu Shimpo* with the headline "Huge Conversion Rate at the Research Center for Spiritual Culture of Japan." The article read, "In the seven years that the research has been established, almost 1,000 elementary school teachers have attended intensive training at the wonderful six-month extended study seminars held at the center. Moreover, at similar research centers in every prefecture, 9,000 young school principals and teachers who have completed the one-month lecture series have had their lives turned around by being exposed to major educational theories and teacher training. In all, this brings the total throughout the nation to 10,000 people . . . the centers can be quietly proud of the fact that the spiritual fortitude of these 10,000 has made it through, as instructed, educational training during the protracted years of war."

The move by middle schools to a war footing began in 1938 as a result of the "Matters Associated with the Implementation of the Collective Labor Movement," a directive from the undersecretary. Even so, as Maeda explained of a time when things were still quite relaxed, "Up until the voluntary labor idea at Kin in 1939, teachers and students all cooperated as one group. During the day we worked and during the evenings we mixed socially. It was very pleasant." However, things became much more serious when the Outline for the Implementation of the Increase in Food Production by Students was decreed in 1941. As a result of that plan, physical labor was "to be handled as a part of the normal curriculum." More and more, Maeda and other experienced middle school teachers led groups of pupils out to farms around Haebaru to help with farm laboring work. "Gradually, study had less and less to do with the curriculum. Education had become a stop-start affair as middle school study came to an end with more things being done outside the curriculum."

Eventually, teachers were also mobilized, thereby creating a teacher shortage. "At that stage, unqualified teachers were in the classrooms, but even worse was that in many cases senior students were teaching their juniors," explained Maeda. In April 1944 when things were becoming increasingly desperate, Maeda found himself transferred to the prefecture's education unit. "When the matter was first mentioned, I was really enjoying the direct contact I had with my students. Also, people like Matayoshi Kowa advised me, 'What a waste if you leave the classroom,' so I declined the transfer. However, I decided to make the move on their assurance that after two years I would be able to come back as a school principal. The first of April 1944 was the very day that the statutory declaration was invoked by the commander of the 32nd Army to give the military total authority.

In April 1944, Maeda was transferred to the Prefectural Education Unit, leaving behind his teaching position at the Prefectural Middle School where laboring for the war effort was still voluntary. Maeda remembers that around November or December 1944, a soldier in army uniform, gold braid on his epaulettes, arrived at the education unit. The unit head was away at the time so Maeda had taken over the reins. That soldier was Lt. Col. Miyake Tadao. Miyake cut straight to the chase and announced, "The army is short of manpower. So, to boost our numbers we need to train middle school year one and year two students in signals and the top pupils from the girls' schools as emergency nurses." This request was totally different from the labor contributed to build army emplacements, which they had been doing up to that point. His request really meant that the students were to become full-fledged members of the regular army. "What he was saying was of major significance and had come right out of the blue," recalled Maeda. "I shrugged it off by saying that I would pass it on to my superiors and quickly arranged a meeting with the head of the internal affairs section."

He had a meeting with the head of the internal affairs section and the head of the education unit where they agreed that it was not something the prefecture could give a ruling on. Even though things were becoming desperate, the reality of giving this type of labor contribution priority over school study was not a decision they could make lightly, especially when they thought about what the families would want. In the end, ". . . given the state of affairs, we simply could not force students to undertake military training. If Okinawa became embroiled in war, all citizens would have to stand up and fight together. In that case, students would be no different. It was a case of 'if student mobilization is urgently sought during a time of crisis, then it's a matter for the nation to decide.' But mobilization for the military is an important request at government level so the prefecture is in no position to make a judgement." According to Maeda, Lt. Col. Miyake was duly informed of the prefecture's response and subsequently visited a number of classrooms at the First Prefectural Girls' School (which had already been taken over by the military). Maeda has no recollection of any further communication with him on the question of student mobilization. He did, however, ask Miyake, "If these students were to be drafted into the military, what would their status be?" Miyake replied, "It would be too tough on them to make them soldiers, so I guess they'd be military employees." Thereafter, Maeda had no further involvement regarding the mobilization of students.

The issue of Okinawan evacuees first came up the following year, 1945. It was said that Okinawans were unable to adjust to local customs and were treated by locals in Japan as uncivilized. To resolve this, it was decided that guidance should be given by the teachers who had been evacuated with their young charges. In order to allocate teachers as advisors in each region, Maeda traveled to Miyazaki Prefecture in Kyushu on 11 February, Japan's National Foundation Day. He did everything he could to get a ride on an army plane, although by then American aircraft were launching repeated attacks. Only after he arrived at Miyazaki did Maeda discover that a friend who had flown out the previous day had been shot down by the enemy over Sesoko-jima off Motobu. Although his work at Miyazaki was over in about ten days, Miyazaki was the target of a huge air raid and he was unable to get a flight home. Even the sugar cane he had taken with him to use as a bribe didn't help him find someone to organize his trip back. When one of his friends told him of a high speed vessel which could get him back to Naha in seven hours, he made his way to Kagoshima, only to be told, "Nothing like that exists. Even if there were one, civilians would not be allowed to use it." It was a time when people were hoping for some good news from the war and rumors were rife.

Maeda was eventually repatriated to Okinawa early in November, around three months after the Battle of Okinawa ended, and he was astounded to learn that students had been drafted into the army and that many had been killed in the fighting. "I said *No* to the army," Maeda recalled, "but, because I was initially involved in the discussions, I do feel some sense of responsibility. Once the fighting broke out, educationalists ended up cooperating with the war effort, and it was really difficult to remain independent in that environment. For me personally, I feel that I was weak in not opposing the war on an ideological level. But in those days, even the teachers were swept along by the surging tide."

In September 1943, Nakayama Koshin moved from his role as principal at Iwa Kokumin School into the Prefectural Department of Education. His new role was prefectural representative in charge of social education. "I used to teach them about supporting the war effort," Nakayama explained. The boat service to the Sakishima islands could no longer be relied upon so he concentrated on moving about the main island of Okinawa encouraging people everywhere to do their bit for the war effort. He spent around twenty days of each month away from home. At each kokumin school in each region, he would assemble groups of local women and "encourage" them to do their bit. Then, each evening, he would walk the almost eight kilometers to the next school where he would stay the night.

Raising people's awareness of Japan's "war footing" was an important job. Nakayama traveled about instructing people to reduce their daily consumption and to increase production. He preached "mental preparedness" to those who had to stay at the home front by urging them to save money and donate their precious metal items to the war effort. Also, he encouraged those families who had not done so to send their family members away to take part in the fighting.

Training women to fight with bamboo spears was seen as another essential aspect of preparation. Nakayama explained, "It was a time when nobody harbored any doubts at all about what was going on because it was all being taught with such unwavering consistency from elementary school level. The plan was that the whole of society would be "spiritually" educated. Textbooks focused on the emperor and the nation, events focused on the Imperial household. Anybody standing back was regarded as unpatriotic, so civilians joined in with real commitment and even felt proud of their participation. Therefore, no matter how tough things might become, they all believed that a "divine wind would save their nation." Nobody ever questioned the concept that Japan was a sacred nation." *National Unity* was certainly the slogan of the day.

The following year, Nakayama's job changed slightly. Preparing the land became an urgent task, with runways and army emplacements being set up in every area. Then the order came through from the military that he had to assemble a work force. Using a network of Imperial Rule Assistance Association support organizations across the island, he rounded up the necessary workers, and even Nakayama himself set to work with a hoe. Just as he was settling into that task, he was suddenly faced with the issue of the evacuation of children. The Education unit was chosen to oversee this task. Evacuation groups were set up, with each group containing forty children brought in from the various cities, towns, and villages in the prefecture. A teacher and a dormitory matron were assigned to each group.

Maeda explained, "Because we had been teaching that there would be a final showdown, the idea of evacuation was not widely understood. The better educated people were, the greater this was. Some school principals went around insisting 'defending the nation is the responsibility of every citizen . . . where does evacuation fit into defending one's country?' Things became really heated and the chief of police exclaimed angrily, 'Anyone who opposes the national strategy is a traitor and we'll throw them in jail.'"

After the requirements of Nakayama's job were decided, things took a real downturn. The police were in charge of organizing the evacuation boats and announced an approximate departure date. After notifying schools, towns, and villages about where and when their evacuees were to assemble, Nakayama was flat out trying to organize accommodation for them at local inns. "It was my job to look after everything once they had assembled, including even carrying their luggage, so I had no time to rest." But that wasn't the end of it. The departure date and time were top secret so, in the meantime, everybody had to wait on standby in their own homes. When the final word came through in the middle of the night, Nakayama had to call at the inns to let them know and then gather up all the luggage. "The port was teeming with students, plus their families who had come to say goodbye. We had to get their luggage on board as quickly as possible which only added to the confusion. In some cases, people got on one boat but their luggage was put onto a different boat. For some of the children who boarded the *Tsushima Maru*, only their luggage made it to Kyushu." The seas around Okinawa were full of American submarines and, when Naha was reduced to ashes as a result of the 10 October air raid, the army issued instructions that the evacuation strategy was to change from shifting people out of Okinawa altogether, to moving them to the northern part of Okinawa itself. In the Prefectural Office at that stage the Demographics Section had just been established and Nakayama, together with Kan Nagayama, a school inspector, moved into that section. Most of the people working in that operation came from the Police Department, where they had been responsible for transport issues.

In order to accommodate evacuees from central and southern Okinawa, people throughout the towns and villages in the northern part of Okinawa banded together and began building huts up in the hills. Nakayama's work at the Demographics Section was to systematically dispatch civilian evacuees from the various cities, towns, and villages. The task of compiling separate schedules for towns and villages required long hours of work which often lasted until late in the evening. The walls of his house were covered in timetables. In 1945, evacuation to the north was in full swing. On 31 January, Governor Shimada Akira, who had just taken up his new posting, assembled the staff at the Demographics Section to give them their instructions. "Gentlemen," he began, "If the enemy does land, there is no point in you taking up weapons to fight. Do what you can now organizing behind the scenes for the cause!" The Battle for Okinawa was almost upon them.

In March, when the first evacuation schedule was completed, Nakayama traveled around the northern region of Okinawa checking on conditions there. He planned to return to Naha on the 23rd after completing his inspections as far as Haneji, but because an unprecedented level of air raids had started that week he was forced to stay put and spend three days in an air raid shelter. On the evening of 27 March, he eventually tracked down a truck heading for Naha and was able to catch a ride.

As the truck was approaching Uenoya, however, Nakayama couldn't believe his eyes. A brilliant light stretched as far as he could see and, following the 10

October air raid, there was barely a building still standing in the city of Naha. The brilliance of the light was such that Nakayama had never seen anything like it. Although it did not take him long to work out that the concentration of lights was, in fact, the U.S. invasion fleet offshore, he remained struck by its sheer brilliance.

For two days, staff from the Prefectural Office gathered in the underground shelter at Shuri Girls' School before continuing their journey north. "The bank safe still had all the prefectural funds in it but the bank manager had gone and taken the key with him. Police inquiries revealed that he was at Misato and I was told to bring him back to Naha at once and I got all the way to Misato carrying the governor's name card with me. It was pouring on the night I left and I didn't arrive until dawn." After that, he had no need to return to Naha, so Nakayama made his way to the Imperial Photograph Guardian Unit at Oshittai in Hane-ji. All the photographs of the emperor that had been displayed in Okinawa's schools were gathered up and solemnly and securely stored in a concrete bunker. A dozen or so teachers then set up the Imperial Photograph Guardian Unit to guard the collection.

"Back then, if any of those photos received even a tiny scratch, the school principal would be fired. At the time of the 10 October 1944 air raid, some principals were seen fleeing, having abandoned their families but still clutching the emperor's photograph in its display frame. Once a week, each principal would don his white gloves, open the secure unit, and check on the photographs' condition. They would then note the date and report their findings back to prefectural administration." Just one of those photographs back then had huge significance. Nakayama joined the other teachers but, in less than a week, the photographs were no longer safe.

Around 11 April, American troops were seen in the vicinity of Oshittai, and Nakayama also had to flee into the hills. "Twelve of us carried rucksacks with the photos in them but they were so heavy that they cut into our shoulders. It was hard going along those mountain tracks and the talk soon turned to 'what do you think about dumping them?'" recalled Nakayama. The governor had earlier given the members of the Photograph Guardian Unit the secret command that "If the Americans invade this part of our island, make sure you dispose of the photographs." And now, having been forced into the hills, the governor's words were again the topic of conversation. However, because it was so serious a matter that they could be strung up if they were found out, it wasn't quite as simple as that and they could not bring themselves to dispose of them. In the end, they agreed, "We are going to win this war. Imagine the shame if we no longer have the photos then. In the meantime, the least we can do is to protect the emperor and his wife." Inside the bags there were photographs of Emperors Meiji and Taisho, plus imperial edicts and rescripts, which they decided it was acceptable to discard. However, the bags were still heavy, so they then pulled away the cardboard backing and retained just the actual photos.

Up in the hills, they built a makeshift hut, using logs for pillars and then attaching timber onto them to make a roof and walls. They then placed the bags with the photographs safely inside the hut. Each morning, they would hang the photographs up on a tree, face the Imperial Palace and bow reverently. Around 23 June, Nakayama left the photograph group as food supplies were running low, and he decided that he was becoming a hindrance to the men. Several others had also departed by that point. Nakayama was captured by the Americans on 7 July and heard about the end of the war in the POW camp from an American soldier yelling out the momentous news. Nakayama's earlier hopes of the Japanese forces rallying and turning the tide evaporated into thin air when he saw the resources that the Americans had at their disposal. As for the photographs, only after the war did Nakayama learn that they had been disposed of.

Building of fortifications commences

"Just as a wild rabbit tries to disguise the location of its warren, the entrance to the Headquarters cave certainly wasn't an impressive concrete entrance or anything like that."

Miyagi Kokichi, who had been a teacher at the Normal School in 1945, pointed at a concrete structure near Enkanchi Pond, which a tour guide was explaining as the entrance to the Command Post Shelter. "The No. 1 entrance to the shelter was over there," said Miyagi, pointing to the slope below the Sono-hyan-utaki (sacred location), a spot completely covered by grass and bushes. On closer inspection, there was a hole there, with no concrete surrounds. It is said to have led to the main tunnel 30 meters in. Construction of the 32nd Army Command Post Shelter, referred to by Lt. Gen. Cho as the "Heaven's Grotto Battle Headquarters," began in earnest on 9 December 1944. The 2nd Field Construction Duty Company was in charge of the construction with students of the Normal School called in to work on it at the start of January 1945.

Inferior to the enemy in every respect—including those most crucial issues of firepower and manpower—in order to survive the incredible barrage from both the sea and the air, the 32nd Army focused on the construction of cave-type fortified shelters that aimed to take advantage of the Ryukyuan limestone. This is why the shelter was constructed from around July 1944 in Tsukazan in Haebaru.

However, overall strategy and the planned deployment of each unit had to be changed when the elite 9th Division was moved to Taiwan. The Command Post was relocated to Shuri, which meant abandoning the shelters that had been purpose-built at Haebaru and starting to build new ones under Shuri Castle.

The Americans started their attack on Iwo Jima around the time that work began on digging the shelter, so it did not take long before rumors started to circulate among the soldiers of the Field Construction Duty Company that Okinawa would be next. However, progress was slow, due to the extremely labor-intensive nature of the digging and the fact that it was difficult to make an impression on the hard rock with pickaxes. Miyagi, who was in charge of the student work gangs, remembers seeing Lt. Gen. Ushijima come in to look at how the work was going. "I got the impression that Command Post staff were very unsettled at that stage."

On 23 March 1945, U.S. air raids suddenly intensified. The landings were obviously getting close, so the 32nd Army Headquarters Unit moved its base of operations underground. Despite the digging continuing around the clock, at this stage the main tunnel that was to link No. 1 and No. 3 shelters and the shelter entrance on the Kinjo side were incomplete, as were vertical shafts linked to tunnels. Those in the Headquarters Unit found themselves hurled into the fray with their complex of shelters and tunnels far from complete.

CHAPTER 3

EVACUATION

With the fall of Saipan imminent, on 7 July 1944, an emergency meeting of the Japanese cabinet ratified the request from Lt. Gen. Cho Isamu, chief of staff of the 32nd Army that the elderly, as well as women and children, should be evacuated from Okinawa, Miyako-jima and Ishigaki-jima.[1] In the course of the following week instructions were issued by the Japanese government to evacuate 80,000 people from the main island of Okinawa to Kyushu, and a further 20,000 from Miyako and the Yaeyama Islands to Taiwan.[2] It has been suggested that the figure 100,000 was chosen because that is the number of soldiers who had been deployed to Okinawa, so acquiring food supplies for them meant that the same number of locals needed to be removed.[3] That was particularly pressing given that most livestock on the island had been slaughtered and eaten.[4] Also, the military decided that in an island prefecture as small as Okinawa reducing the number of civilians who could not assist the IJA to conduct the battle.

There were several reasons why evacuation did not go smoothly. First and foremost was that the military saw the civilian population only in terms of what food resources they could supply (or consume) or what tasks they could carry out to aid the defense of the island, either in construction or combat roles.[5] With this being the case, regardless of any plan for evacuation, civilians were kept working as long as possible building airfields and then digging tunnels and fortifications.[6] By March 1945 the military and able-bodied civilians had assumed one integrated purpose [*gunmin-ittaika*] and evacuation to safety did not fit in with this philosophy.[7] Statements in the early months of 1945 by Lt. Gen. Cho were blunt and to the point—those who were not capable of contributing to the military effort were expected to remove themselves from locations where they might hinder military operations, and those who remained were expected

1.   Tsushima-maru Memorial Museum Official Guidebook. 2010: 8.
2.   Hayashi, H. 2010: 59.
3.   Okinawa Heiwa Network. 2008: 30.
4.   Feifer, G. 1992: 92.
5.   Oshiro, M. 2007: 78.
6.   Oshiro, M. 2007:183.
7.   Kunimori, Y. 2010: 4.

to give their lives for the cause. At an address that he gave in Shuri on 10 January 1945, he is reported to have said, "To the people of Okinawa, as Japanese citizens you are expected to come forward to do your utmost to defend your homeland ... The young and the old are to cooperate by evacuating so that they do not interfere in the fighting."[8] Second, soldiers often discouraged people from evacuating by denigrating the act of relocation to Kyushu, where food was already in short supply, as cowardice.[9] Third, because the IJA talked only in terms of certain victory over the American forces, the civilian population did not sense the need to evacuate.[10] Fourth, the main premise upon which evacuation was carried out was that the people going to Kyushu had relatives or friends upon whom they could rely for support.[11]

In the background to this, while the military did its best to stop information circulating about the tragedy, was the sinking of the *Tsushima-Maru* by the submarine USS Bowfin on 21 August 1944 with the loss of 1,375 lives, including 777 children. This even highlighted just how dangerous the waters between Okinawa and the main islands of Japan had become by mid-1944, and this of course discouraged parents from sending family members away.[12] While it did not become widely known in Okinawa, less than a month before the *Tsushima-Maru* met its fate, the *Toyama-Maru*, carrying the 44th Independent Mixed Brigade to reinforce the 32nd Army was also torpedoed and sunk in the same seas between Okinawa and the main islands of Japan. Over 5,000 troops were lost on the *Toyama-Maru* in what was to be one of the world's worst maritime disasters.[13] The Japanese military authorities' ability to hide information on the sinking of merchant vessels was illustrated by the fact that the tragedy of 577 Okinawans (mostly young volunteers preparing to join the *Yokaren* Naval Aviator Preparatory Course, but also including 61 civilians) who were killed when the *Konan-Maru* was sunk by an American submarine in December 1943 on its way from Naha to the main islands of Japan, was not revealed until mid-1982.[14]

A total of approximately 4,500 Okinawans lost their lives on vessels moving between Japan and its outer islands or occupied territories. As was the case with the *Tsushima-Maru* bringing soldiers of the 62nd Division to Naha from Shang-

8.   *Okinawasen Shimbun*. 2005: 16.
9.   Urasaki, J. 1965: 46.
10. Hayashi, H. 2001: 103.
11. Hayashi, H. 2001. 104.
12. Tsushima-maru Memorial Museum Official Guidebook. 2010: 8.
13. Feifer, G. 1992: 81.
14. Okinawa Heiwa Network. 2008: 32.

hai, when we consider that the same vessel transporting soldiers and munitions on one leg of its journey would on the next leg carry civilians seeking the relative safety of the main islands of Japan, it was extremely difficult for submarine commanders to differentiate one from the other.[15] Other vessels carrying evacuees were attacked by American warplanes. For example, the Senkaku Islands Shipwreck Incident, which is covered in detail in this work, was caused by an attack by U.S. warplanes on the *No. 1 Chihaya-Maru* and the *No. 5 Chihaya-Maru* on their way to Taiwan in early July 1945.

It was only after the large-scale air raids of 10 October 1944, which destroyed 90 percent of Naha, that many Okinawan families were prepared to take the risk of removing family members from harm's way.[16] A total of 60,000 people (including around 6,000 children) were evacuated to Kumamoto, Oita, and Miyazaki prefectures in Kyushu and a further 20,000 to Taiwan. [17]

The military also encouraged civilians to relocate to the northern region of the main island of Okinawa, which was not expected to be the scene of fighting, but the logistical reality of moving north and the lateness of the start of this evacuation (in March) meant that when the U.S. forces quickly cut the island in two by seizing control of the Ishikawa Isthmus, many of the civilians who had started to head north were forced to retrace their steps southward.[18] One reason for the late start to the evacuation proper was that the governor of Okinawa, Izumi Shuki, abandoned his post and fled to mainland Japan in December 1944. The month of total inaction that followed until Shimada Akira was appointed as Izumi's successor was a factor in leaving so many of Okinawa's civilian population in areas where fighting was to occur.[19]

Life for those who did make it to Kyushu was particularly harsh over the winter of 1944–1945. Three things that surviving Okinawans say when reflecting on those times in Kumamoto, Oita, and Miyazaki are that they always felt cold, hungry and lonely.[20] These people, after the war ended, changed from having fled from the fighting to waiting months in repatriation camps for the situation in the devastated homeland of Okinawa to recover to the extent that they could

---

15. Tsushima-maru Memorial Museum Official Guidebook. 2010: 10.
16. Senkaku-shoto senji-sonanshibotsusha Irei-no-hi Kensetsu-jigyo Kiseikai. 2006: 160.
17 Okinawa Heiwa Network. 2008: 30.
18. Hayashi, H. 2010: 61.
19. Yomiuri Shimbun War Responsibility Reexamination Committee. 2009: 66.
20. Okinawa Heiwa Network. 2008:31.

return home.[21]

As Hayashi states: "Even during wartime in those days, designating and announcing a specific area as a safe-zone for non-combatants to prevent such people from being caught up in combat was recognized as an option under international law. However, taking such a course of action did not occur to the Imperial Japanese Army or the Japanese government. Whether it was in Okinawa, or on the main islands of Japan, the IJA had no intention protecting the lives or ensuring the safety of civilians."[22]

Measures to evacuate civilians

"Civilians are to move as far north as they can." This one order was issued in Lt. Gen. Ushijima's name as the preliminary bombardment began before the landing of American forces on the main island of Okinawa. Araki Minoru, who was in the 32nd Army's Command Post Staff Unit, recalls, "I relayed this evacuation order from the Command Post to Governor Shimada Akira."

Japanese predictions of where the U.S. forces would land were more or less spot on. The military decided that civilians living in the central area of the island, which was destined to become the scene of heavy fighting, should move north. However, the actual number who evacuated in the period up until one week after the fighting started was no more than one third of what had been expected.

A-san, who was living in the southern part of Okinawa when the fighting started, relied on assistance from relatives to be evacuated with his mother and siblings to a shelter in Untamamui, a strategically crucial location to the east of the headquarters at Shuri. The 24th Division was deployed here, and this area was expected to see fierce fighting. A-san and his family were oblivious to this.

He left the shelter and headed south with his family and relatives when American illumination rounds began to go up over Benga-dake. On their way south, his grandmother, mother, youngest brother, and aunt were killed by artillery fire, leaving him, his four sisters, and two cousins alive.

"We were all just children, so we had no idea where we should go to escape. We also had next to nothing with us in the way of food," he recalls. They began to wander around the battlefield, strafed by American warplanes and avoiding artillery shells as they went. They came across some Japanese soldiers one day, but when they tried to follow them, one of the soldiers drew his sword and told

---

21. Dower, J. 1999: 55.
22. Hayashi, H. 2010: 63.

them "Don't come near us!"

Araki says that he relayed just the one evacuation order from the military command to the prefectural authorities. "The American advance was so swift that the civilian evacuation did not go well at all," he says, acknowledging that the order was issued too late. He continues, "The military stance was that all Japanese, including civilians, should take up arms. There weren't enough soldiers to call on the civilians to evacuate or lead them to safety. It just wasn't possible."

About one month after American forces had landed on the main island of Okinawa, Lt. Adaniya Ken, who was attached to the 32nd Army's Headquarters Unit, met with a man who came to visit the Command Post. His name was Sato Kiichi. Adaniya talked to Sato after his meeting and was told that he had come on the orders of Governor Shimada. Sato said, "I'm here to find out what stance the military is going to take. The civilian government will decide upon its position once that is clear." He continued, "The military says that it will hold the Shuri Line, so I will convey that to the prefectural authorities."

However, the Shuri Line was breached less than a month later. With manpower dwindling day by day, the 32nd Army launched two failed offensives before it started to be pushed inexorably southward, something that was to see the civilian population caught up in a truly tragic situation.

After they had withdrawn as far south as they could go, Adaniya recalls an unforgettable scene he witnessed in a shelter in Mabuni. It was around mid-June, by which time he was totally desensitized to the piles of dead bodies that lay everywhere.

In the chief of staff's office space, the flickering candlelight projected two men's shadows on the wall. One was Chief of Staff Cho. The man of short stature standing in front of Cho, with his back to Araki, was wearing a khaki National Uniform. This was not a place that civilians could enter freely, and the number of people who could gain an audience with Chief of Staff Cho was of course limited. "It must have been Governor Shimada. Maybe he had come to say his final farewells." No one knows what actually happened to Shimada in the end.

Adaniya says, "Yahara was a very talented man, thoroughly dedicated to the defense of Japan, but civilian losses would have been much lower if he had not opted for a battle of attrition and had instead supported a last stand at the Shuri Line." Thirty-second Army Headquarters Air Liaison Staff Officer Jin Naomichi commented, "The prefectural authorities are the ones who should be putting measures in place to cope with non-combatants. The military cannot give orders to civilians. Before the fighting started, we requested through the prefectural governor that the civilian authorities issue notices and cooperate in getting the civilian population to evacuate to the north. There were civilians who chose not to move, plus others who had only started to do so in a panic once the fighting had commenced."

He continues, "They [the civilians] didn't seem to think that things would become quite as bad as they did. Moving to the south with the Army was the cause of the huge losses." No doubt it would have been difficult for civilians who had been fed a constant diet of propaganda from Imperial Headquarters about how Japan was winning victory after victory to believe that the Americans would actually land on Okinawa.

Command Post at Tsukazan

Just like the 32nd Army Command Post at Shuri, there is another shelter complex destined to be forgotten with the passage of time—the Tsukazan Command Post. Under Takatsukazan, in Tsukazan, Haebaru, this complex of dugout shelters that was accessed from the northwest corner of the hill was going to be the Command Post for the 32nd Army before its replacement shelter was constructed at Shuri. In December 1944, it was decided to abandon the tunnels in Tsukazan and to construct a new Command Post at Shuri. The main reasons were that the scale of the shelter at Tsukazan was thought to be too small and that Shuri would provide a better view of the battlefield.

The construction section of the Accounting Division of the 32nd Army and the No. 2 Fortification Construction Unit started work on the Tsukazan Command Post complex around summer 1944. Large numbers of locals from southern Okinawa were also recruited as workers. It was hard manual labor, digging away with shovels and pickaxes by the light of oil lamps and candles. Dynamite was also used to help get through the hardest bedrock.

Units of the 32nd Army moved to Tsukazan following the Naha air raid of 10 October 1944. With about a third of the local residents' houses being requisitioned to accommodate soldiers, Tsukazan became a garrison town full of military personnel and civilians. The Naha Branch of the Bank of Japan, which had been burned out in the air raid, also relocated its operations to Tsukazan. The local school had been taken over by the military, so lessons were carried out without a blackboard, the children sitting on chairs lined up in open, grassy spaces, just listening to the teachers.

By around November, the time of year when ears of maiden grass filled the fields, most of the Tsukazan tunnel complex—a total of about 2,000 meters—was complete. The tunnels of the Command Post provided a marvelous playground for the local children. Oshiro Yurayasu, who lived near its southern entrance, was one of the children who played in the Tsukazan cave complex. "I remember going in there with twenty or thirty kids, using bundles of dried grass lit as a torch, instead of a candle. It was huge, with passages leading everywhere. It was like a maze," recalls Oshiro.

The 32nd Army Command Post was subsequently moved to Shuri, with only a small number of personnel from units such as the Accounts Section being left in the Tsukazan complex of caves. The safe of the Bank of Japan was moved into the shelter at the end of March. By that stage, neither the children who had previously played in the caves nor the local residents were permitted to approach the shelter without good reason.

There were fifteen young girls of the First Prefectural Girls' School Himeyuri Student Corps stationed in the shelter as administrative workers. Three teachers accompanied the girls.

At the end of March 1945, the Himeyuri Student Corps was deployed to the Army Hospital in Haebaru and, after a short time, they were then sent to field hospitals in locations such as Ichinichibashi and Shikina. The Army Surgeons' Unit in Tsukazan was also one of the places that accepted the girls.

Arasaki Masako was one of those fifteen girls. She remembers being surprised by the scale of the complex of caves when she entered the shelter at Tsukazan on 28 March. There was an electric generator, and light bulbs illuminated the tunnels. "We thought that it was quite something in comparison to the shelter at Haebaru, but then again that was because it had been constructed as the Command Post."

The duties for the girls in the Student Corps were mainly tasks such as fetching water and carrying food supplies. From mid-April, they were required to help look after wounded soldiers.

Miyagi Kikuko, one of the other Himeyuri members, found going to fetch water the most frightening job of all. "In the middle of the bombardment, wearing a steel helmet on my head, I would go to Tsukazan with a barrel on my back to fetch water. I'd launch myself at the ground face first when I sensed a shell coming in. It was the time of year when there was a lot of rain, so I got all covered in mud."

Into May, large numbers of wounded soldiers began to arrive at the Tsukazan Army Surgical Unit and the Himeyuri girls were worked to the bone. It was around that time that the generator broke down, forcing them to work by the light from candles and oil lamps.

Arasaki recalls, "I was too scared to go to the Army Surgical Unit by myself. There was a place where we had to climb up or down a ladder, in the dark. It'd take 30 minutes to get from the sentry's post at the entrance on the southern side to the Surgical Unit on the northern side."

Almost all of the badly wounded soldiers ended their days inside the shelter. Among them were men who had gone mad. Miyagi, then just sixteen years old, witnessed the death throes of many mortally wounded soldiers.

"There were soldiers who had lost their minds and had to be tied to wooden pillars. Others would rip their bandages off and strip naked however much they might be bandaged up. I remember one soldier, not long before he died, saying, 'Whatever you do, don't get wounded. It's a miserable way to go . . .'" The 32nd Army Headquarters Unit stopped briefly at Tsukazan on their way south from Shuri, and the remaining units in the shelter at Tsukazan followed them on or after 31 May. Trembling with fear, the members of the Students Corps left the shelter and trudged southward through the pouring rain.

Banquet on the evening before the 10 October 1944 air raid

The Japanese Ground Self-Defense Force Staff College paper, *Japanese Imperial Army Strategy: 32nd Army*, explains the 32nd Army's thinking as: ". . . if the main body of the enemy force were to head south after landing on the Nakagami coastal area which had been abandoned, the strategy would be to enter into a battle of attrition taking advantage of the favorable terrain to the north of Shuri."

But why fight a battle of attrition? The objective was simply to hold the American forces in Okinawa for as long as possible while preparations for the defense of the main islands of Japan were being carried out. Okinawa was used as a *sute-ishi*, a sacrificial stone in the Japanese board game *go*. The elite 9th Infantry Division had been redeployed to Taiwan by Imperial Headquarters, so it is fair to say that the only option for the 32nd Army was to fight a battle of attrition. Imperial Headquarters—the organ of supreme command under the emperor's direct control—was not at all concerned about the fate of Okinawa, nor about protecting the lives of its people. The morale of the 32nd Army was also low.

About two months prior to the 9th Infantry Division's departure for Taiwan, Naha was razed in the 10 October 1944 air raid. Horikawa Kyoyu was a first-year student at the Shuri No 2. Kokumin School at the time and watched the air raid from a spot near Shuri Castle. "U.S. warplanes circled the skies over Shuri Castle, then large numbers of them headed off to attack Naha. They were flying so low I could see the pilots' faces. Our soldiers could have shot them with their rifles . . . but they just hid and watched." It seemed as though the low sorties of the enemy planes caused some Japanese soldiers to lose their will to fight.

On that day, Okinawa was bombed five times from around 7:00 AM to early evening, with the attacks concentrating on Naha. According to U.S. military records, 1,396 carrier borne planes took part in the raids, dropping 541 tons of bombs and firing 652 rockets. In the fierce attacks, almost 90 percent of Naha was burned to the ground, with casualties throughout Okinawa totaling approximately 600 soldiers and civilians killed and around 900 wounded.

Tamaki Masakiyo was attached to the 32nd Army's Veterinary Unit and looked after Lt. Gen. Ushijima's horse. He remembers Ushijima's casual remark at the time of the 10 October air raid, "So they've finally come." That was the response of the man who was overall commander of the 32nd Army, which was charged with the defense of Okinawa. Moreover, on the previous evening, 9 October, ". . . all the divisional commanders and the Independent Brigade commanders attended a lively banquet held at the Okinawa Hotel in Tsuji, a district of Naha. After dinner, the staff officers all headed to an exclusive restaurant in the city center for another round of drinking."[23] Such behavior suggests that they felt little genuine commitment to defending Okinawa.

On 1 April 1945, the U.S. military landed on the main island of Okinawa and pushed south. Compared with the Japanese 32nd Army's force of around 86,400 officers and men, the U.S. 10th Army numbered approximately 238,700 officers and men. Moreover, while the American forces were able to spread out in all directions, the Japanese troops were confined to staying in caves where the atmosphere was one of impatience, fear, and hopelessness.

Disagreement about operational strategies had developed between Imperial Headquarters and the 10th Area Army on the one side, both supporting an all-out attack, and the 32nd Army on the other, which advocated a battle of attrition. The argument went back and forth, suggesting that Imperial Headquarters' idea of launching a "do-or-die miracle" attack would only increase the loss of life . . . bringing the debate back to the idea of a war of attrition.

Chinen Kiyoshi, a member of the Blood and Iron Student Corps, explained, the "final showdown" offensive strategy was attempted several times, but they could never make up for the overwhelming odds against them. The Japanese military's countermeasures using suicide attacks and night raids all failed. They

23. Yahara, H. 1995: 31.

were literally powerless and were forced to pull back time after time."

On 4 May, the 32nd Army launched its biggest counter-offensive. Adaniya Ken, the only commissioned officer from Okinawa with 32nd Army Headquarters, explained, "The plan was to defend the Shuri Castle line to the last man and, when we launched our all-out counter-offensive, we were pretty optimistic. In reality, however, the 62nd Infantry Division was almost completely wiped out in the attack and from then on we could barely deploy the remnants of the 24th Infantry Division." The 32nd Army was clearly headed for defeat, so the tension at the strategy meetings was only to be expected. The students from the Okinawa Normal School engaged in digging caves in the Field Construction Company were also fully aware of the situation.

One day, 20 meters of the passageway on either side of the strategy office inside the 32nd Army Headquarters shelter was blocked off while a military strategy meeting was held. Miyagi Kokichi, who was nearby because of his role as works overseer for the Fortifications Construction Unit, remembers, "It was around May because that was when the 62nd Infantry Division was wiped out. The meeting ran from around 10:00 AM right through to about 9:00 that evening. Then, at around 10:00 PM, I could hear one of our captains in a separate room phoning each unit and yelling out orders to them. For almost 40 minutes we could also hear him quite clearly on the phone saying, 'Unit ABC head for Ahacha! Unit DEF will repair the bridges you have to cross by such and such a time tomorrow morning, so Unit GHI will move out after that.'"

These comments provide a useful insight into how the 32nd Army was being forced into a corner by the Americans.

More than 1,100 students die in the name of "National Defense"

Many of the students drafted from almost all of the prefecture's middle schools and girls' schools died in the Battle of Okinawa. Boys aged between thirteen and eighteen years of age carrying improvised explosive devices hurled themselves at oncoming tanks, while exhausted young girls worked in dimly lit caves tending to the needs of wounded soldiers groaning in pain or delirium. We hope that this series of articles, based upon the testimony of survivors, will help people understand why those pure-hearted young people did not hesitate to make the ultimate sacrifice to "defend the homeland."

According to the "Account of Students in the IJA in the Battle of Okinawa" issued in 1959 by the Social Affairs Relief Division of the Government of the Ryukyu Islands, a total of 2,312 students were mobilized from sixteen middle schools and girls' schools. Almost half of that number, 1,105 young people, died in the battle.

Believing that Japan was a Divine and Immortal Land [*Shinshu Fumetsu*], these young people died certain that, however unfavorable the tide of war may have become, "a divine wind would come to save the day." These young boys and girls were prepared to sally forth from caves armed only with hand grenades to defend the homeland from an enemy whom they had been taught to regard as "American and British devils."

Sesoko Seiken, the sole survivor of the twenty-two boys from the Prefectural Fisheries School who joined signals corps units, explains the feelings of the boys: "We wanted to be of use to the country as quickly as we could. We were consumed by a burning desire to offer our lives in defense of the nation. We had no fear of death whatsoever. That is how we had been educated and we accepted this without question."

An unashamedly dark era commenced when the state required its citizens to hold "shared values." Education joined the media in falling into line, playing a key role in maintaining the tone of the times.

In 1938, with the issuing of the official report from the Vice Minister of Education regarding the Collective Labor Service, wartime structures began to encroach upon education. In 1941, the year that hostilities commenced with the United States and its Western allies, schools were affected first by the Outline for the Implementation of the Increase in Food Production by Students, then the Outline for the Mobilization of Students during Wartime, the Outline for Emergency Policies for Mobilization of Student Labor, and the Outline of the Implementation of Student Mobilization based on the Outline of Decisive War Emergency Measures. With this, student labor became an "important extension of education," and preparation for the last decisive struggle through education was complete.

Maeda Yoshimi, who worked in the Prefectural Academic Affairs Division back then, states, "When I look back on those days, I realize my inability to oppose the ideology thrust upon us. Educationalists were also swept along by the times." Nakayama Koshin, who was in the same division, recalls that "Everyone was brought up with the idea of protecting the country firmly in their minds and no one doubted it in the slightest. We weren't permitted to harbor any doubts. Anyone who questioned the way things were done would have been taken to task by the authorities for being 'unpatriotic.'"

Higa Tokutaro (then principal of the Prefectural Technical School) states that, "In those days, most principals considered that getting their students to work for the military was the best way to fulfill their professional responsibilities."

Military education teacher's memories

Onaga Jikei of Sobe, Naha, took up his position as a teacher of military education at the Second Prefectural Middle School in April 1944. It was his own former school where he had studied for five years from 1930, although things had changed greatly since his time there. The white summer uniform and the black attire for winter had changed to something in khaki made from rough natural yarn. Little did Onaga know that by this stage, in many respects, the whole of Japan was colored khaki.

"When I was a pupil at the Second Prefectural Middle School, Japanese society still enjoyed the vestiges of Taisho Democracy and we led peaceful and free lives. Military education was seen as just another subject." But things were very different in 1944. "Students were expected to 'Do their utmost for the country' . . . the attitude to everything had changed. We sensed that the war was about to affect us directly and that our fate hung in the balance."

The militaristic approach to life that had been the order of the day for some years by 1944 determined that the future of children would involve joining the military. For this reason, the pass certificate in military education meant so much more than it had during Onaga's time as a student.

"There were two levels of pass, which had an impact on what happened after someone joined the army. Those who managed a Type A pass were able to become officers after two years, but the Type B passes meant going only as far as corporal or sergeant." The type of pass was decided by the officer attached to the school, then reported to the headquarters of the regimental district where it would be recorded on the enlistment list.

Military education in schools commenced with the establishment of the School Regulation Law in 1886. In those days, it was nothing more than the inclusion of what was called "military gymnastics" in the gymnastics curriculum.

In 1917, however, the Special Teachers' Committee issued a "Recommendation for the Promotion of Military Gymnastics," and based on this, in 1925 the Ordinance for Appointing Serving Army Officers to Schools was promulgated and the military education syllabus was set. The next year, the Ordinance for Youth Training Centers was also put in place, which would extend as far as technical continuation schools.

This meant that the sound of army boots was now to be heard in schools, which were transformed into places for fostering thoughts of loyalty and patriotism. This kind of thinking reached its zenith in society in 1944, the year that Onaga became a military instructor.

There were four military instructors in the school, including Onaga, and above them there was an army officer attached to the school. Onaga recalls that "Military training was mainly infantry-related, so my artillery background meant that I was the odd one out. That both Regimental Headquarters and the school still asked me to instruct was an indication of how tight the personnel situation had become. The officer attached to us was also looking after the Normal School. Maybe they saw the Normal School as their main source of soldiers, I don't know, but he didn't spend much time with us, so I ended up being the main instructor."

During the classes they would have practical lessons such as learning how to use a rifle and learning drill, as well as subjects based on the infantry manual and the Imperial Rescript to Soldiers and Sailors. "Reading out the Imperial Rescript to Soldiers and Sailors would take a full 30 minutes, but passing the course without memorizing it wasn't possible."

The students spent most of their days constructing emplacements and shelters, but they still were serious about their studies. Every day they came in contact with regular soldiers and came to know what the army was about. "Until we joined a unit we had no idea that soldiers were physically hit as a matter of routine, so it was very different from what we had expected."

Because the emphasis was on whether or not the students possessed leadership ability, during unit training the teachers overseeing them kept a close eye on the disposition of each of the students. There was leadership training in squads in which the fifty students of one class were divided into three sub-groups, as well as when the entire class was handled as one platoon and then the whole year group as one company. "The issue was how well a student could get the group to do what he wanted it to do. The senior students had outdoor training too, with the key point being assessing the terrain around them really quickly and whether or not they could take appropriate action on that basis."

It was an age when scenes of groups of boys outside the school grounds with rifles following shouted commands were not regarded as out of place. Indeed in those days, most young boys thought such activities were something to be proud of.

Seeing the students going out every day as "volunteer labor," Onaga, in his role as military instructor, knew that the war was closing in on Okinawa. During his four and a half years in the army, he had participated in the landings at Mindanao and Borneo, had been surrounded and cut off in China, and had seen other units commit themselves to suicide charges at the enemy. These experiences led to him to suspect that these preparations "were not designed to create a base for an attack launched somewhere in the South Pacific." A development that clarified this beyond any doubt was the deployment of the 9th Division to Okinawa in July of 1944. "This was a unit made up of hardened soldiers who had been in Manchuria. They were an elite unit with their own Regimental Colors listing their battle honors. When these guys arrived in Okinawa I realized that something big was going to happen here." Before too long, the 9th Division would go on to be re-deployed to Taiwan, but by that stage it was clear to Onaga that the war was closing in on Okinawa.

Shortly after his appointment in April 1944, having worked for just a short time, he had to leave. "During the summer holidays that year, in preparation for introducing it as a subject in the curriculum in future, there was glider training for military instructors. A handling error by the pilot saw our glider drop straight into the ground from a height of 10 meters, breaking the glider in half and leaving me knocked out so badly that I was taken to hospital unconscious on a stretcher." The injury was so bad that it took one month for him to recover, so at the start of September, when he was recuperating at home, he was contacted by regimental headquarters to find out how he was. They said "You can walk now can't you?" and urged him to do some work for the Reservists Association. The principal of the Second Prefectural Middle School, Yamashiro Atsuo said, "Take your time recuperating. The school is responsible for you until you have made a full recovery," but regimental headquarters did not have the leeway to leave him be. As a military instructor with five months teaching behind him, he was sent back to the same workplace he had been after being discharged from his unit.

So in this job he would go around the towns and villages supervising early morning reservist training, plus out on the road he instructed students how to use bamboo spears and conduct bayonet drills. "There was an inspection of reservists, in which discharged soldiers and those who were yet to be called up would train for two or three hours each morning for two or three weeks at a time. This was designed to establish whether or not they were physically and mentally capable of enduring military service." The net was constantly being cast to see if the people behind the front lines were ready to be sent to fight.

Onaga remembers the end of January 1945. He was appointed unit commander for the Southern Area Home Guard newly formed at the First Prefectural Girls' School. Approximately 1,000 Home Guard recruits were called up from the southern area of the island with what was known as a "blue paper."

"The 'blue paper' was different from the 'red paper' in that there was a waiver available to the likes of doctors or policemen, people who were judged as essential in their workplaces or areas, but the degree of compulsion involved was the same. They all had to put on uniforms and were dispatched in accordance with the requirements of each unit. The main tasks were constructing fortifications and emplacements, digging out shelters and carrying ammunition. The 1,000 members of the Home Guard were allocated tasks based on a list that would be sent from 32nd Army Headquarters every day detailing the required numbers of people and the day's tasks.

In March that year, Onaga was sent to work with the Home Guard in Haneji. "It was designed to fill the gap left by the departure of soldiers from the 9th Division, but among the 1,000 Home Guard recruits only one third would have had some degree of military experience. We had fewer than twenty of the old Type 38 infantry rifles, one machine-gun and two grenade launchers. The only other weapons we had were bamboo spears." Armed in this manner, Onaga's group readied themselves for battle.

They launched two attacks aimed at infiltrating American lines. "I knew that we wouldn't get anywhere, but it was necessary to keep morale up. We went out just before dawn, and we pulled back immediately when their machine guns opened up." Only one member of their unit was killed.

Onaga was taken prisoner in November. He and other officers were given a room to themselves, but there was one officer, Capt. Murakami Haruo of the 3rd Guerrilla Unit, who stayed out in the barbed wire compound with the lower ranks. "He refused to eat 'food from the enemy,' cooked for himself, and spent his days without taking a bath offered by the enemy. He was a fine soldier. He turned down the chance to be discharged, saying that 'I'm not going anywhere until I find all the remains of my men and hold a memorial service for them.'"

It was not until several days after the end of the war that Onaga found out that the students of the Second Prefectural Middle School had been mobilized. In two minds about his own involvement in the army, Onaga says, "It's really hard to believe that those young boys were actually involved in combat."

CHAPTER 4

COMPULSORY MASS SUICIDE

Incidents of "mass suicide" represent the most tragic example of civilians suc-cumbing to the horrific pressures brought to bear on them during the Battle of Okinawa.[1] Apart from the many who took their own lives without being part of a group, there were approximately thirty cases of multiple suicides and fam-ily members killing loved ones, with the tragic escalation of panic and fear on Zamami-jima and Tokashiki-jima in late March claiming the lives of 234 and 329 people, respectively.[2] The majority of mass suicides occurred early in the battle and either involved direct coercion by the Imperial Japanese Army or their functionaries to prevent civilians being taken captive by the Americans, or indi-rectly by the fear of capture that had been instilled in civilians through contact with units of the Imperial Japanese Army. Many of the Japanese soldiers who had fought in China had told locals of the terrible excesses that had occurred during the fighting there and suggested that American troops would behave the same way towards any Okinawan civilians whom they captured. Fear of execution as "spies" by the Japanese forces also served to heighten the sense of despair among the civilians who, having failed to escape northwards, had been caught up in the merciless U.S. naval bombardment.[3] To most Okinawans being pushed south-ward by the American advance, death must have seemed an inevitable outcome. It is significant to note that in many cases, hand grenades distributed by the mil-itary or Home Guard provided the means to commit suicide or kill loved ones, but in addition, poison, razors, farm tools, knives, pieces of wood were used, and in some cases bedding was set alight to cause asphyxiation.

At a deeper level, since the Meiji period Okinawans had been educated to show total devotion to the emperor, and therefore to the nation, so their de-sire to obey military orders as though they had been given by the emperor him-self meant that any form of coercive message from the Imperial Japanese Army carried a weight far stronger than can be imagined in modern times. By April 1945, Okinawans had been so inculcated with the need to serve the emperor

---

1.   Ota Peace Research Institute. 2010: 3-4.
2.   Ienaga, S. 1978: 185.
3.   Aniya, M. 2007: 3.

that death at their own hands was preferred over surrender. The acceptance of *gunmin-ittaika* (that the military and civilians had a shared purpose and destiny) meant that it was only natural that civilians in close contact with the IJA would accept death at a time and manner decided by the military.

The most famous cases of mass suicide occurred on Tokashiki and Zamami and in Chibichiri-gama in Yomitan. Comment from a survivor of the tragedy at Chibichiri-gama is covered within this work.

The cases at Chibichiri-gama and the nearby Shimuku-gama in Yomitan that occurred in the first few days of April 1945, directly after the landing by U.S. forces, provide a clear contrast in terms of how panic and fear could lead to mass suicide or be mollified to avoid a tragedy.[4] At Chibichiri-gama, the worst-case scenario occurred, with eighty-three people of 140 in the cave committing suicide or being killed by panic-stricken family members.[5] However, at Shimuku-gama, a huge cave located less than one kilometer away from Chibichiri-gama, the lives of over 1,000 people were saved because two local men who had returned to Okinawa after living in Hawaii persuaded the terrified locals that the Americans would not commit atrocities against them.[6]

The degree of compulsion from the Japanese military on local people who either took their own lives or killed family members became an issue of national significance when in 2007 the Ministry of Education ordered the amendment of passages in several history textbooks stating that coercion by the military was behind the mass suicides during the Battle of Okinawa. The references to the Imperial Japanese Army driving civilians to commit suicide were subsequently reinstated, but in some cases using less forthright terms. This will no doubt be an ongoing issue.[7]

It is important to understand the background of the widely used Japanese expression *shudan-jiketsu*, which was originally used to imply that the acts of suicide were self-determined and spontaneous.[8] From 1953, the Relief Law, officially known as *The Relief Law for Individuals and Survivors of Individuals Killed or Wounded at War*, came to be applied to grant pensions to Okinawan civilians judged to have been killed or wounded while either cooperating or participating in some way in the combat activities of the Imperial Japanese Army. People who

---

4. Hayashi, H. 2001: 158.
5. *Gama—Okinawa-senseki Bukku*. 2009: 31-32.
6. *Okinawa no senso iseki*. 2008: 15.
7. McCormack, G., & Norimatsu, S. 2012: 31-32.
8. Aniya, M. 2007:7.

had been infants when their parents died during the battle became eligible to apply for bereaved family pensions, so the tone of the Relief Law encouraged a perception that defining war deaths as having occurred for the sake of the nation matched the logic of the law. It is suggested that this in turn helped lend momentum to the use of the expression *shudan-jiketsu*, and contributed to perverting the stance on historical records of the civilian experience of the battle.

Compulsory mass suicide in the Kerama Islands

The more ghastly someone's experiences of war are, the harder it is to talk about them. In the Battle of Okinawa the Kerama Islands became known as the "islands of tragedy," and people who witnessed the *shudan jiketsu* or compulsory mass suicide there have been reluctant to talk about what happened. It is claimed that a total of between 600 and 700 civilians took their own lives, and the memories of that living hell of all those years ago are still vivid in the minds of the survivors.

Kinjo Shigeaki, a professor at Okinawa Christian Junior College explained, "It took me more than twenty years before I felt able to talk about it." He was there when his own mother, younger sister and brother were among those who took their own lives on Tokashiki-jima. The war occurred in abnormal times and, when normality returned to society following Japan's defeat, the realization of what had happened brought enormous pain for Kinjo Shigeaki. He spoke of the "victims of policies for subordinating people to the emperor," and talked to us about what happened back then.

On the 23 March 1945, in contrast to what the IJA had expected to happen, American forces commenced their attack on the Kerama Islands. Three days later, on the 27th, they landed on Tokashiki. Stationed on the island at that time were 104 men of Japan's 3rd Special Boat Battalion, under the command of Capt. Akamatsu Yoshitsugu. The unit was equipped with 100 special attack speedboats, known as *Maru-re*. Each craft was manned by one person, weighed one ton and carried a 250 kg depth charge at the stern. The idea was to get close to an enemy ship and attack it from the stern by launching the depth charge under the vessel. The Japanese military had high hopes of what the unit could achieve, but in the end none of these special craft ever put to sea on an actual mission. In order to maintain secrecy over the scheme, they were all destroyed and the role of the 3rd Special Boat Battalion finished before it really started.

Kinjo had just turned sixteen. His family comprised both parents, an elder brother aged nineteen, a sister aged ten and a younger brother aged six. His eldest brother was away working somewhere far south of Okinawa. On 27 March, the date of the American landing on Tokashiki, Kinjo's family and the other civilians in Aharen Ward were ordered to move to Tokashiki Ward. "By this stage, the civilian population was beginning to feel that their fate was intrinsically linked with that of the soldiers," Kinjo commented.

"As far as we civilians were concerned, we thought that we had the soldiers to protect us, and if the worst came to the worst, we were prepared to share their fate. From the army's point of view, if the civilians were scattered all over the place, they thought that we may end up cooperating with the enemy. As a result, they felt that it was better to keep us all together in one place." To start with, Kinjo's family was opposed to the order to move because they thought that if they were going to die, they wanted to die in their home villages. But in the end, they decided to go with the others out of fear of being the only family left alive.

They headed away at night and were caught in a torrential rainstorm. As they were lashed by the pouring rain, they were constantly on the alert for enemy soldiers. Even now Kinjo remembers the flashing red trail of American tracer rounds as they zipped across the pitch-dark sky. Some of the group slipped on the muddy mountain track and fell down to the valley floor, their pitiful calls ringing out as they rolled down the slopes. Although Kinjo stayed awake all night in the assembly area near the IJA base, he has no recollection of how he passed the time. All he can remember is that he was soaked to the skin from the rain, but that he didn't care. It was a night of anxiety. Kinjo explained, "We saw the grim reaper in our mind's eye and believed that death was the only possible outcome for us." As dawn broke, civilians all over the valley were herded into a single area. A terrible chapter of history of the Kerama Islands was about to unfold.

Everybody was resigned to the fact they were going to die. But even so, Kinjo clearly remembers that the women did up their hair and tidied themselves. On the morning of the 28th, civilians from every corner of the valley were gathered together. It is thought that there were between 700 and 1,000 of them there. "I can't remember how long it was after we were all rounded up. Maybe it was a few minutes . . . maybe it was few hours." That was when the order for mass suicide came. The Home Guard soldiers had about thirty hand grenades. As soon as the order for the mass suicide was given, the sound of grenades exploding one after the other from within groups of people gathered in circles could be heard. However, not only were the grenades available never going to be enough for all the people gathered there to kill themselves, many of the grenades were duds. This led to an even greater tragedy.

Probably because they were startled by the explosions of the grenades, the American attack began immediately, and the pandemonium escalated to total chaos. Kinjo was all but knocked out by the shockwave of a grenade which just missed him as it was hurled in. Stunned by the blast, he pinched himself to see if he was still alive. Then, as he gradually regained consciousness, he was aware of something bizarre taking place before his very eyes. The man who had once been ward chairman of Aharen Ward was frantically tearing a branch off a tree. His eyes still not focusing properly, Kinjo watched the man's odd behavior but was astounded by what happened next. The man used the branch as a murder weapon to bash his own wife and child to death. "That bizarre, suicidal environment had turned him into a madman."

Those people who had not been able to take their own lives with grenades were worried about being left alive. They had to find other ways to kill themselves, and the former ward chairman's behavior had set the example. Some used scythes and razor blades to slash themselves, while others strangled themselves with lengths of rope. As the mayhem unfolded, they found all sorts of ways to kill, included bashing others to death with rocks and sticks. Men bashed their wives and parents bashed their children, young people killed the elderly and the strong killed the weak. What they all felt in common was the belief that they were doing this out of love and compassion. Before they knew it, Kinjo's father became separated from the rest of the family and they never found out where he died.

Kinjo and his elder brother also had to fulfill their role. Everything that was happening around them made them understand that they had to carry out their duty as well. Kinjo said, "I think it was our mother we hit first." As he and his brother began bashing her in the head, Kinjo screamed out until she became a blur through the tears flowing from his own eyes. For the first time in his life he wept uncontrollably. "I have never wailed like that since," Kinjo explained.

The brothers used sticks to rain blow after blow on their mother. Watching her from behind as their pounding sent her step by step toward her death is still a vivid image in Kinjo's mind. However, he has no recollection of what he did to his sister and brother after that. They were constantly afraid of being left alive and, after killing his entire family, one distant relative tried to take his own life by hanging himself from a tree. He failed, however, and just wandered around aimlessly for quite some time as though he was sleepwalking. Eventually, he was shot and killed by American soldiers at the bottom of the hill.

The place where those people who lost their lives in so many ghastly ways was filled with corpses. Blood ran into the stream below, staining the water red for days on end. Although they knew they were about to die, it was the thought that they were sharing their fate with the military that drove them to take their own lives. Therefore, when the order to commit suicide was given, everybody naturally assumed that it was because the soldiers must have all been killed already.

The insane mass suicide was almost over but they could still hear the groans of those who were not quite dead. They heard one person who could barely manage to call out his last request of, "Finish me off." Kinjo was both afraid and worried about being the last one left alive. "Who was now going to kill whom?" His mother, sister and brother were already dead, and he and his elder brother now had to decide which of them would be next. As they were discussing it, two people from the same year at elementary school on Maejima stepped in between them and said, "Look, if we're going to die, let's die attacking the Americans."

They had no idea what might befall them if they were taken prisoner. Maybe they chose the ghastly option of mass suicide in order to escape that panic and fear, or thought that to go out and launch a suicidal attack against the Americans would be best way to die. "As the last living citizens of the Empire, we thought that we each had to take an enemy soldier with us when we died. With that, we agreed on an infiltration attack, challenging ourselves to an even more frightening death. For whatever reason, two sixth grade elementary school girls joined them." Five others aged between twelve and nineteen also found themselves included in the infiltration squad, armed only with sticks. It goes without saying that the children in that attack group, going out to take on American soldiers with their bare hands, had no military objective in mind. As he wandered aimlessly about, Kinjo was stunned to see that the first living person he came across was a Japanese soldier.

Kinjo said, "I just couldn't believe it. We'd chosen to take our own lives because we thought they were all dead. That was when our sense of solidarity with the military came crashing down around us." Then the soldier added insult to injury when he said, "You civilians are over there." Kinjo explained, "Group suicide was the ultimate display of our solidarity with the military and our sense of unity with the people of the Empire of Japan." Kinjo's shock was even worse as he realized that his sense of solidarity and national unity had been mere illusions. Thereafter, he and the others lived in the hills until they became prisoners of war, but not once did he ever feel glad to have survived. "All I did was stay alive in preparation for dying. All hope that any members of my family might still be alive was gone. In that atmosphere of total despondency, we just looked after ourselves and took it easy as best we could."

After the war, Kinjo suffered horribly from feelings of guilt. His terrible anguish grew ever deeper once he was freed from the abnormal psyche of war and rediscovered the person he had once been. "I was the biggest victim of those policies designed to make people subservient to the emperor and what he stood for. Growing up as a naïve boy of sixteen, I never questioned what was going on." While discovering Christianity finally set his soul free, it was still more than twenty years before he was able to talk with anyone about his truly horrific experiences. Kinjo gave three reasons for the mass suicide: the ideology of obedience to the emperor, the presence of the Imperial Japanese Army, and being on an island some distance from the mainland with no means of escape. "Back in those days of 100 million Japanese citizens supposedly being prepared to fight to the very last man, everybody was prepared for death. The doctrine of total obedience to the emperor emphasized death and made light of life. The willingness to die for the emperor on a faraway island resulted in a whole new sense of identity for them."

Three hundred and twenty-nine people are believed to have died in the compulsory mass suicide on Tokashiki-jima. According to the Defense Agency's archives section, twenty-one of the 104 men stationed on the island as part of 3rd Special Boat Battalion died, as did thirty-eight of the 161 men of 3rd Battalion's base unit. Furthermore, the only official record of the men press-ganged in Korea and brought to join the Marine Labor Corps is listed as "fate unknown." In Okinawa, civilians were executed by the military on suspicion of spying for the enemy, and there were also incidents of massacres of Korean military laborers. Kinjo commented, "War turns normal human beings into savages."

Incidents of Group Suicide during Battle of Okinawa

Region	Location	Date	Those involved	Method	Number
Ie-jima	Ahaja-gama	22 April	Civilians and Home Guard	IED from Home Guard	Approx. 100
	Sandata shelter	Around 20 April	Civilians and regular soldiers	IED and hand grenades	More than 50
	Tabaku-gama	Around 16-20 April	Civilians (Chinen family)	Dynamite	5
	Cave	Around 16-20 April	Civilians (Oshiro family)	IED	47
	Gusukuyama fortifications	21 April	Women	Explosives	6
	Tiigishi shelter	23 April	Civilians and regular soldiers	Explosives	22
		April	Civilians	Explosives	2
Onna-son	Afuso (Shitakachaa)	6 April	Civilians	Hand grenades	11
Yomitan-son	Chibichiri-gama	2 April	Civilians from Namihira	Suffocation from smoke and injection of poison	83
	Namihira air raid shelter	1 April	Civilians from Namihira	Hand grenades	14
	Sobe Kuragaa shelter	1 April	Civilians	Drowning	8
	Nagata	1 April	Civilians	Hand grenades	2
	Iramina Kunii shelter	3 April	Civilians	Hand grenades	14
Okinawa City	Misato	Early April	Residents of Misato Hamlet	Burned, stabbed or slashed to death	33
	Misato	Early April	Refugees from Naha	Burned, stabbed or slashed to death	Approx. 30

Incidents of Group Suicide during Battle of Okinawa

Region	Location	Date	Those involved	Method	Number
Uruma City	Gushikawa Castle shelter	4 April	Local young people	Hand grenades	14
Chatan Town	Heianyama Emplacement (Ukamajii shelter)	1-2 April	Women's Volunteer Corps	Hand grenades	17
Itoman City	Komesu Kamintou shelter	2 June			
	Maezeto				2
	Kanegusuku			Hand grenades	2
	Arasaki Coast	21 June	Himeyuri girls	Hand grenades	14
	Kyan, Gushikawa Castle remains	Unknown	Family of refugees	Poison	4
	Ahagon	11 June	Young woman	Hand grenade	1
	Unknown				18
Nanjo City	Itokazu Cave (Umaakueeabu)	3 June	Civilians	Hand grenades	9
			Family of Itokazu residents	Unknown	3
	Maekawa air raid shelter	30 May	Civilians	Hand grenades	7
Zamami Village	Zamami-jima	26 March	Civilians	Hand grenades, razors, poison	234
	Geruma-jima	26 March	Civilians	Hand grenades etc.	53
	Yakabi-jima	26 March	Civilians	Hand grenades	Approx. 10
Tokashiki Village	Tokashiki-jima	28 March	Civilians	Hand grenades etc.	329

Induction ceremony

It was the evening of 31 March 1945, less than a day before the American forces landed on the main island of Okinawa. In the area in front of the Ryukon shelter dug out within the grounds of Shuri Castle, a graduation ceremony for the students of the Okinawa Normal School was held, followed immediately by an induction ceremony into the ranks of the IJA.

School principal, Noda Sadao, addressed them saying, "We certify that all students have completed the requirements to progress from their current year of study and therefore graduate." The ceremony took just a couple of minutes.

As soon as the students were deemed as having graduated, the ceremony changed to one of induction into the IJA. Major Komaba advised the boys standing in ranks that "The staff and students of the Okinawa Normal School have been called up for service in the Blood and Iron Student Corps. The enemy will soon land upon these shores. You must give your all to defend the homeland." With this, the Blood and Iron Student Corps was formed.

The 386 staff and students of the Normal School Boys' Division were assigned to the 32nd Army Command Post Blood and Iron Student Corps Headquarters (16), the Chihaya Unit (22), the Infiltration Unit (57), the Special Company (48) and the No. 2 Field Fortifications Construction Unit (243). All of the students were given the rank of private second class.

"I wonder if there is any way that their lives can be saved, even by getting them to flee somehow?" thought Normal School teacher Miyagi Kokichi, his heart aching as he watched his students being handed their army uniforms.

A supervisor of the students' efforts to dig shelters, Miyagi has never been able to forget the scene of those young boys working assiduously "for the sake of the nation."

"We left the boys to dig as they saw fit. We didn't really give them any instructions. They gave their all without having to be told what to do. Not one of them slackened off and that made me worry even more about them."

It was as though the teachings of military education had seeped into the very marrow of their bones. In poorly fitting uniforms, some outrageously large on the boys, they were all totally committed to doing their bit to defend the nation.

"I thought that the stage was set for me to give my life for my country," said Chinen Kiyoshi, who was assigned to an infiltration unit. "I think all of us felt that way. I was afraid, but the education of the day had taken over. The militarist education had affected every sinew of my body."

In keeping with the orders they had been given, some attempted to break through the front line and others tried to infiltrate enemy encampments. Two hundred and twenty four of the 386 boys conscripted were killed in action.

The landings

Early in the morning of 1 April 1945, a fleet of 1,300 vessels landed American forces onto the beaches at Chatan and Yomitan on either side of the mouth of the Hija River on the west side of central Okinawa, signaling the start of fierce fighting that would last three months.

The IJA unit that faced them was known as the Gaya Detachment, named after its commanding officer, Lt. Col. Gaya Kokichi. It was deployed ahead of the main defenses to fight in isolation, and by 6 April was deemed to have completed its mission. By that stage, it had lost six officers and 232 soldiers of other ranks.

A youth unit comprising local children under eighteen years of age was assisting the Gaya Detachment. "We were attached to the Murakami Unit, and the duty for the boys was to carry ammunition, while the girls were to help the nurses," said Yagi Seiei, who was then seventeen years old. The fourteen or fifteen people in this youth unit had been thrown together one day after an order was suddenly given for them to assemble.

"Cpl. Murakami, a wild character to say the least, was in charge of the unit. It was a light machine-gun squad made up of about twenty men." Before the youth unit was organized, Yagi had been drafted into an agricultural unit and sent to the Ginowan Agricultural School. From there, he went to work for a family that was struggling to get all the jobs done on its farm because they had a son fighting at the front. "There was a Japanese flag flying from a pole in the middle of the fields, and every day we worked on the land. Maybe for about two months . . . our job was to carry ammunition from a shelter about 200 or 300 meters from an emplacement set up on high ground. Normally we spent time in the local civilian shelter before going out at night to do our shift carrying the ammunition." At that stage, in Kiyuna where they were, each family had dug its own shelter, and for a while he spent time in one of those. However, when the air raids increased in intensity they decided that the family-made shelters were not safe enough, so they moved to the five caves in the area. The sea in front of Chatan was full of warships which had been there for about four or five days before the American landings, so Yagi was close enough to sense that the landings could happen any day. The shelter where the gun emplacement was located is in what is now Camp Zukeran, and has a panoramic view of the Chatan coastline. "On the evening of 31 March, I'd just gone on duty," said Yagi. Early the next morning, the vessels out at sea started to move toward the beaches. "Cpl. Murakami watched this through his binoculars and after checking his watch shouted 'Landing commences at 6:48 AM!'"

According to various books on the Battle of Okinawa, the American forces landed at 8:30 AM, but Yagi says, "There is no mistaking the fact that it was 6:48 AM. The corporal checked his own watch and then shouted out for someone to check the time. The position of the sun in the sky also meant that it couldn't have been after 8:00 AM," insists Yagi.

He describes the landings as follows. "In those days there were railway tracks running between the coastline at Chatan and the prefectural road [now Route 58]. The unmanned Chatan Railway Station was located centrally between the two of these. There were smaller roads branching off from the railway station, one going along the prefectural road and the other connecting the prefectural road with the coastline. The landings started with three amphibious tanks in the vanguard and behind them waves of troops came ashore from the warships sitting off the coast. The three tanks took the narrow road toward the main prefectural road, where one turned toward Naha, one toward Nago and one headed for Zukeran."

When the American troops first came ashore they expected to come under fire so they immediately took cover, but they relaxed and started to walk around when they realized that no one was shooting at them. "They marched along the nearby riverside, just like the Imperial Army used to do," said Yagi. That day, when Cpl. Murakami heard that American forces had entered the settlement of Aniya, he flew into a rage and said that the unit would launch an infiltration raid on the enemy.

On the night of 1 April, after having waited in a shelter with ammunition ready to carry, Yagi was ordered to go to a fortified shelter. Just when he got to the area below the plateau where the position was, the ground was shaken by the force of a direct hit on the very position he was heading for. He scrambled up to the emplacement but there was nothing left, just bloodied pieces of uniform on the remaining wooden supports of what had been the shelter. "The guys who had been killed were a lance corporal and a first-year recruit. I'm pretty sure that I'd heard that the young soldier was from Shikiya in Chinen," said Yagi. The lance corporal had been firing his machine gun and the young guy had been beside him feeding in the ammunition belt.

Yagi hurried back to the shelter where he'd been waiting before he went out to carry the ammunition, and when his duty shift ended for the day he was relieved and returned to the shelter for local civilians.

On the evening of 2 April, when Arakaki was on his way to the cave where they used to wait for orders to carry ammunition, he quickly hid himself when he heard a noise from the field beside where they were walking. A few moments later he heard people talking. It sounded like there were two people there, one speaking in a loud voice and the other in much quieter tones. He listened hard to pick up what they were saying and could tell that they were speaking in the Okinawan dialect, both talking about a noise that they had heard from the field. Yagi joined in, saying that it was probably the enemy that they had just heard. "I'd say that the enemy heard them talking," said Yagi, because in just a short time, bullets rained in on them as they scurried back to the local civilians' shelter.

"The American soldiers had dug a hole in the field and were hiding there," said Arakaki Masahiro, another member of the youth unit who was there helping the Murakami Unit. The boys in the youth unit were divided into two sections with Yagi and Arakaki being in separate groups. For that reason, Arakaki was to head for the civilian shelter to change with Yagi's group on the evening of 1 April.

"I remember hearing a strange sound from the middle of the field, so I headed back to the shelter. I heard later that American soldiers had been hiding in that field so turning back probably saved my life."

For this reason, on the evening of 2 April, the day after the U.S. forces landed, Arakaki went to the shelter to await his orders. It was there that he received a wound to his left thigh. "We were standing in a line, one behind the other, a young recruit called Teruya at the front, then LCpl. Sakuma and me, when a shell landed right in front of us. Teruya and Sakuma were killed instantly and I was hit in the left thigh." Just moments before that, another young soldier called Shimabukuro had been killed when a piece of shrapnel hit him in the chest.

Dragging his wounded leg, Arakaki headed for the shelter at Nodake. On 4 April, he was taken prisoner and put into a camp at Chatan. "The camp was within what used to be the Hamby Airfield, but many of the people there died, so they dug large pits with caterpillar tractors and buried them.

Yagi said that at around noon on 3 April, a second generation Japanese-American came to the shelter where the local people had sought refuge and persuaded Yagi to surrender together with about 250 other civilians.

The cave that the Murakami Unit operated from, and the civilian shelter at Kiyuna, are now inside Camp Zukeran. Yagi and Arakaki guided me to where I could see them through the wire. There is a tomb across from the base and the road. Yagi said, "I remember some American soldiers cooking food where that tomb is." The tomb was only a very short distance from where we were stand-ing, so the shelter was obviously very close to where the American soldiers were cooking. Almost all of the locations that they talked about are now inside Camp Zukeran.

"The young recruits Teruya and Shimabukuro were killed right in front of me; all I know is their surnames so there's nothing I can really do to link to any-one with just that. The families are probably searching for information about them too . . . In those days new recruits in their first year of service were treated just like any other soldier. They were older than me and I was afraid of them, so I never had a chance to ask their first names. I of course wish that I had . . . "

Yagi, who witnessed the American forces landing, said, "The U.S. fleet out there was just huge. The scale of their flotilla meant that the result of battle was never in doubt."

On 1 April, the American forces landed with no losses, and before the end of that day had occupied the northern (Yomitan) and central (Kadena) airfields and issued Proclamation No. 1 (The Nimitz Proclamation) to set up the U.S. Military Government in Yomitan.

Defensive fortifications in Ginowan

The location is now within the boundaries of an American base and as such is off limits to anyone not connected to the U.S. military. The remains of twelve soldiers are still inside the United States Marine Corps [USMC] Air Station at Futenma. Futenma Air Station in Ginowan, to the east of the Chatan area. On 1 April 1945, on some slightly higher ground where there are now lines of houses, a company of soldiers of the 62nd Infantry Division was wiped out.

"The actual exchange of fire was over very quickly, maybe in fifteen minutes. Lt. Kawasaki's company was equipped with heavy machine guns but they had no chance when the Americans used accurate mortar fire against them," said In-amine Masahiro who witnessed the last moments of Kawasaki and his men.

Inamine was eighteen years old at the time and was living about 500 meters from where Kawasaki's men had set up their position. He said, "Twenty-five of them, including their commander, had been stationed there from the previous year. There were six Okinawan recruits among them. My elder brother had just been conscripted so I had a good idea of what their circumstances were. I used to take them sugar and potatoes so I mixed with them regularly."

When everyone realized that the fighting in Okinawa was not far away, the company started to construct pillboxes and machine gun nests, and Inamine helped them with their work. They built six such positions to house machine guns, each of which was dug out to create between 6 and 7 square meters inside strengthened with a wooden frame and camouflaged with pine trees.

On 1 April 1945, after an unopposed landing, American forces soon advanced as far as the position held by Lt. Kawasaki and his men. U.S. warplanes filled the skies, and fighting commenced in the area around the Futenma River. Inamine had been asked the previous day to help carry ammunition for them, so he was with Kawasaki's men at this time. Lt. Kawasaki was killed instantly that day, 31 March, when a naval shell landed right beside him. The remaining twenty-four men were divided into groups of four in the six machine gun positions where they waited for the enemy to approach. There was one Okinawan recruit in each of the positions. When he was handing ammunition to the soldiers operating the machine gun in his position one of the men suddenly said to him, "Morihiro, it's getting dangerous, let's get out of here!" Their position took a direct hit just seconds later and he was thrown through the air. "I was in a daze from then on. I don't know how I got down the 20-meter slope beside our position. That evening I went back to have a look, but it was an awful sight." The next day, 2 April, Inamine took his cousins aged five and two years old to a shelter at Futenma Shrine, where they were found and taken captive by the Americans.

In the early 1960s, when the American forces were constructing a building on the base, they found three shelters with the remains of Japanese soldiers inside. They found the bones of Tonaki Kosei, with whom Inamine was on particularly friendly terms, and interred them in the Nodaka Cemetery. However, the remains of Kishimoto from Nago, Uehara from Itoman, and a man from Sashiki-cho [now Nanjo City] whose shop was named Agari Chinen, plus those of the other Okinawan recruits, are still on the other side of the base fence.

"This unit was made up mainly of veterans who had fought in China. They often spoke of how they expected to die in Okinawa. They even asked us to look after their remains after the battle was over. When I think of this, I'm really eager to try to do something to recover them. Ten years ago, around 1973, I made a request to the Ministry of Health and Welfare but never heard back. If I could go in and dig for myself I certainly would," said Inamine somberly.

CHAPTER 5

STUDENT SOLDIERS

A s the Battle of Okinawa loomed, male middle school students over the age of fourteen were conscripted into either the Blood and Iron Students Corps or the signals corps of various infantry and artillery units. There were nine schools on the main island of Okinawa from where upward of 2,000 boys were conscripted.[1] Those schools were, in order of the number of boys conscripted, the Okinawa Normal School (386),[2] the Third Prefectural Middle School (363), the Second Prefectural Middle School (270), the First Prefectural Middle School (254), the Prefectural Technical School (134), Naha Municipal Commercial School (117), the Prefectural Agricultural and Forestry School (130), one private school, Kainan Middle School (81)[3] and the Prefectural Fisheries School (48). Half of the boys conscripted were killed during the battle.[4]

In terms of duties, the younger boys among the new privates second-class in the Blood and Iron Students Corps were initially allocated to signals units or worked digging shelters, carrying ammunition or food supplies, but before long were often given the extremely dangerous tasks of crawling out into the field to reconnect communication wires or running messages from one shelter to another.[5] Many older boys were required to actually take part in combat, sometimes on suicide missions to destroy enemy tanks with improvised explosive devices tied to their bodies.

Okinawa First Prefectural Middle School Blood and Iron Student Corps

The American naval artillery booming away ominously in the distance showed no signs of letting up. As evening set in, close to 100 students had gathered in the central garden of the Yoshu Dormitory. One of those students was Higa Shigeto-mo who had heard from a friend just the previous evening that their graduation

---

1.   Oshiro, M. 2008: 76.
2.   Ota, M. 2000: 252-283.
3.   Hayashi, H. 2010: 158.
4.   Okinawa Heiwa Network. 2008: 59.
5.   Hayashi, H. 2001: 122.

ceremony was being held. At the time, Higa was a fourth grader at the Okinawa First Prefectural Middle School.

With the passing of the Outline for Emergency Policies for Mobilization of Student Labor the previous year, Higa's five-year study program had been shortened by a year and the graduation ceremony had been moved up to the evening of 27 March 1945. For the students attending the solemn graduation ceremony, the bombardment that shook the very ground they stood on made them all the more tense.

The Yoshu Dormitory had been built five years earlier to commemorate the fiftieth anniversary of the establishment of the boarding school. On an elevated section of ground in the central garden, Principal Fujino Norio and a number of his staff members were lined up with their backs to the dormitory. With them were the special guests, the Governor of Okinawa Shimada Akira and Lt. Col. Sano Yoshito from the 5th Artillery Command.

Directly facing them were the fourth and fifth-year students lined up in rows. A single lamp flickered faintly between the students and the staff, who looked like dolls on a tiered stand. But however it might have seemed, the fact that several fifth-year students stood on one side of the lamp to prevent it from being seen from where the American ships were lying offshore made it painfully clear that they were in a war zone. The light of the lamp was very faint, but it was enough to show the strained looks on the faces of the teachers and students.

Higa is not quite sure whether it was just before the graduation ceremony or during it, but in contrast to the naval shells that had been falling in the distance, suddenly one landed with a resounding "thump" near to where they were all standing. But just as he thought, "Let's get out of here," an angry voice boomed out across the school ground. "Don't move! Nobody is to move!" It was Lt. Shinohara Yasushi, the officer attached to the school.

"All I can say is that the effect of Shinohara's order was quite amazing. The officials and the students were all trembling but, when they tried to move, the immediate and thunderous roar from the lieutenant meant that nobody moved a muscle, not even the governor. By the time the ceremony was over, I think that two, maybe three more shells had landed almost on top of us, but not a single soul had moved." Shinohara tried to appear calm and composed throughout the whole ordeal, but he was clearly nervous as well. When he introduced Lt. Col. Sano, he mistakenly said, "From now on, you are under the command of *Mr. Colonel* Sano." He obviously didn't realize what he had said as he made no attempt to correct himself at any stage. There was quite a large group, including Principal

Fujino, standing on the raised area but Higa recalls little of what they said. In fact the only thing he remembers is how impressed he was when Governor Shimada said, "This graduation ceremony is the most important one in the whole of Japan." But Higa was disappointed to learn after the war that he had said the same thing at every school graduation.

Higa started at the Okinawa First Prefectural Middle School in 1941 when the mood of the times was clearly reflected throughout the school. "In my first year," recalled Higa, "there was the 'Tomikawa Kiyoshi incident' and in my third year it was 'Be like Captain Omasu—the senior boys' war hero.'" Tomikawa Kiyoshi was a boy known as the top student of the First Prefectural Middle School. He was accepted into both the Faculty of Arts of the First Higher School [now Tokyo University] and the Imperial Japanese Army Academy but in the end decided to go to the First Higher School. The army officer attached to the school was so enraged at Tomikawa's decision that he canceled all of the First Middle School's passing grades into the academy. The issue was even taken up in the newspapers. It was a time when the media played a major role in influencing public opinion on issues such as the army being able to control an individual's future.

"When I started school under Principal Goya Chosho, the atmosphere was quite free and relaxed, reflecting the Taisho democracy that was still in vogue there. However, when Principal Fujino replaced him in July 1942, wearing our military caps to school and militarist education were strictly enforced," explained Higa. Then in 1943, Capt. Omasu Matsuichi, a former student of the First Prefectural Middle School and the Military Training Academy, was killed in the fighting at Guadalcanal. When he was awarded the highest personal citation for gallantry, "Be like Captain Omasu" became a fanatical call to arms. The "Legend of Captain Omasu" appeared in the *Okinawa Shimpo*, with teachers Tabata Isson doing the research and Ono Shigeo writing the article. In 1943, in the growing mood of militarist austerity the Naminoue Festival was canceled. "We young boys had very few opportunities for contact with girls, so it was really unfortunate that they called off the festival," recalled Higa, his face still showing the disappointment he felt about that decision decades earlier.

In 1944, Higa's course of study was cut short because of the implementation of the Emergency Student Mobilization Outline. "My father read about it in the paper and when he told me I was really shocked. I thought I still had two years to enjoy at school but now I had only one. The thought of becoming a soldier after that didn't appeal." There was a feeling of antagonism between Higa's fourth-year group and the year-five students that started shortly after the new academic year began in 1944. The trouble started when year-four students were called over by the year-five group to walk the "gauntlet of fists," an annual middle school ritual at the time. The year-four students responded by telling the fifth-year boys, "We're graduating at the same time as you so we demand to be treated the same as you," and they all boycotted classes for three days. "I just followed the others but I definitely agreed with them." Each morning they would gather on the embankment next to the tennis court, refusing to go to class even when the principal called them in.

Their demands were met, maybe because of the hard line they had taken. "There was a huge difference between going out into society after experiencing the senior year at school, and missing out on that year. I don't know whether they took into account the combined graduation, or whether the decision was made by the school after considering the various relevant authorities and the declining number of year-five students due to those moving on to the Naval Aviator Preparatory Course. However, while they did agree to our demands, it certainly didn't mean that we were treated like equals right away. That one year's seniority was just so important under the old system."

Most classes were canceled and the boys' days were given over to working on the airfields and emplacements. The war was obviously not going well. The following summer, after the fall of Saipan, Higa was in the schoolyard of the Prefectural Technical School listening to Lt. Gen. Watanabe Masao, who was then commander of the 32nd Army. Watanabe was giving instructions to the crowd assembled in front of him, including students from the First Prefectural Middle School, the Technical School, the Normal School and the Youth School, together with members of Shuri's civilian population.

The commander seemed to be concentrating his whole body and soul on the message. "Soldiers and civilians alike must work together, more than ever, and take on the enemy." He was almost yelling. "There is no doubt that the enemy will land in Okinawa," he continued, "and, when that happens, every civilian must share the same fate as our soldiers, so I am asking you to be ready to die a glorious death in the name of the emperor." Higa was amazed at the sight of Watanabe imploring his audience, tears in his eyes, as he screamed and thumped the desk in front of him. Having always believed that Japan was simply winning one battle after another, Higa was also amazed to hear one of the military's highest ranking officers speak in terms which meant only one thing: defeat for Japan.

The unexpected reduction in the length of Higa's course of study meant he had only one year left at school. Keen to get the most out of the time remaining, he immersed himself in music. Of course, he only played songs popular at the time, describing it as a way of "holding on to my fleeting youth." One of his classmates, Kuwae Ken, was really enthusiastic and went over to Higa's house almost every day. For some reason, he seemed to collect every available record, one after the other. Snacking on brown sugar, he became almost intoxicated as he sensed himself sliding into the unknown of an adult world.

In January 1945, the meeting at which Shuri's tripartite Student Council Group [the Sanseikai] would be dissolved, was held at Higa's house. Somebody took some *awamori* along to the meeting, which naturally became very noisy and of course the popular songs were soon playing on the gramophone.

There was an army unit stationed near Higa's house, with a sentry on duty. From inside the house, they could suddenly hear the sound of his army boots approaching . . . thud . . . thud . . . thud. They all assumed he was annoyed about the noise at the party but, although the sound of the man's boots stopped at the fence outside the property, he never ventured inside. Rather, he stood there listening to the music. He must have been attracted by it as he stood there on guard, probably thinking back to his hometown on the main islands. As tension over the decisive battle for Okinawa was building, everybody was searching for just a little bit of calmness.

Around February 1945, Higa's home at Sakiyama in Shuri became the dormitory for the boys in the Second Prefectural Middle School Signals Unit. In the nearby Sakiyama Church, they took their lessons by correspondence. "I think there were about eighteen third-year students. Our house was made out of yew plum and I can remember students from the Second Prefectural Middle School trying to hammer nails into the wood and my father rushing about and making them stop."

The better rooms were taken by Higa's Second Prefectural Middle School "adversaries," leaving him a six tatami room [about 7 square meters] at the back to live in. On that same day, he was listening to his records when he suddenly decided to play each school's own special song. The First Middle School's song finished and was followed by the Second Middle School's anthem. "I set the record player going, wondering how they would react," explained Higa.

He sensed someone in the doorway behind him as the door began to open. Very gradually, just a few centimeters at a time, five or six students entered the room. The Second Middle School song suddenly stopped and at the same time the Second Middle School students, looking very uncomfortable, snuck out of the room. "I was from the First Middle School and one term ahead of them so, with schools being fiercely hierarchical, they were in no position to say anything," Higa explained with a wry smile.

On 28 February, Higa's father Kazuma was drafted into the Home Guard. He had had an inkling about being called up a few days prior to that but hadn't said anything about it to his son. It was drizzling on that particular morning and, holding some of his medicine for a chronic illness he had, Higa's father simply announced, "Right. I'm going." All Higa could say in reply was, "What do you mean . . . going?" Kazuma held out his call-up letter in front of his son. In an effort to memorize his father's unit number in the 24th Infantry Division written on the document, Higa stared hard at the letter, but his father quickly put it away.

On 23 March, the day that the Battle of Okinawa started, about the time the air raids ended—Higa and his close friend Kuwae Ken set off to take part in the *machi-mawari* street parade, hoping they might see some female students. However, most of the girls had already been mobilized as nurses's aides.

The shutters on the windows of the houses were closed, covered in newsprint posters with slogans written in black ink. The soldiers had probably written them because they read "Beautiful Okinawa is where the Americans and the British will be wiped out." After the air raids, the city fell quiet again, but the posters that had been blown inside out were a sad sight, flapping in the breeze. However, before long the naval bombardment became so intense that they couldn't leave their shelter during the day. From inside, they simply had to endure the noise of the big guns which sounded like distant thunder and occasionally the shaking and the reverberations. Then on 27 March, it was their graduation ceremony.

During the formalities, shells occasionally fell quite near them. Maybe it was because of the warning shouted by Lt. Shinohara, but the ceremony ended without incident and without anybody trying to make a run for it. After the ceremony had concluded, Shinohara faced the graduates and informed them that they were about to form a Blood and Iron Student Corps Unit. He ordered them all to write down their address, full name, school year, and blood type and hand the information back in. Some of the younger students who were bustling about bidding farewell to the graduates also handed in their details in the hope of being allowed to join up, but Shinohara just yelled angrily at them to go away. That evening, those who lived in greater Shuri went home to their families, while the other boys stayed in the Yoshu Dormitory.

That day, Higa's mother had specially prepared a cabbage stir-fry with egg which she brought for him. Without acknowledging the food, he said, "Tomorrow I'll be heading away with my school group." His mother didn't ask anything and just nodded in response. The two of them ate their meal in silence, although racing round inside Higa's head was the thought, "This is probably the last time we'll ever see each other." Just a month earlier she had bid her husband farewell and now she was having to say farewell to her only son. When Higa thought about how his mother must have felt, he couldn't bring himself to say anything.

The following day, 28 March, the number of fourth- and fifth-year students assembled at the Yoshu Dormitory was greater than it had been the previous day. They were each issued with an army uniform but had been told to provide their own leggings. The uniforms had already been worn for four years, winter and summer, without changing, so they were patched up and tattered. While the boys felt no attraction to them at all, they hesitated to throw away their field caps with their single white stripe and official school badge. Having been forbidden to take any items of personal clothing with them, they buried their own clothes nearby hoping to come back and collect them once the war was over.

Shinohara announced to the boys that their unit would be called the Blood and Iron First Middle School Unit. The unit was made up of a number of separate platoons. No. 1 Platoon had thirty-two members, No. 2 Platoon had twenty-eight members and No. 3 had thirty-three. There would also be nineteen boys assigned to the prefectural office and approximately ten boys to the unit kitchen. Higa was in No. 2 Platoon. On that same day, eight members of the 5th Artillery Command, including Cadet Officer Watanabe, arrived to take the boys for training and education.

Each uniform had a single star attached, plus on the chest a floating chrysanthemum denoting a Blood and Iron Student Unit. [The chrysanthemum insignia were subsequently removed.] That evening, the students staying at the Yoshu Dormitory joyfully put on their uniforms for the first time. Many could not shrug off their teenage mentality altogether, however, and wore their hand towels attached to their waists. "How do I look?" they asked each other excitedly, making sure they looked the part. But they failed to notice some regular soldiers who had come into the room.

"So you little pricks don't salute your superiors, eh?" one of the men barked as two or three of his colleagues slapped some of the boys across the face. "Just a while ago we were all digging shelters together and the next thing they were looking down on us because of our lower rank. The difference a single star badge made became clear as soon as we put on our uniforms," explained Higa. "But we were naïve and not aware of it until we'd been warned that higher ranking soldiers were a bit like an extension of the emperor himself." Between 4 April and 14 April, the boys' farewell letters were written and handed in. "I think I wrote mine on about the 8th or 9th," recalled Higa.

The boys were confined to the shelter as the bombardment intensified. In the evenings, after the shelling had stopped, they enjoyed being able to go outside and chat among themselves. That was when they were told by the school to write their farewell letters. Higa spent some time just holding the scrap of paper he had been given, thinking to himself, "What a waste of time writing these letters when we don't even know if the people they are for are going to live or die anyway."

As dusk approached, Higa hurried to use the remaining time to write his letter. "Dear Mother and Father. You have looked after me for sixteen years but now the time has come for me to leave. Even if you hear that I have been killed in the fighting, please do not feel sad. As your only son, I will be sorry to die without repaying the debt I owe you [next four and a half lines illegible]. I am so grateful to you both and thank you from the bottom of my heart for all you have done for me." When he continued with a note to his grandparents—so many people's faces appeared in his mind's eye that the tears started to flow.

Higa says that he did not write the propaganda expected of him such as "dying for my country" or "meeting up at the Yasukuni Shrine," but one letter left behind included the comment, "When it's my turn, I want to die a glorious death for my country. If you should hear that Shigetoshi is dead . . . smile for me." Higa explained with a strained smile, "We were only sixteen but the militarist education we had received had gone to the depths of our very souls."

They boys enclosed nail clippings and strands of hair in with their letters. They had to bite the nail clippings off with their teeth and, because they had been digging for days on end, the soil was wedged in behind their nails, which made a snapping sound as they bit them. Their hair was close cropped and only about two centimeters in length so they had to pull some together at the edge of their forehead and cut it with scissors. Higa thought to himself, "After I'm dead, I wonder if there will be anyone left in my family to get these?"

It was around 4 April that the First Middle School Blood and Iron Unit registered its first fatalities. The Yoshu Dormitory was razed to the ground in the bombardment and the burned bodies of two of the boys were found inside. On 30 March it was decided that the three platoons of boys would move into shelters because of the danger involved in staying in the dormitory. However, the air inside the shelters was so stifling that two of the boys slipped out to sleep in the dormitory. At dawn the next morning, someone came and reported what they had seen to those in the shelter where Higa and the boys of No. 2 Platoon were. Lt. Shinohara ran outside calling the boys to go with him, but none of them went. "We had sort of given up. None of us thought that we would survive, or that there was any point in going to look at the bodies."

Shinohara wrapped the boys' remains in a blanket and buried them in open land on the eastern side of the dormitory. Their two grave markers, each about ten centimeters square, were still there almost twenty years after the war ended. But at that point, Shinohara, the school's army officer, underwent a dramatic change. In front of the teachers and students inside the No. 2 Platoon's shelter, he pulled out his wallet and started burning the banknotes it contained, muttering as he did so, "We can't win this war. We're going to lose."

It was the first time the word "defeat" had been used in front of a group of people who believed absolutely in Japan's ultimate victory, so news quickly spread among the students. An experienced soldier who had already tasted defeat in the Pacific was given the job of leading the students. Shinohara summed up the situation objectively and told the boys honestly what was happening. Looking back, Higa explained, "I think that was an act of resistance to the principal because of his militarist ideals."

One of the features of the First Middle School's Blood and Iron Corps was that Lt. Shinohara discharged a total of twenty-nine of its students on medical grounds. On the night of the graduation ceremony, three boys were first told that they did not need to turn up the following day and were then discharged from the unit on medical grounds. They were then told to go home to their parents. Out of all the boys who were discharged, the thing that left the deepest impression on Higa was when his good friend Ken Kuwae and six others were discharged on 26 April.

That morning they were all assembled and the announcement was made about the seven boys being discharged. American spotter planes were flying high overhead but Shinohara ordered the boys not to move, explaining how that would make them easier to be seen from the air. So they were all forced to remain in their ranks, glancing fearfully up at the sky. Out in front were the seven boys in question. Looking directly at the seven, Shinohara said, "While you may want to fight valiantly and selflessly for your country, your health has deteriorated and unfortunately I have no choice but to discharge you on medical grounds." Higa looked at Kuwae's face. His mouth was pulled tight and he looked distraught as he tried to give the impression that he was upset. Higa explained, "Just as I was jealous of him, he was obviously doing his best to hide his satisfaction." By

14 May when three boys answered "yes" to Shinohara's question as to whether they wanted to return home, a total of twenty nine students had been discharged from the Blood and Iron Corps. Lt. Shinohara was killed in the Kyan area on 4 June after being hit in the temple by a piece of shrapnel from a mortar round. He lay dead under a tree, looking as though he had simply fallen asleep.

The 12th of April was a beautiful day, not a cloud in the sky. For a change, the U.S. naval bombardment was focused on distant targets and there were no spotter planes flying overhead. That was the day when Higa's father, who had been drafted in the Home Guard, came to visit his son in the No. 2 Platoon shelter. They both left the shelter and walked about twenty meters where they sat down beneath a large tree. Higa's father was the first to speak. "So, you're Okay then?" he asked. Higa nodded but said nothing. In fact, for the next ten minutes, barely a word was said between them. Watching the man sitting there in front of him, a man who was already over forty when he was conscripted into the Home Guard, Higa knew how tough things were for his father. And his father, too, by looking at his only son, would have certainly understood the harsh existence the young boy was having to endure. That was forty years ago but the scene is still vividly etched in Higa's mind. Suddenly, our conversation stopped. Higa looked up but tears were already rolling down his cheeks. "If he'd come home alive, we could have had talked about all that had happened, but I don't even know where he died . . ." He wiped his eyes and fell silent again.

On 20 April, the First Prefectural Middle School's building was destroyed. "It was about 5:00 PM. A shell fired from a U.S warship offshore from Naha Port scored a direct hit on the school building. The thunderous explosion even shook the ground in the shelter where the boys of the Blood and Iron Corps Unit were. Sheets of flames leapt out of the second story windows and lit up the early evening sky as the dazed students lined up in front of the building. A place of learning boasting sixty years of tradition, the building crashed to the ground, its final gasps sounding like cries for help.

The previous day, Higa and two staff members had been in the school's assembly hall, removing floorboards to use in the shelter. The area had been under attack from around that time and the hall's wooden window frames were ablaze. The noise of their footsteps resounded around them as they walked through the concrete-built hall in their army shoes. The window frames were burning fiercely, and Higa felt like the leading character in war movies he had seen. He even felt a strange sense of excitement, although the two teachers with him were feeling quite the opposite. Because the boards were easy to rip up, around one third of them had already been taken, and without proper tools they were unable to get the remaining ones out. However, they persevered with their bare hands until the two teachers decided it was too dangerous and that they should go back to the shelter.

By May, the Japanese front line was beginning to crumble and the area around Shuri had reached a critical juncture. On 12 May, a second lieutenant and some soldiers arrived at the No. 2 Platoon's shelter from Takushi. "Get out of here, you lot!" they screamed. When a teacher nearby explained, "This is the Blood and Iron Student Corps' shelter." But the lieutenant snapped back, "Iron Corps? What the hell's that? Anyway, we're using this shelter now," and began to force the boys outside. But at that point, Shinohara appeared and, because he was an army officer attached to a school, he held the higher rank of first lieutenant. "You prick. You're nothing but a second lieutenant," Shinohara pelted the man with a volley of backhand and forehand slaps to the face, with which the second lieutenant and his men left the shelter without saying a word.

As the situation deteriorated, the First Middle School's Blood and Iron Student Corps Unit came to be needed in a combat role. While the teachers and students had operated together since the unit's formation, they were to separate on 14 May. However, Principal Fujino Norio's address to the boys about developments seemed to go on forever. As he spoke, artillery shells were landing off in the distance, but flares hung in the air much closer and from time to time shells targeting Shuri Castle whistled overhead.

Facing the twenty seven boys who had been allocated to the No. 1 Heavy Field Artillery Regiment, Principal Fujino's address continued. "During war, circumstances are always changing, hour by hour, minute by minute. Things can become extremely difficult, and don't necessarily continue in our favor. Keeping all of you together in the Blood and Iron Corps has become impossible." The emphatic way he uttered the words "hour by hour, minute by minute" was a habit of the Principal whenever he spoke, so it drew a chuckle from the boys assembled in front of him.

The decision as to which boys would be sent to which unit was made around midday that same day. The nineteen boys who had been attached to the Prefectural Government the day before were recalled and reallocated along with the others. Higa remembers that about twenty boys were sent to the Blood and Iron Corps Headquarters, ten to the No. 5 Artillery Command, twenty seven to the Heavy Field Artillery 1st Regiment, twenty to the 100th Independent Heavy Artillery Battalion, twelve to the First Prefectural Middle School Independent

Survey Unit, and twenty to the 66th Independent Engineering Battalion. Also, six others were killed in the fighting at Shuri and twenty-nine had been previously discharged.

Higa was disappointed to be attached to the No. 1 Regiment of the Field Heavy Artillery. "As soon as I heard the news, I felt the weight of a cannon on my shoulders. I thought that this would put me in harm's way and compared to that, the survey unit was far more attractive. I was really envious of them."

Ironically, not one of the twelve boys attached to the field survey unit survived the war. In the artillery, the survey unit was sent right up near the front line where their job was to identify where Japanese shells were landing and report that information back to the artillery emplacements. Needless to say, their work was extremely dangerous because it required them to be out above ground, but of course Higa didn't know that at the time.

After being addressed by the principal, the twenty-seven boys allocated to the artillery unit were led away by the soldiers who had come to meet them. They were sent to join the No. 6 Company working in the medical section of the No. 1 Regiment of the Field Heavy Artillery at Shitadomari in Kochinda.

On the way, four of them had to carry a wounded officer from that artillery unit on a stretcher which made the journey seem to last forever. When the boys were sorted into their various units, Higa was issued with a steel helmet, a combat knife and a Type 38 Arisaka rifle. He was also given just fifteen rounds of ammunition, but he was already so exhausted that the weight of just that number of bullets made him feel as if he was going to pitch forwards. Higa had handed his rifle to another student to carry but, although he had to bear only one quarter of the officer's weight on the stretcher, it was a terrible strain on his shoulder.

The wounded officer they were carrying complained about the pain the whole way, but the boys couldn't do anything to help him. They had run out of energy and every step was a struggle in the cloying mud. Somewhere just past Haebaru, when some shells landed very near to them, in their panic, the boys dropped the stretcher and threw themselves to the ground. As they did so, the wounded officer rolled off down a slope.

Once the shelling stopped, the boys put him up on the stretcher again. "Who the hell dropped me down like that?" the officer screamed, but nobody replied. They were all too exhausted to care about what he was saying.

Higa quickly changed his mind about his new posting. Compared with Shuri, the new location was much quieter, only attracting the occasional shell from the U.S. warships offshore. Two- and three-tiered bunks had been installed for the boys to sleep on and, while some were annoyed that their blankets got wet from water dripping on them, life in the shelter was relatively comfortable. The murmur of a small stream running in front of the shelter was peace itself to their ears and the war almost seemed to be off in a different world.

Higa recalls that it was 15 May, the day after they arrived at Shitadomari. "Does anyone know the area around the Shikina Shrine?" a sergeant called out to the boys. Higa had often gone to the Shikina Shrine as a child to collect insects. His ancestors' tomb was near there and he also used to go for the Ushimi Festival. As happy memories of his times at the shrine came flooding back, Higa called out "Yes" and put up his hand. He immediately wished that he hadn't for, when he looked around, the others all seemed very relieved. Higa had forgotten all about the war and to make matters worse the area around the shrine was under heavy artillery fire. But it was too late. Their job was to take messages up to the command unit located near the shrine and the sergeant, Higa and one other unfortunate boy from the Blood and Iron Corps had drawn the "short straws." By the time they drew near the shrine, incoming artillery fire had become heavy and, as they approached Shikina Gardens, it was so intense they couldn't move ahead at all. Throwing himself face down onto the ground, Higa thought, "I knew I shouldn't have volunteered." Even after the shelling stopped it was still hard going. They had been heading for the forest near the shrine but by now that had already been wiped off the landscape. Higa had no idea which way to go and the sergeant snapped at him, "What the hell did you bring us here for if you don't even know the way?" What a mess. Just for putting his hand up, Higa now had to wander around on his own, as shells poured in, looking for the Command Unit shelter.

Starting the following day, the Blood and Iron Student Corps members took turns running messages to the Command Unit. On 27 May, it was again Higa's turn to head out. That was the same day the Command Unit pulled out, which meant that Higa had in fact acted as a messenger for them on their first and last day at Shitadomari. At the same time, the Shuri Line was on the brink of collapse and signs of imminent defeat were everywhere. On his way to the command unit, Higa saw a man who had lost both legs. Propping himself up on his hands, the man was able to move by dragging his buttocks along on the ground. A thin trail of feces, some fifty centimeters long, from around the man's buttocks, lay in the thick mud covering the road. On his way back the following day, Higa noticed that the trail of feces was almost three meters long.

After crossing the Ichinichi Bridge, they approached the slopes of Shikina when Higa heard a voice calling, "Shigetoshi . . . is that you?" He recognized the voice: it was the mother of his best friend Kuwae Ken and, as he looked up, he saw Kuwae standing there beside her. The two were fleeing south.

Although the bombardment was relentless, with some shells landing close by, Higa stood and talked to Kuwae and his mother for around thirty seconds until a lance corporal yelled at him to get a move on. These two good friends had spent time together listening to records and drinking *awamori*—trying to enjoy the youth that had now been taken away from them. They parted company, one going up the hill and the other down. When Higa said to his friend to make his way to their shelter, Kuwae smiled and said, "I will . . . I definitely will." Those were the last words Higa heard his good friend utter. Kuwae and his mother never made it to the shelter. After the war, Higa learned that just a month after he left them, they were both killed near the ruins of Nanzan Castle.

When Higa's group pulled out of the main shelter at Shikina, the hillside to the south was littered with wounded soldiers lying where they had fallen. Higa and the others had to step carefully to make their way through all the bodies. They could feel wounded men tugging at their trousers, while those who were still well enough pulled at the sleeves of their jackets. "Take us with you," they pleaded, but to no avail. Higa and the others tried telling them that the medics would be there soon, but the wounded soldiers had heard it all before. "You bastards telling us that bullshit too?" they said, as they let go.

There were also many wounded soldiers at the Shitadomari shelter, where one of the jobs allocated to Higa and his friends was disposing of amputated arms and legs from the "operating theater." That meant going as far as the little stream running in front of the shelter but they were so exhausted from the endless toil that they ended up tossing the limbs into a hollow along the way.

On 1 June, a truck brought five or six wounded soldiers to the medical annex at Aragusuku. Although the wounded soldiers were fortunate to be transported by truck, the road, if you could still call it a road, was more like a mass of shell craters. The truck would make a little headway, get stuck in a hole then move forward again. The shells almost seemed to be pursuing the truck before landing on the muddy road, making them feel very uneasy. Eventually, the vehicle became bogged down in the mud and the boys from the Blood and Iron Corps had to push it out. But, just as they thought that they had got it moving again, a shell landed very near them and they instinctively threw themselves face down. When they were greeted with painful cries of, "You idiots . . . what the hell are you doing . . . ," they realized that they had thrown themselves on top of the wounded men. "We were trying to protect you from the shells," they said, embarrassed at what they had just done.

It was another hard job getting the wounded soldiers from the truck into the medical annex because the shelter entrance was on a steep slope part way up a hill. The wounded men did not know how hard it was to carry them so they yelled at the boys for the slightest slip. By the time they had carried all the soldiers up the slope, the boys were exhausted and stopped for a rest at the shelter entrance. However, the sergeant who had already gone inside came back out with an announcement that almost finished them off. "We've got to take the wounded back to Shitadomari." Transporting the wounded men had been in preparation for the withdrawal of the No. 1 Regiment of the Field Heavy Artillery, but now the medical station itself was also getting ready to withdraw. He said he was told, "We're going to pull back as well, so why the hell did you bring them here?" They headed back along the same steep road they had come, burdened with the weight of the stretchers and again having to push the truck each time it slipped into a shell crater.

The shelter at the medical annex was where Higa first saw female students. Two girls from the Second Prefectural Girls' High School were gallantly tending to some wounded soldiers. Some nearby medics saw Higa's group arrive and joked to the girls, "Hey, the middle school boys are here. Your boyfriends have arrived!" The girls paid no attention to the comments and continued to work away in silence. They also seemed to be totally ignoring the Blood and Iron Corps boys as well, wrapping their gauze bandages around the same injuries over and over again.

On 2 June, Higa and his unit left the Shitadomari shelter and very early the following morning arrived at Makabe. Higa had no time to rest, however, having drawn the short straw as runner back to Shitadamori where they had just been. He was exhausted, almost to the very limits of his endurance, but no sooner had he left the shelter and walked thirty or forty meters when some high-explosive shells came his way. He hurled himself to the ground but then found himself unable to move. He wasn't wounded, but he couldn't stand up. The lance corporal with him urged him on but still Higa could not move. The private came in beside Higa and said, "Come on . . . get going," then gave him a couple of swift kicks in the ribs. Higa swore at the man under his breath but quickly got up. "As we got near the shelter," Higa explained, "I suddenly thought of a song I knew that was urging me to keep going and not to give up. The song just hit me, I don't know why." By the time he got back from his messenger duties that day, some dried bonito flakes that he had left in his haversack were gone. Food was becoming scarcer by the day.

In Higa's unit there were also several women from the Tsuji [red light] area of Naha who were toiling away valiantly as nurses. One of them was killed towards the end of June when they pulled back to Makabe. As Higa was passing the shelter entrance, the women were weeping as they applied funeral make-up to her face. "You are beautiful," they sobbed as they talked to their friend lying there silently. Higa was taken aback when he caught a glimpse of the dead woman's face. The redness of her cheeks was in stark contrast to the rest of her face, which was covered in pale, white make-up. Higa recalls that she was as pretty as a doll, more beautiful than any other woman he had seen before.

After they had moved to Makabe, the officers appeared outside less and less often. They urinated into pots, which Higa and the others in the Blood and Iron Students Corps had to go and empty. The wounded soldiers also tried to grab the pots begging, "Give us that water to drink." Even when they were told it was urine, they refused to believe it and the boys had to wrench the pots from their hands in order to get away. The wounded soldiers swore at them with every foul word they could think of. It was also around that time that they were told by an officer with a serious look on his face, "If you see a woman carrying a red handkerchief and a mirror, and with her pubic hair shaved, report it immediately." He said she was a spy.

The boys in the Blood and Iron Corps continued to enjoy spending time chatting outside the shelter in between artillery bombardments. Moreover, they became so used to it all that they would stay outside right up until the guns opened fire again. On one occasion, Higa was a little slow getting back inside the shelter and thought his number was up as he found himself caught in a concentrated mortar attack. He hid in a crater and didn't move, covering his eyes with his thumbs and blocking his ears with his fingers. Five minutes went by, then ten minutes, but still the attack showed no signs of letting up. Bullets whizzed across his back, almost touching him. Unable to bear it any longer, he opened his eyes only to see reddish tracer rounds shooting past above him. Absolutely petrified, Higa felt an overwhelming urge to get up and run, but just managed to control himself and stay put. Such occurrences were common, so from then on the lance corporal in charge of the boys always urged them to get back inside the shelter as quickly as possible. The lance corporal was wounded and later died but in his deranged state he babbled over and over again, "Are my Blood and Iron boys safe?"

On 19 June and 24 June, the Blood and Iron Corps unit was divided up into three separate squads and sent out on an infiltration raid. Maybe it was because the dissolution order had been issued by then but during the previous evening the wounded soldiers inside the shelter disappeared. There were seven boys in Higa's squad and an improvised explosive device was prepared for them to take on the raid. However, nobody wanted to carry it so Pvt. Urasaki ordered Higa to take it. Higa's being relatively tall, at 168 centimeters, was the reason he was chosen. "I had no choice so I picked it up," explained Higa. "But as soon as I did, I almost felt a surge of energy and the bomb felt as light as a feather. Maybe it was because my mental state of selfless devotion had surpassed my fear of death." But what did upset Higa was that he also shed a few tears. It was a moonlit night and the most embarrassing thing would be for the junior students to notice, so Higa looked away and wiped his tears.

Improvised explosive devices were widely used in the Battle of Okinawa, and the following comments appear in the 32nd Army Senior Staff Officer Yahara Hiromichi's book *The Battle for Okinawa*.

> If a poor man fights with the same tactics as a rich man, he is sure to lose. Therefore, the Japanese Army has formulated new "patented" antitank tactics. These involve hand-carried makeshift explosive devices containing ten kilograms of picric acid. Our experiments have shown ten kilograms of this powder to be enough to blow up enemy tanks of any size. Delivery of these explosives would be in the nature of a suicide attack, of course. Soldiers assigned to this duty should be promoted three ranks.[6]

In reality, it was mainly the students who were given the job of delivering these explosive devices, although cases of anyone being promoted three ranks for doing so were almost unheard of. The aim of the infiltration raid was to break through enemy lines and create an escape route, but they abandoned the idea when they realized the Americans had been paying far closer attention to the perimeter than they had thought. They had only gone a short distance when several shots were fired at short range and they then also came under sustained fire from heavier weapons. Their only option was to throw themselves to the ground and wait for the firing to stop. The moment he was put in charge of the improvised explosive device, Higa's fear of death vanished completely, although the others felt very differently. They hadn't chosen this crazy strategy of a forced breakout. Moreover, it took a great deal of courage for those boys who had been ordered to launch the infiltration raid to then return to their shelter. But they did, finally

6.   Yahara, H. 1995: 12-13.

making it back just before dawn, Higa having discarded the bomb along the way.

The boys were afraid that the soldiers in the cave would scream at them and send them out on another infiltration raid, so they were surprised when two lieutenants who had stayed behind, one from the medical corps and one from the paymaster's office, actually welcomed them back inside. The other two platoons, which had headed south separately from Higa's group, never made it back and Higa learned after the war that six of them were either killed or missing. Back inside the gloomy shelter, Higa was amazed so see that most of those who had stayed behind were officers and that they still had plenty to eat. They had cans of beef and were using solid fuel for cooking. The boys in the Blood and Iron Corps unit also prepared some of the food and were all treated to a great feast, although Higa couldn't bring himself to eat a thing. He was so exhausted he couldn't bear the thought of food.

In the three months since the fighting started, the attitude of the boys in the Blood and Iron Corps had become rough and unkind. The innocence of their student days had been wiped away as they moved about with the IJA and by the endless shelling they had been subjected to. Around 21 June, a woman aged about sixty with two small children rushed into the shelter looking for help. The others she had been with had all been captured but inside the shelter she was met with nothing but cold, uncaring stares. Some of the boys in the Blood and Iron Corps even told her to get out. Looking back Higa explained, "We were at the stage where we only wanted to look after ourselves. We too were at fault by then."

On 23 June they heard a voice near the shelter entrance yelling *"Dete-koi! Dete-koi!"* at them to get them to come outside. On the previous day when members of the Home Guard had been out collecting water, they were surprised at how close the Americans were and scampered back to the shelter. As they did so, however, they kicked over some tin cans and gave away their location. The next thing, a phosphorous grenade was thrown into the shelter. The boys in the Blood and Iron Corps unit grabbed their gas masks to protect themselves, but the Home Guard members had no masks and were coughing. Higa recalls that he heard one of the boys from his unit scream out "Fuck you!" in local dialect, but other than that, there was no response to the American troops' call for them to surrender. To get ready, he tried to slip a round into his gun but couldn't because the chamber had rusted over. Higa remembers that his legs shook with fear and he felt as though his blood was running cold at the thought that his time was up. He held his bayonet hard up to his throat but it hurt so he could not bring himself to take his own life. Before long, someone who could speak English talked with the Americans and, after making sure they would not be killed, about thirty of them surrendered. The last IJA soldier to come out reported that Lt. Ishikado had committed suicide inside the shelter. A gunshot had been heard just before that.

It was the first time they had seen the outside world during daylight for a long time. Everything looked totally white—the grass, the trees, even the ocean. The whole world seemed to be white, apart from three dead bodies lying near the entrance, black and bloated to the size of cows. Unable to move because of their hideous wounds, the three soldiers had been "dispatched" by medical orderlies. The buzzing of swarms of flies beat out its own tempo as they flew round and round, the sound gradually bringing Higa back to reality. He explained that some IJA soldiers who had also fought in China had described the Battle of Okinawa not so much as a war, but as a "world of insanity." "In a very short time, our whole state of mind had changed. In war, it is always the weak that end up suffering the most," he added.

Agriculture and Forestry School Blood and Iron Student Corps

One of the comfort stations set up for Japanese soldiers was located just a stone's throw from the Prefectural Agriculture and Forestry School's shelter. Toward the end of March 1945, shortly after the start of the Battle for Okinawa, one of the students was resting inside the now vacant building when it was attacked by American planes. He was killed almost immediately but was also so badly burned in the ensuing fire that his face was unrecognizable. "He was in the same class as me during our first and second year. He was very bright and his grades were always in the top five in the class. I remember that he was faster than everybody else doing calculations on his abacus. I'm pretty sure that he was from Yaeyama. I remember that he was one of those people who were always very tanned . . ." Akamine Takeshi who had been in the same Year Three class [the final year] at the Prefectural Agriculture and Forestry School choked with emotion as he recalled his school friend.

The Agriculture and Forestry School, which three years earlier had been the vocational school, was located in Kadena. From around May 1944, staff members and students were being rushed in to help build facilities at the northern and central [Yomitan and Kadena] airfields where they worked day and night. In readiness for the American landing which followed the massive October air raid on Naha of 10 October that year, they were building underground shelters near the headwaters of the Hija River. By the time 1945 arrived, the war was already going badly for Japan, and the IJA decided to enlist students from the Agriculture and Forestry School to bolster the defense of the central airfield. So on 26 March, the Blood and Iron Student Corps was formed and on the following day they were mobilized to help with the construction.

There were around 600 students at the Agriculture and Forestry School, but by this time the number of third year students had dropped to around 100. Akamine explained, "That was because students who volunteered for the Japanese Naval Preparatory Flight Training Program, plus others who were older than me but in the same class, had joined up ahead of us on active service." Students from the Agriculture and Forestry School who had joined up as members of the Blood and Iron Student Corps worked hard carting food supplies from near the northern and central airfields. Their base was an underground shelter near the headwaters of the Hija River, in a place called Makihara in Yomitan, so the students used to call it the "Makihara shelter."

Vegetable fields spread out in front of the Makihara shelter, and out there on its own was the thatch building that had been the local comfort station. The Japanese soldiers had already left by the time of the attack, with the comfort women also leaving several days earlier. "The story we heard was that there had been several Korean prostitutes there," remembers Akamine, who then explained the reason for the attack on the comfort station as follows. "It was suffocating for the students from the Agriculture and Forestry School to stay in the shelter all the time, so occasionally to relax they would make their way over to the empty house which had previously been the comfort station. So maybe the foot traffic between the abandoned comfort station and the shelter was seen by American spotter planes. My classmate just happened to be in there when they attacked it from the air."

Just spotting a building out there in the hills was cause enough for suspicion, but on top of that there was a lot of activity with people moving in and out of it. "Fair enough if they thought Japanese soldiers were in there, so it was only natural that it should be become a target for the Americans."

But who exactly was the student from the Agriculture and Forestry School who was killed in that attack? Akamine saw the charred body with his own eyes but is still not sure of the boy's identity. "The only one unaccounted for at the time was Tamoto Kiyoshi, and I remember how the other students said that it must have been him."

Another classmate who was there at the time was Oshiro Kenki. In recalling the incident, he explained, "Tamoto was the one who died. That building was burning so fiercely that the smoke poured into the shelter where all the students were."

After the former comfort station suffered direct hits from the American planes, the scene turned to chaos. Akamine described what happened. "That building was right in front of us and when it went up in flames the smoke poured into our shelter. It was terrible . . . I thought I was going to die from suffocation inside the shelter. Directly outside, the place was like an inferno, but we raced out of that shelter en masse. Some of the boys suffered burns as they rushed around in confusion. It was complete pandemonium." Akamine said that he saw the charred body of his classmate still inside the burned remains of the building.

That same evening, the Blood and Iron Student Corps Headquarters left the Makihara shelter and moved to what was then Kurashiki in Goeku. After they arrived, they again worked hard carting food supplies from areas around the airfields. However, the air raids grew worse as the days passed, and around a dozen students were strafed and killed as they worked.

On 1 April, the Americans finally landed and moved inland from the coast near Kadena. Lt. Sho Ken, who was leading the Blood and Iron Student Corps, commented that he had so many students in his charge at that stage that there was nothing really that he could do. From the roughly 100 students, he picked twenty third-year seniors who were all gifted sportsmen. "He had a really stern look in his eyes and was stricter than the other officers when instructing the students." One of the twenty selected, Akamine said the following about Lt. Sho. "From that point on, our education was about 'you've got to pick up guns instead of pens and fight for your country.' In other words, it was a sort of spiritual education getting us to understand that we were not to return home alive."

Lt. Sho was the officer attached to the Agriculture and Forestry School. While he was normally strict, surprisingly he sometimes even encouraged the students to smoke. "He used to tell us that it was already okay for us to smoke and actually shared his cigarettes with us. He would tell us that they were Imperial cigarettes he'd received from His Majesty the Emperor and that we could smoke as many as we liked. We were surprised, as it was the first time we'd come across anything like that. Those were the days when you got expelled if you were caught smoking while you were still at school. So not only were we pleased at being able to smoke while we were still students, but it also made us feel like real soldiers in the army."

Together with his twenty students, Lt. Sho headed off toward the airfield at Kadena. However, they were not sure just what the Americans were up to, so he decided that if they just hurled themselves into an attack without consider-ing the reality of the situation, they would run the risk of losing everything and achieving nothing. So for the time being, they pulled back. They arrived at a small settlement called Ikehara, where, "We entered a civilians' shelter located in the middle of a bamboo grove," explained Oshiro, who, together with Akamine, was one of the twenty students chosen by the lieutenant. As they waited inside this shelter for another opportunity to attack, they received the news that the airfield had already fallen into enemy hands and that there was no way a group of twenty or so people would be able to get anywhere near it. They all felt dejected and talked to each other about what to do next.

"At that stage, opinion was divided along two lines. We discussed whether to head down south to Yonabaru and join the unit which was deployed at Untama-mui down by Shuri, or whether we should make our way north and link up with Col. Udo Takehiko's Kunigami Detachment on the Motobu Peninsula. Looking back now, if we'd headed for Untamamui, we'd never have made it back alive. Fate took us in the right direction," said Oshiro solemnly.

The food situation was the main reason the twenty students of the Agriculture and Forestry School from the civilian cave at Ikehara in Misato headed north to the Motobu Peninsula, rather than southwards. Again, Oshiro explained, "The officer leading us was Lt. Sho. He was a nobleman from Shuri, and the story was that he owned an orchard in Izumi on the Motobu Peninsula. So in the end, we concluded that it was best to head for Motobu so that if we ran out of food, we would still be able to find something to eat and survive up there."

In order to join up with Udo's Kunigami Detachment on the Motobu Penin-sula, on the evening of 2 April, the day after the Americans landed, Lt. Sho led the students toward Nago via Ishikawa, Kin, and Ginoza. "We could only move at night so we walked right through the entire evening. It was a real foot slog and we were so exhausted that some of the boys even banged their heads on the branches of trees as they stumbled along in a daze. Half the time we couldn't even tell if we were awake or asleep," explained Oshiro with a wry smile. During the day, the American attacks were relentless so they waited among the trees. As well as air attacks, they were also bombarded by naval gunfire. Akamine added, "While it was light, we weren't able to move at all. Japanese forces had lost all control of the air."

While Akamine and the others were on the move, they witnessed large num-bers of civilians who had obviously fled from the central and southern areas of Okinawa. "On the road at Ishikawa, I saw a little boy who had been hit by something from a white phosphorous shell. Some of the sparks had landed on the back of his head and were still burning him. I thought 'This is awful' and I tried to extinguish it with a cloth I had, but it just wouldn't go out. I remember saying that I couldn't put it out without pushing his head right under the water in the paddy field." On the morning of the 4th, the 20 students and Lt. Sho arrived at the Izumi Kokumin School at Motobu where they gave an update on their movements to Udo's Kunigami Detachment and another unit that had based themselves in the school buildings. They then asked for permission to join those units.

Their request was approved and the boys were provided with army uniforms. Oshiro explained, "Our uniforms didn't have any rank insignia, but some of the students were issued rifles." Akamine added, "Rather than a rifle, I just had two hand grenades." There was an orchard in Izumi that Lt. Sho had some connection with, so they spent the night there.

"Back then, the Sho family owned land in various areas that they had received from the government, and the orchard at Izumi was one of those. It was hidden away up in the hills and I still clearly remember being given a meal there. Well, I say 'meal' but it was really just rice balls. The best part of it was that there was some pork-flavored miso inside the rice. It had been a while since we'd had anything to eat and we were starving, so it tasted marvelous." That was how Oshiro and Akamine recalled wistfully what happened.

In the background to this, the American military was getting closer and closer, landing at Nago around 7 April. Joining a unit of the Kunigami Detachment that was to move to Mabuyama, that evening the students also left Izumi. The fighting that spread across the area around Mabuyama and Yae-dake was fierce, and a number of the students had their young lives cut short there.

Around 16 April, the Americans had advanced as far as Mabuyama on the Motobu Peninsula. Early that afternoon, the unit the boys were with received the order to join the defensive line and immediately prepared for battle. The fighting that unfolded was far more savage than anyone could ever have imagined.

Oshiro, one of the Agriculture and Forestry students who had made it to Mabuyama with the unit, recalls his experiences. "The ferocity of the American air attacks was just incredible, plus we were pounded non-stop by shells from U.S. ships off the coast. American soldiers were obviously just a few hundred meters in front of us, and closing, but we couldn't see them. I thought that if we just stayed there and did nothing, we'd be killed by the bombardment before we even caught sight of their troops."

The Agriculture and Forestry students waited behind the Japanese soldiers fighting on the front line. "From where we were in among the silver grass, I watched as one Japanese soldier was caught by machine-gun fire. He was crawling along on his stomach when the rat-tat-tat of a machine gun rang out. He suddenly stood up and began to run away but he was cut down in another hail of bullets." Oshiro added gestures as he continued, "At one point, our group of students were hiding in foxholes half way up the hill when we heard machine-gun fire from up above our position. 'Maybe it was one of own machine guns,' we thought. One of our guys went to have a look so we all said that we would stay put until he got back. While he was away, bullets began whizzing toward us. The boy who had gone out to look around told us that what we had assumed might be one of our own machine-guns was, in fact, the enemy and that he had only just managed to escape with his life."

"We had no idea where the Japanese army was," Oshiro explained, "We only found out later that they had already pulled back from Mabuyama southeast toward Yae-dake. In other words, they had simply abandoned our student group, even though they had told us that we had to stay and hold that location to the last man. We believed them, and that was what we were going to do. We were simply given hand grenades and told not to throw them until we could see the whites of the Americans' eyes . . . we all felt as if we'd been betrayed."

Several students were killed at Mabuyama. Even today, Akamine still remembers how one of his former classmates Higa Shinsei died. "Before the Battle for Okinawa started, Shinsei had gone back to his home in the country. Even though it was 'in the country,' it was actually a town in Motobu near Mabuyama. Anyway, he could have just kept his head down at home but he heard that the Agriculture and Forestry students had arrived. He wanted to join them so he volunteered but sadly he was killed in the fighting. He didn't even have to go, so it was such a waste, joining up just to be killed," Akamine muttered with a sigh.

In their foxholes, the students finally realized, "We were the only ones left at Mabuyama. If we stayed there, we would obviously be killed, so we broke out." In groups of two and three, one after the other, they pulled out and headed for Yae-dake where they believed units of the Japanese army were located. Having just managed to get out of Mabuyama with their lives, the Agriculture and Forestry students then found out for the first time the difference between the American and Japanese military capabilities.

Akamine talked about one member of the Home Guard who escaped by crossing the stretch of water from Ie-jima. "During the evening it seems that he'd got off the island in a traditional dug-out Okinawan skiff. He was from Okinawa and was twenty-seven, maybe twenty-eight years old. From up on the hill, we could see what was happening out there on Ie-jima; it was completely surrounded by hundreds of American warships. This man said that right from the start there was no way they could offer any resistance. He said that the naval bombardment was so fierce that he thought that those on the island would be annihilated. With so many ships out there, getting back to Motobu without being detected was nothing short of a miracle."

At Yae-dake, having had nothing to eat for quite some time, the students had to endure crippling pangs of hunger. Oshiro recalls the harsh memories of those times. "The IJA unit that had abandoned us was now at Yae-dake. They had plenty of food, including canned goods, which made our mouths water, but they wouldn't share it with us. On the day they pulled back, all of their canned food was thrown out. They wouldn't let us eat any of it. I just felt it was so callous of them . . . I can't understand why they didn't give it to us if they were just going to throw it out." The night they withdrew to Tano-dake, they also shot their army horses. "They told us that the animals were becoming a burden and if they had just left them, they were afraid that the enemy would use them."

Two of the Agriculture and Forestry School students were badly wounded at Yae-dake, so when it was time to withdraw from there, the two had to be placed on stretchers and carried out. Although they left hot on the heels of the army unit, as they drew near to Kogayama in Nakijin en route, the students found themselves unable to keep up with the soldiers who had pushed ahead at a much faster pace.

"Those of us carrying the two wounded students discussed leaving them behind and pressing on. It seemed like an awful thing to do but there was no alternative. We tried to placate the two by saying things like, 'There are refugees close by so it may actually be safer for you to stay here,'" Such was Akamine's bitter recollection of leaving his two buddies behind. One of the students carrying the stretcher, Matsukawa Kanichi, disagreed with what the others had decided to do. "If we leave our two badly wounded buddies here, you know they'll starve to death. I'm staying here with them!"

The others welcomed Matsukawa's comments and prepared to push on. Then, giving the excuse of, "We'll go and see what the enemy is up to. We'll be back soon," they headed off. Oshiro explained, "We had no time to lose. The Army unit was forging ahead with no concern at all for us, so if we didn't get a move on we wouldn't have known which way to go. We simply had to hurry and catch up with them. We didn't know the Tano-dake area so we were getting desperate."

But what about the three who were left behind? Oshio explained, "The two wounded students, Izena and Yonaha, survived, but Matsukawa who stayed behind to look after them was killed in the fighting. I subsequently caught up with Izena who had been taken prisoner at Mihara in Kushi [now Nago] and asked him what had happened. He said he thinks Matsukawa must have been found and killed by the enemy. It seems that he went out looking for food but never returned." Akamine added, "It's tragic that the two who were wounded and couldn't even walk were lucky enough to have made it out alive, while Matsukawa who was not injured is the one who got killed . . . just because he stayed to care for his buddies . . ." His voice faded with emotion.

The group of students who had been left behind when the Japanese army unit hurriedly pulled out continued their search. As they approached a small settlement called Kogayama in Nakijin, one of the students happened to spot a long wire like a telephone line on the ground in front of him. "If we follow this line, it just might lead us to the soldiers . . ." Immediately, the students looked around at each other and almost leapt for joy.

"We had searched so hard for those soldiers who had simply disappeared that we were too quick to jump to conclusions," Oshiro chuckled as he remembered the occasion. "But now when I look back, we couldn't have been more wrong."

The telephone wire ran from in front of them to a nearby river. The river had no water in it at the time so one after the other the students hurried into its dry bed and followed the direction of the wire. But when they reached the "end of the line," they were in for a real surprise, as Oshiro explained. "Somehow, attached to the end of the line were cans of fish. I'm pretty sure they were salmon, if I remember right, and they were in a container a bit like a wire basket." Even as he spoke all those years later, Oshiro still had the same look of amazement on his face.

"I bet this is a trap the Americans have set," said Akamine. "The fish will have been laced with poison."

But when they took a closer look, it appeared that the cans were Japanese. The students agreed that, if the cans were Japanese, they didn't have to worry about them being poisoned so with great excitement they opened some. The fish tasted marvelous, especially because of the canned food they had missed out on earlier at Yae-dake.

Just then, they heard the clatter and rumble of an approaching truck. "The enemy's here!" they said. The whole group of students, still holding onto the cans of fish, looked around for somewhere to hide.

They found themselves in a valley within a gorge with a river running between the road and a steep slope. There was a thicket of vegetation on the side of the slope that looked as though it might hide a number of people, so they all quickly clambered across to it. Oshiro explained what happened next.

"As we glanced out from the thicket toward the road, American military trucks rumbled past one after the other. Obviously, if they spotted us we were done for so we clung on and waited, hardly daring to breathe. Some couldn't hold on any longer and slipped down the slope, but then desperately crawled back up. That tension lasted until nightfall."

Eventually, dark fell. In a cold sweat from fear, once the students made their way down to the river, they crawled up the road on the other side, which was when Oshiro spotted a civilian, rolling a bale of rice along past them.

"When we asked him, 'Where did you get this bale of rice . . . where are you taking it?' he told us there were Japanese soldiers in the area and that they had asked him to carry the rice. What? So there are Japanese soldiers around here?' we yelled with joy, asking him again if it was true."

With directions from this civilian, the students were finally able to rejoin the Japanese soldiers. So, led by Lt. Sho, the Agriculture and Forestry School's Blood and Iron Corps moved from Kogayama, then crossed the Isa River and made it to Tano-dake where the IJA were engaging the Americans. Akamine has no recollection of the actual fighting, although he was staggered when he realized the difference in the quality of the weapons the two sides were using. "Some said that there was a dead American nearby, so I went over to have a look . . . he'd died with his rifle in his hands. That was the first time I'd been that close to a dead enemy soldier, but it was his weapon that surprised me most. It was a rifle, but it was very high-powered and could shoot rapid-fire, round after round. The old single-shot rifles our soldiers had were no match for them. I thought there was no way our army could match that."

The students all moved together as far as Tano-dake but after that, because they were to withdraw even farther, they were divided into two groups. Those in Oshiro's group, who had been issued with rifles earlier at Izumi Kokumin School in Motobu, remained with Udo's Kunigami Detachment. It was decided that Lt. Sho would lead Akane and the other students without rifles off in a different direction.

"By the time we got to Tano-dake, several of my former classmates had been killed in the fighting. While we were on the move, however, other local students from the Agriculture and Forestry School joined us, so the actual number in our group was still around twenty, about the same as when the Blood and Iron group was formed. Also, we'd been split into two groups so I guess there would have been about ten in each group."

Akamine then spoke of the terrible developments that unfolded next. "From Tano-dake, we were led by Lt. Sho towards a place called Uchifukuji in Higashi-son. On our way there, a number of Agriculture and Forestry School students who had heard that we were in the area came rushing over from a nearby settlement to join us, boosting our group to fourteen or fifteen. Before the fighting had even begun, they had fled into the countryside but now they were really keen to join up with their schoolmates."

When they got to Uchifukuji, they were on the receiving end of a ferocious American attack, costing Lt. Sho and seven or eight of the Agriculture and Forestry students their lives. That was around the end of April 1945, and Akamine then explained the events of the previous evening which he has never been able to erase from his memory.

"That evening, it seemed as though the moonlight was much brighter than usual. We could only move at night when there was a lull in the American attacks, and that night we were making our way along beside the river at Uchifukuji. The weather was good. It was really hot and I remember that we took off our shirts and uniforms and washed them in the river."

The following day, just as the sun was at its peak in the sky, all of a sudden two rifle shots rang out. The Agriculture and Forestry students who had been resting on a tree on the steep slope leading down to the river looked out to where the shots had come from and saw twenty or thirty American soldiers. A fierce firefight quickly broke out.

"The distance between us and the enemy was barely 20 meters. All we had to use against their automatic weapons were a couple of hand grenades each, so we didn't make much of an impression. One of my buddies threw a grenade, but it hit a tree and bounced back and exploded, killing him. We didn't have a chance, so I just turned and ran away up the hill."

Akamine gestured excitedly as he explained the horrific scene. The American soldiers were unable to get a clear shot at Akamine because the hills were covered in dense vegetation, so fortunately he managed to escape. A bullet grazed his back as he scrambled up the hill. "I still have the scar from that," he explained.

Lt. Sho was killed in that fight, and at that point the now leaderless Blood and

Iron Student Corps from the Agriculture and Forestry School split up and the boys went their own way.

After his escape, Akamine made his way to Arime, a small village in Higashi-son where he came across Lt. Takayama, an officer attached to the Second Prefectural Middle School. By then, the area around Arime was full of refugees. Maybe he had heard it from one of them, but Lt. Takayama said to Akamine, "I understand that Lt. Sho, the officer assigned to your unit, was killed at Uchifukuji."

"I was ordered to go and get something from his person . . . 'A lock of hair would be okay' I was told. So I went back to the scene of the fighting but, when I got there, I wanted to turn and look away." Almost three weeks had passed since the fighting, so the corpses on the hillside were now half-decayed, with mostly just the bones remaining. They were so badly decomposed that he could barely tell which body belonged to which student. Lt. Sho was the only one Akamine could be sure of because of his beard. He used a razor to take a lock of the lieutenant's hair.

The upper reaches of the Fukuji River in Higashi-son, the site where the Agriculture and Forestry students of the Blood and Iron Corps fought their last battle, lies deep in the hills which today lead down to the Fukuji Dam. Akamine recalled the time he returned to the site just twenty days after the battle and took a lock of hair back from Lt. Sho's body.

"Of all the bodies scattered about, the only one I could clearly identify was Lt. Sho because of the beard on his cheeks and chin. Even though his hair and beard were still there, it felt as though they were just barely attached to his skull. He would have been about forty and he was very strict. I have no real memory of ever hearing him speaking in a friendly manner. He was the sort of man who would never tell a joke. He was apparently an important nobleman from Shuri, and I heard that he had something to do with the Imperial Rule Assistance Association."

The scene of the fighting was so tragically hideous that Akamine could barely look, but he had no time to feel sad about the corpses.

"I didn't know if the Americans would come back and attack again. As ordered by Lt. Takayama, I'd gone out and collected something from his body. The sun had gone down and it was already dark when I left. I could also still feel the pain where the bullet had creased my back so I was tentative about being back there."

With the lock of Sho's hair in his hand, Akamine wanted to get out as quickly as he could. Forcing himself to stay calm, he looked to see if there were any other personal relics that he should grab, but the officer's sword was missing—maybe the Americans had taken it. The dead students were so badly decomposed that he couldn't tell one from the other. "No matter how dangerous it was back there, I should at least have dug a hole and buried my buddies," said Akamine remorsefully.

Two of his classmates killed at Uchifukuji, Ashimine Yukihiro and Oshiro Kiko, were among the original twenty who had been with the unit ever since it was established at Kurashiki in Goeku [now in Okinawa City].

"Yukihiro was a good athlete. He used to do 100- and 200-meter sprints. He was quite slender and tall but fairly reserved. Yoshitaka, on the other hand, was good at kendo. He had something wrong with his leg, but he was still good enough to come first or second in the class."

Nakazato Kansho, Hirata Kiyoshi—who was in his second year, a year below Nakazato—and Taira Keishun who was in his first year subsequently joined the unit when it was on the move, up north. All three were killed. Keishun was really skilled at bayonet drill . . . he was always the best, but I remember that Kansho always got top grades.

Akamine recalled much happier school days before they got caught up in the war. One by one he recalled the faces of his good friends still in their prime, unable to hide the loneliness he felt from having lost them. He never thought for a second that he would survive the war. "When the twenty of us were picked and our special unit was formed, we each gave the junior students things that we wanted them to take back to our families. I entrusted one student with a photo of myself. I'd scribbled on the back, 'I don't expect to make it home alive.'"

The students were totally convinced that Japan would win the war. Akamine explained the effect of Japan's militarist education by saying, "We always felt that, however grim things seemed, there was no way that our divine nation would lose the war. Letters home from the Agriculture and Forestry High School students who had been called up earlier contained nothing but statements like 'We'll all meet at the Yasukuni Shrine.' That's because we were all more than happy to die for our country . . . I wonder if Lt. Sho's lock of hair was returned safely to his family."

Akamine was still concerned about what happened to the lock of hair he had risked his life for. Shortly after receiving it from Akamine, Lt. Takayama moved to a POW camp and from there it seems that he returned to mainland Japan relatively quickly.

"Amid all the chaos of the months immediately after the war, I guess he didn't have time to go and track down Sho's family, but I assume he still had the hair when he went back to the mainland. Takayama would have been in his mid-twenties back then, so I imagine he had just completed his officer cadetship. I saw his death notice in the newspaper about four or five years ago."

Forty years later Akamine visited Higashi-son in search of the site where the fighting took place. He remembered it being somewhere near the Fukuji Dam at the headwaters of the Fukuji River, but was not 100 percent sure. When a local resident told him, "Uchifukuji is further inland, but I don't think anybody lives there now," he drove farther up the hill beside the river.

Around 10 July, shortly after the fighting ended in the southern part of Okinawa, Akamine was taken prisoner at Sedake, which overlooks Oura Bay on the eastern coast of northern Okinawa. He described what he saw in the camp.

"Among the huge numbers of refugees was a boy who'd been two years ahead of me at school. He was preparing food with a black American soldier. We'd been taught about the 'American and British foreign devils' so I wondered if what this guy was doing was okay. He'd even put on weight because of his work preparing food, so I gradually became envious of the way he was getting on so well with the Americans. It was a time when everybody was starving so I soon realized that there was no other way to survive."

Several days later, a ship crowded with refugees from down south arrived in Oura Bay. When Akamine went down to have a look, there were quite a number of people on the boat from Haebaru, Akamine's own home region. He found someone he recognized and soon learned that those down south had been literally decimated.

"They told me that my mother, grandmother, two sisters, and other relatives had been killed. It was a real shock to be told that my whole family had been wiped out. I felt completely helpless."

Somehow managing to pick himself up, Akamine soon heard that his sister-in-law had been evacuated to Matsuda in Ginoza. He headed there and did some work as a day laborer in return for one rice ball per day. "While we were up in the mountains, all we had to eat was Sago palm [*sotetsu*, the food eaten as a last resort in Okinawa at times of famine] so that rice ball really tasted good."

"It's often said that competition for food changes a person," and during the Battle for Okinawa, Oshiro learned about that the hard way. "Students who had been best friends ended up fighting each other over food ... it was a terrible experience."

At Tano-dake, the members of the Agriculture and Forestry Blood and Iron

Corps split into two groups and went in separate directions. Oshiro and the others who had been issued with rifles went with the IJA soldiers heading for Kesashi in Higashi-son. They never saw the other group led by Lt. Sho again.

"When we came to the small village of Kesashi, the first thing we did was hunt for food. But there was almost nothing edible to be found . . . we struggled to find just a few potatoes. That was about the time we heard the obviously false rumors that our soldiers down in the south of Okinawa were winning their battle with the Americans. We felt really envious, thinking they probably had plenty to eat down there."

Even though they managed to find some potatoes at Kesashi, they couldn't eat them as they had hoped. Oshiro explains how frustrating their personal struggle was.

"While we were cooking the potatoes over a fire, some Japanese soldiers approached us. Commenting that the potatoes were already cooked, one of the soldiers poked a chopstick into the fire and helped himself to part of our meal. Students were second class privates so we couldn't say a word."

"With soldiers like that, it wouldn't matter how long you waited, you'd never get anything to eat." The students became increasingly frustrated until finally they talked about leaving the soldiers and heading off on their own. They resolved to break through to the south where they had heard there was plenty of food.

The students snuck away from Kesashi and followed the eastern coastline south until they reached Oura Bay. However, at Oura they discovered an American position in front of them, making it too dangerous to try and push any further ahead.

Oshiro explained their predicament. "There was only one road. On the left was the ocean and even if we had tried to swim out past the American position, we would have been in serious danger of being spotted and shot at in the water. Then, on the right side of the road was a very steep slope. In order to keep moving, our only option seemed to be to try to get through along the road."

One of the boys slipped away to take a look at the American position and to size up their chances. He soon returned, waving his hands and shaking his head. "There's no way through at all. It'd be all over as soon as they see us." He told the others that the Americans had set up camp and that many of them were sitting round an open fire in a grassy area not far from the road, which was clearly visible in the light of the bonfire. Obviously the boys would be spotted if they tried to go along the road.

The moment the boys abandoned the idea of breaking though the American lines the adrenalin-fed tension that had kept the group going dissolved. Deflated and exhausted, they headed back into the Sedake hills.

"By that stage, there were about ten of us Agriculture and Forestry School students and we had started fighting among ourselves over things to eat. We were too exhausted to go and look for food, so if one of the boys found something edible, the others would try to take it from him. Back at Kesashi when the soldiers stole our potatoes, we all held back, but when it happened among our group it was a different story—fights broke out. In the end it seemed better if we each went our separate ways." That was when Oshiro and two of his closest buddies headed away.

Akamine explained, "I don't talk about my wartime experiences much at all these days. I guess it's because when I tell the young ones, all they can say is, 'I can't understand why you only ate potatoes . . . fighting wars seems a pretty dumb thing to do . . .'" He seemed to keenly sense the effect of the passage of time.

No. 1 Surgery Unit Nurse

When the Okinawa Army Hospital was established in June 1944, Okumatsu Fumiko did not hesitate to put her hand up to work there. One reason was that such displays of cooperation with the military were almost an inherent requirement in society in those days. But Okumatsu says that it was more than that for her— she wanted to create the opportunity to get to the place where her older brother had lost his life. Her brother had been killed in the fighting around Nanking in 1938. The situation on the Asian continent had worsened considerably, but, she says, "I thought that if I signed up to be an army nurse I might be sent to that part of China."

As it happens, her boss in the Prefectural Office persuaded her not to go. "You're too young to be going off to war," he said. With no idea of the horrible experiences that awaited her as an army nurse, either way, Okumatsu certainly had no intention of staying home and working for the Prefectural Office.

Absorbing the Nakagusuku Bay Fortress Hospital, the Okinawa Army Hospital was established in May 1944 under the auspices of the Kumamoto Army Hospital with Army Surgeon Lt. Col. Hiroike Bunkichi as its commander. When it commenced services it had its headquarters, internal medicine and infectious diseases departments set up in the Kainan Middle School. Surgery was set up at Saiseikai Hospital. The barracks were in the Second Prefectural Middle School.

Okumatsu remembers that there were about eight nurses working there when she was put to work in the operating theater in the Saiseikai Hospital. The head nurse in charge of the theater was Uehara Kimiko, and the nurse in charge of the ward was Nagata Noriko.

"The ship bringing medical equipment to use at the Army Hospital was sunk off Oshima, so we borrowed drugs and other requirements from the Prefectural Hospital and the Hamamatsu Hospital. At that stage the only operations that were being carried out were appendectomies and surgery for hemorrhoids." However, this changed dramatically after the 10 October 1944 air raid. On that day they had just finished five appendectomies and, tired out from the day's work, Okumatsu made her way from Saiseikai Hospital in Izumisaki back to the barracks near the headquarters. She had had a bath and was going to take a rest when she heard some loud booms off in the distance. There was a soldier walking past the barracks and when Okumatsu asked him what the noise might be, he casually replied, "Maybe an exercise or something like that." But that soon changed as people started to yell "Enemy planes!" It took her less than 15 minutes to get from the barracks back to the hospital where there were wounded soldiers being treated left, right, and center. Until that day, while it may have been called an Army Hospital, apart from the rigid military discipline there had been little difference from a civilian hospital. But now things were very different as the flood of wounded effectively transformed it into a field hospital.

They also had to move the patients, who were divided into three categories according to their degree of mobility. Those with less serious wounds were deemed to be capable of walking unassisted. Then there were the patients who needed assistance to walk, plus the most serious cases who needed to be carried on a stretcher. "The patients capable of walking, either by themselves or assisted, were made to do so, and we even told some among them who had just been operated on to hold their midriffs in place as they walked. Moving the twenty-six patients who assembled at about 8:00 AM took until that evening. The location they moved the Army Hospital to was the Haebaru Kokumin School. Haebaru is a place that evokes many memories for Okumatsu because she was the first public health nurse to be stationed there. She had acquired the necessary qualifications to work as a public health nurse during her time at the Hamamatsu Hospital, and her boss had asked the hospital to take her on. When they agreed, she started what was to be a six-month stint as the resident public health nurse at Haebaru, where she cycled around spreading the word about public health issues.

In March, the Army Hospital set up at Haebaru Kokumin School moved into dugout shelters. "The shelters weren't completed, so the one used for surgery had virtually no room on either side of the operating table," recalls Okumatsu Fumiko.

"On 23 March there was a large air raid and from that point on we became really busy," she said. In one day they would have to attend to between seventy and 100 patients. There were only two doctors, two nurses and two medics, so there was no time for them to rest between operations. By this stage, all the different sections covering the various branches of medicine were carrying out surgery. Okumatsu explained, "When people are under pressure psychologically, it is not uncommon for illnesses and contagious diseases to occur, but when people are totally focused, their bodies can display quite remarkable resilience."

Okumatsu still clearly remembers two of her patients. One of them managed to get to the hospital cave unassisted. "When I looked closely, I saw that the bone in his leg was smashed and the bottom part was just dangling there. I just couldn't imagine how on earth he could have got there by himself. I suppose he had managed something that would have been impossible in normal times, because in an emergency he was able to ignore the pain and focus his body and soul on just getting to his destination," she said. She also remembers a soldier who was hit in the belly in the fierce fighting in the Shuri area. He somehow managed to push his intestines back through the wound in his belly, put on the jacket of his uniform, tighten his belt and walk to Haebaru. He was operated on as soon as he arrived. It was a time when there was not enough anesthetic to go round so the only conversation the medical staff had with this wounded soldier was, "Do you want to live?" to which he replied, "Yes, I want to live and be useful to my country." Instead of anesthetic, two medics held him down so the surgeon could operate.

The operation lasted two hours by the light of oil lamps. "Considering the lack of proper equipment, I think that the doctor did a great job. He probably felt his way through the procedure. This patient was a man by the name of Nakandakari. He was from the Kerama Islands. Okumatsu worked in the operating theater space so she did not have many opportunities for contact with patients in the "wards" of the hospital cave. But even so, she cannot forget the sight of patients whose wounds were covered in maggots. "At first we thought that it could not be any good for wounds to be covered in maggots, but then one of the doctors used the term 'maggot treatment.' They say that maggots eat even the toxins in the wounds."

The Army Hospital withdrew from Haebaru at the end of May. Okumatsu somehow managed to get to Ihara but after about a week she was called to go to Command Post Shelter. "There were five of us. Me and Cpl. Nobutake, LCpl. Kohashikawa, plus nurses Nagata Noriko and Kuniba-san." The hospital head surgeon, Hiroike Fumikichi, ordered Cpl. Nobutake and the others to convey the order to withdraw from Haebaru to the unit left behind to guard the position. Okumatsu and the others were given the task of carrying the remaining medical supplies.

As a matter of routine, Okumatsu and the others were reminded that "Medical equipment and supplies are as important to soldiers as bullets are. It's just like ammunition."

Everyone understood that the situation had deteriorated since they had withdrawn. When she told head nurse Uehara Kimiko about the orders, she was told, "Matchan [Okumatsu's nickname], if you go with them you won't come back alive. You'll be killed." Uehara did her best to stop Okumatsu from going, but she had no choice but to obey the orders they had been given.

Okumatsu was shocked by what she saw when they reached the three-way junction near the Takamine Factory. Three patients left behind at the Haebaru Army Hospital because their legs had been blown off were pulling themselves forward using their arms. In the surgery space in the cave, she knew of people displaying phenomenal strength because they were in extreme situations, but now she was witnessing something incredible right in front of her.

When these three badly wounded men heard that Okumatsu and her companions were heading for Haebaru it was their turn to be surprised. When the men said, "That's madness. You'll just be going to your deaths," the group decided that because Nurse Kuniba was married, and therefore had more to live for, they would send her back to where they had come from. However, when Okumatsu eventually returned to the shelter at Ihara she heard that Kuniba had been killed by shellfire from U.S. warships when she had been out getting water. Okumatsu reflected that "That's the way death in war is . . . just a matter of good or bad fortune."

Nurses with the 62nd Infantry Division

With only the faint glimmer from candles to light the way, three former army nurses ventured into the pitch darkness of the cave, revisiting the site of their nightmare experience of thirty-nine years earlier.

It is a limestone cave beside Komyoji Temple in Shikina, Naha. This is where one section of the 62nd Division's field hospital was located. Nurses from the second intake of the Okinawa Prefectural Nursing School were attached to the 62nd Division's field hospital as employees of the military. There were forty-five nurses in this year's group. At first they were stationed at the field hospital head-quarters in Arakawa, Haebaru, before being sent to the field hospital units located near the front line. Of the group of nurses in question, in May 1945 four were attached to the hospital unit at Shikina—Higa Chiyo, Nakaji Toyoko, Higa Masako, and Hokama Hideko. Until that point it had been a shelter for civilians, but they were ejected by soldiers when it was requisitioned by the army for use as a field hospital.

The entrance to the cave is located on a highland that has a view of the East China Sea and the streets of the city of Naha. Inside the cave there are two or three large open areas where wounded soldiers lay in rows halfway in. The cave has a total length of approximately 100 meters.

The land above it was covered in scrub and trees at the time of the battle but is now a residential area so the entrance to the cave is very difficult to find. To get to it, one needs to walk sideways along a narrow path; moreover a house has been built directly above it. The other entrance at the far end of the cave has been sealed because of construction above it.

Higa Chiyo and Nakaji Toyoko who visited the cave for the first time in thirty-nine years and their classmate at nursing school Yoshino Kazuko who was there for a short time during the battle, reflected on their memories of the place, saying, "I feel sick just thinking of the smell of so many people down there and the stench of the wounds."

When we went in, the air inside the cave was cool, the only sound being from the occasional droplet of water dripping from a stalactite into a tiny pool below. This is where Higa Chiyo and her friends spent their days tending to the needs of wounded soldiers brought there from the front line.

"They'd bring the soldiers in one after another using doors from houses as stretchers. I don't know how many died each day or how many wounded were in there. It was the rainy season, so the ventilation in the cave was poor because of the still, humid air. The wounds of some of the men were infested with maggots. I still remember the men groaning in pain, both night and day. We'd wash old pieces of gauze and bandages to use over and over again. We had no soap, so we just washed them with water. Every day, when it was dark outside after the sun went down, we'd go down to the well, not far below the cave, and wash the blood off the pieces of gauze."

The well is still there. If you come out from the shelter and cross the road there are wells in two locations. Rather than a "well" as such, fresh water just flows from two places on the slope.

"I remember how we'd put water in a bucket and wash the pieces of gauze or bandages. Even at night we'd be able to tell that the water in the bucket had turned red from the blood. We didn't mind washing them like this, but the thought of going back to that smell from the wounds in the cave was something that we all dreaded."

When Nakaji Toyoko was trying to get some sleep in the cave one day, a stalactite fell and injured her right leg. She put a bandage on it for two or three days, but remembers being taken aback when maggots started appearing from underneath it. She was in this cave for a total of about one month. The U.S. forces were slowing edging their way southwards, and at the beginning of June the occupants of the cave were given the order to withdraw to the south. Wounded soldiers capable of walking were each helped by two nurses, but those who could not walk were left behind in the cave.

Higa and her friends left the cave in Shikina at the start of June and pushed southwards ahead of the American advance, which was by now more of a mopping up operation. Moving from cave to cave at night, they went from Taketomi to Ahagon to Komesu and then to Ihara in Itoman. Since the Amerian landing on the main island of Okinawa on 1 April, the IJA had not been able to move forward at all and were now forced to give ground in the face of mounting enemy pressure. It was clear that the army was fighting a losing battle, but Higa and the other army nurses were not permitted to voice such thoughts. After they left the cave in Shikina, during the retreat southwards they did little that could be described as nursing duties.

"When I think about it now, we were only in that cave for about a month, but it felt like years," said Higa. The things that she experienced as an innocent young eighteen year-old are still vividly etched in her memory. "I am amazed that I was able to live through all that," she said.

They remember Higa Masako, who was in the same unit as them, being with them until they left the cave at Shikina, but on the way south she went missing. They heard nothing of her after the war either. Also, while in a cave at Ihara, Hokama Hideko was killed when a piece of rock fell and hit her on the head during a naval bombardment. Hokama's elder sister, Arakawa Fumiko, had been with her the whole time during the retreat. Knowing where her sister had died, she was able to collect Higa Masako's remains not long after the war ended.

Higa Chiyo and Nakaji Toyoko were taken prisoner in front of their cave in Ihara on 19 or 20 June. When they peered out from the cave, they saw some soldiers who had gathered together and were dancing to music. For a moment they thought that the soldiers were Japanese, but there was clearly something quite different about the scene. Before long, the American soldiers called out "Come on out" to the young women and gestured for them to come out of the cave. When they ventured out, terrified of what might happen next, an American soldier offered them water from his canteen. Conditioned to think that the enemy might poison them, the girls did not accept it, so the soldier drank some himself to show them that it was safe to drink. Only then did they take the water, and were taken into captivity.

Of the forty-five young women in the second intake of the Okinawa Prefectural Nursing School, twenty-five worked as army nurses in field hospitals. Ten of those were killed during the battle. When the remains of fifty-five people were found in June 1983 during road works near where the field hospital was located at Arakawa in Haebaru, the remaining eleven nurses decided to get together for the first time since the war. Most of the women had continued working as nurses in the post-war years.

The fifty-five sets of human remains were located close to the 62nd Infantry Division field hospital in which Higa and her friends had been working. Upon reading in the newspaper about this find, Yoshino Kazuko quickly went to the site and told the people working there of one more location where they had disposed of dead bodies and, just as she had said, there were also more remains there.

"I don't want to remember the things we went through back then, but we cannot remain silent about this forever," said one of the women who had come together almost forty years after the battle. On 14 June 1983, a memorial service was held at the site where the bones were found. The former army nurses who gathered with bereaved family members at the scene of fierce fighting thirty-nine years earlier offered sticks of incense and prayed, tears flowing down their cheeks. There were family members who asked Yoshino and the other former nurses if they knew any details of the last moments of their father or elder sister, and the ladies did their best to pass on what details they could remember.

The spot where the memorial service was held had remained undeveloped in the years after the war, and people living nearby said that occasionally men who looked like tourists from the main islands of Japan could be seen praying in front of where the field hospital had been. The ladies surmised that "Maybe they were soldiers who had survived the battle."

Special Student Units

In preparation for the expected invasion of Okinawa by U.S. forces, in January 1945 the IJA organized units using locally recruited high school students. These units were known as *Gakutotai* or Student Units, and records have it that they comprised 1,685 boys and 543 girls (of whom 731 and 249 were killed, respectively).

Fukuhara Choei was one of the boys who joined the Student Units. He was in his final year at Kainan Middle School at the time, and around January 1945, when the student draft order was given, he joined a signals unit in the 24th Infantry Division.

Signals units were divided up into the three sections of codes, wireless and cable, with Fukuhara attached to the code section. His main duties were working with the codes used within the division. "We deciphered codes using a random number list, adding and subtracting four-digit numbers."

But those duties only lasted for about one month. After that he was transferred to the 24th Division's Special Operations Unit. When asked about what his new duties were, Fukuhara hesitated, saying, "We'll leave that one as it is. I don't really remember, and there are some things that I'd prefer not to talk about."

"But in that unit there were also tasks like this . . . well, things that aren't that well known . . ." He focused on one point off in the distance as he concentrated, choosing his words carefully and deliberately.

Their job was to somehow get in behind enemy lines and cause confusion. Their base of operations was the first floor of an old two-story hospital that had been damaged in a bombing raid and looked as though it could fall over at any moment. The building was located in Tomigusuku. Fukuhara says that they stayed in it until just before the Americans landed, spending their days there being briefed on how to carry out their mission.

They started at 6:30 AM each day when they were woken by *reveille*, commencing study after going for a run. There were chairs behind long desks, with each subject being taught by a different officer from Divisional Headquarters who would each focus on his own specialty. The emphasis was on English conversational skills, but they were also taught to walk somewhere at a fast pace, and then draw a map or take a quick look at the topography of a location and commit that to memory. They were instructed in a diverse range of things from methods for gathering information in front of someone without taking notes, to clambering up steep slopes wearing a gas mask.

There were around forty-six members in the unit and the average age was about twenty-three. "I was the youngest. There were only two of us from Okinawa—a man called Taira aged twenty-four or twenty-five from the central part of Okinawa and me. The others were all from the main islands of Japan. With our duties being what they were, at first our unit commander wasn't even told our names." To the maximum extent possible, the members of the unit were required to avoid contact with people outside their group.

"Our job was to get in behind enemy lines where we were supposed to steal weapons and destroy enemy supplies, so we could be called a kind of 'Sabotage Unit.' If it looked as though we might be captured, we were to disguise ourselves as civilians and try to gather intelligence. The training for this was really tough. Learning English vocabulary was the hardest thing for us. We had a quota of ten words that we had to learn each day and the instructor would hit us if we couldn't remember them." On just two small meals a day, hunger was a constant distraction for them.

At the end of March 1945, just before the U.S. forces landed on Okinawa, Fukuhara was ordered to go to Makiminato. Each member of the unit was told his destination individually and, while they were organized into special mission pods of three to five, beyond that they did not know where their other comrades were to go. Those in each pod would make their own way to a predetermined rendezvous point. All that they were to carry with them in terms of weapons was one hand grenade. Everything they needed was to be procured in the field.

"But when we got out there where the fighting was, what we had been taught was of no use at all. Of course, we'd only had a short period of training and the unit was far from ready. In our case, we were sent to a location right on the coastline, so we could hardly get in behind enemy lines from there." After the Americans landed, the IJA was slowly pushed southwards. With that, Fukuhara withdrew from Makiminato to Kakazu, Aja, Asato, Sobe, Tomigusuku, Yoza, and finally Mabuni in June.

"As we moved south, we were pulled in to join various units and on several occasions we came very close to being used on infiltration raids." When they were operating in the field, members of the Special Unit wore a uniform with no rank insignia attached. The only thing they had on them to prove their membership in the unit was a piece of paper that they kept in their pocket. On that paper, in addition to the name of the 24th Division and their serial number, it said, "Awaiting further orders," which effectively meant "on a mission." Fukuhara remembers that, "Even that tattered piece of paper was very useful."

When he arrived at Mabuni, after staying several nights in an abandoned house he moved down to a shelter near the coastline, close to where the Peace Memorial Hall now stands.

"It was a two-story shelter with as many as forty people inside—soldiers and civilians. I think that it would have been about 10 June when I went in there." Fukuhara recalls that the area around the shelter was littered with dead bodies and that hand grenades seemed to be flying in all directions, with enemy soldiers now right there in front of them.

On 20 June, he was finally taken prisoner and joined the crowds of others in an open space near the shelter. He remembers that it was about 10.00 AM. It was there that Fukuhara saw American soldiers separating those badly wounded but still alive from the clearly dead.

"They were checking the pupils of the eyes of each of the bodies scattered everywhere. There were old folk in there whose wounds were covered in maggots, and they must have been on the verge of death, but the Americans separated them out from the corpses, probably to get them to a field hospital." This effectively occurred while the battle was still going on; Fukuhara remembers this as an example of the humanity displayed by the American soldiers. After about an hour, he was put on a truck and taken to a camp in Gushikami, but then as the truck moved away, he remembers seeing a large pit full of countless corpses in civilian clothes.

"The pit would have been 30 meters long, 5 meters wide and about 2 meters deep. It was really large. I'd say that there would have been about 100 bodies in there." Beside the hole was a tank fitted with a bulldozer blade. "The corpses that the American soldiers had sorted were going to be buried in there."

After the war, every time Fukuhara went past that spot he remembered those corpses. When there was finally a move to recover the remains of the war dead, he drew a map of the area as it had been back in 1945. Those who saw it were surprised by its detail and accuracy, testimony to the training he received in the Special Unit all those years ago.

Chihaya Unit

Tomimura Moriteru, a member of the Normal School Blood and Iron Corps Student Corps' Chihaya Intelligence Unit, still has a list of names of members of that unit: *Current Circumstances of Male Students at Okinawa Normal School.* In June 1946, at the suggestion of staff at the Normal School, student teachers assigned to Okinawa Bunkyo School compiled the list. Tomimura's finger follows the names of the twenty-two members of the Chihaya Unit on the list, now tattered and yellowed with age. "It was forty-seven years ago but, as soon as I see this list, my mind returns to what happened back then."

Members selected for the Unit were from the second and third year regular course—outstanding students who excelled at both writing and speaking, plus those with experience as class captains and vice-captains. According to the Normal School Unit records left behind by the group charged with winding up the 32nd Army's affairs, the basis for selection into the Chihaya Unit was to be "principled and resolute." In other words, the unit was exclusively for the archetypal militarist youth. "At our joining up ceremony, we were the first to be organized as a unit. We felt so proud to have been chosen from the whole school," reminisced Nakada Seiei who had also enrolled in the Chihaya Unit.

Operating under the command of the 32nd Army's Intelligence Section, the Chihaya Unit's role was to report on the current state of the war to civilians who had fled from the fighting and taken refuge in shelters. They also gave locals advice so that they wouldn't be taken in by misinformation. It was also the Unit's job to distribute copies of the Okinawa Shimpo Newspaper, which was produced in one of the shelters. Nakada explained, "Our ultimate role was in underground operations, sort of like spying really. We had to report on how the battle was progressing and devise how to get information from the military to the civilians. At the same time, an important part of our job was to report on the fighting and keep the civilians' spirits up." Tomimura added, "We used to try to encourage the civilians in the shelters by telling them that the enemy were scared and on the run."

The twenty-two-man unit was split up into squads of two or three members, each visiting the various shelters in Shuri and the southern area of the island with information about the fighting they had received from the Intelligence Section at Command Headquarters' shelter. At the start, the central area of Okinawa was also included in their area of operation, but the American landings soon ruled that out. They went from one shelter to the next, dodging enemy shells along the way. They would attempt to cheer up the civilians with comments like, "Hang in there. We're going to win for sure." The boys in the Chihara Unit really did believe they were going to win. Nakada explained, "I was so determined to get the information to them . . . I never thought of questioning the validity of those war reports."

In charge of the 32nd Army's Intelligence Section and providing information to the Chihaya Unit were Intelligence Staff Officer Maj. Yakumaru Kanenori and Lt. Masunaga Tadasu. In the main, the Chihaya Unit did its rounds of the shelters on the orders of Lt. Masunaga. Tomimura's impression of Masunaga was that "He wasn't the archetypal military man. He was more of a mild-mannered, academic sort of person, but at the same time he had real backbone and a steely look in his eyes." Nakada Seiei also commented, "We didn't have a bad impression of him at all. He was a nice person."

The Chihaya Unit was made very welcome in the civilian shelters, and sometimes its members were also given food, which made them the object of jealousy among the other Normal School units. But while they may have had some privileges, on their rounds they were constantly hounded by reconnaissance aircraft and exposed to the relentless enemy shelling. The Unit was an important source of news for the civilians for whom daily life was fraught with worry and who had no other way of obtaining information. But some civilians, almost beside themselves with worry, were also suspicious about the Chihaya Unit, asking "Are we going to win this war . . . is it really true that we've sunk some of their battleships?" To dispel their concern, the Chihaya Unit continued to try to cheer them up by telling them, "Of course we are going to win! Please cooperate with us to the very end."

However, the battle situation was rapidly deteriorating, something that the Chihaya Unit was now experiencing first-hand. Tomimura explained, "In the Command Post shelter everyone was running around frantically, as though panic was starting to set in . . . but we did our best to disguise the fact that we were losing the battle. We told the civilians that many enemy planes had crashed, that lots of their ships had sunk, and that we were winning. We couldn't let on how many on our side had been killed." When they withdrew to the south everybody in the Chihara Unit began to feel that Japan was going to lose the war. "That was about the time we stopped going round to the shelters."

After heading south toward Cape Kyan, some members of the Unit were killed or captured. Some ignored American calls to surrender and remained hidden until September, waiting for the war to take a different turn. Of the twenty-two members of the Unit, nine were killed. Although the Unit was exposed to constant danger, the figure of 40.9 percent of its personnel being killed was lower than the other units (the average for all units was 58 percent). Nakada explained it as, "We were constantly out in the open so we got used to the firing. I think that more of us survived because we became what you might call 'battle-savvy.'" That their experience of such incredible dangers helped these young people to stay alive is both ironic and tragic.

Ryukon Shelter

Below the observation point in the grounds of Shuri Castle there was a small cave in which civilians sheltered. The shelter that the students of the Okinawa Normal School dug around was known as the Ryukon shelter. It was designed by one of the students, Moriteru Tomimura. Using his plans, as they dug their way into the hill they hung three plumb-lines from the top of each post to check if it was straight. Tomimura remembers that there were days when they only managed to make twenty or thirty centimeters progress.

Kawasaki Masanori says, "I think that we finished it on about 20 March 1945. I remember how we sang Army songs and our dormitory song as we were working. "We were absorbed by the desire to do our bit in wiping out the 'American and British devils.'" In the shelter next to theirs, also dug out by the students, the *Okinawa Newspaper* produced the *Jinchu Shimbun* [Fortress Newspaper].

The teachers brought tatami mats from the school and before they were laid down in the cave the students covered the floor with bishopwood branches and other things to make it level. Tomimura recalls that about 200 people could be accommodated inside. The students in the Fortification Construction Unit commuted the 300 meters from the Ryukon Shelter to where they worked digging out the 32nd Army Command Post cave complex. However, as there were 386 students, each working on one of three eight-hour shifts, at any one time only two-thirds of the students would be in the cave. Miyagi Kokichi, who was a teacher at the Normal School, explained that "Because that number of people could not fit in the shelter properly, a system of two twelve-hour shifts was adopted."

Most of the students spent their waking moments digging in the 32nd Army Command Post cave complex, but for these sixteen- and-seventeen-year-olds, the Ryukon Shelter was the only place where they could relax with their friends. Moromi Moriyasu recalls, "We used to look forward to getting to the shelter and competing to count how many lice we could find in our clothes." Such simple pleasures would also soon be taken from them. After the U.S. forces landed on the main island of Okinawa on 1 April 1945, they would be stricken by the mortal fear that came with living on the edge of life and death.

In the early days of April, Kuba Yoshio became the first fatality suffered by the Normal School students. He lost a leg when hit by a piece of shrapnel from a shell fired from an American warship. Tomimura recalls that "We were panic-stricken when we saw blood for the first time like this."

An army surgeon treated young Kuba, and his friends prayed that he would survive, but before long he died from loss of blood. From that day on, students from the Normal School were killed one after another. Those who died were promoted two ranks from private second class to lance corporal, but of course all that remained for their school friends was a feeling of emptiness and loss.

Kunii Hill Shelter

The locals hid in the shelter the whole day, hardly even daring to breathe. Terrified that the American soldiers would find them, they hadn't used their only means of lighting—a kerosene lamp—since the previous day. Only when the sun's rays finally entered the shelter were they able to barely make out the faces of the people next to them.

All of a sudden the silence was shattered when a gas canister was thrown into the shelter by the American soldiers outside.[7] Children cried out and mothers screamed as smoke poured in, creating a scene of utter pandemonium. Unable to bear the acrid sting of the gas, many of the people ran outside yelling, "Let's die outside in the light of day!" Another group ran outside to join them, followed by yet another group. These people were all rounded up by American soldiers, and their lives were spared. But there were others—around thirty apparently—who refused to go outside, having been indoctrinated with the mantra of "white devils."

Kunii Hill is in Iramina in Yomitan. Although many people have provided information about the site, to date it has never been cleared of human remains. The reason for this is that by the time the civilians were released from the American internment camps, the entire area was already part of a U.S. base. Cordoned off with wire mesh fencing, the area is off limits. Today, the shelter lies within the grounds of the Chibana Ammunition Depot.

Chairman of Iramina Ward, Uechi Seiyu, was only two years old at the time. He escaped from the ordeal at Kunii Hill cradled in his mother's arms. Other family members in the shelter with him were his grandparents and five of his brothers and sisters. His father and two elder brothers were in the military and were away with the Home Guard. They never returned.

There has been much discussion about Kunii Hill shelter, but it is only since February 1983 that the talk has included the issue of clearing the human remains from the site. Uechi commented, "To be honest, I'm flabbergasted. I'd just as-

---

7.   There is no record of the U.S. military using poison gas in the Battle of Okinawa, but they did use smoke and white phosphorus grenades and projectiles, so "gas" is likely to be either of these.

sumed that it had all been done . . . maybe it was the collection of remains on Ie-Jima that stirred them into action. Maybe they'd just given up because it's on the U.S. base. I guess that means that there are still human remains inside the U.S. bases."

About ten years after the war ended, Uechi himself discovered the skeleton of a soldier at Yomitan-dake. The skull was still wearing its steel helmet and the soldier's boots were completely intact. Beside him lay his Type 38 infantry rifle. "I couldn't believe it and ran home as fast as my legs would carry me. There must be lots more like that up there." Because the base is completely off limits, we have no idea whether the Americans are doing anything to collect human remains.

The Kunii Hill shelter was specifically dug out by the Japanese military. Bolstered by pine logs, the inside was relatively spacious. Civilians with little more than a few household effects occupied the shelter after the Japanese military abandoned it and retreated.

Uechi's elder brother Seijiro is one of the survivors who very clearly remembers what happened, but he finds it difficult to talk about. "Even today, it suddenly flashes through my mind . . . it's not a nice feeling. I knew lots of those people up there . . ."

On the third day after the Americans landed, there was a group suicide in the Kunii Hill shelter. Many people have talked about how some of them killed themselves with hand grenades, while family members found other ways to kill their own parents, siblings or children. On the morning after the landing, 2 April 1945, the tragedy of Kunii Hill shelter began. Most of the people inside were from Iramina Ward, but there were also civilians from nearby Sobe and Owan. The tragedy was exacerbated by the presence of two Japanese soldiers who had become separated from their unit. The shelter was discovered by American troops on the evening of the second. The people inside were surrounded and could do nothing but remain absolutely silent and wait. At one stage, some American soldiers entered the shelter to have a look around but according to those who survived, there was no indication that the Americans were actually attacking the shelter. On the contrary, they seemed to be checking on the well being of the civilians inside.

Those civilians remained hidden in the darkness of the shelter, petrified. Then it happened. One of the Japanese soldiers shot and killed one of the Americans. The other Americans withdrew from the shelter immediately, leaving the civilians in the cave to sit out hour after oppressive hour until the next morning.

Goya Masayoshi from Iramina Ward in Yomitan lost his father inside the cave. His wife Toshi also lost her eldest sister and child, plus the wife and child of their eldest son. Goya talked hesitatingly about what happened. "The next morning, there was a really strong smell of petrol. Even today I don't know exactly what it was from, but when we stepped out of the cave, the whole hillside had been burned."

Later, gas canisters were thrown into the cave, which caused screams of pain from all over the place. About two hours would have passed, so it must have been around 10:30 AM. Then one of the Japanese soldiers yelled out, "All those who want to die now, get over here!" Almost as if they had been waiting for his command, one after another, a group of civilians formed a circle around the soldier. Then there was the sound of a hand grenade exploding. All the people in that circle had committed group suicide.

Goya continued, "I can only remember hearing one grenade and I don't recall anybody screaming so they must have died instantly." Those who took their lives in that incident had been in the front group in the cave. They included relatives of both Goya and his wife. Toshi subsequently tried to strangle herself by tying a rope around her own neck but was unsuccessful and was taken prisoner. Neither Goya nor his wife Toshi can remember, but apparently some family members actually helped each other commit suicide.

In all, five relatives of Goya and his wife died in the hand grenade incident. "There were two soldiers there as well," Goya continued. "They had both returned from the fighting in China. One was from Iramina, while the other one was born in Namihira. But I don't really know anything about him. I don't know the person's surname, but there was also a woman called Yoshi. Her husband had been killed fighting in China."

"There were also two old women inside the shelter, both almost blind. All I can tell you is that one was from Iramina and the other was from Sobe. There were also three families with the same name and another person who had been in Toshi's class at school. None of those people made it out of the cave alive."

So Goya and his wife knew of fourteen people who died there. The inside of the shelter was so dark and large that it was almost impossible to establish exactly who was there, so it is likely that the actual number who died was even higher. Goya added, "We had the thirty-third year memorial service years several ago and I thought that would be enough, but I don't want to leave them like this . . . I guess they'll no longer be able to identify whose bones are whose anyway."

And yet, his wife Toshi was much more certain about one thing: "There'll be no problem identifying my sisters' remains." What she meant was that both of her elder sisters will have been lying there in that cave all these years since the war with their babies cradled in their arms.

Fortification Construction Unit

The "Historical Records of the Normal School Blood and Iron Student Corps in the Battle of Okinawa," issued in March 1947 by those entrusted to wind up the affairs of the 32nd Army, records how, "In the belief that victory for the Empire of Japan was nigh, the Normal School students carried out their duties without complaint, working both night and day to construct shelters in the midst of relentless bombardment." Through a hail of incoming shells, the students ran the 300 meters from the Ryukon Shelter where they slept to the Command Post shelter where they worked. They were frequently on the verge of collapse from fatigue and hunger.

"We would leave the Ryukon Shelter between 8 and 9 o'clock in the morning and run to the Command Post shelter. Boys were often wounded as shells from the bombardment from the American warships exploded all around them," said Uehara Seitoku, who had joined the Fortifications Unit after completing his second year of Yokaren training. (Japanese Naval Preparatory Flight Training Program). It was obviously extremely dangerous moving from one shelter to the next.

When the bombardment became increasingly fierce, Uchima Takeyoshi and Yonabaru Harutaka, a boy one year his senior at school and who rotated shifts with him, dug a foxhole near the No. 5 shelter. On 16 May 1945, it took a direct hit and Yonabaru was killed. That day, young Yonabaru had a fever and was unable to work. The fatal shell came hurtling in moments after Uchima placed a damp towel on his friend's forehead and moved away from the foxhole.

"I remember crying as I scrambled to dig away the stones and soil that had slipped into the hole. As I dug away, a blackened hand appeared from under the soil. That night, when it was pitch dark, I went back with some wild flowers and gave Yonabaru a burial. Just thinking of it now brings tears to my eyes," said Uchima in hushed tones.

Despite losing their school friends in the battle, the Normal School students continued to do their utmost to help dig the shelters. There was no room in their day for any thoughts that may have made them question the logic of the war.

Moromi Moriyasu, who dug on the No. 3 shelter side toward the shelter extending in from the Kinjo side, recalls, "I was sixteen years old at the time. I had no concept of war at all, certainly nothing like the thoughts that it brings up for me now. All I was thinking about was getting that shelter finished, nothing else . . . " Higa Yoshio from Yomitan stresses this point, saying, "At that stage, I didn't see anything strange about the war at all. Without education in its truest sense, people just don't see things for what they are."

"In the belief that victory for the Empire of Japan was nigh . . ." These words are testimony to the frightening nature of the education and the circumstances that those young students found themselves in in those days.

"I reckon that it was around here. I'm sure it was." Tokuyama Chosho, who had worked digging shelters as a member of the Field Fortification Construction Unit, looked around for the Kinjo-side entrance to the shelter.

The place that he was visiting forty-seven years after the event is on the southeast slope of the hillock where the campus of the Okinawan Prefectural University of Arts is located. The roots of a banyan tree cradle the rocks under it in an area that is otherwise overgrown. There is a creek flowing through a concrete-lined open channel and nearby is where the Normal School's rice paddy used to be. The area is now completely transformed into a residential area.

When Tokuyama visited the shelter, he was undaunted by the rain which was pelting down just as it had done forty-seven years earlier. Memories of that time all those years ago came flooding back.

"As the soldiers made progress with their pickaxes, we students shoveled the rock and soil into a wheelbarrow. When it was full, we pushed it out of the cave and tipped it out. We were up to our ankles in water dripping from the ceiling of the shelter. Our skin became waterlogged and all wrinkly as we were wet through the whole time. The tunnel in the shelter was really humid, so the soldiers stripped down to their loincloths when they worked."

The construction of the shaft that was still incomplete when the U.S. forces landed was pushed ahead at a furious pace amid bombing and strafing attacks. The shaft that was to be connected to the main tunnel was being dug on the right side facing the Kobiki Gate of Shuri Castle, just below the castle wall.

Shells fired from the American artillery on the uninhabited Keise Islands off Naha Port hit the walls of Shuri Castle, causing ammunition stacked up along the wall to catch fire and explode. Soldiers and students working close by were blown over by the blast with some killed as they fell down the vertical shaft.

The digging of the tunnels was fraught with difficulty. The No. 2 and 3 tunnels located on the Josei Elementary School side met up with the No. 1 tunnel and, after forming the main tunnel, divided into the No. 4 tunnel. The main tunnel then extends to the Kinjo side where it connects with the No. 5 tunnel.

Digging down on an angle to connect up with the No. 5 tunnel was particularly problematic, with gas building up and the air being so thin that the workers' candles would often go out.

"So as not to suffocate, those working in the main tunnel would be lowered down by rope, swing their pickaxes two or three times and then be quickly pulled up again. Next, another student with a basket would be lowered, shovel some soil and rocks into a basket before being pulled up as fast as possible. That was repeated over and over again," recalls Miyagi Kokichi, a Normal School teacher who was in the Field Fortification Construction Unit.

"I think it was around the end of April when we finally cut our way through. We held a little ceremony and everyone was overjoyed," said Uehara Seitoku. Toyosato Yasuhiro remembers it the same way, saying, "I was right there when we broke through to the other tunnel. It was quite emotional for all of us."

Prefectural Technical School Student Unit

In January 1945, ten officers and enlisted men from the 5th Artillery Command Unit visited the Prefectural Technical School in Shuri to set up a student unit. In preparation for the defense of Okinawa, national policy required students to cooperate with the IJA and help lead Japan to victory. Aptitude tests were quickly held and over 2,000 male and female students from the boys' and girls' Okinawa Normal Schools, plus from the First and Second Prefectural Middle Schools, were drafted into the student units, of whom fifty percent died in the fighting. The Technical School suffered the greatest casualties, losing around ninety percent of those students who joined. In other words, passing the aptitude test was tantamount to signing their own death warrants. In those days, the Technical School, where the principal was Higa Tokutaro, was located in Shuri, but after the war it became the campus of the University of the Ryukyus. It offered a three-year program with the first and second years involved building and chemistry, with civil engineering taught in the third year.

At the request of the military, from around June 1944, classes were canceled and the students were put to work building facilities at Oroku Airfield and constructing anti-aircraft emplacements at Ameku in Mawashi. Many of the students were from places such as Nago, Ie, and Katsuren. They had been boarding in Shuri but when classes were canceled some returned to their homes in the country. Because second-year students from the building course and third-year students were responsible for surveying the areas for military installations, only the first-year students and students from the two-year chemistry course, plus around 300 from the introductory course actually sat the aptitude test. The test itself was basic and all those who looked fit and seemed as though they would cooperate with the IJA were selected. However, many of those who sat the test were far too young, and only 107—fewer than half—actually passed.

The No. 5 Artillery Command Unit under Lt. Gen. Wada Kosuke set up its headquarters in the First Prefectural Middle School [now Shuri High School]. Students who passed the aptitude test were quickly put into the Command Post signals unit and separated into three separate sections, namely wireless, wire telegraph, and encoding. They also took classes in the First Prefectural Middle School gymnasium. While studying, they were billeted with families near Kanegusuku in Shuri, which meant commuting between where they lived and the Command Post each day. The telegraph section was under the command of a Lt. Kosugi and studied wiring above ground and how to repair breaks, memorizing names, and semaphore. The wireless unit was led by a Lt. Kubo and concentrated on receiving Morse code, while the encoding unit (Lt. Nakamura) studied random digit sampling and the alphabet set used for code encryption. Finally, their induction ceremony was held in the grounds of the First Prefectural Middle School. According to one edition of the Prefectural Department Relief Division Records during their period of study some students were evacuated and some succumbed to accidents. So a total of seventy-six were officially signed up, of whom forty-two were in the wireless unit, fourteen in the wire telegraph unit and twenty in the encoding unit. As they stood and listened to the officers speaking, the innocent young faces of the boy soldiers showed the tension they were feeling.

Among those boyish faces were Nagamine Katsumasa (signals section), Yamakawa Munehide and Arakaki Anei (wireless section), and Ishikawa Naesuke (wire telegraph section). They thought it would be an honor to be enshrined at Yasukuni.

"When we were told that we would have the honor of being immortalized at Yasukuni ... I guess what they meant was that if we were killed we'd be enshrined at Yasukuni just like real soldiers. For some reason, that's the only bit I can still clearly remember," explained Nagamine. Only sixteen at the time, decades later Nagamine has never been able to forget those words. As they signed up, the boys were each given the rank of private (second-class) and issued with uniforms, caps, boots and rifles. A white cotton flash bearing the words Special Communications Unit was sewn onto the left side of their tunics at chest height. Prior to their induction ceremony, the army handed out enlistment permission slips to each student soldier and sent the boys off home to get their parents' consent.

Several days later, the forms with the required seal of permission were returned, but there were also some forms where consent had not been given.

According to Student Military Records, Lt. Kubo ordered a student from the wireless section to gather up any permission slips which did not have the parent's seal of consent, go to the stamp shop, get the appropriate stamps made, stamp all the forms and hand them back in. Also, around the time of the induction ceremony, every student had to provide a lock of hair and some fingernail clippings as human mementos in preparation for the worst-case scenario. Nagamine explained, "I also wrote a farewell note. I can't remember what I wrote but I know that it included 'I will do my absolute best for my country.' We then put the locks of hair and the nail clippings into envelopes, wrote our names on them and handed them to our section leaders. The envelopes were then buried all together in the ground. I went back after the war to get them but I couldn't find them." On the evening of 22 March 1945, the boys were told that they were having live firing practice early the next morning and were each given five rounds of ammunition. That would be the first time they would actually fire their guns since the weapons had been handed out. "When the fighting begins, you guys will have to use these," they were told. After that they all cleaned their rifles. Early the following morning, 23 March, they collected their packed lunches and headed off for the firing range along the main road. That's when it happened.

The air raid started with a massive explosion that caused the ground to vibrate as though the earth was being shaken off its very axis. The attack took them completely by surprise and the live firing practice was immediately canceled. The boys fled to the nearby Toraju Hill, from where they could see out over Naha Port. Nagamine explained that out to sea, swarms of U.S. warplanes in formation were attacking a Japanese destroyer. The Japanese were firing back from their anti-aircraft emplacements at Ameku, and the boys watched as the Japanese destroyer tried to escape the bombs. "When the ship finally went down, a bugler at the Shuri Command Post played a very doleful tune." The air raids on Naha continued for several days and, as almost every house in the city had been razed, the boys moved to another shelter that the Command Post had prepared in case of emergency. That was the start of life in the shelter for the Technical School student soldiers. The Command Post main shelter was man-made and located near the back of what is now the Okinawa Annex of the Japanese Arts and Crafts Center in Kinjo in Shuri. The shelter used by the students, on the other hand, was a naturally formed cave located nearby. Unfortunately, the cave took a direct hit from U.S. naval guns, which caused a huge rock to fall inside rendering it uninhabitable. From that point on the student soldiers slept in the Command Post Shelter. There were several hundred soldiers in the Command Post Shelter, which was well equipped. It had two entrances camouflaged with trees and earth. Duties for the Technical School Student Unit began in earnest. However, because the code section's studies had been interrupted by the air raids, that group was given a range of other jobs. The main responsibility for the wireless section was to crank the generator used for sending messages, while the wiring section laid telephone cables to connect the Command Post with the front line. Yamakawa's job was to crank the generator in places such as Maeda and Takushi.

"I used to observe where the shells were landing and crank the generator for wireless transmissions, but I was amazed at the difference between Japanese and American firepower. Every time our guys fired one or two rounds, the Americans would reply with dozens back. I remember how the evening sky was bright red." The Americans landed on 1 April. The fighting grew even more vicious, especially at Kakazu in Ginowan and Maeda in Urasoe. By that stage, wounded soldiers were being brought into the Command Post shelter. The torrential rain also continued for days on end and, as more and more wounded soldiers were carried into the shelter from the rear, it became a seething mass of groaning men.

In the torrential rain, young Arakaki in the wireless section was told to wait near an artillery emplacement to the north, ready to deliver wireless instructions from the front line to the gunners. "I had to decipher all the coded messages from the front line, rewrite them in ordinary sentences, put the messages in my inside pocket, and deliver them. It was the same, day or night. On several occasions I went out in the middle of the day and was attacked by American aircraft. About five minutes after I left, one of my friends arrived. But he was not there to help me. He was there in case I went down, in which case he would take the message from my pocket and deliver it to the gun emplacement himself."

"It was tough for us as well," explained Ishikawa who had been in the telegraph wire section. His job had been to lay phone wires between Urasoe where the fighting was intense and the Command Post shelter. "We had to lay phone lines as the shells flew all around us and, just when we finally thought we'd finished, they would lose contact and we'd have to struggle back along the wires inspecting them and repairing the breaks. We did that over and over again." At the same time, some of his classmates were going out to attack with improvised explosive devices made from wooden boxes stuffed full of dynamite and with only the fuse sticking out. The idea was for the boys to carry the charges strapped on their backs like a school bag, crawl in underneath an enemy tank, pull the fuse wire and blow themselves and the tank up at the same time.

More and more of their classmates were killed once these kinds of attacks began. Some of the students went crazy with fear. "They ran wildly all over the place inside the shelter and danced up and down as the shells poured in. Then all of a sudden, they would collapse motionless into a corner," explained Nagamine and Ogawa. The ferocious American attacks eventually forced the 32nd Army to abandon the fight at Shuri and begin withdrawing towards Mabuni. The artillery Command Post followed suit by also pulling out of Shuri. That was at the end of May. When they withdrew, they blew up the shelter entrance so the Americans would not be able to use it. However, some of those students who had gone crazy shut themselves inside and absolutely refused to leave. Even though their friends carried them out, they struggled violently and ran straight back inside. In the end, the cave was blown up with some of the students still alive inside.

The withdrawal from Shuri followed a route through Shikina, Ichinichibashi, Nagado, Yoza, Komesu, and Mabuni. Young Nagamine went back and forth between Shuri and Mabuni over and over again carrying box bombs and food. On his first visit to Mabuni, it was green with lush vegetation. To young Nagamine, who had just come from the battlefield at Shuri, it seemed like a different world altogether. But in the short time it took him to complete three or four return trips, the area became a battlefield and the greenery had disappeared, leaving behind the stench of gunpowder and blood. He has never been able to forget what he saw as he made his way back and forth along that road.

"I was passing through an area which had just been under an intense attack and the whole area was covered by the smell of gunpowder and there were things still burning. In one place, several members of one family lay dead, piled one on top of the other. The body of a young woman was propped up against the rear wheels of a Japanese army vehicle. On her back she had a baby in a sash. The baby was dead, its head slumped over. The woman was obviously the baby's mother. She was the only one of the family still alive but her leg had been hit and the white of the bone was protruding. She was holding the shattered bone and moaning in agony. There were bits of flesh and human innards lying everywhere. That was when I thought to myself that this must be what hell is like."

Not far from the various prefectures' memorials in Mabuni in Itoman is the Okinawa Technical School Memorial to Young Students. The remains of 124 staff and students from the high school are enshrined there. On the same site is another small plaque, bearing the following inscription:

At 7:00 AM on the morning of 4 June 1945, the Tokumura residence in Mabuni suffered a direct hit from a U.S. naval gun. Nine classmates from the second year advanced group at Okinawa Prefectural Technical School were killed instantly.

All nine were members of the code section and at the end of the inscription are the names of the four who were able to be identified. The memorial was erected by the bereaved families of the deceased students. Two people survived the direct hit on that dwelling—Nagamine and Yamagawa. The house had a thatched roof and the walls were made of stones and earth, but the floor boards had been ripped out. Nagamine explained, "The night I carried the last of the box bombs from Shuri to Mabuni, I went into the house. I was absolutely exhausted. Inside the house were about twenty soldiers and some people I knew. A good friend of mine Uehara Seigi and I went to sleep leaning against a pillar in the middle of the kitchen. Others propped themselves up against walls and went into a deep sleep, almost as if they were dead.

The following morning, Nagamine was woken by the sound of shellfire and he quickly realized that the house next door was under attack. This was followed by screams, crying, and the sound of shellfire. As he was thinking, "Ah, I've been hit," a little girl from next door came into the kitchen. Just then, although he was not sure how many minutes had already passed, everything went totally black as soot from the kitchen covered the entire area. Only when the soot settled did Nagamine start to wonder what on earth was happening to him. They had received a direct hit a by shell fired from an American warship. It had smashed a hole through the roof.

Nagamine looked at Uehara who had been asleep beside him, but he was already dead. He was covered in blood and his skull had been split in two. Nagamine had also been hit in the leg in two places. He moved away lumps of thatch, rock, and dirt that were strewn about and almost in a daze headed for Mabuni Hill. Only when he got to the hill did he actually realize that blood was oozing from the wounds in his legs. Arakaki also looked inside the house that had suffered the direct hit. "That house was where we did the cooking," he explained. "I think I'd gone there to get some food ready." That was when he saw a Normal School student lying among the dead bodies scattered about. "He had no head . . . it had been blown clean off."

Nagamine's leg wounds were not too serious, and in a tomb halfway up the hill at Mabuni he found himself caring for a badly wounded soldier. He went to a nearby pool of fresh water to fill his water bottle, only to find there were dead bodies floating in it. The water was thick with weeds and smelled bad. He managed to avoid throwing up, held his nose and drank some of the water. "By that stage, we were all thinking that, if we were going to die anyway, then just one last time we wanted to eat some beautiful white steamed rice and drink our fill of cool, sparkling water." The Americans eventually attacked the tomb, so he shifted to an artillery command shelter near the top of the hill. It was a basic shelter, just taking advantage of a large crack in the rock face. Ishikawa was also there. Around the same time, Yamakawa and Arakaki from the wireless section were in a naturally formed cave just behind where the Technical School Memorial to Young Students is today. The enemy were now on top of them and before dawn on 23 June the order came in that all surviving soldiers and student soldiers were to go out on an infiltration attack.

Based on what Nagamine and the others said, it appears that two infiltration raids were launched at about the same time, one from the artillery command post shelter, the other from the wireless section shelter. After a final meal, they listened to their section commander's impassioned words. "Die for the sake of our mother country, fight like hell to protect your homeland. Let's meet up at the Sanzu River on our way to the afterlife," said Lt. Kubo inside the wireless section's shelter. His subdued voice filled the shelter with an air of nervous anticipation. Ishikawa who was in the command post shelter explained, "To be honest, by that stage everybody in that shelter was utterly exhausted." They were each given two hand grenades. They were to be used on the raid but if anybody was taken prisoner then they should use them to kill themselves. Some wore *hachimaki* scarves around their foreheads and some carried ceremonial swords. There were around thirty of them in total, crawling along a path lit up as bright as the middle of the day by overhead flares. But once the flares stopped, the area was as black as pitch and, as they moved forward, some of the soldiers became separated from their comrades.

Nagamine was one who became separated. "When I got back to the shelter, the soldiers who were still there were just about to leave so I joined up with them and set off again." Ishikawa also set off from that shelter. "We were the last ones to go. We headed off with the unit commander, Gen. Wada, but on the way we lost track of him."

The enemy position was very close but it took them until morning to reach it. Nagamine took up the story. "We all gathered in a large rocky hollow. We were so close we could hear them speaking English. I thought 'This is it' and got ready. But then one of our soldiers said something to our medic corporal and immediately aimed his pistol at his own forehead and killed himself. At the sound of the shot, our hiding place attracted withering gunfire from the Americans." Inside the rocky hollow it was utter chaos, with some people screaming out "Long Live the Emperor!" and others committing suicide. Those who survived headed back toward the coast. They climbed down the cliffs and hid beneath a rocky outcrop. There were only six of them left.

A while later, the announcement "The battle is over!" could be heard from the loudspeakers set up in the American encampment. On the night of 23 June, the survivors tried to break through to the north by following the coastline, but ended up remaining in a cave in Yoza until August. In their group, however, Yamakawa, Arakaki, and some soldiers headed for the enemy position but, as they drew near, one of them touched the trip line made of something like piano wire, which resulted in another furious volley of gunfire. So Sgt. Watanabe called out "Follow me!" and edged forward, checking each wire he found as he went. The soldiers first, and then the students, moved slowly forward.

"He obviously felt there were no more trip wires," explained Arakaki, for suddenly Sgt. Watanabe stood up and, waving his sword in the air, ordered "Charge!" But they got no more than a few paces when a land mine exploded and the soldiers at the front of the charge were blown up into the air. The rest waited for things to quiet down then slowly pulled back and waited in some bushes. Only seven were still alive and, before they realized what was happening, the Americans had surrounded the whole area.

A student named Teruya who was holding a hand grenade was hit several times. "I'd say that it was because he was about to throw the grenade," explained Arakaki. But almost immediately the other Japanese soldiers also came under heavy fire. It was such a fierce hail of bullets that only the two boys Yamakawa and Arakaki survived.

As to why 90 percent of the Technical School students were killed in the battle, Nagamine points unequivocally to the infiltration raids. "There are several reasons, such as the fact that our main duties were with the communications unit and that there was no dissolution order for us. But however you look at it, the main reason was the infiltration raids. Classmates dropped in front of my eyes, one after the other, launching those raids where death was the only possible outcome. They went on those raids simply to get killed. That's how war is."

Normal School Infiltration Squad

At the very end of 1983, I visited Itoman High School in the southern part of Okinawa to ask a staff member about events that had happened forty years earlier. When I entered the career guidance office early that Saturday afternoon, several students were looking through some materials.

Hiranaka Koei from Kochinda took a break to talk to me. A man of solid build, Hiranaka was in charge of health and physical education at the school as well as providing the students with careers advice.

"In my day, career advice had only one meaning: 'join the army.' Whenever the officer attached to our school back then saw us, he'd urge us to 'go and volunteer!'"

Hiranaka smiled wryly as he recalled his own student days and began to tell his story. As I listened, I watched his students poring keenly over the brochures outlining their university and employment options, and it occurred to me that they were all about the same age as Hiranaka would have been back then.

During the Battle of Okinawa in 1945, Hiranaka was a second year student in the boys' division of the Okinawa Normal School. In the final few days of March, he was drafted into the 62nd Division, which meant that he eventually ended up taking part in some of the most horrific fighting at the Maeda Escarpment in Urasoe.

Hiranaka had started his secondary school education four years earlier, in the spring of 1941, at the age of fourteen. Two years into his study in the secondary course at Kochinda School, he dreamed of becoming a teacher. In order to fulfill that dream, he decided to sit only the entrance exam to the Okinawa Normal School because it served as the prefectural teacher training facility. "We were farming people but because we only farmed a sub-holding, we were not well off. So rather than gradually narrowing my options down to the Normal School, it was really a matter of studying where it wasn't going to cost us a lot of money."

Hiranaka explained another reason for choosing the Normal School. "In those days, there were also the prestigious schools such as the First and Second Prefectural Middle Schools, and a lot of children from families that were quite well-off went to them. But there were a lot of other kids who wanted to study, but simply couldn't afford the tuition fees. They used to take the Normal School entrance exam in the hope of studying without paying too much."

Hiranaka's grades were good and it was his teacher at Kochinda School, Teruya Nagashige, who really encouraged him to sit the Normal School entrance test. (Teruya subsequently taught at the Shuri Girls' School but was drafted into the militia and was killed in action.) Teruya was very supportive of Hiranaka. "You'll definitely pass the entrance exam," he told the boy, urging him, "Go and talk to your father about it." When Hiranaka wrote to his father who was away working in the Philippines at that time, his father wrote back, "Have a go ... we'll support you with an allowance."

He eventually sat and passed the Normal School entrance exam, overcoming the various difficulties he faced. His joy was all the greater because, "Throughout the whole prefecture, only about 110 students actually passed that exam, which meant that about one student per school was successful." Looking back at his success, he commented, "The only thing I can really say is that I was just lucky. Students who passed the exam received a government grant of 25 yen to pay for their fees. At that time, the boarding fees were about 13 yen, which was a lot of money. I was absolutely overjoyed."

In April, Hiranaka walked through the gate of the Okinawa Normal School in Tonokura in Shuri on his first day, something that he had so looked forward to. But his original resolve of, "I want to be a teacher" soon began to waver under the daily brainwashing by the army officer attached to the school, who constantly urged him to become an army officer rather than a teacher. Eventually, he ended up thinking, "Once I graduate, I *will* become an officer."

The buildings used by the Okinawa Normal School that Hiranaka attended were in Shuri, near Ryutan Pond in Tonokura. In 1943, three years after he started there, the school was upgraded to the status of a government-run vocational college and divided into separate divisions for boy and girls. From that point on, the whole nature of the school changed from its original and very simple purpose of being a place for training teachers to one of creating instructors capable of carrying out the education of the Empire of Japan in Kokumin Schools.

For two or three hours every week, the students had to attend drill classes held by the school's army officer. Also, under the so-called military instruction, activities such as how to fire a rifle, how to launch an attack, and general military discipline were relentlessly hammered into the boys. The school drillmaster was a commissioned army officer on active service and, in the eyes of Hiranaka and the other boys, he was "like a god."

"We always did our very best because if we got into his bad graces, come graduation day, we were afraid that we wouldn't receive our military certificates. Once we'd graduated, that military certificate was a passport to getting an officer's commission. So we actually put more effort into that than we did into our regular classes." In some ways, army officers attached to schools had greater authority than the school principal.

A process was then set up by which students could train to become commissioned officers once they had graduated from the Normal School. After their graduation, they could sit the Class A exams as part of the officer cadet scheme, and almost everybody who took the test, passed. The fighting in the South Pacific was becoming increasingly intense and, as more and more Japanese soldiers were killed, the army was running short of trained officers. That was the basis for the newly established Special Class A Officer Cadet Scheme. Boys who passed the exam under that scheme could then take the one-year course at the Military Reserves College on the mainland. From there, they would spend another six months as cadets and finish up with the rank of second lieutenant.

Compared with the usual four years at cadet school, the appeal of being able to obtain a commission in just a year and a half was considerable. Even more appealing to the boys was the special arrangement of being able to sit their cadet exams while still at school. Hiranaka reflected. "I guess the army's purpose of addressing its officer shortage by putting the dream of a commission in front of all those young guys was an attempt to strengthen their will to fight."

He had observed other young men who had passed through that elite training course and who were subsequently doing their cadetships under the watchful eyes of fully commissioned officers. He was full of admiration and longed to be one of them.

"As far as rank was concerned, they were still non-commissioned, but their uniforms were the same as fully commissioned officers and they were allowed to carry swords. Also, their collar badge was different from other cadets in that it featured a round metal washer. They looked terrific."

Day after day the boys' minds were filled with militaristic ideals. Whenever they came face to face with the school's army officer, he would urge them, "Set your sights on becoming an officer!" It was hardly surprising that the boys' ideas started to change, and all too soon most of them had completely forgotten that their original ambition was to become a school teacher.

"It wasn't just the courses that we did under that army officer that pushed us in that direction, the teachers in our other subjects also kept telling us we should become army officers rather than school teachers. As my best friends at school signed up one after the other, I very quickly came to the conclusion that I had to sit that exam as well."

That was about the time the bombing raid on Naha of 10 October 1944 occurred. Hiranaka was visiting his hometown of Kochinda from Shuri where the school was. Three days after the raid, he got a call from school to head for the assembly point at Naha Port. When he arrived at the train's final destination of Naha Station, near what is now the Asahimachi bus terminal, he couldn't believe his eyes.

"I could see the all the way to the ocean. The buildings had all been destroyed in that bombing raid . . . the whole area was just scorched, bare earth. It was then that I really wondered whether Japan could win this war, which I had previously always believed." This was a great shock to Hiranaka, who by that stage had abandoned his dreams of becoming a teacher and had set his sights on an officer's commission.

There were very few classes held at the Okinawa Normal School in the days either side of the 10 October air raid, and instead the students were sent out as part of the construction team building military facilities. One month before that raid, in September 1944, Hiranaka had been allowed to graduate early, just one term into his third year of study. "We didn't expect to receive our graduation certificates," he recalled.

It was early in 1945 and the fighting was creeping ever closer to the islands of Okinawa. As the clouds of war gathered overhead, Hiranaka's own feelings began to waver. His dreams of becoming a teacher, even back when he graduated from elementary school, had changed to pursuing a commission in the army, but seeing the terrible results of the October 1944 air raid meant that he was no longer so sure. Yet it was neither the time nor the place to voice doubts as to whether Japan could win the war, so he re-gathered his thoughts and told himself that he was going to sit the examination to join the special Class A Officer Cadetship scheme.

His resolve was almost matched by his feelings of resignation to whatever might lie ahead. But, before he had time to even sit the entrance exam, Hiranaka found himself caught up in the Battle of Okinawa. The students from the Normal School were drafted into the newly formed Blood and Iron Student Corps. Hiranaka was put in an infiltration unit and sent to battle, immediately ending his dream of becoming an officer.

As the Battle of Okinawa entered its second or third day in the last week of March, Hiranaka joined 1st Platoon of the 1st Company of the 15th Independent Mixed Regiment. The thirty men in the platoon were based in a fortified shelter in a graveyard below the Tomari water reservoir in Naha.

"I was the only one from the Normal School in that platoon and I was assigned to assist Lt. Seo, our platoon leader, who had also attended a Normal School somewhere up in Tohoku. He was very kind to me."

Hiranaka has never forgotten how the lieutenant often used to say, "Japan is going to win this war! At some stage you'll be able go back to school if you want to, so make sure that you do your absolute best."

Just eighteen years of age at the time, Hiranaka was the youngest soldier in the platoon. His role was to man the observation post to keep a lookout around the area and to issue emergency alerts. His lookout area was from the shelter they had dug, out to about 40 or 50 meters to the top of some low-lying hills by the entrance of the reservoir. By standing up and looking straight out to the west, Hiranaka could see the ocean and Kamiyama Island, one of the Keise Islands just west of Naha, where the Americans had already landed. The Americans had deployed field artillery on the island and from there, the relentless bombardment continued through the day and into the night, almost without stopping, targeting Japan's military command post over toward Shuri. As he stood there on guard, he felt that the arch of trajectory of the artillery shells was at its peak directly overhead as they hurtled towards Shuri.

He recalls that the Americans launched their attacks in salvoes of eight. "They'd fire off eight rounds, then pause, and then eight more rounds. It's funny but I can remember quite clearly that number sequence." Not until 1:00 AM did the barrage come to an end. Immediately, the Japanese defenders set about preparing their evening meal.

"Most of the houses around the village of Tomari were completely deserted because the residents had already evacuated. That meant we were able to find good quantities of things like potatoes, canned foods, white sugar and cooking oil. We split up into small groups and gathered up everything we could. The people in the area seemed to have stocked up and had even hidden food under the floor."

Being the youngest, Hiranaka was ordered around a lot. That didn't upset him so much, but there were other things that did annoy him. Because he couldn't keep watch all day on his own without a break, sometimes privates were sent to relieve him. Some of them would try to pressure him with comments such as "You little prick . . . just because you're a student—that's no excuse for having it easy. If *you* don't protect your own island . . . who the hell will protect it, eh?"

One night, the duty officer was out checking the man on sentry duty. Still some distance away, the officer called out through the darkness, "Identify yourself by your name and unit!" When Hiranaka yelled out the name of the private who had forced him to stay on watch duty, the officer called back "Well done!" The platoon leader was an easy-going guy and afterward Hiranaka heard that the officer was impressed with his nerve.

Just a few days later, Hiranaka witnessed the results of the bombardment and destruction of Shureimon, the second of Shuri Castle's main gates, built in the sixteenth century. With this, the immediacy of the conflict became even more apparent. His unit was ordered to the front line with the specific instruction to attack immediately to recapture the area where the ruins of Urasoe Castle were. They started moving from their position at Tomari in Naha in mid-April 1945, with the men finally arriving at the front line on Maeda Escarpment after making their way through Sueyoshi and Ohna to Kyozuka in Urasoe. Maeda Escarpment is still remembered for some of the fiercest fighting of the entire Battle of Okinawa. Hiranaka also played his part in that terrible conflict. In the area around the ruins of Urasoe Castle, the battle with the U.S. forces, often just a stone's throw away, was a truly desperate struggle.

"At night, we launched a surprise attack and finally took the ruins, but they recaptured it the next day; things hadn't gone as we'd hoped."

Even today, his memories of his role in the battle trying to infiltrate the U.S. lines are still vividly etched in his mind. "We set off on a surprise attack at around 4:00 AM, but they launched all these star shells which lit the place up as though it was the middle of the day. We crawled along on our stomachs, inching our way forward to attack the enemy. Unfortunately, they worked out what we were up to and we took a real pounding from their withering fire. It just rained down on us. I managed to somehow avoid getting hit but, when rounds flew just above my back, I felt as if I was already as good as dead."

Hiranaka was able to work out where the shells were coming from and where they were landing by the retorts of the guns as they were being fired. In the course of his experience in action he developed the ability to differentiate between the types of enemy ordnance. They were to hold fire until given the order, but he remembers one occasion when a Japanese soldier hugging the ground could not hold back from returning fire in the face of this one-sided barrage from the enemy. As soon as he did, shells rained down on the area where he was hiding and clouds of dust rose into the air above them. When he realized what had happened, it was clear that the soldier had been blown to pieces.

Also, the enemy's tanks were huge and the Japanese soldiers' guns and hand grenades were almost useless against them. The most effective thing they could do was to get right up close with their own improvised explosives. Carrying satchel charges of at least 10 kgs of explosives over their shoulders, the men would get right in beside the tank tracks. Then, as quickly as possible, they had to throw the explosive charge under the tank. Needless to say, however, there were many occasions when it didn't end up as the men had intended and countless Japanese soldiers were killed this way attempting to achieve "One man for one tank."

Although the number of soldiers left alive was by now very small, several of the men among the remnants of the unit formed suicide groups to launch themselves directly at the enemy. With their white symbolic *hachimaki* wrapped tightly round their foreheads, those men of the suicide groups had accepted their fate of certain death when they set off. None returned.

Lt. Seo, who had been very kind to Hiranaka, also led a group out to attack and was killed. "We heard a rumor that he'd been shot through the left temple and killed instantly. Lt. Seo was a real gentleman—not your typical soldier, if you know what I mean. At that time, many of the other men used to show off screaming out their orders with "hey you!" and "oi!" and so on. He wasn't like that."

Unfortunately, light rain was falling the day that Hiranaka guided us to the battle site. Nevertheless, we sat down in a secluded forest behind the Chayama Housing Complex in Urasoe and listened as he shared his ghastly memories of the war with us.

Maeda Escarpment, which overlooked the ruins of Urasoe Castle, was pounded day after day until the entire area was nothing more than a burned wasteland. Even after they had lost their platoon commander Lt. Seo, Hiranaka and his fellow soldiers in the unit fought tooth and nail to drive the Americans back. During the day they stayed in their cave shelter, barely daring to breathe in case they were detected. But once it was dark, they would head out to launch surprise attacks on the enemy. However, these tactics proved to be a complete failure and, as the number of men around him continued to decrease, Hiranaka accepted that his fate also would be to die in battle.

Next, the order came from the rear that they were to pull back to Shuri. It was now just after mid-May, about one month since they had arrived at the Maeda Escarpment.

"We lost countless soldiers in every attack. They were in a different unit, but many of the student soldiers from the Normal School were killed, their young lives coming to an end far too soon."

Hiranaka also saw many civilians get killed. "On one particular evening, I thought I would stretch my legs so I left the shelter and walked toward the Nakama area. Outside a big old house there were so many dead bodies lying around. I found a smoke-blackened house that looked as though someone was still inside, and I remember being given some sweet potatoes. The person there was very understanding, saying that it must be tough for me as I was just a student."

With tears of regret, he and the others pulled out of the front line at Maeda. They withdrew through Shuri toward the southern part of the island. By the time they reached the area near Kochinda, the 62nd Division had almost disintegrated, losing most of its cohesion. Together with a corporal and five or six lance corporals, Hiranaka worked his way through the town of Gushikami and finally arrived at Makabe. While they were walking through a village called Maehira in Makabe, Hiranaka came to a fence, whereupon someone called out "Koo-ee-ii!!!" Wondering who on earth it could be, he entered the old house but, as he looked toward the kitchen where the woman's voice had come from, he couldn't believe his eyes. Holding onto her right leg and in obvious pain, was his own mother.

"I became very emotional . . . I'd heard nothing about my family since I signed up. And then, just like that . . . I felt so relieved to see her right there with my own eyes."

A piece of shrapnel had struck her in the right leg. Hiranaka took some medication out of the first-aid box the corporal was carrying and gave it to his mother. Looking on, the corporal said sympathetically, "You've done enough with us. Stay with your mother and look after her." Then he left with the others.

As well as his two younger sisters, several other relatives were sheltering nearby, and for a time Hiranaka stayed there with them. One day, however, while he was out collecting water, he got caught up in an air raid.

"Hours later, I managed to get back to where my family were supposed to be waiting, but there was no sign of any of them."

So for the second time he had been cut off from his family. Totally bewildered, he headed away and arrived near Giizabanta Cliffs in Gushikami. Almost immediately, the first familiar face he saw was Lt. Zamami. They concealed themselves among some pandanus trees but were quickly discovered by American soldiers. This occurred toward the very end of the Battle of Okinawa, on 19 June 1945.

Even as he was being made to walk along the coast to Minatogawa in Gushikami, the word "death" was already firmly in his mind. "This is it . . . finally I'm going to die crushed beneath an American tank."

When they got to Minatogawa, there were already a couple of dozen other prisoners assembled there. Under the instructions of the American soldiers, some Japanese-American interpreters were conducting the interviews.

"Once the interpreters had finished their questioning, the prisoners were divided into two groups, those who had actively taken part in the fighting and the civilians who had not. I strongly denied that I had been a member of the Blood and Iron Student Corps. They tried hard to make me confess, but my lies worked and I managed to get put into the civilian group."

The prisoners who had been herded into Minatogawa at Gushikami were all interrogated there. The people conducting the interrogations were second generation Japanese-Americans whose job was also to find out whether or not Hiranaka had taken an active role in the combat. At first, they suspected that he had been in the regular army but he steadfastly denied this. Next they pressed him [to confess] that he had been in the Blood and Iron Student Corps. His heart skipped a beat but, quick as a flash, he came up with this reply.

"Of course I'm a Normal School student. But I spent a lot of time absent from school as I was quite sick, so I was never drafted into the Blood and Iron Student Corps at all. By the time the fighting started, I was feeling better and I thought that I'd better do something to help, such as preparing food. So, I headed off to assist one of the nearby units."

Hiranaka just said anything that he could think of on the spur of the moment, but was resolute in his denial of any role in the Blood and Iron Student Corps. One of the interpreters pushed him harder with the threat, "They'll shoot you if you're lying," but he soon gave up in the face of Hiranaka's attitude and unrelenting denials. In the end, he was separated from those who had fought against the Americans and put into the civilian group.

The day after he was taken prisoner, a group of several dozen civilian prisoners was taken away to Hyakuna in Tamagusuku where they wandered off in all directions as though they were on a mass migration. Hiranaka wandered around looking for somewhere to live. He made his way through to the Yamazato area of Chinen and couldn't believe his eyes when he bumped into an old acquaintance. The two of them teamed up and managed to build a hut, which they then moved into. It was not much, but it was enough to protect them from the elements.

"Whenever I think back to our time in Yamazato, I always remember how the Americans made us get rid of all the dead bodies. We were herded away to Gushikami to pick up the bodies of the dead Japanese soldiers. The area was just covered with them, and we had to gather them into shallow depressions in the ground and cover them up with stones. I'll never forget the sight of those corpses all riddled with bullet holes."

The prisoners loathed this task right from the start. At one stage, there was an incident where the soap disappeared. The Americans guards tried to make out that the prisoners had stolen it, which made them so furious they refused to work. Their only pleasure was brewing "*dobu-zake*" by fermenting dried grape juice mixed with yeast. It was so strong that even when the next morning came around, they were still slightly inebriated. Hiranaka explained, "Getting drunk helped us forget about our situation."

Nearby lived the chief of Yamazato Ward, Minei Fujimasa, whom Hiranaka had got to know quite well. "We're going to open an elementary school,' Minei said. "So how would you like to be the teacher?'" This offer was like a dream come true to Hiranaka who could barely control his excitement.

"Right from day one, my heart was set on becoming a teacher, so there was absolutely no reason to say no. I was invited into the Chinen Municipal Office where I was handed a letter of appointment by the mayor at the time, a Mr. Oyakawa. I was so excited I was literally shaking."

On 21 July 1945, Yamazato Elementary School opened for the first time and Hiranaka began his work as a teacher there. All they had for classrooms were U.S. army tents pitched in the middle of an empty area of land. Of course, they were no books, nor even pencils. But there was hope—the school was buzzing with the hopes and futures of around fifty children. Hiranaka was placed in charge of teaching Japanese and math.

"I became totally absorbed with teaching those kids everything I knew." During recess, they had the time of their lives playing with a volleyball they had been given by the American soldiers.

"I will never, ever forget the innocence of those children back then. I was driven by the belief that we must not teach them the 'learn to kill' education we had received. And forty years on, I am still a teacher."

Kainan Middle School Signals Unit

Before the war, the only private middle school in Okinawa was located at Mawashi Village in Higawahara [currently Higawa in Naha]. Kainan Middle School—opened in April 1936, brought its history to a close as the war ended. It was established thanks to the efforts of famous public administrator Shikiya Koshin and others in an attempt to do something about the fact that Okinawa had the lowest ranking among Japan's prefectures in terms of advancement to middle school education. However, the political climate in the late 1930s did not help these educators make progress toward their ideal. Darker forces were taking an ever-stronger grip on education and, a victim of the times, Kainan Middle School was to have a short and sad history, closing after graduating only four classes that year.

These days, the area known as Kainan, where the school was located, is the only reminder of its existence. With no students graduating since the war, little is said about the school's unfortunate history. Of the seventy-one Kainan students mobilized for service in the Battle of Okinawa, sixty-seven were killed. A second grade student at the time of the mobilization, Kinjo Kazuo, was one of the few survivors.

Kinjo has no clear memory of when the Signals Unit training began. "What I can remember is that there was an aptitude test when we were in the second or third grade and that we were divided into one of the three sections of wireless, telephone [cable], and codes. I was in the wireless group, but thirty or forty of us were all trained in the one classroom." Kinjo also remembers that before the aptitude test, they were told that, "For the defense of the nation, our school will also form a Signals Unit."

Cpl. Murata and LCpl. Imai were dispatched from the 24th Division as instructors. Cyclostyled teaching materials explained the basic structure of a wireless and how to use it, and Morse code. "We used mnemonics to remember them and mastered the code in about two weeks or so."

The goal was to be able to send 120 characters in one minute. There were students among us who could work at that rate, just like the trained soldiers, and normally we managed at least seventy characters a minute. "There were competitions between schools and a rumor went round that the Kainan representative came first, but I think that that was probably just a lie circulated to lift our morale."

Kinjo commuted to school from Itoman by bike, taking about one hour each way. Rubber was no longer available so Kinjo used old inner tubes he got from a friend's bicycle shop to create a "comfortable ride."

The air raids began to get heavier. "The venue for training was switched to Shikina because the school buildings we were using were large. This meant that we were a target from the air. Shikina was a broad, open space surrounded by pine trees. It overlooked the city of Naha."

On 23 March 1945, the bombing seemed to be far more intense than normal when he headed off to Shikina for training, so Kinjo turned around and went home. However, there was no respite, with the bombing continuing the next day and the day after that.

"I was being looked after by some relatives at that stage, but after about four or five days I heard that the *Kempeitai* (military police) were rounding up young people [to press into service] and I thought that I'd be best joining a unit where I could put what I'd learned so far to use. So, I headed off toward headquarters of the 24th Division."

When he got to the headquarters at Yoza-dake he met up with three other students from Kainan Middle School and heard that they would be assigned to the 32nd Infantry Regiment. That evening, accompanied by their instructor, LCpl. Imai, they headed for the Regimental Headquarters shelter in Ufugusukumui.

As they stood rigidly to attention in front of the Regiment's commanding officer, they felt that they had somehow come of age. They were issued with uniforms and other kit, plus ammunition, but there were no rifles for them. Instead, they were given bamboo spears with sharp metal spearheads. Kinjo was 160 centimeters tall, so the spear was a full ten centimeters taller than him. "I thought, 'Is this what I'm supposed to fight with?' but I knew that once the fighting started, I'd be able to pick up a rifle from someone that might be killed around me." From that day on, polishing the head of his spear became one of the highlights of young Kinjo's daily routine.

Kinjo's wireless company was stationed in a dugout shelter on a hill on the northern side of Ufugusukumui. The three tunnels facing eastward were connected by a tunnel running parallel to the front, creating an E-shaped complex. The open area in front of this was covered by the branches of cedar trees, hiding it from potential detection from above.

They spent about one month here, with their wireless radio training continuing every day. When they were to be attached to the unit, their platoon commander said that "You have been mobilized to help in the defense of the nation even though you are still students. You are not regular soldiers, so you will not be required to do [dangerous] tasks such as carrying food and water." Nevertheless, the students came forward to carry out these duties.

Kinjo and his student comrades were ordered to relocate to Shuri when the fighting became intense around Maeda.

Armed only with hand grenades and spears, they were forced to carry the radio equipment and portable generators, so the longer they walked, the deeper the equipment seemed to dig into their shoulders. Kinjo remembers seeing dead bodies everywhere as they headed toward Shuri. When they asked if it was all right for them to pick up the weapons of dead soldiers they were given permission to do so, but soon realized that the extra weight made their march even tougher.

That night they stayed in a shelter not far down the road toward Shuri just beyond the Haebaru junction. Not long after they arrived, Kinjo was ordered to go and fetch food supplies from a field kitchen, a journey of 5 kilometers there and back.

"It was around that time that bullets started to whizz past me. I ran through that fusillade carrying eight empty rice containers to have filled." Going back was even tougher with them full but, because the cook said, "Today there isn't any soup to carry," Kinjo could run even faster without worrying about spilling any soup. When he got back to the shelter and delivered his load, he saw that he'd been carrying *botamochi* [sweet rice and sweet red bean paste], which was like a dish sent from heaven for those out on the battlefield. They were each given four or five portions of a size that would take two bites to consume. For Kinjo, it was the sweet red bean paste covering on the outside rather than the sticky sweet rice that had his mouth watering.

Then at that very moment, his platoon leader said, "Kinjo! From today you're assigned to our section," and handed him some dried noodles. But the next thing the platoon commander said made Kinjo go weak at the knees. "So give that *botamochi* back."

He was assigned to Section No. 1 of the Wireless Platoon. They moved around Kubagawa in Shuri and near Ishimine for a week waiting for orders. There was a large banyan tree near the shelter in Ishimine, and horses and cattle were tied up there. These animals were often killed by incoming artillery shells, but the following day it was only ever the meat from the cattle that would disappear without trace. "The horses were Army property so no-one dared touch that."

Kinjo remembers seeing pieces of shrapnel flying through the air. A long whistling sound was followed by the thud of it sticking into a paddy field and then disappearing. When he went over to have a look, he saw that it was sharp like the blade of a razor. He remembers cold sweat running down his back inside his shirt at the thought of what such shrapnel could do to someone.

The section that Kinjo and the other student signalmen belonged to was dispatched to a nearby battalion. Their role was to transmit reports from that battalion to Regimental Headquarters about the combat situation, but the battalion commander would not let them send or receive messages. He said that transmissions would be picked up by the American radio-detectors on spotter planes, bringing artillery rounds down onto their coordinates. The battalion commander was right—five or six shells would come hurtling in the direction of their shelter as soon as a wireless transmission was made. "Section leader Lance Cpl. Tanno said, 'The Commander is a coward for not letting us send this vital information.'"

But it wasn't long before they were able to transmit. When they went to Regimental Headquarters to report on their predicament, they were told in no uncertain certain terms, "You can't just opt out! Messages are to be sent at regular intervals!" From then on, they tried to time their transmissions when no spotter planes were about, but even so, without fail a barrage of shells came in as soon as they transmitted.

Kinjo was stationed at the frontline, but the first of his Wireless Section schoolmates from Kainan Middle School to be killed was a student who was actually holed up in the Regimental Headquarters towards the rear. Including Kinjo, there were six students from Kainan Middle School in the Wireless Platoon. When the first student was killed, Kinjo just happened to have come back from the frontline to Regimental Headquarters to deliver a report.

"I was in a dug-out shelter nearby when I heard a huge explosion outside. A short while later I realized what had happened when one of our platoon yelled out, 'Oshiro's been hit!'" He had been killed by a shell [that hit] about 50 or 60 meters from the shelter that they were in. "We rushed over to him, but his body had been smashed by the blast and pieces of shrapnel were sticking out of his flesh. In the dim light, Kinjo remembers discerning that his schoolmate's uniform was in tatters and that the boy was covered in a frighteningly dark shade of blood.

The other five Kainan students attended to the boy's burial. They found a place nearby that was covered with thick undergrowth. However, the soil was so stony that they couldn't dig a hole, leaving them with no option but to pile rocks on top of their friend's body to form a sort of burial mound. Kinjo remembers that "Oshiro was the son of a watch dealer who had a shop near Tsukazan Station."

Kinjo also cannot forget the wounded private from the telephone communications platoon. He had a wound on his leg. "He didn't have maggots on the wound, but had gas gangrene and so had no hope of recovering." At the field hospital near Shuri, Kinjo had witnessed nurses handling patients with maggots on their wounds and those who didn't have maggots. The nurses would pay no attention whatsoever to those without maggots. "Those patients had gas gangrene. Before too long they would drift into a dream and start talking to themselves. Most of the time they seemed to be talking about their families."

Kinjo and one of his schoolmates were ordered to move the wounded private to a nearby graveyard. Normally four people would carry a wounded soldier, but there were only the two of them to carry the man. To make it even more difficult, the private was of a heavy build and enemy shells were coming in thick and fast. He was too heavy to carry properly, so they had to drag him along the ground, with the man's lower back hitting against rocks jutting out of the ground as they went. Each time he thudded into a rock he wailed like a child saying, "That hurts, that hurts . . ."

When they got to the graveyard, and gave him two bags of dried bread and a canteen of water, the private looked up at them and said, "You're going to leave me here to die aren't you?" They felt terrible leaving him there in the graveyard to await his death, but they had no choice.

Kinjo's section spent the next month moving from place to place between Ohna in Shuri and Ishimine or Maeda. The topography of the area changed from one day to the next. In the course of one night, the incredible barrage saw roads and earthen banks disappear and fields transformed into quagmires.

Kinjo and his comrades became thoroughly exhausted from having to move from one location to the next. By now they were fatalistic, thinking that "Getting hit and dying would actually be a way out from all the suffering." They could no longer be bothered crouching down when they heard artillery shells coming their way; they just kept on walking. Kinjo remembers how his section leader screamed at them, "You bastards! If you want to get killed, I'll do the job for you!" The boys immediately lay flat in the sea of mud.

When they were on the move near Maeda, the section found themselves in the field of fire of an American sniper. A veteran soldier among them said the sniper was hiding in a slit trench and pointed out where the enemy must be. He said for Kinjo to slowly raise his steel helmet up on the end of his rifle, which he did. Just as the helmet appeared at the entrance to the shelter they were in, a bullet hit it and knocked it off the end of his rifle. Kinjo still remembers the jarring feeling in his arm from the bullet's impact.

One day, the roof of a house near the Regimental Headquarters was blown off. Kinjo went over to see what was there and remembers finding that there were many ceramic jars inside. When he took the lid off one he realized that it was alcohol. He put the lid back on straightaway, but soldiers walking by immediately recognized the smell, so the cat was out of the bag.

That night, all of the soldiers at Regimental Headquarters filled their canteens with *awamori* and had a party. Before long, drunken soldiers started to pick fights with their superiors. Kinjo remembers one soldier saying, "I'm older than you, so once we get home, it'll be me who's higher on the pecking order." There was no way that sort of comment was allowed between ranks in a such a fiercely hierarchical system as the Imperial Japanese Army, so in a flash the offending soldier had two buckets of water poured on him and everything went ominously quiet. Kinjo never heard what punishment was meted out on this occasion but it was clear that the soldiers' nerves were becoming strained to the breaking point in the face of the inexorable American advance.

Clearly outnumbered and straining to hold the line as it stood, the 32nd Infantry Regiment withdrew from Ishimine to Ufugusukumui. At the front at this stage, Kazuo Kinjo's section was also ordered to pull back. "By the time we reached Regimental Headquarters most of the soldiers had already gone. Inside the shelter there were piles of canned food that the Headquarters staff had not been able to take with them and I remember gulping down the contents of two cans of pineapple."

They stayed one night in the Headquarters shelter before departing southward the next morning. It was raining on and off but for some reason there were no incoming artillery shells. "It was the first time that we had relocated during the day."

The early summer rain transformed the fields into something resembling rice paddies. Each time they stepped into such open spaces they sank in up to their knees and when the four of Kinjo's section lost their way, they had no option but to try to keep going through these wretched conditions.

This was hard going for a sixteen-year-old boy. To make it even worse, Kinjo had to carry vacuum tubes and other communications equipment on his back. By late morning, when they reached the Haebaru Junction, he was thoroughly exhausted, so tired that he couldn't even crawl any farther. Their section leader screamed at him but it made no difference.

The other three gave up on Kinjo. Taking the vacuum tubes and other radio parts off him, they set off again. After a while, he regained enough strength to get to his feet and start walking. Kinjo recalls, "I was desperate, so I carried only my rifle, throwing all my other equipment away. After I'd taken just two or three steps I saw four or five potatoes on the ground right there in front of me. I wiped the mud off them and ate them, then and there, and felt a lot better pretty much right away."

He walked a little farther and, when he approached the Haebaru Junction, he saw a soldier who had lost both legs dragging himself along the ground. Kinjo recalls, "I thought that if he was a higher rank than me, he'd order me to help him, which I wasn't capable of doing," so he decided to avoid the Haebaru Junction and instead headed toward Ichinichibashi. "I felt sorry for him, but there was just nothing I could do. There were wounded soldiers everywhere, and I was only barely capable of keeping myself going, let alone helping anyone else." From Ichinichibashi he went back to Ufugusukumui via Kochinda.

Maybe that route worked out to be shorter, or maybe it was because he was only carrying a rifle, but Kinjo arrived at Ufugusukumui ahead of his three friends. They got there just as Kinjo was down by a nearby river washing the mud off his body. When they saw him, they all shouted, "Kinjo! You're alive!"

While the Regiment had been away from Ufugusukumui, dignitaries such as the prefectural governor and the police chief were said to have sought haven in that shelter. "Itoman Police Chief Inoha was there too. I remember that he was carrying a pistol. When we asked him, 'What's this for?' he told us that he was protecting the governor. When the soldiers of the Regiment came back into the shelter, the governor and those with him headed south."

By now, the Signals Company was down to about thirty men. In the Wireless Platoon, there were five Kainan students still alive, with just one having been killed. However, Kinjo had no idea how many of his schoolmates in the Telephone Communications Platoon had been killed while out reconnecting wires during enemy bombardments.

When the boys from the Kainan Middle School Wireless Platoon talked among themselves, it was mostly about food. Occasionally they talked about the fighting, but Kinjo remembers that no one was ever optimistic of a change in the way the battle was going.

They weren't able to stay at Ufugusukumui for very long either, and in no time at all they again withdrew toward the south. The Signals Company was deployed in a dug-out shelter in Kuniyoshi (beside which the *Shiraume-no-To* memorial now stands), Regimental Headquarters was set up in a shelter in Maezato (where the Yamagata Memorial now stands) and each of the battalions took up positions in the area surrounding these locations.

Kinjo and the others in his squad spent just two or three days in the company shelter before they were sent to a battalion deployed in the defensive line on the western side of the small settlement of Maezato.

The Americans were visible out there in front of them. Soldiers in the forward observation posts could see the faces of the American lead scouts. The defenders communicated to the remaining artillery units that they wanted fire support, but were told that there was no ammunition left. By this stage, the 32nd Army had lost most of its troops and had few weapons left with which to carry on the fight. The army units flooding toward Cape Kyan were to cause countless tragedies for the thousands of civilians already seeking safe haven in the area.

Kinjo knew that the Japanese army's combat capabilities were rapidly disappearing. American scouts were coming closer and closer, "But we couldn't shoot at them, "he said. "The small arms that we had left didn't have the range to shoot more than a short distance."

Observation planes seemed to be in the air all the time. "The spotter planes would circle overhead then go back out toward the ships just offshore. They would circle around a warship for a short time then come back over us, but at a higher altitude. Then, without fail, the warship would open fire on our positions with its deck guns. I imagine that the crews of the spotter planes were letting the ships' gunners know where their shells were falling, but there was nothing at all that we could do about it." By that stage the U.S. forces could do whatever they liked.

One day, Kinjo saw something dropped from an American plane drift slowly down to the ground suspended from a parachute. "It was supplies for the American soldiers, attached to a colored parachute. We saw it land in a nearby rice paddy and a few of us ran there as fast as we could to try to get to it first. When we got there, we ran straight into a group of American soldiers who had come to get it. Neither group was carrying any weapons, so when we came across each other we just panicked and ran back where we had come from. It wasn't long before we saw the Americans return armed with submachine guns and claim their supplies. When I think about it now, it even seems quite comical."

Another day, he heard a voice he recognized in the darkness of the shelter. "Lt. Kinjo reporting for duty." It was Lt. Kinjo, who was also from Itoman and had been a teacher at Naha Commercial School. He'd been wounded at Shuri from where he was taken to the Army Hospital at Haebaru and now had made his way back to his unit after the caves at Haebaru were abandoned.

"I couldn't see his face, but there was no mistaking that lively voice as he reported to the battalion commander. I remember feeling lifted by the thought of his bravery, managing to find his way back to his unit alone and wounded," said Kinjo.

On his way to Regimental Headquarters to deliver a message, Kinjo met one of his seniors from school who was attached to Signals at Divisional Headquarters. "His name was Oshiro Gensei, and he was a big, well-built young man. He was well-known at our school." He remembers how a schoolmate said to him, "Good to see that you're well. Let's both do our best to get through this." That was all that was said, but on a battlefield, that more than sufficed as a conversation. Kinjo never saw the boy again.

After being attached to the battalion at Maezato for two weeks, when Kinjo was in a shelter that had its entrance facing south, a white phosphorus shell fired from Itoman to the north landed right by them.

"I was trying to get some sleep after I'd finished my wireless duties. A white phosphorus shell hit a rock right by the entrance to our shelter and bounced straight in." Smoke started coming into the shelter. Kinjo woke up when he started to find it difficult to breath but by now the shelter was rapidly filling up with smoke.

He quickly put on his gas mask but he couldn't stop coughing. He remembers hearing a voice beside him saying, "Your mask isn't on properly!" It was their section leader, LCpl. Tanno. But the coughing wouldn't stop as he had already inhaled too much smoke.

By this stage, the chief cook had died and Kinjo was in a bad way. It was now painful for him to breathe. "I was breathing as though my heart had somehow gotten smaller and I could only take small breaths." After a while, LCpl. Tanno couldn't bear watching him like this any longer and so told Kinjo to go outside to breathe some fresh air.

That day, Kinjo lay motionless in the lee of the large rock just outside the entrance to the shelter until the sun went down.

After night fell, someone came and called him back inside the shelter, but he still struggled to breathe normally. "I didn't want to go back inside, but it was an order, so I had no choice." About ten or twenty minutes later, the shelter was rocked by a tremendous noise and the thudding of large caliber shells hitting the rock above them. The impact of the explosions was such that the shock waves even extinguished the lamps inside the shelter, although incredibly, no one inside was killed.

That night, Kinjo lay still in the shelter, but the next day he started to feel worse and asked for permission to go outside. As he stepped out, he gasped at what he saw. The large rock, behind which he had lain down to rest the previous day, had been blown away without a trace. "If I had stayed out there just a few minutes longer . . ." he thought, cringing as he again realized how close he had come to death.

Kinjo Kazuo was in the Wireless Platoon, but when he was with the battalion in Maezato he also helped the Telephone Communications Unit.

"I offered to help because I thought that I might meet someone I knew if I went outside, but I didn't meet anyone out there." It was then that he realized just how dangerous their work was. "We would go out in pairs to reconnect wires that had been cut in the bombardment. One would attend to the wire, while the other would watch from a safe distance, ready to report if the person doing the repairs had been killed. It goes without saying that wherever we were at that stage was immediately targeted by enemy artillery, so the chances of being killed were high." Many students carried out these dangerous duties.

After his brush with death in the attack involving the white phosphorus shell, Kinjo's section was attached to the battalion deployed just to the west of the settlement at Kuniyoshi.

The U.S. forces were now not far away at all. Indeed, they even walked boldly close by the shelters in which Kinjo and his comrades hid. It increasingly seemed as though it was just a matter of time before they too would be killed, and maybe it was this thinking that eventually affected the battalion commander's judgment.

All of a sudden, the battalion commander yelled out, "All those with weapons will go outside and engage the enemy tanks!" Just then, in the silence of the shelter, they could make out the eerie rumble and clatter of tanks moving above them. Kinjo doesn't know if that was exactly when the attack occurred, but it was obvious that the enemy in the tanks knew that they were in the shelter. The Americans blasted the area with flamethrowers to burn away the surrounding low bushes and scrub and then withdrew. The entrance was now clearly visible.

That evening, the battalion commander ordered them all to go on an infiltration raid. The plan was to go out with a heavy machine gun spearheading the attack. Kinjo and his comrades destroyed their wireless equipment with hand grenades and prepared themselves for the raid. But the attack was to end in failure.

"In the darkness, we could hear what sounded like voices, but we had no idea whether they were from the enemy or friendly troops. To make things worse, the machine-gunners who were supposed to lead the way just disappeared, so we had no choice but to withdraw."

The next day, the enemy used a flamethrower to attack them. "Our shelter was L-shaped, so the three in our section who didn't receive a direct blast survived. But the Battalion Headquarters was just one long tunnel straight back from the entrance, so . . ." During the rest of that day, they sat tight, but at night they could hear groans coming from the Headquarters shelter.

When they went to see what the situation was, they found the battalion commander and his adjutant still alive but with awful burns. The other ten or so soldiers were there, but had all been burned to death. After a while, the two survivors managed to get up and walk, so they decided to take them to the Regimental Headquarters.

After a short time, Kinjo and the private next to him suddenly realized that they had been separated from those in front of them. They had been crawling in the dark with a 10-meter gap between them, but the private lost sight of the person in front of him. It was almost dawn.

"We were astonished in the morning when we saw that, after walking all night, we were only three or four hundred meters from the shelter. And in front of where the shelter was, we could see that the Americans were piling up ammunition and food supplies. They were stripped to the waist, singing or whistling away as they stacked up boxes. It certainly didn't look as though they were at war." During the day, Kinjo and his comrade hid in a ditch, motionless as though dead.

They reached the Regimental Headquarters shelter around noon the next day. Wounded soldiers were made to lie near the entrance. Kinjo remembers overhearing a soldier saying that the wounded were placed there so their bodies would serve as a buffer against blasts from explosions. There were also more wounded at the back of the shelter. They were the officers and were using wooden boxes as beds.

Kinjo remembers that, as he was looking around the shelter for LCpl. Tanno, maybe just a few minutes after he got inside, there was a tremendous boom from an explosion. The area around the entrance collapsed inward and the blast put out the lamps, so the shelter was thrown into darkness. Maybe someone had been crushed under falling rocks because terrible screams came from over by the entrance. Further inside no one said a word. They were all speechless as they considered what might happen next. All that could be heard was the whimpering of badly wounded men. However, that day, there was only the one attack.

Kinjo Kazuo found LCpl. Tanno outside, more or less right above the shelter. He was lying face up, between two rocks. His steel helmet had been blown off, and half of his head was missing. His brain was exposed, but incredibly, considering his wounds, he was still alive.

He was breathing, but didn't respond to anything that was said to him. "This guy's done for," said the medical officer. The officer took the lance corporal's arm and gave him an injection. There was no change in his breathing after one injection, so the medical officer gave him a second, but he showed no signs of dying.

"He's done for. Bury him." Having given up on killing LCpl. Tanno himself, the surgeon ordered Kinjo and his comrades to do it for him.

They buried him beside a field below a bluff. Tanno was a well-built man, so they had to dig for quite some time to try to create a hole big enough to accommodate his body, but the ground was so hard that they couldn't dig very deep at all. On his way back to the Regimental Headquarters, Kinjo had picked up a bottle crammed full of cigarettes, so he used one of those as an offering of incense for Tanno. As he lit one and placed it by the shallow grave, he almost sensed that the earth piled over Tanno's body was rising and falling as though it were breathing.

They buried Tanno's body in a spot close to a rock as a point of reference, but when Kinjo went back after the war to collect the bones he found that the area had already been developed. He was relieved to hear that the bones had been collected and taken to the village's mausoleum, but regretted not being able to return the bones to LCpl. Tanno's family.

The entrance to the Regimental Headquarters shelter was sealed off with a satchel charge and two or three days later another shelter was closed off when the Americans used a bulldozer to push large quantities of earth in on the entrance.

It was not difficult to clear the entrances, but those in the Regimental Headquarters shelter were effectively buried alive for several days. They had food and water in the shelter, so Kinjo thought, "They were probably feigning death to get the enemy to turn their attention elsewhere."

The Headquarters shelter was opened up "a week or so later, maybe even longer." They dug a hole just large enough for one person to get through. The first person to go in was a civilian who had fled south to that area. He took in some American canned food, which he explained seemed to be lying around all over the place.

The Americans certainly did seem to be well supplied. When they looked for a spot where the American troops had set up camp, there always seemed to be canned food buried just under the ground. Some of it had been burned and the contents of the cans had spoiled, but for those who had been living on a diet of dried bread, the canned food was a welcome luxury. The first night, all of the people in the shelter who ate the cans of food suffered from diarrhea, but they gradually got used to the food.

Kinjo and the others in the wireless company, plus some women employed by the Army, around ten or so in total, were told to go to Maezato because of the lack of food where they were. It was August 29 before he and his comrades realized that the war was over. The 32nd Infantry Regiment still had its internal organization in place, and its officers would go on and sign the instrument of surrender.

Including Kinjo, there were six students from Kainan Middle School in the Wireless Platoon. Kinjo was attached to a section away from the Headquarters, so he does not know the details of what the five students there did during the battle. The only one about whose death Kinjo knew the details was Miyagi, his senior at school.

"The other four were Uezato, my senior at school, Kanda, who was my year, and Inamine Seijiro. For the life of me, I can't remember the name of the fourth student, but I think that he was one year older than me."

The last time Kinjo saw those four was when he was about to go from the battalion at Maezato to the battalion at Kuniyoshi. One of them had succumbed to the stress of the circumstances and was behaving strangely. He would say, "My family's here to see me," or "A friend has come," and try to go out of the shelter during the day, so someone would keep an eye on him all the time. The other three were well.

The next time that Kinjo went to Company Headquarters was just before the Regiment surrendered. The rock face around the entrance of the Company Headquarters was burned jet black where it had obviously been attacked with a flamethrower. They called out to anyone who might be there but there was no reply, so they did not venture inside. When he got to a POW camp, Kinjo heard that no one from the Signals Company had survived the battle.

Of the sixty-two students from Kainan Middle School who joined the 62nd Division, fifty died. A total of seventy-one Kainan students took part in the fighting, but only four survived. When the war ended, all that was left behind of the school was its unfortunate history.

Third Prefectural Middle School Signals Unit Code Section

As in other schools, when the third term began in January 1945 a Signals Unit was formed in the Third Prefectural Middle School [now Nago High School]. All of the students involved were third year students, thus in their last year of secondary education. Designated to the Cable Section (15 students), the Wireless Section (15 students) or the Code Section by the officer attached to the school, the student soldiers slept in either the school hall or the martial arts hall as they underwent rigorous training.

If we don't count two students who were unwell, the Code Section actually comprised thirteen people. The training in this section was mainly carried out by LCpl. Tokumaru Haruo, who had been a teacher in Miyazaki Prefecture, and LCpl. Nagatomo, with assistance from a Pvt. Goto.

"Lt. Tokumaru was a sickly character who always seemed to be complaining. LCpl. Nagatomo was always sullen and, if we made a mistake, he'd yell at us saying something like, 'Do you think you'll survive under fire if this is the best that you can do?' Private Goto was so laid back that it was hard to believe that he actually got by as a soldier. He was really friendly with all of us students," said Kuniyoshi Shinsho.

Kuniyoshi continued, "I had no particular reservations about joining the Signals Unit. Everyone around me wanted to join the military, either to go to officer training school or to become *yokaren* [flight reserve enlisted trainees], so it was the natural thing to be doing." On one occasion, a non-commissioned officer took them to see a movie and he recalled how, when they marched through the streets of Nago, "We were proud to be looked upon by the people there in a respectful manner."

The training in the Code Section was demanding, starting with how to write numbers in a very specific way through to learning how to decode messages. However, they felt a kind of superiority over the members of other sections in the Signals Unit because the other sections only went as far as dealing with the numbers in the messages, whereas the Code Section was able to fathom the content of the message.

"They constantly reminded us that we were handling secret information. We were not to have any contact with outsiders and they kept on at us about how awful the U.S. forces were. They said that if we were taken prisoner, we would have our ears ripped off and be skinned alive, so we were scared stiff," recalled Maeda Yasuhiro and Shikina Moritoshi.

At the end of January 1945, the location for their training was changed from the Third Prefectural Middle School martial arts training hall to headquarters of the Kunigami Detachment (otherwise known as the *Udo-butai* due to the fact that it was commanded by Col. Udo Takehiko) located in a valley near Yae-dake. From that point on, the training effectively ended as they ceased to be involved in anything related to codes, instead spending most of their time carrying timber to be used in constructing barracks or digging shelters.

Digging the shelters was hard work. The two of them started at 5:00 AM and after breakfast all of the student soldiers were dragged off to work, continuing until around 10:00 PM. They hauled timber from the sawmill at Izumi or were made to cut down and carry trees that would be used as pillars and beams in the shelters.

The hills around Yae-dake were cold, even if they used the two blankets the Army provided on top of the one each of them carried themselves. The hard labor during the day and the poor food took its toll on the young boys who were at an age when they needed to be eating well to sustain their growth. "We were only fed enough rice to fill the lid of our rice bowls. They said that there was enough food stored to last three years, but we were never given more than measly amounts to eat," said Shikina.

Maeda said, "We looked forward to the NCOs' turn to eat." He was irritated by their demands about how to lay the bedding down, but the boys were able to eat their leftovers, so that more than made up for the NCOs' unwelcome comments. On their half-day off on Sundays, they also used to look forward to going to a merchant in the hills. It was so far away that it was always dark when they got back, but the opportunity to buy Calpis sweet drinks or *oshiruko* [red bean soup] was just too good to miss.

They may have been worked hard and been hungry all the time, but their days spent in the wooded hills were still a far cry from the awful realities of the battlefield. On 10 March, Army Memorial Day, Professor Kochinda Keii of the Normal School came to visit their unit and, after standing on a wooden box, he directed the first performance of the *Song for the 2nd Infantry Unit* that he had composed himself. They were not to know that just two weeks later the Battle of Okinawa would commence and that in the course of the battle they would lose six of their school friends.

As everyone else was struggling with the effects of hard labor on empty stomachs, Kuniyoshi Shinsho spent most of his time in the Command Post Code Room. He said, "For me there are no memories from those days of carrying timber, or of being constantly hungry. I just remember that the large rice balls that I was given for dinner tasted very nice." But at the same time, every day, the officers who crammed into the Command Post shelter were all clearly on edge. On top of that, protocols surrounding secrecy meant that they were forbidden to even converse with the students.

"But when we used to stand at attention and salute Col. Udo, he would acknowledge us without hesitation. He was as big as a sumo wrestler and we hardly ever saw him in uniform in the headquarters shelter. He was pretty much always naked from the waist up and dressed with no account for formality. I often heard that women were seen going into his room, and to be honest, he didn't really seem to have much backbone."

Those in the Signals Unit wrote out rows of numbers. There were several types of random number charts to use, but first of all they were "given instructions as to what line and what number across to start from." From there they would convert the message into sentences. To communicate with the 32nd Army Headquarters they used units of four digits, but three digits to connect with positions at Tano-dake and Onna-dake. "There were three different types of code: military code, unit code and intelligence code, but the most exciting to decode was the intelligence code because it included reports on the battle situation."

The Battle of Okinawa effectively began on 23 March 1945 with the opening phases of the conflict featuring fierce pre-invasion bombing raids on targets in the northern part of the island. Kuniyoshi climbed a tree to get a view of the sky, but all that he could see through the dense foliage of the trees was one Curtiss warplane. "Our training finished around 25 March and we were told that we would be able to make a trip home to visit our families, but I did think that the 'balloon going up,' so to speak, would prevent that," said Kuniyoshi.

Two or three days later, Lt. Tokumaru Haruo told them all that they could return home. They all needed consent forms from their parents in order to join their units, so they were basically ordered to go and get these.

Most were back by the end of March, but Shikina Moritoshi was late getting back because his home was further away, in Katsuren. He returned to his unit at night on or about 2 April. Unaware that sentries had been posted on the perimeter, he was suddenly challenged from the darkness by someone saying "*yama*" [mountain]. He immediately responded "*kawa*" [river] only to have a bayonet thrust in his direction. The correct response to "*yama*" was "*yama*." Still suspicious, the sentry questioned him as to why he was late.

When Shikina finally managed to explain his situation and was let past by the sentry, he did not get far before he was stopped again, to be asked the same question this time by an officer on horseback accompanied by a soldier on foot. He mentioned the name of LCpl. Nagatomo, who was in charge of them, and was allowed to proceed. Shikina knew from the officer's rank insignia that it was Maj. Sato Tomio, commander of the 2nd Battalion of the 2nd Infantry Unit.

Lt. Tokumaru assembled the boys in ranks in front of their lodgings to announce that "You are now all officially given the rank of private second-class." They were issued with a uniform, army shoes, underwear, and puttees. Their caps were simply the ones from their school uniform, but with the three stripes signifying the Third Prefectural Middle School removed. From the group one year ahead of them, the school uniform had changed to a khaki cap, which for all intents and purposes was the same as an army cap.

Once the fighting started in the Battle of Okinawa, the work digging shelters stopped and the boys were put on half-day shifts in the Code Section. Occasionally they were given two-hour stints on sentry duty, but otherwise their tasks were decoding messages and running messages to the wireless units. Maeda Yasuhiro remembers, "We believed it when they said Japanese soldiers were ready and waiting in every nook and cranny of the island." The boys were to be surprised at the news that the U.S. forces had landed.

At night in the hills, the sound of kamikaze planes flying overhead toward their targets had a plaintive ring to it. "It was quite different from the frightening sound of the U.S. warplanes that we heard during the day," said Maeda. They interpreted lights flickering on the horizon south of Cape Zanpa as kamikaze "successes." Maeda recalls how they believed in the supposed "one-person-one-ship" success rate of the kamikaze to such an extent that "When U.S. troops landed in Nago, to start with, we accepted the official line that they were the crew members of U.S. warships that had been sunk by kamikaze attacks, who had survived by swimming ashore."

However, the truth of the matter of course was that U.S. forces had landed and were making steady progress as they headed both north and south. American efforts to block the wavelengths that the Japanese Imperial Army used for communication were effective, so receiving messages became increasingly difficult. Shikina Moritoshi remembers a piece of incoming communication that he was unable to decode. "We realized afterward that it was the order initiating the attack of 8 April. We were able to make something of it from context before and after the key part of the message, because the blocking of the wavelength stopped for a short time, but at the time we were unable to decode it to mean anything. Subsequently there was an order to 'Carry out the previously communicated mission' but we didn't know what that mission was. It was only later that we understood that it was the order to 'Attack the enemy in the Nago area with all the forces at your disposal.'"

On 8 April, the Unit Headquarters relocated from a valley near Yae-dake westward to Mabuyama. Maybe it was because the Command Post at Mabuyama had received no information at all from the front lines and that American troops had suddenly appeared right in front of them, but their relocation was carried out at a frantic pace.

Kuniyoshi Shinsho saw his father for the last time that day. His father was a policeman working out of the Nago Police Station but, as Shinsho had been born in Naha, his parents decided to send him to the Third Prefectural Middle School, something that would lead to many unhappy experiences for the Kuniyoshi family. The previous year, his mother and six siblings had been evacuated out of Okinawa. Being a member of the Police Force, which at that stage was encouraging evacuation, meant that Kuniyoshi Shinsho's father was obliged to override his wife's desire to stay in Okinawa rather than be evacuated. On top of this, the Kuniyoshi family's decision to go influenced many other families in their neighborhood to evacuate.

That the boat that the family had gone on was the *Tsushima-Maru* was to cause his father enormous grief.

"Dad knew that the *Tsushima-maru* had been sunk, but his desire to maintain military secrecy meant that he said nothing about it to me. I had sort of heard about what had happened, but seeing my father in such anguish meant that I couldn't bring myself to bring the matter up." Kuniyoshi remembers how one night, one of his father's police colleagues visited and could be heard quietly trying to raise his father's spirits. Another time, he remembers how he woke his father up when the man was lying on the verandah after coming back home after a few drinks. Kuniyoshi still clearly remembers how, obviously profoundly troubled, his father uttered a deep, plaintive sigh as he sat there staring blankly into space.

The day came when Kuniyoshi Shinsho, the only surviving member of the family, was to be moved to Mabuyama. His father told him, "We evacuated the civilians to a safe place up in the hills." The two didn't talk much to each other but he remembers how his father went on to say, "Don't do anything stupid," as though to discourage the young man from casting his life away recklessly. Kuniyoshi remembers that his father also spoke to Lt. Tokumaru, possibly to ask the officer to keep an eye on his son.

They parted ways and only after the war ended did Kuniyoshi hear that his father had been killed at Gabusoga on his way back to where he was working. "By then, the Americans had landed. If he hadn't come to see me, and had stayed with those civilians who had been evacuated, we would probably have both survived and been able to meet up again after the war." The Battle of Okinawa left Kuniyoshi as the only surviving member of his family.

After the relocation to Mabuyama, the Code Section originally located inside the wooden-walled barracks at the Command Post in Yae-dake set up in a dugout shelter. It was a construction that had been dug out in no time at all and seemed as though it would be able to withstand a substantial amount of punishment. "The smoke from the oil lamps used in the shelter meant that our nostrils were black, so you can imagine how we used to enjoy sitting out in the sun in the time between each period of bombardment," said Kuniyoshi. The stories they heard in the shelter from the men were all upbeat. "They told us how we might be taking a pounding where we were, but that our soldiers were dug in as far as

Ishikawa and that the Imperial Army had landed in San Francisco and was at that very moment marching toward New York." They hung onto every piece of this kind of "information" and could feel it lift their morale.

They picked up the news of President Roosevelt's death on 12 April on the radio. Maeda Yasuhiro remembers hearing how that night an infiltration unit was formed in an attempt to get huge numbers of printed fliers into the American soldiers' camps to let them know about the death of their leader. "Restrictions on intelligence information and news meant that we were operating with only a limited knowledge of the real situation, so I imagine they thought that the shock of this news would reduce the American troops' will to fight. Needless to say, these fliers had no effect whatsoever on the U.S. forces whose open system with regard to information meant that they already knew about Roosevelt's death.

On 15 April, the Code Section was also ordered to launch an attack. It was to be their first time in combat. "From the time when we had been in training we had been told that the Code Section would be the last to go out to fight, so I must admit that I thought that we were done for," said Kuniyoshi. He remembers how he felt himself shaking with fear as they left the shelter.

As they climbed up the slope toward the top of Mabuyama, he caught sight of Col. Udo sitting on a rock beside the road, now in uniform and holding a sword in his hand, looking far more dependable than on those previous occasions when he had been naked from the waist up and surrounded by a bevy of young women.

The boy soldiers did not have rifles, but had each been given several handgrenades. They set up the front-line position at the top of Mabuyama while it was still light and waited there until nightfall. Fierce fighting was going on down on the southern side of the hill. They could hear the relentless firing from machine guns, interrupted only by the explosions of shells from the naval bombardment, some of which occasionally landed near them on the top of the hill. Incoming shells cut branches from the trunks of pines trees in a flash, as though they had been severed by the sharpest of axes. That night there was no sign that the boys were to go into action. Trees burned on the southern slope and illumination shells exploding in the sky meant that they could clearly see the faces of those beside them. The fighting raged below, and boy soldiers from the likes of the Third Prefectural Middle School must have been involved down there. But for some reason, they were not hurled into the fray that night and before long all were ordered to pull back.

On the way back from their position atop Mabuyama they saw U.S. warships anchored audaciously in the waters between Motobu Peninsula and Ie-jima. Kuniyoshi remembers saying, "Look at the size of that warship!" Born and bred in Naha, he had seen Japanese naval vessels in Naha Port, but what he saw out there off Motobu was far larger than anything he had ever seen before. The scene he witnessed that day was all the more frightening considering that during his time living in the barracks and the dugout shelter they had hardly seen anything of the outside world.

The next day before dawn, 16 April, all of those in the Code Section were again ordered to assemble. Among them were some who had not even had one moment of sleep since having been ordered to Mabuyama then withdrawn to go straight onto code duty. There were eight regular soldiers and thirteen boys from the Third Prefectural High School. They assembled in the Code Section Office at the furthest point from the shelter entrance.

"Today the enemy will launch an offensive, so our Code Section will go out to take them on," said Lt. Tokumaru Haruo. He opened cans of pineapple and handed them out to those in the unit, saying to each of the boy soldiers, "Do your best and fight hard." Maeda noticed that Lt. Tokumaru's voice was hoarse. Maybe this young lieutenant, who was by no means a dyed-in-the-wool military man, was struggling to hide the fear he harbored for the impending combat. That evening, the situation on top of Mabuyama was very different from that of the previous day. The fate of those thirteen boys would be decided that night.

The unit was to launch its attack just after daybreak, but LCpls. Nagatomo and Tamaki Kazutomo of the Third Prefectural Middle School Code Section were left behind in the shelter to dispose of the code sheets. This act in itself steeled the others to be ready for their fate in the suicide attack that was to follow. Now comprising seven soldiers and twelve students, the unit started to make its way toward the ridge at Mabuyama.

An American reconnaissance plane flew so low over the boys that they could even make out the face of the pilot. Guided by the coordinates provided from the plane, naval guns offshore poured shells on them as they made their way through the little valley. Off in the distance, the whole island of Ie-jima looked as though it was in flames, with plumes of black smoke streaming into the sky.

They crawled up toward the top of the hill, trying to find shelter behind rocky outcrops as bullets whizzed past their ears. Before they knew it, the students were by themselves, left behind by the regular soldiers, whose progress was much quicker up the slope.

"Don't bunch up! Keeping moving!" someone yelled at them, but after trying to spread out they would again instinctively group together. In the course of this happening several times, with them bunching up then trying to spread out, someone yelled, "I've been hit!" Several ear-splitting explosions were heard one after another and the area around them was suddenly potted with numerous holes 1.5 meters across.

As this barrage of shells landed, Maeda Yasuhiro was in his own world trying to make his way to the top of the hill. When he gathered his senses and looked around him, he saw Kinjo Isamu sitting in the lee of a rocky outcrop. Maeda asked his friend, "Isamu, what's the matter? Have you been hit?" but Kinjo merely sat there without giving any response, a deathly pale look on his face. It didn't look as though Kinjo had been wounded, but Maeda was unable to move him anywhere by himself, so he just left him where he was in the shelter of the rock and continued on his way forward.

Further up toward the top of Mabuyama he joined the rest of the Code Section, but among those who had made it that far, only four students were to be seen, Shimabukuro Takehisa, Arashiro Harutoshi, Kuniyoshi Shinsho, and Kuba Kenkichi. Oshiro Motoden and Gibo Sakae were never seen again.

U.S. troops were advancing up the other side of the hill. Without a rifle to shoot, Maeda hurled hand grenades at them. He does not remember how long he was engaged in combat, but he soon came to understand that the situation was deteriorating. All around him increasing numbers of Japanese soldiers were retreating down the slope past them into the little valley behind the hill, so before too long it seemed that only the Code Section was near the top of the hill fighting the enemy. As though he sensed that things were nearing the end, Lt. Tokumaru gathered them together, saying, "We're all going to charge the enemy."

With no weapons to use, those around Maeda gave him a scabbard for an officer's sword and a large pocketknife. There weren't even any bamboo spears for him. Armed only with such "weapons," the idea of hurling themselves at the enemy through a hail of bullets was designed merely to grant them a gallant death.

Bullets rained down upon them during the moments before they received the order to attack. One of their schoolmates was crawling forward with blood pouring from a wound to his leg. Another two had been hit in the arms and legs. When Maeda moved to tend to his friends' wounds, Lt. Tokumaru yelled at him: "We're all going to die! Leave them alone!"

"That's right. We're going to die anyway," Maeda told himself as he looked off into the distance toward Ogimi, but he remembers that he couldn't make out the hills around his hometown.

All of a sudden, Lt. Tokumaru stood up and yelled out "Charge!" The other soldiers followed him as the officer ran down the slope toward the enemy, brandishing his sword. With Shimabukuro at his side and an empty scabbard in his hand, just as he Maeda started to get up and join the attack there was a tremendous explosion as a shell landed just meters from them. Black smoke filled the air and the sound of machine-gun fire continued for some time before an eerie silence took over, not a sound to be heard. The two of them sat there dazed, having lost their chance to leap up and join in the attack. The only energy they had left was focused on gripping their hand grenades ready to detonate and kill themselves if the enemy appeared in front of them.

From there, somehow the two of them managed to get back to their unit. Decades after the event, Maeda commented, "I don't think that a real army officer with combat experience would order his troops on such a reckless attack. I can't help but think that with him having been a teacher, he felt responsible for the sacrifices that the student soldiers from the Third Prefectural Middle School made and decided that death was the only option." Decades later, Maeda still cannot rid himself of the sound of bullets whizzing past his ears.

During their advance up Mabuyama, one of the students from Third Prefectural Middle School who yelled out, "I've been hit!" was Shikina Moritoshi. When Kuniyoshi Shinsho looked at him, he saw blood flowing from a wound in the boy's left arm. They stopped the blood by tying a towel around the arm as a tourniquet, and with help from Maeda Takatoshi and Nakazato Kunio, who were nearby, took him to a field hospital at the foot of the hill.

But there was only one medic there. "Take him to the field hospital at Command Post. Take him on a stretcher," the medic said, also telling a member of the Home Guard to help so they would have four people on the stretcher. "But that guy simply let go of the stretcher and ran for cover every time an enemy plane appeared overhead, meaning that Shikina would be spilled out time and time again. "That's how we carried him, trying our best to placate him each time he was dropped on the ground," said Kuniyoshi. Shikina started to complain of pain in his arm as they carried him through the uneven ground of some terraced fields. From there, the largest of them, Kuniyoshi, carried their wounded friend on his back. After a three-hour journey to the Command Post located in the valley at the foot of Yae-dake, the three set off back to their unit.

Shikina recalls, "I was left on my stretcher lying in an open field by the field hospital, with no attempt by anyone to give me any treatment. When I couldn't stand it any longer I asked someone walking past to call an army surgeon for me and remember that a medic came and just applied a tourniquet again. After that, I know that I was taken to the toilet by a nurse's aide from the Third Prefectural Girls' School, and that's where I passed out."

When he came to, he found that he had been sleeping with his head on the thigh of one of the nurses. Only barely conscious, he remembers that he could make out the character *shiro* [white] on the name badge on her uniform. When he was finally taken inside the shelter, he had bandages applied to his wound and remembers that the nurses brought him sugared water during the night.

That evening the nurses became increasingly agitated, talking in small groups. Before too long, the army surgeon could be heard adding his opinion. "A Japanese man would slit his belly and end his life," he said. A corporal was facing the doctor as he said tearfully, "So you're going to leave us behind?" The sound of men weeping eventually echoed around the dugout shelter. They were about to withdraw from the Command Post and leave the wounded behind.

The next morning, Shikina recognized a sergeant major lying asleep in the same ward. He had been the one who had summoned the medic when Shikina was lying unattended in the open space near the field hospital. He remembered the sergeant major because of all his gold teeth. When he thanked him for his kindness, the man nodded and said, "So that was you then." It seemed that the man had been hit in the lower back, and Shikina still remembers how the next day the sergeant major was lying there dead with his mouth open.

When dawn broke on the morning of 17 April, there was no one else in the dugout shelter except the wounded soldiers. Many of the men thought that they had simply been abandoned. "It's time to take our own lives! Does anyone here have a hand grenade?" said someone. Shikina had a grenade hidden in his shirt pocket but was not prepared to kill himself. He quietly left the shelter and, after making his way to the field hospital's storeroom, was surprised to find that it was full of food. He opened some of the cans with a bayonet and stuffed himself full of types of food he hadn't eaten for a very long time.

About two days later, he saw someone heading in his direction. The soldier must have been hit in both legs and one arm because he was sitting on his backside pushing himself along the ground with his one good arm. His face looked old but Shikina thought that he recognized him from somewhere so he asked, "Are you related to Isami Kinjo from the Third Prefectural Middle School?"

Shocked by the question, the wounded soldier said, "I am Kinjo Isamu! Who are you?" When Shikina replied, "It's Oyama" (Shikina's name before he got married), Kinjo burst into tears. "Only about four days had passed since the attack at Mabuyama. He'd taken part in the fighting there and then taken four days to drag himself a distance that would normally take about one hour on foot. The hardship involved in being caught in the no-man's land between life and death must have aged us terribly," said Shikina.

The U.S. forces were now getting close, so the two went their separate ways again. Shikina did his best to get clear of the area and could hear bursts of machine-gun fire behind him and the awful crackling sound of burning followed by the muffled boom of what could only have been explosive charges going off inside the shelter. As he ran, he looked back over his shoulder and was relieved to see Kinjo being carried away on the back of a civilian, but that was the last he was ever to see of Kinjo. Shikina was taken prisoner by the Americans in mid-May.

The three boys who carried the wounded Shikina Moritoshi to the field hospital on a stretcher—Kuniyoshi Shinsho, Maeda Chozen, and Nakazato Kunio—all headed back with the intention of doing their bit in the fighting at Mabuyama, but retreating soldiers they met on the way back told them, "They've all been wiped out. Don't go back there."

With no other option but to return to the part of the shelter where the Code Room was, after waiting for a while, Tamaki Kazumasa who had been left behind, disposed of the codes. Before long, LCpl. Nagatomo also appeared, but he seemed to be absolutely terrified. Kuniyoshi commented, "Someone who'd been such a tyrant during our training seemed to have lost his courage altogether. Until we turned up, it was obvious that he wasn't capable of doing anything to help with the codes. He saw us as he tried to gather his senses and help, but just as I was pouring gasoline over everything, he suddenly threw a match on it. I was really lucky not to have been burned alive. It was obvious that Nagatomo had lost his grip of things altogether." After that, the lance corporal left the student soldiers and wandered off by himself.

The Command Post at Yae-dake thronged with people. Not just soldiers from Col. Udo's unit, but soldiers from the central and southern areas as well as the Home Guard and fleeing civilians. They could hear people in the crowd saying, "Our troops have withdrawn from Yomitan," and others saying that, "Reinforcements aren't far away." The four of them were then reunited with Maeda Yasuhiro and Shima Takehisa and the others there. When he heard that there was to be a night attack on the enemy positions at Mabuyama, Maeda confidently said, "We students now have our chance to get revenge."

But things didn't turn out that way. They were ordered to assemble in front of the Command Post but when they joined the hundreds of soldiers gathered there around Col. Udo, their commander made an announcement that ran contrary to what they had heard from the other men. "We have lost many of our number so, rather than just sit here and await our fate, we are going to withdraw to Tano-dake and regroup."

His next words were an even greater shock. "Those of you who can walk will do so, but the wounded will be left behind. Those in the Accounting Section and the students will stay too. Anyone who disobeys this order will be taken aside and executed."

The student soldiers were about to be left behind in a situation where they had already lost their commanding officer and where their surviving members had been scattered all over the place. The enemy was fast approaching and they had no idea what do. If they obeyed the order they would more than likely be killed when the Americans attacked, but if they disobeyed they would be killed by their own side. They had no choice but to sit there under the trees and watch the soldiers march off. After several lines of soldiers walked past, a group carrying wireless radio equipment appeared in front of the boys. Just as they noticed the radiomen, they heard one of the soldiers call out to them, "Hey, what are you guys doing here?" It was a sergeant whom they knew.

When they explained their situation, he just said, "Come with us then." To prevent them from standing out they were given steel helmets to wear and radio equipment and field generators to carry, and they were positioned to march between the regular soldiers. The officers stood by the entrance to the encampment with their swords drawn, looking for men who had disobeyed the orders, but the sergeant just saluted the officers calmly as he walked past, and the boys were not discovered. After that, the unit was attacked by U.S. troops near the herb farms of Haneji, and the survivors were scattered. Maeda says that he has forgotten the sergeant's name, but Kuniyoshi remembers there being a "Sgt. Dekita and LCpl. Wada."

Kuniyoshi added that, "The sergeant was probably killed in that firefight in those gardens, but there is no doubt that the six of us owe him our lives."

Maeda visited Mabuyama not long after the war's end. When he stepped into the long grass and scrub he found two bodies here. One was lying as though he had fallen down across the other's knees. On the ground beside them was a pair of spectacles and a personal seal. He left everything where it was but said, "The seal had the name 'Ueyama' on it, so it would have belonged to Sgt. Ueyama, while the glasses must have been those of Pvt. Sakaguchi."

These days, the hill called Mabuyama that was the focus of such fierce fighting in April 1945 is covered with impenetrable scrub and vegetation, so the old battlefield can only be viewed from afar.

Second Prefectural Middle School Signals Unit Wireless Section

Moromizato Yasuhiro entered the Second Prefectural Middle School in 1942. He recalls, "My navy-style uniform changed to a khaki student one and the white leggings were replaced by army-style puttees."

Normal lessons were being held when he started at the school so it was still what could be termed the "good years." However, he was taken aback when he saw his first class in military instruction. "I hadn't been told at the elementary school that middle school students marched in ranks with rifles over their shoulders."

There was a well-known military instructor at the Second Prefectural Middle School, Mr. Oshiro Yu. He was an older man, known for using dialect in his lessons, plus for Moromizato and the fact that they were both from the same town of Gushikawa created a feeling of closeness. His pet phrases uttered in Okinawan dialect used to relax the boys in what was otherwise a tense atmosphere in the classes.

The amount of volunteer labor that they were expected to do increased in their second year at high school, while in the third year, two-thirds of their time at school was devoted to such tasks. They were sent to work on the anti-aircraft emplacements at Amekudai and Gajanbira, in addition to being mobilized to work on the construction of the airfield at Yomitan. They were involved in digging so many shelters that Moromizato has forgotten where they all were.

"The work was tiring but we were glad to do it. We thought that we were offering ourselves for the sake of the Empire and the Emperor. We had been told that foreign nations had ganged up on Japan and that war was unavoidable, indeed that the very survival of the nation was at stake. We felt both fear and loathing of what to us were 'American and British devils,' and we longed to take up arms. Because we couldn't fight, we were prepared to do what we could away from the front line." Many of their seniors had gone on to the Army or Navy Officer Training School and *Yokaren* [Japanese Naval Preparatory Flight Training Program], and these older boys were looked upon with awe.

One day in 1944, when Moromizato got to school, he found several dozen soldiers lying in their wet uniforms in the school gymnasium. He thought that this was rather strange but wasn't told any more. In the name of "military secrecy" the students were not told that a freighter heading south had been sunk off

Kume-jima.

On the morning of the air raid of 10 October 1944, as Morimizato ran to school he heard the sound of tremendous explosions near the port at Naha. That day, the air raid commenced just as he was heading out to work on the construction of the gunnery emplacements at Amekudai. When he got to school he found that there were already many teachers and students there, all worried about what was happening. Someone yelled, "Let's go and help put out the fires!" and a dozen or so students ran out into the streets as the bombs dropped. Needless to say, the fires caused by the incendiaries were raging too fiercely for a few young people to put them out. By that stage, an area stretching as far as Izumisaki was engulfed in a sea of flames.

Left with no option but to go back to the school, there the students were told by their teachers to go to the shelter at Jogaku. When they got there they found that it was crowded with local residents. Terrified by their first experience of a major air raid, they waited for the bombing to stop.

The Second Prefectural Middle School buildings burned down in the bombing during the afternoon. The students and teachers watched from the shelter, but there was nothing they could do to stop the fire so they merely waited as the U.S. warplanes continued to attack with impunity.

By the time the bombing raid had finished, the only part of the school left standing was the Memorial Hall. The lush verdure that had surrounded the school grounds had all been burned away, so the Hall standing alone in the midst of the burned out ruins further highlighted the devastation. Moromizato's eyes filled with tears as he surveyed the piles of burned rubble in front of him.

It was late in 1944 that the Signals Unit entrance examination test was held in the Memorial Hall for Moromizato and his fellow third-year students and the second-year group.

"I remember before the examination being moved by the instructions given by Captain Sunagawa, who was also from Okinawa. I don't think we were given much advance warning of the exam. I had always wanted to join the Army so I didn't mention it to my parents."

Several days later, written notification came in the mail that Moromizato had passed the examination and he was ordered to report for duty early in the New Year. Parents' consent was required but, considering that his mother was the President of the Gushikawa Women's Association, there was no way that she was going to stop him. That, plus the fact that the news of the "suicide attacks" by the IJA in Saipan, where his father had worked, meant that his family had a strong animosity towards the U.S. military. "I wanted to avenge my father, who at that stage I thought had died in Saipan." In actual fact, although Moromizato did not yet know it, his father had survived the fighting in Saipan.

He joined the Wireless Section of the 62nd Division's Signals Corps. They held their entrance ceremony for the thirty students from Second Prefectural Middle School in a church in Akata, Shuri. They were all issued with new uniforms and the third-year students were given old style Arisaka Type 38 rifles. At not even 150 centimeters in height, Moromizato was among the smallest in his class, so his uniform was too big for him and his rifle felt very heavy. But, he had the uniform adjusted so that he could wear it and felt proud of the one star of a private second class that sparkled on the red background of his collar.

"We were freed from volunteer manual labor after we officially joined the army, and the food was much better, so it was enjoyable." Occasionally the boys were called upon to help dig out shelters, but most of their time was spent on signals training. They were pushed hard by the veteran soldiers to master Morse code as quickly as possible. They had learned about half of the requirements to serve in a wireless section when the Battle of Okinawa started. Shuri began to be bombarded at the end of March, so they relocated to a nearby shelter. Their lives changed dramatically from that day.

Because Moromizato and his friends were still not proficient enough to be of use with communications, their main jobs were helping to carry food and manning the hand-powered generator, an exhausting task that involved them working in pairs turning the handle on the radio transmitter. Occasionally, they would also be sent out as far as 100 meters from the entrance of the cave on dangerous missions to reconnect the wire to the antenna after it had been cut by artillery fire.

Because it allowed them to breathe the fresh air and escape from the dark, foul smelling confines of the cave, carrying food was something they looked forward to. In the early stages of the battle, the shells from the American ships' big guns sailed overhead into the distance, so it was not such a dangerous task.

From their vantage point up on higher ground, in the evening, once the U.S. naval bombardment stopped, they were able to look out over the port of Naha to the west and Nakagusuku Bay to the east, but all they were able to see out there were row upon row of American warships. They often saw "special attack" (kamikaze) planes hurtling down towards the U.S. ships, but most were blown to pieces by the thousands of anti-aircraft rounds hurled up at them from the American armada. Occasionally, a plane would get through the withering hail of fire and smash itself down onto one of the ships, from which pillars of flames and smoke would shoot skyward. At each such "success," Moromizato shouted out "*Banzai!*" in chorus with his comrades, but the elation was mixed with feelings of sadness.

Moromizato was among the first students in the Signals Unit to be wounded when enemy shells began to land very close to them on 26 April. That evening, he was assigned to cooking duties with a first-year soldier by the name of Takayoshi who was from the south of the island and had been to the Second Prefectural Middle School. After washing the rice pots, on the way back to the shelter the two boys rested for a while against a stone wall, looking out over the sea full of American warships. As they headed back toward the shelter, all of a sudden a shell exploded ahead of them just a few steps away from the entrance. They heard a scream as everything went dark from sand and stones hurled into the air. One of Moromizato's seniors from school was lying on the ground groaning in pain.

Still in a daze from the blast, Moromizato moved to help his fallen comrade, but the noise from the explosion had attracted soldiers out of the shelter, so he let them carry the wounded boy back inside as he picked up the rice pots. After taking several steps his leg felt hot, as though someone were holding a heated iron rod against it and, when he looked down, he saw that it was covered in blood with the flesh torn away and the bone exposed. At that same moment, he fainted.

When he came to in the medical treatment area of the shelter, he saw that his left thigh had a tourniquet on it and that that the leg was suspended from the ceiling. Beside him, his senior was lying groaning in pain from shrapnel wounds to his chest and leg. The sentry standing at the entrance to the shelter had been killed instantly by the blast from the shell that had wounded Moromizato, while another soldier who happened to be outside going to the toilet was also hit in the jaw by a piece of shrapnel. That soldier and Moromizato's senior were taken to the Army Hospital in Haebaru the following evening and Moromizato would also spend the next month there in the shelter for the badly wounded.

Around 20 April, just a few days before Moromizato was wounded, a young second lieutenant sought shelter with them in the Signals Unit. He had been apprehended near the entrance of the shelter after withdrawing from the Urasoe area and the next evening was executed as "a spy who had deserted from the front line."

There was no doubting the fact that what the sentry saw was out of the ordinary. The officer had been running around waving a white flag as he fled from an American warplane. As soon as he came into the shelter the U.S. bombardment commenced and the cloth that he'd used for his flag looked as though it was from an American parachute or the like. It was certainly of a sort that they had never seen before. After an interrogation, it was decided that he was "a spy trying to inform the enemy of our positions." He was executed in a shell crater outside the shelter. Moromizato recalls later being told that the man was shot with a pistol before being beheaded with a sword. "It was painful to think that we were killing each other before we had even engaged with the enemy." It is too long ago to allow us to ascertain exactly what had happened, but Moromizato thinks that, "the officer's cowardly behavior probably resulted in him being mistaken for a spy."

Maybe this officer fled from the front line when he could no longer stand the bloodshed occurring before his very eyes in the fierce fighting in the Urasoe area, a battle fought as though the very existence of the nation was at stake. But in those days when people where brainwashed into thinking that their lives were disposable for the cause, the young officer's actions were unforgivable. And for those who fought believing in the "immortality of the divine land," the easiest way to interpret such mortal reactions to the rapidly deteriorating situation at the front line was to label those who tried to flee as "spies."

Moromizato spent just over a month in the medical treatment area of the shelter. There was no army surgeon so a medic treated his wound, but all they could do was to apply iodine tincture and bandages. His wounded left leg swelled up to twice its normal size and he ran a fever and was unable to eat for several days.

The situation in the battle became increasingly tense during the weeks that Moromizato was laid up in the shelter. The area around Shuri also began to attract the attention of the U.S. forces and the naval bombardment became even more intense.

Toward the end of April, the Second Prefectural Middle School's wireless section saw its first member killed. His name was Ageda Shigeru, one of Moromizato's classmates. "He was from Goeku, so we often ended up going to or from school together. I felt it when he was killed. It was a terribly sad feeling." Moromizato was told by one of the other student soldiers that Ageda has been posthumously promoted two ranks. From that time on, student soldiers died in ever-increasing numbers.

In early April, Moromizato heard on the radio that the battleship *Yamato* had left on its mission to attack the U.S. forces off Okinawa, news that considerably lifted the spirits of those in the shelter. But the situation in the battle showed no signs of improving. In fact, it was steadily deteriorating. Feelings of betrayal manifested themselves among those inside the shelter who now were openly making comments like: "What's happened to the *Yamato's* attack?" or "What's Imperial Headquarters actually doing?" There was of course no way that they would have known that the *Yamato*, the world's largest battleship, had been sunk on 7 April.

A friend of Moromizato's, Uehara Yasuei, one year younger at the same school, was also in the Wireless Section. When volunteers for a "suicide attack squad" were called for in late May, Uehara put his hand up, only to be turned away for being "too short."

"The mission was to carry a 10 kg improvised explosive device and detonate it when we got close enough to a tank. About twenty volunteers came forward from among the student soldiers, and their mission was to destroy 'one tank with one man.' I was turned away, but for some reason the mission was canceled." Uehara was told that many of his schoolmates in the Code Unit and the Telephone Cable Unit had already been killed.

The order to withdraw from Shuri to the south was given at the end of May. Making their way through the relentless naval bombardment was no easy task. Already badly wounded, Moromizato Yasuhiro and his comrades in the 62nd Division Signals Corps were dicing with death as they made their way south.

The company commander stood in front of the ten or so wounded soldiers and said words to the effect of "We are now going to withdraw toward Yamagusuku. If you can walk, come with us. If you can't, . . . then you are to take your own lives!" They were each given a hand grenade, a sock full of rice, and two small bags of dried bread.

Moromizato and another private could not walk, so the company commander's words were in effect an order to commit suicide. "I felt horribly alone and afraid of being left behind."

But then the company commander got soldiers to help the two of them. "I'm still grateful for that. There were plenty of men left behind but, for some reason, two able-bodied soldiers were ordered to help us. LCpl. Sakurai was told to help me and a private helped the other wounded soldier"

The early summer rainy season was at its peak when Moromizato left the shelter for the first time in a month. Shells from the artillery and naval bombardment seemed to be falling almost as heavily as the rain. The ground was so slippery that Moromizato lost his footing and fell down time and time again, and the walking stick that LCpl. Sakurai had made for him was next to useless in the cloying mud.

He managed to negotiate his way down the slopes by sliding on his backside, but it was impossible for him to make his way up an incline. It took him a long time to get across a 10-meter wide river as he made his way toward Shikina. "Maybe 20 or 30 minutes, or even an hour . . . I remember that it took an incredibly long time to cross that river." But even so, the urge to survive kept him going when he thought that anything less meant ending up dead among the piles of corpses on the side of the road.

"Once we got across the river there was a slope for us to climb. We eventually got to the top, but by that stage I was absolutely exhausted and struggling to stay awake. I was about ready to give up and told LCpl. Sakurai to leave me and go on ahead himself, but he yelled at me, saying, "You don't want to die out here, you fool!" Every time I started to doze off, he'd slap me in the face to keep me going, and from where we were beside that river, he took me to a little hamlet close by."

As they made their way forward, Moromizato sucked on pieces of dried bread and some rice, by now covered in mud from when they had crawled through the quagmire. "On the way, we stayed one night in an Army Hospital Shelter at Ichinichibashi where there were still student nurse aides working. I remember being really happy when one of those girls gave me a rice ball to eat."

Not far from Makabe, Moromizato found himself pursued by an American warplane. It was at dawn as he was making his way along the path on top of an earthen bank, raised above potato fields on both sides. There was effectively nowhere to hide and he thought, "I'm done for." From his right, the machine-gun bullets from the U.S. warplane tore up the ground in a line toward the bank, so he leapt over and hid on the left side. But then the plane turned around and started to dive down at him from the left side, so he dragged himself over to the right side of the bank. "The American pilot made five or six determined runs, but in the end he gave up. Maybe because he'd lost interest or just thought I was dead."

"But after that I found some chunks of brown sugar in a deserted house where I stopped to rest. For the first time in several months I was able to sleep on a floor. The joy of that and having somehow survived the attacks by the warplane was exquisite."

On his way south, Moromizato saw Japanese soldiers eject civilians from shelters at bayonet point. Around this time, the threat of force by Japanese soldiers toward helpless civilians became a common occurrence.

Moromizato linked up with his unit at Namihira, just short of Yamagusuku. Already over a week had passed since he last saw them. They were not in a shelter, but instead each squad had simply fashioned a crude place to hide using rocks camouflaged with tree branches. The place where they were was so quiet that it seemed to be in a totally different world from the battle not so far away.

"I had nothing to do during daylight hours so every day I just watched the maggots crawling around in my wounds. They attended to the parts that were itchy and cleaned out the wound. I did nothing more than apply vine leaves to it but, thanks to the maggots, the swelling went down and I was able to walk again."

The quiet did not last long and soon the landscape was devastated in the same manner as that around Shuri. As the battle entered its final stages, the ferocity of the destructive forces brought to bear was to become even more terrible.

Two of the Second Prefectural Middle School student soldiers were killed in Namihira. One was a year younger than Moromizato. He was killed instantly when he was hit by one of the heavy caliber tracer rounds that started to rain down on Namihira around this time. When he fell to the ground beside the well, half of his skull had been blown away. Morimizato remembered how just a few days earlier he had been envious on seeing the boy reunited with his elder sister, a student at the same Second Prefectural Girls' School that his own sister attended.

The second death was that of Tengan Kenji, a close friend from his hometown. Moromizato recalls, "Our squad had only a makeshift "shelter" from a pile of rocks, but Tengan and his squad had found themselves a real "shelter" by using a big crack in the rock on the other side, the northern side of the hill." However, U.S. troops accompanied by tanks attacked from that northern side and one of their shells scored a direct hit on the rock, causing the upper part to completely collapse and crush all those below it.

On Coming of Age Day, 15 January 1983, Moromizato visited Namihira. When he looked out to the south at the expanse of sea he muttered how that same vista all those years ago had been so horrible to see. The memory of the sea being so full of American warships that there was no clear line of sight through to the horizon is etched into his mind.

When he finally found the well that he was looking for, he confirmed that it was still just as it had been back in 1945. "Here it is! This is the well!" As he slowly scooped up some water, he said, "This is the water that kept us alive." Twenty or thirty people would come down there in the evening to get water when the naval bombardment stopped for the night. He remembers how there were bodies piled up in the area around the well.

The rocks where his friend Tengan was killed are still there to be seen. As Moromizato went through an explanation of what happened that day, all of a sudden, he stopped speaking. He pressed his hands together in prayer as he looked at the rocks in front of him where his friend had died, and then took out a handkerchief to wipe away the tears.

In the face of fierce attacks by the American forces, Moromizato and the remaining members of his unit withdrew toward Yamagusuku. Soon after they arrived there, they heard the news that Lt. Gen. Ushijima had committed suicide, so it must have been the end of June.

"The shelter at Yamagusuku was a constructed fortification with five entrances. By that point, my leg had recovered and I was carrying messages both inside, and occasionally outside, the shelter." There was already another unit in the shelter but Moromizato's unit crammed themselves in. The bunk beds along one side of the passageways inside the shelter were full of wounded men in obvious discomfort.

Two or three days later, American troops appeared outside the shelter. A group of around thirty regular and student soldiers exchanged fire with them twice from near one of the entrances to the shelter. The defenders had only small arms which meant that there was a clear difference in their firepower and the enemy's who were so well-equipped with machine guns and mortars.

Uehara Yasuei, one year Moromizato's senior, was there running messages for the officer in charge of the combat unit. He explained, "The fighting started around 10:00 AM and by about 2:00 PM there was no one left alive. Lt. Fujita told me to run and get reinforcements from elsewhere in the shelter. But when I got back, we could see that shells fired from tanks were raining down on that particular entrance to the shelter."

The entrance had been hit and rocks had blocked it to the extent that one person could only just squeeze through to have a look. When Uehara turned back with the soldiers who had come to provide support, there was no sign of Lt. Fujita. So small that he was not even given a rifle to carry, Uehara hid in a depression in the rock face and watched the fighting. From there he could see Japanese soldiers going down like tenpins as they tried to move from behind one rock to the next.

The fighting stopped in the early evening when, as was always the case, the Americans withdrew for the night. The five of them who had survived gathered among the trees at the top of the hill. Oshiro Morishin, one year his senior at school, was also there. When they looked back toward the shelter they could see some U.S. troops, stripped to the waist, standing on top of it. "Their sunburned, pink skin made me think that they really do look like the devils that we thought the Americans and British were."

The Americans were obviously going to launch a "horse-back attack" from on top of the shelter so the boys decided that it would be too dangerous to go back inside. The only option they thought they had left was to take their own lives.

They formed a circle and, just as they had readied the percussion cap on a mortar round, someone said, "Kunigami is still holding strong. If we don't kill ourselves, and survive, we can still be of use to the nation." The percussion fuse was soon put back in its place and they withdrew into the shelter where the eerie sound of a rock-drill up above reverberated off the walls in the semi-darkness. They all knew what was going to happen next but there was absolutely nothing that they could do.

At this point, the sick and badly wounded soldiers lying in the bunks were given the order to take their own lives. One of the wounded men hurled the grenade he had been given to use to commit suicide with at a squad of soldiers just about to go out on an infiltration raid, killing several of them. Moromizato said, "Back at Shuri, I too had been told 'Kill yourself!' so I knew how the sick and wounded felt."

Uehara remembers that not long after he got back to the shelter, the sound of the rock drill stopped and there was a huge explosion. Soldiers were killed and wounded all through the shelter, and groans could be heard everywhere.

By this stage, four of the five entrances to the shelter were blocked with fallen rocks and the Americans were attacking the fifth using a flamethrower. The wooden pillars in the shelter and the beds were burning and the air was thick with the smell of gun smoke. A group of them wearing gasmasks gathered near the shelter's middle entrance where they started working away to unblock it.

Then Uehara lost consciousness. "When I put a gasmask on, it felt as though an anesthetic was starting to take effect and I fainted."

Eventually they cleared the collapsed entrance. Their company commander ordered them to go their own ways, saying, "The Empire will not be defeated. You are each to infiltrate enemy lines wherever you can and ensure that your meet an honorable end."

Now with a gasmask on, Moromizato looked around for Uehara but couldn't see him anywhere. Faint voices called out to him in the eerie darkness of the shelter, "Please help me," "Give me some water." There were corpses everywhere so he had to walk over them to get to the entrance. He heard someone say, "Who's that standing on me!" but didn't stop.

Uehara had been carried as far as the entrance where he regained consciousness just before they fled from the shelter.

The two of them left the shelter and headed off to the right where they could see someone standing in the dark. When they went closer to have a look, they realized that it was a man carrying a Japanese sword. The man made it clear that he did not want them with him, saying, "Follow me and I'll cut you in two!" They turned around and headed back, but soon linked up with the unit led by Sgt. Yoshida, who had been in charge of their training.

All fourteen of them set off on an infiltration attack that night, but were met with fierce fire from an American machine-gun, so they hurried back to where they had started from. They claimed to have accounted for one of the enemy at a forward observation point, but the response was so overwhelming that, with flares lighting up the sky, they had to crawl on their bellies with machine-gun bullets zipping just above their heads.

Just before dawn they reached a field of sugarcane overlooking the sea. Moromizato and Uehara sat down to one side of the field, a short distance from the rest of the unit. They moved away so they could open a container that they had taken from the rucksack of a dead American soldier just outside the entrance to the shelter. Moromizato recalls: "We'd never seen anything that shape before. But, I'd seen a can of food once that used a sort of key-type opener, so I had an idea that it might be canned food, but all the same, we were afraid that it might be some type of explosive device."

If it was an explosive device, the two of them would be killed when they opened it, but when they nervously peeled back the top of the can, a beautiful aroma was released from inside. Uehara remembers that, "It was potato and corned beef. I'd never eaten anything as delicious as that in my life."

The sugarcane field was being surrounded by American troops as the two of them were sharing the canned meal. The enemy opened fire as one member of the unit woke up and grabbed his rifle. In just a few seconds the screams from those hit in the hail of bullets abated. Thrusting their hands in the air to surrender, the only ones to survive were Moromizato, Uehara, Yamashiro Yoshinori, and Shirado.

The four of them were stripped down to their loincloths and lined up with their hands on their heads. The American soldiers finished off those shot in the previous minutes and still groaning as they lay in the sugarcane field. Sgt. Yoshida, from Hokkaido, was among the dead. Higa, a classmate from the Second Prefectural Middle School, had also been killed.

One of the American soldiers who came over to the four of them started speaking in English, probably asking questions. When they didn't answer the soldier prodded them in the chest with a pistol. Moromizato then blurted out

"I-cannot-speak-English" which had the opposite effect of bringing the soldier over to him, smiling as he started to question him. Still unable to understand what was being said, Moromizato clammed up, which angered the American, who now pointed his pistol at the side of his head. When Yamashiro said "schoolboy" they turned around to him. They were again saying something in English but the boys could not understand a word of it. Moromizato then thought that they might be asking how many had been in the unit, so he said "ten four" [in Japanese the words ten and four are added together to mean fourteen], so the Americans turned to him. When he traced the number 14 in the ground they finally seemed to understand him.

They saw dead bodies piled high at many spots along the way on their one-hour trip to the POW camp. The Americans made them carry captured Japanese weapons, and Moromizato was made to carry an American military wireless the 1 kilometer to the holding camp.

They hadn't eaten probably for several days so they weren't steady on their feet but, even so, Uehara thought about nothing but escape. When they came to a place where there was a ditch, Uehara says that he even said, "Let's go," and was about to make a run for it, only for Moromizato to dissuade him. "We were weak and I'd seen the Americans' firepower, so I stopped him, saying, 'There'll be another chance soon.'"

At the holding camp, they were relieved when they saw a second generation Japanese from Kunigami eating something. They felt better after eating some chocolate but were soon moved on to a POW camp at Iraha.

On the way to the POW camp, they saw piles of bodies along the sides of the roads. Maggots teemed from the corpses' eyes and mouths and some of the bodies had swollen to the size of a cow. But Moromizato thought that the sight of him having become a prisoner of war was far more miserable and pathetic than anything he was now seeing lying dead on the side of the road. "We seemed to be the only ones alive," he recalled, feeling totally ashamed that the corpses seemed to all be staring accusingly at them.

But this thinking lasted only until they arrived at another holding camp where there seemed to be an incredible number of soldiers. Two of the officers in Moromizato's unit were sitting there with totally unconcerned looks on their faces. One, he thought, was the man who had threatened them with his sword and an intense feeling of anger welled up at the sight of these men.

Moromizato was sent from that camp to Kadena and two or three days later, to a POW camp at Yaka. They spent the next week or so at the camp in Yaka before being assembled and put on to trucks. Uehara and Morimozato were together as they moved from Yaka on one of dozens of trucks packed full of POWs.

"I thought that we were probably going to be killed because there were too many POWs for them to handle," said Moromizato who, as though to signal his departure from the world, threw his hat with his name written on it from the truck as drove along the road. He was not to know that someone then picked up that hat and that it eventually was handed over to his mother.

They were told to alight from the trucks at Sunabe on the coast just west of Kadena. There were hundreds of POWs there, and from the shore they were transported by landing craft to ships anchored offshore, still thinking they would be killed and their bodies thrown overboard.

Once onboard the ship, they were made to take a shower and were treated with DDT. The sizes were far too big, but they were each given a white running-shirt and shorts, as well as a spoon and a bowl. Only then did Moromizato finally realize that they were not going to be killed after all.

However, they had no idea of the ship's destination. Below decks there were about ten separate levels of bunk beds and, apart from the time allocated to sun themselves on deck, they lived below in the hold. Uehara remembers that the meal served just once a day was a type of mutton stew.

Moromizato remembers being told several days into their voyage by a second generation Japanese-American that they were headed for Hawaii. On the way, they stopped at Saipan, which gave him an opportunity to pay what he thought were his last respects to his father (who in actual fact had not died), so he gained some satisfaction from that part of the journey.

Once they arrived in Hawaii, they were transported by truck to a camp with bare red clay which they called Akancha Camp (Honouluili Internment Camp). They heard that a survivor (Sakamaki Kazuo) of the midget submarines used in the attack on Pearl Harbor was also being held in this camp. Uehara said, "I'd always wondered why the song, 'Five vessels and nine crew that were never to return from Pearl Harbor' spoke of nine people, when each of those midget submarines had two crew members. When I got to Hawaii I realized what had happened. They had just hidden things that didn't suit them to be made public."

With Moromizato and Uehara both being shorter than 150 centimeters in height, the American soldiers and other staff at the camp used to call them "Shorty."

They spent three months at the Honouliuli Internment Camp on Oahu Island. They were not made to work and there was plenty of food, so their malnourished bodies soon recovered. Moromizato and Uehara had a comfortable existence in the camp, but three months later the two boys who had been through so much together would be separated. Moromizato was in hospital recovering from an operation to have a piece of shrapnel removed from his leg when Uehara was repatriated to Okinawa. The groups that returned to Okinawa were the "Boys Group" and the "Filaria Group" which were interned separately from the other POWs. If he had not been in the hospital, Moromizato would have been repatriated with the Boys Group.

Soon after he was discharged from the hospital, Morimizato was sent to the Sand Island Camp at the entrance to Honolulu Harbor. "The quality and quantity of food was worse than what we got at the Honouliuli Internment Camp and we slept on camp beds in tents. We had one blanket each and, because it was quite cold at times, if we fell out of bed when it was raining, we'd be wet and unable to sleep for the rest of the night."

They were also required to work at cutting grass at airfields or by roadsides, and there were also laundry or cooking duties. Their daily wage was 80 cents, from which food costs were subtracted, but they were given coupons representing the remainder which they could use in shops within the camp. Moromizato was moved to the camp in Kaneohe where he worked in a medical clinic, although he spent most of his time at Sand Island.

During his time at the internment camps he heard the unexpected news that his mother was alive and well. When he was being transported from the camp at Yaka, and had despondently thrown his army cap with his name on from the truck, someone had picked it up and passed it on to people who would deliver it to his mother to let her know that he was alive. In turn, a letter from his mother was passed from one American soldier to another, eventually reaching a second generation Japanese-American of Okinawan descent living in Honolulu. "I had thought that she was probably dead, so when I heard that she was alive and well, it certainly helped me get through my days as a POW in a much better frame of mind." But it was clear that other POWs were concerned about whether or not their relatives were safe. They all seemed bright and cheerful, but he knew that many were in despair. As a distraction from their concerns, gambling was rife in the camp.

Around this time, they were permitted by the U.S. military authorities to engage in some form of recreation, and the thing that they all did was Okinawan theater performances. There was a professional performer among their ranks, so that person took charge and they all got involved in making the necessary wigs and other stage props. The shows they performed in the camp were of course very amateurish, but nevertheless they were a great hit among the POWs. Each scene played out on stage allowed the POWs to release the full range of pent up emotions. Living as prisoners of war in a foreign land far from their homeland, they would have watched the performances with complex feelings going through their minds. There were even people on the outside of the wire fences watching with tears in their eyes. They were first or second generation Japanese-Americans living in Hawaii. Their feelings of nostalgia were even greater than those of the men in the camp.

The first people from the outside who started making contact with the POWs in the workshops were the first and second generation Japanese-Americans. At first they moved stealthily behind the backs of the MPs but before too long there was open interaction. There were many POWs who were given rice balls, fountain pens, and watches by relatives among the Japanese-Americans.

Moromizato was working in the camp clinic, but one of the POWs assigned to work outside the camp told him that there was a first generation Okinawan immigrant who was looking for a POW with the name Moromizato. He took a day off from his work at the clinic and joined an outside work crew. Once he got to the worksite, he sneaked behind some bushes when the MPs were not looking and met the man who, it seemed, was a distant relative.

"He wanted to know how the war in Okinawa had been and if any of his relatives had been killed, but I had been sent to Hawaii so quickly after the fighting stopped that I wasn't able to tell him anything," said Moromizato. But even so, when they parted, the man gave Moromizato his wristwatch—a warmhearted gift from a distant relative who had lived in the internment camp during the war.

Moromizato returned to Okinawa in November 1945. The bottom of the trousers he had worn when he arrived had been at his ankles, but now they were 15 centimeters too short for him. "This was due to the fact that I'd had a real growth spurt and been eating nutritious food in Hawaii," he said. When he arrived back in Okinawa, even his mother couldn't pick him out from among the crowd.

Later going on to run a clinic back in Okinawa, Moromizato described his awful experiences as follows: "As someone who survived, my job is to pray for the repose of the souls of my comrades and all those students who were killed. I have a hatred of war and an understanding of the precious nature of peace that is based on such terrible experiences. When I interact with patients, I do so in the knowledge that human life is weightier than the Earth itself."

During the interview, Moromizato brought out the treasured wristwatch that he had been given in Hawaii all those years ago. When he wound it, the hands started to move again just as they had forty years earlier. As though remembering the events of those years gone by, Moromizato sat there silently, his eyes following the second hand move around the face of the watch.

Okinawa Fisheries School teachers

Oyakawa Mitsushige took over his new role as physical education teacher at the Fisheries School in Okinawa in November 1941. He explained, "At that time the school was dominated by its military officer and drill instructor. The other school subjects were not taken seriously." The drill instructor would strut around the schoolyard holding a bunch of "Official Completion" certificates in his hand, making a great display of fanning himself with them so that everybody would notice. "They were even more important to the students than their academic graduation certificates. Without them, even after joining the military, we couldn't have become commissioned officers and, at a time when joining the military was a top priority, that was a matter of personal shame," Oyakawa continued.

The Fisheries School had the youngest principal in the entire country. Barely six months before Oyakawa joined the staff, thirty-seven year-old Ochi Michiaki took up his new role as principal. "By nature he was an honorable man, fair-minded and passionate about education." He was a second lieutenant in the Army and he would often wear his uniform at school. "He was also strict with the students, but handled them with a sense of compassion. If a student was messing around, he would deal with it as a matter of collective responsibility by making a whole group of them line up and slap all of them, one after the other. Then as soon as he got inside the staff room, he'd add a humorous dimension to the episode by rubbing his 'slapping' hand and exclaiming, 'Ahhh… that hurt!'"

To a principal who had a third dan in kendo and wore a military uniform, obedience and unity were the essentials of a school whose ethos was "Educated to be crew members." Oyakawa explained, "The military influence was strong in every middle school, but the Fisheries School had the most obvious military ethos of them all. We were the first school to introduce saluting. The Army and prefectural government thought highly of us." The first time the clouds of war gathered over the Fisheries School was 21 December 1943 as a result of the sinking of the *Konan Maru* southeast of Palau. Around ten students enrolled at the Fisheries High School at the time had volunteered for the Class B Army Cadet Air Corps. They passed their course and were aboard the *Konan Maru* on their way to active duty when the ship was sunk after being hit by two torpedoes from an American submarine.

Everything about them, including their departure, was top secret so nobody at school knew anything about it. Outside, however, news of the sinking got around and local residents soon learned what had happened. "Only one person from the Fisheries High School, a boy named Toma Shijiro, survived. Because of the nature of the school, they were all good swimmers and after the first attack five or six of them were rescued by the *Kashiwa Maru*. However, because it was very cold swimming in the wintry sea, they had all crowded into one cabin and were not as fortunate when the *Kashiwa Maru* was attacked. Only Toma was picked up, but that was after he'd spent six hours in the water. He went back home and, in between his tears, told us what had happened." The school was gripped by a mood of despair and staff visited every household to offer their condolences. However, they could not find the words to console the sobbing mothers and relatives and soon found themselves weeping in sympathy.

As news of the defeats at Saipan and Tinian in the Mariana Islands got around, a change came over the warrior-like principal. At a staff meeting he burst out, "The war is a lost cause. Now that I understand what is happening, as a school we have to face up to reality." After that, he sent those of his teaching staff who were from outside Okinawa back to their homes and encouraged his local teachers and even his students to evacuate. Oyakawa was urged many times to leave but, while he was still deciding what the best course of action might be, they were caught in the air raid on Naha of 10 October 1944. Without even any bedding left among his belongings, just as Oyakawa was accepting the inevitable, he was called by the school principal who again urged him to evacuate with the words, "It is now obvious that there is going to be fierce fighting here in Okinawa." Unable to spend a winter on the main islands without anything to keep him warm, in response, Oyakawa said, "I'll stay. There's no other option." The principal replied, "So, are you ready for what lies ahead of us then?"

Around September 1944, the military officer attached to the school, Lt. Nakagawa Sanzo, finished his duty there. His place was taken by the military drill officer, Lt. Ueno Minoru. On his first day, Ueno was trying to decide whether or not to enter the principal's office to greet him when he heard the principal shouting, "Japan has already lost the war, but this young man turns up here as a lieutenant, a drill officer . . ." Stunned by what he heard, twenty-three year-old Ueno, fresh out of university, was lost for words and simply walked away. In the context of the media control that was in place, the principal had a much better idea than most about how badly the war was going and was unable to hold control his anger.

When Oyakawa Mitsushige was teaching physical education at the Fisheries School, he also taught at the privately run Kainan Middle School where the principal, Shikiya Koshin, was also weighing the course of the war. From around the time that the Japanese defending force had been wiped out in the Mariana Islands, Shikiya had started responding to Oyakawa with comments like, "Our army no longer has the nerve to take the initiative and put up a decent fight." From the beginning of 1945, he had been pleading with his students, telling them that "We are really in an impossible position. Please don't do anything silly, whatever happens. Don't do anything foolhardy just out of bravado."

"The principal was called to Command Headquarters almost on a daily basis, so maybe he heard detailed information that way. I also sometimes wondered if he might have been an enemy spy," explained Oyakawa, since a statement like that was unthinkable for people to make at that stage. The school buildings at the Fisheries School at Kakinohana in Naha escaped the fires caused by the 10 October air raid but had been damaged in the bombing and still could not be used. They looked as though they were going to collapse at any moment. As a result, the school briefly used private dwellings in Kamiizumi but after a while shifted to a rural martial arts training hall in Ginowan. However, while on one hand the students were getting correspondence lessons from the Army, they also found themselves being roped in to work for the 62nd Division. There had originally been as many as 300 students, but by then the number was down to just forty or fifty. "There were so many from the outlying islands who'd returned home, so that reduced our losses," Oyagawa explained.

In January 1945, the principal, Ochi Michiaki, left for Kagoshima on a very small boat called the *Nichirin Maru*. Since the loss of Saipan, Ochi had become so weak as to be almost unrecognizable, and had also been urging his staff and students to flee. However, considering that until then he had been so full of bravado and had received high praise from the military itself, when the local newspaper reported him as having "fled," there was a rush of inquiries from people associated with the school criticizing him. Rumors flew in all directions.

Oyakawa explained, "I didn't know what to do. Together with the assistant principal, Arasaki Hirotaka, I visited Maeda Giken at the Prefectural Education Offices to find out if it was true. I was told that the principal's letter of resignation had been submitted and his replacement had been appointed. When Mr. Maeda said, 'I've taken the necessary action,' we accepted that Principal Ochi had fled so we went home." (Maeda has no recollection of this discussion.) "But," Oyakawa continued, "I am glad that the principal fled. If he'd stayed in Okinawa, being the man he was, of course he would have had to head for the battlefield and would have just meaninglessly added to the death toll." Oyakawa only found out after the war that he had worked under a principal who, as he was putting students in harm's way, was also betraying them by leaving himself.

"At the POW camp, there was a female student with a wound to her forehead. When I asked her what had happened, she got angry at me for making her tell her story. It seems that down in the southern part of the island she had no idea what to do or where to go. Then she found the principal and some teachers of one of the girls' high schools so she followed him, only to be yelled at for doing so. They even threw rocks at her and one hit her on the forehead. That's not how people in education are supposed to behave. Remembering how they strutted about in their army uniforms before the war really made me angry."

With regard to the students who were mobilized for the Battle of Okinawa, Oyakawa said, "Anyone with even a little bit of military experience should have opposed that. The head of the department of education, Asato Noboru, would say, 'Why on earth are you using students to fight the war?' How were they being drafted? Even now, I'd still like to know the truth." The general call up for the Blood and Iron Student Corps came through to the Okinawa Fisheries School in late March after the school had moved to the hall in Ginowan.

The names of Lt. Gen. Ushijima and Governor Shimada were written on a sheet of stencil-copied paper. That paper was an official document stating the names and sections of the signals unit members of the Blood and Iron Student Corps. On 25 March, two days after the start of the Battle of Okinawa, an army truck pulled up to the Fisheries School, which had already shifted to the hall in Ginowan. An NCO got out and held up the document. On that particular day, he let them all go home explaining that they wouldn't be falling in because of the air raids, but two days later on the 27th, he was back. Assistant Principal Arasaki and drill instructor Nakandakari Morio were both at a loss for words.

The NCO said that the army was going to take the students away immediately. Oyakawa replied, "I can't agree with my students just being taken away like this. I want them to go home and visit their parents before they go." He knew that his comments might draw an angry response, but surprisingly, the NCO agreed. So after telling everybody to be back by 1 April, he went on his way. Oyakawa was reluctant to send his students to the war zone straight from school. "The Blood and Iron Corps members were with their teachers but those in the Signals Unit were just students on their own. Following the military's orders in sending young kids away without draft papers, and not even as official soldiers, weighed heavily on his mind." That evening, he held what was to be the final staff meeting for the Fisheries School. Furious debate raged, with opinions being divided along two very different lines: which units of the Blood and Iron Corps the boys were to be attached to, and whether or not they should head for Kunigami.

Drill Instructor Nakandakari and an assistant teacher called Susumu Komine were uncompromising, arguing fiercely, "What's the point of them going north where we've got no units deployed? They've got to head south where they can support our troops and fight alongside them." But Oyakawa was totally opposed. "The army's deployment orders are the same as call-up papers. Heading south means a certain and needless death."

On the first evening, the hard-liners had the upper hand. On the second day of the meeting, however, Oyakawa's counter-argument was so convincing that the assistant principal, who had been following the debate with a neutral stance, then supported the principal's case and said the Army's orders were to be followed. The evening of the twenty-ninth of March was moonlit. The students were lined up in two rows in front of the training hall. On the right were those in the Signals Unit bound for Shuri, while lined up directly opposite them on the left was the Blood and Iron Student Corps bound for Kunigami. Assistant Principal Arasaki addressed the students, urging them on by saying, "At this time of emergency for the Empire, even you students must now put down your pens and take up arms to protect your country." Oyakawa then rose to his feet. Turning to the students in the Signals Unit who did not have a staff member in charge of them, he told them in no uncertain terms, "Before you do anything, go home and talk it over thoroughly with your parents." On 1 April, the students in the Signals Unit all assembled at Command Headquarters at Shuri. Except for a very small number, they had cast a deaf ear to Oyakawa's advice, brushed aside their parents' objections, and hurried away from their homes.

That evening, Oyagawa, together with his staff and the students in the Blood and Iron Corps left for Kunigami, where they were to take up their position. According to the official departure register, while there should have been sixty-to-seventy people in the Blood and Iron Student Corps, there were actually only a dozen or so, including staff members. The road to Futenma was choked with civilians. It was a chaotic scene, with some heading north and others trying to make their way south where the soldiers were. In the middle of it all, the group lost its cohesion and Assistant Principal Arasaki and Iroha Choyu, a clerk, became separated. Arasaki was never heard of again.

As they left the hall, drill officer Nakandakari who was also supposed to be in charge of the Blood and Iron Corps unit, together with a teacher, Komine, broke away saying, "We're going to get our families from Haebaru and make our way north." That was the last sighting of the two men whose departure left the Blood and Iron Corps group with only Oyakawa in charge of them. Nobody knew where the unit at their destination of Kunigami was and when Oyakawa, who only knew of Headquarter's Kunigami Detachment, sent one of the students out to scout around, that boy got nowhere. He was told by soldiers that they had no idea where the unit was and asked what they were doing there without any weapons or food.

At that stage, word spread that the Blood and Iron Corps from the Agriculture and Forestry School which had gone on ahead had dispersed without finding the unit they were supposed to meet up with. The Fisheries School group then left their contact details at Kochiya in Ginozan (now Matsuda) and also dispersed. After that, they learned from some students that the group they were looking for was a squad of the 2nd Guerrilla Unit and several joined ranks with them. As a result, only one member of the Blood and Iron Corps was killed there. "The Fisheries School unit had already moved to Ginowan in the north and taken up a position there. Also, because they had been unable to find the other unit, they ended up with only light casualties," explained Oyakawa.

Right after the war, Oyakawa became involved in the administrative recording of the student involvement. He explained, "That really brought home to me the terrible disregard for human life that occurred and how Okinawa was just abandoned." He then voiced another doubt he had been harboring, "The Military Conscription Law was passed in March 1945. So without any legal foundation, the Signals Unit and the Home Guard were set up on Okinawa. Why didn't the newspapers of the day expose such an illegal process?"

Fifteen-year-old signalman

Among the third- and-fourth-year students of Naha Municipal Commercial School lined up in ranks in the schoolyard at No. 2 Ozato Kokumin School on 4 March 1945 was a young boy conspicuously smaller than the rest of the children. He was wearing the army uniform that he had been issued but it was so big on him that the sleeves covered his hands and the trousers were clearly several sizes too large. Similarly, his field cap and his steel helmet both covered his eyes. Barely 150 cms in height, this fourteen-year-old's uniform was so large that it looked comical rather than awkward.

"I think that there were around sixty students. I was about the second shortest of the lot. My voice hadn't even broken yet and I was even mistaken for an elementary school pupil. There were three sizes of cap: large, medium and small, and the small size was still far too big for me."

A third-year student back then in March 1945, Kuniyoshi Shin'ichi smiled as he began to tell his story. "I didn't feel sad to be joining the army. I was really happy to be wearing that uniform, with its rank badge showing me to be a private second-class. I was thrilled that even someone as small as me was being recognized as a soldier. We were full of pride and confidence as we bowed to each other."

In addition to the uniform, he was given a rifle and 120 rounds of ammunition. Kuniyoshi spoke of how proud he felt to be among the young "soldiers," listening to a general telling them that their country needed them in this time of crisis.

However, what he was to experience during the next three months was far worse than what he could have ever imagined. He would see units totally destroyed in fierce combat with American forces, and Japanese soldiers and civilians killed in droves in the U.S. bombardment, the typhoon of steel that was to epitomize the Battle of Okinawa. Many of his friends headed out to the front line to engage the enemy, never to return.

Toward the end of the battle, he also witnessed Japanese soldiers shooting their comrades from behind as they stepped out to surrender to the American forces, plus scenes in which American soldiers cornered and raped Okinawan women—unspeakable scenes that etched themselves into the mind of a young boy not yet halfway through his teenage years.

We asked Kuniyoshi, miraculously the only one to survive a rock-drill and explosives attack from above a cave in Nakaza, Gushikami, to tell us about his experiences in the Battle of Okinawa.

Accompanied by their principal, Nakazato Chosho, and other teachers, Kuniyoshi was among the children taken to the No. 2 Ozato Kokumin School where the 44th Independent Mixed Brigade, commanded by Maj. Gen. Suzuki Shigeki, was stationed. He joined their Intelligence Unit wherein the boys were separated into three groups, to be attached to the Wireless Section, the Code Section, or the Intelligence Section.

His training as a signalman in the Wireless Section began from the next day, 5 March. Kuniyoshi applied himself diligently to his task and, with age on their side, the teenage boys' progress was so fast that their instructor said, "You boys are bright! Two weeks and I'll have you master what a new recruit takes six months to learn."

"Kase, the officer in charge of instruction, Sgt. Shinyama, and LCpl. Furugen. They were the main three instructors who looked after us. We had tests every day; so many tests that sometimes we didn't even have time to eat, but we were prepared for this and didn't find it tough."

On 10 March, the students were told that they could return home. It was only for one day and they had to be back that night, but Kuniyoshi was full of pride when he returned to his parents' house in Sobe, Naha. "I was so keen to parade myself to my family in that army uniform," he said. That evening he was met by his mother Kamado and younger brother and sister with whom he enjoyed dinner. "It was the last time I saw my mother. I later heard that she died of malaria and malnutrition up in the Yambaru where she had been evacuated. When I think back to dinner that night, while she didn't say anything, I had a feeling that she was sad that her son was leaving the family." That day was Kuniyoshi's birthday. He turned fifteen years of age.

"You bastards are eating Army food, so you'll be treated just the same as new recruits. You're not going to get spoiled here!" they were told. In just six months they could send and receive messages in Morse code. "Kuniyoshi says: "I can still remember that '*i*' is dash and '*ro*' is dot, dash."

The U.S. invasion force appeared off Okinawa on the morning of 23 March 1945. The next morning, the 24th, the naval bombardment of Okinawa began.

The school buildings of the No. 2 Ozato Kokumin School, where the 44th Independent Mixed Brigade had set up its headquarters, were hit and burned down, so the headquarters staff moved to the shelter located in front of the school. The students of Naha Municipal Commercial School who had joined the Signals Unit went with them. Their training as signalmen, carried out under the U.S. naval bombardment, was now complete, so the following day, 26 March, they were split into three groups and formally attached to the 44th Independent Mixed Brigade Communications Section, the 2nd Infantry Wireless Unit (operating under the auspices of the 44th Independent Mixed Brigade), and the 35th Independent Mixed Regiment.

Kuniyoshi was attached to the 2nd Infantry Wireless Unit, stationed at Ozato in Nishihara. Together with two boys from the same year at school, he was sent to the Wireless Section of No. 3 Company, commanded by Capt. Ozaki. The Wireless Section was led by Sgt. Inagaki who set the ten soldiers in the section to work operating the generator, sending and receiving messages, as well as carrying out a range of routine duties in the shelter.

About one month later at the end of April, the American forces had already landed and were engaged in fierce fighting centered on the approaches to Maeda Escarpment in Urasoe. It was decided that as one of Japanese army's main units, the 44th Independent Mixed Brigade would be thrown into the fray, so Capt. Ozaki's No. 3 Company was sent to the front line. The ten members of the wireless unit were then provisionally stationed to the area near Benga-dake, just to the east of Shuri Castle.

"Our section's job was to ascertain exactly how the battle was going, so we were always operating with the enemy's tanks not far away from us. We went as far forward as Maeda Escarpment but were simply overwhelmed by the ferocity of the enemy's firepower. I think we were only there for about three days."

Kuniyoshi's section relayed back coordinates to artillery emplacements in the rear that then concentrated their fire on the advancing U.S. armored units, scoring direct hits on several tanks. There were occasions when Kuniyoshi and his friends were elated with the successes of the artillery, but the disparity in firepower was clear for all to see. From around around this time, he started to think that it was going to be impossible stop the enemy.

The 2nd Infantry Unit continued to send soldiers out to infiltrate the American lines but they lost more than two thirds of their strength, almost 200 men, in the process. Signalmen of the Commercial School who had been attached to several different units involved in the fighting also lost many of their number. In the series of combat actions that occurred at that time, Kuniyoshi lost two of his friends in the Wireless Section, Arakaki Moritaka and Oshiro Kiko.

"I think that it was at the end of April. We were running around all over the place carrying messages for Company Headquarters and the two of them went out, one after the other, but never came back. Moritaka was an uncomplicated boy. I remember how he used to amuse himself by taking potshots at Hellcats as they flew low over us. Kiko wasn't afraid of anything and would say, 'There's no way I'm going to die' as he went out with messages."

Kuniyoshi went quiet as he remembered his friends who died. He recalled how Sgt. Inagaki was so upset that the teenage messengers had been killed that, even if it involved relaying orders from the Company, from that point on he stopped sending Kuniyoshi on dangerous tasks.

Early in May, Capt. Ozaki's No. 3 Company was ordered to withdraw to the Command Post at Shuri. Their fighting strength had dropped by half so they merged with the 15th Independent Infantry Battalion. The Wireless Section removed the urns from an old tomb near the Command Post shelter and hid themselves in the space roughly as big as one small room. Plagued by insects and drained by the heat and lack of food, many of them became badly dehydrated. Communication duties were almost impossible.

"The U.S. forces used a really powerful signal to block ours. We had the equipment but could neither send nor receive messages, which meant that messengers often had to run around out amid the hail of fire. Sgt. Inagaki told us "Don't do anything stupid!" but we were all keen to do our bit. Some even went out at night on infiltration raids."

Kuniyoshi continued to relate anecdotes of those days when little frightened him. "One day, I was ordered to go and get some water. The section leader decided not to go, but I rushed out of the tomb as though there was no way that enemy shells were going to hit me. In hindsight, it was no surprise of course that I was knocked head over heels and my buckets and carrying pole were sent flying in all directions by the blast from a bomb dropped by a Hellcat." He was knocked unconscious but came to a short time later. The buckets were lying nearby and the air was full of the smell of gunpowder. When he stood up, he hurriedly scooped up some water from a hollow in the ground and ran as fast as his legs would carry him back to the tomb.

"When I got back inside everyone was really pleased to see me back. The section leader was amazed that I hadn't been killed, but I was just happy to have been of use to the others."

At the end of May 1945, the Command Post at Shuri started to relocate southward. No. 3 Company, to which Kuniyoshi was attached, moved from Shuri to Shikina and then as far as Gushikami, to the east of Yaese-dake, where they split up to go into several different shelters. Kuniyoshi and Sergeant Inagaki moved from one shelter to the next, trying to flee from the American soldiers' attacks using rock drills and explosives.

"We finally settled into a cave on the slope of a hill known as Hill 108. There were six of us left in the Wireless Section: Sgt. Inagaki, Cpl. Yamada, LCpl. Ishimaru, Pvtes. Goya and Seki, and me."

The American attacks were relentless and, one after another, caves were destroyed with the loss of everyone inside. The cave that Kuniyoshi was in had a steep slope leading up to the entrance. Once you clambered down a ladder it went back for about 30 meters so it there was plenty of room to accept the flow of soldiers fleeing the maelstrom outside.

"There were about fifty of us in there, crowded tightly together inside that cave. Maybe it was because I was among the youngest, but the other soldiers would order me to go out to gather food. I remember often being praised for go-ing out and cutting chunks of meat off dead pigs that had been burned to death out on farms. This of course was something that I could have easily been killed doing, but I was so keen to be praised . . ." When Kuniyoshi thinks back on those days he sees it in another light: "I know now that they were just buttering me up so I'd go out and get more food." Even so, the way the battle was developing, however determined he may have been, it was becoming increasingly difficult for Kuniyoshi to venture outside the cave. Before too long the cave he was shel-tering in would be engulfed in flames.

Kuniyoshi says that he clearly recalls that day on which he alone survived while those around him were wiped out. "I ended up being pinned under the bodies of those killed and blown backward on to me by the blast. I was small and didn't have the strength to get out from under the bodies. But an officer, whose name I never knew, saved me. When I looked at his face, I saw that his eyeballs had come out of their sockets and he seemed be struggling to breath. His face was covered in blood and he died soon afterward."

Several years after the end of the war, Kuniyoshi visited the cave and was sur-prised at what he found. It was exactly as it had been when he made his miracu-lous escape. There were skeletons everywhere including one that seemed to have been almost mummified as it lay there, still in uniform, reclining against a rock.

The nightmare ensuing from the *uma-nori* attack [horseback attack] occurred on 19 June 1945. Such attacks were used frequently by the U.S. forces toward the end of the battle with the objective of killing all of the Japanese soldiers hiding inside a cave or shelter. A satchel charge of TNT would be hurled in through the entrance, followed by a blast from a flamethrower—a terrible method of neu-tralizing a cave. If resistance continued, a rock drill would be used to drill a hole from above, through which even more explosives would be dropped.

Early in the morning of 19 June, those inside the cave with Kuniyoshi in the Nakaza area of Gushikami sensed that American troops were approaching. They warned each other in hushed tones to stay alert. The two or three Japanese sol-diers nearest to where the American troops might appear aimed their rifles up at the entrance, some five meters above where they were all waiting with bated breath. Out of the darkness down below, they stared up at the one sliver of light that leaked in through the entrance.

How many minutes must have passed like that, Kuniyoshi muses, before all of a sudden they saw the silhouette of an American soldier peering into the cave? At that moment, the Japanese soldiers fired at the enemy at the entrance.

He thinks that they then heard the American soldiers shouting something that sounded like "Okay" before seeing several objects that looked like hand grenades come sailing through the air.

"What an awful scene it was. The soldiers who had shot at the American were blown backward by the blast, killed instantly. We had no time to react as the explosions continued one after another. The last one, really big, probably a satchel charge of TNT, really shocked the cave right back to the farthest point from the entrance."

Not knowing what to do, he just stayed still, cringing in fear. Before he knew it, just fifteen years old and only 150 cms tall, Kuniyoshi was lying pinned under the bodies of the soldiers killed in the blasts. "I just tried to brace myself against the blasts, but soldiers' bodies came tumbling on to me from in front and behind. I was pinned on my side with maybe five or six bodies on top of me, so I couldn't move at all. Blood from the wounds of the dead soldiers came dripping down on me, all over my face and even into my mouth."

Kuniyoshi said that he grabbed a hand grenade as soon as he sensed that the American soldiers were just outside the shelter.

"A few minutes earlier, I had grabbed a grenade so I could be ready to take my own life . . ." said Kuniyoshi. But now that he found himself pinned under the pile of bodies, he was doing his utmost to free himself. But whatever he did, he couldn't move. Maybe an hour had passed since the "horseback attack" and by now he was struggling to breathe under the weight of the bodies. A wave of sadness came over him as he thought: "I'm going to die pinned under here."

Silence reigned, so he wondered if everyone was dead. But at that moment he heard a faint groan from somewhere further back in the cave. "Is anyone there?" someone called out. When Kuniyoshi yelled back, "Private 2nd Class Kuniyoshi!" a wounded officer started to slowly make his way over on all fours toward Kuniyoshi and the pile of bodies.

"He felt his way over to where I was, so I'd say that he had been blinded. He had been hit in the face by a piece of shrapnel and his eyeballs were hanging out on his cheeks. They hung down loosely as he crawled over toward me. His face was covered in blood, an awful, ghoulish sight." But thanks to this unknown officer, Kuniyoshi would be the only one to escape from the cave alive.

The badly wounded officer made his way over and, one by one, removed the bodies piled on top of Kuniyoshi. Freed from the weight of the men killed by the blasts, Kuniyoshi stretched his aching limbs before getting to his feet and bowing deeply as he thanked the officer for saving his life.

Then after a while he said, "Lieutenant, you've been hit in the eyes . . ." The officer did not respond. He did not ask Kuniyoshi to do anything for him, but simply breathed hard as though in real pain. Then, after a period of silence, the officer suddenly put his hand out, offering Kuniyoshi his pistol. He told Kuniyoshi to leave the cave and make his way to the Command Post shelter, which was about 200 meters to the rear. Kuniyoshi agreed, but knew that trying to cover that distance in broad daylight would be suicidal.

About an hour or so later when the sun had reached a point in the sky almost directly above the cave, Kuniyoshi shook the now motionless officer by the shoulder, saying, "Lieutenant. Are you all right?" but there was no reply.

"He didn't seem to be wounded apart from his eyes . . ." said Kuniyoshi, still remembering the officer who saved his life. "I didn't know his name, so I just called him 'Lieutenant.' If it hadn't been for him, I'd have died a horrible death . . . not killed by the blasts but under a pile of corpses. I wish that I could meet his family and express my gratitude, but I never found out his name, so I haven't been able to."

Maybe the officer had only been partly conscious and had saved the young soldier almost on instinct, but whatever the case may have been, there is no doubting the fact that his presence was the difference between life and death for Kuniyoshi.

Night fell as Kuniyoshi pondered his plight, but before long he shook himself into action and fled from the cave, heading as fast as he could toward the Command Post shelter. When he found it and stepped inside, he was met by a wall of heat. Flames were visible from something burning toward the back of the shelter, while the scorched bodies lying everywhere were testimony that it had received a blast from a flamethrower. While Kuniyoshi had intended to report that everyone in his cave but him had been killed in a "horseback attack," obviously those in the Headquarters cave had met a similar fate.

Quickly leaving that shelter, he spent the next few days on the run, with the sole aim of avoiding capture by the Americans. By now he hadn't eaten for several days and slated his thirst by drinking his own urine.

"Along the way, when I needed to, I hid among the rotting corpses in the ditches beside fields of sugarcane. Sometimes I could hear the footsteps of American soldiers approaching. It seemed as though they were looking for Japanese soldiers who might still be alive. I didn't budge and, for all intents and purposes, I became one of the 'corpses.'"

The rotting remains of dead soldiers were covered in flies and maggots. Kuniyoshi says that he had to endure them trying to crawl into his ears and nose, and even into his anus. Making slow progress with periods hiding like this, eventually he found his way to Mabuni where he met up with several members of the Blood and Iron Student Corps. "Like me, they too had been desperate to get out alive, but Army officers said 'All those who are physically capable will attack the enemy'. We were ordered to go out on infiltration raids so that's what we did."

Kuniyoshi lost consciousness somewhere out in no-man's land.

Eventually, the feeling of maggots crawling over his body brought him back to his senses. It seemed that almost immediately he heard the footsteps of someone approaching. He grabbed his hand grenade, but immediately felt a sharp pain run through the palm of his hand as a large boot came down on it. A second later he was pulled to his feet to find himself standing face to face with an American soldier. "I struggled as much as I could for the little guy that I was, wanting to shout 'Kill me!' but the words wouldn't come out."

Kuniyoshi Shin'ichi was repatriated to Japan from a POW camp at the end of January 1947. After landing at Uraga in Kanagawa Prefecture, he boarded a different ship and headed home to Okinawa.

Not long after he arrived back, the mother of one of his friends from the Naha Municipal Commercial School came to visit him. Kuniyoshi recalls what his friend's mother said. "Shin-chan, when is our boy coming home? I heard a rumor that you saw him in Hawaii."

Kuniyoshi had seen that friend die right in front of his eyes, so the question left him speechless. The boy had been among the people killed in the American soldiers' "horseback attack" on the cave in Nakaza, Gushikami. At that stage, apart from the six signalmen in the cave, including Kuniyoshi, many soldiers from different units had flooded in, including some student soldiers from the Commercial School. Kuniyoshi thought that it would be just too heartless to tell the boy's mother that in actual fact her son had been killed in the blast from a satchel charge of TNT, so he held back from telling her the truth. But later he came to the conclusion that not telling her was actually even crueler, so several days later he told the woman about her son's death.

At first, the dead boy's mother was at a loss for words, but then said, "Can you take me to where my son died? I want to see it with my own eyes."

A few days later, Kuniyoshi took several members of bereaved families whose sons had attended the Commercial School to Nakaza in Gushikami. Only a few years had passed since the war, so the area around the cave was still bare ground. Kuniyoshi found the one-meter diameter entrance to the cave and dropped a rope in so he could clamber down inside. It was dark, so he used a flashlight. There were likely to be poisonous *habu* snakes around too. This did not deter those with Kuniyoshi, but the scene that met their eyes would no doubt have made their hearts miss a beat.

"It was just as I had left it. Many of the bodies were now just skeletons, but there was one soldier who looked as though he had somehow been mummified. He was lying back against a rock in his uniform, with his rifle by his right shoulder."

Having been forced to look at those dead soldiers scattered around the cave for one entire day as he lay pinned under the pile of corpses meant that the scene was indelibly etched on Kuniyoshi's mind.

The mothers whom Kuniyoshi had guided to the cave said that they would recognize their sons from the shape of their skulls or the alignment of their teeth, so Kuniyoshi did his best to help them. "Your son was somewhere over here. He'll be one of these five skeletons," he remembers saying to one mother.

When a mother found her son's skeleton, she would pick up the skull and sob. The boy soldiers had been in their mid-teens. Kuniyoshi remembers how mothers collapsed down onto the ground holding a small skull to their bosom, weeping uncontrollably. "I had no idea what to say to comfort them. Often, the boys had shouted out '*Okaa . . .*' [mother] before they died, so it was a really heartrending scene."

The leader of their signals team, Sgt. Inagaki, was one of those who lost their lives in this cave in Gushikami. His wife visited Kuniyoshi from Oita in Kyushu thirty-five years after the war, bringing their second son with her to visit the site of her husband's death. She stood outside the cave and said, "*Otouchan*, we're here! Look how our son has grown up." They pressed their hands together and prayed.

A taxi driver later in life, Kuniyoshi says, "Young couples sightseeing here laugh in the back of my cab saying 'There wasn't a battle here was there?' I do my best not to get angry, and just tell them the way it was."

Laborers from Korea

"Apart from the comfort women, there were also Korean military laborers in our shelter. Our senior officers used to insult them by calling them "peninsula peasants," so I did the same," explained Kuniyoshi Shin'ichi, who had been a member of the Blood and Iron Student Signals Unit. Unaware of the background regarding their being forcibly brought from Korea to Okinawa, his attitude toward them came from observing his officers.

There are many statements about the comfort women in the Command Post shelter, but very few about Korean laborers. According to one of the staff officers, "There were some Koreans at the Kanoya Base (in Kyushu) but I don't know about Okinawa. The whole issue had nothing to do with us while we were fighting and working out strategies." Kuniyoshi's testimony to their existence is one of the very few we have.

The most shocking incident of ill-treatment of Korean conscripts that Kuniyoshi witnessed was during the Japanese retreat. One of the Koreans had been brought into the army hospital at Haebaru with a smashed knee but, with nothing to relieve the pain, he was screaming in agony. At the height of the fighting, the casualties had formed a queue and the Korean man had no choice but to join the end of the line. When his turn finally came, a voice from behind yelled "get out of the way!" as a Japanese soldier tried to push his way into the queue. Just then, one of the high school nurses helping the surgeons shouted back at the man, "You wait your turn!" Even today, Kuniyoshi remains full of admiration for her because of the laudable way she reacted.

Eventually, the Korean man was thrown roughly onto an operating table, which was really like a table-tennis table and, without any anesthetic, his right leg was amputated. In all, it took no more than ten minutes, after which he went into shock. Turning to the man who had been so roughly handled, the surgeon simply threw the amputated right leg away. It is claimed that a total of as many as 400,000, even 500,000, Koreans were forced into service for Japan in all theaters of the Pacific War as soldiers and military workers. But the real figure has disappeared into a depressing dark hole so as to hide the reality of this shameful part of history.

The number of Koreans brought to Okinawa is uncertain. After the war, about 3,000 of them were held in a compound for Koreans at the Yaka POW camp. Always given the most dangerous tasks, always being spied on by the Japanese and equally at risk from Japanese and American bullets, their death rate was far higher than that of the Japanese. Accordingly, it is not difficult to see why the actual figure possibly should be counted in the tens of thousands. Most of the Korean laborers who survived the war and made it back to their homeland have kept their terrible experiences locked away in their hearts. It's the same with what happened in the now sealed off 32nd Army Command Post shelter—we've still not heard it from the Koreans themselves.

Distribution of Korean Laborers during the Battle of Okinawa

Region	Number of locations	Number of people
Northern Region	12	1,063
Central Region	5	621
Southern Region	14	862
Naha	7	1,300
Miyako	1	70
Yaeyama	8	617
Total	47 locations	4,533 (at least)

Exact numbers cannot be confirmed. These are rough estimates to indicate distribution.[8]

Communications blocked

On 1 April 1945, the day that U.S. forces landed on the main island of Okinawa, Kuniyoshi Shin'ichi, a third year student of Naha Municipal Commercial School, was attached to the 32nd Army's Signals Corps as a member of the Blood and Iron Student Corps. He remembers how, at the induction ceremony, his group leader, a regular soldier by the name of Inagaki gave them their first orders. "From today, you are full-fledged soldiers. Your duties are to run messages, fetch water, and do various other tasks." By this stage, the instruction in Morse code and the relevant terminology carried out at Ozato Kokumin School was complete. Before long, they were to carry their wireless equipment and go out to the front with the regular soldiers to observe and communicate details of the point of impact of Japanese artillery shells or to convey target intelligence and requests for fire to the gunnery officers. However, the crucial equipment, their wireless radios, were of no use to them. "The Americans would block our signal with powerful jamming transmitters when we started to send a message, so we struggled to get the information through, and even if we did, the Americans could get our coordinates from the transmission, so we would be bombarded immediately," says Kuniyoshi.

So instead of using wireless equipment, Kuniyoshi and the other boys in his

8.   Ota Peace Research Institute. 2010: 11.

unit ran through the hail of fire on the battlefield delivering messages. Shrapnel from exploding shells clattered against their steel helmets as they went and shell fragments and splinters cut into their flesh. Seven of Kuniyoshi's young comrades lost their lives at the Maeda Escarpment, where some of the fiercest fighting of the Battle of Okinawa occurred.

IJA units withdrew from Maeda to Shuri on around 2 or 3 May. From that point on the boys received their orders in the Command Post Shelter and on occasion even had to dash out from the cave to deliver messages.

When they received their orders in a coded message involving a series of numbers, they took these to the decrypting section. Kuniyoshi remembers how they used special ink that disappeared when it came in contact with water. There were several signals corps caves in the vicinity of the Command Post at Shuri. Shimabukuro Ryotoku was communicating with the garrison on Tokunoshima, in the Amami Islands north of Okinawa from a shelter built using tombs on the south side of the Memorial Park (now the Shuri Castle Park rest area and carpark).

Even there, the jamming of radio frequencies by the Americans made it difficult to send or receive messages. To make things worse, the telephone wires that linked the Command Post with Shimabukuro's shelter were constantly cut by U.S. artillery bombardment and bombing, so any incoming messages from Tokunoshima, as well as replies from the 32nd Army Headquarters, had to be delivered to the Command Post on foot and collected from there to send back to Tokunoshima. "All communication with Tokunoshima was severed early in April. We couldn't use our wireless equipment so we couldn't really function as a signals unit. The military called on us to adopt an attack-oriented mindset, with each warplane taking out one warship and each soldier destroying one tank, but given our circumstances, there was no way we could achieve that," said Shimabukuro.

Yamashiro family wiped out

Brushing the silver grass and leaves on the trees aside, Ward Chief Yamashiro Mitsunori and another survivor, Uehara Tokichi, made their way forward. Behind them was a steep ridge. Treading carefully, they climbed to a spot on the ridge—the Miyamoto Shelter—where the family of Yamashiro Kamado lie in repose. The shelter is on a highland that locals have nicknamed the "high forest." From the Buckner intersection on Route 331, which leads towards Hyakuna, the shelter is located behind the Futenma Internal Medicine Clinic, which is on the prefectural road. These days, the area is completely overgrown and nobody would know that there had ever been a shelter there. The view is superb, with the gentle waves of Nakagusuku Bay lapping against the shore down below.

"The Miyamoto shelter was buried by a direct hit during the naval bombardment shortly after the Battle of Okinawa began, around 15 April. My father, grandfather and I were hiding in a hole under a massive boulder about 20 meters along the north side of the shelter as dirt and sand rained down. I was shaking and thinking I was going to die." That was how Uehara recalls the occasion, while Ward Chief Yamashiro added, "Acting on the Army's advice, women, children and the elderly at Tsuhako were evacuated up into the Yambaru area in the north before the Americans landed. The only ones to stay behind were some young people and those who had been unable to leave. They included three little girls under the care of a five- or-six-year-old, plus Kamado's family who were also caring for their grandmother. It was a pitiful situation. I wish that I could dig them out but I can't do anything by myself." Uehara still hopes that the government will come and retrieve their remains.

At the time of the fighting, the Imperial Japanese Navy was using the port at Baten. When they tried to store torpedoes and other materiel in a building beside the port, they found the existing jetty was too small for their needs so work began on a new one sometime after 1943 or 1944. Ward Chief Yamashiro explained, "Contractors arrived and a lot of people worked on that project." Following the Naha air raid on 10 October 1944, one of those contractors—the Miyamoto Construction Company—built the shelter in which the remains of five members of Kamado's family are still buried. It was U-shaped with two entrances and approximately 2.5 meters in height. Originally, the Miyamoto Co. used it for storing food but, by 1 April—around the time the Americans landed—the company workers had moved on, so it was then used as a shelter for local people.

However, this same highland that offers such beautiful views in peacetime was a dangerous place during the war because it stood out so clearly. The fact that its entrance faced directly out to sea made it a prime target for the U.S. Navy, thereby inviting disaster. Uehara explained, "So, when the Americans looked up here from their ships, the entrance must have been very obvious to them."

At that stage, the American approach from the sea was to move warships into position each morning and then pull them back before nightfall. They did that over and over again, almost as though it were a regular scheduled service. "The daily routine of the people whose houses had not yet been burned down was to move between their home and the shelter, while those whose homes had been destroyed stayed permanently inside the shelter," explained Uehara. A hail of shells from the American bombardment began to fall around 10:00 AM on that fateful day. The Miyamoto Shelter took a direct hit and in no time at all both entrances were sealed off. Uehara called out "Aunty Kamaru, Aunty Kamaru!" but the shells that destroyed the shelter also killed all of Kamado's family.

Takaishiburi serves as a headstone

The area of Arakaki near the foot of Yoza-dake in Itoman, southern Okinawa, was one of the many places where large numbers of civilians fleeing southward from Naha lost their lives. In the neighboring area of Maehira there was also an incident in which IJA troops killed local civilians.

To the northwest of Arakaki, on the side of the road outside the settlement, there is a four- to-five- meters high coral rock that is referred to by the local people as Takaishiburi. It is surrounded by a lush green swath of torpedo grass. Uezato Sachiko came to this spot regularly for decades after the war to pay her respects to those, including two family members, who are buried beneath it.

In June 1945 Uezato's family of eight was attempting to flee from Shikina in Naha to Tamagusuku in Chinen. They were heading south as part of a group of several dozen civilians when they realized that the way forward was blocked by what looked like a line of people. They moved ahead carefully to a point almost close enough make out the faces of whoever was blocking the way but, as soon as they heard a voice, they turned and scattered in the opposite direction.

Straightaway there was a volley of fire from behind them and they could hear bullets whizzing past their ears and the screams of people who had been hit and had fallen to the ground. Running as fast as they could, Uezato's family soon arrived at the settlement of Arakaki. Their father had been hit in the lower back by a bullet so he stopped and gathered the family together behind an old thatched house. Seconds after he had checked that everyone was there, a shell landed right behind him.

Uezato describes the scene, "My father was killed instantly, as were several other civilians. There were bodies of soldiers and local people everywhere around us. The shells were coming in thick and fast whereupon my older sister, two younger sisters and I found that we had somehow managed to tumble into a cave in front of the ruins of the house."

"I remember that it was really dark inside the cave and that it went back maybe five or six meters from the entrance. There would have been a total of seven or eight people in there—wounded soldiers and civilians. We stayed there one night." The next day, Uesato's older sister, who had a wound on her neck, went out to get some water but did not return, so Uesato left the cave to try to find her and to get water. That was to be the last time she saw her two younger sisters. About 180 meters from the cave, she found her older sister lying dead beside the spring known as Soojigaa. It was then that she saw a truck slowly approaching through the hail of shells and, close to exhaustion, Uezato was taken captive by the Americans.

She was taken to a POW camp in Chinen but, concerned about what had happened to her two younger sisters whom she had left behind in the cave, every day she went to Hyakuna to ask if they had been found. "My mother and other younger sister had been found hiding in a tomb and had been taken into captivity, but the two younger sisters who had been with me were not among the people being held at Hyakuna."

After the fighting ended, Uezato asked a friend to go with her to the cave in Arakaki. Americn soldiers were still all around the area and when they found the cave they saw that it had collapsed from above. The one next to it had also been destroyed. The remains of her father and older sister had already been taken away from where they had died so she was unable to claim them.

The bodies of approximately 10,000 IJA soldiers and civilians were collected in the Arakaki area after the war and interred at *Jokon-no-To* to the west of the settlement. However, local ward chief Oshiro Hideo comments that, "I didn't know about the caves near Takaishiburi until quite recently. It seems that they were used to dump rubbish in. Even older people whom I've asked don't seem to know anything about remains being recovered from there."

"My two younger sisters are probably still in the cave. It's strange how I came to survive. Since the war, I've often thought that if I'd done something differently they might even be alive now. I have regrets . . . It's no good . . . war . . ." Tears welled up in Uezato's eyes as she tried to smile. For her, Takaishiburi will always be a headstone for her two beloved sisters.

Unexploded ordnance

"It was sheer hell. That unexploded shell buried there in the dirt was even more terrifying than the war itself. Anybody who doesn't take unexploded ordnance seriously is courting disaster. I don't want anything like that to happen again."

Working her way back through her memories of that terrible experience, Uehara Yoshi was talking about the time she was caught up in a ghastly incident involving unexploded ordnance in front of the Seimatai Kindergarten in Oroku, Naha, on the morning of 2 March 1974. Uehara suffered injuries to her left arm in the incident.

Piles were being pounded into the earth as part of the work involving the laying of the new water mains in front of the Seimatai Kindergarten. At precisely the same time, around 400 children and parents had gathered at the kindergarten to celebrate Japan's annual Dolls' Festival. Although distracted by the noise of the pile driving, the children were singing the traditional doll's festival song. They were just reaching the end of the final verse when suddenly they heard an almighty *boom*, as a massive explosion rang out.

Sand flew everywhere and the steel pile the men had been driving in at the time, around seven meters in length and forty centimeters in width, was hurled almost a hundred meters. The crane was blown to pieces and the man who had been operating the pile driver was killed instantly, along with three of his workmates. In the grounds of the kindergarten, a little girl about to turn three was playing in the sandpit and was buried in the sand, which the explosion had hurled in every direction. In all, the explosion left four people dead and thirty-two injured. The tragedy was worse than most people would ever witness in a lifetime. Uncontrollable anger wells up in the hearts of the Okinawan people at the realization that the war is still not over for them.

Oshiro Mitsu from Iraha in Tomigusuku was also caught up in the incident, along with her second daughter, Yoshiko. Mitsu said that she doesn't like thinking about the incident, although she did talk to me about it. At the time, her eldest daughter was attending Seimatai Kindergarten, and on that particular day Mitsu had gone to meet her. Yoshiko pestered her mother, so the two of them went to play on the swings when suddenly, there was a massive boom like a rumbling belowground. In a split-second, Mitsu was buried in sand, while Yoshiko had been hurled more than 10 meters by the explosion. Mitsu was saved from certain death only because people nearby came to her rescue. Her daughter Yoshiko escaped with minor injuries. "Even now," she explained, "whenever I hear the sound of piles being driven into the ground, it really upsets me." She has never been back to the kindergarten grounds.

Nine years after that terrible incident, the water mains project was restarted at that same location after a thorough check of the area using metal detectors. The kindergarten, the swings, the slide and so on have all been replaced since then and the children are innocently playing in the kindergarten grounds again. Looking at it now, it is hard to imagine the ghastly scene that occurred there in the past. Moreover, during those nine years, people's awareness of the dangers of unexploded ordnance has steadily faded. Certainly, to the untrained eye, it often seems impossible that a rusty old piece of metal could explode. That's why it is important that we don't forget that ghastly event at Oroku and that we think again about the horrors of unexploded ordnance.

The discovery of unexploded ordnance in the main shopping district of Makishi in Naha was no different from the bomb that exploded at Seimatai Kindergarten.

The issue of unexploded ordnance is an aspect of the Battle of Okinawa that is far from being fully resolved. The U.S. bombardment of the Japanese 32nd Army from warships off shore, warplanes and land-based artillery and mortars was in turn met by the heaviest concentration of artillery under a single Japanese command in the Pacific War. Not all of the several million shells fired by both sides exploded as intended. Even today, decades after the end of the war, bombs and shells lying hidden in the ground are a reminder of the dangers of war and continue to jeopardize civilian lives. Traffic was temporarily halted along Kokusai Avenue as the work to remove the unexploded ordnance at Makishi in Naha was carried out. According to information gathered by Okinawa's Fire and Disaster Prevention Unit, 200,000 tons of shells and bombs were used during the Battle of Okinawa, of which an estimated five percent (10,000 tons) did not explode on impact. Up until the time that Okinawa was handed back to Japan, civilians disposed of around 3,000 tons and the U.S. Army about 2,500. Between Okinawa's return in 1972 and 1981, Japan's Self-Defense Force removed a further 600 tons. It is estimated that more than 3,000 tons will remain buried beneath the surface forever. According to the Bomb Disposal Squads in Japan's Ground Self-Defense Force, the simplest calculation is that it will take another sixty years to remove what is recoverable. That is a frightening prospect.

Working through the police, the Ground Self-Defense Force Bomb Disposal Squad recovers and disposes of unexploded ordnance. The recovered items are placed temporarily into secure containers and then disposed of through controlled detonation or by being dumped at sea by the Maritime Self-Defense Force. The Okinawa Unexploded Ordnance Strategy Organization was established in May 1949 in order to determine how to conduct preliminary investigations, excavation, and removal of unexploded ordnance. During a water mains renewal project at Mikuro in Naha in March 1949, over thirty people were killed or injured when an unexploded bomb blew up, so the organization was created to devise a range of measures to prevent such a tragedy from ever happening again.

Each year, based on information from locals, the organization draws up plans for exploratory excavation and then clears any unexploded ordnance it finds. Between 1949 and 1954 there were 354 such disposals. Incidents of unexploded ordnance removed between 1947 and 31 October 1962 by city, town and village, were as follows: Naha (50), Itoman (43), Uehara (36), Hirara on Miyako-jima (23), Ishigaki (21), Nakagusuku (21), Tomigusuku (18), Kochinda (13), Urasoe (12), Nishihara (10), and Gushikami (10). It goes without saying that most of the unexploded ordnance is in the southern part of Okinawa. Ground Self-Defense Force figures show amounts of recovered ordnance (in tons) as follows: 1947 (6), 1948 (54), 1949 (78.3), 1050 (48.9), 1951 (51.4), 1952 (63.6), 1953 (52.5), 1954 (58.3), 1955 (50.4), and 81.5 tons during 1956.

Similarly, Ground Self-Defense Force figures for the removal of heavy ordnance show that in 1949 a one-ton bomb was removed from Kochinda. During the excavation, 2,500 residents were evacuated from the area. In 1952, a 500 kg bomb was retrieved, one in 1953 and another in 1956. Two 350 kg bombs were recovered in 1949 and three in 1950, bringing the total of heavyweight bombs to eight. By far the most common were 250 kg bombs, with 100 such bombs being recovered between 1949 and 1956. Moreover, 155 50 kg bombs have also been dug out, along with seventeen 16-inch naval shells, seven 14-inch naval shells, one 500 kg torpedo, a 1-ton mine, and three 250 kg mines.

On 13 May 1974, just over two months after the nightmarish incident in the grounds of Seimatai Kindergarten in Oroku, the Okinawa Unexploded Ordnance Strategy Organization held its inaugural meeting. Prior to excavation work being undertaken, the new committee's primary focus was on conducting preliminary site investigations to determine whether there actually was unexploded ordnance present. Since then, various companies have been set up throughout Okinawa using metal detectors to check for unexploded ordnance, and before long eleven such companies, large and small, were up and running. If such preliminary investigations had been carried out at Seimatai Kindergarten, that tragedy would have been avoided. Sadly, no such investigation was carried out and the buried ordnance exploded without warning when hit by heavy machinery. In another incident, work was being carried out on a site at Makishi in central Naha on 16 May 1983. No preliminary testing had been conducted and live ordnance on the site was only discovered when heavy machinery hit it.

Magnetic detection equipment is now used to check for live ordnance on all public work sites involving building homes, installing sewer mains, and the like. Detectors are used that ascertain the presence of large metal objects both just below the surface and at a deeper level. Metal detectors available in the 1980s could detect a heavyweight 250 kg bomb two meters below the surface and smaller bombs a meter below. If the excavation work needs to go deeper than that, preliminary checking is done by drilling boreholes and using a detector from that point. Great care must be taken when working around any area where shells landed during the war. Of course it is also possible that site inspection might not uncover any live ordnance, but that is the luck of the draw as the whole of Okinawa was embroiled in the fighting to one extent or another.

Since the Seimatai incident, people have become more aware of the dangers of unexploded ordnance, and those in the business of magnetic detection have responded to the demand for detection equipment. For example, when all 25,000 square meters of a public park at Iso in Urasoe were checked, the contractors uncovered twenty hand grenades and 5-inch shells. Also, when they checked the 41,000 square meters of land being prepared for a high school in Kadena, they unearthed 100 rounds of armor-piercing anti-tank shells and nineteen hand grenades and naval shells.

Unexploded ordnance is not just left over from the Americans. Japanese mortar rounds and land mines are also frequently discovered in areas formerly used by Japan's military as army emplacements and weapons stores. Recovered Japanese ordnance is mostly smaller caliber, while U.S. ordnance is generally larger. In 1953, in the grounds of Itoman High School where the Imperial Japanese Army had a munitions depot, a total of forty-eight 5-inch naval shells, 81mm mortars and hand grenades were discovered. A subsequent recovery operation was also carried out using information from people who had observed a cave near the school being used to store ammunition during the fighting. That cave was between 40 and 60 meters long and, until the recovery, as a precaution, student campfires were banned at Itoman High School.

As with the Itoman High School discovery, even in areas where we know there is unexploded ordnance lying buried beneath the surface, there are very few people alive today who can remember where such munitions were dumped, either during the war or immediately after Japan's defeat. Moreover, like the site of the discovery at Makishi in Naha, large caliber ordnance has turned up in locations which have been built on several times since the war finished. The men operating magnetic detection equipment are adamant that we must treat every part of Okinawa as though it contains unexploded ordnance.

On the main island of Okinawa itself, clearly most live ordnance is in the central and southern regions, with many such discoveries in places like Naha, Itoman, Nakagusuku, Tomigusuku, Kochinda, and Osato. In particular, In October 1981, thirty disposal operations were carried out in Tomigusuku where a task force was set up to evacuate the locals. In 1981 alone, there were three substantial discoveries. When a heavy-duty 500 kg bomb was unearthed in Tomigusuku on 11 May, 3,287 households (11,551 people) within a radius of 800 meters were evacuated. Then, on 30 July 1983 at Nakachi, a modified land mine was discovered, and on the day of its recovery, 1,677 people from 384 homes within a radius of 500 meters were evacuated. Subsequently, on 21 August at Kakazu, a 50 kg bomb was detected which resulted in the evacuation of 1981 people from 444 houses within a 60 meter radius. At Nesabu during March, April and May 1983, fifty-eight rockets were discovered. In the 1980s each month there were around three instances where unexploded ordnance had to be dealt with.

Various items have been discovered throughout the entire village, including artillery rounds, rockets, large calibre shells, rifle and machine gun ammunition, mortars, modified land mines and hand grenades. When some large-calibre unexploded ordnance was discovered, the fire service informed the local population of the disposal date. Their reaction of "Oh, another one?" shows just how accustomed they have become to such events. Village Chief Kinjo Riichi explained that there had been an army shelter and a naval hospital at Tomigusuku, plus a military emplacement behind the Tomigusuku Apartment complex and council office. "The Americans closed in on the IJA site and laid a minefield there," he explained, "so there was a lot of unexploded ordnance left behind, especially around the naval shelter." By the 1980s, around two thirds of the land in the village of Tomigusuku had been cultivated and a lot of live ordnance was discovered while they were using diggers to prepare the soil there. In the old days they would have simply used hoes and shovels. In modern times, however, it is all done by mechanical diggers which go down much deeper, thereby uncovering a lot more live ordnance.

When something was found during site preparation, council staff had the task of securing the surrounding area with sandbags. Each time something is found, they are dispatched to carry out their work. When a large item of ordnance was discovered in Tomigusuku, prior to its recovery by council staff, the police and fire service closed off access roads and advised residents what to do. Kinjo explained, "There's a lot of time and effort involved but people's lives are at stake so keeping them safe is always the top priority." Only twelve years old when the war finished, he fled from one place to the next around the southern part of Okinawa until he was captured by the Americans at Itoman. "The Americans pulled out without removing the shells, so disposing of unexploded ordnance is going to be a major task for the village in the future," Kinjo added.

After Okinawa was returned to Japanese control, good progress was made in disposing of unexploded ordnance. The vast majority (93.5 percent) of all discoveries are made by sheer chance during building construction, with the remainder (6.5 percent) of finds being the result of people informing the authorities. Many items of live ordnance were recovered during and immediately after the fighting because of information from the public. In 1977 at a housing complex at Asato in Naha, 661 items of ordnance were discovered at a single location. The man who reported that find was Masayori Yamashiro from Asato.

Yamashiro remembers that during the war there was a Japanese anti-aircraft installation set up near his home. That site today is an apartment complex but during the war it was bombed by American aircraft and a pond of around 10 meters in diameter formed in one of the huge bomb craters. Straight after the war, the pond was used as a dump for unexploded ordnance and shortly after that it was covered over. When construction of the apartments began there, Yamashiro remembered that ordnance had been dumped there and immediately reported it to the police.

Almost everybody today understands the dangers of unexploded ordnance but, prior to Okinawa being returned to Japanese control, theft was commonplace. Rumor has it that in some cases people removed the gunpowder from stolen shells and bombs and used it for poaching fish.

Unexploded shells and bombs found throughout the prefecture have included most types of ordnance used by the Americans and the Japanese. Finds have included illumination rounds, smoke grenades, phosphorus grenades, flares, armor-piercing rounds, anti-tank shells and incendiary shells, while propellants have included artillery shells, naval shells, mortar rounds, rockets, bombs, hand grenades, rifle ammunition and land mines. Because of the simplicity of the fuse design in items such as hand grenades, they can explode very easily. The normal process is that munitions finds are either reported by members of the public, or discovered by magnetic detection and then reported to the police. They, along with prefectural agencies, then enlist the help of the Ground Self-Defense Force [JSDF], which dispatches a special disposal squad to remove the ordnance. Thereafter, it is disposed of by the JSDF. In May 1983, a new temporary storage facility inside the United States military ammunition store at Kadena was completed, while prior to that, a private facility in Itoman had been commissioned to store the unexploded ordnance.

In 1983, an unexploded 250 kg bomb was discovered by chance on a building site in the central shopping area of Makishi 2-Chome, Naha. Fortunately, the bomb was removed without incident but, when we consider that unexploded ordnance of all types has been discovered in just about every part of Okinawa, surely it would have made sense to check the site with a metal detector before they began working there? The fact that there are at least eleven companies using magnetic detectors on Okinawa alone speaks volumes about the terror of unexploded ordnance. Discoveries made by chance are extremely dangerous, but it would be fair to say that live ordnance which does not explode when struck by machinery is also a matter of chance.

As of June 2011, some 2,200 tons of unexploded ordnance is said to remain undetected in Okinawa, and each year an average of approximately 30 tons are located and dealt with. At this rate, clearing the prefecture of all remaining unexploded ordnance will take another seventy or eighty years.

Unexploded ordnance in Tomigusuku

On 18 July 1984' during the construction of a bridge at Taira in Tomigusuku, locals were shocked at the discovery of large quantities of unexploded artillery rounds and cartridge cases. By the time the site was cleared the following day, 293 rounds and sixty five cartridges of 75 mm shells, 667 cartridge cases for 155 mm shells, and 271 fuses had been found. To date, this is the biggest single discovery of unexploded ordnance in Okinawa, just one more reminder of the scars left behind by the battle.

Oshiro Kamado, who was the mayor of Taira Village at the time of the fighting on Okinawa, described what happened. "I don't remember the exact date, but when we realized that there was no option but to evacuate, the head of the village ordered us to send the children up north. There were 4-5 dozen households in Taira and, having received that order, I went around to each one. Personally, I did not want to let the children go but the way things were I had no choice and said goodbye to my eldest son who was eleven and my second son who was ten. I think about twenty children headed north. Those who stayed behind fled Taira as the fighting intensified and most just ended up wandering around the southern part of the island."

Following the Naha air raid of 10 October 1944, local villagers dug caves in about ten locations near where this latest unexploded ordnance was found. Initially, the 9th Infantry Division was stationed in this area but, because the

Japanese believed that the Americans would invade Taiwan, the division was shifted there. A naval unit subsequently arrived and set up some emplacements. Two guns were installed but, according to Oshiro, for every two or three rounds that they fired, around a dozen American shells would come flying straight back.

In preparation for the American landing, the people of Taira set about digging shelters. Most of them were never used, however, because the villagers fled southward to Namihira and Kyan in Itoman as the fighting intensified. According to Oshiro, those who did take refuge in the shelters were mainly old people and those who had been wounded. It appears that these people were captured by the Americans after the IJA retreated to the south. When the Taira villagers fled south to where the fighting was at its fiercest, they took their tools with them to dig new shelters. Most families lost somebody at that time. Some families were completely wiped out and their homes have been left unoccupied ever since.

Oshiro fled to Namihira with three families from his own village of Taira and another family originally from Oroku. While seeking shelter in an empty house, they came under fire from American forces and thirteen members of their group were killed. They immediately returned to Taira. Oshiro explained, "We originally intended to flee toward Gushikami but we heard that that area was already under attack so we just kept moving from place to place. All the while American shells were coming in but amazingly nobody was wounded. Many of them were killed later on . . ."

The villagers of Taira helped the military prepare for the impending struggle but they had no idea about how the war was progressing and were unable to ask the soldiers themselves. The locals fled in all directions but it seems that none of them went with a military unit, so it is not known what became of the naval unit that had deployed there. When this most recent pile of live ammunition was discovered, nobody had any idea about what had gone on there; nor did they know where the guns had been located or where the ammunition was stored.

As a result of the unexpected discovery, Oshiro recalled his wartime experiences, repeatedly saying, "War is a terrible thing." At a recent meeting of elderly people at the community center, as the topic of conversation turned to the discovery of ammunition, each of the people present spoke of how they only just managed to get through the *typhoon of steel* alive. Civilians were not allowed inside proper shelters because they were monopolized by the military so they had to dig their own as they wandered around the southern part of the island. The discovery of the unexploded shells meant that images came flooding back to all those who had experienced the fighting. They also decided to use this discovery as an opportunity to explain to the local young people what had happened during the battle.

CHAPTER 6

LIST OF POSTWAR ACCIDENTS INVOLVING UNEXPLODED ORDNANCE IN OKINAWA[1]

Aug. 1948   An American ammunition transport vessel about to carry unexploded ordnance off the island of Ie-jima exploded in port, killing 106 people, injuring seventy-three, and destroying eight buildings.

Oct. 1996   A woman picking up cartridges at the U.S. Marine exercise area in Kin was killed when one exploded.

Mar. 1974   An explosion occurred beside a private kindergarten in Oroku, Naha, during work on sewage pipes. Four people were killed and thirty-four injured. Eighty buildings and forty-one vehicles were damaged to some extent.

May 1975   White smoke was seen coming from the top of a 2 m revetment in Chinen (now Nanjo City), which then exploded. Two elementary school children suffered burns to the face.

Sept. 1975   One person was killed when attempting to remove the gunpowder propellant from a piece of unexploded ordnance in Sawada, Irabu-jima, in Miyako City.

Jul. 1976   Four children were injured in Uchima, Urasoe, after the object that they were throwing stones at exploded.

Apr. 1978   One person was injured in an explosion while burning off some grass and bushes in Ganaha in Tomigusuku.

Jul. 1978   Two firemen were injured when an explosion occurred in an area of scrub in Arakawa in Haebaru that was being burned off to clear the land for development.

Nov. 1984   An explosion occurred in Mizugama in Kadena when a piece of unexploded ordnance was tossed into a metal drum storing items for disposal by burning. A young child suffered cuts to the leg.

Jan. 1987   One person died in Nagata in Naha when an IJA artillery round exploded while being taken apart.

---

1. *Ryukyu Shimpo* electronic edition. 14 January 2009.

Apr. 1989	One person was killed in an explosion while mowing a lawn on Higashieue in Ie-Jima.
Dec. 1991	In Ozato in Itoman, one person was injured in an explosion that occurred when waste construction materials happened to be burned above a piece of buried unexploded ordnance.
1995	A 50kg bomb exploded in a housing area on Miyako-jima, destroying the gatepost of a house.
Nov. 1997	One person was injured in an explosion while mowing a lawn in Mizugama in Kadena.
June 2001	A workman using a jackhammer on land improvement work in Asato, Gushikami (now Yaese-cho), found a piece of ordnance still smoking after having exploded underground. No one was injured.
June 2001	A U.S. 2.36-inch white-phosphorus rocket exploded when crushed by a bulldozer during work on reclaimed land in the Marine Town Project in Nishihara. The driver incurred light injuries to his head. On this site, a total of four incidents were reported that same month.
July 2008	Emergency services were called when something that appeared to be a piece of unexploded ordnance began emitting smoke on a construction site in Sueyoshi in Shuri.
Jan. 2009	A workman operating a heavy caterpillar-tracked jackhammer in Kohagura in Itoman made contact with an American 250 kg bomb, which exploded. The operator suffered serious injuries to his face. A nearby resthome had more than 100 panes of glass broken with one resident injured. Thirteen vehicles and one piece of heavy machinery were damaged to some extent.

Fierce fighting in the Urasoe area

Many civilians in the Nakama area of Urasoe died alongside defending Japanese troops when they found themselves caught up in the fighting during what was undoubtedly the critical phase of the Battle of Okinawa. One family affected in this way was that of Miyagi Tomiko, who was living in the village of Yafuso, in Urasoe. Tomiko lost both parents and her elder sister in the maelstrom, and her recollections of the fighting offer a poignant illustration of the hair's breadth between life and death for those caught in her situation.

Her mother, Nahe, then forty-four years old, was the first of her family to die.

The roof of the cave near Nakama where her family had sought refuge collapsed when attacked from above by the Americans using a rock-drill and explosives. Nahe miraculously escaped the cave-in, but died of exhaustion soon after extricating herself from the cave. Tomiko thinks that this took place around 6 April 1945, just a few days after the American forces landed on the island. She remembers seeing "things like landmines . . . clattering down through both entrances to the cave, followed by a massive explosion a few seconds later which caused parts of the cave near the entrances to collapse." The cave was known as Ufuguchi-gama [large-mouth cave] because of the size of the entrances, but after the explosion, both entrances were completely blocked. Civilians had fled to that particular cave around the end of March in an attempt to shelter from the increasingly fierce bombardment from U.S. warships. In April, IJA troops arrived from the Shimajiri area to provide front-line support. At any one time fifty to sixty soldiers were in the cave, but once night fell, they headed out toward the enemy positions hoping to infiltrate their lines. Most never came back.

The day the cave was attacked from above, there were approximately fifty soldiers inside, together with around 100 civilians, including Tomiko's family who were huddled together deep into the cave. "It all happened so suddenly . . . they shoved the explosives in and the top of the cave collapsed, one section after another. I saw so many people crushed by the huge rocks . . . there must have been 100 of them buried alive . . ." Before she had time to catch her breath, the area where she and her family had been sheltering also began to collapse. Although they were all together in an area of about 160 square meters and 30 or 40 meters back from the entrance, it was no safer there once the Americans began using explosives directly overhead. "They were obviously using dynamite directly above us . . . each time we heard another blast go off, pieces of rock rained down on us from a height of four to five meters. We were terrified, absolutely terrified . . . too scared to even touch the walls in case that caused more cracks to open up."

The rocks eventually stopped falling on them several hours later. When Tomiko finally managed to sum up what had happened, she realized that only thirty or so civilians had somehow avoided being buried alive. But the whole area around them had collapsed and there was no way out. Aged just fifteen at the time, Tomiko felt the blood drain from her face as she looked at her parents and elder sister, thinking "We're going to suffocate in here."

Before long, the plaintive cries from under the rubble of "Corporal, help me, please . . ." stopped. Maybe those caught in there had died, crushed by the weight of the huge rocks, or maybe they had just resigned themselves to their fate. Either way, the cave fell silent. Thirty women and children were left alive inside the murky darkness. Trapped with no way to escape, Tomiko thought, "We've survived the cave roof collapsing but we're all going to die in here anyway."

Then, she noticed three soldiers among the civilians. One of them took some matches from the bag over his shoulder and lit one. "Yes!" a young officer shouted. "The flame hasn't gone out! That means there's an opening somewhere letting oxygen in. Listen everyone . . . I think we'll be able to get out of here. It's going to be all right." His words of encouragement echoed around the cave. It was very dark but smiles must have lit up on the faces of the thirty survivors.

The officer took his sword from round his waist and began poking at the cave walls as Tomiko and the others watched with baited breath. Then, at last, he discovered a hole big enough for a person to crawl through. Casting her mind back, Tomiko says, "I had already accepted that I was going to die of suffocation or starvation, so I was just so thankful. Even now, I shudder when I think about what would have happened if they hadn't found that hole . . ."

The group, including Tomiko's family, followed behind the officer, crawling out through the hole one by one. Just as Tomiko was about to get out, a voice behind her made her stop. When she turned round and went over to have a look, she noticed a man whose lower body was buried beneath the pile of debris. Only his upper torso was protruding from the rocks, so he was able to speak.

"I'm a recruit. I graduated from the Normal School. My parents live on Ojima in Tamagusuku. Could you please go and let them know that I died here in this cave. They are the only coach drivers on the island so you'll have no trouble finding them." As the young man spoke, he handed over his personal seal and his wristwatch to Tomiko's father, Yoshime, who was forty-six years old at the time.

"He didn't ask us to help him. He must have already given up hope because he didn't say 'please don't leave me here' or 'please finish me off.' That's how it was—it was terrible because however much we might have wanted to help him, we'd never have been able to move those big rocks pinning him there." Even now, Tomiko says that she can still remember his face. "It tears me apart every time I think about how I just left him there, still alive, in that awful darkness . . ." she said, her voice choking with emotion.

Tomiko's father was later killed in the fighting in the south and there is no record of what happened to the young man's personal seal and wristwatch. Even long after the war was over, Tomiko continued to worry about what might have happened to them. She eventually resolved that "Even if I can't return his belongings, I have got to tell his family what happened to him."

In 1972, when Okinawa was returned to Japanese sovereignty, Tomiko visited Ojima. "The young soldier's parents had both passed away and, while his older brother and wife were still there, he didn't want to talk about it, explaining, 'We have heard that my brother passed away in a cave somewhere in the Shimajiri area, and we've been there to bring his spirit home. We don't want to hear now that he was buried alive.' I asked if I might be allowed to light some incense in his memory and had them let me pray in front of their Buddhist altar." Stunned as she looked at the dead boy's photo, Tomiko says "It was the same face that I saw in the cave back then . . ." She was lost for words. The photo was taken when he was about twenty years old, his young face happy, smiling . . .

They began to extricate themselves from the cave, with no choice but to leave behind those buried beneath the rubble from the collapse. The small opening that they had hoped would lead them to the outside was only about 70 centimeters in diameter, so they had to get down on their stomachs and drag themselves out. Needless to say, it was very tough going.

"Dad did his utmost to help us. With my being just a young teenager, he decided that I wouldn't be capable of getting out of the cave by myself, so he attached one end of the rope he had around his waist to my wrist. Then he explained, 'I'll go first—you just keep up and follow me.' The hole in the rocks was too narrow for me to use my feet, but I managed to pull myself through the narrow opening using only my arms . . . almost as if I was swimming." Tomiko finally managed to get through the opening, with her father Yoshime pulling her along by the piece of rope. When she recalls being back in that tunnel among the rocks, she remembers, "It just seemed so incredibly long . . . it felt like it must have been 70 or 80 meters long." The look on her face explained what an incredible feat their escape was.

Behind Tomiko and her father, Tomiko's elder sister Kamado, then aged twenty-two, made her way through the opening unassisted. Once he was sure that his two daughters were safely outside, Yoshime went back into the cave to rescue his wife, Nahe. Eventually, the whole family made it outside. Tomiko thinks that it must have been just before dawn the following morning. "The last of our family to get out was Mum, pulled along by my father. She was already recovering from a previous illness, so she was very weak. Being starved of oxygen inside the shelter for so long had weakened her even more."

Once all thirty people had made it outside, they hid behind a rocky outcrop, doing their best not to make a sound. Among the group was a woman with four children, a boy of about sixteen years old out in front. Tomiko witnessed them fall victim to two hand grenades. "The rocky outcrop was far too small for all thirty of us to hide behind, so some of the group stuck out and were exposed. When the first grenade exploded, the sixteen-year-old boy screamed out, 'My eyes . . . I've been hit in the eyes!' Immediately, a second grenade was hurled straight toward the sound of his voice, killing the woman and her three daughters instantly."

Tomiko's father, Yoshime, immediately realized that it was too dangerous to stay where they were and decided they had to try to get away, but his wife, Nahe, had neither the physical stamina nor the mental will power to go any farther. It was clear that death for her was not far away. "C'mon, Dad, we've got to get out of here!" Tomiko urged her father. She also remembers how her mother reacted to all her crying and yelling by gasping out the words: "Tomiko, we aren't going to let you die. It's too late for me, but you've got to get away with your father."

"I'd been told about the evacuation of school children before the fighting became too fierce, but Dad had said 'no.' So, I guess that my mother always thought that 'If we'd gotten the children out then, they'd have avoided all this.'"

Nahe was particularly concerned about young Tomiko, but she said to her elder daughter, Kamado, "I want you to stay here with me until I die." Tomiko could never forget the sight of her mother clutching Kamado's kimono, determined not to let her go. In the end, the elder daughter resolved to stay with her mother. Tomiko's father faced a truly heart-rending choice. "It was so hard for Dad to leave my mother and sister there, but I was relentless as I urged him to get moving . . ." After promising each other that they would meet again, the family split up. Nahe passed away not long after her husband and daughter left Ufuguchi-gama.

After listening to Tomiko's story, we visited Ufuguchi-gama where we assumed things to be as they were after the cave-in.

The location was within Urasoe Castle Park, to the north of Urasoe Elementary School. Tomiko's uncle, Higa Hideo (Nahe's brother), led us there. As soon as the war ended, he had gone there to collect Nahe's remains, so he knew exactly where it was. The surrounding area, known as Shiima Hill, was now basically a small forest, completely overgrown with trees and vegetation. Tomiko explained wistfully that ". . . for quite a while after the fighting ended, not even a blade of grass grew here." She then added that the whole area was covered with the bones of those who had died.

The entrance to the cave was just as it was when Tomiko and the others made their amazing escape. "It doesn't look as if anyone has tried to dig their way in," she explained. "I imagine the remains are still buried inside. I certainly haven't heard anything about anyone removing them."

Higa explained that he came to get his sister's remains at the end of 1945. The remains of the woman who, with her four children, fell victim to hand grenades as they tried to hide behind the rocky outcrop were still there. That was the same explosion as when the boy who was hit in the eyes. He survived and remembered that outcrop—the area around the cave entrance—very clearly so had been able to tell Higa exactly where it was.

Tomiko's sister Kamada was captured by the Americans shortly after their mother passed away. Her memories of it all are so horrific that, since the fighting ended, she had never gone anywhere near that cave entrance until this day. "When I think about it," she explained, smiling ruefully, "I realize that our amazing escape was due to the fact that the Japanese soldiers shoved us all to the back of the cave. Back in those days, I was angry about everything Japanese soldiers did, but it was thanks to them that we didn't get caught in the cave-in and escaped with our lives."

Tomiko, her father, and the others who managed to get away from the cave fled from one place to another until the war was over. On one occasion, others in their group were cut down like nine-pins by machine-gun fire as they were making their way through the valley between the Maeda Escarpment and Chayama near Urasoe. They were killed instantly. "We could hear their cries behind us, but we didn't do anything to help. In fact, we couldn't even bring ourselves to look back because the entire area around Urasoe was crawling with American and Japanese troops. We had no idea what was going on. There were bloated corpses floating in pools of water all around us, looking like pieces of tempura in a bowl."

By the time they finally made it to Gibo in Shuri, Tomiko and her father were by themselves. "I think that was about 10:00 PM. There was a huge moon shining up in the night sky, but every time I thought how that beautiful moon would have no idea what a terrible war was unfolding down here on earth, tears rolled down my cheeks."

After Tomiko and her father rested, they set off again, heading for an army field hospital in Kochinda where Tomiko's other sister Tsuruko was supposedly working. Tomiko and her father eventually managed to make their way to the Garabi Cave at Aragusuku in Gushikami. The cave was being used as part of an army field hospital and Tomiko's elder sister Tsuruko was working there as a nurse. She had been called up from her job in a civilian hospital and posted to various military hospitals. In the Garabi Cave, she was working flat out in the operating theater, but was also teaching the fundamentals of patient care to the schoolgirls who were there as nurse's aides.

Tomiko, Tsuruko, and their father met up at the cave entrance. "When I told my sister that our mother had died at Urasoe, she was so shocked that she couldn't speak for some time. After she managed to regain her composure, she said, 'I'll go and ask if they'll let you stay here,' and took us to where the medical officer was. Although Tomiko's father was forty-six years old and had narrowly avoided being drafted into the army, he was suddenly asked by the medical officer, "You're still young and fit enough to contribute . . . how come you've been running away? It's not too late though, so go over and help out with the food preparation." Fifteen year-old Tomiko was also put to work helping the nurses.

"At the time, I actually felt pleased that I was doing something to support our army," Tomiko recalled. But life in that cave was way out of the ordinary. Caring for a soldier whose jaw had been shot away, she'd had to insert a syringe down a rubber tube from his throat to his stomach to get some rice gruel into him. "Disposing of urine and pus was not so bad. What I really hated was changing their bandages, which were crawling with maggots." The cave was over-crowded with more than 1,000 wounded soldiers, so there was barely room to walk. In fact, although they were all working in the same cave, Tomiko, Tsuruko and their father were so busy that they barely saw one another.

"About a month into the rainy season," that is, probably at the beginning of June, Tomiko's father was suddenly ejected from the cave. The army's explanation was that their food supplies were exhausted and that "they didn't have enough rice to make into gruel so they didn't need him in the kitchen any longer . . . they just had no further use for him."

The three of them hugged one another and sobbed. Their father had decided to make his way to a friend's house in Komesu. As he bid his daughters farewell, he urged them, "you two follow me later on, when you can."

"The two of us bawled our eyes out. After he left the cave, Dad kept looking back at us, over and over again, waving until he was completely out of sight." That was the last time Tomiko saw her father.

A few days later, the Dissolution Order reached the Garabi Cave field hospital where Tomiko and Tsuruko were working. Those patients who couldn't move were poisoned with potassium cyanide and the like, while the other civilians gathered briefly in the Tomori Cave at Kochinda, where they were told, "From now on, you're free to go. You're on your own."

"My sister's job was to look after all those sobbing young girls. There were about 100 of us under her care. I was the youngest at the very front and she brought up the rear. We all paired up, held hands and just walked away."

Even though it was night-time as they approached Yaezu-dake, the boom of artillery fire suddenly rang out. "It sounded like that huge gong they use to start a tug-of-war . . . the whole area was just swarming with people and not only was it pitch black, but it was also raining." The hundred or so of them scattered in all directions, but afterward nobody knew anything about what had happened to Tomiko's sister Tsuruko.

At the end of June, Tomiko was captured by the Americans as she was coming out of the 32nd Army Headquarters' Cave at Mabuni. At the place where she was held prisoner, she came across one of the girls who had been with her father in the cave in Komesu. That was how Tomiko learned that her father had been killed. "Dad used to have his own barber shop. According to the girl, the soldiers recognized his skills so he ended up giving them haircuts before they went out to try to infiltrate the enemy lines. But while he was getting some sleep early one afternoon, he was killed in a shell blast. Apparently he'd said to the girl, 'my daughters are supposed to be heading this way so please look out for them.'"

So many civilians found themselves caught up in the crossfire and lost their lives. As Tomiko Miyagi fled desperately from place to place, she lost several members of her family, one after the other. After she had explained to us the details of the cruel hand that fate had dealt her, she mumbled wistfully, "Those caves reeked of death. I still can't believe that I am actually alive."

Infiltration squads

Capt. Hirose Hideo, a specialist in guerrilla warfare dispatched from Imperial Headquarters, studiously appraised the group of Blood and Iron Student Corps soldiers from the Okinawa Normal School who had assembled in the 32nd Army's Headquarters shelter. The teenage soldiers stood ramrod straight as they listened to him address them. It was the evening of 27 May 1945.

"Will you all gladly go to your deaths?" Hirose asked the boys. "The Army's main units are to steadfastly adhere to the policy of fighting a strategic war of attrition," he explained. "We will relocate to Mabuni so as to force the enemy to shed yet more of its soldiers' blood. Infiltration squads will be deployed throughout the southern region of the island from where you will slip through enemy lines and cause confusion in their rear." The strident response of the young soldiers—"Yes, Sir!"—rang around the cave.

Infiltration squads had been ready to go into action since the formation of the Blood and Iron Student Corps, but the opportunity to deploy them had not presented itself. The U.S. forces pressing hard against the Shuri Line meant that under the circumstances the 32nd Army was unable to properly assess its strategic options and order the infiltration squads into action.

Halfway through May, Kinjo Fukuichiro was ordered to "Put explosives on rafts and push them in front of as you swim from Yonabaru to Kin." From there they were to "carry out guerrilla activities behind enemy lines." But by this point, the U.S. forces had advanced as far as Ishimine, near Shuri Castle, so this plan was also canceled.

Infiltration squads were equipped with about 10 kgs of yellow explosive powder, fuses (lines), and detonating cord. Kinjo recalls that "Our mission was to approach enemy lines without being detected and then lay out detonating cord around their positions, setting fuses as we went. Then we were to detonate the cord and attack the enemy as they rushed around in confusion at what was happening, but this was never carried out."

The order given on 27 May for them to move south was the first example of forward planning being put into action. The fifty-seven members of the Infiltration Unit started their march southward. Because Shuri Castle was surrounded by the enemy the only corridor open to the south was the road that linked Shikina and Ichinichibashi.

Chinen Kiyoshi's squad comprised twelve or thirteen boys. An enemy shell exploded near them soon after they left Shuri, wounding Shiroda Sakae in the leg. Thereafter, most of his friends were also hit at Takamine in Ozato. Other sections suffered the same level of casualties, so of the fifty-seven who set out, only eight survived the march south.

Chinen recalls, "I was envious of my school friends who died. I thought that it was just a matter of time before my number was up too . . . I really thought that it would be easier to die sooner than later."

Husband killed in battle

In July 1944, an evacuee ship left Naha Port bound for Kagoshima. Only those with relatives living on the main islands of Japan were able to get berths on the vessel. Passengers were packed into the narrow confines of the ship's hold, now divided into two levels. That's where Oshiro Yoshiko was with her children, including an eight-month old baby. Oshiro watched over the sleeping faces of her five children as she worried about what would become of her husband whom they had left behind in Okinawa.

Yoshiko's husband Yukio had told her about their impending evacuation only three days before the ship's departure and, while she doesn't recall the exact date, she does remember that it was the day on which the soldiers came to stay in their house.

Yukio was a doctor in Fusato, where he was also working as the head of the Shimajiri *Yokusankai* Young Men's Corps, so he regularly did the rounds of local villages urging residents to produce more food and extolling the virtues of patriotic fervor with the phrase "One hundred million fireballs!" For that reason, members of the *Yokusankai* often visited and occasionally high-ranking officers from IJA headquarters even turned up. Using the map of the world that they had on the wall, the men would discuss the ever-changing fortunes of the units at the front.

After the soldiers left, Yukio spoke to his mother and then called in Yoshiko to break the news. She knew that he was going to tell her something important but never imagined that it was going to be that they were to be evacuated in just a few days' time. As though to persuade her, Yukio told his wife, "Lt. Gen. Ushijima intends to die a glorious death here, and he's talking about the whole island of Okinawa doing the same. It's quite possible that Japanese soldiers will resort of the same type of behavior as those foreign devils." Yoshiko was dumbfounded, thinking that if death were now inevitable surely it would best if they were all together when it happened. Yet she didn't say anything.

Yukio continued to try to persuade her, saying, "The food supplies on the island need to be left for the military. Women and children will just get in the way." Yoshiko didn't agree with this, but Yukio's mother did. She also told her that being evacuated was the right thing to do.

In the end, Yukio finished the conversation by saying, "I am pleading with you to do this so as to keep our family line intact." Decades later, Yoshiko reflected on the situation saying, "In those days, the word of the man of the family was absolute and just could not be disobeyed. When my husband pleaded with me like that, there was nothing I could say. I had no choice but to do as he said."

The night before they departed, the family had dinner with their close relatives, a meal that was to literally be their last supper together. Yukio ate none of the food that had been prepared and said very little. After the meal he just sat staring out of the window. Later that night he said to Yoshiko, "Maybe you could leave one of the girls behind?" but when she replied, "The boys and girls are all the same, they will go or stay all together. Being indecisive about this does none of us any good," he clammed up as though he had given up hope. "It was so painful to see my husband torn like this, but there was no way I could leave any of our children on an island that was doomed to destruction. We did trade a few words on that, but the only option was for me to leave with all the children."

Yoshiko's house in Tamagusuku Village (now Nanjo City) overlooked Ou-ji-ma. The well-maintained garden had a 180-degree panoramic view out over the sea. In one corner, there was a large magnolia tree with a portion of its trunk that seemed to have been violently scooped out. She said that it was the scar from a shell ripping through the tree. It offered a raw, painful contrast to the verdant and vigorous growth around it.

On the day that they were to be evacuated, Yukio and Yoshiko carried out the *mizu-sakatsugi* custom of exchanging cups of water on the basis that they did not expect to ever see each other again. "Thinking of that sort of thing these days, it almost seems funny that it was all so dramatic," she said. Yukio had to undergo his army entrance examination in Chinen Village, so he promised that as soon as he had finished his test he would go to see Yoshiko and the children off from the port. They bid each other farewell before busying themselves in preparation for their next move.

In contrast to their mother's concern about what was to become of them all, the children were excited about their trip to Kagoshima on a ship. Naha Port was crowded with family groups, with husbands and wives everywhere obviously worried about what their fate would be.

Yukio had still not appeared by the time the ship left port. After the war, Yoshiko found out that at that stage he was almost at Naha.

The hold of the ship was hot and the air smelled bad from the dozens of people in the confined space. "It smelled like the inside of a silkworm rearing hut," said Yoshiko. On top of that, she suffered from terrible bouts of seasickness. "Part of the area in the hold containing the evacuees was divided into two levels. We were on the lower of the two. At times, urine from small children on the upper level dripped down on us and we struggled to get much sleep because of the crying of babies or the sound of air raid alarms. It was horribly uncomfortable."

Once they arrived in Kagoshima, they stayed with relatives for a while but, when Yoshiko thought that they had overstayed their welcome, they started moving around, to places like Miyazaki and Oita. That December, Yukio was called up into the IJA and spent his days working between military hospitals at Haebaru and Itokazu.

Yoshiko heard about her husband's death when she was in Miyazaki Prefecture. Concerned about his safety, she went to several of the military liaison offices in places where evacuees were living. At first, they told her, "It seems that he may have been killed, but it's not confirmed yet." However, after she visited several of the liaison offices she found that the reply had changed to "Killed in action."

"Oshiro Yukio, forty-one years old. Killed in action in June 1945." She had known that that was a likely outcome, but still, the shock of losing her husband was huge. As tough as she was, the news left her totally despondent. There was no information on where Yukio had been killed. She considered not returning to Okinawa, but then heard that her husband's remains were still in the family shelter in Tamagusuku Village.

In December 1946, Yoshiko and her children returned to their homeland, to find it laid waste by the ravages of war. She claimed Yukio's remains and buried them herself. "I was glad to be reunited with him in that way. I had no time to mourn though as from that day on I was too busy trying to bring up our five children. But when the worst comes to the worst, women are capable of toughing it through, and I suppose that's just what I did."

In August 1983, when Yoshiko visited Mabuni she couldn't get over how green it was. During the last weeks of the battle the area was covered in the powder of fragments of white coral rock blown apart in the bombardment, so she saw a totally different scene from what had been the case in June 1945. On seeing a leafy banyan tree, she wrote a line to commemorate the day.

> The roots of the banyan tree grow thick and strong
> on the anniversary of defeat in the war.

Kamiya Kinei

As Kamiya Kinie started to recall his wartime experiences, he pointed at the photograph of him as a boy soldier in Ota Masahide's book *The Battle of Okinawa*. "I'm the one whose face is only partly visible," he said.

Kamiya joined the Home Guard in Kochinda in March 1945. His main duties were carrying ammunition. They lugged large caliber shells from their base in Kochinda to the fortifications in Shuri and on the way back acted as stretcher-bearers to get wounded soldiers to the field hospital in Kochinda.

"It was too dangerous to move about during the day so we only went out at night, but because we were carrying live ammunition, every day was really tough." The boys carried large shells on their backs, threading their way through the sugar-cane fields as they made their way toward Shuri.

After fierce fighting, the IJA was gradually pushed back, with all units along the front line beginning to withdraw southward. Kamiya's unit also retreated as far as Arakaki in Itoman. By that stage most units were losing their cohesion. Kamiya tagged himself on to a squad of men led by a sergeant. The first thing the group had to do was find themselves a shelter, so the sergeant entered a cave already occupied by civilians and ejected them. "There were about fifteen civilians in there. They obeyed the sergeant's order, but they clearly didn't want to leave the safety of the shelter. I think that it was during the morning."

Kamiya remembers there being U.S. spotter planes up in the sky. That night he went to get some water from a nearby well and found an old man and what may have been his two daughters, dead there. "I recognized their faces. I'm pretty sure that they had been in the shelter that the sergeant and his men took over."

The Japanese soldiers did not allow Kamiya inside the cave. "The sergeant said, 'Find somewhere else to shelter' so all I could do was pile up just enough rocks around me to hide myself if I squatted down in the middle of them. At that stage the boy soldier in that photograph was also there with me."

Kamiya remembers using a futon as a roof on his makeshift shelter, but he knew that the pile of rocks offered no real shelter from the shells that seemed to fall like monsoon rain.

"That's why I went into the cave that's visible in the background in that photograph. It's near the Himeyuri Memorial. There were many civilians and wounded soldiers in there." The day he entered that cave it was attacked by American soldiers using "blowtorch and corkscrew" tactics and then three days later a gas canister was thrown in. "I thought that I was done for, so if I was going to die anyway, I wanted to get outside and breathe some fresh air first. There was a small hole in the roof of the cave, so I went out through that." As soon as Kamiya got outside he found himself faced with about ten American soldiers pointing their weapons at him. The other boy soldier followed him out through the hole, creating the scene in the photograph. Kamiya says that the white powder on their clothes is from the smoke in the cave.

The boy soldier was taken away by the Americans. "I didn't even know his name. I think that he was about two years younger than me."

Kamiya was kept alone at gunpoint for several hours until a Japanese-American appeared. The man asked, "Is there anyone else in this cave? The Americans are going to blow it up pretty soon, so can you get anyone who's inside to come out quickly?" Kamiya went inside and told those in there what the Japanese-American had said. "They were suspicious, but then again, that wasn't surprising, because so was I. But still, between twenty and thirty civilians went out to surrender." However, when they stepped out of the cave they were immediately faced with American soldiers pointing guns at them, "So they turned around and went back into the cave. I spoke to the Japanese-American and persuaded him to get the soldiers to hide, then I went back in the cave." Only then did the civilians come out and surrender.

There were still IJA soldiers inside the cave. Kamiya went back in to talk to them, but there was no way they were going to surrender. "You bastard! You're a spy!" said one, drawing his sword. "There was very little room in the cave, so he couldn't swing his sword, but I got out of there very quickly."

Kamiya spent four days with the Japanese-American going around caves and calling upon the people inside to surrender. Many came out and were taken away to camps, thereby avoiding a terrible death in the caves, but Kamiya recalls that, "It was only afterward that I found out that my parents and brothers, and cousins, and others whom I knew, were killed near where I was. How ironic is that . . ."

After that, Kamiya was taken by the Americans to a camp at Yaka in Kin, in the eastern part of central Okinawa, but he only stayed there for a few days before being put on a ship bound for Hawaii. "It was a long voyage on that boat," he recalls. Life as a POW in Hawaii was far more comfortable than what he had just experienced in Okinawa. "We had three meals a day and were even allowed to have seconds. That in itself kept us happy. There were many people from Okinawa there."

Two months later, Kamiya was taken via San Francisco to the camp at Angel Island in California. The facilities on Angel Island had originally been a military prison, the Angel Island Guard House, and the place where Kamiya entered had been used to hold Italian POWs.

"It was an easy life there too. We were not made to work. There was nothing to do other than eat our three meals a day. We made pipes, but that was really just to kill time. In comparison to Okinawa, it was heaven. There were a few people there from Okinawa and we always talked about things back home. We were all concerned about how members of our families were. We thought of Okinawa every day."

Six months later, he was returned to the camp at Yaka, where he was officially demobilized.

"Many things happened on Okinawa. I saw people get their arms and legs blown off. I imagine that no one who experienced war as I did wants to talk about it. I certainly don't enjoy it. But at the same time, there are things that need to be passed on through the generations so that our children or grandchildren will never have to experience what we did."

Shuri Castle

The inscription on the Bankoku Shinryo-no-Kane bell [The Bridge Between the Nations Bell] hanging in the Seiden [main hall] is "The Kingdom of Ryukyu is a splendid place in the South Seas." The symbol of that Kingdom, Shuri Castle, was not only the political and administrative center of Okinawa, but in military terms, it also occupied an excellent strategic location.

Located on the highest ground among the hills just to the east of Naha, it is protected by two natural moats in the Makabi River and the Kinjo River. To the north there are the hills of Sueyoshi and Urasoe, while to the east stands Ben-ga-dake. Looking southward, Shuri overlooks the southern region of Okinawa and to the west the city of Naha and the South China Sea are visible.

Maj. Jin Naomichi, a staff officer with the 32nd Army, rated the location of Shuri Castle very highly, comparing it to 203 Meter Hill, the scene of fierce fighting in the Russo-Japanese War of 1904–1905.

"In the war against Russia, Gen. Kodama Gentaro moved the headquarters from their location far from the front line to right up close to where Gen. Nogi was fighting. That served to lift the troops' morale, and what had seemed like an impregnable fortress fell. In the same way, the Command Post cave complex at Shuri was a classic example of a frontline base of operations," said Jin.

In other words, Jin explained, "The commanding officer being in Shuri provided a level of unspoken support to the frontline soldiers that 'We can't move back, can't withdraw from Naha,' and this in turn was effective in terms of combat strategy."

In 1879, when the Ryukyu Islands were annexed by the Meiji Government of Japan to become Okinawa Prefecture, the curtain was brought down on 500 years of history in which Shuri Castle had served as the administrative and cultural center of Okinawa. That same year, the barracks for soldiers dispatched from the Kumamoto Garrison was set up inside the Castle, from which point it came to be viewed as a military base.

From December 1913 to the following January, the *Ryukyu Shimpo* newspaper ran a series of articles in which it covered scenarios for military exercises for the 6th Division Mixed Units fighting a land battle in Okinawa. In those hypothetical scenarios, the Okinawa Defense Force Headquarters was set up at Shuri, so the scene was set for Lt. Gen. Ushijima's 32nd Army to build its Command

Post under Shuri Castle.

On 25 February 1945, only weeks before the Battle of Okinawa commenced, the U.S. 10th Army issued a *Technical Bulletin* stating, "There is no need to destroy important public property." Jin Naomichi harbors doubts about this statement. "There was no way that they could manage that. Whether they had important cultural significance or not, both the U.S. Army and the Imperial Japanese Army were obliged to attack locations of strategic significance." So after being transformed into a military strongpoint by the IJA, Shuri Castle was destined to be totally destroyed in the course of the battle.

32nd Army Command Post at Shuri

Many sightseers from the main islands of Japan and from other countries come to visit Shuri Castle Park. There is a large, burned bishopwood tree with a strangler fig growing in it near Enkanchi Pond where fighting occurred during the Battle of Okinawa. Tour guides often pause here to explain the battle to busloads of tourists.

"Because the Command Post cave complex of the 32nd Army was underground near here, Shuri Castle was destroyed in the fierce fighting that occurred in this area." About 20 meters further on is a concrete structure closed off by steel mesh. "This is the entrance to the Command Post cave complex," said the guide. But that is not actually the case. All of the entrances to the 32nd Army Command Post cave complex in this area were sealed off.

The 32nd Army Headquarters Unit directed operations in the Battle of Okinawa from this cave complex. Some 243 students from the Normal School were mobilized from December 1944 to work on the construction of the shelter, toiling right through until the end of May 1945 just before the IJA abandoned the complex and withdrew to Mabuni.

It is said that there were six entrances and that the total length of the underground tunnels was between one and two thousand meters. The tunnels varied in depth from 15 to 35 meters below ground and were about 4 meters in width and over 2 meters high. They were totally impervious to the fiercest bombardments that the U.S. forces directed at Shuri.

There were two or three bunks for soldiers on both sides of the tunnels, as well as kitchens, baths, toilets, and plentiful supplies of food. It was a totally different world from the outside, which had been transformed into something akin to a lunar landscape by the U.S. bombardment. While Shuri Castle has been restored, the Command Post cave complex of the 32nd Army, and the bodies that it entombs, remains to this day basically as it was left in 1945.

Life in the Command Post Shelter

Life in the 32nd Army Command Post Shelter was a constant battle with heat, humidity, and smell. Without fail, people with any knowledge of the Command Post Shelter all comment on the oppressive heat, the debilitating humidity, and the terrible smells emanating from putrid matter.

Makiminato Tokuzo, who had cause to frequent the Command Post as a writer for the *Okinawa Shimpo* newspaper, likened the heat and humidity to "something like mist or steam hanging in the air." "Glasses would constantly fog up and match heads would crumble when we tried to light a cigarette." This unbearable heat and humidity affected the commanders, soldiers, and student corps members of the 32nd Army all to the same degree.

Soldiers and members of the Student Corps would put their faces out through the ventilation holes in an attempt to get fresh air. Some soldiers even stripped down to their loincloths in order to survive the heat. Many of the Normal School students in the shelter remember Chief of Staff Cho getting women in the shelter to fan him as he sat in his loincloth. Makiminato remembers how "they rigged up a kind of wind tunnel made of cloth from the entrance to the shelter to the chief of staff room. Chief of Staff Cho would stick his head into this at times to breathe."

According to the "Regulations for Combat Headquarters Shelters" there were to be three meals a day, served at 8:00 AM, 1:00 PM and 9:00 PM. There was plenty of food, with bags of rice being stacked along the sides of the passageways and used by soldiers to sleep on.

The meals used canned ingredients so "there was some quite tasty food cooked up," recalls Makiminato. However, the students who worked so hard building the shelters were only fed twice a day. Inadequate meals and hunger was part of their lot. Moromi Moriyasu, who worked in a construction squad, recalls painfully that "Although there was plenty of food, we were never fed properly. All we wanted was to get enough to eat."

There was a little stream near the cooking area close to the No. 5 entrance to the Command Post shelter, so that is where they got their water to cook the rice. Unfortunately the heat inside the shelter caused the cooked rice to spoil, so they often had to cook it again.

From mid-May, heavy rain started to fall on Shuri, dripping through from the ceiling of the dugout shelter and leaving the floor awash with water. That water then got into the bags of rice, which had absorbed perspiration from the soldiers lying on them so before too long the rice in the bags started to ferment. "The smell was just awful," recalls Makiminato.

The "Regulations for Combat Headquarters Caves" were issued on 5 May 1945 in the name of Chief of Staff Cho Isamu. The wording of these regulations clearly indicates the suspicion the military harbored toward the Okinawan people. "It is forbidden for military personnel or employees to use any language other than standard Japanese. (Those speaking the Okinawan language will be deemed to be spies and will be punished.)"

Anyone who uses an Okinawan dialect is a spy—this perception of Okinawans would subsequently lead to the tragic murder of many civilians. The Normal School students say they knew that the soldiers would be suspicious of them if they spoke in dialect, so they made a conscious effort to avoid it.

The regulations were formulated to keep order in the shelters and to help maintain the morale of the soldiers but, as the Japanese situation in the battle worsened, the regulations lost their effect. Makiminato Tokuzo, who had cause to go into the Command Post shelter as a newspaper reporter, said, "The soldiers were all doing their own thing. There were men among them who did nothing but chant sutras all day long."

The regulations also paid close attention to matters of hygiene, but the relentless bombardment from the U.S. warships off shore meant that those in the cave could not use the toilet by the entrance to the shelter, so there were piles of excrement everywhere.

The soldiers' emotions were also put under enormous strain. Takara Yoshio, a member of the Normal School construction unit, remembers listening to soldiers lying in their loincloths on top of the bales of rice that lined the sides of the passageways. "They bravely talked about how they were resigned to dying in Okinawa and talked longingly of their hometowns."

Uchima Takeyoshi, also a member of the same construction unit, saw many soldiers who faced death in a land far from their homes. "Many of the soldiers wished us students well and told us about things back home such as the rivers where they caught carp and where they used to run around in the hills and fields. They often talked of their hometowns."

These soldiers sat illuminated by tubular lanterns fitted with electric light bulbs. On the lanterns were written brave-sounding expressions such as "Shoot them down" or "Graveyard at the end of our guns." On one side of the passageway there was a line of light bulbs which, according to Makiminato, looked just like those strung up on the stalls at festivals in peacetime."

Women in the Command Post Shelter

Nohara Hironobu remembers watching some women—referred to as "Korean chicks"—use sticks to pick brown rice out of the 1.8 liter bottle it was packed in. Some people also witnessed the women snap back at the Japanese soldiers who teased them with the term "Korean chick." Seeing Nohara exhausted from his efforts excavating the Command Post shelter, day after day, night after night, sometimes the girls would call out to him kindly, "Don't work so hard." One of them offered him some canned fish cake to eat. "Maybe I reminded her of her own little brother back in her home village. Anyway, I was so grateful. I divided it up among four or five of us and we ate every last morsel. I'll never forget that act of kindness."

Moromi Moriyasu had heard about some women from the Tsuji area of Naha visiting the senior officers' quarters. He was surprised, explaining, "I noticed them on several occasions. I could smell their perfume and, although they had on *monpe* baggy Japanese pants, they were well dressed. Can you imagine how strange it was, such pretty women in the middle of a war . . ."

It was humid inside the cave. "During the midday meal, the girls would gather around the general and fan him to keep him cool," recalled Uehara Seitoku. "Even though the soldiers were supposed to protect the civilians, they used to make fun of the Okinawans by telling them that it was their island and they had to protect it themselves." He felt angry watching one of the army's most senior officers behave like this. Tokuyama Chosho was staggered when he saw a group of several girls working with shovels right next to a group of Japanese soldiers clad in loincloths. Some of the girls were from Nara Prefecture and, even as the soldiers kept touching them, giving them lecherous glances and directing obscene comments at them, the girls said nothing and just kept going with their physically demanding work.

On the 32nd Army Headquarters daily orders dossier inside the shelter was a section covering *female employees*. It included the words *women's bath time allocation* and a series of statements setting out their bath times in detail. In a map produced by the U.S. military, the women's accommodation area was identified as being 85 meters in from the entrance to No. 5 tunnel. It also specified the presence of twelve Japanese and ten Okinawan females.

On the evening that they finally abandoned the Command Post shelter and headed to the south of the main island, one of the Korean women called out to Takara Yoshio, "I'll give my body to you . . . take me with you." There was no way he could, but he couldn't just refuse her desperate pleas, so in a flash he thought up a fake withdrawal time for his unit, saying, "We're pulling back around 7.30 PM!" and snuck away without her. After the withdrawal from the Command Post shelter, it is not clear where the Korean women from the shelter ended up. Nohara Hironobu, however, confirms that he subsequently saw a group of Korean women further south, exposed to the shelling as they wandered aimlessly through the hellish fury of the battlefield, which by that stage the rain had churned into thick mud.

Observation Post in Shuri Castle

In early May 1945, a Japanese kamikaze plane scored a direct hit on one of the U.S. warships off Aja near Naha. Sesoko Shoken watched from the 32nd Army's Command Post observation point as sheets of flame from the sinking vessel shot up into the air. He and his fellow soldiers danced with joy at the sight.

As a member of the Okinawa Prefectural Fisheries School's Blood and Iron Student Corps, Sesoko was posted to the Signals Unit of the 32nd Army's Intelligence Division as of 1 April 1945. He was one of twenty-two from his school attached to various Signals Units. From March 1945, they underwent training in telephone (cable) communications at a rural martial arts hall in what was then known as Ginowan Village.

The Cable Signals Units, assigned to maintain around-the-clock surveillance, comprised one NCO, one regular soldier, and three or four students. Their observation post was on top of a wall at Shuri Castle. The NCOs would confirm the number and movements of American naval vessels and fighter aircraft, plus where their artillery shells were landing and so on, while the students would use the portable transmitters they carried over their shoulders to report that information to the communications base inside the Command Post shelter.

On one particular day, Sesoko climbed up a vertical shaft in the Command Post shelter and made his way to the above ground observation post where he carried out his assigned duties. "There were U.S. ships anchored out there as far as I could see, so I thought Okinawa was already done for. Our kamikaze planes arrived every two or three days but all were shot down on their way in. I saw some of our planes succeed at the start, which made me feel great."

Because the United States increased its air defense capability after the initial success of kamikaze attacks, most subsequent sorties failed. Sesoko watched Japanese aircraft being chased away by American fighters and then trying to touch down near Makiminato. Furious at what he regarded as "Opting out without smashing into anything . . . they're just cowards," he immediately reported his observations back to the communications base. However, when his superiors heard his report, they ripped into him with, "You idiot. You don't need to report that sort of thing!"

The worst part of manning the observation post was seeing civilians become victims of the war. As Sesoko was doing his usual lookout duties toward Aja, an artillery shell landed near a factory and ripped the building apart. After the smoke had cleared away, he saw that the landscape had changed completely and there was no trace of the people who had been working inside the factory.

Unlike inside the Command Post shelter, which was said to be able to withstand bombs of up to one ton, those manning the observation post, which was constantly exposed to artillery fire, were perched on the edge of life and death. Only after they had finished their duty and made their way back to the shelter, did they check with each other that they were actually still alive. It was a miracle that nobody was killed out in the observation post. "Our observation post was inside Shuri Castle, so I guess our Ryukyuan ancestors were protecting us," Sesoko remarked gratefully.

5th Artillery Command Post Shelter

The 5th Artillery Unit, as part of the 32nd Army, constructed its command shelter inside the southern slope of what is now the Shuri Castle Park Rest Area. There were other fortifications located in the vicinity of Shuri Castle in addition to the 32nd Army Command Post Shelter, making the area into a veritable fortress. The 5th Artillery Headquarters accepted eighty-six students from the Prefectural Technical School Blood and Iron Student Corps into its signals unit. These boys were divided up into three groups to be trained in wireless, telephone (cable), or coded signals from early January 1945. Yet without gaining sufficient technical skills in these areas, they were hurled into the Battle of Okinawa. One of the Technical School signals corps boys, Katsumasa Nagamine, recalls, "We weren't any use as signalmen so we were made to do all sorts of jobs such as repairs inside the shelters, carry food and other things."

The Command Post shelter was about 100 meters long with a shaft of another 50 meters heading north of it. According to Nagamine, work was underway to connect it with the 32nd Army Command Post Shelter to the east, but this was canceled when the U.S. forces landed.

There were always more than eighty soldiers and students in the shelter where the atmosphere became increasingly tense as the American forces got closer to Shuri. Wounded soldiers were often carried in, and operations were carried out in an area of the cave designated as the medical room. The cries of, "Kill me! Please kill me!" from the badly wounded soldiers still ring in Nagamine's head. The hellish scenes that these teenage boys witnessed were so shocking that they were scarred for life. For some it was too much to bear, with the worst cases breaking down completely and rolling around on the ground outside the shelter.

Soldiers and student signalmen were not the only people living in the shelter. There were also comfort women attending to the officers. Technical School student soldier Arakaki Anei remembers seeing comfort women in the officers' quarters, saying that, "The soldiers didn't really let us see them, but we had heard that there were comfort women there. I could tell from their facial features that they were Korean."

At the end of May, when the 32nd Army Command Post Unit withdrew, the 5th Artillery Command Unit also pulled out of Shuri. On the day that the soldiers were to withdraw, the comfort women are said to have left the shelter ahead of the men of the Command Post Unit, their belongings wrapped in a *furoshiki* as they headed through the hail of incoming shells in the direction of the cobble stone streets of Kinjo.

The situation awaiting the Technical School students in the southern part of the island was a scene from hell. That only nine of the eighty-six Technical School students survived is testimony to that.

62nd Division Engineers

Several IJA shelters were built on the eastern side of the area around Shuri Castle, under which the Command Post cave complex of the 32nd Army was located. Students of the Okinawa Normal School were mobilized to help dig these shelters. The shelter occupied by the 62nd Division Engineering Unit was among these, although its entrance which was then located on the northern slope of the hill where the Daruma Temple now stands has been buried by soil and sand.

Iraha Nagafumi, who had been working as a conductor on the light rail trains, was one of the thirty young Okinawan men who joined the Engineering Corps on 1 March 1945. He was still nineteen years old. "I was not afraid of death," said Iraha, describing himself as a typical product of a militarist society.

Iraha and the other new recruits were given the task of hindering the advance of the U.S. forces. Basing themselves at the military storage facility built on the hill known as Akamuya, in Kubagawa, Shuri, they worked digging foxholes and laying minefields. It was Iraha and his fellow engineers who brought down the large metal tower at Benga-dake in an attempt to block the way of American tanks.

The number of casualties among the Engineers Unit increased as the U.S. forces approached Shuri. The area just inside their shelter was crowded with wounded soldiers. For Iraha, death was "something that was an expected outcome." He recalls that "If death was inevitable, I wanted to go quickly, without any pain."

On 23 May, there was a disaster in the Engineers' shelter when ammunition stored there exploded. Earlier that same day, Iraha had been transferred from the Engineers' shelter to that of the 13th Independent Infantry Battalion which occupied the next shelter. Explaining the incredible force of the blast, Iraha said, "The whole cave seemed to lurch sideways and soldiers lying in their bunks were thrown out onto the floor by the blast from the explosion. Pieces of rock as big as your fist came falling down from the ceiling of the cave."

Iraha remembers dashing out of the shelter he was in and looking toward where the engineers had been, but there was no sign of an entrance. They managed to drag out several men who must have been close to the entrance at the time of the explosion, but they were all near death. "More than 100 men died in that accident and I would have been among them if I had been in there."

The Engineers withdrew to the Mayoral Hall in Tomigusuku on 27 May. The following day, ten of them set off for Shuri with orders to blow up the 32nd Army Command Post there, but they were never seen again.

After the end of the war, efforts were made to recover the remains of the Engineers from their cave shelter, but fears of further disaster in the cave meant that only three bodies were recovered with nothing having been done since. "Is that the way it has be I wonder? It's a real shame," says Iraha.

CHAPTER 7

EXCESSES COMMITTED BY THE IMPERIAL JAPANESE ARMY

In the last year of World War II, sixty-six years after Okinawa had been incorporated as a prefecture of Japan in 1879, Japanese interpreted the cultural differences they found on Okinawa as a reason to look down on the locals as second-class citizens. By and large, Okinawans were judged to be unconcerned about the fate of the nation and unable to be trusted to contribute to the protection of the Empire in its time of greatest need.

Their innate prejudice against any form of ethnic difference, fanned by the strain of knowing that the battle could only have one outcome for the defending force, produced a mindset among Japanese soldiers that led to a range of excesses against Okinawan civilians. That such acts were committed against local people by troops ostensibly there to defend them is one of the features of the Battle of Okinawa.

In the early stages of the campaign there were instances of locals being killed for "impeding the war effort" by failing to cooperate in a satisfactory manner with the military.[1] As the situation in the battle steadily worsened, many civilians were murdered by the IJA on the pretext of being "spies."[2] Anyone who had been in contact with the American forces or held a flier giving instructions to civilians on how to surrender ran the risk of summary execution. In a famous case on Kume-jima in the last two months of the war, the killing of civilians continued after the main island of Okinawa was secured by U.S. forces, with the last murders of locals on Kume-jima occurring in August, after Japan had surrendered.[3]

By 1945, the combat units of the IJA were made up to an ever-increasing extent by older conscripts including men who just a few years previously would not have passed the physical tests for entry to the military.[4] As the quality of new recruits dropped, the IJA increasingly relied on fear and brutality to maintain order in the ranks. Following the withdrawal southward from Shuri, discipline

1. Oshiro, M. 2007: 104-107.
2. Saki, R. 1982: 32-33.
3. Hayashi, H. 2001: 179.
4. Hayashi, H. 2010: 41-42.

within the units of the 32nd Army deteriorated rapidly and there were many in-stances of theft of food from civilians and rape of local women. There were occa-sions when infants sheltering in caves with their mothers were killed by soldiers who feared that the child's crying might give away their location. Civilians were also killed for refusing to go out into the maelstrom on what were effectively suicide missions to collect water or carry boxes of ammunition.

In the final stages of the battle, Japanese soldiers often ejected civilians from caves, effectively sending them to their deaths in the U.S. bombardment. In the final two or three weeks of the battle, literally thousands of Okinawans were killed in the "Typhoon of Steel" directed at the remnants of the 32nd Army fol-lowing the withdrawal toward Cape Kyan and Mabuni, with over 10,000 chil-dren under the age of fourteen dying in this manner.[5]

Execution of a "spy"

"There is something that I haven't been able to talk about since the war. It's about Uehara Tomi, a young woman from Tomigusuku." The face of lawyer Kawasaki Masanori, who had been a member of the Blood and Iron Student Corps, as-sumed a pained expression as he readied himself to tell the story. He had had to wait almost fifty years before he could talk about what had happened.

One day in May 1945, Kawasaki remembers that the sun was going down and it was starting to get dark. Some *Kempeitai* [military police] men dragged a woman out of the 32nd Army's No. 6 Tunnel. Her name was Uehara Tomi and she was about thirty years old. She wore an army issue short-sleeved jacket and shorts and her hair had been shaved very short. The name uttered by one of the *Kempeitai* men etched itself in Kawasaki's mind. "All spies will receive the same punishment as Uehara Tomi."

The *Kempeitai* man said, "We will now execute a spy." Uehara Tomi was now in a kneeling position, tied to a power pole some 20 meters from the tunnel entrance. Four or five Korean comfort women from the tunnel complex were standing in front of the woman, each wearing *hachimaki* headbands emblazoned with the rising sun and each holding a 40-cm long bayonet.

As the *Kempeitai* man controlled the timing by barking out orders of "next," "next," the comfort women took turns stabbing the kneeling woman. The *Kem-peitai* man then cut the rope tying Uehara to the pole and forced her into a sitting position. Kawasaki said, "He was either a first or second lieutenant. I remember that as he held out his officer's sword he said how he wasn't very good at swords-

---

5.   Ota Peace Research Institute. 2010: 8.

manship." The officer stood behind Uehara and swung the sword down onto her from above. He severed her head with the second blow. At that moment, some soldiers or young members of the Blood and Iron Student Corps who had been watching came running over, picking up clods of soil or stones to throw at Uehara's now decapitated body—human beings ceasing to be human. Caught up in the maelstrom of war, those young people who had lost classmates took their feelings out on Uehara's body.

"I'll never forgive myself for that," Kawasaki said, still tortured by his conscience. Fourteen or fifteen years after the war's end, Kawasaki visited the spot where it had happened. "As one of the people who witnessed her last moments, I am obliged to say something. With circumstances as they were in Okinawa at that time, there was no way that people would act as 'spies.'" For more than twenty years, Kawasaki had thought of writing about the fate of Uehara Tomi, but the "pain of just thinking about it" meant that he could never bring himself to put pen to paper.

This year, in the days before *Irei no Hi* [June 23, Okinawa Memorial Day], Kawasaki again visited the place in Kinjo, just south of Shuri, where Uehara Tomi is believed to have been buried. He prayed for her soul to be at peace, but in his heart the turmoil of the Battle of Okinawa continues unabated.

Fires on the Battlefield

The hills of Shuri burned bright red. Around the end of May 1945, Ahagon Reiko remembers gazing from Kakazu in Tomigusuku at the fires that cast a red tinge on the sky. "It looked as though a large building was on fire and I imagine that it was probably Shuri Castle. The flames slowly moved from one level to the next, as though crawling their way up the castle walls." The developments that day spurred Ahagon and those around her on to evacuate southwards toward the Shimajiri district of the main island of Okinawa.

Things were obviously not going well on the battlefront. Then a second year student at the First Prefectural Girls' School, Ahagon remembers the words of one of her teachers who suggested to the students that "If the Americans are to attack from the south of Japan, Okinawa is a far better prospect for them than Taiwan. Supplies are plentiful in Taiwan, so it would be a drawn-out struggle. Okinawa is smaller and not as well-supplied, so it would be easier to force a result in a shorter time."

The cautionary tales doing the rounds of the classrooms reminded them of the *gyokusai* [suicidal attacks] in Saipan, the shame of being taken prisoner and to be prepared for *jiketsu* [an honorable suicide], but the teacher's words were a shock to the girls. They realized that the arrival of the American forces on their homeland was imminent.

The image of fire is an enduring part of Ahagon's memory of the war. She clearly remembers seeing flamethrowers being used when she was desperately trying to make her way south. "A thick jet of flame would stretch out and then disappear as though being sucked back in. It was actually quite beautiful," she says, but was quick to add that the bodies of people burned to death by the flamethrowers were a horrible sight to behold.

The streets of Naha were also on fire when Ahagon fled from her house with just one bag of belongings at the time of the air raid on 10 October 1944. When their house in Naha burned down, they fled to Kakazu, from where they looked back at Naha being slowly consumed by the fire. The evening sun that night seemed to be an even deeper red than usual as it arced its way down toward the sea that within six months would be full of U.S. warships.

Before too long, they would soon see *tokkotai* special attack planes falling from the sky toward that same sea off the coast from Naha. At first, they viewed them with the hope that the *kamikaze* attacks would help turn the tide of battle but, faced with overwhelming American firepower, as the planes fell out of the sky as harmlessly as leaves falling from the trees, she remembers that the scene became increasingly sad to witness. Ahagon remembers how the *tokkotai* aircraft also left their mark on the evening sky as they burst into red balls of fire.

After the air raid of 10 October 1944, Ahagon spent her days traveling to and from school, and contributing her labor to the war effort. She remembers that 11 December 1944 was spent helping to dig a shelter at the hall of the Mayor of Tomigusuku. It was a pleasant day, not so cold at all for December, and certainly not a day on which anyone would have thought a disaster could happen.

At that stage, Ahagon was living with her grandmother in Kakazu, but a shortage of food meant that she also occasionally stayed with an uncle in Itoman. Students living further away were allowed to commute by train.

The train's departure time meant that two of her classmates, Yogi Tsuruko and Kinjo Sadako, finished work early. They came over to Ahagon, asking if she was going to return by train with them, but when she told them that she was going to stay in Itoman that night they hurried off to catch the train at Tsukazan Station.

"Twenty or thirty minutes later there was a tremendous explosion. When we looked over to where it came from, we saw great plumes of black smoke going up into the air. It was obvious that there had been some kind of accident," said Ahagon. She remembers that a short time later she saw a carriage that must have been blown free from the train come roaring into Tsukazan Station as a ball of fire.

Two days later, Ahagon heard that her two school friends had been killed in the explosion when she was at her uncle's house. According to people involved at the time, the details of the accident, from which the explosion could be heard as far away as Naha and throughout the entire Shimajiri district, are not well known. The military hushed it up so it did not become widely known among the local residents.

The accident occurred when the train had gone through Kyan Station and was heading for Inamine Station. The explosion destroyed six carriages loaded with ammunition, one carriage full of gasoline and medical supplies, as well as setting fire to and exploding several hundred tons of ammunition stacked in a nearby field. More than 200 people, including civilians, lost their lives in the accident. It occurred when the gasoline being carried in the front carriage ignited, with the flames reaching the carriages behind that which were carrying ammunition and which then exploded. Transporting munitions and gasoline together in open carriages is an incredible lack of common sense. "Despite it being wartime, I cringe at the stupidity of carrying ammunition and passengers on the same train," says Ahagon, who heard how pieces of human flesh were found stuck to sugarcane in the fields near where the accident happened.

Ahagon Reiko and her grandmother left Kakazu in Tomigusuku and headed for the sugar refinery in Takamine where her uncle worked. It was difficult making progress with an old person on roads that were now slippery and muddy due the early summer rain. "We only really carried food with us, but the weight of that was tough to carry. I remember leaving things like pork oil on the side of the road, saying to my grandmother: 'I'll just leave this here and come back and get it later.' I remember how she scolded me for being 'no use at all.' But it just couldn't be helped." They couldn't move by day, so it took two nights to reach their destination. The roads were jammed packed with civilians trying to get away from the fighting.

A shelter had been dug out in the hill in front of the sugar refinery at Takamine. "There were about 200 people in there, workers from the refinery and their families. Among them were my uncle and his wife, my cousin and his wife, and their son and daughter." It was only a short time after they entered the shelter when disaster struck.

There was a brook flowing past the front of the shelter, a place there where transport corps soldiers would water their horses. That day, one of the soldiers looking after the horses had dashed into the shelter where Ahagon and the other civilians were, but unfortunately this had been spotted by a U.S. reconnaissance plane. Before long, a white phosphorus shell landed right by the entrance and the flames from the fire it started spread all the way to the back.

"I rushed as fast as I could toward a separate entrance. I thought that I'd be burned alive if I stayed inside, so I just wanted to get outside. But a person standing at the entrance stopped me, saying, 'You'll be seen by enemy planes.' That's when I fainted," said Ahagon.

When she regained consciousness, she found that she had been carried to a house nearby. "I remember one of the tank corps men who were in the house saying 'This one's alive.' I knew that two days had passed, but not why they had carried me to the house. I don't know what happened to the others. I heard after the war that my cousin had been killed, leaving behind his wife and daughter.

"When I think about what happened then, it makes me miserable to think that my grandmother and uncle left me there and fled like that. I had no food with me and no one to rely on. By that stage, I was pretty much ready to die, so I just started wandering around with no particular destination in mind." Ahagon had no idea of what direction might be safest, but recognized that while some people were going north the main flow seemed to be heading south. She joined those walking southward.

Ahagon remembers it as being somewhere around Maezato. The road at night was occasionally lit up by illumination shells, which highlighted the awful scene of corpses on all sides. Among them, she remembers seeing something white that stood out from the others. "When I looked closely, I saw that it was a woman's naked body. Right in the middle of the road, there were no clothes on her at all. Maybe they had been ripped off her in a blast from an explosion, but I've never forgotten the whiteness of her body lying there on the road."

As she approached the town of Nashiro, she remembers seeing a man wearing a palm frond hat, dead, but in a sitting position with a carrying pole over his shoulders. Next to him, lying dead on the ground, was his wife. Her long hair was tied up at the back and she wore a relatively short kimono, so maybe they were a couple from a local farm. Ahagon remembers that there did not seem to be any blood on either of them. Her attention had been attracted to the dead couple by the cries of their baby, crying for all it was worth as it scrambled to feel for its mother's breasts amid the noise of the explosions from the U.S. bombardment.

She was mortified by the pitiful sight but there was nothing she could do. Her loathing of war surfaced when she thought, "That baby was probably doomed to follow its parents."

Ahagon was wounded while she was sheltering behind rocks near the coast at Mabuni. She had managed to meet up with her aunt, who had been in the headquarters of the 32nd Army, but every day was spent cringing in expectation inside the cave.

All of a sudden, there was a burst of machine-gun fire. One bullet hit her behind her left ear, so her left shoulder and arm were soon covered in blood. Another went through Ahagon's left leg and hit the knee of a girl called Shikina, who had been sitting next to her. She only realized that she had been wounded when her leg swelled up and her trouser leg became tight. "The bullet went through my leg, but the person beside me had a bullet that lodged in him and killed him," said Ahagon.

But the bullet that hit her behind the ear had to be removed, so Ahagon was carried to a cave behind where the *Kenji-no-To* Memorial is now located to be operated on. "The operation was carried out by the light of a candle without any anesthetic. About ten people held me down, but I still managed to yell out in pain. I think my screams were probably louder than those of a pig about to be slaughtered."

"After the unit I was with broke up, I hid in a gap in the rocks for quite some time and was eventually captured by the Americans on 10 July. She has never regained full use of the leg that sustained the bullet wound. Being a woman, it's been tough not being able to kneel down. I'd like to learn the koto or the shamisen, but . . ." says Ahagon. The wounds of the past still affect her.

Shuri Castle burned to the ground

Shuri Castle was burned to the ground in April 1945. It is said that, until very late in the day, U.S. forces were of two minds about attacking this precious cultural treasure. However, with Japanese 32nd Army troops hiding in a complex of shelters under the castle, in the end the Americans had little choice but to bombard it.

This must have been a shocking development for Okinawan citizens. But then again, it seems that different people responded in different ways. In the context of people being killed everywhere around them, many had no leeway to be concerned about the destruction of Shuri Castle.

"I think that it was about the 20th of April," recalls Kawasaki Masanori. "I remember the crackling noise as the fires raged. In the morning, all that was left were the smoldering ruins."

Kawasaki had played in the area around the castle as a child but says, "At that stage, it didn't feel as though a cultural treasure had been burned down. With my school friends being killed one after another around me, I had no room for sentiment toward the castle."

Toyosato Yasuhiro saw the tragic scene of the ruins of Shuri Castle after the fire had died down. "I can clearly remember how the huge wooden pillars were lying there smoldering away. But there were enemy bombers in the sky so staying alive was my main priority. I suppose I just thought that 'Shuri Castle is burning,' and that was about it."

However, once Toyosato got back to the Ryukon shelter, he started to feel the loss, as though his soul had been grabbed and was being squeezed by something. "It was an indescribable feeling. I remember suddenly feeling a huge loss."

Moromizato Moriyasu recalls that he was asleep back in the Ryukon shelter when Shuri Castle was on fire. Earlier he had been out digging inside the 32nd Army Headquarters. "I woke up when someone yelled, 'The castle's burning!' It was a strange feeling to see such a cultural icon on fire. Some local people came out and stood watching for a while, but they soon moved away when the bombardment started up again."

Shuri Castle has been burned down three times through the years, but 1945 was the first time that the castle walls were brought down. The trees around it were all burned and its structures all destroyed without trace. The third reconstruction was carried out between 1712 and 1715, but that structure, which had become a cherished symbol of Okinawan history and culture for over 200 years, was totally destroyed due to acts of folly that come with war. In 1992, the main building of the castle was reconstructed.

Last days of a Shuri Girls' School teacher

The date of the death of Teruya Eihan, a mathematics teacher at the Shuri Girls' School before the war, is recorded as 20 June 1945. However, it is not known if that date is accurate. After his wife Masako returned to her hometown of Haebaru from Miyazaki in Kyushu to where she and their three children had been evacuated, she submitted the documents stating this date to the local authorities based upon hearsay from a number of people. Masako had of course not received any of her husband's ashes or bones, or any of his belongings, or she still does not know where he died. Every year without fail Masako attends the remembrance ceremony held at the *Zuisen-no-To* memorial in Komesu in Itoman for those members of the Shuri Girls' School nurse's aide corps who lost their lives during the Battle of Okinawa, but she avoided any conversations about her husband with students who survived. "I don't know, maybe it's because I was afraid of hearing about his last moments," she said.

The Society Section of the *Ryukyu Shimpo* newspaper received a letter from Teruya Masako. In it she wrote, "I wonder if there is anyone out there who might know something about my husband's last days, or someone who might have anything that belonged to him? I have heard that to get a wound to his arm treated, he came to a hospital shelter where some of his students were acting as nurse's aides and that that shelter was attacked the same night he arrived, but I have no idea where that might have been. Does anyone out there know where the Shuri Girls' School shelter was?"

Masako's memory of her husband had not dimmed with the passage of time. "I came to realize that as the years elapsed I would have less and less chance to ask members of bereaved families or actual survivors for information about him. I just couldn't help wondering what actually happened to my husband," she said. She started trying to get leads to information about the details of her husband's fate, but failed to find anyone who could help her.

In March 1945, six months after seeing his wife and three children evacuated to Miyazaki Prefecture, Teruya (then thirty-five years of age) was drafted into the Home Guard in Shuri. After that, the 100 or so newly recruited members of the Home Guard who were made to wait at the Yonagusuku Civic Hall, were given duties collecting food for the soldiers or carrying ammunition. They were divided into a number of separate units, and several of Teruya's former students later said that they remember seeing him running around busily as a member of the Home Guard.

Masako asked those members of the Shuri Girls' School nurse aide unit who had somehow managed to survive the war if they had any memories of her husband. Nakanishi Yukiko told her, "Mr. Teruya's mathematics classes were really easy to understand." She continued, "I remember that he had large, friendly eyes, and so was quite different from the normal foreboding impression we had of mathematics teachers. He was a nice man." Three other survivors, Makiya Tomiko, Okawa Toyo, and Nakasone Kiku all nodded in agreement.

Makiya remembers seeing Teruya near the shelter they were in at Ihara in the south, around 20 June 1945. "I think he was on his way to deliver a message to the Headquarters shelter at Komesu. He asked if Shimabukuro Fumiko and

I were well. I thought that we should go and see him the next day to have a chat but that was the last we were to see of him. There were rumors that where we were would also be attacked with flamethrowers in the next two or three days, so it must have been around the 20th. I think that maybe Mr. Teruya was killed somewhere near Komesu. I don't think that he got down as far as Mabuni."

If Masako's deciding upon the date of 20 June is correct, it means that it is likely that Teruya met his fate not long after exchanging greetings with Makiya and the other girls.

When she was in Miyazaki, her husband Eihan appeared in a dream she had. "In the dream, I had returned home from Miyazaki, but when he saw me he ran outside as though he was trying to get away. I tried to follow him, but he'd gone. I remember how I burst into tears and that woke me from the dream." With this, she had a premonition that her husband was no longer alive.

Approximately 13,000 members of the Home Guard were killed during the Battle of Okinawa. It is estimated that around 22,000 people were recruited, so that means that 60 percent lost their lives in the fighting. Of the three months of fighting, that which occurred in the southern part of the island toward the end of the battle was particularly horrific, and people who had received no military training at all were thrown into the breach. Many older "soldiers" lost their lives simply because they had no idea what to do on a battlefield.

The recruitment of Home Guard units began around October 1944. At first, they were assigned to duties related to the construction of airfields or fortified emplacements or shelters, but early in 1945, the mobilization dragnet started to bring in all and sundry to supplement the fighting force. As the situation at the front worsened, the stipulation that Home Guard recruits needed to be "between seventeen and forty-five years of age" was ignored. It is said that even disabled and sick people, plus those between thirteen and seventy years of age were recruited into the Home Guard.

"Teruya Eihan really did his best to help these people. They really trusted him." This is what Minei Goiei, former principal of Shuri Girls' School, said to Teruya Masako one day, about a year after the end of the war, when he visited Teruya's parents' house in Tsukazan.

Principal Minei said that Teruya's being recruited into the Home Guard was a problem for the school. Minei went to Army Headquarters and requested that Teruya be released from his military service, which the military authorities actually agreed to. But Teruya then had to ask the principal not to make him leave the Home Guard because so many people there wanted him to stay.

"My husband said to Mr. Minei, 'I can do my bit for the country wherever I am.' When I placed the notice in the Uruma Newspaper asking for information about my husband, he saw it and came to visit me."

Two members of the same Home Guard unit commented on Teruya's character. Nohara Koei, said, "Because I was so small, he would always be there behind me, ready to help me." Nohara Hiroji whose eyesight was not good, was also helped by Teruya.

"I'm pretty sure that it was about the 20th of June, but that evening the Home Guard was disbanded. At that stage, the fourteen or fifteen of them, including Teruya, were among some trees at Makabe in Itoman. That was the last I saw of him, but I remember how he told me that we should perk up because our troops were approaching."

After saying this to Nohara Hiroji, Teruya and his comrades disappeared. "They had been planning what to do, so I thought that they had managed to get away, but by that stage, the area that we were in was such that just lighting a cigarette would see bullets come flying in from the enemy, so I don't know what happened to them."

Turning the pages of the name list of the Zuisenkai, or old girls' association, of Shuri Girls' School, we see that the words "killed in battle" are written beside many of the names of girls who graduated in March 1945. But beside the name Teruya, in the column for members of staff, it merely states, "died." Maybe this is because there were no witnesses to verify that he died in battle.

In January 1945, Teruya sent a long, caring letter to his wife and children who had evacuated to Hoshiyama in Miyazaki Prefecture. At the end of the letter he wrote:

> Eiko. Are you going to school every day? Make sure you practice your writing and reading at home too. Is it very cold where you are? Strong boys like you play well despite the cold. Your dad wishes that he could get on a boat and then a train and go to see you in Hoshiyama.

This letter was written two months before Teruya was drafted.

CHAPTER 8

How Strategic Decisions in the Battle of Okinawa Affected Civilians

With the fall of Saipan and the other Marianas Islands in mid-1944, the Absolute National Defense Zone created by Imperial General Headquarters [IGHQ] for the defense of the main islands and the continuation of the war was compromised.

As the situation in Japan's Pacific defense perimeter rapidly deteriorated, in February 1945 the emperor rejected Prime Minister Konoe Fumimaro's advice to end the war immediately, insisting instead that Japan fight on in the hope of achieving one last military success. His hope was that this would force the United States and its allies to offer peace terms that would allow Japan to maintain its national polity, which of course hinged on the status and institution of the emperor.[1] Had the emperor heeded Konoe's advice that the United States and its allies were not leaning toward abolishing the Imperial system, and pressed IGHQ to sue for peace, it is possible that there may never have been a Battle of Okinawa, or atomic bombs dropped on Hiroshima or Nagasaki.

However, the emperor's belief in the need for one last victory and military hardliners' intransigence meant that Okinawa would be sacrificed in an attempt to save the main islands of Japan from the disaster that invasion would visit upon the hierarchy as it stood in 1945.[2] The decision to engage in a battle specifically designed to be drawn-out to cause maximum losses to the enemy and the approach that demanded that civilians also be prepared to make the ultimate sacrifice doomed the people of Okinawa to a level of suffering clearly outside the concern of those in IGHQ.[3]

From the American point of view, airfields on Saipan, Guam, and Tinian allowed U.S. B-29 bombers to attack key targets in the main islands of Japan. The next step was to invade either Taiwan or Okinawa, but the lack of sufficient troop numbers to be confident about subduing the Japanese defense force on Taiwan

---

1. Hayashi, H. 2010: 212.
2. Hastings, M. 2008: 483.
3. Hayashi, H. 2010: 214.

meant that Okinawa loomed as the better option of the two.[4] Its location south of Japan also meant that its airfields and anchorages needed to be secured by U.S. forces before the planned invasion of Japan could be launched. In response to the loss of the Marianas, as part of Operation Sho-Go II, the Japanese also recognized the significance of projecting airpower from Okinawa, but from the unrealistic standpoint that the American invasion fleet could be destroyed at sea by Japanese air and naval forces, and that the 32nd Army would then repel any U.S. forces that did manage to land.[5] In late 1944, work to complete a total of fifteen airfields in Okinawa went ahead at a frantic pace.[6] However, in the end, because Japanese air power had been dramatically reduced in the battles off the Philippines, IGHQ could not muster the aircraft to operate from this "unsinkable aircraft carrier," and months of concentrated effort to create the platform for the air-defense of Okinawa came to nothing. The defenders destroyed the airfields with their own hands before the American landings.[7]

In November 1944, after reinforcing Okinawa with powerful army units, in response to U.S. forces having landed in Leyte Gulf in the Philippines the previous month, IGHQ then opted to withdraw the 32nd Army's best division, the 9th, which represented one third of the 32nd Army's infantry strength, for redeployment to Taiwan.[8] The elite 9th Division, with its large numbers of Okinawan recruits, was not replaced. By this stage of the war, movement of troopships on the seas south of Japan was a perilous operation, as evidenced by the sinking of the *Toyama-Maru* on 29 June 1944 in which the 44th Independent Mixed Brigade, bound for Okinawa, lost over 5,000 men. In addition, the increasing fixation on strengthening homeland defenses saw Okinawa effectively left to its own designs within a new plan, Operation Ten-Go that focused heavily on so-called "Special Attack Units," including of course the kamikaze offensives of early April and the suicide mission of the battleship *Yamato*.[9] In mid-February, six weeks before the U.S. landings on the main island of Okinawa, when Lt. Gen. Ushijima announced the battle slogan of the defense force as "One Plane for One Warship, One Boat for One Ship, One Man for Ten of the Enemy or One Tank," it was clear that all were expected to give their lives in order to cause maximum

---

4. Sloan, B. 2007: 12.
5. Huber, T. 1980:2.
6. Kunimori, Y. 2010: 4.
7. Oshiro, M. 2007: 193.
8. Oshiro, M. 2007: 190.
9. Feifer, G. 1992: 18.

damage to the enemy.[10]

The redeployment of the 9th Division and the subsequent cancellation in late January 1945 of the dispatch of the 84th Division required the 32nd Army to review its approach to the defense of Okinawa.[11] Rather than spread its depleted resources all over the main island, it decided to concentrate them in the southern region in order to fight a strategic delaying action from static defensive positions.[12] The lack of a replacement unit for the 9th Division meant that locals were required to fill the gap so that after two rounds of conscription, by February 1945, 110,000 Okinawans, almost one quarter of the prefecture's population, had been called up.[13] This irrevocably linked the fate of the local people to that of the 32nd Army, which had by that stage effectively been abandoned by IGHQ as it focused its attention on preparation for the coming decisive battle on Japan proper.[14]

Before the U.S. invasion of the main island of Okinawa on 1 April 1945, the Japanese military did evacuate 80,000 of Okinawa's 435,000 indigenous residents to the main islands of Japan or to Taiwan.[15] In addition 60,000 very young and old people went to the scarcely populated northern region of the island, but this still left around 300,000 local people firmly in harm's way.[16]

After the failed offensive of 4-5 May, the commanders of the 32nd Army weighed their options on 22 May and decided that they could earn more time and inflict more losses on the Americans by withdrawing southward rather than committing their remaining forces to a fight to the death at Shuri.[17] Helped by days of torrential rain, by the end of May the remnants of the 32nd Army slipped away from the noose closing in on Shuri and retreated toward Cape Kyan in the southwest corner of Okinawa. That the 32nd Army commanders chose to prolong the battle for as long as possible by its 30,000 survivors retreating to an area where 100,000 civilians had already converged was the underlying cause of 80 percent of the civilian deaths in the Battle of Okinawa.[18] The U.S. artillery and naval bombardment was so intense following the withdrawal from Shuri that key

---

10. Hallas, J. 2007: 6.
11. Tobe, R., et al. 1984: 236.
12. Huber, T. 1980: 9.
13. Oshiro, M. 2007: 193.
14. Ota, M. 1988: 120.
15. Okinawa Heiwa Network. 2008: 30.
16. Huber, T. 1980: 13.
17. Arasaki, M., et al. 2002: 143.
18. Okinawa Heiwa Network. 2008: 14.

crossroads and bridges flooded with fleeing civilians and soldiers became tar-
gets for concentrated enemy fire. Bridges south of the Shuri Line at Madanbashi,
Ichinichibashi, and Yamakawa became known as the "Bridges of Death," and the
Haebaru Junction as the "Crossroads of Death."[19]

While the Japanese Army decision to not to make a last stand at Shuri and
instead to withdraw toward Cape Kyan ultimately led to the terrible civilian casualties of mid- to-late June, it should be noted that U.S. commander Lt. Gen.
Simon Bolivar Buckner was also criticized for his conservative strategy and costly approach to using the forces available to him.[20] Had he been able to bring the
battle to a conclusion earlier, the civilian death toll would not have been as high
as it was.

After Lt. Gen. Ushijima's refusal to respond to Buckner's plea for a Japanese
surrender on 17 June, and then Buckner's death in action at Maehira the next
day, the ferocity of the American forces' "mopping-up" operations intensified
to the extent that some commentators attribute the merciless slaughter of thousands of Japanese soldiers and civilians in the Kuniyoshi and Maezato area as
revenge for the death of the American commander.[21]

As the carnage continued outside, in the Headquarters cave at Mabuni on 18
June Ushijima issued his last order, "The battlefield is now in such chaos that all
communications have ceased. It is impossible for me to command you. Every
man in these fortifications will follow his superior officer's orders and fight to the
end for the sake of the motherland. This is my final order. Farewell." To this, his
chief of staff, Lt. Gen. Cho added: "Do not suffer the shame of being taken prisoner. You will live for eternity."[22] After urging their troops to "fight to the end,"
within four days, both the commanders of the 32nd Army, Ushijima and Cho,
had taken their own lives, thereby removing the opportunity for the remaining
Japanese troops to carry out an organized surrender which would have helped to
avoid the final "mopping-up" operations that claimed so many civilian victims.[23]

Choice of strategy

The choice of which strategy to use in the Battle of Okinawa created conflict
within the 32nd Army's Command Headquarters between Col. Yahara Hiromi-

19. Yoshihama, S., et al. 2010: 35.
20. Hanson, V. 2003: 28-29.
21. Okinawa Heiwa Network. 2008: 14.
22. Yahara, H. 1995: 134.
23. Hayashi, H. 2010: 212.

chi, who advocated a war of attrition, and Lt. Gen. Cho and the junior staff officers who wanted to go on the offensive.

Air Liaison Staff Officer, Maj. Jin Naomichi, also supported the more aggressive stance, explaining, "At that stage [ahead of the Battle of Okinawa], between our army and naval forces [including kamikaze units], we still had a substantial amount of airpower left as well. I was the 32nd's air officer, so I was strongly in favor of making this the decisive battle. In terms of air force strategy, attack is the only option."

The first attempted counteroffensive took place on 12 April 1945, and the second on 4 May. Both failed, with the 32nd Army suffering heavy losses. Jin explained, "Even if we hadn't launched those attacks, we'd still have lost significant numbers of men increasingly quickly. I still believe that we weren't much better off in terms of losses by opting for a drawn-out battle of attrition."

As the Japanese Army's first offensive failed, the Americans launched attacks on the key position of Shuri, sending the 32nd Army reeling. When the Japanese second offensive was aborted on 5 May, Lt. Gen. Cho indicated to Lt. Haginouchi Kiyoshi, the head of the *Kempeitai* [military police] in Okinawa, that the remaining Japanese forces were ready to move to the southern part of the island, and he sought an assurance from the *Kempeitai* that they would protect military facilities in the south.

After Headquarters had weighed the three options of (1) withdrawing to the Kyan Peninsula, (2) withdrawing to the Chinen Peninsula, and (3) holding the line at Shuri, on the evening of 22 May Lt. Gen. Ushijima opted to withdraw to Kyan. Headquarters knew that this option would result in a heavy toll among the civilian population in the south. Despite those predictions, the withdrawal was implemented.

Looking back on the decision to abandon Shuri, Haginouchi felt that "Military common sense compelled us to move south. We had to prolong the fighting, even for just an extra day, to earn time for the preparation for the final showdown on the mainland." However, Adaniya Ken, the only locally born officer at Army Headquarters, laments, "If we'd held Shuri as our last line of defense right to the end, far fewer civilians would have died."

The withdrawal from Shuri began in earnest on 27 May. Officers and enlisted men alike left the Command Post shelter one after another. They were divided into two groups, one heading directly for Mabuni, the other making its way to Tsukazan. Senior officers such as Lt. Gen. Ushijima, Lt. Gen. Cho, and Col. Yahara set off for the army shelter at Tsukazan in Haebaru to lead further operations. Uezu Anei saluted his farewell to Lt. Gen. Ushijima as he left the shelter. "It was about 10:00 PM. He put on his cape and headed off on foot, plodding wearily through the heavy rain. There was a tragic air about him. Maybe he'd accepted that he was going to die. I couldn't help but think to myself, "Was this really our commander-in-chief?'"

On 27 May, during the withdrawal, Takara Yoshio was given an improvised hand grenade made by stuffing gunpowder into an empty tin can. He buried it in a paddy field after musing angrily, "Are we supposed to fight a war with this sort of thing?" Most of their available weapons and ammunition had been used up by that stage. The seriously wounded were left inside as the officers and enlisted men made their way out of the shelter in a steady stream. "What are you going to do with us? Take us with you," one of the badly wounded men whose legs and arms had been amputated implored Shin'ichi Kuniyoshi, weeping. But there was nothing Kuniyoshi could do.

As for dealing with the seriously wounded, it seems that Lt. Gen. Cho instructed them to take their own lives with his words, "Do not suffer the shame of being taken prisoner. You will live for eternity."[24] Once the withdrawal was complete, Japanese troops destroyed the Command Post shelter. American military documents confirm that the cave had been detonated in eleven different places, including entrances, exits, shafts, tunnels, and connecting points. During investigations carried out in Naha in about 1965, the equivalent in volume of two truckloads of human remains were found at the shelter entrance. Some people have suggested that the shelter was blown up with the seriously injured soldiers still inside.

On 29 May, American forces moved in from the west side of Shuri to reach the ruins of Shuri Castle and by the 31st, Shuri had been taken. When Lt. Gen. Buckner, commander of the American 10th Army, received that information, he commented, "It's all over," effectively judging that organized resistance by the Japanese army was at an end. For the Americans, the fighting that remained was to be little more than mopping up operations.

Imperial Headquarters' focus switches to final showdown on the main islands

As the remnants of the 32nd Army were attempting to hold out around Mabuni, Air Liaison Staff Officer Jin Naomichi slipped out of Okinawa. On 15 June, he reported on the battle situation to Imperial Headquarters, requesting, "For the

24. Yahara, H. 1995: 134.

sake of Okinawa, I want us to launch another attack." On the evening of the 17th, he repeated his request for an air attack, this time to the vice chief of staff, but was rebuffed with "That's out of the question." The focus at Imperial Headquarters had already switched from Okinawa to a final showdown on the main islands of Japan.

At about that time, the American forces had advanced to within a few hundred meters, on the eastern side of Mabuni. By now, communication between the Command Post and all operational units had ceased and, having almost run out of ammunition, the Japanese army was reduced to launching repeated suicide infiltration raids. On 19 June, Lt. Gen. Ushijima Mitsuru issued his final order to all Japanese units before committing suicide several days later.

"The battlefield is now in such chaos that all communications have ceased. It is impossible for me to command you. Every man in these fortifications will follow his superior officer's order and fight to the end for the sake of the motherland. This is my final order. Farewell."[25]

On the 18th, the Chihaya Unit of the Blood and Iron Student Corps received its own orders. According to Tomimura Moriteru, the order was "Head north toward the Yambaru. You must not throw your life away. Even if you are taken prisoner, stay alive and somehow disrupt their communications." He seriously thought about trying to break through the enemy lines but was sternly rebuked by his brother-in-law Miyagi Kokichi, a teacher at the Okinawa Normal School, and gave up on the idea. Some soldiers also chose to stay alive by ignoring the orders to sacrifice themselves in suicidal charges.

Head of the Okinawa *Kempeitai*, Haginouchi Kiyoshi, was in a shelter in Tamagusuku in charge of a group of men, but surrendered on 3 June. He was taken prisoner and subsequently took part in the operation calling on officers and men in the IJA to give themselves up. "I kept thinking, I will die today . . . I'm going to die today, but then I decided that with things having reached the stage they had, I thought that if I could help stop some of soldiers from committing suicide and stop any more Okinawan civilians from dying . . ."

On 25 May, Haginouchi was required by the American military to officially identify the bodies of Generals Ushijima and Cho in the Command Post shelter at Mabuni. He confirmed that "Both men committed suicide on 22 June." With respect to Lt. Gen. Ushijima having ordered everybody to "fight to the end," but then having taken his own life, Haginouchi's comment was, "He had overall re-

---

25. Yahara, H. 1995: 134.

sponsibility and, even though he knew we were beaten, there was absolutely no mention of surrender. If he hadn't committed suicide, the only option for him was to be taken prisoner."

However, because the IJA did not surrender, countless numbers of Okinawans citizens lost their lives in the fighting. "The army's job is to fight. Protecting civilians was never part of the plan . . . so they couldn't protect them. Civilians are important but, in terms of strategy, they just get in the way." Such are Naomichi Jin's memories of the 32nd Army as commanded from beneath Shuri Castle during the Battle for Okinawa.

From a decisive struggle aimed at victory to a battle of attrition

Takara Yoshio, then a second-year student at Okinawa Normal School, describes the situation leading up to the battle. "I had never expected that Okinawa would be somewhere that the Americans would land. But I began to sense that something was up when the Japanese Army started stationing soldiers here. Then things got really hectic after talk of evacuation started going around."

The dark clouds of war were starting to gather even over normally peaceful Okinawa. The construction of airfields commenced in May 1944, requiring over 2,000 locals to be mobilized on a daily basis. Almost all were required to work—males and females, regardless of age, even including elementary school pupils. In August 1944 there was great loss of life when the *Tsushima Maru*, a ship evacuating children from Okinawa, was torpedoed and sunk by the submarine *USS Bowfin*. The air raids of 10 October 1944 razed most of the buildings of Naha, Okinawa's largest city.

That day, Takara was in the little town of Bise, in the northwest of Motobu Peninsula, visiting family. When he returned to Naha two days later in an IJA truck, he found that the city had effectively been reduced to ashes. "I went back to Shuri from there, but I remember strange smells of what could only have been burned corpses. There's no doubt that I then started to feel a sense of impending disaster."

The 32nd Army was created on 22 March 1944. Japan's position worsened dramatically following the crushing defeat at the Battle of Midway, making the defense of the Ryukyu Islands a matter of urgency. The commander of the 32nd Army at the time of the Battle of Okinawa was Lt. Gen. Ushijima Mitsuru, who had been involved in the fall of Nanking in December 1937. His chief of staff was Lt. Gen. Cho Isamu, who was known as a larger-than-life, eccentric character. Cho had also been in Nanking.

Just as units were flooding to Okinawa one after another, there was a sudden development that rocked the preparation of the 32nd Army. In November 1944, the elite 9th Division was redeployed to Formosa. The disappointment among the military in Okinawa was palpable and was soon followed by a sense of impending doom.

Teruya Masayoshi, of Zakimi in Yomitan, joined the 9th Division in October 1944, receiving his training in the area around Shuri. "On 27 December, we were woken up in the middle of the night, formed into ranks, and headed for the port at Naha where we got on a troop ship. We weren't told of our destination."

He heard that the U.S. forces had landed on Okinawa when he was on Formosa, digging shelters every day. "Those of us in our company who were born in Okinawa got together and talked about things over a few drinks. We thought about us Okinawans getting a boat and trying to get back home to help, but of course, that wasn't possible. It was almost as though the 9th Division had evacuated to Formosa," recalls Teruya.

The loss of the 9th Division saw the strategic approach of the 32nd Army change dramatically from seeking a decisive victory to a battle of attrition designed to bleed the enemy dry.

Retreat

In Japanese there is a word "*tenshin*," which is a euphemism for retreat by saying "advance in a different direction." In the document compiled by those entrusted in winding up the affairs of the 32nd Army after the war, the movement southward of the army was described in this manner, not as a "retreat," but as an "advance in a different direction." It was a "relocation" to enable the army to continue its battle of attrition against the enemy, but the move that occurred with soldiers and civilians, by now mixed together, would only lead to awful tragedies all over the southern part of the island.

"It brings tears to my eyes. I don't want to remember," said Hashimoto Kichitaro, a former soldier from Hyogo Prefecture as he started to describe the withdrawal.

"I was wounded in the fighting at Kochi, and after being treated at the Army Hospital at Haebaru I went into the Command Post shelter. Psychologically I was struggling at this stage, and I don't really want to talk about that time in the shelter. The withdrawal was just chaotic. A defeated army on the run really has it tough. As the rain lashed down, we had no time to stop for a rest. We were under the gun so much that we even urinated on the move."

After leaving the Command Post shelter on 27 May, Japanese commander,

Lt. Gen. Ushijima Mitsuru and his staff arrived at the Tsukazan shelter, where they stayed for two days.

Former member of the Himeyuri Student Corps, Miyagi Kikuko, who was at the Tsukazan shelter as an administrative assistant, wrote in diary form describing what happened at Tsukazan when she was in captivity in a camp in September that year. She recorded her memory of Ushijima's arrival as follows: "In the evening, General Ushijima and his chiefs of staff arrived from Shuri. We had been frantically busy from the previous day getting ready for them. The unit commander's room will be switched to the high-ranking officers' room so his excellency can use it. The soldiers on duty and the women cooks were busy carrying luggage from one room to the next."

The army commanders left the shelter at Tsukazan in the rain late at night on 29 May, arriving before dawn at Mabuni on the 30th. Miyagi and her Student Corps friends lined up at the exit to the cave and bowed as Ushijima and his staff set off. On 31 May, those in the Student Corps also left the shelter. Miyagi continues in her diary:

"Without a word, everyone gets their belongings ready to move. At about 8:00 PM, we leave the shelter that we have become used to, heading for who knows where. The roads are really muddy because of the rain in May that has been falling constantly for a week. The occasional flare illuminates the path for us with an eerie white light."

The southward withdrawal by Command Post staff meant that the southern part of Okinawa would soon become the scene of fierce fighting. It was in this context that such features of the Battle of Okinawa as the annihilation of entire families and the massacre of civilians occurred. In Komesu, Itoman, of a total of 270 households, some 120 were wiped out during the battle—a scenario from hell brought about by the Japanese army's suicidal strategy of attrition in order to win time for the defense of the home islands.

Tsuken-jima—Arakawa Castle Shelter

Tsuken-jima is a small island located to the south of Katsuren Peninsula which juts out into the Pacific Ocean from the eastern side of central Okinawa, approximately 5 kilometers from the port of Yakena. It has a population of about 500 people. It is hard to imagine that this quiet, little island with a small economy based on agriculture and fishing was the scene of fierce fighting during the Battle of Okinawa.

However, the fact is that those nightmare days actually occurred. Traces of the fighting still exist, and many remains are still entombed in the former Imperial Japanese Army shelter located among the ruins of Arakawa Castle on the south side of the island.

"The first attack happened around 10 April, not long after the U.S. forces had landed on the main island of Okinawa. I remember the sea being just full of American ships putting landing craft into the water." Three Tsuken-jima residents, Asato Yoshizo, Midorima Haruko and Oishi Toyo, conscripted by the Japanese Army just before the battle began to carry out Home Guard or nursing duties experienced the battle with the Japanese soldiers on the island.

At that time, the garrison on the island totaled some 350 men. In addition to the soldiers under the command of Capt. Teishima Hideo and the seventy members of the Home Guard there were about sixty men from the 15th Independent Mixed Regiment who came to the island after the large-scale air raids of 10 October 1944 to help with the construction of fortifications. The defending force was split into groups to work on three different fortified emplacements.

The Arakawa Castle Shelter, where the three Tsuken-jima residents claim that many bodies still remain unrecovered, was originally a natural cave where locals paid their respects to the spirits of members of the ancient warrior class. They constructed a three-story structure inside the hill that is the only protrusion on the otherwise flat island. It had a wooden staircase linking the floors and, while the lower level had an entrance which had been covered over before the American attack started.

Oishi says, "The Americans attacked a total of four times. They would land, fight, and then return to Okinawa by ship, once every three or four days. In the end, the defending troops launched a banzai suicide attack when the Americans landed for their fourth assault, but thirteen of us nurse's aides were still right down on the bottom floor of the shelter with some wounded soldiers. The American soldiers poured gasoline in from the third floor part of the structure and lit it. Fortunately the gasoline didn't flow down as far as where we were, but the shells stored in the shelter exploded above us one by one and the wooden ladders and floor started to burn, so the interior was full of smoke. Thinking 'This is enough for me,' I pulled the pin out from the grenade I'd been given and was ready to strike the percussion cap and kill myself at any moment."

After the Americans withdrew, the island residents who had been hiding in the civilian shelter dug out the entrance that had been covered over, thereby saving the lives of Midorima and Oishi. Apart from just two or three, the people inside the shelter who had been burned or crushed to death were almost all wounded soldiers. After the third round of fighting Capt. Teishima gave the order that "All those who are of sound body will meet up again at Divisional Headquarters in Yonabaru." They got into twelve Okinawan fishing boats, known as *sabani*, and left Tsuken-jima. Left behind were about forty wounded soldiers and thirteen nurse's aides, with just a handful of able-bodied soldiers to help look after the wounded.

"We thirteen nurse's aides worked in sub-groups of four, four and five, but you could not call what we did medical treatment. We just tried to stop the flow of blood. We didn't have many bandages, so at night we went down to the sea and washed used bandages in seawater. Our job was to then apply those bandages to wounds . . . It was just awful," said Oishi and Midorima. Asato, who was in the Home Guard, also said, "We went to the main island of Okinawa with Capt. Teishima and his men and when I think how we were then ordered to go back to Tsuken-jima to rescue the wounded soldiers who had been left behind it all seems like a strange dream. I have talked about this with my children and grandchildren in the hope that they will never have to experience anything like this."

Asato and about ten other members of the Home Guard returned to Tsuken-jima on 24 April about one week after the third assault by U.S. forces. It was a journey fraught with danger as they carefully rowed the *sabani* boats forward or even back toward Okinawa, depending on the brightness of the U.S. flares in the sky. At this stage, about thirty or forty wounded soldiers were living by candlelight inside the Arakawa Castle Shelter with the nurse's aides.

"It really was an awful situation that we were in, but the soldiers were all very nice to us. They'd tell us about their hometowns and about their families, but as they came closer to death, they'd shout 'Get me some water, put me out of my misery . . .' They seemed to be envious of their friends who had already died and were now being spoken of in glowing terms," said Oishi, obviously pained by the memories. "Before and during the war, we were told that as dying soldiers went to meet their maker they said 'Long Live the Emperor,' but none said that. Most cried 'mother!' as they died. Even if they wanted to die, they couldn't, and I couldn't do anything for them," said Midorima quietly.

It was after 8:00 PM on 24 April when Asato and his comrades arrived back on Tsuken-jima to rescue the wounded soldiers who had by that stage been living quietly in the shelter for a week without attracting an attack from the American troops. They arrived under cover of darkness at the beach about 500 meters to the north of the shelter. Straightaway they started carrying out the wounded soldiers. There were Japanese army stretchers and some left behind by the American troops, but still there were not enough, so they cut branches from trees to use as makeshift stretchers. All able-bodied people were mobilized to take part in the desperate attempt to carry the wounded to the boats. But time was ticking away . . .

The beach that these days is always busy with tourists was farther away for them than the actual distance as the crow flies. "We had to go all the way around the mine field that had been laid by the Japanese Army," said Asato. "We were also told to walk in a way than made no noise, so that slowed us down too," said Oishi. Before they knew it, it was already 3:00 AM. They calculated the time they had left and came to the conclusion that "Even if we got all of the wounded in the boats and set off for Okinawa in the time left before dawn, we would not make it before daybreak," so their efforts had come to nothing. They carried all of the wounded men on the beach back to the shelter and laid them on the second and third floors close to the entrance, but ironically, that was the same day the Americans made their last attack. Everyone was exhausted and dozing off when it happened.

The previous three attacks had all been launched from the beach in front of the shelter (now the fishing port), and the Americans lost many soldiers using this approach. This fourth attack was launched from the north, heading southward. "The previous landings on the beach near the shelter had been made in the face of a Japanese machine-gun post positioned on the edge of the bay, so this had been effective in blunting the attack. The 150 meters of sand from the water's edge was stained red with the blood of American troops hit by the machine gun's fire. I think that is why they launched this fourth attack from the north," said Asato, who that day did not go into the Arakawa Castle Shelter. He recalls that there were so many people just inside the entrance to the shelter that he couldn't get in, so he went to a cave near the shelter, where he dozed off.

The fighting did not last long. Only a very small number of soldiers were physically capable of resisting. The firefight soon ended with the Americans clearly in a position of advantage in firepower with eight tanks leading the way for the soldiers behind them. The American troops surrounded the shelter and started calling for the people inside to surrender, yelling "*Dete-koi* and *dete-ki-nasai*" [meaning "Come out!"] in through the entrance. Before long, one of the American soldiers peered into the shelter, an action that was to end in tragedy. A wounded soldier near the entrance stabbed the American soldier with his bayonet. Immediately, the calls for those in the shelter to surrender stopped and the Americans started pouring large quantities of gasoline through the myriad of small holes at the top of what had originally been a natural cave. They then lit the gasoline, which immediately burst into flames, with the wooden floor, the staircases, and the superstructure also starting to burn. Piles of ammunition exploded with the heat and rocks started to fall from above as the wooden beams burned and collapsed. The inside of the shelter had been transformed into a veritable scene from hell.

Of course Asato, who was in a different cave at this time, plus Midorima and the nurse's aides with Oishi who had been made to flee to the lowest level in the same shelter, did not witness the death of the wounded soldiers on the second and third levels. However, we do know that the remains of many of the dead soldiers either crushed under the large rocks that fell or burned to death still lie in there. Three stupa were set up in the dark inside of the collapsed shelter by old soldiers, including Nagamine Masao, a survivor of the fiery hell on the third floor with severe burns all over his body who went to live in Osaka after the war. It is still painful to look at them knowing what lies beneath the rocks.

A memorial overlooking the ocean has been placed on top of the shelter by the Tsuken-jima Bereaved Families Association. On it are inscribed the names of the people from Tsuken-jima who lost their lives fighting in China or the Pacific, together with the names of the garrison soldiers led by Capt. Teishima, who fled the island only to be killed in Okinawa. This memorial overlooks the playground of the Tsuken Elementary and Junior High School where young children are educated without a care in the world. However, other than on 23 June, Okinawa Memorial Day, hardly anyone comes to pay their respects at the site.

Maezato in Itoman

The Yamagata Memorial at Maezato in Itoman was erected where the last remnants of the Yamagata 32nd Infantry Regiment met their fate. Few people visit this spot because it is some distance from Mabuni where the majority of monuments to the fallen from each prefecture stand. Directly under the memorial is the site of the Regimental Headquarters shelter where the bones of many dead soldiers still remain, untouched since they fell in 1945.

"There is a large crack in the rock at the very back of the shelter, creating a hole several meters deep. That is where we threw the bodies of those who died. I remember that there were at least ten in there. I left the shelter before the end so I'm not entirely sure of the numbers in there, but I'd say twenty to thirty bodies," says Professor Matsuda Sadao of Okinawa Christian Junior College.

Matsuda joined the 24th Division in October 1944. The following April he was put in charge of divisional stores, and in June he moved to Maezato where the Divisional Accounting Section's shelter was located. On 2 July, he was ordered to leave the shelter and head north toward Kunigami. During the month or so that he was at the shelter, however, he saw many badly wounded soldiers die there.

On the night of 4 June 1945, Regimental Headquarters moved from the fortified shelter at Ufugusukumui to the shelter at Maezato. The shelter filled with wounded and sick soldiers as the fighting intensified. In the beginning, they buried the dead outside not far from the entrance, but when the Americans surrounded the shelter and attacked it from on top they could no longer dispose of the bodies outside. From that time on, they placed them in the deep crack in the rock at the back of the shelter. The scene is described as follows by Takashima Yunosuke in his book, *The End of the Yamagata 32nd Infantry Regiment.*

"Once the Americans sealed off the entrance, the shelter was pitch dark through the whole day. There was no ventilation so the limited supply of air for several hundred people to breath, plus the terrible humidity, meant that the badly wounded died one after another. Unable to carry their excrement or urine outside, the smell of putrefying feces and urine and the bodies of dead comrades was overpowering. It was a hellish environment, which spawned tens of thousands of flies . . . Some of the badly wounded men went insane, suddenly yelling out despite enemy soldiers being just outside.

"I stepped inside the dugout shelter with Matsuda. There in front of us was a large 'room' of between 60 and 70 square meters. As we shone our torches around, the first thing that struck me was that there were army shoes strewn everywhere, plus a large broken water vessel. We headed down the pathway on the right. The ceiling was low and it was difficult to walk because there were rocks of all sizes everywhere. Great care was also needed so as not to bang one's head on the rocks protruding from the ceiling. There was not a sound to be heard, and water dripped from the rocks above our heads. The area above where they obviously did their cooking was blackened with soot. At the back of the large 'room' we found the crack in the rock that Matsuda had mentioned. We shone our flashlights into it, lighting up the soil that covered the bottom part of the fissure."

After Okinawa reverted to Japanese sovereignty, Matsuda confirmed the location of the shelter with some staff from the Okinawa Prefecture Relief Division who said that in order to retrieve the remains, evacuation machinery would be needed to work on the very hard rock face and the narrow crack in the rock wall. Since then, there has been no report of any attempts to recover the bones from the cave.

Saito Chujiro of Yamagata City in Yamagata Prefecture, the regiment's standard bearer back in 1945, comments: "There won't be many bodies in that hole; maybe those of about ten people. It couldn't be helped. The enemy was right outside and we couldn't just leave them lying dead where they were, so it was the only option left to us. We didn't just throw them away." When it is put that way, considering that they were unable to go outside and with the awful smell and the hordes of maggots and flies, maybe the only option they had was to throw the bodies in the hole.

The Maezato shelter was basically a natural cave that was dug out and enlarged to make it into a shelter. The local people and the soldiers in the unit that used it spoke of having "made it ourselves."

In the book *The End of the Yamagata 32nd Infantry Regiment*, the situation when the advance party from regimental headquarters relocated from Ufugusukumui to Maezato is described as follows: "The Imai Unit of the 24th Division, their women, and some displaced local civilians had already occupied the shelter. When the advance party from the 32nd Infantry Regiment arrived and announced that they were to take it over, Capt. Imai refused to give it up, claiming angrily, "This shelter was constructed by our 3rd Company. We will let you use one corner of it but you will leave all the remaining space to us!"

At the same time, local people claim that they were "forced out by soldiers of the 24th Division." Kuniyoshi Masako, who had been living in Maezato before the war, said the same. "That shelter was originally found and prepared by local civilians. It wasn't used very often normally, but we went in around May when the fighting grew more intense. Then, all of a sudden, we were thrown out by soldiers of the 24th Division who had come from Ufugusukumui."

Most of the civilians who left the shelter tried to seek safety in the hills and fields around there, but Kuniyoshi's family headed toward Kyan. Or maybe more to the point, they "went with the rest of the flow of people and ended up in Kyan." They spent about two weeks there. Twenty-six years old at the time, Kuniyoshi Masako made her way forward through the barrage of shells, holding her ten-month old son in her arms and pulling her four year-old daughter along by the hand. Her grandfather was killed along the way in the bombardment.

"By that stage, I was resigned to the fact that I was going to die, and if that were the case, I wanted to die in the place where I was born and brought up. That's why I went back to Maezato."

But when she returned to the village, she found that her house had been destroyed, so she hid for two or three days in the corner of a field. Some Japanese soldiers told them that if they stayed there they would soon be killed in the crossfire, so they went to the Maezato shelter to see if they would let them in.

"Grandma and my husband went to ask if we could enter the shelter, but because only a few days had passed since the enemy troops had pulled back after attacking the shelter from above, at first they were accused of being spies. Luckily, because there was a soldier in the shelter who had met them before, they weren't treated as spies, and we were let inside the shelter," said Kuniyoshi Masako. "Every night we went out to search for food, foraging for American canned food that might be lying around and potatoes in the fields. We spent almost two months living in that shelter."

Now Kuniyoshi lives just a stone's throw from the Maezato shelter, but since the war she hasn't been near it, let alone gone inside. "I imagine that that awful smell is still in there. I can't bring myself to go back inside. I've had enough of war. All I want to do is forget. I survived because I had children with me to drive me to live through each day. I did my best for the sake of the kids. If they hadn't been there it would have been so much easier to die. It really was a time when life was so sad."

Matsuda Sadao talked about his memories of witnessing the death of Lt. Gen. Simon Bolivar Buckner.

The U.S. commander, Lt. Gen. Simon B. Buckner, was killed on Maezato Highland in Takamine (now part of Itoman) at 1:15 PM on 18 June 1945. United Press reported this as follows: "Lieutenant General Buckner sat down on a rock on the top of a small hill, observing the movements of the U.S. 8th Marine Regiment. Suddenly, two Japanese artillery shells flew through the air. The first landed near where Buckner was sitting, a piece of shrapnel piercing his chest. He died ten minutes later."

"It was just shortly after lunch, so I remember the time and location very well. He was shot by a soldier at a forward observation point. No doubt about it," said Matsuda.

That day, after having something to eat inside the shelter, Matsuda went outside "to get some fresh air." The soldier at the observation post, Pvt. Ono, immediately signaled for Matsuda to be quiet by putting his finger to his mouth. Then, without saying a word, he pointed toward a small rise several hundred meters in front of them. Three American officers were standing beside a jeep that had stopped by the hillock. "Shall I shoot them?" said Ono casually. Matsuda stopped him, saying, "Not without orders to do so."

Of the three American officers, the one who looked the most senior in age took his hat off and wiped his brow with a handkerchief. At the same moment that Pvt. Ono said, "I'm going to get the one who looks the highest rank among them," a flash shot out from the muzzle of his rifle. As the two other American officers leapt to the aid of the older man who had fallen, Ono said, "I got him!" They put the fatally wounded officer in the jeep and drove away at speed.

In March 1952, seven years after the end of the war, Matsuda learned that the fatally wounded officer was actually Lt. Gen. Simon Bolivar Buckner. "I was traveling around the old battlefields in southern Okinawa with my younger sister and her husband when we stopped at what is now called 'Buckner's Hill.' There was a bronze plaque with an explanation on it, including the date of his death. It was an exact match with the time and the location when Pvt. Ono shot the American officer. Needless to say, I was rather surprised."

Matsuda said that Pvt. 1st Class Ono, who was from Tokyo, was killed the next day, 19 June 1945. When we inquired with the Ministry of Health, Labor and Welfare about Pvt. Ono, they replied that they could find no record of such a soldier from Tokyo with that name and rank.

Tears welled up in the eyes of all of the people whom we asked to recall their wartime experiences. Matsuda Sadao and Kuniyoshi Masako both became tearful as they recounted their tales to us.

Matsuda then talked about his wife Sonoe's wartime experiences. "My wife survived her time in the Himeyuri Nurse Aide Corps. She had the same sort of experiences as me, around the same time and in the same places. When I talk about the war with someone like her who has experienced it, all of those awful memories come flooding back. That horrific world reappears in my mind's eye." Matsuda recalls that he could not sleep for several days after they talked about their wartime experiences, and about how he had to see a doctor to help him cope. Since then, the two of them decided never to talk about the war again.

At first, Kuniyoshi refused to speak to us. "All I want to do is forget. Why do you ask me about these things?" she said. She lost three close relatives in the Battle of Okinawa.

Yamane Unit's Medical Shelter

During the Battle for Okinawa, the Yamane Unit was the key naval unit deployed in the Oroku and Uebaru districts of Naha. Under the command of Maj. Yamane Iwao, the unit had a force of 3,000 men and was made up of three companies and a headquarters unit. No. 226 Construction Unit's main task was to build facilities, including the construction of a secret airfield which was never used. Because of its role, it was the most lightly armed unit in the navy, its only weapons being three 25 mm, twenty-five 13 mm and eight 7.5 mm machine guns, plus two rocket launchers.

Morine Tetsuo was a squad leader in the 3rd company. "It's concerned me for a very long time. Right up till now, I've come here over and over again searching the area," he said as we walked along the streets of Oroku looking for the shelter. An American attack on the Yamane Unit's medical services shelter left many of the seriously wounded soldiers and nurses dead. Morine and the others moved the dead to one room within the shelter and estimated from the pile of bodies that around forty people had been killed.

We found ourselves on the other side of the main road where buses ran, a street lined with houses and shops. Dressed in a suit, Morine quickly swapped his leather shoes for a pair of rubber boots and, with a large flashlight in his hand, began searching. "Please be careful as there are lots of *habu* snakes around here," he warned. I sensed his determination as he chuckled, "But they won't bite me." The shelter was completely closed up and the surrounding area was also covered in trees and undergrowth. It was rather tricky locating the cave, but not as difficult as we had thought. "I think this is it here," Morine said.

Some of the people living directly in front of the caved-in shelter shared their stories with us. "It was a long time ago," one of them explained, "but I did notice some junior high school pupils go in there . . . maybe they were just trying to see how brave they were. We've been here for a very long time and have never seen any attempt to recover the remains . . . haven't even heard anyone talk about it." Another resident explained, "When they were building the old house which was here even before this one went up, I was really surprised at the large amount of human remains that were unearthed." It was *that* story which convinced Morine beyond all doubt that the cave was right there, as an explosion had blown a huge hole to the left of the entrance and the remains of twenty or thirty people had been buried there.

Arasaki Takemori, who had been chairman of Kagamizu Ward thirty years ago, began by explaining, "That particular area is not actually within the ward boundary, so I'm not really sure. Mind you, there are a lot of shelters around Oroku. Even when they built the Kagamizu Community Hall, they came across a number of human remains." So it would be no surprise if the shelter was in that area and there were still human remains lying there. "I've never heard of any attempts to remove remains from around there," he added.

Even though we knew where the shelter was and that bones had never been cleared away, there was a major problem regarding their removal. Not that far from the cave entrance, houses have been built directly above the spot where the bones are believed to be, and other houses are currently under construction. Standing on the hill where the shelter was, Morine gazed out across the landscape. "Some people committed suicide on that hill over there," he said, pointing out an area and adding, "Some of my friends were killed there. I often used to watch the sun go down from this hill, but there were also times when I felt I would die. I've really had enough of war."

The medical treatment shelter was about 3 meters wide, 3 meters high and some 30 meters deep. Entering the shelter from the direction of the road where the buses go, was the "ward" with its three-tiered wooden bunks on the right. Next to that was the army surgeons' area, while on the left was the NCOs' room. Further into the shelter, the operating table stood in the center of the room, although general medical treatment was also provided there. To the right were numerous passageways, while on the left was the accommodation for the nurses. Two army surgeons were based in the shelter, Capt. Kimura Hisashi and Lt. Sadamura. Both of these young men in their late twenties died in the fighting. There were also four regular nurses and a number of orderlies, bringing the full complement of the medical team to around twenty.

Because the shelter was connected to the Yamane Unit's No. 3 Company's shelter, Morine often used to go there. Although it was deemed a "medical surgery shelter" until around April 1945, much of the treatment was for people with only minor wounds. Most of them made their way between the medical shelter and their own shelter several times, so it was really like a sort of out-patient facility. However, sometime in April, while the men were making hand grenades in the Headquarters Company shelter, some of the gunpowder ignited, causing a massive explosion. Suddenly, the medical shelter was jam-packed with forty-to-fifty seriously wounded men. At the end of May, the naval units moved down to the south. Some days later, they returned again to Oroku, but they now had a large number of civilians and men from other units with them. They had walked for days on end in rain that had never let up. They had slept standing up and, as they walked, their urine ran freely down their legs, the warmth from which being the only sensation they had of being alive. Then one day, not long after they got back from down south, explosives, white phosphorous canisters, and tear gas were suddenly hurled into the shelter. Those who were near the entrance would have died instantly. Because the Red Cross flag was flying in front of the shelter, indicating that it was a medical station, very often civilians would go there as well, believing it was safe.

Morine talked about the scene inside the shelter. "I got there just as they'd been hit. A lot of people had collapsed in the passageway, but it wasn't the time or place to feel sad or mourn for them. Their bodies were making it difficult for us to move about so we shifted them all into one corner of the shelter. I think that space was about six square meters so we stacked the bodies, one on top of the other. Just then, I happened to glance down as the hand of one of the 'dead' bodies, whose head and arms were sticking out to the side, moved. I thought 'What the . . .' and pulled the body back out of the pile. It was a woman. Her body was completely blackened and her hair was all gone."

The woman was Uesato Toshiko, one of the nurses in the shelter. Her injuries were not as bad as they had first appeared and she had almost recovered in the few weeks after that. "But they were serious injuries at that time," one of the other nurses, Kusumi Fumiko, told me. "The skin on her head was hanging off," she explained. "I quickly bandaged her up but I felt it was already too late." Toshiko has no recollection of the explosion and what followed. By the time she regained consciousness she was already being treated by Fumiko. She was actually unconscious when her hand had moved, the deciding factor between life and death for her. Within a few days, the bodies they had piled up almost to the ceiling had started to give off a terrible stench, so they covered them with blankets. Referring to the human remains in the hospital shelter, Morine said, "It has troubled me ever since. It's possible that, even today, the whole place is just as it was back then."

During the final week or so of March 1945, the artillery units of the invading American forces began to pound Oroku almost every day. Once the Americans had established their heavy artillery battery on Kamiyama Island in the Keise group of islands, since Shuri was also within range, there were regular bombardments. The serious burn victims from that shelling and from bombing raids were taken to the medical shelter. "It really was horrendous," Toshiko and Fumiko said. A white zinc oxide ointment was spread over their injuries, turning their scorched faces pure white. Only their eyes stood out and they looked very odd, quite eerie.

The American artillery bombardment continued throughout April and May, so at the end of May, the naval units moved temporarily down south. There were many seriously wounded men in the shelter, and those who were unable to move by themselves were euthanized with potassium cyanide. At the start, it was mixed in with their food. The wounded just lay there, writhing in agony. After one of the group ate some of the food and died, none of the others would eat it. So, the next method they tried was injection, many men dying from what were passed off as injections for "the good of your health." After watching one of the wounded men die from his injection, the other patients struggled violently and were held down by several staff while they were given their injections. Toshiko talked about this as the most horrific of her war experiences. "They died almost immediately after the injection. They just let out a little sigh or groan before both hands started to twist and contort . . . like this." Her sad voice became even sadder. After the war, she suffered endless nightmares about it and even when her own husband died, "I felt I was being punished for what I'd done." She suffered mental health problems for some time after his death.

By the time they returned from down south, the shelter in the hill-face was giving off an appalling stench. The bodies had decomposed rapidly due to the incessant rain. The humidity in the shelter, together with the flies and stench, stopped anybody from entering. The whole scene was so terrible that we placed ladders on top of the dead bodies and walked on them." Their first tasks included gathering up the corpses and putting them all in the nurses' room. These were included in the total of forty bodies. Also, there were swarms of flies in the shelter, so many that they smothered the light. "At that stage, the only lighting we had was a wick dipped in some oil. But as soon as we lit it—quick as a flash—more flies than you could imagine swarmed in and extinguished the flame." Just hearing that story was enough to make me choke.

On 4 June, the American landing started from the direction of Cape Sakibaru on Oroku. As well as the Japanese defenders having very few weapons, their supplies of ammunition were almost exhausted. Also, the only outcome of the unit's infiltration attacks in which each soldier was armed with a single grenade was to lose more of their own men. "If we'd had more weapons, we may have even won that battle," Morine said. "As it was, all we had was one rifle, one machine gun and 300 rounds. That was our lot." The frustration they felt must have been overwhelming as, right in front of their very eyes, they saw many of their friends being killed, one after another. "And yet, the navy still had reasonable supplies of food so there was very little squabbling among the men. From the unit commander down, they were all very good men in that Yamane Unit." On 10 June, close to the time of the naval unit's suicide attack, the company commander announced, "Local people, please head south and look after yourselves as best you can. Please do everything you can to get back to your own homes and villages."

Morine explained that whenever anything came up, Yamane would also stick up for the folk of Okinawa. "And war? Never again. I don't want our children to ever experience that."

Commanding officers of the 32nd Army

"He should have been a teacher." Kuniyoshi Shin'ichi, who was attached to the 32nd Army's Signals Unit as a member of the Blood and Iron Student Corps from the Naha Municipal Commercial School, said this when he had an opportunity to meet the widow of Lt. Gen. Ushijima Mitsuru after the war. Many people who had had dealings with the 32nd Army said that Ushijima had a humane side to him that was far from anything normally associated with members of the Imperial Japanese Army.

Ushijima was born on 31 July 1887. Both his father, who was a lieutenant in the army, and his mother were members of the Shimazu clan from Kagoshima Prefecture in southern Kyushu. In 1908, he graduated second in the class from the Infantry Officers' Course at the Imperial Japanese Army Academy, and in 1916 he graduated from the Army Staff College. In March 1937, he assumed command of the 36th Infantry Brigade, seeing action in many battles in China.

In 1941, he became commandant of the Non-commissioned Officers' Academy and from 1942 to 1944 was commandant of the Imperial Japanese Army Academy. On 8 August 1944, he was posted to Okinawa as commanding officer of the 32nd Army.

Moromi Moriyasu, who was put to work digging out the shelters used for the 32nd Army's Command Post, said that when he was working he often saw Ushijima. "He was a pleasant character. When I bowed to him, he'd say 'You're doing good work, young man.' One day, when I was working barefoot because my shoes had split, he asked me, 'What's happened to your shoes?' and when I explained the situation, he got me a new pair right away." Among the awful stories of the war that Moromi told us, only with this single incident did his expression brighten.

Tamaki Shosei, Ageda Kamesaku, and Arakaki Masatachi, who all worked in the veterinary section helping to look after the horses used by the top officers in the 32nd Army, all said, "General Ushijima was a good man."

At given times, the men in the veterinary section had to take horses to the executive officers from the stables at the bottom of the hill on which Shuri Castle stands. One day, Arakaki arrived late at the designated place with a horse for Ushijima who was already there waiting. "I am very sorry that I'm late," said

Arakaki, expecting to be dragged over the coals. Yet rather than getting angry, Ushijima smiled as he replied, "It's OK. I must have arrived early."

While Ushijima's reputation has been tarnished by allegations of involvement in the Rape of Nanking, some people who met him have spoken favorably of his character.

However, in stark contrast to the reserved nature of Lt. Gen. Mitsuru Ushijima, his chief of staff, Cho Isamu, was a tempestuous, larger than life character, not at all liked by the people of Okinawa. Many who crossed his path were on the receiving end of acts of violence for the slightest indiscretion.

Arakaki Masatachi and Nakandakari Kokichi of the 32nd Army's Veterinary Section recall Cho's idiosyncrasies with little affection: "On one occasion when he got on the horse I had prepared for him, the length of the stirrups didn't match the chief of staff's feet and he immediately yelled at me, 'You bastard! You're going in the brig!' There were also times when he punched and kicked some of us."

One of the staff officers of the 32nd Army familiar with Cho's temperament and behavior said, "He was belligerent by nature. He was always looking for a fight and constantly clashed with Senior Staff Officer Yahara Hiromichi, who advocated a defensive war of attrition. His short temper resulted in many of the younger officers freezing in his company. Before the second offensive launched by the Japanese forces in early May, he did a lot of groundwork among those younger officers to ensure that his opinion would be accepted."

Chief of Staff Cho's difficult character meant that he was without friends among staff officers. The staff officer quoted above continues, "When we were carrying out map exercises, the commander of the 24th Division was enraged at Cho's comment 'I'll have each division dancing a merry tune once the fighting starts.' He replied, 'We take orders from the Army commander, not from you.' Cho often overstepped the line between chief of staff and commanding officer and, as a result, his was a negative influence in terms of overall strategy."

Agena Kamezaku, a member of the veterinary section, said, "At first, there were Navy staff in the Headquarters tunnel complex, but Vice-Admiral Ota Minoru did not get along with Chief of Staff Cho, so the Navy people soon left."

There are many anecdotes that reflect the character of Chief of Staff Cho. Moromi Moriyasu who worked on digging out the shelters said, "Cho seemed to be drunk most of the time. I remember how he'd grab a weapon from a medic and pretend to shoot at American planes up in the sky." Miyazato Sadami, who was then manager of the Okinawa Hotel where the 32nd Army held its planning meetings, recalls that "Cho was a rather strange man who often walked around in a red loincloth. About the way the war was going, he'd say things like: 'Don't worry. It's going to be OK. We've got a secret weapon up our sleeves.'" Cho was also known for wearing out women workers with his slave-driver approach.

While the chief of staff had many rough edges, there was also a surprisingly contrasting side to his abrasive character. There are people who remember him for his skill with the written word, and as a singer, and how he composed poetry praising Ushijima.

Right to the end, Chief of Staff Cho was a larger than life figure. Just before he and Ushijima committed ritual suicide in a cave in Mabuni, he made those around him laugh with his comment: "Since your Excellency is going to heaven and I'm going to hell, I'm afraid that our separate destinations mean I will not be able to guide you along the way."

Home Guard

It was two or three days before the last large-scale attack launched by the 32nd Army, which makes it early in May 1945. In a shelter dug into a low hill south-west of Untamamui, a small gathering was held to celebrate the promotion of Home Guard soldier Nagata Saburo. Then eighteen years old, Nagata was in the 89th Infantry Regiment. His squad leader was a soldier by the name of Aizawa Isamu. That day, the seven Home Guard soldiers under Aizawa's command were treated to *sekihan* [festive red rice], a dish very rare on the battlefield.

Nagata remembers, "The meal began with Squad leader Aizawa saying, 'Nagata you've worked hard, so I'm going to promote you to private first class.'" He talked of festive red rice, but his expression suggested that this was not normal *sekihan*. When he explained I understood his unease.

Nagata pointed out a small stream that flowed from the east past the hill. "It was there back then too. We got water from it and used it for drinking and cooking. From a certain stage the water was tinged red, probably because so many Japanese soldiers were killed farther upstream and fell into the stream, so the red color was from the blood of dead or dying men. We used that water to cook our rice, so it became a gruesome type of *sekihan*."

Nagata joined the Home Guard from the Mabuni Youth School. In October 1944, he was sent to join the No. 2 Company of the 26th Sea Assault Squadron based at Nashiro in Itoman. "It was a unit in which, when the boats were to launch their attack, they had two metal drums full of explosives attached to their hull. We worked in squads of thirty, and our main task was moving the boats into and out of the water. Our daily routine was to put the boats out at night and then at dawn to hide them in holes that we had dug in the beach or camouflage them with branches and leaves. Around the time that the battle started, we were holed up in our shelter, getting reports of how the fighting was going."

But as it happens, the boats were all destroyed in the U.S. naval bombardment and the surviving members of the unit were ordered to disperse. "When that happened, they gathered us together and asked us who was capable of working as a messenger. I was among the first to put my hand up." With that he went from Nashiro to Untamamui Hill.

His work as a messenger only lasted a few days. He was shown where the roads were and the topographical features of the land, but beyond that the only instructions he received were about carrying ammunition. He must have made upward of ten round trips every night to the front line at Untamamui Hill. "I'd say that those boxes of ammunition must have weighed about 60 kilograms," said Nagata. The distance to the front at Untamamui was almost one kilometer each way, so at the end of a day's work his shoulders were marked with red lines from the rope attached to the ammunition boxes.

The first death of one of the Home Guard soldiers transferred from Nashiro occurred around 3 May. In the evening, just as they left their shelter to start carrying ammunition a shell fired from a U.S. warship landed near them. Nagata was hit by a piece of shrapnel and his left hand swelled to twice its normal size, but a young man from Itoman called Uehara was killed instantly when he was hit in the head by a shell fragment.

Nagata recalls, "Of the seven Home Guard soldiers, five were killed and nobody knows anything about what happened to one. That I survived was thanks to Squad Leader Aizawa."

At the end of May they withdrew from Untamamui and headed for Yoza-dake. What they saw on the way made them give up on any thoughts of final victory that may have remained. They made their way south, often having to step on the bodies of wounded soldiers who had fallen in the mud. Many of the soldiers, who used pieces of wood as walking sticks, had wounds covered in maggots.

Just before dawn, when they arrived at Yoza-dake, Nagata saw soldiers chasing local civilians out of places where they could shelter safely. Nagata and his comrades were also ordered to wait in a turtleback tomb already occupied by some civilians.

"There were five or six of them in the family and they said that they were from Takue in Goeku. They had a gramophone, so I suppose they were quite well off. I remember that there was a young woman there whom they called

Chiiko," said Nagata.

As the civilians were evicted from the tomb, Nagata told them, "If you go to Mabuni and announce yourselves to my family they will look after you," but he never heard anything about them making it to Mabuni. "Maybe they were all killed in the American naval bombardment," Nagata surmises. Around that time, it was not uncommon for families caught out in the open to be wiped out by one shell fired from the big guns on the U.S. warships offshore.

On the second day after their arrival at Yoza-dake, Nagata Saburo and the other members of the Home Guard were ordered to ready themselves to go on a night infiltration raid. "But Squad Leader Aizawa ignored this order and told us 'Go and visit your families.' We were all from that area, so our families lived relatively close. With this, effectively our unit dispersed, which meant that thanks to Aizawa I was able to survive," says Nagata about the man to whom he owes his life.

They each headed off to where their respective families lived, and Nagata left Yoza-dake with Squad Leader Aizawa and another member of the Home Guard, a man called Kinjo from Makabe. They had no idea what lay ahead for them as they headed roughly south through the U.S. bombardment, eventually reaching the vicinity of Mabuni Elementary School just after daybreak. "Another unit had already occupied the shelter on the eastern side of the school, but we got them to let us stay there during the day and we went out to look for shelter that next night."

Almost all of the caves and shelters were full of people, so the three of them kept on going south until they reached the coast by Komesu. There were already soldiers and civilians in a stand of ironwood trees, but they found space to rest there. The trees were dense enough to provide cover overhead to remain concealed from the American spotter planes that seemed to be constantly up in the sky during the daylight hours, but Nagata was soon to realize that it was not at all a safe place to be.

Near where they sat down to rest was the body of young mother, her head and legs blown off. Too young to realize that its mother had been killed, her baby was still trying to suckle at its mother's breast. "It's still etched in my mind. I wanted to do something for the child, but I had no idea how long I'd survive, so I wasn't able to do anything," recalls Nagata.

They were all starving by this point. On his way south, a friend gave Nagata some rice tied up in two socks, which he used as a pillow when he lay down to sleep down by the coast at Komesu. When he woke up the next morning, both bags of rice had disappeared.

By that time, the IJA had lost all cohesion as a fighting force. When he was at Yoza-dake he was not afraid to sneak past a sentry to steal food and clothing from a storage dump. He took a jacket with a lieutenant's rank insignia on it and put it on when he got to the coastline near Komesu.

"I think that the fact that military discipline had fallen apart by this stage made me more daring, but as we made our way I witnessed so many instances of heartless behavior toward civilians by people in uniform that I wanted to use the authority that came with an officer's uniform to help civilians if I could." But Nagata was only eighteen years old and small for his age, so his attempts to pass himself off as a second lieutenant were soon seen through. When he was digging for potatoes with an officer's sword that he found along the way, he was yelled at by a warrant officer to "Take that rank badge off!" and was hit on the back with the sword. Yet Nagata left the rank insignia on.

With no idea what lay ahead for them, the three parted ways down on the coastline near Komesu. Squad leader Aizawa, whom Nagata had recommended to join him in going as far as his hometown of Mabuni, tried to break through American lines and was killed. He heard that the Home Guard soldier called Kinjo who went back to Makabe was also killed. He also heard after the war that the other two Home Guard soldiers took their own lives with their family members. "At that stage I wasn't afraid of death at all. But so many people went to their deaths because of the mistaken education that we received. Unthinkable these days . . ." he said with a sigh.

Home Guard on Ie-jima

The bitter struggle between Japanese and American forces on Ie-jima occurred during the early stages of the Battle for Okinawa. During those six days from 16 to 21 April, some 2,000 IJA soldiers and 1,500 villagers were killed, as were most of the locals who had been recruited into the Home Guard.

In October 1944, the Ie-jima Home Guard had 500 members, but in November a further 200 had joined and by March 1945, just before the battle, a further 100 recruits brought the total strength to 800 men. Led by Lt. Gibo Toyotake, the force was divided into three companies to defend the area from the airfield in the central part of the island and the area to the west. Because their main role was to maintain and repair facilities at the airfield, they were relatively poorly armed. Each company was equipped with around ten rifles and one grenade launcher, plus there were only two light machine guns for the entire battalion. Apart from that, the only other weapons they had were hand grenades and bamboo spears.

In March, as the American landing looked imminent, the unit received orders to destroy the airfield. After that they were to withdraw to the main island of Okinawa, but there were no boats, so they had no choice but to stay and help defend Ie-jima. The Home Guard was made up of people recruited from the villages located from Onna-son to the north, but other members, such as Tamaki Tokumoto, also recruited from Ie-jima, stayed on and worked the land there in the decades that followed the war. He recalls, "After the Americans landed, they occupied the part of Ie-jima surrounding the airfield. That meant the island was divided from east to west, but we had lost all communication with the Japanese main force who were defending the eastern side, so we fought on with no idea what was happening."

After arriving off Okinawa, U.S. forces immediately started pounding Ie-jima from the air. Then on 25 March, enemy ships appeared off the coast of the island itself. A large number of warships hove to in between Ie-jima and the Motobu Peninsula and from 14 April, two days before the landing, their guns bombarded the island non-stop. Ie-jima was utterly devastated. Just before dawn on the 16th, around 6,000 soldiers of the U.S. 77th Division under the command of Maj. Gen. Andrew Bruce began to come ashore. From that moment on, for the next six days Ie-jima was locked in a desperate struggle.

A deadly battle raged on the western side of the island, defended by Tamaki and the others in the Home Guard. "Throughout the day of the landing, we were given a pounding by waves of American soldiers led by tanks. Our unit was all but wiped out so we stayed hidden in the foxholes we'd dug along the ridge. Only under cover of darkness did we crawl back to launch a raid, armed only with the two grenades we had each been given." That went on for almost four days.

After their fourth night attack, which they launched on the 19th, they arrived at the southern tip of the airfield to launch a mass suicide charge when an argument broke out between the commander, Lt. Gibo who favored a night attack, and his NCO. The NCO urged, "Whatever we do, we're going to die here, OK? So let's make it a daylight attack." In the end, the NCO lost out and the daytime attack idea was abandoned. However, concluding that there was nothing more they could achieve together as a unit, Lt. Gibo ordered them to split up into small groups and try to break though the enemy lines. "Once you get through you should look to join up with Igawa's unit" (1st Battalion, 2nd Infantry Unit, 44th Independent Mixed Brigade), he said.

Tamaki explained, "In those days, we thought that to die was the only thing that we could do for our country. We were even proud of the notion, with none of us even thinking about trying to make it out alive. In fact, we felt the obvious thing to do was as the NCO had suggested. The fact that we burned everything, from Battalion Headquarters' important documents to the last bank note, gives you an idea of the state of mind we were in."

However, after being ordered to break into small groups and join up with Maj. Igawa's main force—effectively an order for the unit to disperse—Tamaki lost all motivation to fight. The drive he had felt until then simply disappeared and he explained his change of heart at the time as, "It was unbelievable the way I had thought about nothing but dying out there for the cause, and then we were just told to go our own way! We felt hugely let down." The Home Guard, now reduced to around 200 members, split into small groups that headed off in various directions. Everything Tamaki did from then on had a new focus—to stay alive.

Tamaki moved about with three or four of his friends, but they never gave a thought to joining up with Maj. Igawa's 44th Independent Mixed Brigade and fighting desperately for the school plateau, which is now Ie Junior High School at the foot of Gusukuyama. Instead, they escaped to the Maja region in the northwest of the island and, on 22 April, after spending two days in a cave on a coastal bluff, they saw the Stars and Stripes flying on Gusukuyama, the central peak of Ie-jima.

"From my time fighting in China, I knew that the Americans would soon commence mopping-up operations," so Tamaki and his friends moved to a point near the lighthouse on the western side of the island. From there, they continued to move around the island until they were captured.

Tamaki was thirty-two years old at the time. In addition to both his parents, he had a wife and children. His elder brother Noriyuki had been killed on Ie-jima, but his parents, wife and two children were evacuated to Nakijin early in March. Tamaki had already been called up at that point and, busy making improvised explosive devices at battalion headquarters, he had not been able to bid farewell his wife, who was almost due to give birth, or their two children.

On 12 April, as a precursor to the battle on Ie-jima, American forces and the IJA had clashed on Motobu Peninsula with Col. Udo Takehiko's Kunigami Detachment, engaging the Americans in fierce fighting. When Tamaki heard about the fighting, he looked across the water to the opposite coast. Everything seemed to be ablaze in a mass of red flames. "My parents . . . my children . . . my family have all been killed," he thought, and from then on he did his best to forget about them.

But Tamaki was wrong. His family was still alive, although they had all been captured and were being held at a camp in Kushi. Initially worried sick about Tamaki's safety after hearing about the savage fighting on Ie-jima they abandoned all hope that he might have survived. His was one of those tragic "ships in the night" scenarios which happen in war, but for those people who were involved in the fighting, it was probably nothing out of the ordinary.

Captured on Ie-jima, Tamaki was taken with 2,100 other survivors to a POW camp on the Kerama Islands in early May. They were split into two groups, with about 400 prisoners going to Zamami and around 1,700 going to Tokashiki. Tamaki was held on Tokashiki and spent the next twelve months—until April 1946 when captured villagers being held on the Keramas were repatriated to the main island of Okinawa—agonizing over his future alone in the belief that his family had all been killed.

Tamaki finally made it back to Kushi-son (as it was called then) in the northeast of the main island of Okinawa where he had a dramatic and very emotional reunion with his family. Both parties were so convinced that the other was dead that they were speechless when they first met. Tamaki first saw his third son. "With things like that, if I hadn't been there in person, I'd never have believed it. I just can't explain what it was like," he recalled emotionally. "Being away from my family like that is something I never want to go through again."

"All I can say is that back then, people—including me—and the world in general had all gone mad. That is how we got into such a terrible war," lamented Tamaki, who never talked to his own family about the fighting on Ie-jima. In some respects, Tamaki not wanting to talk about his experiences is in itself an indication of the horrors of war.

Tamaki's war took him from working on airfields to making explosive devices, from night attacks to fleeing for his life, from being taken prisoner to living in a POW camp . . . and finally to an emotional reunion with his family. But another part of his story is that out of the 800 members of the Home Guard on Ie-jima, only about 180 survived the war, so over 600 lost their lives. The remains of many of those killed are still lying in unknown places around Ie-jima, but in 1983 the Ministry of Health and Welfare began the task of recovering them. They retrieved the remains of 195 bodies from 130 separate shelters and enshrined them in the *Hokon-no-To* Ossuary. The remains may even include members of the Home Guard who suffered alongside Tamaki.

In the steady rain, an elderly man watched as Ministry of Health and Welfare staff carried out the recovery operation. The shelter is situated on a small hill several hundred meters from the coast, with Gusukuyama visible off to the north-east. The elderly man, Shimojo Shuei, was one of the survivors. The next day he was joined by another survivor, Shimojo Ryugen, and together they stared intently at the very shelter where they had both endured their nightmare four decades earlier.

As members of the Home Guard, Shimojo Shuei and Shimojo Ryugen—who had both been called up in October 1944—were ordered to go to a shelter in the defensive line. They arrived while preparations were under way to counter the U.S. landing which occurred ten days later. From then on, the construction of fortifications began. After cutting through a mass of limestone day and night without a break, the fortification and its escape tunnel, just larger than 1 meter high and wide and about 40 meters long, was completed in four or five days.

It was constructed to incorporate a burial tomb—which faced the coast where the enemy would be engaged—as its front. Only 50 centimeters high, the entrance to the tomb was like the gunport in a pillbox. Shimojo Ryugen had set up a light machine gun inside the tomb but, as he waited for the attack to begin, he knew it was of no use in the face of the ferocity of the U.S. attack. "If I fired once, thousands of rounds poured back in," he explained. Shimojo's situation was, "Not a fight at all . . . It was more like a mole living underground and not daring to move. I felt so pathetic to think that I'd been born just to come here and die . . . it was such a despairing thought."

On the 17th, the day after they landed, the Americans began attacking the shelter from the front as well as via the escape route over the hill. There were fourteen or fifteen Japanese soldiers hiding inside the shelter at the time and they detonated some dynamite that had been placed near the entrance to block it off and prevent the Americans from getting in. The blast ripped the soldiers' clothes to shreds, creating an awful scene with blood pouring from their noses. But there was nothing else that they could have done. "We were trapped in a hopeless situation," recalls Shimojo Shuei.

Then, because the Japanese soldiers had blasted the shelter entrance, the Americans moved round to the back of the shelter to carry out their "blowtorch and corkscrew" procedure. They pumped petrol in and then ignited it with a flame-thrower.

Shimojo Shuei just managed to survive the attack by pushing his face down into the dirt. In the evening after the Americans pulled back, he suggested they all leave the shelter, but none of the others was prepared to go with him. In the end, Shimojo Shuei headed off alone. He remembers that as he ran off he was shot at by an American soldier with a submachine gun, but he made good his escape. Finally, Shimojo paddled across to Motobu Peninsula in a small dugout.

Shimojo Ryugen, on the other hand, was still holed up in the shelter with the fourteen or fifteen IJA regulars. When the Americans attacked the shelter again on the following day, he scurried out on his hands and knees. "I was in a total frenzy, just focused on getting out of there," he recalls. "I think that some of the soldiers followed me, but it seems they were killed where they came out of the shelter or near the entrance." In desperation, Shimojo Ryugen headed for Gusukuyama to join the main force. He survived several infiltrations raids with them, even the final night attack. "There were about 100 of us on that final attack, including girls, but they were all killed as well. I ended up on my own and, as I was walking along the coast, I saw the Stars and Stripes flying on Gusukuyama." Shimojo Ryugen explained, quite matter of factly, that his only thought at the time was, "So that's that. We've lost."

Shimojo Ryugen and the others who had been taken prisoner returned to Ie-jima in March 1947. With no locals living on the island for two years, the Americans had been busy retrieving their own dead, carrying out airfield repairs and constructing main roads. However, the bodies of dead Japanese soldiers and local villagers had been left where they fell, exposed to the elements. For Shimojo Ryugen and the other returnees, retrieving those human remains was the first task in helping with the reconstruction of Ie-jima. They collected many bodies and held a funeral service for them but, every time he passed by the shelter, Shimojo Ryugen commented sadly, "There must still be more bodies inside." He did not know many of those who died there as he had been with them for such a brief period. Also, they had come from other parts of Japan as well as from the main island of Okinawa itself. Yet for a long time he wondered, "I wonder if it was that guy, or maybe this other guy who had been inside." As two sets of bones were brought out from inside the shelter, Ryugen dabbed the corner of his eyes as he said, "That's good. I'm glad they're out . . ."

Ie-jima Women's Cooperative Unit

The tragedy surrounding the Himeyuri Student Corps is famous. So many of those girl students ended their young lives in the awful conflict that was the Battle of Okinawa. Units made up of young girls and women existed all through the islands that make up the prefecture of Okinawa. One example is the Women's Cooperative Unit on Ie-jima, formed in January 1945 from unmarried young women between the ages of seventeen and twenty-four.

Oshiro Shige, who survived the fighting on Ie-jima from 16 to 21 April, even joining the soldiers on an infiltration raid, recalls those days: "From around 1943, youth group lessons were held several times a week. The army surgeon stationed on the island, and others, taught us about first aid, but in January 1945, when the war really started to get close, the Cooperative Unit was formed and we were forbidden from being evacuated."

Oshiro remembers there being about 100 women in the Unit. They waited to face the landing of the American troops with the Women's Cooperative Unit, made up of women twenty-five years of age and older who helped cook and do odd-jobs for the soldiers.

Oshiro was attached to a squad in the Independent Anti-aircraft Battalion commanded by Capt. Moroe Harumi. From around March they were holed up in a dugout shelter located at the foot of Gusukuyama (or "Tacchu" as it is known locally), the 172-meter peak that dominates the island. While they were designated as a medical unit, the only medical equipment that they were given was some tincture of iodine, gauze and bandages, so they weren't capable of actually treating wounded soldiers. Oshiro recalls that their main duties were to carry ammunition and help bring soldiers wounded on infiltration raids back into the shelter.

"After the Americans landed, most of the girls who had been attached to infantry units went out on raids with the soldiers and so ended up being killed in the fierce fighting, but for those of us in the Anti-aircraft Battalion our main task was carrying ammunition, said Oshiro. Her words offer a chilling reminder of the good and bad fortune that manifested itself among the young women in the Unit.

On 18 April, the third day after the U.S. landings on Ie-jima, Oshiro's unit carried out its first infiltration raid as part of the fighting around the school grounds. Needless to say, Oshiro joined the soldiers on the raid. Not long into the action, she was ordered to help carry wounded soldiers back to the shelter, and that brought an end to her one and only experience of such a raid. On 21 April, when the last attack was to be launched, she was again left out when the order was given for "Everyone still alive will take part in the attack." A LCpl. Sato from Fukuoka Prefecture who had wounds to his legs and couldn't walk stayed behind in the shelter, as did Oshiro, and about thirty civilians.

Oshiro recalls, "They all went out, but none came back. I will never forget the soldiers who had been hit in one leg. They limped out there too."

LCpl. Sato had been ordered by Capt. Moroe to take his own life and had set himself up by a box full of artillery shells. Oshiro linked hands with her younger sister and friends as they confirmed their readiness to die, saying, "Tonight will be the last night for all of us," but LCpl. Sato overheard them and told them, "You aren't soldiers, so there's no need for you to die." Thanks to Sato's interdiction, they decided against suicide and survived. Oshiro sadly recalled that the man to whom so many owed their lives, ". . . returned home after the war but later died in a mining accident." She continued, "Too many good people died in that battle."

"The soldiers were all very kind; they did their best to look after us young ones. It was awful for us to have to put tincture of iodine in their open wounds when they came back from fighting," said Oshiro as she recalled such painful memories. She remembers with particular sadness one soldier in his mid-twenties saying, "I just want to fall asleep and never wake up." Thinking back, it was almost as though he wanted to say something more to her before he died, but Oshiro recalled painfully, as though her conscience was weighing upon her, "They all ended up dying . . . so I didn't really listen to him."

According to Ie Village records, some 160 young women were drafted into the Cooperative Unit, but almost all were killed, with only nine, including Oshiro, surviving the battle. "My youth was dominated by the war. There wasn't one good thing about it," said Oshiro, her voice fading as she recalled her suffering during and after the war.

Nageera Cave

Arakawa in Haebaru. Few people know that the 62nd Infantry Division's field hospital was located in this settlement during the Battle of Okinawa. Those who were associated with the cave back then have steadfastly maintained their silence and refused to talk about the tragic events that occurred there. Consequently, while it is a man-made structure, it is one of the best-preserved lateral tunnel cave shelters in Okinawa. In fact, few people know of its existence and it remains shrouded in mystery. Commonly referred to as the Nageera Cave, the area around the entrance is now overgrown. Looking at it from a distance, you would never suspect that there is a cave there at all. Even right up close, it is still difficult to find the opening that forms the entrance.

During the Battle of Okinawa, there were sixty-one fourth-year students from Shuri Girls' School working here as nurse aides. These girls in the Zuisen Student Corps worked non-stop looking after wounded soldiers, seeing many of their patients die. As well as IJA personnel, Home Guard members, regular nurses, and girls from the Showa Girls' School who were working in the same nursing corps also died there from the effects of explosions or fever.

More than half of the Zuisen Student Corps, that is thirty-three of the girls, were killed in the fighting on Okinawa, but three of them actually died inside this cave. Ever since, the girls who managed to survive the ordeal have continued to worry about what became of the remains of their three friends. However, when they made their way back to the area, even as they looked from a distance, they couldn't bring themselves to go inside.

A powerful bond had developed among the girls of the 41st class of Shuri Girls' School. Shortly after the war, some of the survivors erected the *Zuisen-no-to* memorial where their old high school sports ground had been in Tobaru in Shuri, in memory of their dead friends. The monument has since been moved to Komesu in Itoman, but apart from those associated with the school itself, hardly anybody goes near the place.

So one day almost four decades after the end of the war, five of the Shuri Girls' School survivors decided to visit the old hospital cave. "I couldn't bring myself to go on my own, but think that it will be okay if I go with some others," said one of the women as they set off for Nageera Cave in search of some form of closure.

A narrow track from Sakiyama in Shuri leads down to the secluded area where the shelter was located. The women's recollection of the location was accurate. On that particular day, the ground was muddy from the steady drizzle but the women did not hesitate as they followed the track between the fields toward the cave's front entrance.

"It was around here that we had our graduation ceremony," said Hoshino Masako as though she had just recalled the occasion. The area she indicated had been a grassy area in front of the hospital shelter entrance, but is now fields of vegetables. "Back then, there was an A-framed barracks building there and we had our graduation ceremony in a tent set up in front of the barracks. That was 27 March, at about 8:00 PM."

Kohatsu Tsuruko added, "But it certainly wasn't a happy occasion, that graduation ceremony." Nakanishi Yukiko explained, "We were away from our parents and felt very uneasy." Held by the flickering light of candles, with the school principal, the prefectural governor's delegate, and an army officer present, it was a strange graduation ceremony because none of the girls' parents were there.

Hoshino's voice faltered as she added, "We sang the school song but, halfway through everybody started to cry and you couldn't hear the words. We all felt that there was just no hope."

The day after their graduation, 28 March 1945, the girls from Shuri Girls' School were officially assigned to the 62nd Infantry Division Field Hospital Cave. During the war, the water in the Kinjo River (near the upper reaches of the Asato River), which forms the boundary between Arakawa in Haebaru Cho and Sakiyama-Cho in Shuri, ran fresh and clear. Hoshino, who had worked in the medicine preparation area, explained, "Apparently they used to collect the clear water from there and use it for preparing medicines." The cave was on the Haebaru side of the river, with the Sakiyama side being used only as a site to dispose of dead bodies. Looking across from where they used to dispose the bodies, an even smaller stream divides it into two separate chambers, one to the left, the other to the right. The rock formation near the shelter's main entrance, where their graduation ceremony was held, is unstable, so the women decided to cross the river near where the bodies had been dumped.

"There used to be a bridge across here about a meter wide," said Tomiko Makiya.

"Another girl and I often used to put the dead bodies onto a stretcher and carry them across. It was heavy work for just two girls. Then we'd count "one . . . two . . . three" and hurl the body into the large shell craters from the naval bombardment. Disposing of the bodies was the most frightening job."

These days the creek is barely a flow of muddy water so they bent the reeds downward and used them as a platform to walk on. They each held the hand of the person behind and crossed safely over to the Haebaru side. From there they continued wading through the grass alongside the little stream when, right in front of them, was the unmistakable sight of several gaping holes in the ground.

"Wow! I never imagined there would still be any left," exclaimed Nakanishi. The others also stopped in their tracks. Then, her face still wracked with pain, Hoshino recalled one of her dead friends. "It was where the people with contagious diseases were put. Typhus was going around. I remember now that Kinjo Ikuko caught something and eventually died from encephalitis as a result."

However, because they had journeyed back to the shelter as a group rather than by themselves, they were able to keep each other's spirits up. These women then decided to go inside the very shelter where no Zuisen Student Corps survivor had set foot alone since the war.

Perhaps the land had slipped away due to the effect of years of heavy rain, but the small stream was farther down the slope than it had been during the war. The shelter entrance was about the same height as the women themselves. Once again, only by holding each other's hands were they able to climb up the slope.

The surface was uneven because some rocks had fallen inside the cave, but the women were adamant that it had barely changed since the war. Several torch beams lit up the walls in the darkness. The marks left by pickaxes were a reminder of how they must have dug as if their very lives depended on it.

The women chatted away to avoid the eerie silence. Makiya pointed to a wall and explained, "One of the wounded soldiers killed himself with a hand grenade … pieces of flesh splattered all over the cave wall. I was ordered to use tongs and remove the bits that had stuck to the wall. Picking it off one bit at a time was just ghastly."

At their graduation ceremony on the day before they went into the cave, the Shuri Girls' School Nursing Corps got some idea of what lay ahead when the officer in charge of the 62nd Infantry Division Field Hospital announced, "You girls will all die with me in battle." Also, while they were not issued with official nursing uniforms, they wore a unit tag with 62nd Infantry Division, their serial number, and blood type on their chest. They were what were known as *gunzoku* [civilian employees of the military], and despite telling themselves that they were "ready" for what lay ahead in the cave, the things they witnessed were too horrific for girls still in their teens.

Hoshino recalled how she happened to go from the medicine room past the surgical area. "I was given a lamp and told to shine it directly on the wound of the soldier they were operating on. I was terrified at the start. I couldn't bear to look at the actual amputation and when I shone the light on his face by mistake the surgeon screamed at me, 'What the hell are you doing! What section are you from?' Holding the lamp was actually one of the better jobs though. When I was ordered to hold a patient's leg down, I thought I was going to faint. I was scared stiff disposing of the legs after they'd been cut off."

Makiya was another who had helped during leg amputations. "They did the operation at the cave entrance, and I was so frightened that I could only hold the leg between my thumb and the tips of two fingers. As they had finished cutting it away, I actually tumbled into the little stream behind me, still clutching the leg. They had no anesthetic so it was just awful for the patients."

Nakanishi spoke about her friend Sotoma Masa, who died of her wounds. "I came back to this cave with Masa from the Shuri Girls' School cave (a naturally formed cave in Tobaru-Cho) where we had been assigned. She had been hit in her left thigh by a piece of shrapnel from a bomb blast. The wound had swollen up and turned purple, so she ended up having her entire leg amputated. Initially she didn't want them to do it, but she finally agreed and said, "Doctor, please do your best."

The smell of blood filled the shelter. As wounded soldiers were brought in one after the other from the front line, other soldiers stepped nonchalantly over them as they lay there unattended. One of three nurse aides assigned to ninety wounded soldiers, Makiya explained, "Basically we worked around the clock, trying to get some sleep standing up leaning against one of the pillars in the cave. In the evening, I remember that it was really busy after we finished our work removing dead bodies, and then after 9:00 PM it got even harder."

At around 1:00 AM on 22 May, a mortar shell landed near Makiya as she was outside the cave clearing up after the evening meal. She recalled that occasion. "Cpl. Oishi was killed instantly by shrapnel, and three regular nurses and I were wounded. Two of them had the sides of their faces ripped away by the blast and they died, groaning in agony, shortly after. For some reason, Cpl. Oishi remembered my name and I actually feel a bit sad when I think back to how he used to call out to me 'Makiya . . . come over here . . .' and get me to do some little jobs for him." Makiya's own wound was also serious. "When I checked it by candlelight, my pants were stained bright red with blood."

Daily life in the shelter was completely different from anything they had experienced. Everybody ended up mentally ground down by the mayhem that confronted them every day. Makiya said, "That reminds me, I don't remember ever going to the toilet." Also, from when they first went into the cave, the girls' menstrual cycles suddenly stopped. "When I think about it now, I still can't believe it, but maybe it was due to malnutrition," added Nakanishi, still struggling to come to grips with the horrific experience.

They have never forgotten their three classmates whose young lives were cut short in the shelter. Tawada Yoshi and Kinjo Ikuko both contracted a contagious disease, while Yamazato Tomiko died from shrapnel wounds to the abdomen. The group who had taken chrysanthemums to the shelter, talked about their three friends' final moments.

Toward the end of April, Tawada Yoshi went down with some form of contagious disease and was put into the isolation area of the cave. The girls went to visit but were not allowed to see her and eventually heard that she had died from encephalitis. "She was a strong but quiet person," explained Kohatsu.

Shortly after that, Kinjo Ikuko also went down with a fever and died from encephalitis. "Ikuko was a very serious girl. She didn't really have any time for jokes," said Hoshino with a wry grin as she recalled their student days. "At the end she kept sitting up in the bed and saying, 'I'm just going over to see Mom . .

.'" Hoshino's voice faltered.

Kohatsu took up the story. "She was from Kin and had a really strong accent. She was always being teased about her distinctive way of speaking." The others nodded as they remembered.

Because they had not been allowed in to visit, none of the girls' nursing corps friends were with them during their final hours. Although it was very rare, Makiya did have cause to go to the isolation area of the shelter on one occasion and was actually asked to help. "I took the bedpan over to one of the patients with encephalitis, but he washed his face with his own urine. I was so frightened I ran off."

Every day, shells poured in around the Field Hospital. One day, a shell landed near No. 3 Surgery Cave, killing Yamazato Tomiko who had been out fetching water. She became the third Shuri Girls' School victim of the Nageera Cave. Makiya, who was at Tomiko's side as her friend died, described what happened. "A piece of shrapnel had sliced right through her abdomen. I tried to comfort her but just touching her made the pain worse. So, I yelled out, 'Quick, get a doctor!'"

Hoshino did hear that Ikuko's family had gone there to collect her body as soon as the war ended. On the first day that the newspaper began publishing the story of the Nageera Cave in serial form, Ikuko's younger sister, Higa Masako, who was living in Torihori in Shuri, asked the staff in charge of the series of articles to look into the matter. "Around 1949, I went back to the area with my father and aunt to try to recover my sister's remains, but we couldn't find the actual shelter so we just gathered a few stones from a nearby field and placed them on my sister's grave to commemorate her life. But when we checked a sketch map, we had obviously gone to the completely wrong place," she explained, adding that if there was anybody who knew what happened during her sister's final moments, she would like to hear from them.

Tomiko's wounds were so serious that she was beyond help and, before the day was out, she passed away on the operating table, just a few hours after being hit by the shrapnel.

"When she died, four or five of us removed her bloodied clothes and dressed her in a brand new military uniform. Disposing of dead bodies was one of my jobs, but of course I couldn't bear the thought of burying one of my own friends. I got one of the army medics to take her away and just quietly said my farewells. I remember how Tomiko had such long legs and how she had always looked so attractive in her volleyball gear."

As Makiya talked, she pressed her hands together in the direction of where her dead friend lay. Then Hoshino explained tearfully, "It's been all of thirty-nine years since the war ended and I've never been able to bring myself to visit and burn a stick of incense for you . . . I am so, so sorry." The women all felt that it was as if the faces of their deceased friends had appeared before them. They offered a silent prayer then felt an eerie chill in the air. Maybe it was not just from the cool change in the weather heading toward Okinawa.

Many died in the Nageera Cave including the three girls from the Shuri Girls' School Nursing Corps. But what happened to the remains of those who were disposed of outside the cave? The women once again visited the small settlement near the cave in search of remains that have never been returned to the bereaved families.

As previously mentioned, the site where the bodies were disposed of was at Sakiyama in Shuri, an area which locals call Shichaara. In fact, the name Nageera refers to a place in a slightly different location so its correct name is actually the Shichaari Cave. However, according to survivors from Shuri Girls' School, the men of the 62nd Infantry Division referred to it as Nageera and that name seemed to stick.

It was already completely dark by the time they met Uza Tokusei, who explained that one section of the disposal site had been cleared soon after the end of the war.

"I'm pretty sure that it was around 1948. When this part was cleared to grow vegetables, we came across lots of bones. I remember there being nine skulls so there must have been the remains of at least nine people out there. We contacted the municipal authorities who sent someone out to get them. They said that they would take them to Shikina, so they'll have placed them in an ossuary there as unidentified remains."

Uza came to Okinawa from Kumamoto, in Kyushu, after the war. He acquired that piece of land of around 3,300 square meters and grew potatoes, sugar cane, and burdock. From time to time, former members of the 62nd Infantry Division who had been in the cave during the war stop by while sightseeing in Okinawa. "It hasn't changed at all, has it," they say before pressing their hands together in prayer.

According to Uza, as they were cultivating the ground, they discovered a body still lying on a stretcher. Perhaps the body had been thrown into the hole, stretcher and all, or perhaps the people carrying it had been hurled in there with it by a shell blast. "If we were to write an epitaph, it would be that we regret not being able to return the bones to their bereaved families . . ."

At first, it was assumed that there may also human remains inside the cave. Today, however, it is believed that the internal timber supports were all removed and that locals actually went inside the shelter as soon as the war finished. Uza explained, "I imagine they would have removed the bodies then. Back then it was common to go into the caves to try salvage things. It was a time when people used any wood they could gather up for building houses."

In any event, they expected to find more than just nine bodies. According to members of the Zuisen Student Corps, several hundred people died in there. Much of the area where their bodies had been disposed of has since been cultivated, so it is mainly vegetable fields. However, there is still one overgrown area that has not been touched since the war. Uza explained, "Various real estate agents handled it, so that particular piece of land changed owners a lot after the war. Probably nobody knows what became of any remains that were up there." Judging from the look on his face, Uza could not understand why anyone would be looking for remains after all this time.

By the time they heard the end of Uza's story, it was 8:00 PM and pitch dark outside. Aware that they were back at the place where their graduation ceremony had been held all those years ago, they set off in the direction of the cave. They felt a shiver run down their spines as they recalled Uza's story, "There was a rumor that when it gets dark up here, an apparition appears . . . of nurses in white coats, carrying stretchers."

To offset the redeployment of the 9th Infantry Division to Taiwan, which began at the end of 1944, the 62nd Infantry Division arrived to defend the area around Shuri. The school buildings of Shuri Girls' School were commandeered for the 62nd Infantry Division to use as their headquarters, with the pupils reduced to having their lessons in private dwellings.

Hisataka Tomoaki, who taught Japanese as his specialist subject at the school during the war, remembers to this day the 41st girls' class who were subsequently assigned to the Nageera Cave. Hisataka was not in the cave himself but, whenever he sees the names of girls he taught listed on the alumni name list as "killed in action," he imagines them back in his class during happier times. He spoke to us about the three girls who died at the shelter.

"Tawada was very reserved . . . a lovely girl. She was never one to push herself forward at all, but she was always happy and smiling. Yamazato was tall and good at sports. Kinjo's parents were very education-oriented. She was a well-organized, sensible girl. The girls who died were the quiet ones."

In spite of the demanding work the girls had to do day after day, the mental image Hisataka has retained of the 41st intake is that they were all very cheerful. "Even on those scorching summer days, they dug away in that shelter from morning to night without a break. It must have been incredibly tough, yet they laughed and joked . . ." Hisataka remembered sadly. Shortly after the war, Minei Goei, Principal of Shuri Girls' School, together with a number of staff, visited the homes of former pupils who had died. After that, they went from one place to the next to confirm the exact time, date, and place the girls died. Hisataka, who was one of those staff, explained, "In January 1946 when we visited the ruins of Shuri Girls' School, we found the school flag in tatters. Near the bleachers at the sports ground was the cave that the school had used as a shelter. It was big enough to hold about 400 people and we started our investigations there. Then we heard that some remains had been found around what had formerly been Shuri when the land was being prepared for farming or building houses, and that the locals had collected them and placed them in a repository in Tonokura in Shuri. So I imagine that any remains from Nageera would also have been taken there."

In January 1953, at a meeting of the Zuisen Alumni organized by the staff and former students of Shuri Girls' School, a panel discussion was held to which members of bereaved families from Tsuboya in Naha were also invited. As a result, they were able to piece together the circumstances surrounding the deaths of the thirty-three members of the Zuisen Student Corps based on the former students' statements. But apart from the girls in the Zuisen Corps, forty-eight school committee members and fifteen former staff members were also killed in the fighting. The Zuisen Memorial was built to commemorate the souls of all ninety-six.

"We pray for the repose of the souls of the thirty-three members of the former Prefectural Shuri Girls' School Student Corps, sacrificed due to the misguided adventures of the defunct Japanese military. They were young girls whose graduation ceremony was held in front of an air raid shelter and who immediately became the first Student Nurse Aide Corps to stand at the front line in defense of their homeland, only to have their dreams and their young lives taken from them."

Nunumachi-gama

During the war, a military field hospital was set up in a naturally formed cave near Aragusuku in Gushikami. Teams of investigators and university research groups often visit the cave which locals refer to as Nunumachi-gama, although it is widely known as the Garabi shelter. The entrance to the military hospital, however, was not the Garabi shelter at all, which was on the eastern side, but over toward Nunumachi-gama, on the western side. The official title for the 1st Field Hospital of the 24th Division, which was located in this cave in Tomori, Kochinda on the slopes of Yaezu-dake, was the Aragusuku Field Hospital. As the battle was drawing to a close, some 800 wounded soldiers in this natural cave took their own lives using hand grenades or poison. Any who were still breathing were then shot by medical orderlies.

We forced our way through the thick undergrowth to the Nagata entrance to the cave, treading very carefully, one deliberate step at a time, so as not to slip. Then we arrived at what I guess you would call the main entrance to the lower cave. It was a comparatively wide, flat area and looking upward, we could see shafts of sunlight filtering through the leafy canopy above. We would have been several meters below the ground.

Zakabi Yoshi led us to the cave. She stopped at the entrance, clasped her hands together and prayed. When she opened her eyes again, memories of what had happened almost four decades earlier obviously came flooding back and the look on her face showed how traumatic it had all been. She recalled a man holding a souvenir lock of his wife's hair and weeping. A soldier named Hamamatsu from Hokkaido drifted into mind. Realizing he was about to die, she said that Hamamatsu had removed his wristwatch with his other heavily bandaged hand and held it out to Zakabi saying, "This is for taking care of me."

"When I put the food beside their beds, some of them would just stare blankly at it. They were so weak they simply couldn't eat anything. Others nearby saw this and would grab it and eat it. I felt so sorry for them but there was nothing I could do."

We knew from the maps drawn up by the excavation teams from Aichi University that the entrance to the cave was divided into two separate passages, one leading to the left, the other to the right. The passage on the right continued into the Garabi shelter and with our flashlights we could see the remains of approximately six cookers right in front of us. This was the exact spot where Zakabi Yoshi used to work as a cook, preparing food for the wounded soldiers. They had the enormous task of providing for around 1,000 soldiers and, when it was dark, they would sneak out and make their way through the bombardment to collect vegetables from the surrounding fields. Initially, they were able to prepare a watery form of miso soup, but before long the food situation was such that the best they could do was make rice balls. Zakabi's mind drifted back to the days in the cave when she had been so busy handing out the rice balls and carting water.

Then, near where the cookers had been, she suddenly spotted a container overflowing with human bones. The bones had obviously been collected by one of the investigating teams, but a large number of them had fallen out of the container and were once again partially buried beneath the soft earth. The whole area was supposed to have been completely cleared, yet we also saw bones at the back of an indentation in the cave wall which had been used as a food storage area during the war. So even in the well-known Garabi-gama, where the prefectural council had completed extensive surface clearances, pieces of human bone are still being found. We asked Oshiro Shoho for his opinion. A member of the Prefectural Historical Society, Oshiro has been up to the cave on numerous occasions, guiding visitors keen to see the old battlefield site and others intent on gathering data.

"People have often found human bones sticking out from between the rocks. They always contact the Prefectural Historical Society and get us to come and gather them all up. But I'm sure there are lots of bones still completely buried. There must be plenty entombed under the rubble forever." Oshiro himself has also found various items of surgical equipment including a pair of tweezers, a hypodermic syringe, and a saw.

Next we decided to follow the cave on the left, into the area which used to be the operating theater and where the items Oshiro found would have been used. With Yoshi leading the way, we headed into the cave where the operating theater used to be. Our boots sank right down into the mud, making progress very difficult. Large amounts of soil and sand had been washed in by the heavy rain over many years and had built up so that the overall size of the cave was much smaller than it had been during the war. To prevent drops of underground water showering down on us, a tarpaulin had been stretched over the ceiling and walls like a tent.

With our flashlights, we watched Zakabi looking all around. Then her hands stopped. "Yes, this is it. This was the operating theater all right." We turned toward the sound of her voice. She was indicating an area which had been excavated and considerably enlarged. Our flashlights lit up the sole of an old army boot half-buried in the mud, but we did not find any surgical equipment.

One survivor from that cave was Nakachi Masako. Nakachi was a member of the Shiraume Student Nursing Corps from the Second Prefectural Girls' School and had been sent to help in the "operating theater" in the cave. She takes up the story.

"Whenever the soldiers' wounds became infected, the flesh would putrefy, turn purple, and swell up. We had to hold down the patients' arms and legs while the doctors used their saws to perform one amputation after another. We were just terrified and many of the girls fainted outright." They got almost no sleep but still had to continue helping as the procession of operations continued almost non-stop. Having to make do with nothing more than a quick nap each day, Na-kachi Masako and the other girls became completely exhausted. Also, the girls became drowsy as the temperature in the operating theater rose from the heat of the candles. "When we dozed off, our hands would start to shake. Then the army surgeon, scalpel in hand, would laugh at us with comments like 'Ah . . . the candle dance has started.'" The ghastly memories of being in that operating room area of the cave are still vivid in her mind.

Following behind Zakabi, we pushed on further into the cave. A quick look into the right-hand passage revealed swarms of centipedes that had attached themselves to the walls. In that same area of the cave, wounded soldiers would certainly have just lain there waiting to die. I felt a cold shiver run up my spine as I could almost hear their desperate groans in the darkness.

The back of the cave was a dead end. When the mass suicides occurred, some of the men retreated to that part of the cave and died there. We guessed that there could still be human remains lying about and wanted to get to the very back of the cave to find out. However, we were forced to stay out because the whole area was in danger of caving in.

On an earlier occasion after Zakabi had visited the cave, she developed a very high temperature and slept almost non-stop for three days. "I remembered how the wounded soldiers would grab my hand, tears pouring down their cheeks," she muttered. "Even though years later they were only a pile of bones, it really unsettled me, as though their spirits were still here." She refused to go any further into the cave.

During the Battle of Okinawa, there were many instances of civilians being killed on suspicion of spying. One such tragedy occurred in the cave. A civilian by the name of Kuwae was picked up while trying to escape to the south of the island. Suspected of being a spy, he was beheaded with a sword. Zakabi explained that "Rather than actually having any reason to suspect him at all, it seems they were just hell-bent on making him out to be spy. They threatened us saying, "If you try to stand up for him, we'll kill you."' Before he was executed, she took his personal name seal and returned it to his family after the war.

As the conflict intensified, the task of digging graves to bury the dead couldn't keep pace with the scores of bodies that were piling up day after day. Before the wounded soldiers were brought into the cave, those who were beyond help were given lethal injections and rolled to one side.

The 3rd of June was right in the middle of the rainy season. When the news came through that the American forces were very close, it was decided that those wounded soldiers who could still walk should make for the Shimajiri area. The order was given that any who could not move were to take their own lives so that they wouldn't give away information. As they headed off, Zakabi, Lt. Sato, and Sgt. Kaneyasu buried the remaining money held by the 24th Division and a list of the men's names and home towns. Lt. Sato said to Yoshi, "If you're alive and well when the war is over, you can use this money. But make sure you also check the list of names and contact their families." When the war ended, Yoshi went back to retrieve the buried items, only to find that they had deteriorated badly over the years because of the damp conditions.

Because Zakabi's home had a very large garden, an army food store had been built there. At the tender age of fifteen, she had been forced to help, her lot being to work alongside the others at the cave. She said that she cried every single day as she carried out her duties.

The groans of patients and angry shouts from wounded men filled the air. A wounded officer shouted: "Hey, get over here, nurse. My bandages haven't been changed for a week. What the hell are you lot doing?" Amid the terrible stench of sweat and pus, the nurses raced frantically back and forth to keep up with their tasks. They worked like zombies despite being exhausted from lack of sleep.

"During the day, we never got the chance to stretch out and have a proper rest. The best we could manage was to snatch two or three minutes whenever the opportunity arose. There were even times when we felt so envious of the soldiers lying there asleep that we honestly thought that it would be good to be somehow injured, just so that we could also get some sleep." That is how Nakachi Masako remembers those endless, humid days during the rainy season. At the entrance to the cave is a cairn with the inscription "Shiraume Student Nursing Corps Cave." For about a month and a half from the end of April 1945, Nakachi Masako was among that group of student nurses from the Second Okinawa Prefectural Girls' School working in the cave.

Oyadomari Masako also survived the war and told us that, "Some large rocks crashed down on top of one of the wounded soldiers lying there. He was killed instantly but nobody had the energy to shift the rocks." Omine Tomoko added her own details to the story. "There was also a soldier with brain damage who used to rant and rave for no apparent reason. He got caught in the fallen rocks and fell down. He screamed his lungs out, but nobody could help him."

As those girls worked for all they were worth, things deteriorated further. When the Dissolution Order arrived at the field hospital, it was decided that any soldier who couldn't move would be required to take his own life. Four or five years after the war ended, Nakachi Masako recorded her memories of those events.

"The night before the Dissolution Order was to take effect, a sergeant and two or three others were preparing individual doses of powdered potassium cyanide mixed with glucose powder. They didn't say a word. With only their hands moving as they went about their task, they were not in the least concerned about what was going to happen thereafter or what they should do. In total silence they went about packaging up the doses of the dreadful poison. Then all of a sudden, the sergeant let out a raucous but hollow laugh, as if to cheer up the others."

The next morning, the lethal poison was administered to all the badly wounded soldiers who were still alive. This was to prevent the wounded men from giving information about the Japanese army's strategic plans if they were taken prisoner by the Americans. Outside the cave, the rain continued to pour down. The tragedy of mass euthanasia had finally begun.

"The demeanor of those men as they waited to die was amazing. They were totally calm, as if they had resigned themselves to it all. And yet, I wonder what grief and torment they were really feeling inside . . . about their hometowns, their families, and the like. When my mind goes back to how they must have been really feeling . . . well, I just can't bear to think about it. When they called out things like, 'Hey, nurse . . . I'm going to beat the others to Yasukuni . . . please just make sure you get it right for me,' somehow I could actually sense a hint of cheerfulness."[26]

One by one, they were given their dose of poison, while those who were incapable of drinking received lethal injections. Any still alive were finished off by the sergeant with his knife. Nakachi's diary continues.

"'From Ueno to Kudan . . .' What had been faint singing gradually increased in volume. I ran out of the cave, screamed, and burst into tears. Then I heard someone shriek 'Banzai!' followed by the sound of a gunshot. One of the officers had taken his own life. A short time later when I went back inside the cave, some of the wounded men were already struggling to breathe, while others

---

26. Yasukuni Shrine was established to commemorate and honor those who dedicated their lives for their country.

were lying there with nothing but the roof of the cave reflected in their vacant eyes. They were so calm as, one by one, they waited for death to take them. An air of almost God-like spirituality pervaded the cave. Ahhh . . . we abandoned all those men . . ."

Oshiro explained that people have got to be told the history of these caves. "It is imperative that we preserve what is left of these caves as war memorials. In spite of that, the Ministry of Health and Welfare and the Prefectural Relief Department have simply not done enough to collect all the old bones and relics. Consequently, we've never been able to get our hands on all the wartime relics. Even though we've got mountains of surgical items and the like, and we've confirmed that there are many more items partially buried under the rubble . . ."

44th Independent Mixed Brigade Engineers Shelter

"Until I finally realized that the American soldiers had pulled back after their tanks had unleashed an absolutely terrifying attack on our shelter, I felt totally stunned, almost as though I was no longer actually alive," said Yoshikawa Masahiro, as he began to describe the demise of his unit, the 3rd Platoon of the 44th Independent Mixed Brigade Engineers.

Established in Kyushu, the Brigade suffered huge losses on 29 June 1944 when its transport vessel the *Toyama Maru* was torpedoed and sunk on its way to Okinawa by the submarine *USS Sturgeon*. In September that year, the Brigade was reconstituted with men recruited locally in the Nago area, and from there it was deployed to shelters located in the ruins of Itokazugusuku in the Tamagusuku area where it would play its part in the Battle of Okinawa.

After hostilities commenced, the 44th Independent Mixed Brigade's main force left the caves in Itokazu and advanced toward Shikina. It took part in the fighting at Shuri but withdrew after sustaining significant losses. From there, its remnants headed southward, turning to fight in several locations along the way until it reached the fortified shelters in Asato in Gushikami, where it would meet its ultimate fate. Yoshikawa remembers that fateful day as being around 4 June. The shelter that his No. 3 Platoon was in had been constructed by the IJA, and Yoshikawa and his comrades had occupied it after its previous occupants had moved elsewhere.

The shelter was constructed with its entrance facing north. It was about 2.5 meters in height and width, going back about 20 meters into the hill before turning to one side, making it L-shaped. The ferocity of the American bombardment caused the entrance to collapse. These days the area around the entrance is thickly overgrown, with the huge rock that smashed down inside during the fighting still lying there unmoved since 1945. The remains of the approximately thirty members of the 3rd Platoon are still waiting to be excavated.

Yoshikawa recalls that the tragic developments began to unfold on 13 June, the day before the U.S. attack, when his comrades shot at an American scout. "The enemy had no idea that we were hiding in the shelter, so our shooting at their scout triggered a response that would see the whole platoon wiped out. It was a furious assault by the Americans and, even if some of the guys managed to live through that, I don't know what happened to them afterward. Some surely must have survived . . ." said Yoshikawa, his voice tinged with emotion.

Until that fateful moment when their presence was discovered, the day had passed uneventfully. They moved to a different cave that evening, meaning dozens of them might have been given at least a temporary reprieve. On 12 June, American troops passed by the cave. Lt. Ikawa, the officer in charge of the 3rd Platoon, saw the enemy advancing southward and issued orders not to move. No doubt he had already decided that where they were was as good a place as any to die.

Yoshikawa remembers that "If that was the platoon commander's decision, then everyone in the platoon accepted it without question." But then on that fateful day, 14 June, Yoshikawa and two others were ordered to station themselves in a foxhole near the platoon's shelter. "If I'm going to die, I want it be with my friends who joined up with me," protested Yoshikawa, but Lt. Ikawa would have none of it, so Yoshikawa took first-year soldier Sakiyama from Sakimotobu and new recruit Nakasone with him to set up in the foxhole outside the shelter. This move was to save Yoshikawa's life. Around noon that day, U.S. troops, led by three tanks, advanced toward them along a narrow path between fields.

Yoshikawa recalls that just after 10:00 AM there were two booming sounds as the lead tanks fired their cannons in the direction of the 3rd Platoon's cave. The explosions caused fourteen or fifteen soldiers immediately dash out from the cave but they were all immediately mown down in front of the entrance by American machine-gun fire. Watching closely from his foxhole, Yoshikawa recalls thinking, "If they'd stayed in the cave they would have been OK. I tried to will the others not to come out." But there was nothing he could do, other than watch in dismay. "It was so sad," he said wistfully.

Before long, the cave ceiling collapsed and a large rock tumbled down the slope outside the cave, hiding the foxhole where Yoshikawa and his two comrades were hiding. "That saved my life," he said, but with the American soldiers showing no signs of moving away after dealing with the cave, Yoshikawa, now in pain from shrapnel fragments in his right arm and chest, told the other two to sit tight. They must have waited for seven or eight hours until the Americans withdrew in high spirits.

The battlefield went quiet. When the three of them crawled out from their foxhole, they saw the bodies of their comrades lying in front of the shelter entrance, now cruelly blocked by a huge rock. Toward the top of where the entrance had been closed by rocks and soil there was a small hole, probably just big enough for someone to get through, but there seemed to be no sign of anyone alive inside. "I remember thinking that there must be about thirty people inside, including Cpl. Ishihara, from Kakinohana, who had a wounded leg and couldn't move, as well as Pvt. Nakasone Katsumasa, from Motobu, but I thought that there was no way they could have been still alive." Reluctantly, the three of them fled south. Yoshikawa was subsequently separated from Sakiyama and Nakasone and has no idea what happened to them.

Yoshikawa is not the only person to return in later years to have a look at the scene. Nakasone's son Takashi has also been there. When Yoshikawa visited the Nakasone family's home in Motobu and told them about the demise of the men in 3rd Platoon, the Nakasone family all went to the visit the site in Gushikami and, although he was just a child then, Nakasone Takashi does remember that the upper part of the cave had collapsed. He says, "We couldn't collect my father's bones so instead we picked up a stone from the cave entrance. We still have it on the *butsudan* [family Buddhist altar] and every year on 23 June (the date of the memorial events held to mark the anniversary of the end of the Battle of Okinawa) we go to the site of the cave. My grandmother, who was always concerned that Dad's bones had not been recovered, passed away twelve years ago. We know that the remains are definitely in there and we want them to be dug out as soon as possible."

The *Banda-no-To* Monument to the 44th Independent Mixed Brigade Engineers Unit was erected in 1968 near the location of the 3rd Platoon's cave. The bones of more than 200 members of the unit are enshrined there.

14th Independent Infantry Battalion of the 62nd Division

In Okinawa, while the bones of over 10,000 people are buried where they died in 1945, far greater numbers than that have been interred in mass graves because it was not possible to establish their identities. Many do not know when, where and how their relatives, friends or comrades in arms were killed. But at the same time, there are many people who have that information and would like to let bereaved families and other related parties know what they saw or heard.

"I heard that he was from Kuwana in Mie Prefecture. He was a nice young man, about 170 cms tall with a pale complexion. I'd say that he was about twenty-five or twenty-six years old," said Nishihara Hiroshi about Sgt. Nakamura Kentaro.

Nishihara's house was requisitioned when the 14th Independent Infantry Battalion of the 62nd Division set up a base of operations in Gusukuma in the summer of 1944. A member of the company cooks section, Sgt. Nakamura, was around the same age as Nishihara, so the two men got on well, talking everyday about all sorts of things.

With both fond memories and sadness, Nishihara continued to recall his friendship with Nakamura: "When he first arrived he was a corporal, but was soon promoted to sergeant, so we celebrated that together. He was always smiling, a really pleasant character."

Early in 1945, the 14th Independent Infantry Battalion moved to a natural cave in Azanishihara in Urasoe. It was small, going back into the hill less than ten meters with three separate spaces inside, the middle of which was used by the cooks. Apart from army cooks, there were also local home guard members and women who helped to prepare food. Teruya Yasuko, a relative of Nishihara, was one of those women. Nishihara says that there were ten people in the cave on that fateful day.

"I think that is was 16 April. I was asleep at the back of the cave when I heard this tremendous explosion. Everything immediately went dark, so I felt my way toward the entrance. Light was coming in through a five-cm gap in the rocks and soil that had collapsed at the cave mouth, so I frantically tried to make that bigger," said Teruya, who was the only one to survive the explosion. "Sgt. Nakamura, LCpl. Tone, who was also from Mie Prefecture, Pvt. Iwase, who I think was from Iwate Prefecture, Miyagi Kameko from Gusukuma, and my older sister, Miyagi Sumi, were all killed."

The explosion was from what had been an unexploded shell at the entrance of the cave. Some soldiers had been trying to dispose of that shell when another round came in from the naval bombardment. The three trying to dispose of the shell were blown to pieces, and ten people in the cave—soldiers and women helping with the cooking—were killed instantly and the cave entrance was sealed over.

Nishimura comments: "I think it was his fiancée, but Nakamura was especially fond of a photograph of a young lady who looked very smart in her kimono.

She was very attractive. He was so happy when he showed that photograph off to us." Nishimura felt his friend's death so much that after the war he tried to find the young sergeant's next of kin through the Mie Prefectural Office and central government files to let them know how Nakamura had died, but got nowhere.

Nakamura's bones were gathered up by local people after the war and interred at the *Urawa-no-To* memorial, which is within the grounds of the ruins of Urasoe Castle. This memorial accommodates the bones of 5,000 soldiers, workers employed by the military, and civilians. Nishimura has been there many times to pray for the repose of Nakamura's soul. Every time he goes he again feels that he wants to contact Nakamura's family.

Ufugusukumui Shelter

Ufugusukumui shelter, in Koshihara, Ozato, Itoman, was used as an operational base for the 32nd Infantry Regiment set up in Yamagata Prefecture and is said to have the remains of between three-to-four hundred people still inside. As the extensive recovery of bones and remains carried out by the Ministry of Health, Labor and Welfare in 1956 made no mention of this shelter, none of these remains have been recovered.

The younger brother of Yokoyama Seiichi, of Sagae City in Yamagata Prefecture, Yokoyama Seiji, is one soldier whose body is still in the shelter. His older brother Seiichi heard of this decades later.

We heard from Hirao Masao, of Yamagata City, who was the commander of the rear guard at the Ufugusukumui shelter, that Seiji had been wounded in the arm in some fierce fighting and had then had that arm amputated in the shelter. But no one seems to have actually seen Seiji die in the shelter. With hundreds of sick and wounded men inside, it must have been a scene straight from hell. Hirao said that he came to know Yokoyama Seiji after happening to recognize that they shared the same Yamagata accent. He then matched the two brothers up upon hearing from Yokoyama Seiichi that his younger brother Seiji had died in that shelter.

Seiichi made his fourth trip to Okinawa, where he went to the Ufugusukumui shelter to pay his respects to his younger brother. After going their separate ways in 1944, forty-four years later he stood outside the shelter and called out to his brother, now at rest under the ground. Seiichi brought a photograph of his brother with him from Yamagata and placed some flowers on the ground with an apple, some rice, and saké. He lit some incense and turned on a cassette recorder, quietly playing recorded voice messages from friends and his younger sister as well as their old school song. "Seiji, I know how lonely you must be down here in distant Okinawa. The mountains back home that we used to climb, Gassan and Zao, are just the same as when you knew them." The recorded voices calling out to Seiji from the cassette recorder are all tinged with sadness. "Is there no way that we can recover his remains?" said Seiichi, picking up a stone to take home instead of his brother's bones.

Entrusted with the defense of part of the southern sector of Okinawa, the 32nd Infantry Regiment, commanded by Col. Kitago Kakuro, decided that, because of the terrain, Ufugusukumui would be the best place to make a stand. Seeing it as "Our place to die," they worked frantically to construct appropriate defensive emplacements and shelters. When finally completed, the shelter had its own power generator and water supply system and a total of 1.3 kilometers of tunnels.

As the U.S. offensive through April and May 1945 took its toll, for all intents and purposes the shelter was transformed into a field hospital as it filled with wounded soldiers carried from the battlefields of Naha and Shuri and displaced civilians. One army surgeon and five or six nurses were the central figures as they attended to hundreds of sick and wounded soldiers. The work was shared—one person would stem the flow of blood, another would apply iodine, and several people would put the bandages on. The only medicine available was iodine, so all burns and other wounds were treated just by applying iodine. Hirao describes what it was like: "Four or five out of every ten people had tetanus. They would develop a strange swelling in their abdomens that was obviously really painful. Their jaws would lock shut so they couldn't drink water properly. We soaked pieces of cloth in water and put them in behind their lips to let them drink. Lots of people died every day."

Early in June, the shelter was attacked from above and, despite having been referred to by high ranking officers of the 32nd Army as being "capable of withstanding the rigors of modern warfare," it was abandoned as its inhabitants relocated to the Kuniyoshi shelter, 1.7 kilometers away. By that stage, the inside of the cave shelter was overflowing with dead bodies, while the badly wounded soldiers who were incapable of moving were being given doses of potassium cyanide.

One person who took a particular interest in the attempts to locate the remains was Maeda Seiichi. He was the last person to see the inside of the shelter after the regiment retreated. He actually spent almost ten months in the shelter by himself from June 1945 until April 1946, after the war was over.

On the evening of 18 June, when Maeda entered the shelter with four friends from his unit, he was met with a scene of countless bodies and a terrible number of badly wounded soldiers. As the army surgeon left the shelter to join the regiment, he said, "We have given these patients syringes and drugs, so things will quiet down in about ten minutes time. I'll hand everything over to you guys now." Maeda continued: "What a load of rubbish that was! They were still alive after much longer than ten minutes had passed. When we said to them, 'As long as the country is still in one piece we will get you out of here'; they grunted replies to us to the effect that that was just what they wanted . . ."

It was not long before two of Maeda's friends died of tetanus and the other two were captured by the Americans, leaving him there by himself. He started to check out what was in the shelter and discovered a spot for personal belongings where there was a pile of *yanagi-gori* willow basket trunks, seven of which he opened to see what was inside. They contained all sorts of things such as photographs, swords, and bits and pieces of army uniforms. At night he would leave the shelter and collect U.S. Army food and other provisions. He even walked as far as Mabuni, saying that he was surprised to be able to pick up items such as coffee and cigarettes discarded by the Americans.

The inside of the shelter was full of rotting bodies covered in maggots, but Maeda says that he did not notice the smell at all. He continued to base himself in the shelter. His elder brother Nobuta came to the cave several times to urge him to surrender but he would have none it. When he finally came out of the shelter in April 1946, his hair was down to his waist, which he said obviously surprised a black American soldier—but probably not as much as Maeda himself was surprised because that was the first time he had seen an African American.

Maeda made the following comments about the war: "However much I explain the situation back then to people, they just can't understand if they haven't experienced war firsthand. It's the same for the victors and the vanquished. And the soldiers actually had it easier than the civilians . . . they had it tough."

Arakaki Shelter

The greenery so violently torn from the ground has grown back in the southern region of Okinawa now that almost seventy years have passed since the turmoil of the war. Yet, there are many people who still do not know what happened to family members who disappeared during the battle. Despite knowing roughly where a loved one spent his or her last hours, for the bereaved family, the fact that they have been unable to confirm the identity of their remains is something that troubles them to this day.

It goes without saying that there are also many people who only know that a loved one was killed during the battle, but have no idea how or where that occurred. This is despite the Battle of Okinawa being the only land battle to be fought within the prefectural boundaries of Japan.

In this context, there is something that Kinjo Kishin just cannot forget. In mid-September 1945, while they had noticed that the bombardment had come to an end, they were unaware that the war was over. Kinjo and four members of his family were sharing a shelter hidden in a small forest at the back of Arakaki with another five local civilians. They avoided starvation by gathering enough food to survive from fields of the unoccupied villages nearby.

One day, Kinjo met a Japanese soldier when he was on his way from looking for food beyond the bounds of the settlement still littered with corpses. It was the first time in a while that he had seen an IJA soldier. Then nineteen years old, the two young men talked for some time, with the soldier telling him all sorts of things, including that there was a young girl who had become separated from her family living in the same cave as him.

The next day, Kinjo and his younger brother visited the cave where the soldier was living. Located on the eastern edge of Arakaki from where Yoza-dake was visible, it was a vertical cave four or five meters deep. The soldier and a girl about ten years old were living in this cave known by the locals as Nanachu-gama. Although the girl's hair was long and unkempt and she had lost a great deal of weight, Kinjo's younger brother still recognized her as being from Arakaki.

The girl's name was Kinjo Emiko. When they were about to leave, Kinjo said to the soldier, "She's from our area, so we'll take her and look after her. There isn't much food to go around, so that would be better for you too." But the soldier said, "No, I'd be lonely by myself, so I want to look after this child." With this Kinjo and his brother gave up on taking the girl away and left Nanachu-gama saying, "We'll come and see you every so often."

Not long after that, some American soldiers came to where their cave was and attempted to persuade them to surrender. Interaction with the Americans continued for several days until finally Kinjo and his relatives decided to leave the cave and be taken captive. When they visited Nanachu-gama almost two weeks after meeting the soldier, they found Emiko there, dazed and sitting alone. They asked her about the Japanese soldier, but she told them that he had gone missing the day Kinjo and his younger brother had visited. She was saved from certain death from starvation by going into captivity with Kinjo and his family.

Kinjo said, "I later heard that Emiko emigrated to Hawaii. The soldier we met would have been about twenty-four or twenty-five, but I don't remember his rank, unit, or name. Emiko's family treated me as though I had saved her life, but I wonder what happened to that soldier."

After the Battle of Okinawa ended, almost 9,000 IJA refused to surrender and were killed in mop-up operations by U.S. forces. It weighs Kinjo down every time he hears that more bones have been found.

"Maybe Emiko knows that soldier's name. I haven't seen her since then." So the only clues to the identity of that soldier are with Emiko, who now lives overseas.

It is unclear just how many caves and shelters exist in the Arakaki area. According to Kinjo Kishin, who was among the very last people to leave one of these shelters, there were five that the IJA used and many others used by civilians, often in family groups, including Nanachu-gama where young Emiko was found in the last stages of starvation, and Minkehabugwa which sheltered the largest number of people from Arakaki.

At the end of 1944, Kinjo was drafted into the Home Guard and served as a messenger in the 32nd Army's Sea Raiding Unit (based at Nashiro in Itoman) and then the 24th Infantry Division (at Untamamui Hill in Nishihara). In late May 1945, his unit was forced southward by the ferocity of the American attacks, eventually being smashed to pieces near Yaezu-dake. "I was brought up very close to here, so I knew the lie of the land. Just about fifty meters from the U.S. lines, I crawled on my belly to the shelter where I knew my family would be. Somehow I managed to get there without a scratch on me," he recalled.

In that cave, Kinjo found his younger brother, two younger sisters and his grandmother, as well as some other relatives. There was a total of just ten people in the cave, but there were about 200 hundred others, mostly from Arakaki, living in Minkehabugwa, located right next to where Kinjo and his family were.

In May, the U.S. bombardment was so fierce during the day that it was impossible to venture out of the shelter. Into June, Kinjo would go out at night during short breaks in the bombardment and head through the ghost towns to the coast at Nashiro where the unit that he was first assigned to was based. There were many people out that night and it wasn't long before Kinjo realized that he could not get through to Nashiro, so he turned back.

"They were mainly just moving without saying anything, but there were many fleeing soldiers with swords in their hands mixed in among the civilians, and they were checking others with the password 'yama' [mountain] and its response 'kawa' [river]. It was a really ominous atmosphere and I got the impression that anyone who said the wrong thing when challenged would be killed on the spot. It was a scene from which I could easily imagine the terrible sacrifices of civilians." Kinjo recalled how in his case being in the Home Guard is what saved him.

They were always short of food in the caves and shelters. "None of us was really afraid of dying, but I can still remember those terrible pangs of hunger. We ate anything. We mixed starch with water and drank it, and there were many days when the only thing we had to eat was a very small amount of rice and water, with whatever edible wild-grasses we could find. My grandmother died from malnutrition because she'd been hiding in the cave from the U.S. attacks all that time without proper food."

The chronic shortage of food was what made Kinjo and his brother go around each of the caves in Arakaki. When the relentless bombardment dropped off in intensity toward the end of June they went to Minkehabugwa. It was full of civilian bodies, so many that it was difficult to walk without stepping on them. "They hadn't been burned or killed by a blast. There were many corpses of people who seemed to have all been killed in one go by something like poisonous gas." There was no food left in the cave.

They also went to the shelter where the IJA had set up a fortified emplacement. There seemed to be a particularly large number of dead soldiers between the shelter on the eastern side where the *Jokon-no-To* Memorial currently stands and the shelter beside the source of water for the settlement. It was dark, so they could not avoid stepping on dead bodies as they walked through this area. The farther they went, the more bodies soaked with water there were, causing them to slip when they trod on them. But they were undeterred in their search for whatever iron rations the dead soldiers might still have had on them when they were killed.

"Not long after the war, we planted potatoes in the fields, and in some places the plants would grow large leaves and potatoes as big as softballs. When we dug down under those plants there was always a corpse there. I also found several bodies in the fields on the east of the settlement, two of which seemed to be the remains of civilians." Many of the people of Arakaki had the same experiences as Kinjo with bodies still being found thirty years later in their area.

The Battle of Okinawa came to an end about one week after the fighting ceased in the area around Arakaki. Before the war there were about 600 people (120 households) in Arakaki, but that dropped to just 250 people, with the bodies of local people lying everywhere in the houses, fields, roads, and shelters. The surviving residents of Arakaki came together many times to recover remains, and by 1957 when the *Jokon-no-To* Memorial was erected, the bones of approximately 10,000 people had been recovered. However, it is unlikely that this figure represents the total number of people killed in the Arakaki area.

"The collection of remains from that area was carried out as part of the recovery process to improve the environment for living in the area, rather than for funeral purposes. First of all, we hurried to remove those in houses, then on roads and in fields, to clear the way for people to attempt to get on with their lives, to produce food, and to get somewhere on the roads," said Maeda Masatoshi, who was involved in the collection of remains at that stage.

With many of the shelters, except for those in which it was clear that family members or relatives had been killed inside, only the bodies scattered around by the entrances of those near fields or roads were cleared. In Arakaki's largest civilian shelter, known as Minkehabugwa, apparently the bodies of many people from areas other than Arakaki and those of defeated soldiers still remain uncollected. Maeda said, "The dead from the local area were retrieved by surviving family members, but the others are still there, maybe another forty or fifty bodies."

After the war, the word *go-sagui* [Okinawan dialect] was commonly used in Arakaki to mean rummaging through caves and shelters. Many local residents went in armed with oil-fired lamps to look for materials to use in their daily lives, such as for repairing or building houses. They also went into the shelters built by the military as emplacements. In the Arakaki area, there are still many shelters that were used by a range of different units during the battle. The shelter on the eastern side of where the *Jokon-no-To* Memorial currently stands was the largest of the emplacements used by the IJA. Maeda also went deep into this shelter after the war.

"After going a fair distance inside, there was a lower level again in which there were tracks on the floor and beds set up on the side. There were syringes scattered everywhere, so it may have been a hospital cave. There were quite a lot of boards and logs down there. Conservatively speaking, I'd say that there were at least 100 bodies," said Maeda.

Most of the shelters have not been visited by the local people for quite some time because there is no longer any need to try to find useable materials in the shelters, but also because of the risk of rocks falling from above and the existence in the caves of unexploded hand grenades. Also, with the likes of Nanachu-gama, work on the land to enhance agricultural production means that many shelters are destroyed as the land is developed.

In the winter of 1947, many locals came out to help collect bones at Agarib-aru on the eastern side of the settlement. When the shovel a woman was using struck a hand grenade, it exploded, killing one person and wounding several more. The locals were again reminded that retrieving bodies in areas where there was fierce fighting is a dangerous business.

On 6 December 1979, a nearly complete set of remains was discovered in a hollow in a field behind Arakaki at Namisatomonchubaka. "He had a hand grenade in his left hand and was wearing long leather boots. He'd been shot in a trench and had lain there ever since," said an official from the Itoman Municipal Office.

On 4 August 1982, Ward Chief Oshiro Hideo said that hand grenades and little bottles of oxygen for use with gas masks were scattered on the ground near the spot where remains were recovered at a little forest called Ufunimoo. When we went to visit on 16 September, near the *Jokon-no-To* Memorial there was a red plastic container sitting there full of bones from arms and legs.

Cave at Tahara

We headed toward Naha Bridge, then down the slope at Tahara. I was told, "Left there," so I drove down past a gasoline station where, on the other side of a sugarcane field, I could see a small hill covered in wild tamarind trees. "This is it. Without a shadow of a doubt, there are three bodies in there," said Uehara Yoshiko and Takara Kamado.

The two women explained that at the base of the hill known as "Tumuinusera" there are three entrances to a dugout shelter with a depth into the hill of about 5 meters, with each entrance joining up inside. Parting the tamarind bushes we looked for the entrances, but in the end could not find anything.

It was June 1945. A grenade thrown into the dugout shelter transformed it into a scene from hell. "I think that it was about the 20th of June, around noon. I remember how there were American soldiers outside with their shirts off, sunbathing and talking to each other," said Uehara. Inside the shelter she had eight of her family, all except her father, and with Takara and some others there were sixteen in total.

"I remember how an American soldier outside called out 'Teruko.' Just as I was thinking 'that's strange, there is no-one in here called Teruko,' someone shouted 'look out!' as a hand grenade was thrown in. Afterward I thought that what sounded like 'Teruko' was probably some kind of warning in English."

Those who survived the blast of the grenade hid in a pocket in the wall of the shelter. The American soldiers who came in dragged the survivors with long hair out of the cave, but the men with short hair were judged to be soldiers and were kept inside where they were then killed with a blast from a flamethrower.

Uehara may have told us her story in a dispassionate tone, but her words still conveyed her obvious feelings of anger and sadness. "It all happened in the blink of an eye. There wasn't even time for the little children to cry . . . All of a sudden my two year-old brother had disappeared, blown to pieces I suppose . . . At least the relatives of the people whose bones are in there can gain some solace from them. But it must be tough not having them for decades."

At the time we were out looking for the dugout shelter. The only one of Uehara Yoshiko's siblings still alive and well was her younger sister, Sumi. Looking at a family photograph taken in 1943, she explained what had happened to the other members of her family, one by one. "Chogoro and Chohachiro died inside the shelter, Jiro died in hospital in Goya, Taro and Mitsuko died just outside the shelter . . ."

One of the people whose remains will still be in the shelter is Uehara Kame, then forty-one years old. Her son, Koshin, said, "I had already been evacuated to the Yambaru region, up north, so I wasn't there, but I heard about it from Yoshiko and Kamado. My mother passed away, but before she died, she said, 'Make sure that you come and collect our bones.'" Before we met and talked about the shelter and what had happened there, the area surrounding it was fenced off within U.S. Army controlled land. "But now, we can get in by car, and I don't think that excavations would be particularly difficult," said Koshin, obviously keen to recover the bones of his deceased relatives as soon as possible.

Uehara Yoshiko's closing comment was, "I never want to experience war again. Best not even to have war memorial days. Those days just bring those horrible memories flooding back for all of us who have lost relatives."

Kohatsu in Nishihara

During the Battle of Okinawa, in an attempt to avoid the barrage of American artillery shells, many soldiers and civilians crowded together inside a shelter on the western side of what is now the Kohatsu Apartment Block. I visited the site guided by Toma Choei, who said, "My grandmother Toma Kamado is said to have died inside this shelter.

"It's over there," said Toma, pointing to a place just above one of the family tombs lining the side of the road. The spot that he was indicating was about 3 or 4 meters above ground, but there did not seem to be anything there resembling an entrance to a shelter. However, when Toma clambered his way up, parting the grass and ferns as he went, sure enough, there was a small hole just where he said the entrance would be.

When I said, "A place hidden like this is unlikely to have had any remains removed from it," Toma replied, "I'd say that no one knows that it's here so the remains of whoever died inside are probably still in there." Maybe the roof inside collapsed in the artillery fire, or because the passage of time had weakened the shelter, but the entrance went less than 30 centimeters into the hill. The space inside is said to have been no more than 10 square meters and it was too dark to see anything. It certainly was not the sort of place that humans would normally venture into.

Toma only found out about this shelter in 1977, when he attended a memorial service to mark the anniversary of his grandmother Kamado's death. He explained that Kamado's daughter Ushi guided him to the location. Ushi told Toma that it had been decided that the family would flee from the fighting and head toward the Shimajiri region but, realizing that age was catching up with her, Kamado said to her daughter, "You go and make sure you survive. I'll stay here in the cave and if things work out, we'll meet up later." They divided up the small amount of food they had left and tearfully separated.

Ushi is said to have left the shelter in mid-April 1945 and, judging from the fact that she only had two or three days food supplies with her, they assume that Kamado would have died from starvation soon after that, so the date 20 April 1945 is written on her grave tablet. Just a few days before that, a shell landed near the entrance to the shelter close to where her sixth son Choboku was sitting at dawn. He was killed instantly by the blast, and it seems that Kamado then decided that her life was no longer worth living.

Several caves and shelters existed in these hills that are known as Tsukinta-magusuku, and large numbers of fleeing civilians came there from places such as Naha and Yonabaru. I asked Yonabaru Choei, who was boarding at Kamado's family house near what is now the Yonabaru Police Station, about his recollections of that shelter. "If the remains haven't been recovered, I'd really like to see something done, even if it costs money to make it happen. It makes me feel really sad to think that that an old lady like that starved to death with no one to help her."

American POWs

The U.S. bombardment that had stopped around dinner time started once again. Between barrages, Taira Kichitoshi, then a member of the First Prefectural

Middle School's Blood and Iron Student Corps, was shoveling soil to help camouflage the Signals Unit facility near Sonohyan-utaki when he caught sight of something dark-colored moving under a tree halfway between Enkanchi Pond and the spot where he was working.

Upon closer inspection, he saw that it was an American pilot who must have been shot down earlier that day. The man was lying on his side, tied to the tree. In a weak voice the airman pleaded: "Water, water . . ." I went and got some and brought it over for him to drink. "After guzzling down the water, he said 'Thank you very much.' At a time when we had been taught that they were 'American and British devils,' when I came across a captive American airman, rather than hating him, I felt that I should be doing something to help him. It was just something that I felt I should do," said Taira.

Taira remembers this as having been in April 1945, and Tokuyama Chosho also saw an American airman tied up in the same spot around the same time. He says that the American was sitting facing the Enkanchi Pond.

"The upper part of his body and his face were badly burned and covered in festering sores that smelled really bad. There was a swarm of flies around him. I'd say that they had put him out there with the intention of having his own countrymen kill him in their bombardment. When, out of curiosity, I asked him in English his name and age, he replied 'Goodbye.'"

According to Uchima Takeyoshi, around March 1945, anti-aircraft guns shot down a U.S. plane, and two pilots landed by parachute near the No. 4 entrance to the Command Post tunnel complex. He said, "The two panicstricken men were shot and wounded by Okinawan recruits. Forty or fifty enraged soldiers and civilians then rushed over to where the men had come down and immediately took to them with pieces of wood and stones, killing them in no time at all."

Kuniyoshi Shin'ichi remembers seeing a dead American flier near the No. 5 entrance to the Command Post tunnel complex. It was in early May, around the time of the failed Japanese counteroffensive.

"His arms and legs had been tied to a stake and it seemed as though he had been used for bayonet practice. His head hung limply on his chest and he was covered in blood. I remember how there were people throwing stones at his body too," says Kuniyoshi. "Everyone had gone crazy. We were losing the war and, having our friends and family killed by the American forces, when people saw an American soldier they probably thought 'you bastard!' and wanted to get some form of revenge."

Makiminato Tokuzo, a reporter for the *Okinawa Shimpo* newspaper and then attached to the 32nd Army Intelligence unit says that he saw intelligence officer Capt. Hirose interrogating an American POW at the Shuri Police Station. He remembers this as having been around March 1945 and that the American pilot had a moustache and was about thirty-five years old.

Around April or May, another POW was brought into the Command Post tunnel complex. Makiminato remembers that "He had been pummeled by the soldiers on the bunks on one side of the tunnel and was dazed by the time he reached the interrogation room."

After the POW had been interrogated, the Japanese soldiers retreated to the safety of the tunnel complex and he was left alone. They tied him to a tree near Sonohyan-utaki and left him exposed to the American naval bombardment. Rumor has it that he was later killed in the Memorial Park (now Shuri Castle Park Rest Area).

Makiminato recalls hearing from an Okinawan medic that the POWs were only given food left over after the Japanese soldiers had eaten. That medic said to Makiminato, "They may be the enemy, but I don't think it's OK to be only feeding them leftover food and mistreating them."

Chapter II, Article 4, of the Hague Convention on Land Warfare concluded in the Netherlands in October 1907 clearly states: "Prisoners of war must be humanely treated." Article 7 states that ". . . prisoners of war shall be treated as regards board, lodging, and clothing on the same footing as the troops of the Government who captured them." Japan ratified this Convention and it was still in force during World War II.

While the Japanese Imperial Army in Okinawa was therefore obliged to adhere to the provisions of the Convention, Makiminato states, "In my experience I do not think that POWs were handled the way they should have been."

After the war, a number of people were sent from Okinawa to Hawaii as prisoners of war. Tokuyama Chosho was one of them.

"At first I thought that we would be killed, but it wasn't long into our lives at the POW camp in Hawaii before we realized that wasn't going to happen. The food was better than what we were used to in Okinawa, and the work wasn't too arduous. There were some Japanese POWs who refused to work until the food was improved, but if we look at that from another angle, it actually means of course that we were free enough to go on strike."

In the Military Tribunal held in Yokohama from 1947 to 1948, members of the Japanese Naval Militia on Ishigaki Island were tried for the brutal murder of three captured American pilots, but the events that occurred near the Command

Post tunnel complex in Shuri were not brought up.

Letters sent to evacuated family members

Many things give us an idea of what life was like during the war—letters are one of those. While they may have been sent at a time when correspondence was censored, they still give us an indication of many aspects of life back then. The sixteen letters sent by Hamamatsu Akira's father to his family who had been evacuated to the main islands of Japan are an invaluable testimony to the experience of a family caught up in those tumultuous times.

The Hamamatsu family managed to get everyone together in April 1942 for the first time in quite a while. Second son Iwao had graduated from Showa Medical College and was about to start his cadetship as an army surgeon in a military hospital, and third son Shigeru had returned for a break from his studies at the same institution. But that was the last time they were all to be together. The next year, 1943, their fourth son Akira entered the Tokorozawa Army Aviation Maintenance School in Saitama Prefecture and mother Emi and daughter Tamiko were evacuated to Minamata in Kumamoto Prefecture, meaning that only the father, Tetsuo, was in Okinawa working in a hospital. As the wartime situation steadily worsened, Tetsuo began to write letters to his wife and daughter from September of 1944.

> 2 September 1944
>
> I'm worried because I've had no other contact other than the telegram in which you wrote, "We've settled in, send the family register documents." I'm concerned at what might have happened because that very night that the telegram came I heard that the western parts of Kyushu had been bombed . . . It seems that the age criteria for evacuation from Naha have changed and that from now on, for both men and women, only seriously ill people can be considered. Also, the fact that the ship [the *Tsushima Maru*] that left on the 21st to evacuate children did not arrive has got the school authorities in a fix as to what to do.
>
> Received 23 September.
>
> Dated 7 September
>
> Other than the one telegram in which you wrote: "We've settled in, send the family register documents," I haven't heard anything from you at all. Worried at what your situation might be, I sent a telegram four days ago

asking, "Have the children started at new schools?" but have had no reply. I know that the western part of Kyushu has been the target of air raids, so I'm desperately worried about what might be happening. If it's difficult to get letters through, maybe it's possible to send a telegram on some pretext to let me know that you are all safe and sound. Not hearing anything just makes me worry. I wonder if one of you is sick . . . A postcard sent from Manchuria on the 21st of last month arrived here on the 31st but nothing else.

Things have settled down here and seem calm now after a hectic period, but people are being evacuated at a frantic pace. At first it seems that people left in a hurry without doing any preparation for being away during winter, but now community groups are collecting old *tabi*-socks and cushions. I suppose that they intend to use them to make futons to send to evacuees. The government says that it will look after us, but it makes me mad to see the lack of action. It's awful to think how these people will embarrass us in the eyes of other prefectures . . . I went to bed but couldn't sleep, so I got up to write this.

Received 22 September.

The father, Tetsuo, had worked in a medical practice in Siberia when he was young, so during the tumultuous times of the revolution, he had experienced street fighting on several occasions. Son Hamamatsu Akira said, "For that reason, he didn't really seem to be afraid of the prospect of war. He was just worried about his family who were living far away from him and was frustrated with the difficulties involved in communication." His father sent one more letter with the same content by another route. (Sent 11 September and received 15 September).

The Hamamatsu family as of September 1944 (age at the time)

Father: Tetsuo (52) Managing the Hamamatsu Hospital in Uenokura, Naha

Mother: Emi (51) Evacuated to Minamata in Kumamoto Prefecture in August 1944

Eldest daughter: Tamiko (27) Evacuated with her mother

Son-in-law: Hisada Tomoyuki (30) Army surgeon serving in China

Second son: Iwao (23) Serving in Burma as an army surgeon. Caught malaria, and killed when the ship that he was on was bombed on the way back to Japan

Third son: Shigeru (21) Studying to become an army surgeon cadet at the Tokyo No. 3 Army Hospital. (Subsequently was stationed in Okinawa, where in June 1945 he took his own life in the last stages of the battle.)

Fourth son: Akira (17) From August 1944, studying at the Tokorozawa Army Aviation Maintenance School

Fifth son: Hiroshi (15) After being evacuated, he entered the Hofu Naval Signals School in Yamaguchi Prefecture

Third daughter: Midori (13) Evacuated

Sixth son: Ken (12) Evacuated

Granddaughter: (4) Hisada Yumiko evacuated

Granddaughter: (3) Hisada Ryoko evacuated

Grandson: (1) Hisada Hideki evacuated (Died of illness at the end of 1944)

Nephew: (11) Kanari Kenichi Evacuated

Aunt: Higa Tsuru (76) Remained in Okinawa with Tetsuo. Died of natural causes in April 1945

Eldest son and second daughter died in their infancy.

In August 1943, following in the footsteps of his two older brothers in studying in the main islands of Japan, fourth son Akira joined the third class of the Tokorozawa Army Aviation Maintenance School. He left Naha Port on 13 July 1943 and describes his departure as follows: "The day before I left, a really large unit of soldiers arrived. The trees along the main road in Wakasa [near the port] had yellow communications wire strung through them and horse-drawn carts moving back and forth on the road carrying army supplies meant that there was a real hustle and bustle out on the streets. When we departed, the port was full of military vessels so we went from the shore to the *Kaijo-Maru* by barge."

His mother, Hamamatsu Emi, also recalls that time, saying, "Naha at that stage was just full of soldiers; there seemed to be units from Manchuria everywhere. There was real tension in the air."

The arrival of such a large number of troops affected the life of local residents. The already worsening food shortage was exacerbated by the priority now given to the military, and vegetables from the Naha area were no longer available elsewhere. "As it happens, the officers staying with us wanted for nothing in terms of food. Dinner every day was a banquet. They'd even use a military plane to go and get the specific alcohol they wanted to drink. I remember how they even had piles of vegetables that were starting to rot. Tamiko recalls, "I even complained to the unit commander that they were living like this while local people were struggling to find anything to eat." It was around this time that the family decided to evacuate to Kyushu. Even the local mayor recommended evacuation in the context of there being such a shortage of food. However, they were optimistic, thinking that things would improve and they would be able to return to Okinawa in two or three months. Mother Hamamatsu Emi planned to go to Kyushu with the children and then come back to Okinawa to be with her husband. They left in mid-August 1944.

They intended to send some luggage afterward, so they too had very little with them. "I just took three pairs of *monpe* baggy work trousers. In Okinawa, I was told off by a policeman for not wearing *monpe*, but I was surprised at what I saw people wearing in Kagoshima," said Tamiko.

> Sent 11 September 1944
>
> Yesterday, a month since you left, we were all really pleased when Muta-san (an engineer on the *Kaijo-Maru* with whom they had become friends) dropped in unexpectedly to see us. It was great to hear from him that you had arrived safely, but those air raids in Kyushu of 20 August have had me worried sick. We are rapidly becoming cut off here, with maybe one boat coming in each month. It's hard to handle the flood of government propaganda that we get here . . . With regard to luggage, I intend to ask Muta-san to take some winter clothes that you might need. He kindly said that rather than my sending two suitcases as freight, he could take them for me, so I asked him for the date and time that the *Kaijo-Maru* will sail . . . I have no thoughts of evacuating and, considering what I might be able to do as doctor when things do happen here, it would be irresponsible of me to leave Okinawa. But in saying that, don't worry because I don't think that there is going to be any great danger involved. Since the time you left, things have settled down and we can be a little more relaxed about things.
>
> Received 15 September.

Hamamatsu Emi was unable to get back to Okinawa by boat, so she had no choice but to remain in Kyushu for the rest of the war. The winter clothes that her husband sent for them arrived, but the warehouse in Kagoshima where they were stored was hit in an air raid, so they were never delivered.

While Emi had relatives in Kagoshima, it was not easy for a mother and her children to get by as evacuees. Daughter Tamiko recalls, "We collected driftwood from the shore to use as firewood and got access to a small plot of land to grow vegetables. We cut down a cedar tree in a forest and pulled it on a cart for about 12 kilometers. That was when I realized just how heavy freshly cut trees are."

Emi's own family there in Kagoshima were farmers, but said, "There was always a policeman standing on duty just outside the village, so we couldn't bring any food away from the farm. We were hungry all the time." Emi would turn down food offered by local people, and disliked the children accepting food. Tamiko said, "It was where she had been brought up, so I think she had her pride to deal with. So as a result we were hungry everyday—so hungry that we even picked up scraps of food left over by other children."

Back in Okinawa, Hamamatsu Tetsuo still knew nothing of his family's circumstances at that stage. He had given them some cash when they left and, while in his letters to his wife and children he made comments about going to hot-springs and to the sea and mountains to "broaden your horizons" or told them not spend money on meals out, his real concern was about their safety.

"It was certainly no situation for us to be going to a hot-spring. We did nothing but dig for potatoes every day. At a time when there was nothing available to buy, the money we had was really of no use to us. When we were sheltering during air raids, the children were so hungry that they would hide from me and eat their emergency rations. We were on the path to starvation." While they were living in Kyushu, Tamiko lost her one-year old son, Hideki. "It was really cold. He caught pneumonia and died within a day."

The Hamamatsu's fourth son, Akira, who had entered the Tokorozawa Army Aviation Maintenance School, was also finding life a struggle. They had run out of coal, so the barracks had no heating. In rooms in which the temperature plunged to minus four degrees, their closely cropped hair meant their scalps felt as though they were going to split from the cold, so to get to sleep they had to curl up under the futon and cover their heads completely.

There were many at the school who had collapsed from malnutrition. "We were twenty years old and there was no way that we could be made run to around all day on just one bowl of rice a day. We survived by stealing seed potatoes and radishes from nearby farms," said Akira.

He heard about the 10 October air raid the next day from a section leader at the school who often traveled to Taiwan. The man called together all the students from Okinawa and told them that Naha had been burned to the ground and that the Maruyama Department Store was the only building left standing. "About twenty of us from Okinawa went to the company commander to ask if we could be posted back to Okinawa, but were told that our duty was to complete our studies at the Aviation Maintenance School."

Their father wrote a postcard informing them about the air raid on 21 October 1944.

"After the air raids on 10 October, by midnight that same day we had safely moved all the staff and patients to Mawashi in Hantagawa and now are managing fine, getting food brought in from Asato. I won't be able to send anything to you in for a while, so you'll have to somehow get by yourselves until I can. From the 14th we have been running a temporary medical center here and are seeing patients. Don't believe all that you're told about what's happening here. Grandma is well and helping to make food every day. The insurance procedures are all underway so there is nothing to worry about."

This postcard arrived eleven days after the air raids on Naha and, while the content seems to suggest that Tetsuo was unperturbed about developments, the letter that arrived after that makes it clear that he was shocked by the way things were going. Akira recalls, "Dad always used to say that the Americans and the British were cowards, so that's why they dropped bombs from a great height or fired shells from a distance and that they never hit anything. Yet he must have been shocked when he saw the effect of the air raid on Naha." Their father had now sensed that the day when Okinawa would be transformed into a battlefield was close at hand.

Not long after the postcard about the air raid of 10 October arrived, a letter from Tetsuo was delivered by a friend. In pencil, he wrote, "There was an air raid from 7:00 AM on the 10th. There were so many enemy warplanes dropping bombs that unfortunately Naha was basically burned to the ground. I can't write the details, but don't worry, we are all safe. When things have settled down, I will start to think about how to get things up and running again." The previous bravado had disappeared and a sense of despair had clearly set in. After that, a long letter dated 30 October was received. It gives a useful picture of how things were following the air raid of 10 October 1944.

I'm not free to write about things over here, but the hospital and our house have been completely burned down, so I managed to get away with nothing more than what I had on me. At about 2:00 AM we arrived at Shikina Shrine where we set up camp and the next day the ward chief helped us set up a temporary clinic at a place called Jinnoji, so we are trying to see patients here.

Other doctors have fled north to Kunigami so I'm the only one attending to the needs of wounded people down here. Even so, it seems that rumors are going around up north that I was killed in an explosion or burned to death in a shelter. This is probably because when the first wounded were brought to my hospital, I was so busy tending to them that I lost the opportunity to get away.

It seems that the health authorities are very grateful for my efforts. In the newspapers it says that 700 people were killed or wounded and that more than 10,000 buildings were burned down. Basically, Naha has been razed to the ground, but with these local sacrifices in mind, the people of Okinawa are really proud to hear the marvelous achievements of our fighting men off Taiwan and the Philippines.

We have been worried about the air raids on Kyushu by the U.S. Air Force based in China, but have you been affected at all? Please do your best to look after the children while you're away. I had wanted to send you some raw sugar and other things on the *Kainan Maru*, but that's no longer possible.

Okinawa has been bombed to an extent that you would probably struggle to imagine. But people here are not showing any signs of folding and in fact seem more relaxed now that hostilities have actually started. I also feel better now. It's almost as though the terrible tiredness that I'd felt previously has been swept away.

The next letter dated 18 November arrived on 20 December 1944.

We are sure that there will be further air raids so we can't settle down and plan what to do to get things back on track. The newspapers suggest that the areas burned to the ground will be converted into fields to grow more food and that the construction of buildings to the regular building code will not be allowed. But we can't just sit around doing nothing, so we are thinking of trying to set something up in Makishi in the suburbs of Naha. It seems that this is where the new city center will be located.

This year has been very warm, but it is not long before it will get cold again, so people's lack of warm clothing is going to be a problem.

The American bombers based in China will probably really start to crank things up soon and the factories in Minamata will no doubt be a target, so I want you to spend some money on getting a really strong air raid shelter made. Also, even if the house is destroyed, please make sure that your entrance to the air raid shelter won't be blocked. In the air raid here on 10 October, most of the people who were killed had put too much faith in their shelters and were crushed when their houses collapsed on top of them. Apart from the great damage to Naha, Toguchi in Motobu has been totally destroyed and almost all of the ports and islands of the prefecture have been damaged to some extent. But the people are holding up well and working toward rebuilding things, so there is no need for you to worry.

It must have been a letter written with very uncertain feelings about how things were to develop. It is interesting to note from this letter that the same Makishi area that grew without any particular plan from the black market located there after the war, had been thought of during the war as the new center of Naha.

On 18 December 1944, Hamamatsu Akira was visited at Tokorozawa Army Aviation Maintenance School by his younger brother Shigeru. "I really got a surprise. When I was told that he was waiting for me in the school's meeting area, I went there to see him and was so impressed with the way he looked in his officer's uniform with his sword. I even remember saluting him as I went into the room."

They soon engaged in normal sibling conversation in which Shigeru said happily, "I'm going to be posted to Okinawa!" Akira said, "I was so envious. My older brother said how he'd be working with our father for Okinawa so there was no need to worry, but I was keen to get back there. From then on I remember how we used Okinawan dialect so we could say what we liked about the Army."

The letter that Hamamatsu Tetsuo sent 2 December 1944 was delivered to his wife a considerable time later, on 25 January 1945.

I'm worried that I haven't had any letters from you for more than two months. Has your mother returned from Korea yet? Not knowing if Hiroshi has safely joined up is also a worry that I could do without. But it sounds like the air raids by the B-29s are happening all the time over the main islands of Japan, and I think that we have seen the worst of things here. Anyway, if things do heat up further here, I'll make sure that I survive it, so don't worry. But considering that I send letters as often as I can, not getting anything in return makes me angry. Whatever is happening over there, I know it's wartime so I won't be surprised, so please let me know . . . Quite a few of the other doctors here still don't have a fixed abode and so are living out in the countryside. But there are others who seem to have forgotten the nature of their vocation and have fled to other prefectures to save their own skins. Those of us who have remained are amazed how they could leave old people behind like this and just think of their own safety."

It was around this time that, on his way to his posting to Okinawa Hamamatsu Shigeru visited his family who had been evacuated to Minamata. His elder sister Hisada Tamiko commented, "He was on his way to serve in Okinawa, so we used all the precious sugar that we had to make some sweet things for him. That was the last time we saw him." Akira and the others knew that circumstances in Okinawa were worsening to such an extent that being posted there as a soldier was akin to being given a death sentence. But their father back in Okinawa was overjoyed to hear that his son would be coming to fight there.

> 31 December 1944
>
> At first I didn't realize who he was talking about when at about 8:00 PM on the 27th Tamaki yelled out from the entrance to the house, "Shigeru-san's here!" Then when I thought, "He means our Shigeru!" and went to the entrance I found this fine looking man standing there in uniform. I had thought that he might be posted to Okinawa so it wasn't entirely out of the blue, but I had no idea that he was going to turn up that day.
>
> Grandma was so surprised that she couldn't even stand up. It was great to see him looking so splendid as a military man.
>
> We sat and talked from that point on until about two the next morning. I had been worried about all sorts of things, but was relieved to see him, but of course was truly saddened to hear about our grandson, baby Hideki, passing away. But we are at war. Adults and children may be killed at any time so I'm at least pleased to know that little Hideki was being held by his mother when he passed away. Shigeru doesn't know where he will be posted to, but for the time being it seems that he will be with the top brass in the Command Post Medical Section. He seems rather pessimistic about things, but we were given quite a bit of New Year's pork by the Akamine family, so we certainly had a good meal thanks to them.

The Hamamatsu family evacuated to Minamata in Kyushu understood from the fact that letters were not getting through that Okinawa was rapidly becoming cut off. In the early stages of their evacuation, mail reached its destination sometimes as quickly as four days, but after the New Year in 1945, it sometimes took up to two months. In Tetsuo's letter to his family in Minamata when he described his joy at seeing Shigeru back in Okinawa, he also described the onset of winter after the air raid of 10 October 1944.

> Many of the people who have lost their homes are feeling the cold because they don't have any winter clothes. Shuri and Naha are now a terrible mess, like Tokyo would have been after the Great Kanto Earthquake. As far as clothing goes, ordinary men in the street are wearing items of summer clothing over the top of their winter outfits. They have leggings on and wear straw shoes or even workmen's *tabi* on their feet and don't seem remotely embarrassed to be carrying bundles of vegetables about. In fact, it's the people wearing expensive clothes and make-up who will be embarrassed by the looks they get. At this stage, our only concern is to put food in our bellies and to keep ourselves warm. There's no point wishing for decent clothes and good food as there is none. People have just given up on those kinds of things. But, this is war and we will hold out and wait patiently until we win."

In spite of Tetsuo's delight at seeing his son Shigeru back home in Okinawa, the pessimistic tone continued throughout the letter. He tried to cheer up his family but it was easy to work out that with each passing day things in Okinawa were becoming increasingly difficult. His next letter included comments about financial matters such as the balance on their savings and buying and selling property.

> Dated 6 January 1945
>
> We are already part of the front line. Whatever happens, my only hope is that if I am to die, at least it will be in my hometown. The 400,000 people on Okinawa are different from the people in Saipan and the Philippines. We are absolutely determined not to let the enemy set foot on our home soil but, in readiness for the worst-case scenario, all sorts of shelters and emplacements have been set up. My first thought is to avoid doing anything stupid like dying needlessly. Anyway, my only concern is what's happening with you all in Minamata.
>
> Emi and Tamiko, stay as relaxed as you can. Don't worry, because this is what war is like, so instead of feeling down because the family has been split up, cheer yourselves up by going for a soak in the hot pools, even though there's a war on. It's just silly to worry about things you can't control.
>
> Received 13 January

On 10 January he wrote a similar letter. It was entrusted to Toma Shigetami who was flying out to attend a meeting and was safely delivered to his family. Also, following a letter dated 15 January and received on 10 March, one further letter was sent on 17 January.

Surprisingly, a special delivery letter dated 3 March arrived in under two weeks, on 15 March. It was the third of the eagerly awaited letters. One was sent to Kagoshima following the evacuation, one was brought by a family friend, while Shigeru brought the other one with him. All the other letters posted from Okinawa obviously went missing en route. Of course, that's how things are in wartime.

However, I never think that I won't see my wife and children again and I refuse to feel pessimistic thoughts such as we will be apart like this forever. And it's not just me. Tens of thousands of others are also separated from their families or pupils so try not to think too deeply about what is happening. Instead, cheer yourselves up with a good soak in the hot pools. Of course, I just feel really upset when I think about the hard times I've given you since we got married, the fact that we have nothing left and no home to go back to. I certainly don't think that I'll stay on Okinawa in my old age. I'd like to buy a house somewhere in Minamata and spend my days relaxing and fishing.

The fate of Japan will already be decided should Okinawa happen to fall into enemy hands. Even if I were to flee to some isolated little backwater somewhere in Japan, as a Japanese there would be nothing left for me to live for. If the army decides to issue an evacuation order, that's different, but I won't be fleeing of my own accord. And that is how the entire Okinawa population feels as well. So everybody here has cast aside their worries about the war and we are all working as hard as we can on increasing production for the war effort.

Received 10 March

Tetsuo received only three letters after his family was evacuated. Accordingly, he knew little about how they were faring in Minamata and, right to the end, his own letters reflected the frustration this caused him.

31 January

Once we get used to the air raids, things will be OK. They arrive as regular as clockwork and all I have to do it grab my emergency kit and head for the shelter. It cost almost 200 yen to build the shelter but for that I can manage two or three days at a time of living in safety.

We've organized emergency food there as well. There was also a large alcohol-fueled lamp in the shelter so we can cook rice and prepare soup as well.

It appears that the enemy have also been rethinking their strategies lately as they are not bombing the built–up areas as much. They've been concentrating on our military installations, which means that civilians have been able get out of the city without too many problems. Some soldiers are also in our shelter, from where we just sit and watch the American troops waste their shells, but there's absolutely nothing for you to worry about.

Received 15 March

The last family member to see Tetsuo's second son Iwao was his mother Emi who visited him around October 1943 while he was in Kofu before his departure. At that stage, he knew he was probably being sent to Burma, so he and his mother only managed a quick catch-up. Thereafter, he sent only one letter from the battlefield and his family never saw him again.

His fourth son Akira said, "I heard from my aunt and uncle in Tokyo that there had been an NHK Radio program about my older brother, Iwao. The program was called *A Note From Burma* and it was about a Lt. Hamamatsu, an army medical officer who was teaching Japanese to the local kids. I knew it had to be my brother."

Although he died in battle on 22 September 1944, the family did not receive notification of his death until after the war. Just before he died, a relative saw him lying on a stretcher in Burma suffering from malaria. He eventually died at a place called Kalaw during the retreat when he was caught in a bombing raid by the Royal Air Force.

Akira explained, "At that stage we couldn't imagine that an army doctor would get killed, as they were always supposed to be well back from the fighting. We received no letters—maybe because his unit's movements were secret—but Mother always worried about him."

Written 12 February

The 11th of February is Empire Day as well as our National Anniversary Festival. It is also the anniversary of the opening of the Hamamatsu Hospital and New Year's Day on the traditional lunar calendar. But this is the first time in my fifty-four years on this earth that I have had to spend the day as an evacuee, so I hardly feel like celebrating. I was sitting alone in a cold room when letters arrived telling me that Iwao was safe and sound. Although I had always tried to remain cheerful by telling myself that no news was good news, I was feeling quite despondent at getting no letters for over a year. So when I got news that Iwao was all right, I was more excited than I had ever been about anything in my life. I immediately put his letter in with this and sent it off to Shigeru. He had moved quite close to here and spent two nights here before heading back to his unit after purchasing medical supplies.

Little Yumi seemed rather sad reading the note in Minamata dialect from little Reiko. I realize that because there's a war on we simply have to endure all these hardships. At the same time, however, I also feel somewhat sad at the way life can change so quickly. If I start to think that all these hardships are part of winning a war, I need to just grin and bear it. And then those feelings get mixed in with a longing for how things used to be before all this started."

Maybe this will be my last letter. With things as unsettled as they are in the war, I don't think it's a good idea to send civilians away. It's not going to make any difference; our situation is just how things are in wartime.

It's absolutely impossible for me to send you anything from here. Also, you cannot imagine how things have changed from when you were here. Everything is so totally different from how it was before the war. We think about nothing other than finding enough food to stay alive, and all I can do is pray that this letter reaches you safely. All the middle and elementary schools here have abandoned teaching classes so when I hear about the children in Minamata still attending lessons, it sounds as if they are in a foreign country."

Received 10 March.

The postal service was falling apart, so although Iwao had already been killed in battle, subsequent mail excited the family with the false news that he was still safe. As Tetsuo had predicted in his letter, this was indeed his final contact as he found himself caught up in the turmoil that followed the American landings. He attempted to commit suicide by taking morphine, while his third son Shigeru shot himself. And that is how the Battle of Okinawa ended for them.

The only letter Shigeru sent to his family in Minamata still exists. In it he describes how Naha had changed completely as a result of the 10 October air raid.

Naha has been razed to the ground! As I walk among what are literally the ruins of our hometown, I am overcome with emotion. Nothing is as I remember it: not the town, nor the houses or the roads. Yesterday I went back to our home in Wakasa but if there was even a single wall left of that house that we all loved, I saw no sign of it. Among the pile of rubble was what looked like the pieces of my kendo mask from when I was at middle school plus bits of an old bowl that I also recognized. My blood boiled over with uncontrolled hatred for the American bastards."

Shigeru was also forced south after the Americans landed, and on 20 June he took his own life inside a shelter to the east of Nakaza in Gushikami. The whole area was surrounded by American tanks, and as Shigeru had already been hit in the leg and was unable to walk, he shot himself with his own pistol.

After the war, the Ministry of Health and Welfare sent their mother Emi a piece of a branch in a small, plain wooden box together with the official notification of Shigeru's death. She complained angrily, "Why on earth did they send this from mainland Japan when he was killed on Okinawa?"

Iwao's remains have never been recovered from Burma where he died, but the mother's resolute determination to retrieve Shigeru's remains from where he died on Okinawa endured for more than a decade and eventually led her to the site of that bloody battle in the southern part of the island. Her fourth son Akira explained, "I think she searched for his remains almost every day for seventeen, maybe eighteen, years. I wonder how many of the remains from down there have been honored in commemorative monuments."

It was also difficult to find survivors who could provide reliable comment, and just as difficult to piece together even the slightest clues. They erected a memorial cairn, but then came to the conclusion that it was in the wrong place. In the end they came across a woman who had been a cook in the shelter at the time Shigeru was killed and from there they were able to recover his remains. Akira told me what his mother said when she found her son's remains after the war. "She picked up each of the bones in the shelter then pointed to the teeth and said, 'Yes. This is him . . . no question at all. I recognize Shigeru's teeth.'"

During the Battle of Okinawa, the father Tetsuo also decided to take his own life inside a shelter at Makabe. He took five grams of heroin, far more than any lethal dose, but he was then found by some American troops who worked quickly and managed to save his life. His eldest daughter Hisada Tamiko described her father as a ". . . typical militarist but after being saved by the Americans, his outlook changed after the war."

As Tetsuo fled to south of the island, the appalling treatment of civilians by

Japanese soldiers that he witnessed really changed his thinking. At one stage he was sheltering in a cave when some Japanese soldiers arrived and yelled, "You civilians, get out of here. This place is just for soldiers." Tetsuo was furious and yelled back at them, "Your job is to protect the civilians, isn't it?" Then, before they could respond, he continued, "One of my sons is a first lieutenant and the other a second lieutenant in the Japanese Army." However, they replied with, 'Shut up you stupid old bastard.' Dad never forgot that incident," Tamiko continued. "He felt that the inhumanity of the soldiers meant that Japan could only lose the war. My father always had such respect for our soldiers so it was a massive shock for him."

As well as his two sons who were army surgeons, Tetsuo's fourth son Akira had progressed to the Army Aviation Maintenance School and his fifth son Hiroshi was also a cadet at the Naval Signals School: the Hamamatsus were certainly a "military family." Only one of the letters sent from the family at Minamata still exists today. It was written by eleven year-old Kanari Kenichi whom Tetsuo and his family had raised as one of their own.

"When I heard that you have nothing to eat down there because of the air raids on Okinawa from those American and British devils, I thought, Right! I'm going to get revenge for Okinawa at any cost. But you mustn't worry Dad. Hiroshi has already joined up so the house is now completely empty. Our Special Attack [Kamikaze] squadrons are doing fantastic work and we are going to get our revenge. Look after yourself, Dad."

Tamiko said that ever since Akira was a young boy he had loved airplanes. When he decided to go into the Army Aviation Maintenance School, he lamented that he was not going to become a pilot. "Our two elder brothers were army surgeons so, right from the start, our father always told Akira that he could do whatever he wanted. In those days, joining the armed forces was regarded as the number one public duty, so Akira volunteered to join up."

"However, after reading in the newspaper that the Americans had landed on the Kerama Islands he lost all enthusiasm. He stopped obeying his officers' commands and just became *lackadaisical*. To him there didn't seem like anything left, including his family, to defend," she explained.

CHAPTER 9

NURSE AIDES DURING THE BATTLE OF OKINAWA

In early March 1945, elected schoolgirls were formally mobilized into Okina-wa's new Student Nursing Corps. Following the 23 March air raids, the girls were issued army-style uniforms and dispatched to various medical caves and shelters, many of them so confident of a rapid Japanese victory that they took their school books with them in anticipation of a speedy return to school.[1] Furthermore, many saw the opportunity as an honor and an opportunity to contribute to the nation's cause,[2] believing in "Victorious battle . . . our army is always superior . . ."[3] Prior to their enlistment, most classes had already been canceled, and the girls were instead building gun emplacements and airfield facilities.[4] In spite of their long hours of physical labor, they pursued their basic nursing studies every evening, so tired they could barely stay awake. As with all wartime casualty lists, reported numbers in the nursing units vary. However, it is generally accepted that the total number of girls and teachers in Okinawa's Student Nursing Corps was 521, of whom 206 (including thirteen teaching staff[5]) were killed.[6]

After the Americans landed on the main island of Okinawa on 1 April, the girls were urgently dispatched to help in various army surgical units. However, rather than the basic nurse aide work they had anticipated, they were quickly allocated gruesome and dangerous tasks beyond their wildest imagination. They often worked round the clock carrying soldiers' food and medical supplies while exposed to enemy fire, excavating caves, holding candles for surgeons during operations, holding limbs during amputations which often lacked anesthetic, changing maggot and pus-saturated bandages, euthanizing and giving injections, all the while enduring torrents of abuse from doctors and patients alike.[7]

---

1. Himeyuri Peace Museum. 2004: 58.
2. Feifer, G. 1992: 183.
3. Cook, H, T., and Cook, T. F. 1992: 359.
4. Oshiro, M., 2007: 207.
5. Only Showa Girls' School and Showa Normal School included teachers in their student nursing units.
6. Hayashi, H., 2001: 272.
7. Himeyuri Peace Museum. 2002: 16-17.

Student Nursing Corps Fatalities During the Battle of Okinawa

School Name	Nursing Unit's Name	Number of Draftees		Number Killed	
		Girls	Teachers	Nursing corps	Not nursing corps
Okinawa Normal School	Himeyuri [Princess Lillies]	157	13	81	
First Prefectural Girls' School	Himeyuri [Princess Lillies]	65		42	
Second Prefectural Girls' School	Shira Ume [White Plum]	56		22	
Third Prefectural Girls' School	Naagoran	10		1	
Shuri Girls' School	Zuisen	61		33	
Showa Girls' School	Deigo [Deigo Blossoms]	31*		9	
Sekitoku Girls' School	Sekitoku	25		3	
Miyako Girls' School	No specific name	40**		0	
Yaeyama Girls' School	No specific name	16		1	
Yaeyama Agricultural School	No specific name	60		1	
Totals		521	13	193	13

Table 1: Based on Himeyuri (2004:38-39) and Hayashi (272).
*Himeyuri (2004) gives this figure as 17 ** Himeyuri (2004) gives this figure as "unknown."

Cleaning up patient feces, being splattered with diarrhea and preventing patients from drinking their own urine were further trauma the girls had to endure.[8] In spite of their innocence, they soon found themselves emptying bedpans and even "... holding the penises of double amputees to help them urinate." Before long, most of the girls were themselves seriously ill and "painfully weak" from lack of sleep and food.[9] Many were given hand grenades by the military or phials

8.   Himeyuri Peace Museum. 2004: 68.
9.   Feifer, G. 1992: 187.

of potassium cyanide by medical staff so they could take their own lives rather than risk capture.[10] Ironically, one survivor later explained, "... I hated and feared those Americans, but they treated me with great care and kindness, while my classmates, my teachers, left me behind."[11]

But worse was to come with the Dissolution Order of 18 June by which the girls were each given a small supply of food and ordered to leave the relative safety of the medical shelters. Even the badly wounded and injured girls were ordered to leave, some taking their own lives with hand grenades to avoid capture.[12] Prior to this, only nineteen Himeyuri students had been killed, but their horrific experiences in the hospital caves were now surpassed by what awaited them outside. Caught in between the retreating 32nd Army and the pursuing Americans, 80 percent of all the Himeyuri victims subsequently died in the chaos.

A month later on 19 June, many more Himeyuri students died in an early morning smoke grenade[13] attack on their No. 3 Hospital Cave at Ihara. As American troops repeatedly called the terrified occupants to surrender, Japanese medics and soldiers inside forbade them to move, insisting that they risked being raped, having their ears and noses cut off, and being flattened under tanks and bulldozers. When the Americans finally attacked the cave, there were ninety-six people inside. Many of these were Himeyuri students, of whom forty-two were killed outright, with more dying later of their wounds.[14]

Sekitoku Girls' School

It was the end of June. With the rainy season having ended, Okinawa was experiencing seemingly endless days of oppressive heat. As the tourist season approached, downtown Naha was full of young women from the mainland islands of Japan. In among them were small groups of local high school girls still in their school uniforms after the day's study. They were at an age when everything was interesting and a source of joy. In contrast to these young girls who were enjoying their teenage years, a group of women had gathered in the grounds of a temple in Naha. Because of the war, they had lost the years of their youth and now were paying their respects to their friends who died during the battle.

The people holding a memorial service on 23 June, Memorial Day [*Irei no*

---

10. Feifer, G. 1992: 471.
11. Cook, H. T., and Cook, T. F. 1992: 359.
12. Himeyuri Peace Museum. 2004: 89.
13. Probably white phosphorous as survivors recall the tell-tale signs of white smoke and choking (see Cook, H.T., and Cook, T.F., 1992: 357).
14. Feifer, G. 1992: 473.

Hi] at Daitenji Temple in Matsuyama in Naha were classmates from Sekitoku Girls' School. About 150 classmates and family members gathered to pay their respects to the forty-nine students and five staff members who lost their lives in the Battle of Okinawa.

"When I think back, we entered school with such great expectations and a good deal of pride, but our dreams faded away when the military education system made us quit our studies and become nurse's aides for the army, which then dragged us into the front lines of World War II. It makes me so sad to think that if it hadn't been for that awful war, our friends who were killed would have grown up to enjoy creating their own beautiful families . . ."

Irei Chiyo, who graduated in March 1945, spoke on behalf of the survivors, but her voice faltered as she remembered her former school friends in the days before their lives were cut short. The students at Seitoku Girls' School were attached to the 24th Infantry Division's No. 2 Field Hospital in a man-made shelter located in what had once been Tomigusuku Castle grounds. When the IJA gave ground as the American forces advanced, they subsequently withdrew to a cave in Itosu in Itoman where they were subject to an attack using a rock-drill and explosives from above, inflicting unspeakable horror on the girls.

As it happens, in comparison to the somewhat better organized prefectural schools, this private school does not have a memorial in Itoman. Despite its students having served as nurse's aides at the front in the same way as the girls from the prefectural schools, because very few who survived the ordeal spoke up about it, it seems that little was known about them. It was not until November 1957 that the Mie Old Girls' Association of survivors set up a memorial at Daitenji Temple where memorial services have been held every year since then.

But before we trace the steps of the "Seitoku Unit" during the battle, let us briefly touch upon the history of the school. Sekitoku Girls' School did not publish any yearbooks, so not only is its general history not very well known, but there are not even any lists of its students. Because of this, I spoke to Kugai Kiyo who graduated in March 1942 and went on to become the head of the Old Girls' Association. Sekitoku Girls' School was a home science girls' school established by Buddhist priests at Daitenji Temple in May 1918 to teach Japanese dressmaking, home science, and practical arts. In 1932 it relocated to Miebashi and, after receiving authorization from the prefectural office, became a private home economics girls' school in 1936. In March 1943 it assumed the status of an incorporated foundation, changing its name to Sekitoku Girls' School.

Delivery of almost all regular classes was suspended after the 10 October

1944 air raid, with the school providing its students for work constructing anti-aircraft emplacements at Kakinohana, Ameku, and Shikina or dug-in tank emplacements.

In February 1945, all fifty-five fourth-year students commenced rudimentary nursing studies, undergoing practical training in the No. 2 Field Hospital set up on the Kochinda Kokumin School. In mid-March, this training was stopped as the dark clouds of impending battle settled on the horizon, and on the night of 31 March the girls were posted as a nurse aide unit to the field hospital located in what had once been Tomigusuku Castle grounds. Their graduation ceremony was canceled.

The other day, I visited this shelter with three ladies who survived the battle. There I was told about the extreme experiences these girls had in their teenage years and which in many cases affected them physically to the extent that they ceased to menstruate.

In early April, not long after the girls were stationed at the hospital shelter in Tomigusuku, they were permitted to go to see their families, and about thirty students returned home to do so. However, because the fighting intensified from that very time on, only a few were then able to rejoin the unit in the shelter.

In the end, the nurse aide unit was made up only of the most senior students, in their fourth year of studies. These girls looked after wounded soldiers in this hospital shelter for about two months until 27 May when the order was given to withdraw to the south. Inside the shelter there were so many wounded men carried in from the fighting in Shuri, Urasoe, and Nishihara that the girls hardly had any floor space to step on as they moved around. At any one time there were about 600 wounded soldiers to attend to, far beyond the capacity of the shelter, so treatment was carried out around the clock.

Because candles were the only source of light, the wounded men were only barely visible, creating an eerie scene in the shelter. It was so humid that sweat dripped off everyone inside even without any exertion.

Nashiro Fumiko, who worked in the infectious diseases ward, still remembers the groans of agony from the men everywhere around her in the shelter.

"I remember a Sgt. Saito jumping on top of a badly wounded young soldier who was groaning in a bottom bunk and yelling at him to 'Shut up!' Eventually that same sergeant contracted tetanus and his jaw locked shut." Nashiro Fumiko remembers forcing the man's jaws apart in order to pour some food into his mouth.

There were also many soldiers who developed what they termed brain fever, plus others who walked around the shelter with bandages on the stumps of both arms that had either been amputated or blown off. Nashiro remembers a man who had clearly gone mad, saying again and again, "I'm to blame for all the power-poles being too high."

Then there were the typhoid patients who flew into a rage when they were fed rice porridge, hurling the bowls of food at the girls. Other Japanese soldiers would yell, "Get me some water!" and there were men among the wounded who would insult the girls by saying, "I hear that Okinawan girls are hooking up with the Americans now that they've landed. Maybe you girls should get out there with them too." Nashiro remembers thinking, "Why on earth are we doing our best for people like this?"

Also, the wounded soldiers who arrived at the hospital shelter day after day brought many unwanted creatures with them. The most notable of those were lice. Toshiko Uehara said, "They would latch onto the bottom of our work pants if we stopped moving. Knocking them off was hard work." She continued, "The patients who waited to have their bandages changed had wounds full of maggots. We'd grab them and throw them away as they stuck their heads out above the bandages. When we took the bandages off, the deeper part of the wound was always full of countless maggots. If we administered some disinfectant, some of them would disappear inside the wound while others would wiggle their way out and fall onto the ground. It took too long to pull each one out using tweezers, so more often than not, we rubbed the wound with a piece of gauze to get them out."

Bandages and gauze that was used from one day to the next smelled ghastly and, of course, acted as a breeding ground for more maggots. "In one night, we'd remove the equivalent of four or five bucket loads of maggots," said Kohatsu Teruko.

The girls washed the gauze in a nearby river or well early in the morning or in the evening. Often, American warplanes would attack if they spotted the girls outside the cave, so this task was fraught with danger. The place where they buried the bodies was hit by a large caliber shell, creating the macabre scene in which pieces of body parts hung from the branches of trees. But in the midst of this scene from hell, the young girls found some white lilies, which they then placed by the beds of wounded soldiers in the shelter. The women said that the fragrance of the flowers even seemed to make the wounded men forget their pain for a short time.

The No. 2 Field Hospital shelter where the girls from Sekitoku Girls' School were posted as nurse aides is located on the northern side of Tomigusuku Castle-Ruins Park, at the bottom of the slope facing the Kokuba River. It runs from south to north and overall is approximately 300 meters long. There were several entrances of about thirty meters in length connecting with the main shelter but they have mostly collapsed through the years since the war.

The first discussion of erecting a memorial near the site of this shelter was in 1980. Wheels started turning when former Army surgeon Lt. Futa Shimao, from Ishikawa Prefecture, visited Okinawa and said to Makishi Yoshiko and the other surviving Sekitoku Girls' School nurse's aides, "I can't get the people who died in this shelter out of my mind. I'd like to build a memorial so people can pay their respects to those who died in there."

After that, the women who guided me to the shelter on this occasion busied themselves talking to a range of people about having a memorial erected to those who perished in the shelter. A memorial was eventually erected in 1982, while work to restore the shelter also began at the same time and was completed in August 1983.

In stark contrast to the heat outside, it was cool inside the shelter. There were light bulbs every few meters, but they provided only dim light. Water dripped from the ceiling of the shelter onto their backs.

More than 600 wounded soldiers were in this shelter at any one time. The unit commander, Lt. Koike Yusuke, had a total of 170 army surgeons, medical orderlies, and student nurse aides carrying out treatment under his command.

The restoration of the shelter saw several survivors contribute their notes to the project. Nakazato Haru wrote, "Morning and night the treatment areas rang out with cries of pains from the wounded men and the angry yelling of the army surgeons. We just worked through this and did our best."

Onaka Kiku wrote, "I remember holding the hand of a wounded soldier as he cried out 'Mom, it hurts. Mom . . .' then he died. When I asked soldiers who had gone quiet how they felt, there was often no reply—they were already dead. When I think of these things now, it sends a shiver up my spine."

Miyagi Toyoko said, "I still cannot forget the scene in which the unit commander told us to survive and do our best for subsequent generations of Japanese people, then killed himself. Now that I have become a wife and a mother, I am really grateful to have been able to survive and enjoy the preciousness of life."

At the end of May, they were ordered to withdraw southward. Those wounded who were capable of walking were given walking sticks and told to head out, but the badly wounded men were given some water and dry biscuits and left behind.

Tears welled up in Kohatsu's eyes as she recalled the scene when they left the field hospital shelter. "It was raining heavily that night. The badly wounded patients who were to be left behind knew what was going to happen. They were resigned to the fact and just lay there in their beds, saying nothing as we left. I wanted to stay with them if I could, and while it hurt to leave them like that, I couldn't disobey orders."

Tears welled up in Kohatsu's eyes as she recalled their reluctant departure from the shelter. As they walked in single file through the pitch-dark night, she remembers crying as the faces of the men they had left behind appeared in front of her.

Through the cloying mud, they set off for the shelter in Tomigusuku for Mabuni, well before dawn on 28 May. They were thoroughly exhausted but continued to help the wounded soldiers in their care through the shellfire of the naval bombardment to go through Namihira, Yoza, Takamine, and Makabe before finally reaching their destination of Itosu in Itoman. They forced themselves to cover this distance in the space of just one night.

The relocation southward was to become a nightmare experience for these young nurse aides.

Uehara still remembers a soldier saying to her, "Nurse, how can I stop this wound on my head from bleeding?" As she trudged on without even looking back, all she could do was tell him to tighten the bandage. It was heart-rending scenes like this that forced their way back into their memories. However, back then they had no leeway to be sad about anything they were doing—their every thought was focused on survival. The place they were to seek shelter at in Itosu was a naturally formed cave known as Todorogi-no-go.

Maps created subsequently show that this cave extends as far as Ishiki and to a considerable depth. To start with, they assembled in the caves to the south such as Ukkaa-gama and Unjaa-gama.

According to Kohatsu, there was plenty of room inside the cave, but there were many stalactites hanging from the ceiling and there was thigh-deep water to wade through.

"The first thing that we did was go to the nearest village and collect some boards from deserted houses. We put those boards on top of the muddy areas beside the water, creating just enough space for the wounded soldiers to sit on. After we arrived at Todorogi-no-go with the men in our care, a constant steam of wounded soldiers arrived at the cave. The humidity inside weakened everyone and there were men everywhere with diarrhea and awful fevers."

The nurse aides also suffered from athlete's foot. They were never able to take off their *jika-tabi* [split-toed boots], so the skin on the bottom of their feet was rubbed raw.

"The soles of our feet were red and swollen. Rather than merely itchy, however, they were actually painful," said Kohatsu.

Some girls from the Second Prefectural School came to Todorogi-no-go and asked to be allowed inside. There were wounded soldiers with them so Kohatsu and the other Sekitoku girls asked the section leader what to do, but he said, "We haven't got enough food to go round so we can't look after people from other units."

Nashiro said that she will never forget a young recruit from her hometown. "His name was Hamahiga and he was one year ahead of me at elementary school in Koza. He said that he was going out on an infiltration raid so I gave him a rice ball before he left. When I saw him off, we promised each other that the next time we would meet would be under a certain tree at Goeku Elementary School. That was the last time I saw him," said Nashiro as she began to choke up.

Before long, the entire southern part of Okinawa was engulfed in the maelstrom, and by mid-June Todorogi-no-go was the target of an American attack. After the American troops managed to create a hole in the top of the cave, they hurled in gas canisters and satchel charges. The inside of the cave was immediately transformed into a scene of total mayhem.

On 17 June, more gas canisters and hand grenades were tossed into the cave, killing about 100 soldiers. "Surrender! If you don't do as we say, we'll pour gasoline into the cave and light it!" shouted the Americans to the survivors.

Uehara explained, "After that attack we had no choice but to move deeper toward the back of the cave." She continued, "When one of the medics yelled out 'Gas!' we would wet a piece of cloth in the little stream that flowed through the cave and put that over our mouths."

Kohatsu said, "There were many people who saved themselves by putting their faces straight into the water." Nashiro added, "What started as one canister of gas each day was then changed to three. It'd take about 20 minutes for the gas to move through the cave with the water, so breathing during that time was difficult. We could always see a flamethrower up through the hole at the top. The corpses in the cave were starting to rot so I remember feeling as if I was going to choke on the smell. Our food supply was gradually running out and after ten days in there all we had left was about 500 mls of brown rice and two little bags of dry biscuits. By this stage, the girls were beginning to feel that fate was not far from catching up with them. All they hoped for was to "die in an appropriate manner."

About ten days from the first time that gas canisters had been thrown into the cave, the nurse aides were ordered to assemble so that the unit commander Lieutenant Koike could address them.

"Well done for having worked with the Army for such a long time. It goes without saying that soldiers fight to the end. But you are young and have much study ahead of you, and of course you are the generation that must carry our country forward into the future. Death is not the only way to serve your country. I've got children your age and think of all of you as my children, so I can't lead you to your deaths. You have been through an experience that children from other prefectures could not even begin to imagine. I want you to live through this and to tell the young people from other parts of the country what the Battle of Okinawa was like."

Unable to hold back the tears, Lt. Koike then shook hands with each of the girls.

In the end, Kohatsu and the other nurse aides left the cave in twos or threes at intervals of several minutes. The women remember this as being during the night between 27 June and 28 June. Lt. Koike had killed himself by this point.

Sekitoku Girls' School lost forty-nine students in the Battle of Okinawa. Twenty-five had been posted to the No. 2. Field Hospital and of those, Kuniyoshi Kiyo and Yasumura Yoshiko were killed. Kuniyoshi died when she was hit by a shell near the cave in Itosu. She was a kind-hearted, athletic girl, who had been on the school volleyball team. Kohatsu remembered how she always had a nice set of white physical education clothes "ready to wear the day that our team wins the championship."

Yasumura was killed somewhere near Madanbashi after she left the cave. Uehara remembers her as "Always being positive and cheering people up regardless of how tough things were around her."

After recalling the end of the short lives of their two friends, the three women reflected on their experience of war.

As an after effect of her terrible experiences, Kohatsu developed slight asthma symptoms following the war. "The people who were affected the most were the normal people in our society. The word 'sacrificed' could not be more appropriate than for those girls who died in the battle," she said with feeling. Uehara added, "I don't know how I survived to be honest. I don't want there to be any more wars anywhere in the world."

Nashiro later said that she couldn't sleep at all that night after she had talked about her wartime experiences. Not only did the horrors she had experienced during the war reappear in her mind's eye, but so did the struggles she had subsequently experienced as a war orphan who had lost eight family members.

Showa Girls' School

By rights, young girls in their last year of school should be in full bloom; every strand of their hair shining, their cheeks flushed with a delicate shade of pink and their faces pictures of beauty. Without a doubt, they would be dreaming of their hopes for the future. During the war years, however, most of the girls in the student units are said to have had their health affected by malnutrition and stress, with many stopping menstruation until they were taken prisoner and started to receive proper food and care. The war not only took the lives of tens of thousands of people, it played havoc with young girls' physiological well-being.

The 23rd of June 1981, Okinawa Memorial Day—at the *Deigo-no-To* monument erected in Ihara in Itoman to commemorate the students of Showa Girls' School who lost their lives in the war, four women quietly took photos as they remembered their twenty-three school friends who died. On this occasion, the women had come to pay their respects to the souls of their friends who were never allowed to blossom into adulthood, withering instead as young buds on the vine. There were some flowers and a modest offering of fruit by the monument, and the delicate smell of incense filled the air.

The four women, including Takami Yukiko, Inafuku Masa and Moromikawa Mie, had been students in the 12th class at the private Okinawa Showa Girls' School. Moromikawa explained adamantly, "After the war, I saw a movie about the Himeyuri Nursing Corps. The real war was nothing like the way they depicted it. However good writers and directors are, they can't really convey the horrors of war. Only someone who has been through it can understand."

In June 1948, school principal Yamaki Taichi, members of staff, twenty classmates, and twenty members of bereaved families held their own commemorative service at Haneji Kokumin School. Other commemorative services were subsequently held, although not a great deal is known about them. Showa Girls' School was established by Yamaki in March, 1930, to the southwest of Sogenji (now known as Tomari) in Naha. It was a commercial school, specializing in preparing students to work in retail stores, companies, and banks by teaching bookkeeping, typing in English and Japanese, and how to use an abacus. Okinawa prefectural statistics of 1940 show that the school had twelve staff, 177 currently enrolled students, ninety-one students about to enter and fifty-seven students graduating.

On 6 March 1945, thirty-one students of Showa Girls' School's twelfth intake were assigned as nurse aides to the field hospital of the 62nd Infantry Division. The girls were later known as the Deigo Corps after the school emblem which featured a row of beautiful deigo trees and flowers in Sogenji where Showa Girls' School had stood. The school buildings, and all records, were destroyed during the Battle of Okinawa, so they were never able to receive their graduation certificates. The *Deigo-no-To* Monument was originally established by Principal Yamaki at the war memorial in the ruins of the school grounds at Sogenji but was subsequently shifted to Ihara in Itoman by alumni members. The original monument still exists near Sogenji.

The eight girls from No. 7 and 8 squads in the Deigo Student Corps who went south with the 62nd Infantry Division's field hospital unit and lost their lives in the fierce fighting at Ihara are honored at the *Deigo-no-To* Monument, along with fifty-four other students and teachers who were also killed in the battle. Terukina Setsuko, who was with No. 7 squad and accompanied them for part of that journey, lost her father and younger sister in the fighting. "We must never allow war to happen again. It doesn't matter how many years go by, I can never forget those who didn't make it," she sobbed. "Our friends who were killed are still really important to us. We must never let their memory fade." Her voice was heavy with emotion.

Things were still relatively quiet prior to the Naha air raid of 10 October 1944. The thirty-one girls of the Showa Girls' School twelfth intake were in a classroom at Sogenji learning first-aid theory for internal medicine and surgery from an army doctor and four or five non-commissioned officers of the 62nd Infantry Division. After completing their theory lessons, the girls then joined the 62nd Infantry Division in its hospital shelter at Akata-cho in Shuri on 6 March 1945. They stayed in a private dwelling called Yamashiro while undergoing practical training. However, before they could complete their studies, events overtook them and, while still in the middle of their studies, the girls relocated to the Nageera shelter at Arakawa in Haebara. The American forces had still not landed on the Kerama Islands at that point.

We can retrace the movements of the No. 7 and No. 8 squads of the Deigo Unit using records of the experiences of students of Showa Girls' School's twelfth intake, Inafuku Mari and Moromikawa Mie, plus Yoshikawa Hatsuko who was with the No. 7 squad for part of the way. At that stage, the seventeen girls (including Moromikawa) from the school's twelfth intake were in their fourth year. Plans for their practical nursing studies were rapidly brought forward as they shifted from the 62nd Infantry Division's hospital shelter at Akata-cho in Shuri to the Nageera shelter at Arakawa in Haebaru. That was on March 26, just before the Americans landed on the Kerama Islands. At the Nageera shelter, the girls were organized into their No. 7 and No. 8 squads. The No. 7 Squad comprised eight girls—Moromikawa, Yoshikawa, Terukina Setsuko, Gakiya Michiko, Itokazu Yoshiko—plus three more who were killed, Teruya Tamako, Shimabukuro Fumi and Oyama Masako. Of these, Teruya Tamako died inside the Nageera shelter.

Nine girls made up the No. 8 Squad, of whom only three—Inafuku, Takami Sachiko, and Yamakawa Matsu—survived the fighting. Taminato Fumiko, Noha Yae, Oshiro Kiyoko, Kinjo Hatsue, and Nakaema Yone were killed, although nobody from the No. 8 Squad actually died inside the Nageera shelter. On May 1, the Americans moved inland from Chatan, Kadena, and Yomitan but experienced stiff resistance around Tanahara. Up until the beginning of April, the only patients in the Nageera shelter were the unit's own members from its field hospital, so minor surgery for things such as appendicitis was also carried out there. However, as the fighting intensified, large numbers of wounded poured in from the front line at Sakiyama-cho, the three-way intersection leading to what is now Shuri and Haebaru.

By 17 April, the situation at the front had deteriorated and they could not accommodate any more wounded in the shelter. Unable to cope using only the main shelter, Inafuku and the other girls of the No. 8 Squad were sent to a separate, natural cave in Shikina. Moromikawa recalls what it was like: "Even though we couldn't fit any more wounded inside the shelters by then, more and more kept arriving, so all we could do was line them up on the ground in rows using every inch of space there was. There were so many wounded jammed together that we could barely walk between them. We tried to step over them but sometimes couldn't help but stand on them when we changed their dressings." It was obviously not easy for her as she continued: "I suppose the reason so many became infested with maggots is because humans are living creatures and decompose. As soon as we removed a wounded soldier's bandage, the wound would erupt with enough maggots to fill a small bucket . . . so many that we could sweep them up with a broom to clear them away." Every wound was alive with maggots, and the girls used sticks wrapped in gauze to dig them out. Then they cleaned out the pus from inside the wound, disinfected it, and repacked it with fresh gauze soaked in ribanol. However, they could only treat each wound every two or three days, so in between times it would become reinfested with maggots so the girls would have to repeat the procedure over again.

Moromikawa then explained that coping with menstruation was the most difficult thing for them. They had enough bandages and gauze so that was not a problem, but the issue was finding a "suitable place." All they had for toilets were holes in the ground that were hidden by sacking cloth from bales of rice. They never knew when they might come under fire from the enemy, and it was even worse when they were on the move. Showa Girls' School's first victim was Teruya Tamako, who died on 29 April, the night when Japanese people traditionally prayed for the long life of the emperor. It was the day the Americans attacked the shelter for the first time. Also on that day, four or five soldiers from the Accounting and Finance Section had been digging to extend the cave. However, even after Yoshikawa and the other girls had finished their shift, they still could not go inside, so they stayed at the entrance of a smaller cave, chatting and singing. Suddenly, thump . . . thump . . . thump: the ear-splitting boom caused the ground to shake. It was a concentrated heavy mortar attack which saw the girls at the cave entrance fly face-first to the ground. About the time the sound of the incoming shells ceased, Takami heard the distraught voice of one of her friends calling out the names of her comrades, one after the other.

When they lit a lamp they could see that Teruya had collapsed, bleeding profusely. "Blood was pumping from her heart like water gushing from a hose," Yoshikawa recalled. Ishikawa, the squad leader, wrapped a length of bleached cloth bandage tightly round her chest and carried her to the treatment station. However, she died there less than five minutes later from the mortar shell fragment which had sliced straight through her chest. Machida Yoshiko from Shuri Girls' School was also killed in the attack. Moromikawa, Asato Fukiko from Shuri Girls' School, Lt. Hagiwara, and another soldier took both girls outside and buried them. They then lit incense for them. "Teruya had a bright personality," murmured Terukina sadly. "She was quite small, with a swarthy complexion and sparkling eyes." On 27 May, the kamikaze planes they had been expecting from the Japanese military failed to arrive. Also, the Nageera shelter was being attacked by the Americans every day so, realizing that they had no chance of holding their position in the field hospital, they started to make their way south.

There is a naturally formed stalactite cave next to the Komyoji Temple in

Shikina, Naha. The cave was part of the 62nd Infantry Division's field hospital network, and on 17 April, Inafuku and the other members of No. 8 Squad were taken there by truck from the Nageera Shelter. Inafuku told me that with the help of articles published in the *Ryukyu Shimpo* on 25 and 26 June 1984—thirty-nine years after the war ended—she contacted some of the girls who had been in the cave with her. The articles, entitled "Nursing the 62nd Infantry Division," were about the nursing units. I visited the cave with Inafuku and we followed a hillside track to a small highland plateau that a local resident had pointed out. But all we could see were rows of houses, and it did not seem possible that there could be a deep cave in the area. However, we then went down some steps between the houses and, sure enough, we found the cave entrance. We had to bend down low to get inside. Everything was pitch black and, although it was mid-summer, the air inside the cave was cold. The faint glow of our candle lit up the jagged stalactites inside the cave. Trying to recall what is was like, Inafuku explained, "Back then there were thirty tatami mats spread out in here. The student nurse aides, the regular nurses, and the soldiers all slept and ate together here."

"Maekawa Kiyoko and Noha Yae, in the same year at school and from same village, were both killed here on 13 May." There was a beautiful moon on the night of 17 April and Inafuku and the other girls finally managed to get outside for some fresh air, barely able to believe that they were still alive. From up on top of the shelter they could see the ships of the U.S. fleet off Yomitan. From time to time, fireballs would shoot skyward and the girls would clap and yell gleefully, "Great . . . another enemy gone." But their joy was short lived as the girls were soon busy nursing the wounded brought in from the front line.

Inafuku finished her duties very late into the evening of 13 May but could not get to sleep. So, she took her needlework to the field kitchen area inside the shelter, although normally she would have been sleeping between Maekawa and Noha in the large open area at the entrance. Inafuku was wearing the jacket from Maekawa's *monpe* or baggy work clothes, while Maekawa was wearing the pants. Then a soldier came running into the kitchen area, his face as white as a sheet and on hearing him say, "The entrance has been hit!" Inafuku ran straight to the shelter entrance without even picking up her candle.

A piece of shrapnel had flown in through the shelter entrance and hit a hand grenade lying nearby. The grenade had exploded and the open area outside the entrance was blown to pieces. Maekawa was killed instantly, her insides completely exposed. Noha was still alive but the left hand side of her face from her eye socket back had been blown away. Her arms and legs were also broken in four or five separate places. She was originally from Haneji in Kunigami where her parents had lovingly raised her and her two siblings. Inafuku raced to her side, but Noha passed away as her fading voice just managed to utter her final words "If you make it back to Kunigami...." All three girls were from the Kunigami region where Inafuku's home village was in Ogimi while Maekawa was from Haneji and Noha was from Hanji. At the time, Inafuku said to herself, "If I'm the only one who makes it home alive, I'm bound to be asked 'do you know what happened to my daughter?' So that I could tell them, I wanted to bury the two girls, even if I was killed in the process."

Members of the Home Guard waited for a lull in the terrible bombardment, and Inafuku desperately followed them as they went out to bury her two friends. Up above the shelter there was a narrow path leading down to Ichinichibashi and a large pine tree. They dug a hole near the pine tree and, so that those who would eventually collect the bodies would know who was who, they placed one girl with her head facing south, the other facing north. They then wrapped the girls in a blanket and buried them. In July 1946, around the time of the rice harvest, Inafuku visited Shikina with Noha's parents. The shelter was in ruins and the pine tree was gone. Only the bare stump was still there. They turned over the rocks but the burial had taken place in the dark of night and Inafuku could not remember which girl they had buried facing north, and which facing south. Also, the blanket and the girls' hair had rotted away and Inafuku was worried that if she couldn't distinguish between the two bodies, she would not be able to return them to their parents. She carefully brushed away the surrounding soil but only when the remains were completely exposed did they find a scrap of material on one of the legs. It was from Maekawa's work clothes, the top of which she had loaned to Inafuku.

That scrap of cloth provided the clue that allowed Maekawa's parents and Noha's parents to be certain that they had taken possession of their own daughter's remains. Maekawa's voice choked and her eyes filled with tears as she explained, "Even today, both sets of parents still say to me, 'Whenever we see you, it's as if we're looking at our own daughter.' Back then, if I'd been concerned with saving my own life and not gone out of the shelter to that burial, the spirits of both girls would never been able to rest in peace." Inafuku and I looked for the pine tree but the spot is now the garage of a private dwelling and covered in concrete. On 17 April Inafuku and the girls from No. 8 Squad moved from the Nageera shelter to Shikina. Approximately one month later, Moromikawa and her No. 7 Squad set off separately for Taketomi in Kanegusuku. By the time Inafuku caught up with Moromikawa in the headquarters shelter at Itoman in June, three more of her former classmates were dead. Their suffering really began on 29 May as the U.S. bombardment intensified. As a result, the girls were forced to pull out of the 62nd Infantry Division's field hospital at Shikina where they had been working, the two squads setting off independently of each other. The wounded who could walk, walked on their own. Those who couldn't walk were assisted or carried on stretchers. They were forced to travel only at night as they made their way from Shikina to Takekomi, Itoman, Ihara and Ahagon.

The rain continued to pour down and their tired bodies felt as heavy as lead. They trudged forward, desperate to avoid being hit by the shells that seemed to be coming in like hailstones. Occasionally, they got bogged down in the muddy track. Inafuku recalled, "I had no feeling in my legs. If we slipped and fell, our clothes got covered in mud as well and it was so hard to get back up again." The girls just managed to drag themselves to Ahagon, but there they heard that the enemy was nearby so they went back along the same road toward Ihara. The shelter at Ihara was dug beside a coral outcrop but "...looked as though it would collapse if it was hit." One day as they were picking out lice from their clothing, the shelter collapsed when a shell landed on top of it. A huge rock fell and crushed the legs of one of the girls who had been at Shuri Girls' School with Inafuku. One of the nurses rushed over to help, but both were killed instantly when more shells hit.

Only barely functioning by this stage, the field hospital was abandoned when it came under fire from artillery. Inafuku and the other girls had no sooner made it to the village of Ihara then they came under heavy fire from the guns on American ships. "Hundreds and hundreds of red flaming rounds whistled past our ears." With no other choice, the girls decided to head back for the shelter but on the way Kinjo Hatsue and Taminato Fumiko became separated from the others. Inafuku explained, "I still don't know where they were killed," although records indicate that both girls died at Ihara. Inafuku was distraught at what happened but in the days that followed, she lost yet more of her schoolmates.

Under intense mortar fire, the shelter was again ripped apart. Inside, Oshiro Kiyoko, Nakaema Yone, and Yamakawa Matsu were buried alive but one of the soldiers heard the pathetic groan of someone calling out for help from among the rubble. He started digging frantically through the rocks, blood oozing from his fingernails. He found Yamakawa, her clothes ripped to shreds and barely breathing, so he immediately gave her the kiss of life and miraculously she started breathing on her own again. However, Inafuku recalled that because of the shock Yamakawa's eyes didn't focus but just stared blankly into space. "Throughout the evening, thirty mortar shells . . . yes, it would have been that many . . . just smashed the shelter to pieces." A Japanese soldier called Ito took a fragment through his chest, while a Taiwanese military laborer had his insides blown out and was killed instantly. One of the girls from Shuri Girls' School died from appalling injuries, her entire buttocks having been blown away by shrapnel.

Writhing in agony, the soldier asked Inafuku for morphine. Ito had kept some aside for the final attack, so she gave the man his injection although her hand holding the syringe was shaking wildly. "Freed from his suffering, he died peacefully just as if he was going to sleep. Back then, that sort of thing was normal," Inafuku explained sadly. Shimabukuro Fumi, from No. 7 Squad, which they had unexpectedly met up with, also had massive leg wounds. "In spite of the horrific wounds to the bones and flesh in her leg, she still somehow managed to run two or three meters to where I was to get something to stop the bleeding. Even now, I still can't believe that she did that." There was no morphine left, but Shimabukuro kept asking Inafuku, "You gave Ito an injection, why won't you give me one too. Don't leave me in agony like this . . . please give me a shot as well." All Inafuku could do was to watch over her dying friend as she writhed in agony. Inafuku's eyes glistened with tears as he recalled the scene.

The 21st June. Their seemingly endless nightmare of suffering was finally over when they were captured in a sewage ditch at Mabuni. "But I have terrible memories of it all," Inafuku explained emphatically, "Next year it will be forty years since my friends were killed and I'm working really hard on a memorial service to get some sense of closure." She continued, "There were so many bodies out there that we weren't able to carry out a proper burial. There were blowflies all over the swollen, bluish-black corpses. They no longer looked like human beings. But the thing that frightened me most was myself. It was as though I'd become some sort of hard-hearted person who couldn't cry even when I saw a dead body. I felt that I'd turned into a cold human being." Inafuku's words were hesitant and she found it difficult to explain how she felt about her horrific experiences.

Nurses at No. 3 Surgery Unit

Kinjo Shigeko had never been back to the cave shelter where she worked as a nurse at the Army's No. 3 Surgery Unit, but when she visited it with fellow former nurse Adaniya Yoshiko almost forty years later, she found that it had changed dramatically from how she remembered the place.

All those years ago, the sea below had been full of U.S. warships relentlessly bombarding the island, but now it was empty—a pleasant spring scene as waves broke harmlessly on the shore. Forty years had passed since those tumultuous days and the passage of time had seen the area around the shelter completely overgrown as though to seal in the events of the past.

The dugout shelter they took us to was on the western side of the Naha Meat Yamagusuku feedlot, in Itoman.

Kinjo could not remember the exact location of the shelter, so one of the workers from the nearby farm guided them through the thicket of long grass and bushes. They went quiet when they stood in front of the entrance, as though a scene from the past had been thrust in front of their eyes. Four decades earlier, when the two women came here after withdrawing from the shelter near Ihara where the *Himeyuri-no-To* memorial is now located, the only options left to them were suicide or surrender.

We asked Kinjo Shigeko to tell us about the time between her starting work in the Army Hospital and eventually being taken prisoner.

She commenced work at the Army Hospital in November 1944, after it had relocated to the Haebaru Kokumin School. Adaniya had had her graduation from the Prefectural Hospital Affiliated School of Nursing brought forward and was already working there. They both worked in the Contagious Diseases Ward of the hospital, which was to go on to become the No. 3 Surgery Unit.

At first Kinjo was confined to office work. "Chief Nurse Miyazaki took a liking to me and gave me work helping her in the office, but I found it tough working everyday in close quarters with the chief nurse and the army surgeon. I asked several times if I could go out and work in the ward with the other nurses, but they wouldn't listen."

So Kinjo decided to take things into her own hands, going to work out in the wards despite the fact that her job was office work. Section leader Cpl. Arakaki Matsuo told her "You'll end up in the brig if you continue doing this without orders," but she was undeterred and stayed in the wards. Chief Nurse Miyazaki was not impressed, but by the time they moved to the hospital cave shelter at Ihara she regained her fondness for Kinjo.

The fighting had already begun by the time she was out in the ward and wounded soldiers had started to flow in from the frontlines. No. 1 Surgery Unit in the Army Hospital continued as such, Internal Medicine becoming No. 2 Surgery Unit and Contagious Diseases, where Kinjo was, becoming No. 3 Surgery Unit. "The large number of soldiers with typhus or dysentery who had been there when I started going to the ward were sent back to their units," said Kinjo.

In late May, when they were forced to withdraw from Haebaru, we were told that there were more than 3,000 wounded soldiers in the complex of dugout shelters. "The order was for those who could walk well enough to withdraw on foot," says Kinjo. Those who were not capable of walking by themselves were to be left behind.

Kinjo remembers witnessing a strange scene when they withdrew from Haebaru. "Wounded men who until then had been unable to even turn themselves over in their bunk or who had been carried in on stretchers, were coming out of the shelters. There were many badly wounded soldiers following us under their own steam as we withdrew. When I saw that, I really thought that human beings are capable of doing virtually anything when they have to." She continued, "After we got to Ihara, I went back to get the ward diary that I had buried, but there was no sign of any patients there at all."

On their way back to get the diary she remembers how she came very close to death. They went at night so as not to be detected by the enemy, and that night it was raining heavily. It was difficult walking through the mud, but there was a fortuitous side to that. As they struggled to make their way through the quagmire, they heard a sound like something slamming into the deep mud. "About five meters from where we were a very large dud shell was sticking out where the ground had been turned into a sea of mud by the rain. If it had exploded, we would have all been killed." Thereafter, Kinjo would have further experiences in the battle that would see her again escape death by a hair's breadth.

When they were at the Army Hospital in Haebaru, it had been so full of wounded men that it was difficult to walk without stepping on someone, although it emptied out dramatically when the withdrawal southward occurred. Shigeko Kinjo's memories of the patients at the No. 3 Surgery cave in Ihara are unclear. When they retreated, despite it being during the night, U.S. artillery shells were hitting all the main points on their line of retreat. Hospital staff were wounded and killed during the withdrawal, so it was nothing short of a miracle that any of the wounded soldiers from Haebaru actually made it down south.

But even if the wounded men had all made it, there were not enough caves or shelters to accommodate them. Kinjo says of the No. 3 Surgery cave in Ihara, "I think that we ended up requisitioning the cave from civilians who had been sheltering there."

Before long, shells from the U.S. bombardment started falling thick and fast near Ihara. "Every day, we would take turns running to the Headquarters Cave in Yamagusuku to receive orders. Two soldiers and two nurses would go each time to make sure that we had enough people to get the orders despite maybe losing someone on the way. At night we went to get water from a well that was nearby and the section leader would use a drinking cup to give a share to everyone."

Around that time, Kinjo started to wonder what the small towel was for that she had been told to hang from her belt. When she asked, she was told that they should wet it and put it over their noses and mouths if the Americans used gas. That was all very well she thought, "Except that we had no water in our water bottles." They quenched their thirst by soaking up water on the surface of stalactites and squeezing it so it would drop into their mouths.

It was 19 June 1945. "I remember looking toward the light coming in from outside when I saw that something had just been hurled in at us. Just when I thought I'd heard something like 'OK!' something looking like a beer bottle came hurtling in. I remember how a foul smell then spread through the cave and how the section leader was shouting, 'Cover your mouths with a towel and go deeper inside!'"

At the back of the cave was an area about the height of someone standing, so we just headed in that direction, but behind us we could hear more canisters being thrown in.

She thought, "Is this gas?" It wasn't long before she was overtaken by a desire to sleep. When she drowsily said, "Corporal, I'm feeling sleepy," Arakaki yelled at her, "If you go asleep you'll die! Stay awake!" She remembers how Cpl. Arakaki slapped her across the face twice to keep her awake.

But it seemed that many people were succumbing to the gas inside the cave. Kinjo remembers hearing the noise of something being banged against the rock face and Cpl. Arakaki saying, "Shit! Another dud!" She soon realized that what she was hearing was the corporal trying to use a hand grenade to kill himself. Kinjo tried to yell, "No Corporal! Don't do it!" but that was just as she was starting to lose consciousness, so she didn't think that she managed to utter anything intelligible.

Kinjo does not know how long she lay there unconscious; "Maybe it was even a few days," she said. Luckily, every one of the hand grenades that Corp. Arakaki tried to kill himself with was a dud.

She says that she was shaken awake when the others around her were getting ready to abandon the cave. It was night when they started to move outside and, still only semi-conscious, she remembers thinking that all around her white flowers were in bloom. Just this side of death, Kinjo thought to herself, "There were white flowers in here too?"

When she grabbed hold of the ladder, she felt something soft stick to the palms of her hands, something that moved. Bodies lying on the ground near the bottom of the ladder had been there for several days and pieces of flesh had been blown onto the cave walls. She then realized that what she saw as "white flowers" were actually maggots.

The surviving staff from No. 3 Surgery Unit left the cave at Ihara two or three days after the American attack. "We sorted ourselves into a group and, with Cpl. Arakaki leading the way, we headed toward Yamagusuku. So we wouldn't lose anyone, we used twine to tie one hand to the hand of someone else. I was with Motonaga Masako, but it wasn't long before I was walking in the line by myself, says Kinjo.

Without really knowing where she was heading, and by now alone, Kinjo eventually arrived at the location that after the war would become the Naha Meat feedlot. The sun had risen, so it was light. It was the first time she had seen the sun for quite some time. And of course the sea . . . The sea was full of American warships, but the sunshine on her face somehow seemed to make her forget the mortal danger represented by those ships out on the shining water below.

"Oi! What the hell are you doing? Get in here!" she heard someone yell at her. When she looked to see where the voice came from, she saw Cpl. Arakaki's face under a piece of stone about 150cm long covering the entrance to a shelter that she would never have noticed otherwise. She rushed over and jumped in.

"The enemy won't spot a shelter like this," she thought, but later that same day, she was proven wrong. "I think they saw me jump in through the entrance after I'd been standing there looking out at the sea." They heard the sound of a metal object banging against something outside. Those in the shelter froze in anticipation. When Kinjo said, "Corporal! What do we do?" he calmly responded, "There'll be a blast now."

All of a sudden there was the boom of an explosion and Kinjo was thrown backward by the blast. which lifted her from lying on her side to a position sitting up. Her throat was parched, so she soaked the towel she had tucked in her belt in the water flowing along the little channel near where she was sitting. From that point on her memory again faded.

When Kinjo came to, there was no sign of Cpl. Arakaki anywhere. She asked someone nearby how much time had elapsed since the explosion and was told three days. When she crawled over to the entrance, some distance from where she was, it was obvious that the blast had made the hole far larger than it had been when covered by the piece of stone.

When she started to make her way back deeper into the cave, she heard voices which she recognized. There was army surgeon Lt. Tsuruta Motoyuki, Lt. Noguchi Kakutaro, and nurse Fukuhara Tsuru. It seemed as though the three of them had decided that the time had come for them to take their own lives.

Army Surgeon Tsuruta was incapacitated. Lt. Noguchi also had his legs pinned under rocks and was unable to move. Before long, Noguchi pulled out a pistol, saying, "There's nothing left but to kill myself," as he pointed it at his head and pulled the trigger. Tsuruta did not have his own pistol, so he ordered Kinjo to bring him the one that Noguchi had just used.

"There are eight rounds left in the magazine," he said quietly. "I can't do it for you, but I can show you how to do it," pointing the pistol's barrel up at the roof of his mouth. "If you do it this way, it'll be an easy death."

By that stage, Kinjo was not afraid of death. She saw it as an option available to her at any time, but dying in that cave was not for her. She said to Lt. Tsuruta, "I think I know where Cpl. Arakaki is. I want to see him again before I die." To which he replied, "You two have been like father and daughter, but there's nothing that you can do for him now. You don't even know if he's still alive," but there was no hint of him trying to force her to commit suicide. The two officers chose to kill themselves then and there, but Kinjo decided that the time was not right for her.

There was a spring inside the cave, so not only the people in that cave, but from other shelters nearby came to water to drink. One day, she noticed one of the men who came in. "He was dressed in traditional Okinawan clothing and had a belt made of twine tied around his waist." It was Pharmaceuticals Officer Lt. Takatori Shigenobu.

Adaniya Yoshiko says that she met Lt. Takatori around the 2nd or 3rd of July. Thoroughly exhausted, she remembers that when she had collapsed near the entrance to the cave, a rice bowl with water in it was sitting in front of her. She drank it down in an instant, before being asked, "Who are you?" The bowl of water had been placed there, as the man was looking for a chance to escape.

When Adaniya introduced herself as being from the No. 3 Surgery Unit, the man said that his name was Lt. Takatori and that he had been attached to the Miyako Island Army Hospital, but had been unable to return there after coming to Okinawa to transport wounded soldiers. Adaniya remembers: "Water was so precious at that stage that I thought that he would kill me for drinking his cup." The suspense of that moment when she thought that the officer would kill her was such that his name became etched in her mind.

Kinjo Shigeko remembers seeing Lt. Takatori not long before that. She had seen him in the Okinawan garb with the rough rope belt, and asked if he was in fact Lt. Takatori. When he replied that he was, she followed up by asking, "Do you know a Cpl. Aragaki?" "He's inside the cave," replied Takatori.

Kinjo spent the next few nights in that cave. Each day, she heard the sound of explosions in the cave as one after another those hiding there killed themselves with hand grenades.

It was the day that they finally decided they too would die. After dark they went outside the cave to get some fresh air, having decided to take their own lives after seeing the sunrise in the morning. It was still dark when they were woken up. "Someone's calling us." They crawled outside to find Cpl. Arakaki and the others waiting for them.

Kinjo knew that her vision had been affected by the blast inside the cave. "If we had been healthy and strong, we would have buried the dead properly... But we couldn't, so we prayed for the repose of their souls, and left," said Cpl. Arakaki. Kinjo said that she was surprised to hear from Lt. Takatori that the corporal was still alive.

The reason Kinjo had been called out of the cave was because the others were planning to try to escape by raft to Kagoshima. Someone told her that the plan was to get to Kagoshima in southern Kyushu in one night, report to the Army Hospital's unit there before telling the Army exactly where the U.S. forces were so a bombing raid could be launched against them.

When they went down to the shoreline, they saw a raft of about nine square meters made of four logs lashed together. There were over a dozen people standing nearby, including members of the Home Guard. "It'll never carry this number of people," said a soldier from outside Okinawa. When the soldier suggested leaving the women and children behind, Cpl. Arakaki replied, "These children are in my care. I can't leave them behind." In the end, the group of people split into those from outside Okinawa and those from the island, but Kinjo has no idea what happened to the raft.

After giving up on the idea of escaping by raft, the group headed north. At first, they saw dead bodies lying everywhere. Getting through the American lines seemed impossible. They even thought about stealing an American truck to do it but, as the days passed, things seemed to become easier. Their days were spent as quietly as possible in caves and shelters where they also found both clothing and food that civilians must have hidden there before being evacuated out of the area. Also the soldiers in the group managed to steal supplies from

American camps, so they were not short of food.

It happened when they were sheltering in a cave in Ozato. An American unit came to encourage them to surrender. The soldiers paid no heed, sending the women to the back of the cave and opening fire on the enemy. When the firefight stopped, Cpl. Arakaki was nowhere to be seen. They looked around for him in the dim light of the cave and found him lying on his back. He only seemed to have a small wound in his stomach, but his back was soaked in blood. So strong was their bond that Kinjo remembers shouting out, "Dad!" when she saw his body lying there.

Adaniya was captured by the Americans on 28 July, but Kinjo did not become a POW until forty days after that, on 9 September. By then a school had been built and there was a ward office administering the new lives of the civilians.

Haebaru Army Hospital

Kuniyoshi Noboru had been hit in the leg and couldn't move. He spent each waking moment plagued with feelings of hopelessness. "I thought that there was no way I was going to get out of there if Japan were to lose the war." The perpetual darkness of the shelter meant that those inside had little idea if it was night or day. It felt as if all they were doing was waiting for death.

Koganemori in Haebaru. Some forty shelters were dug out of the lower parts of the hill at short notice once they realized U.S. landings on Okinawa were inevitable. The Okinawa Army Hospital, or what was more commonly known as the Haebaru Army Hospital, moved into these shelters on 23 March 1945.

Kuniyoshi came into the Hospital Shelter "at the end of April or the very start of May." Rain turned the soil into mud, so walking through the shelter was like stepping into a paddy field. Wounded soldiers slept in makeshift bunks packed in the shelter.

He is not sure exactly what shelter it was, but Kuniyoshi says that he was placed on a bed 30 or 40 meters into the hill. He said that there were people whose bodies were burned all over, others who had gone mad and were rolling around naked in the mud, some who urinated and defecated where they lay and some who were lying there literally covered in maggots. "All night the air was full of the groans of men deeper in the shelter. It was hell on earth."

There was not enough medicine to treat the wounded so amputations of legs and arms were carried out without anesthetic. "Treatment wasn't possible there and, rather than doing anything to care for the wounded men, it was more a matter of simply keeping them all together in one place."

The only moments of enjoyment were to be found in eating rice balls made from brown rice. The men were given one rice ball twice a day, but there were always some who tried to take two, leading to noisy arguments breaking out.

"People are unpredictable when they are really hungry. Starvation rules out what we think of as normal judgment," said Kuniyoshi. He also occasionally snuck a second rice ball into his hand as he took his proper allocation of one ball. He said that the only way to hide what he had done was to shove both in his mouth at the same time so the others wouldn't notice.

Kuniyoshi said the Himeyuri Student Corps nurse aides "were really dedicated in trying to look after us." But the wounded soldiers felt they had been prepared to sacrifice themselves for the sake of the country. "There were also Himeyuri girls who were reduced to tears by the selfishness of some of the soldiers."

The only time in the darkness of the cave that they actually felt as though they were still in this life and not the next was when the nurses came up to them holding a candle to ask, "How do you feel?" The light of the candle in the darkness seemed to offer the slightest glimmer of hope. Just as all hope was starting to fade, that flickering light gave Kuniyoshi enough desire to survive.

Young girl flees with mother

During the final weeks of June 1945 as the Battle of Okinawa was drawing to a close a woman and her daughter were taken prisoner in an empty house in the village of Fukuji, near Cape Kyan in the southern part of Okinawa. The mother, Makato, was seriously wounded but her fifteen year-old daughter, Tomiko, although slightly built, was a tough young girl and was as well as could be expected in the circumstances. Several days before their capture, Tomiko's mother had sustained multiple wounds as shell fragments ripped into just about every part of her body, including both her arms, legs and her back. It was a miracle that she was still alive, although by the time they arrived at the internment camp she was barely conscious and seemed close to death. The daughter squeezed the juice of sugar cane into her mother's mouth but she was already close to death, and without the medical care she so desperately needed the woman soon passed away. Tomiko Ota is now older than her mother was when she died. She remembers that as her mother passed away, she screamed out "Mother! Mother!" over and over again, cradling the dead woman's head. Tomiko's experience is not uncommon among those who survived the Battle of Okinawa.

Early in April 1945, Tomiko and her mother Makato abandoned their family home at Jitchaku in Urasoe and fled to a shelter at Sueyoshi in Shuri. It wasn't really a shelter as such, however, but rather an old tomb halfway up a rocky outcrop. Already seeking refuge crammed inside the tomb were Tomiko's grandmother Kamado, her older sister Shizuko with five children, including one still being breast-fed, plus her younger sister and sixth daughter Fumiko. Then, when Tomiko and her mother also arrived, things became really cramped as they all had to fit inside the tomb with a floor space of just seven and a half square meters. Another sister Chiyo, who had married into a family at Sueyoshi, was killed by an artillery shell around 22 April. She brushed past her husband as he tried to stop her going out to wash the baby's diapers. But the blast from the shell killed her instantly. Her husband looked around for her right leg but couldn't find it. When the grandmother saw the dead body, she almost went out of her mind. It was the first time Tomiko's family had lost one of their own right in front of them, and the distress was overwhelming. Sensing that the horror of war was closing in on them, they started making preparations to move to the Shimajiri area in southern Okinawa.

The nightmare began on the evening of 29 April, the emperor's birthday. Tomiko remembers the date clearly because she and her older sister's children were singing the emperor's traditional birthday song. During a lull in the thunderous bombardment, Tomiko and her mother went out to the shelter entrance to begin preparing the evening meal on a cooking fire that had been set up there. They pushed away a headstone and were then both able to sit down. The children's faces had grown pale after being inside the dark shelter for days on end. They went outside to urinate but then immediately scampered back into the middle of the shelter, which sloped downward about 30 centimeters from the entrance. Immediately afterward, the roar of an incoming shell boomed out. Tomiko and her mother were facing the entrance as they worked so they did not initially realize that the shell had landed directly on top of the shelter they were in. But the next minute, they could hear the voice of Tomiko's slightly built sister Shizuko calling out "Mother, Mother." Surprised they looked around and as they did so a second shell landed on the same spot. The pressure of the second blast was so great that they couldn't open their eyes and the cooking fire ended up covered in soil that had been thrown up. The shelter had collapsed and there was no sign of any of the family. They had all been buried alive by the second explosion. Tomiko and her mother who had turned deathly pale yelled out the other girls' names, but there was no response.

At a loss as to what to do, Tomiko went to seek help from relatives in a nearby shelter. When the men tried to dig through the rubble with hoes and shovels, an IJA sergeant major who was with them stopped them. "No chance of anyone being alive underneath all that dirt," he said. "It'd be different if you could work safely, but you can't. Leave it as it is and think about the safety of the others." At the time, Tomiko said, "I was sure that they would be still alive and I wanted to dig them out immediately," but she could not disobey the soldier. In that single incident, her mother lost eight family members, and overcome by grief, could do nothing but weep and wail.

Early the next morning—30 April—Tomiko and her mother Makato paid their respects to those who had been buried alive. They stood in front of the shelter and after placing offerings lit incense and prayed toward the earth piled up before them. Makato wept as she called out to her dead family. "Grandma, Shizuko . . . this is the way war is so please try to understand. We want to give you a proper burial, but each time we try to get you out, shells come flying in and it's too dangerous. Please wait. We're going down to Shimajiri now so watch over each other and we'll come back for you once it's all over." That evening, they fled for the second time. Chiyo was already dead, but around ten of her in-laws teamed up with Tomiko and her mother and they all set off on foot on their journey southward.

From Yogi in Naha, they bypassed Kokuba and arrived at Tsukazan in Hae-baru, and from there they slogged their way as far as Shitahaku in Kochinda. They rested for around ten days at Yoza in Itoman before moving on again to Nakaza in Gushikami. That was where Tomiko saw a ghastly sight. "I could hear someone on the muddy road groaning so I stopped to see what it was. There was a Japanese soldier writhing in agony and I realized that one of his eyeballs was hanging out of its socket."

Tomiko then recalled another incident, although she could not remember which village it was. "There was this girl—I think she might have been Kore-an—shouting out over and over again that she was afraid of dying. People who say that are probably very close to death. It was in the middle of the night and everybody was sound asleep when suddenly we came under artillery fire and the girl was blown to pieces. A man picked up what he thought was a rock and found that it was something covered in warm, thick blood. He was horrified when he realized that it was the girl's decapitated head with long black hair attached." Amid all the chaos, Tomiko and her mother then realized that they were now on their own. They eventually arrived at Fukuji after making their way through various villages such as Itoman, Ishiki, and Makabe. It was June by then and everything Tomiko experienced during that time is still firmly etched in her mind. "On the west side of the village there was a large sugar refinery. A few days earlier, when I arrived there carrying my mother because of her wounded leg, the refinery was already inundated with refugees. We had no choice but to go into an empty house nearby surrounded by *gajumaru* [banyan] trees." By then, Makato's leg wounds were full of maggots and the U.S. naval bombardment continued to send shrapnel flying in all directions. The locals from the village had all fled toward Cape Kyan, and Makato urged her daughter to leave with some women from the village, but there was no way she would leave her wounded mother. "It's OK mother, I'm staying here with you," she replied.

The following morning, Tomiko witnessed a grizzly sight. "I heard that the sugar refinery we had tried to escape to the previous day had burned to the ground. I rushed over to have a look, only to find around fifteen dead bodies, all hideously burned. Their upper torsos were sticking out above the rubble of a stone wall, their mouths wide open. Their faces were burned jet black and their black lips were wide apart, I guess because they were screaming for someone to come and help them." The state of the bodies suggests they had been hit by an American flamethrower. As though seeing the ghastly scene again in her mind's eye, Tomiko turned her head away, but has never been able to erase the memory of the refinery and those fifteen bodies, burned beyond recognition.

Several years later when Tomiko was doing some work for the U.S. military, she spotted a photo of that tragic day at the sugar factory. A Sgt. Taylor of the U.S. military had the photo and Tomiko recognized the scene immediately. She begged Taylor to give her the photo but he refused and put it straight back in his wallet. "I still find it upsetting," she explained. "Although it was over thirty years ago, he should have let me have it just so that I could have a print taken from it. I've never seen anything as ghastly as that day at the sugar factory."

Each day the naval bombardment intensified. One evening, an incoming shell shook the ground and the house where Tomiko and her mother Makato were staying started to lean to one side. The kitchen had taken a direct hit and Tomiko screamed out to her mother but there was no reply. A woman grabbed Tomiko by the hand and led her away saying, "Your mother's dead. Come with me and we'll escape to Kyan." But Tomiko's sole concern was her mother. "Okay, I'll just go and get my things," she replied, but in fact went back to where her mother was lying on her back, her face covered in black soot. She opened her eyes and whispered, "I've been hit again." She was obviously badly wounded and lifted up her kimono to reveal multiple wounds where shell fragments had hit her arms and legs. Tomiko recalled the scene. "She was bleeding badly and I didn't know what to do, so I wet a piece of cloth and wiped the soot off her face. I could now see her face properly . . . it was all skin and bone. I remember feeling so sad." Makato kept telling her daughter to get away quickly toward Kyan, but Tomiko had decided to stay with her mother until the end.

That night Tomiko walked about looking for somewhere else for them to seek refuge in the village of Fukuji. Most of the locals had already begun to leave for Kyan, but that journey would be impossible for Tomiko if she was carrying her mother. She remembers that as she continued her search she heard the voices of what sounded to be a married couple coming from inside a house. "So if I die or get wounded," the man was saying," you'll just leave me here and get away as best you can, yeah." The woman replied, "What else could I do? We've got no idea which of us might get hit, so there's no point in talking about it." With the smell of gunpowder hanging in the air, Tomiko, under the eaves of the house, strained to hear the conversation.

In the morning she found a small air raid shelter surrounded by a rock wall in the burned out ruins of a private dwelling. After Tomiko put her mother down she remembers feeling that her back was wet. "Have you wet yourself?" she asked, but received only a faint "Dunno" in reply. Just then, from inside the rock wall where they were hiding, Tomiko spotted an American tank firing round after round into a copse of trees at Yamagusuku. She recalls that before long, from the direction of Cape Kyan a group of people who had been captured walked out in single file, waving strips of white cloth attached to sticks. Some of the prisoners didn't even have loincloths on and so were stark naked. All the while, Tomiko whispered what was happening to her mother lying beside her.

At the same time, American soldiers shot and killed some Japanese soldiers who had not surrendered or were hiding in houses. Finally, an American soldier naked from the waist up approached the shelter where Tomiko and her mother were hiding. Taken completely by surprise when Tomiko walked to the entrance and raised her hands, the soldier leveled his rifle at her. There was no more than ten meters separating the two. Then, with his rifle still raised, the soldier beckoned at Tomiko to move toward him, but she answered, "No; you come over here." She tried to explain with hand gestures that there was another person sleeping inside the shelter but the soldier did not appear to understand. Maintaining the distance between them, the hand signals continued for several minutes. "I guess he was worried in case there were some Japanese soldiers inside. But I started to feel frightened of his suntanned face and his big eyes, so I decided to do as he said and go with him."

Her mother was watching as the scene was unfolding, when Tomiko squatted down beside her and said calmly, "I have to go now. The soldier is getting angry." The soldier then fired a shot, which hit the rock face behind Tomiko and ricocheted away. "I've got to go," she added, "He's just shot at me." Reluctantly Tomiko made the difficult decision to leave her mother behind and go with the soldier. There were dead bodies everywhere and the stench was appalling. When they came to a spot quite some distance from the village they were suddenly joined by a dozen or so others who had also been taken prisoner. One of them, an elderly woman, tried being friendly toward the soldier by offering him some brown sugar. The soldier refused so the woman ate some herself to show him it was all right. He refused again but then took something from his own pocket and held it out to her. This time it was the woman who refused, warning the others, "Don't eat it. It might be poisoned." All the while, Tomiko was concerned only about her mother. Walking at the back of the line of prisoners, Tomiko made sure that the soldier was facing forward and then spun round and ran off as fast as she could. "I was terrified that I might be shot from behind," she added.

She went back to where she had left her mother. Hearing the approaching footsteps, her mother called out "Tomiko!" hoping it was indeed her daughter. "I'm back," Tomiko replied, to which Makato responded feebly, "When you left I was so worried that I would just lie here until I starved to death." So although she had always told her daughter not to worry about her, she must have been overjoyed by Tomiko's return. "When I saw how glad she was, I was just so pleased I'd gone back," explained Tomiko. "I guess it was that sense of duty a child has toward her parents."

Early on the morning of 25 June, some Okinawans arrived outside the air raid shelter carrying a stretcher and accompanied by the American soldier who had been there the previous day. "I was so surprised that I had to look away," Tomiko said. Then he stared at her, the look on his face saying, "This is the girl I supposedly took away yesterday. How did she get back here?" The Okinawans and the soldier lifted Makato up and placed her on the stretcher, while the soldier gave her some canned food to eat. "The fighting has finished," Tomiko explained to her mother. "No more noise from guns and no more shells falling on us."

The captured civilians bounced around on the back of the truck for a long time until they arrived at an internment camp near Zayasu in Tomigusuku where there was a large tent full of wounded people. Tomiko immediately tracked down the soldier in charge of medical treatment and pushed and bustled him over to where her mother was. She pointed out all the wounds on her mother's body, but all the soldier did was sprinkle white powder on them and cover them with bandages and tape. The end was not far away for Tomiko's mother.

Makato was clearly slipping away and was barely able to keep her eyes open. Tomiko opened her mother's mouth and squeezed the juice of some sugar cane inside. It wasn't long, however, before her mouth wouldn't open at all. Fearing the worst, Tomiko immediately fetched the American soldier back and asked him to give her mother an injection. However, the army surgeon looked into both of her eyes and left the tent without saying a word. Tomiko rocked her mother's head in her hands and called out to her over and over again, but there was no response. On two previous occasions Tomiko had thought her mother was already dead, but this time Makato really had passed away. A short while later, an Okinawan nurse arrived and, after feeling Makato's hand and neck for any sign of a pulse, called for a stretcher. Wondering where they were taking her mother, Tomiko tried to follow them but was ordered to remain in the tent. Peering outside, she could see an American soldier digging a large hole this on side of a small hill. Tomiko squatted down, her arms wrapped around her knees. Emotionally dazed, she realized that they were going to bury her mother in that hole. Tomiko was finally alone although surprisingly she shed no tears.

After the war Tomiko visited the spot where her mother had been buried. She approached locals living in the area who told her that bones had appeared from time to time. The area was now densely covered in ironwood trees, so what had happened to the bones that had been recovered? Clearly, Makato's remains would also have been retrieved so Tomiko wanted to know where they were. We asked the *War Victims' Relief Bureau* at the Tomigusuku Council to look into the matter and discovered that some bones had been recovered around twenty years earlier and put into the ossuary at Shikina in Naha. They were later moved to the National Okinawa War Victims' Monument at Mabuni in Itoman.

Sometime later as she was visiting Fukiji in Itoman, Tomiko recalled those days of the war as she walked about searching for the house where she and her mother had sought refuge. She found the place where she had seen the charred bodies, and a young farmer told her that the sugar refinery had been rebuilt after the war but that all signs of it had long since disappeared. The site was now a large field. "Right next to it," explained Tomiko, "was a large, deep well so there was no doubt that it was the site where the sugar refinery had stood." She also picked out the house where she and her mother had taken refuge and where they had both been captured. Kawakado Nobuyoshi's family had lived in the house before the war but had already fled to the coast at Arasaki by the time Tomiko and her mother found their way there. Still drawing on her memory, she went around the back of the house and found the spot in one corner where the air raid shelter had been. "This is where I hid with my mother," Tomiko began explaining to Kawakado and his wife. She looked out at the area now covered with the greenery of banana trees. One by one, the things Tomiko will never forget from the Battle of Okinawa came flooding into focus.

Tomiko lost most of her family during the war. Eight were killed in the explosion at Sueyoshi in Shuri, while her eldest brother was killed on a boat somewhere in the South Pacific and her immediate elder sister was killed working as a civilian for the 62nd Infantry Division. Her father fled via a different route but to this day she has no idea what became of him. When her mother finally died, Tomiko found herself spiritually and mentally exhausted.

Schoolgirls' group suicide

The girls wept as they sat in a circle at the top of the cliff, far from the roar of the waves breaking over the rocks below. As one of them said wistfully, "Before I die, just one more time, I want to be able walk around in the light of day," the others started to sing the song *Furusato* ["Hometown"].

The sound of sobbing was mixed in with the girls' attempts to sing. They were all doing their best, but none had the energy to hold a tune. It was so dark that they could only just make out each other's faces but, even so, they could see glistening tears rolling down their cheeks.

"I'll never forget everyone's voices that night," said Miyagi Kikuko who, by a strange twist of fate, avoided the nightmare of compulsory group suicide that befell her friends. Then she went quiet as she remembered how her friends died.

On 19 June 1945, fleeing from the relentless advance of the U.S. forces, Miyagi and her friends reached Cape Kyan at the southernmost tip of the main island of Okinawa. There were twelve of them altogether. Nine were First Prefectural Girls' School third or fourth year students who had been co-opted into the Himeyuri Student Corps, as well as two graduates of the school who were living nearby and asked if they could join them. The oldest member of the group was a teacher, Taira Matsushiro.

There had been more of them two months earlier when the Himeyuri Student Corps had been divided up as the group was sent to work near Haebaru and Tsukazan at the Accounting and Finance Section of the 32nd Army Medical Corps. They had then withdrawn toward the southern part of the island in the face of fierce fighting, moving to the First Surgery Cave at Ihara, Itoman, where, just over a week later on June 18, they received the heartless order to dissolve their Student Units. This meant that they had to leave the shelter of the caves and go out into the maelstrom. Several of them lost their lives as they made their way to Cape Kyan, and others went missing.

It was dark by the time they arrived at Cape Kyan. Miyagi recalls that scene. "It was raining heavily that night. Just before reaching the cape we had been desperately searching for two teachers, Ishikawa Yoshio and Nakaima Sukeha-chi, who seemed to have had gotten separated from us. We had been walking all around the area in the dark, oblivious to the pandanus thorns sticking into our legs as we went.

"Sensei! Sensei!" the girls yelled into the night, but there was no reply. Again they burst into tears. Rather than easing, the rain intensified. With no sign of the two teachers, the girls' expressions changed to one of resignation, followed immediately by a wave of fatigue.

The next morning, when Miyagi woke up and looked around, she was shocked by what she saw. There were bloated corpses, covered in maggots, everywhere. "Come to think of it, the water I drank last night did smell," she thought. They leapt up and rushed in the direction of the shore.

When the twelve surviving members of the Himeyuri Accounting and Finance Section, including Miyagi Kikuko, hurried down to the shoreline away from the clifftop where they had unknowingly rested among scores of bloated corpses, they saw that the area was already jam-packed with people who had fled from the fighting. There were students there from the Women's Division of the Okinawa Normal School who had been recruited into the Himeyuri Student Corps just as Miyagi and her friends from the First Prefectural Girls' School had been. Hordes of people were resting near the waterline in a large inlet.

Among the crowd, Miyagi caught sight of Nakasone Masayoshi who had been in charge of the group from the Normal School. "He was covered in blood. I'd seen him once the previous night but, in the dark, I hadn't realized that he was wounded. When I saw him in the light of day, I could see that his face was deathly pale. He didn't utter a word and just lay there on a rock looking exhausted." Several of the Normal School students were gathered around him, so Miyagi and her friends felt relieved that there was nothing more that could be done beyond what the girls from the Normal School were already doing.

After a while, Miyagi caught sight of an American landing craft approaching the shore. The American soldiers on board were all waving their arms and shouting something that seemed to be a call for them to surrender. "We won't cause you any harm!" "We'll help you, so come out to us!" Miyagi's recollection of what happened next made her shudder.

"We had it in our minds that if we were caught they would have their way with us . . . that all sorts of terrible things would happen to us. Then they would take advantage of us before killing us by running us over with tanks. We'd been taught from a young age that all Americans were devils incarnate."

The girls huddled over, trembling at the thought that the American troops were about to come ashore and attack them. Holding their breath in expectation, they sat there transfixed with fear. This continued for four or five hours, during which time their terrified trembling never let up. Unable to endure it any longer, they eventually ran away from the rocky shore and went back to the pandanus grove. But, not long after they settled down there, the group came under attack from a flamethrower. Amid the suffocating smoke from the trees that were now on fire, and finding themselves surrounded by a wall of flames, the girls were forced to flee again.

With little or nothing on their feet, once again they clambered down that precipitous slope toward the rocky shore. "By this time, our senior from school, Seragaki Emi, and Tomiko, who was in the same fourth year as the rest of us, were both wounded. I felt sorry for them because they were both clearly in agony as they made their way over the rocks. But of course there was nothing that we could do for them other than encourage them to keep going."

There certainly seemed to be nothing safe about the shoreline either. "We thought that it wouldn't be long before the American troops would pick us off." With this in mind, they thought that the best thing to do would be to try to get through along the coast from Cape Kyan northeast toward Minatogawa in Gushikami. So, terrified at what might be ahead of them, they crawled along on all fours below the towering cliffs on a day that Miyagi still clearly remembers.

"I wonder how far we crawled like that. It's such an unnatural position. It left us absolutely exhausted. When we stopped, we saw Japanese soldiers off in the distance. They were yelling at us. 'Are you idiots or what!' they yelled. 'Do you think that girls, children, can get through from here?' 'You haven't got a chance!' they shouted."

The girls looked at each other. The waves beating relentlessly against the rocks at the bottom of the cliff seemed to be getting stronger. "Now's the time. Sensei, let's climb up the cliff from here," said one of the group. They must have shuddered as they looked up at the distance to the top of the cliff.

"It was an incredibly high cliff, but we toughed it out and climbed to the top. When I think about it now, we must have been unbelievably strong and determined to get to the top. And that was where the group suicide took place . . ."

There were twelve of them in the group, friends who had been together for all of the previous two months. When they had all reached the top, one of the third-year students said imploringly, "Kaneshiro-san (Miyagi's maiden name), it's time to kill ourselves. We've got to kill ourselves." Trying to calm the younger girl down, Miyagi replied, "We can wait a little longer. I'd say that the girls from the Normal School are around here somewhere and maybe we can link up with the teachers because Mr. Nakaima and Mr. Ishikawa are probably looking for us too." Miyagi recalls, "She was a serious young girl. From the previous night she'd been saying that it was time for us to take our own lives."

According to the diary that Miyagi kept, the date that they decided to kill themselves was 20 June 1945.

Night fell and through the murky darkness they could make out countless warships out on the sea below them, no doubt all with their guns pointed toward the coast. But there was no escape to be had across the land behind them. They would soon fall victim to the flamethrowers. There was nowhere left for them to go.

"A message was blaring through loudspeakers on the U.S. warships again and again. The ships and boats were very close to shore and we could see people on them beckoning to us to come out to them. But in our minds, it was as though the devil was inviting us into hell. We were sure that if we were caught, we would all be torn limb from limb."

At a loss as to what to do, the girls sat in a circle at the top of the cliff and looked out to sea. "What shall we do?" said one of the girls. As though there were no other option, someone from the circle replied: "Suicide."

"Yeah, we kill ourselves."

By now, the teacher Taira Matsushiro, who had led the group of eleven girls so far, seemed resigned to their fate. The girls sitting in a circle nodded as they swallowed in trepidation.

However, the fact that there was only one hand grenade among the whole group now became a point of concern as to whether it would suffice to kill them all. "It's something I heard about after the war," said Miyagi as she led into an explanation of how they came to acquire the grenade.

"Not far from where our group was sitting there was a man by the name of Tengan. Hirayoshi, the teacher, had earlier given him a hand grenade with which to take his own life. It seems that Hirayoshi went over to the hole where Tengan was hiding and got him to return the grenade, saying, 'The one grenade we've got won't be enough to kill twelve of us.'"

Hirayoshi brought the grenade over and handed it to Miyagi, saying, "Kaneshiro, you hold one of them . . . This should do. If worst comes to the worst, you are to hold this against your midriff and jump in the middle of the rest of the group. If we do it that way, everyone should be able to die."

Miyagi said that she remembers replying, "OK," in a totally matter-of-fact fashion. With them having decided that they were to take their own lives, they now got ready to discard the last belongings they had with them. One by one, Miyagi took the contents out of the first aid bag she had kept with her since joining the Himeyuri Student Corps and threw the items into the dark sea below. In the bag there was also a rolled-up family photograph taken before she joined up. It too was swallowed up by the waves down below.

Miyagi Kikuko recalls: "But there were some things that even in those circumstances, I could not bring myself to throw away."

One of those was her diary. That she can recall the dates and numbers of people involved so clearly is thanks to the fact that she kept this diary. "I wrote down everything that happened each day. There was just no way that I could bring myself to throw that away."

She also decided to keep her fountain pen and some of the documents she had on her. They were things that she had been looking after for the teacher Ishikawa and, while they were not of particular importance, she stuffed them into the breast pocket of her army jacket. But most of the things that she had with her, she threw away to hide "evidence" from the enemy. "This included the notebook of signatures that all my classmates had signed on our graduation day. Until then I'd been carrying it with me so lovingly . . . " Such things, including her family photograph, were thrown from the top of the cliff and claimed by the sea.

It was pitch-dark. Itarashiki Yoshiko whispered, "I wish I could meet Dad and Mom again before I die." The sound of sobbing could be heard from among the circle of girls.

"Before long, we started to sing *Furusato*. I don't know who started it, but gradually everyone began to join in. We gave it our all . . ." said Miyagi as she recalled that moment. She continued to describe the girl Itarashiki.

"She was an only daughter. She was the same year as me at school, a very attractive young girl. It really hurts when I think back to her saying 'I wish I could meet Dad and Mom again before I die.' It was such a shame."

With the end approaching, that night one of Miyagi's seniors, Higa Mitsuko, laid out all the rice she had left in front of them. "I'll cook this up for you," she said, scooping it into a rice cooking pot and starting a fire with something like pandanus leaves.

"The rice was old and smelled moldy. She cooked it using salt water, so it wasn't something that you'd normally be able to stomach. But we were just so hungry by this stage. Higa Mitsuko told us to eat the rice and gave each of us some in our hands. Everyone did their best to force it down, crying as they tried to swallow, but the smell was just too much for me. There was no way I could eat it all and, while I felt bad about leaving it, I had to leave some."

The girls sitting in a circle soon found a hole in the cliff which they climbed into and lay down. "We were dead tired, but we couldn't really get any sleep," recalls Miyagi.

Eventually, dawn came and the sun came up and shone brightly on them. The hole the girls had found the previous night was quite small and uncomfortable. "Me, third year student Higa Hatsue, and the teacher, Mr. Taira, ended up sticking out from the hole, basically standing up . . ."

The three of them could now be clearly seen by American soldiers, who had closed in on where they were. Where Miyagi stood just outside the hole in the cliff that her friends had squeezed into, she could see Japanese soldiers being fired on in the sea down in front of her.

"This was when the U.S. warships were still blaring out messages for people to surrender. I think that they must have been shouting things like: 'C'mon, swim out to us!' and 'We'll help anyone who swims out.' Hearing that, one of the Japanese soldiers near us started to swim out toward a landing craft. One of the other Japanese soldiers on shore yelled out "You coward!" and shot at him from behind. His shot hit the soldier trying to swim out and immediately the water around him changed to a deep red."

A Japanese soldier shooting one of his comrades—Miyagi describes herself as watching this awful scene "through dispassionate eyes." She explains: "Days on end of being caught up in all the killing meant that I'd become numb to it all. I was not in the slightest bit fazed by a terrible scene like that . . . it makes me think how frightening war is."

It seems that the soldier who had been shot and killed was a Korean military worker. "I knew because he was dressed a little differently, rougher than the regular Japanese soldiers. In those days, Japanese soldiers derogatively referred to Koreans as *Hanto-jin* [someone from the Peninsula], so Miyagi recalls that she just looked on thinking nothing more than that a *Hanto-jin* had been killed.

The sun shone straight down on Miyagi as she sat there in a daze. Just as she absentmindedly thought, "Is it midday already?" things started to happen.

"Enemy!" yelled a Japanese soldier covered in blood as he suddenly rushed into the depression in the rock face where Miyagi and the others were. Three of them were still outside the confines of the hole. The teacher, Hirayoshi, forced his way into the hole where the other nine students were, and Miyagi and Higa instinctively dived into a smaller hole directly opposite the others.

A second later, American soldiers fired wildly in their direction and the small depression in the cliff became awash with blood. Miyagi recalls the horrific scene that seemed to occur in the blink of eye.

"They just shot blindly at us. The hole that the two of us jumped into was where some girls from the Normal School were hiding. A girl called Yoshiko Afuso, who was near the entrance, was killed instantly. She groaned as blood poured out of her mouth and then she toppled sideways onto me. Just as I was saying 'Are you OK?' to Yoshiko, around me, Normal School students Kamiji Ichiko and Nakamoto Mitsu also went down, head over heels."

As people died one after another, those who were wounded but still alive could be heard crying, "That hurts, it hurts . . ." With the groans of the dying and the smell of blood, the small hole was transformed into a veritable scene from hell.

Miraculously unscathed, Miyagi describes the scene in front of her. "I was saved by the fact that I was surrounded by all those around me who were killed instantly because they were on the outside. I survived basically because they were shielding me.

The mayhem that she had just been caught up in distracted her from any concerns about what had happened to her group from the First Prefectural Girls' School. Similarly, she had thought nothing about the teacher Taira, who had jumped in among the other girls.

Some time passed before she saw that in the hole opposite where she was, Taira and her ten friends had killed themselves.

Miyagi came to her senses when someone screamed out, "Get the wounded out!" The person yelling out was Mr. Yonamine, a teacher from the Normal School. "As I was startled out of my daze I realized that I was holding a hand grenade firmly in my hand. Remembering that I was supposed to be with my school friends who were going to kill themselves, I leapt up and headed for the next hole, where they were."

Miyagi dashed out of the smaller hole into which the American soldiers had fired blindly, killing some of the girls, only to be surprised with what was there in front of her.

"There were American soldiers with guns everywhere. When I tried to get past them to go to where my group was, I was surrounded and had guns pointed at me. At this point, Higa Hatsue, who was standing beside me, shouted, 'Kaneshiro-san [Miyagi's maiden name], put the grenade down!' I wondered for a second what I should do, but after looking at the expressions on the American soldiers' faces, I quickly put it down on the ground."

Miyagi explains how the American soldiers then pointed their weapons away from her. But when she looked over toward the hole where Mr. Taira and the girls from her high school had been, she was so shocked by what she saw that she felt as though her heart was going to stop. The teacher and the ten girls with him had committed group suicide.

"When I went over to look, I could see Mr. Taira lying on the ground surrounded by the girls, all lying limp and inert around him. Pieces of flesh were all around. The face of one of the third year students was just covered in blood. I remember that I was so shocked that it didn't seem to register, so shocked that I didn't even shed a tear."

Miyagi stood there for some time transfixed by what she saw, but after a while she regained her composure and started to clamber down the cliff a little way. As she did so, she saw more bodies. This time it was Yoshiko Itarashiki, who the previous night had talked of wanting to see her mother again one more time, and fourth year students, including Miyagi Sadako and Futenma Chiyoko, who were lying there dead.

"They were lying there with their faces undamaged. I remember that they looked beautiful, even in death." In addition to the girls mentioned above, there were others, including fourth-year student Miyagi Tomiko; third-year students Kinjo Hideko, Zamami Shizue and Hamahiga Nobuko; and Higa Mitsuko, who had already graduated, and Seragaki Emi. Higa and Seragaki heard about the Himeyuri Student Corps after its formation and asked if they might be included, but they ended up losing their lives.

Hamahiga was Miyagi's best friend among the group. The night before the girls took their own lives, she had been terrified of what would happen if they were captured, saying, "They'll murder us if we're captured, so the sooner we take our own lives, the better."

Hamahiga Nobuko's father had died when she was very young, and her mother had brought her up doing work around the home until she was old enough to go to the First Prefectural Girls' School. Miyagi says, "I remember how, on the day of the entrance ceremony, Nobuko came to school with her mother who said me, 'Please look after my daughter' when it was decided that we were to be in the same dormitory room."

"Nobuko's mother had centered her life around her daughter so, not long after the war was over when she heard that Nobuko had died, she emigrated to Argentina in South America."

More than thirty years later, when she came back to visit Okinawa, Miyagi guided her to the Arasaki Beach cliffs where her daughter had lost her life. Miyagi recalls how Hamahiga's mother had said, "I thought that if I were to come back to Okinawa, memories of my daughter would come flooding back and that it would be too much for me. That's why I had never been able to return. But I'm now relieved that I've been able to come to the place where she died."

After seeing where her school friends had killed themselves and finding herself unable to move from the shock, Miyagi was again surrounded by American soldiers with weapons in their hands. One of them took her prized fountain pen from her, saying it was an *omiyage*, [souvenir].

"It was precious to me. I'd been looking after it for one of the teachers, Mr. Ishikawa. The previous night, when we had thrown our belongings away, I hadn't been able to bring myself to part with it, so I'd put it away in my pocket."

Miyagi recalls painful memories. "The American soldiers didn't seem to be white Europeans, nor were they black. Maybe they were Hispanic. I still remember their faces clearly, and the fact that they used the Japanese word *omiyage*. I remember them saying 'Hey, school girl' to me."

The girls all had the same bobbed hairstyle and wore the same clothes. Maybe the American soldiers had already heard that they were a student unit. "As the Americans were ribbing me, I started crying and then just couldn't stop the tears." While Miyagi was sobbing, the American soldiers were carrying out the wounded from the behind the rocks. Not far away, a girl she recognized was lying perfectly still. An American soldier holding a syringe came over, about to inject the girl in the arm.

"They're going to kill her!" thought Miyagi, so shocked at what she saw that she instinctively jumped to her feet. The soldier trying to give the injection appeared to be a medic and seemed to be saying that he couldn't get the needle into one of the girl's veins.

"We had only ever been taught that we would be ripped apart if we were ever caught by American soldiers. He may well have been a medic, but I was so frightened that I couldn't watch what he was doing."

As this was happening, one of Miyagi's seniors said, "Let me try it," taking the syringe from the medic and injecting what must have been saline solution into a vein in the girl's arm. "I suppose that saved her life," said Miyagi.

The camp just outside Itoman that Miyagi was taken to was full of displaced civilians. She had thought that all the residents of that area must be dead and that it felt really strange to be walking in front of these people whom she had thought had all been killed.

"I had thought I was the only person to have survived, so seeing these others around me was a real surprise. I wondered what had they been eating to stay alive. They didn't look that well, but there were people there sitting around talking to each other. I remember that there was an area surrounded by wire, in which there were men wearing nothing more than loincloths."

Night fell and Miyagi lay down on the ground. According to the diary that she kept on her the whole time, this was the "evening of 21 June 1945."

That night, one of the teachers she knew, Mr. Yonamine, who had been brought to the same camp, called Miyagi over and told her quietly, "They will ask all sorts of questions, but whatever you do, don't let on that you were in the Student Corps. Just say that you were a normal schoolgirl. It won't be good if they find out that you were in the Nursing Unit," he said emphatically. "I still remember that clearly now," says Miyagi.

Before too long, Miyagi was ordered to move from Itoman to Kushi, in northern Okinawa, so she set off with the others to walk that long distance on foot. "And that's when my days of being treated as an orphan began. I remember how the people around me took pity on me," said Miyagi with a wry smile.

The first work that Miyagi was given to do was in a U.S. Army-run hospital. She helped with the treatment of wounded civilians for a period before being moved around several different camps. When she arrived in Maehara in September, she found herself reunited with her father, a full three months after she had been taken prisoner.

Since the war, Miyagi has been to the scene of the group suicide at Arasaki in Itoman several times, and on each occasion she has taken an offering of some water and *onigiri* [rice balls] with her.

"The last meal that my school friends had was rice cooked in sea water. And that rice even smelled moldy. So when I go, I take lots of rice balls with me to leave in the shadows of the rocks where it all happened. It's as if to say, 'Eat as much as you like.'"

Miyagi was fortunate enough to get married and have children in the years after the war. "I'm happy with my lot. I did have some of what should have been enjoyable young years stolen from me but, after surviving the war, I did manage to lead pretty much a normal life. When I think of my school friends losing their lives at such a young age, how could I see my own life any other way..."

Before the war, when Miyagi Kikuko's father was working as a teacher in Misato Village (now in Okinawa City), she attended Bito Elementary School for six years, before being accepted for entry into the First Prefectural Girls' School. She then left her hometown and went to Naha to board at the Asato Himeyuri Boarding House, where she was to spend the next four years.

"There were girls from all over Okinawa, so not just children brought up in the towns, but quite a few from rural areas as well. It was just a little far for me to commute so I took the plunge and decided to board," said Miyagi.

The boarding houses were divided into South, Central and North buildings, in addition to another separate building—for those days it was a boarding facility of a considerable scale. There were about twenty rooms in total, and each room was about 65 square meters so "They were really spacious," says Miyagi.

The Okinawa Normal School Girls' Division, located beside Miyagi's school, had facilities such as a pool, which meant that the school was particularly well appointed for those days.

"We benefited in all sorts of ways. It was unusual to be side by side like that. Plus, our principal was also a dean of the Normal School so there was quite a lot of interaction at all levels. That's the reason why the teacher Nakasone Seizen taught me Japanese, and looked after me, although he was a teacher employed by the Normal School."

On the subject of Japanese studies, Miyagi says that she liked reading from a young age and always had a book in her hand. During the battle, there was of course no way that she could keep up her reading, but she does remember that there was one book that she read. It was a foreign book, even set in the enemy country America.

"Someone somehow picked up a copy of *Gone with the Wind* and we passed it around the group taking turns reading it . . . When we made too much noise talking about it a very dignified looking soldier said, 'So what are you school girls reading there then?' We got a real fright and I remember how we all looked scared when he spoke to us."

It was a time in Japan when everyone talked in terms of *"kichiku beiei"* [dirty

American and British devils], so the girls knew that it would be uncomfortable for them, to say the least, if they were found with such a book.

"But that soldier wasn't quizzing us in a way that suggested a rebuke. Afterward I heard that he was in fact General Ushijima, the commander of the Japanese Army. The soldiers around us also fooled around by calling each other 'Ashley' [a character from the book]. It wasn't long before they too headed out to the front line to meet their deaths . . ."

Beginning her senior year at high school in spring 1945, Miyagi lost thirty-two classmates during the next few months in the Battle of Okinawa.

"We girls going into the fourth year from April 1945 would really have been the 42nd graduating class, but among those of us who survived, we refer to our year as the 43rd graduating class. To us, forty-two [shi+ni] is a number that represents death. It's bad luck, so we just changed it to suit ourselves," said Miyagi.

Okinawa Region Weather Observatory

On the morning of 10 October 1944, seventeen-year-old Kise Hiroshi was hurrying from his home in Katabaru to the Okinawa Region Weather Observatory. Attacks by U.S. aircraft had started early the same morning and, as the day wore on, they intensified and spread farther afield. Since his graduation, which had been moved up to January that year, Kise had been working at the weather station and, as he scurried across the city as the bombing continued, the words of a senior student were firmly in his mind. "They've been monitoring up there for fifty years—don't let our side down." The weather observatory itself was at the very top of Gajanbira Hill, and Kise had to be there by 8:00 AM to take over from those doing the night shift.

Meteorological observations began in this location in 1890 when the Okinawa Prefecture Naha Meteorological Station was established at Matsuyama in Naha. It was later destroyed by fire but the work continued in a temporary building. Then in 1927, the operation was renamed the Okinawa Observation Center of the Central Meteorological Service and rebuilt on Gajanbira in Oroku, Naha. During the time Kise was working there, it became the Okinawa Region Weather Observatory with a total staff of ninety-eight. As well as a wireless section, monitoring and forecasting, statistics, general affairs/accounts sections, the main building also housed the Naha Aeronautical Weather Observatory.

Kise looked down below him at Naha Harbor where a flotilla of ships lay at anchor. American planes in formations of four or five aircraft each were attacking the ships. They would attack at low level from the east and then fly away to the west. Strafing their targets as they flew in, they dropped their bombs one after the other. Then there was a massive explosion and a huge plume of water soared upward. One of the warships had caught fire, sending black smoke billowing up in all directions until the city of Naha was completely hidden from Kise's view.

Gajanbira was covered in pine forest, and among the trees was an army anti-aircraft unit. When the 10 October air raid on Naha began, the guns sent up a fierce defensive barrage, but before long it became less and less effective. This left the Japanese warships in a hopeless situation, completely at the mercy of the attacking planes. The buildings at the weather observatory were also hit by machine-gun fire but work inside continued as normal. Staff would always begin observing ten minutes before the hour. Then at ten minutes past the hour they would encode the information and send hourly reports to the Fukuoka District Meteorological Observatory. "I wasn't scared or anything like that as I was totally absorbed in what I was doing," explained Kise. That day, however, before he knew it, the time for the night workers to come and replace Kise had already passed, but nobody came. "I kept on working, but by 11:00 PM I was getting pretty scared so I went back to the shelter."

The shelter was about 200 meters to the south of the weather station, and work on excavating it had begun around the time that Saipan and Tinian had fallen. The staff had worked in shifts digging the shelter. One part was designed to store a diesel engine and a transceiver that became the headquarters for the Okinawa Region Weather Observatory during the Battle of Okinawa. The longer and narrower part of the shelter was later taken over by the IJA.

The next morning Kise was astounded as he crossed the temporary bridge where the Minami-Meiji Bridge had once stood. The city of Naha now lay enshrouded beneath a pall of black smoke from the fires in and around the harbor—it had changed completely. As he made his way from Higashimachi to Kumoji, he could not believe the devastation that unfolded before him, the ghastly sight of a city razed to the ground with only the remains of telegraph poles standing in rows.

One day shortly after the 10 October Naha air raid, Kise was called in by the observatory manager. "He asked me in minute detail about what had happened and then at the end he asked me if I'd been afraid. When I said 'Yes,' he replied, 'That's OK.' I've never forgotten that conversation." For the Okinawa Region Weather Station too, the air raid was merely a prelude to the Battle of Okinawa. Staff numbers declined as workers were called up, and staff attendance at work also dropped off. In spite of all that, they continued to send reports to Fukuoka every hour right through until the middle of May 1945.

After the 10 October air raid, the number of staff dropped further as more were called up or transferred away one after the other so that before the Battle of Okinawa even began, the number was down to thirty-seven. The manager also left Okinawa altogether without anyone being appointed to take his place, so for a while the observatory operated without anyone in charge.

Tanaka Shizuo, an engineer and head of the wireless section, took on a dual role when he was appointed to the position of acting manager early in 1945. At that stage, it was clear to everyone that Okinawa would be the next target for the Americans. The appointment of Tanaka, who openly accepted that his new role would lead to his death, was welcomed by the staff.

Kise explained, "Tanaka was a heroic character. The ship he was on down in the South Pacific was sunk by the enemy and he was very lucky to survive." He had no fear of the bombardment even after the battle began and occasionally he would even leave the shelter to watch the shells coming in. Kise remembers how one day Tanaka spotted an army officer running a short distance, hiding, and then running a bit further. Maybe he thought that the officer was running off like a coward for he laughed out loud as he looked on. When the soldiers apprehended him, the officer was accused of being a spy and was beaten to within an inch of his life.

At the start, they received their food from the army. One day, unhappy with the quality of what they received, Tanaka said, "This army food is just awful," and switched their source of supply to the navy. From the next day their diet of rice mixed with barley in thin soup changed to pure white, best quality rice. They also had canned goods as side dishes, miso, powdered soy sauce, and a range of side-dressings.

The activities associated with weather reporting then moved to a shelter located to the south of the main building.

At the start of March, the Okinawa Region Weather Station underwent a change in operational focus. Only six staff remained, namely Tanaka, the acting manager, signalman Uehara Tatsuoki, signalman Maeda Saburo, Yonamine Saburo who was chief clerk for power supplies, observers Yamashiro Shoken and Kise Hiroshi. They were called the "do or die" unit. Twenty other staff members teamed up with the land and maritime weather stations to form a meteorological unit at Ishimine in Shuri. Also, four members of the Oroku Aviation Observatory, including site manager Kasahara Sadayoshi, joined the navy's weather station as employees of the military. Kasahara was given the rank of captain.

On the morning of 22 March as Kise looked out to the west, he was amazed at what he saw. "There were so many ships out there that I couldn't even see the water. But, I didn't feel frightened or despondent at all. We'd picked up bits of information from the naval personnel staff based beside us, so we were sort of expecting this to happen. Plus, I still had some faith in a 'kamikaze' rescue. But even so, I must admit that I was surprised by the sheer number of vessels out there."

Every day from that point on, the U.S. naval bombardment never let up. "The thunder of their guns firing toward Minatogawa was quite eerie. It sounded like a 'thump, thump, thump' rumbling up from the depths of the earth."

Work at the observatory changed to a very elementary form of weather reporting. They stretched a length of wire between two trees, tied a piece of string onto the wire, and judged the wind velocity from the movement of that string and by the feel of the wind against their skin. For the most part they relied on the visual observations and instinct. "We made no allowance for where we were in relation to sea level." The emphasis was mostly placed on monitoring cloud formations. They had to provide accurate information about the shape, density, and height of any cloud formations for the kamikaze squadrons that flew in from far-away Kagoshima.

Because the naval bombardment and the air raids had become increasingly intense, the observatory staff hardly ever ventured out of the shelter. Risking their lives to carry out observations was a real strain on the men, but so too was living in a cave infested with fleas and lice. But one thing that was especially hard on the observatory staff was that it had become impossible to transmit at the designated times. A diesel-fueled generator had been set up inside the cave, but the smoke from its exhaust made them the perfect target for American spotter planes circling overhead. No matter how much they tried to block the smoke with layers of grass, it still got through so they had to complete each transmission as quickly as possible. At this time, staff at the Fukuoka observatory would leave the switches on several of their transceivers on and watch out for incoming transmissions from Okinawa. The weather reports become increasingly important as the bombardments became more intense.

Life in the shelter continued for a number of days. The shells from U.S warships on the western side of the island flew straight over the top of the observatory so were not of any real concern. What they had to be constantly on the alert for, however, were the spotter planes circling overhead. If one of these aircraft detected them, just a few minutes later a massive fusillade would come their way.

Life inside the shelter was uneventful, but one incident does stand out. It occurred when the fighting grew increasingly fierce and they were no longer able to send reports from the observatory. Signalman Nohara Tatsuoki was very worried about his wife and child whom he had made to evacuate to Fukuoka. Not expecting to survive the battle himself, his only concern was for his family.

One day, he sent a coded message to his former wireless operations manager Moriwaki Yoshio who had been transferred to the Fukuoka Region Office. The message read *Please look after Sachiko and Kazuko if worst comes to worst.* Two or three days later, Moriwaki's reply came back saying *Don't worry. Our prayers are with you for the struggle ahead.* After the war, Nohara recalls how he felt at the time. "The second I decoded his message, I was overcome with emotion. Without thinking, I ran straight outside."

A few days later, sometime in the middle of May, the weather station also finally became a target for the enemy. A hit on the navy's munitions store located on the opposite hill with a track running through the middle turned it into a fireball, so the small number of survivors shifted into the observatory shelter. With bated breath, the staff all waited inside the shelter for the maelstrom to pass. Shells slammed relentlessly into the ground overhead and, every time the ground shook and thundered, lumps of soil would break away and fall around them. Before they knew it they had all gathered in front of the transmitter because they hoped that in the event of a cave-in the frame of the transmitter would help them survive the falling rocks. Some of the staff were so frightened that they tried to run outside, but Tanaka stopped them from doing so.

The depressing wait went on and on, with the shock from the impact of each incoming shell causing more soil to break off and fall down. After a while, they all moved away from the transmitter and gathered around a central table where the ceremonial "farewell cups of water" began. There was a thunderous boom just as power-supply section chief Yonamine Saburo moved away from the table. The resulting cave-in left him half buried under rocks and soil. Everybody rushed to help get him out but he was badly injured. Once the bombardment stopped he was taken to the field hospital at the Naval Unit Headquarters.

A new task awaited Kise. Their equipment was rendered unusable in the bombardment and there was no spare vacuum tube on hand to fix it, so Kise was tasked with going to get one from the Naha wireless unit at Jogaku. He was to go with Tanaka and, having already covered that distance once before with signalman Nohara, he was fully aware of the dangers involved. By that stage, the staff had given Kise the nickname of "Mr. Bulletproof" because, in spite of the numerous times he had been sent outside on dangerous missions, he had never once been wounded.

The rain pelted down as they followed the edge of the Manko Wetlands in the direction of Madanbashi. Kise could barely make out the outline of Tanaka in front of him, although from time to time enemy flares were so bright as to light up his entire face if he turned around. They also had to look out for land mines as they made their way along. As well as that, Madanbashi had been pounded by naval bombardment so they had to pick their way across piles of smashed rocks as they hurried on their way. At one stage, Kise saw a dead body floating in a shell crater. He has never forgotten the sight of that body bloated to twice its normal size.

They finally managed to arrive at the Naha wireless unit at Jogaku. When the staff there saw them, they were astonished. After explaining, "We don't want you to throw your lives away. We're also pulling back so don't come here again," they tearfully began smashing their equipment.

They wrapped the precious vacuum tube in a *furoshiki* carrying cloth and headed off again, their return journey every bit as dangerous and difficult as when they had come. When Kise slipped and almost fell down, Tanaka rebuked him, saying, "You idiot! That tube is more important than your life."

Once again, Kise made it back without a scratch on him. But even with the vacuum tube that they had risked their lives to get, the transmitter was beyond repair and never again was their call sign sent out.

The twenty people called up to work in Shuri's Ishimine Weather Observatory from the end of March were issued military uniforms. Their location was named Pinetree Highland. Kuniyoshi Noboru will never forget the instructions they received from Army Command after they had formed their new unit. "When worst comes to worst, the Observatory Unit is to assume a combat role and defend Pinetree Highland to the last man." But the only weapons they had were three hand grenades among five people, plus some flimsy bamboo spears to protect themselves with.

Kuniyoshi joined the weather station in February 1945 so during his time at middle school only his second year was what one might regard as normal. "While I was a third-grader, half my time was spent digging out emplacements, but when I got to the fourth grade I was more or less digging day and night. Then they moved our graduation up." Even when Kuniyoshi joined the Okinawa Regional Weather Observatory—being too light meant abandoning his hopes of joining the air force unit—all that awaited him was the daily slog of digging out shelters. "During the mornings we studied how to transmit messages and in the afternoon we dug shelters. We spent two thirds of each day digging," he explained.

After they shifted to Ishimine, there was no time for digging shelters so they used existing tombs instead. After removing the urns containing ancestral remains from inside, they split up into two groups and moved into the tombs themselves. But there was little space inside the tombs, so the boys used pickaxes to dig farther back to make them a little more spacious. Kuniyoshi was the first of the weather station staff to be wounded.

It was about a month after the move to Shuri. On the day that he was wounded, Kuniyoshi had already come down with the flu and was unwell. Leaving him behind, his two friends went out to look for some boards to use as a floor in the shelter.

The Americans planes arrived shortly after they left. Targeting the open entrance to the tomb, they flew in at low level, hammering the area with machine-gun fire. As soon as one plane had completed its pass, the next one arrived. Before too long there was the sound of a massive explosion.

As the smell of gunpowder filled the tomb, Kuniyoshi knew that he had been hit, but he did not know where. It was only when he tried to walk that he realized where. He simply couldn't walk, as a bullet had gone clean through his right thigh, making a 1 centimeter hole as it entered and leaving an exit-wound of about 4 centimeters.

There was no sign of his two friends returning so he made his way to the entrance of the next shelter, dragging his wounded leg as he went. In there, the wireless staff were busy tapping out their messages. They were surprised to see the wounded Kuniyoshi and took him inside, but there was nothing they could do to treat him.

Then a lieutenant from the Army's weather observatory arrived and said, "Here, use this to sterilize that wound," but all he had was some alcohol in a large saké bottle. The bullet had smashed the bone as it went through his leg. The following day the pain was even worse, but all they could do was sterilize it with the alcohol. Kuniyoshi was in agony, but several days passed before one of the weather station staff asked a 32nd Army surgeon to call. The surgeon simply asked Kuniyoshi how he felt and did nothing to treat the wound. With a cursory, "If it's broken, I'll have to amputate, but I don't have my surgical equipment with me today so I'll do it tomorrow," the surgeon left.

The fighting had intensified by this time and American scouts were even appearing in the vicinity of Pinetree Highland. The night before Kuniyoshi was to have his leg amputated, they made the decision that if they got the chance to leave, they would do so. Kuniyoshi explained, "If we'd stayed there just one more day, I'd be missing a leg today."

It was the start of the rainy season, so the roads were muddy. At night, the moon offered enough light to allow them to watch other units pulling out. Some of Kuniyoshi's workmates made a stretcher, which they covered with a blanket and used it to carry him on their journey. When he apologized for being a nuisance, he remembers that they said, "Get better soon so we can all go out on an attack together."

He had already accepted that he was going to die and entrusted a sum of money and some cigarettes to one of his colleagues asking, "Will you give this to my father for me?" The cigarettes had been an "imperial gift" from the army, while the amount of money was 99 yen, the balance from a crisp, new 100-yen note he had been given a week earlier. He and his friends had each spent one yen on some goat meat, leaving him 99 yen.

Unfortunately, the four who carried Kuniyoshi's stretcher were all killed, as was the friend to whom he had entrusted the money to be passed on to his father. Unable to walk on his own, Kuniyoshi was one of only four staff from the weather station to survive the war. "It's just a toss of the dice as to whether you live or die in war," he mused.

On 26 April 1945, Kuniyoshi and the others in the weather station unit pulled out of Ishimine in Shuri. About one month had passed since their unit had been formed from staff working in the main observatory in Oroku. Communications within the island had already broken down so they continued to use runners to send weather information to the 32nd Army Command Post shelter below Shuri Castle. "We all took turns, with runners scampering back and forth several times each day. It took more than an hour to get to the Command Post from Ishimine," Kuniyoshi explained. "Because communications on the main island of Okinawa were out of action, we only knew about the American landing by intercepting a message from Imperial Headquarters in Tokyo."

That was how life was for them. But with nobody from the weather station unit having been killed while they were at Shuri, and with only Kuniyoshi having been wounded, they set off for Nagado in Tomigusuku. For Kuniyoshi, their departure was most fortunate indeed, for when they got to their destination they found two or three Okinawa Home Guard members still in the shelter that the IJA had been using.

"They treated my wounds with gauze soaked in iodine. They wrapped the gauze around a stainless steel rod and cleaned the area, pushing the rod and the gauze through the wound itself, but I have them to thank for preventing any infection from setting in."

Two or three days later, the first death among the weather station staff occurred when Komine Yukio—one of the team who had helped carry the immobilized Kuniyoshi to Nagado—was killed instantly by a shell burst.

Several others wounded in the same incident were all taken, together with Kuniyoshi, to the military hospital at Haebaru. "The army hospital shelter had been dug out from the distinctive porous soil, turning the place into mud as rainwater dripped through. The wounded were crammed into bunks, and the shelter itself was so dark you couldn't see a thing. It was nothing like a real hospital at all. It was really just somewhere to keep all those who were unable to fight," explained Kuniyoshi.

Men who had been burned by flamethrowers cried out in pain all day long, while those with brain damage babbled the same meaningless things over and over. Some plucked the maggots from their wounds and threw them at other wounded soldiers. The nurses worked non-stop but some of the schoolgirl nurse aids were reduced to tears by the constant unreasonable demands of the wounded men. Because they were close to the age of the soldiers, many of the girls became angry at the unpleasant way the wounded young men behaved toward them.

Two weeks later, around the middle of May, they called for volunteers from among the wounded to be transferred to the Itokazu hospital cave. "If I stay here, I'll be killed for sure," thought Kuniyoshi, so he was the first to put his hand up. They transferred forty or fifty patients, with members of the Home Guard carrying them all on stretchers. The annex hospital at Itokazu was not as unpleasant as the Haebaru Hospital. A hole in the roof of the shelter allowed light to come in, making the place much brighter. Also, unlike the low ceiling at Haebaru where people kept banging their heads, Itokazu was more spacious and the bunks were three-tiered. But the thing which made young Kuniyoshi happier than anything else about Itokazu was that the rice-balls he got to eat there were bigger than the ones at Haebaru. On top of that, there were locals living nearby who gave them potatoes and other vegetables that were past their best.

Inside the Itokazu shelter they received reports about how well the war was supposedly going for Japan, including how many enemy ships they had sunk and how many enemy planes they had shot down. The Japanese military was reported to be well on top and, since around the time that they had been carried to Haebaru, the whole state of the battle was said to have improved dramatically. The American advance had been stopped and the IJA had already launched a counteroffensive. At least that is what Kuniyoshi was led to believe. Naturally, it came as a huge shock when he was suddenly told, "The enemy may be here as early as tomorrow. Everybody who can move must leave the shelter, even if you have to crawl." They were each given one rice-ball, a bag of unpolished rice and a blanket.

Still unable to walk, Kuniyoshi tied a wooden splint around his wounded leg and fashioned some makeshift crutches, but he could not get out unaided. Then he noticed a member of the Home Guard who was originally from Yomitan and who had been wounded in the eyes. Kuniyoshi asked the man for help and, by holding his shoulder, managed to get moving. "I was really only semi-functional, but with the two of us working together, I was somehow able to hobble along," he explained.

As they moved off, they could hear the words of a doleful song coming from the men still inside the shelter, unable to move and abandoned. Even today, Kuniyoshi has never forgotten that melancholy Song whose first stanza was . . . *The little brook in my beloved hometown . . .* He heard that the men who were left behind were given dry bread and some cyanide to take. After the war was over, their dead bodies were found still lying on their bunks inside the shelter.

Once Kuniyoshi made it to Yoza in Gushikami, he became separated from the man with the eye wounds who had helped him on his journey. The man was about thirty years old at the time and of slight build, but Kuniyoshi never saw him again.

At Yoza, they stayed in a barn, keeping themselves alive by eating potatoes taken from a nearby field. One day, a young girl brought some rice and thin soup for them. They ate it without any idea who she was or why she had brought them the food. The following day she returned with more food and continued to call for the next four or five days as well. Thereafter, a woman who was obviously the girl's mother arrived. "My son was in the Second Prefectural Middle School but was conscripted into the signals unit and I've heard nothing of him since. Seeing you here reminds me of him," the woman said, explaining the trays of food. "The enemy will be here before too long. You boys are wounded so you really have to get away as quickly as you can," she continued, handing over some rice-balls as she saw them off. In the midst of the horrors of war, they were touched by her warmth and compassion. Kuniyoshi explained that just a few years earlier he was able to meet up again with the Omija family who had been so kind to them.

At the same time, however, he also witnessed some unpleasant scenes in that house where civilians and soldiers were staying together. One day, a local offered one of the soldiers a potato to eat when the soldier flew into a fit of rage, "Am I supposed to eat a tiny potato like this?" he screamed, "Swap it for a bigger one, now!" He was so wild that he even drew his sword. "Fortunately, somebody had some bigger potatoes so the incident passed without any further ado, but I reckon that local guy would have been killed if there had been no bigger ones for him," explained Kuniyoshi. He also saw instances of high-handed and cruel behavior, including soldiers forcing civilians out of their shelter claiming, "We are the ones who have to stay alive."

By the time he got to Maehira, it was the middle of June. There was no let-up in the bombardment as the shells continued to pour in and, in spite of his wounds, Kuniyoshi had to keep moving. It was at the military hospital in Haebaru where he caught sight of Yoshimasa Kise, one of his fellow workers from the weather observatory but with whom he had lost contact. "So how are you?" was about the only conversation they could manage as the shells flew all around them. Kuniyoshi did notice, however, that the wound in Kise's right arm was full of maggots. That was the last time he saw Kise.

By this stage, the fear of death had strangely given way to the fear of being wounded and having to suffer. On one occasion, resigned to death, they lay down outside in an open field. They screamed out messages for their families, sang songs and yelled out "Long Live the Emperor." Incredibly, not one of them was hit, and that same night they felt both an intense fear of death and a burning desire to live.

Gnawing on sugar cane, they had worked out how to keep themselves alive. "Some locals had more than enough food. We were all hiding in depressions in a rock face, but obviously they felt sorry for us as each time they walked past they would give us some of their food."

Kuniyoshi earned a reprieve from this existence when he met a couple called Kanashiro from Itoman. They were in their fifties and had no children, but they looked after Kuniyoshi as though they had adopted him as their own.

The three of them were together on 22 June, when they were captured. The enemy was very close to them by this stage. The couple were hiding beneath a rocky outcrop and whispering to each other. They had apparently decided to go with the husband's idea that it would be a disgrace to be taken prisoner and that they should take their own lives. But just as they took out their razor blade and were about to commit suicide, an American soldier fired a warning burst into the rocks beside them. Kuniyoshi immediately yelled, "Let's get out of here!" and led the couple out with him.

"It was just how the American leaflets said it would be," explained Kuniyoshi. There was no indication that the American soldiers would hurt them at all. But a second later, the enemy changed when a Japanese soldier fired a volley of shots at Kuniyoshi and the couple. "It was a bizarre feeling to realize that it was the *American* soldiers who pushed us back behind the rocks to protect us."

Kuniyoshi was very keen to rejoin his weather station unit from which he had become separated at Nagado. He got his chance at Maehira when he met Nohara Tatsuoki from the main observatory and discovered that the other members of his former unit were also at Maehira. Nohara promised Kuniyoshi that he would come and get him the next morning. But he never turned up and Kuniyoshi felt let down.

However, Nohara had actually reported back to Tanaka Shizuo, the acting head of the weather station, to ask if Kuniyoshi could rejoin the others in his unit. Tanaka's reply was "No." The reason being that the main unit itself was already short of men and, when the time came to launch an infiltration raid, he could not take someone with them who was already wounded. At that point, Kuniyoshi had no way of knowing that Kise and the others in the unit had protested many times against the infiltration raids and had actually refused to go.

Finally, the day arrived when the staff of the Okinawa Regional Weather Observatory had to withdraw from their shelter at Oroku. It was around 20 May. Their wireless equipment had been damaged when the shelter suffered a direct hit, so it was now beyond repair. Tanaka made the decision, "It will be a waste if we die here, so let's join up with the military weather observation unit and work there."

Saburo Yonamine, the chief clerk for power supplies who had been badly wounded and had been taken to the military hospital in Oroku was also recalled to the main observatory, as was Sato Yoshio, a telegraph operator who had been unable to get back to the mainland after his posting to Sakishima because no boats were available.

They set off that evening after the sun had gone down, bound for Nagado in Tomigusuku where the weather station unit was supposed to be. They placed Yonamine on a window shutter and four or five of them carried him along. For Kise, the pain in his shoulders from the weight of the load paled in comparison to having to listen to Yonamine's groans. The naval bombardment never let up and, whenever a shell sounded as though it was going to land nearby, the men carrying Yonamine would lower him down one end at a time, leave him in the middle of the road and run for their lives to find a ditch or somewhere similar to hide in. After three or four hours they finally made it to the village of Noha just short of Nagado.

From there, they sent out a runner to Nagado, only to find that the weather station unit had already pulled out. Tanaka said, "We've got to get in touch with them as quickly as we can," and left Kise and Nohara Tatsuoki behind with the wounded Yonamine. This was because Nohara and Yonamine were good friends, while Kise was the youngest.

As he left the three of them behind, Tanaka said, "We'll come back for you in two or three days," but they never did and the enemy would soon be upon them. The three who had been left behind were the only three people left in the village of Noha, so Nohara and Kise had to make a decision. Tanaka had told them as he was leaving, "If worst comes to worst, give Yonamine a hand grenade and do your utmost to get to Maehira."

The two talked it through carefully. By now shells were landing relatively close to them. Yonamine had become very thin and there was no way that the other two could carry all that they needed from the hospital and still get away. The enemy was so very close but they couldn't just throw their lives away by dying where they were. "We had no option but to do as Tanaka had told us . . . we gave Yonamine a grenade."

Nohara gave Yonamine two grenades. "I've given them to him," he said to Kise. There was nothing else to say . . . nothing else was necessary. It is not known when Yonamine died, but after the war his remains were retrieved from that shelter.

On the way to Maehira, they saw all sorts of things, especially dead bodies lying scattered everywhere because nobody had the time or the energy to bury them. Fleeing civilians were completely emaciated.

On 3 June the two of them made it to Maehira where they rejoined the Shuri group, bringing their total number to twenty-three or twenty-four. They remained there for around two weeks, during which time the task of running messages to the army weather station, all the while under constant bombardment, fell to Kise. One day as Kise was out delivering a message, a woman with a baby on her back called out to him, "Please help us. My husband has been hit." He went over to check and discovered that the woman's child, aged four or five, had been killed outright. Beside them lay her husband, his entrails spilling from his abdomen and groaning in agony. The woman told Kise they were from Nakagusuku.

"We can't do anything for him," said Miyasato Yoshio, who had fought in China and was now in charge of power supplies. "He's not going to make it so just give him some water and try to make him comfortable." That was all Kise and his friends could do. Then the man's terrible moaning ceased and he stopped breathing.

They buried the father and son next to a banana tree on the outskirts of the village. Miyasato said, "This one is your husband, and that's your eldest son there. After we've won this war, come back and retrieve them." To reassure the woman, he placed a large stone and a small stone on the graves to indicate which was which. After the war, Kise went back to the spot and found that the stone grave markers were gone.

Even "Mr. Bulletproof" Kise was eventually wounded. In the middle of June, the weather station staff moved to Ihara, their number now having dropped to nineteen.

Today the Ryufu Memorial marks the very spot where the weather station staff sought shelter. Unfortunately, when they got there it was already occupied by Japanese soldiers, and there was no room for the observatory staff whose only way to avoid incoming naval fire and stay alive was to huddle beneath a rocky outcrop. Kise was hit soon after he arrived when a piece of shrapnel from a naval shell sliced into his foot, rendering him unable to walk.

Thereafter he was separated from his colleagues and stayed in a private dwelling. Fukushima Hiroyuki, who had been wounded around the same time as Kise, was also in the house, as were a large number of civilians. They brought Kise his breakfast each morning, but he felt very anxious about being in the house and unable to move. He especially hated the "thump, thump" of the enemy's mortars and their shells, which were now falling ever closer.

Eleven years old at the time, Tamaki Minoru had also sought refuge in the house with his mother. His impression of Kise and Fukushima was, "The two of them just sat there calmly, no matter how heavy the shelling became."

One day, a mortar fragment went straight through the roof and embedded itself in Kise's leg. He quickly tried to remove it but it was still very hot and burned his hand. Fukushima grabbed some chopsticks and pulled the sliver of metal out for him. Time and time again, Kise suffered numerous small wounds like this.

Another wounded man was brought in to where the two were. He was Dana Sosei, head of the observation procedures. Dana had massive stomach wounds and groaned in agony for two nights before his cries for help to ease his suffering changed to a direct plea for someone to kill him outright. As the sun went down on the third day, they decided to do as he asked.

Three or four of the weather station staff placed Dana on a window shutter, carried him outside and placed him in a shell crater. They gave him a grenade and then left. The only person to witness what happened was young Tamaki. He'd been told, "Don't look!" but he hid behind a stone wall and peeped over the top. As the grenade exploded, he ducked down and the next time he looked, the agonized groaning had stopped. Dana was dead.

Fukushima then looked at Kise and said, "Depending on the way you look at it, it's better to die now while there are still people around to bury the bodies." Kise did not disagree. On their journey from Oroku, they had seen countless dead bodies along the way. If it was raining, the bodies swelled up grotesquely, while on fine days they turned dark black and were left to dry out and whither where they lay. "Anything but that," was clearly what he was thinking.

On 18 June, the house where Kise and the others were staying took a direct hit from a mortar shell. (This date is Tamaki's recollection, which differs from that of Kise). The blast killed Tamaki's mother who was in the garden beside a water tank made from the clay-like mineral called meerschaum. His uncle was also killed. "The tank just blew apart, and the adults took the full force of the blast, which saved my cousin and the two of us," explained Tamaki. His mother and his uncle were not hit by shell fragments but were killed by the shock of the explosion.

The family next to Kise was from Nishihara. The father was killed instantly when his head was cleaved open by a piece of shrapnel. His wife survived and she quickly gathered up her two children and rushed them away. There was another child, about one year old, but the mother left without it. The child was wearing a red kimono and the story goes that the kimono remained in the house where they had all been staying, right through until after the war's end.

The American soldiers were now very close. By this time there were only twelve fit members of the weather station unit left, so they split into three sections and headed north with the aim of slipping through the enemy front line to safety. Just a short while before that, however, Kise had gone to the rocky outcrop where the others were hiding when a mortar shell landed close by. He was knocked unconscious by the blast and when he came to, he saw that Yamashiro Seiken and Kudaka Kanbin had both been killed instantly. Those with Tamaki were at a loss as to where they should go so they teamed up with Kise's group.

Because the enemy had drawn ever closer, the Japanese soldiers had also moved out, leaving an empty cave nearby. Kise and the others hurled themselves inside. There was already an elderly woman in the shelter, plus two wounded men and two children, who were a great help to all the others. They took some canteens and went off to fetch water, pressing their way in between the adults and pushing aside dead bodies floating in the water to fill the bottles. They also brought back some sugarcane. Then they heard an exchange of gunfire nearby and, after it settled down, they went out to investigate in the hope of finding food and medicine on the bodies of those who had been killed.

Helped by the two children, Kise and the others tried over and over again to slip through enemy lines to safety. After a huge effort, they finally made their way to Odo, where they were taken prisoner. Resting inside a water tank, Kise placed his hand grenades down beside him and fell into a deep sleep for the first time in days. When he awoke, he found American soldiers standing over him. He tried to grab his grenades but one of the soldiers punched him and knocked him unconscious—with that, the Battle of Okinawa ended for Kise.

By this stage, Fukushima Hiroyuki, who had previously been with him, had decided to take his destiny in his own hands.

Kise was the only one to survive of the four weather station staff who made it together to Ihara in mid-June before splitting up.

Command Post in Mabuni

"What? . . . You mean that was Ushijima, the commanding officer?" Tonaki Fumiko was shocked by what she had heard. She'd been listening nonchalantly to the tour guide's explanation, but was suddenly taken aback that her own experience matched so closely the guide's explanation of what happened back then. It all took place in a cave in Mabuni, one of the locations that had been such a nightmare for Tonaki, but until now she had had absolutely no idea that that gentleman who had been in the same shelter was in fact Lt. Gen. Ushijima Mitsuru, the highest ranking officer in the Okinawa garrison.

It was almost twenty years since the war ended, but Tonaki recalled, "Right from day one we were told 'Don't ask the name of this unit . . . don't ask anyone their name . . . don't ask anything.' And right to the end, we knew nothing. Given the position we were in, we didn't know whether we'd still be alive at the end of each day, so it didn't really matter." She had been a nurse with the 24th Infantry Division's No. 1 Field Hospital in the Tomimori shelter until the dissolution order disbanded her unit. Wandering aimlessly about looking for shelter, she came across an army messenger who told her and her friends, "If you're nurses, follow me!" and he led them to the shelter at Mabuni.

Tonaki continued, "There were eight of us so we decided what to do using the 'scissors-paper-rock' game. I can't remember if I won or lost. In addition to me, there were also two others from a student unit, Tamaki Tomiko and her cousin who was known as Sumi-chan." The shelter Tonaki was taken to overlooked the little settlement of Mabuni but just as she was about to enter, she was stopped as a voice called out "Wait there!" "Standing on top of the cave was a lieutenant with a sword on his belt. He then came right up to me and suddenly lifted my hair so he could see my hairline, and said, 'Okay, you're not a spy.' Even now I still don't know what on earth he meant . . ." Then he said, 'Don't ask any questions.'"

She was surprised when she entered the shelter, which appeared to be of sturdy construction. A little farther in it opened to a wider area where a large number of officers were going about their business using boxes of tinned food as tables. They had all placed their swords down beside them, and I thought, "With so many officers in here, this must be an important place." But I was not allowed to ask any questions, so of course I just accepted everything as it was. The shelter seemed very well constructed so I felt quite safe there for the time being," recalled Tonaki.

Near where the officers were conducting their business, shelves had been built against the walls for use as bunks. A second lieutenant with a fever was lying on one of the bunks, and it was Tonaki's job to look after him. "We had almost nothing in the way of medicine so all I could do was keep him cool with water and massage his head. I used a bowl to collect the water dripping down off the rocky walls. I then purified the water by boiling it. But worse than nursing duties was the task of going out into the nearby fields at night to collect sugar cane, potatoes, and garlic. The fields were littered with the bodies of men killed in the fighting and the stench was horrendous." In the cave where Tonaki had been told not to ask any questions, there were two women who appeared to be mother and daughter. An army surgeon explained that they were the wife of a Shuri doctor and her daughter. Tonaki remembers that the woman was around sixty years of age and the daughter about twenty.

Along with the officers were NCOs and enlisted men, one of whom was from Okinawa. "He was obviously an orderly for the lieutenant I met at the shelter entrance, but he was constantly being bullied. The lieutenant would strut around telling him, 'You've been slacking off again!' Then he'd make him pick up a shoe or sword in his mouth and crawl around him like a dog." One day, Tonaki whispered to the soldier, "That an *Uchinanchu* gets bullied like this here in Okinawa is awful. Next time you go out on an errand, you should just not come back. The way things are now, even if you run away, they'll just think you've been killed out there." One day, the soldier did not come back, but Tonaki does not know whether he ran away as she suggested, or had been killed. That's how it was in that shelter, but among her most enduring memories is of one officer in particular, aged around fifty and of solid build, who strolled about the shelter, totally nonchalant. He seldom wore his military uniform but all the officers and men addressed him as "Sir."

This officer always seemed to be relaxed as he moved about; whether the enemy's artillery was pounding away or whether it had fallen silent, his demeanor never changed. Part of his daily routine was to brush aside the bamboo matting covering the shelter entrance and look outside, often commenting, "Ah well, it looks like there are plenty of planes around today." His relaxed approach never let us sense that death was so close at hand. Tonaki no longer remembers the day or month, but suddenly there was a terrific explosion inside the shelter. The smell of blood that followed is etched in her memory. Inside the cave, she was repairing the badges on the officers' caps when this explosion occurred. Tonaki doesn't know whether it was seconds or minutes later, but when she came to, most of the men who had been working behind the boxes of canned food were dead. "Sumi-chan, who had been sitting next to me, was also killed instantly. I couldn't hear anything with my left ear and when I tapped my hand against my head, I couldn't feel a thing." Of the two women introduced to Tonaki as the Shuri doctor's family, the daughter had been hit in the buttocks where the flesh had been ripped clean away.

When she looked toward the back of the shelter, Tonaki saw the army surgeon, barely still alive, beside the man they called "Sir" and pleading with him, "For mercy sake, Sir, please cut my throat and put me out of my suffering." But in response to the doctor's desperate pleas, as though he was trying to reassure a baby, the high-ranking officer just kept repeating, "There, there . . . you'll be soon be OK." Sitting there cross-legged, the way the older man spoke sounded as though he was both crying and suffering. Twenty minutes later the surgeon was dead and, as if waiting for that to happen, "Sir" stood up and put his military uniform on. That was the first time Tonaki had seen him wearing it. After a while he gave his aide-de-camp an order and two wicker trunks were brought in. "Sir" removed some documents from the trunks and placed a military flag neatly over them. The aide-de-camp straightened his uniform and on "Sir's" signal saluted and set the documents and flag alight. At the end of this "ceremony," "Sir" went over to Tonaki and told her, "There's a plane nearby that has come for us so we're leaving here. Until they come to get us, I'm counting on you to do what needs to be done to keep things going." He then left through the entrance on the Mabuni Hamlet side of the shelter.

"I believed him so I waited, but of course they never came. He was obviously just trying to reassure us," explained Tonaki. The wounded officers had been left in the cave. One of them stayed buckled over, unable to move his left knee. It was the lieutenant who had challenged Tonaki and the others when they first entered the cave. "Right from the start he was so arrogant but after he had been wounded he was even worse. We only had to take a step toward him and he'd scream that he was in pain and wave his sword about to stop us from getting past." Several days later, when still in the shelter, they heard the Americans calling for them to surrender. One of the officers who seemed to be in a daze wandered toward the outside as though he was sleepwalking, but the others pulled him back. Then the lieutenant with the wounded knee called Tonaki and the others together and told them, "We're going to commit suicide." Tonaki recalls that "Tomi-chan replied, 'No way,' and ran wildly about. But I said to her, 'We're going to die either way,' and dragged her into the circle."

The thing that made Tonaki agree to commit suicide was somebody's comment, "Let's all meet at Yasukuni Shrine." She had been to Yasukuni Shrine while living in Tokyo studying to become a nurse and she felt quite positive about the idea of her spirit ending up there. The doctor's wife and daughter, Tomi, and the others all stood shoulder-to-shoulder, imagining the beautiful scene at Yasukuni. Outside, all around them, the incredible bombardment meant there was not a tree or even a blade of grass left anywhere but, after all that time hiding in the shelter, she finally felt a sense of peace. They waited and waited, but no hand grenade was thrown among them. In disbelief and absolutely terrified, Tonaki looked up but no sooner had she done so than the lieutenant screamed out, "What the hell are you doing? Hurry up and get me something to eat!" Tonaki recalls that he had clearly lost his mind, and that is what saved their lives.

After that incident, life in the shelter continued as before, although Tonaki witnessed many examples of unsavory behavior by soldiers fleeing from the fighting. Agreeing that if they were going to die anyway they should die outside in the open air, four of them, the mother and daughter, Tomi, and Tonaki ran out of the shelter but almost immediately were taken prisoner. In talking about "'Sir,' Senaha Sakae of the Okinawan War History Publications Society said, "Judging by his age and mild demeanor, it was probably Lt. Gen. Ushijima. Their shelter was attacked on June 22 and Ushijima committed suicide the following day." Tonaki wants to forget the things that happened in the 32nd Army Headquarters shelter, but when she talks about "Sir," the tone of her voice changes. The day she agreed to talk with me, she made her way to this very spot in Mabuni. Then, on the coast side of the shelter where Ushijima took his own life, she put her hands together in prayer and stood without moving for some time.

Adaniya Ken was the only officer from Okinawa in the 32nd Army Headquarters shelter. He had a background in education, but the tide of Okinawan history saw him pulled into Japan's military machine. Accordingly, he is the only officer from Okinawa who actually observed firsthand the organization and the people who controlled the battle, although this is the first time he has spoken about what happened. He personally witnessed many people being killed, and even these days he is unable to sleep for several days as June 23, the anniversary of the end of the battle, approaches. That may be why Adaniya had been reluctant to talk about it for all these years. "There would have been far fewer civilian casualties if we hadn't fought a battle of attrition . . . or if we'd made our last stand at Shuri," he said quietly.

Adaniya was posted to the 32nd Army shelter early in 1945. It was the second draft of teachers from Kadena Agricultural School, and he was given the rank of lieutenant. The city of Naha had already changed dramatically, and things were very tense as the entire prefecture was now within range of the U.S. military machine. At that stage, students from the Normal School were attached to the 32nd Army Headquarters in Shuri Castle, where they were busy day-in and day-out digging the unfinished shelter. It had five separate entrances and contained a construction unit coordinating the digging, a central staff section, an adjutants' section, an accounts section, a medical section, and so on. Although the American landing was expected, there was obviously still a lot of work to be done before the shelter was finished. Once the Americans did land on Okinawa, however, Headquarters was under enormous pressure. "Communication between Headquarters and all the other units was by telephone," Adaniya explained. "As the fighting intensified, the wires were cut so calls couldn't get through. The central staff section ordered me to go out and ask directly how the battle was going and to deliver their orders."

Adaniya's instructions came from Col. Yahara Hiromichi, senior staff officer. Adaniya had two or three NCOs under him and was responsible for round-the-clock communications. The "fighting" had commenced, but they were basically just being pounded by long-range bombardment, with some shells landing very close to where they were. "An NCO called Tanaka had his leg blown off. They got him back to the Command Post but I think he died a short time later. One thing that impressed me about Yahara was that when things were at a crucial stage he always went out to see for himself what was happening, or sent his trusted friend Maj. Nagano Hideo of the General Staff section. Yahara was also wounded in the fighting near Maeda." A little more than a month after the Americans landed on Okinawa they started to edge their way toward the Command Post. On 4 May, the IJA attempted its largest counteroffensive, but as Adaniya described this, "Our strategy was to hold the Shuri Line at any cost and our counterattack was overly optimistic. About 80 percent of the 62nd Infantry Division was wiped out and the 24th Infantry Regiment was so badly mauled that from then on it was barely able to function."

Around the time that the details of the counteroffensive were being planned, there was a visitor in the Command Post shelter at Shuri Castle. It was a man by the name of Sato Kiichi, who was a member of the Special Political Police. Adaniya met with Sato in the shelter under Shuri Castle after he had completed his business. When Adaniya asked him why he was there, Kiichi replied, "Governor Shimada ordered me to come and ask what strategy the army is going to adopt so he can work out what to do with the civilian population. They've just told me that they intend to hold the line at Shuri, so I'll pass that on to the governor." As for the 32nd Army's counteroffensive, however, reports coming into the Command Post did not talk in terms of "glorious victory," but more in terms that for the most part things had gone very badly. The following evening, 5 May, Command ordered all units to call off the offensive and the battle plan again reverted to one of attrition. Because the stated aim of the offensive had been to reverse the tide of the battle, its failure to do so produced a gloomy atmosphere throughout the shelter. Adaniya recalls that "Despite the gloom and doom inside the shelter, Lt. Gen. Ushijima would sometimes try to cheer up his subordinates by joking with them, saying 'So is it day or night at the moment?'"

Two or three times a day he would venture outside to observe the fighting through his binoculars. Ignoring the advice of his adjutants that it was dangerous for him to do so, Ushijima would survey the battlefield as the American shells flew about him. Adaniya summed up Lt. Gen. Ushijima by saying, "His expression never changed whether the battle was going well or badly. Just by looking at him, his subordinates felt that things were going OK." By the end of May, two separate plans for withdrawing from Shuri were being considered by the 32nd

Army Command; the first was to withdraw southeast to the Chinen Peninsula, and the second to move southwest toward the Kyan Peninsula. Historical records indicate that support for the Kyan Peninsula option came from military command, the 24th Infantry Division and the Army Artillery Unit, while the Chinen option was favored by the 44th Independent Mixed Brigade. The Navy's Okinawa Base Force appeared to have no preference. The 62nd Infantry Division was strongly in favor of holding the present position on the grounds that they were already effectively finished as a fighting force, and that the Shuri shelter was crammed with thousands of badly wounded men who lacked the ability to move elsewhere. Adaniya explained that, "The generals held numerous meetings inside the shelter with NCOs standing on guard outside the meeting room. Anybody who tried to get past was quickly ordered back."

In the end, it was agreed that they would withdraw from Shuri, but only a small number of officers including those in the General Staff section knew about this. "Changes in strategy like this were major decisions, so we were certainly not told about them." Nor were they told where the command post was moving to, even as they headed southward. Adaniya explained just how confidential military secrets were as, "I was very friendly with Lt. Col. Kuzuno Ryuichi, a senior deputy staff officer. I asked him, but he wouldn't tell even me." Adaniya pulled out of Shuri on 26 May. "I remember that we said to each other, 'Tomorrow is the Navy's Memorial Day,' so I'm certain of the date that we left," he explained. "An advance party had set out the previous day but, having received word that the some of the enemy were already at Ozato and several other places, they split up, one squad going via Ozato, the other by way of Oroku. I think their job was to look for Americans and clear a safe path for our commanders to withdraw from Shuri."

It was pouring rain when Adaniya and the others left on the evening of 26 May. Adaniya was the only officer among them, leading seventy to eighty men and with no idea where he was supposed to be going. Eventually he received orders that he was to head for the 24th Infantry Division's Command Post, and they finally set off at around nine o'clock that evening, from the south-facing entrance of the shelter. Moving southward from Samukawa and looking at the Shikina Highland to their right, they slogged through the quagmire and down the valley. They climbed to Shikinaen before passing through Ichinichibashi, Kokuba, Tsukazan, and Taira and Takamine in Tomigusuku, as they made their way to the 24th Infantry Division's command post shelter at Yoza-dake. They walked all night and it was light by the time they arrived at their destination. Only then did Adaniya realize that the number of soldiers with him was around half the number that had started the journey. One after the other, men had succumbed to exhaustion from the endless fighting, made even worse by being soaked to the skin by the teeming rain. "When the incoming artillery fire was too heavy, we'd stop for a cigarette and a rest, being very careful, of course. But we kept walking right through the night. It must have been really tough on those poor soldiers who were so utterly exhausted by that stage," Adaniya explained. They simply had to keep walking, but they were at the limits of their endurance and many of them just dropped, one after the other, along the way. Some eventually made it by being carried by their comrades, but most were just left where they fell and nothing more was ever heard of them.

There were many wounded soldiers in the Shuri shelter. When the time came to move out, those who couldn't walk unaided were left there and given phials of cyanide. Some committed suicide by taking the poison, while others killed themselves with hand grenades. Some made a tremendous effort to get up and follow the unit pulling out, but most of them simply couldn't keep up. As they were about to leave, Adaniya ended up having a confrontation with a high-ranking officer over what to do with the wounded men. He voiced his opposition to the idea of just leaving them in the shelter, but the officer would not listen, insisting, "It takes three groups of four men working in turn to carry just one wounded soldier. That's twelve men. There's no food or ammunition where we're headed so if we were to carry these men from Shuri, we would need a huge number of extra soldiers. Therefore, we will leave them here with medical supplies." Adaniya had no choice to but to accept the decision to leave the wounded men behind in the shelter but, even after they arrived at Mabuni, he was still upset about what they had done. He explained the story to his men, suggesting, "Do you think we could save some of those guys." He felt terrible about asking as he knew exactly how tough it would be to go back along the arduous route they had just taken. But without hesitation, his men who must have been totally exhausted took up Adaniya's challenge. Approximately fifteen of them later returned with one of the wounded soldiers from the Shuri shelter. Adaniya was ecstatic and, although the soldier was then entrusted to the care of local civilians, he later died. "After we'd left the Shuri shelter," Adaniya explained, "it was blown up so the remains of those wounded soldiers who committed suicide in the shelter must still be there."

Although many of Adaniya's group died along the way, the rest made it to the 24th Infantry Division Command Post where they were finally able to rest. Most of the 24th Division had already left for the front so there was only a small number of officers and men still there in the shelter, creating a relaxed atmosphere. Only then was Adaniya informed by an adjutant in the 32nd Army Command Post advance party, which had already arrived and was now waiting for the others, that his destination was Mabuni. After resting for just an hour or two and having something to eat they immediately set off again. As they withdrew, they saw many dead and wounded along the way. During their time back at the Shuri shelter, some of the soldiers, in terrible pain after being badly wounded by artillery shells, had begged Adaniya, "Please! Finish me off with your pistol." Barely still alive and moaning and gasping in agony, the situation was truly appalling. Then, en route to Mabuni, they saw civilians in among the dead and wounded soldiers. Witnessing sights such as this on a daily basis had started to take its toll on Adaniya and the others. "People's emotions simply close down in such abnormal situations," he explained. "When we set off for Mabuni there were countless dead bodies scattered along the coastline and the stench was unbelievable, but we felt nothing."

It was already raining before the downpour really started. It was early in the morning when they left the 24th Infantry Division's shelter, taking extra care not to be detected by the enemy, but it was not until around 2:00 PM that they arrived at Mabuni. Once the 32nd Army Command Post staff had completed their move to Mabuni, the first order came through, namely that "Any person who goes up on top of the hill will be executed." The army chiefs of command arrived at Mabuni just before dawn on 30 May, three days after Adaniya and his men. "The military chiefs of command, the general staff section, the medical section and some of the adjutants' section were all housed in the shelter beneath what is now the *Reimei-no-To* Monument. The others were split up and deployed under small rocky outcrops nearby. There were also many Normal School students already there. When we were in the shelter at Shuri, there were seven or eight women from [the red-light district of] Tsuji but I didn't see them again after we got to Mabuni." Adaniya's position was on a slope to the south of the shelter where the commanders were housed. His routine included going from there to the general staff section once or twice each day. There was no clearly formed track however, just a path formed from walking back and forth clinging to the rocks. "What is now the *Reimei-no-To* monument was then a food preparation area where Normal School students were put to work gathering water, collecting firewood, and digging for potatoes. They couldn't prepare food during the day so they worked at night, lugging the food up in buckets. It must have been tough work carrying it up those rocky slopes."

As the IJA withdrew, civilians attempting to shelter from the maelstrom encountered endless problems, including being ejected from caves and having their food stolen by soldiers. On hearing that one of the officers in the 32nd Army Command was from Okinawa, a local civilian approached Adaniya. "Every day the soldiers steal our potatoes and take our sugar. Isn't there something you can do?" he pleaded. "The man's name was Matayoshi, from Mabuni. There were occasions when I went to a shelter and kicked the soldiers out," explained Adaniya. The Americans were close to Mabuni by around the middle of June, and on the evening of 19 June, Adaniya spotted four American tanks from up on his hillside position. The tanks approached from where the Peace Memorial Park is now, stopping just below the village side entrance to the 32nd Command Post shelter. Some American soldiers climbed out of the tanks and spent fifteen to twenty minutes digging holes in the ground with their spades. Adaniya immediately reported back to the adjutants' section, "The enemy knows where our command post is! Surely we can't just stay inside and die. Before they attack, let me go out and attack them first!" But he was rebuked by the adjutants and a staff officer who replied, "No! We won't allow anyone to act on their own." However, he soon learned about their plan of attack. "The plan was for everyone to go out and end their days in hand-to-hand fighting with the enemy as they approached from the village side. Generals Cho and Ushijima would both watch developments from their lookout before committing suicide," is how Adaniya described the plan of attack, which was quickly abandoned anyway.

There were many natural caves around Mabuni with civilians sheltering inside. Around dusk, large groups of them would gather at a water hole just down from the where the *Kenji-no-To* Monument now stands. Dusk was when the U.S. naval guns stopped for a rest and therefore was one of the very few times when civilians could venture out onto the battlefield. But one day, it all changed dramatically. "I think it was around 6:00 PM on 15 June. The Americans now realized that people were gathering at the spring and so the naval guns opened fired on it. Many people were killed, and from then on even the civilians began moving away to other areas." Out at sea, the naval guns fired relentlessly, and U.S. troops waited on the village side of the shelter. So with nowhere to flee, the civilians tied dirty white material up in the branches of trees. Then, waving their hands in the air, they walked toward the enemy. The Americans held their fire as the group of civilians filed out walking in the direction of Gushikami.

The groups of civilians looked absolutely exhausted as they walked along with their children, carrying only a few household items on their heads. Adaniya stared at them from his position up on the hill but, when he looked more closely, he noticed large numbers of soldiers who had taken off their uniforms and were mingling in among the crowds of civilians. "The Americans probably couldn't tell, but for anyone in the army, it was just so obvious. They were wearing army issue shirts and long underwear and carrying children so as not to stand out. But to me, it was as plain as day that they were soldiers," explained Adaniya. They were obviously deserters, but military authority had already collapsed and there was nobody left to stop them.

As each day passed, more and more people from the command post were killed. Before long, the shelter was full of the bodies of men killed in attacks from above or direct hits from shells from U.S. naval guns. Adaniya recalls that around 16 June he was making his usual trip to the staff officers' area and had gone past the entrance to the veterinary section's shelter. "The veterinary unit's shelter was under a ridge on the south side of the command post facing some fields. Anyway, passing by there on my way to the staff officers' quarters, I saw two or three soldiers at the shelter entrance leading to the shaft that connected it to the shelter. It was hot inside so they were sitting out there." It did not take Adaniya long to finish what he had to do in the staff officers' room but, when he came back past the veterinary shelter, it was a burned out ruin, scorched black all the way to a nearby pine forest. "I was at risk of being caught by enemy planes," Adaniya continued, "so I put my hands together and prayed, then quickly took off. They'd poured petrol in and lit it, so I guess all of them had been killed."

Even today, one sight Adaniya cannot forget is what he observed in the chief of staff's room at around the same time. Inside the room, which had guards standing on duty outside, he saw two figures in the flickering light of a single candle. "I looked hard and realized that the person facing me was Chief of Staff Cho Isamu, while the one with his back to me was a smaller man in national uniform [kokumin-fuku]." Cho had a very serious look on his face. The two men were facing each other and, although Adaniya could not make out what they were talking about, he could tell it was something important. Adaniya continued, "The other man was Okinawa Governor Shimada Akira, and I think he had gone there to say his last farewells. Civilians were not allowed near that shelter but I guess Shimada was able to go and talk with Cho like that because he was the governor." Chief of Staff Cho was known for being an outgoing and animated character, and Adaniya summed him up as follows: "He was just the opposite of Ushijima. Even when they were back at Shuri, when things were going badly Cho would rant and rave at his subordinates. But if he received good news, he'd be just the opposite. Then he'd be in a great mood and call out to them, 'Hey, get me a beer.'"

One man who regularly disagreed with Chief of Staff Cho on matters of strategy was Senior Staff Officer Yahara Hiromichi. Adaniya talked about Yahara in the following terms: "Even at military college, Yahara was a brilliant man who stood out as the best of an elite group. As a soldier, he was the reserved, intellectual type. Another officer, Nagano Hideo, was a similar sort of guy and the two got on very well. Maybe the fact that he had been based in America as a *military attaché* was at least part of the reason why he was rather logical in his thinking. The army had sent him into a few dangerous areas and difficult situations, so he always seemed to be disgruntled with his lot. Nevertheless, the fact that he was such a brilliant man meant that he committed himself totally to creating a strategy for Okinawa's defense. The truth of the matter of course is that had he chosen to throw his support behind making a final stand at Shuri rather than the battle of attrition strategy that he advocated, far fewer civilian lives would have been lost."

Adaniya remembers an incident that occurred around the middle of June. As was the norm, he'd been summoned by the staff officers' section and had gone to the command post shelter. Near the entrance, the chief intelligence officer was on the telephone, while over behind him was Commander-in-Chief Ushijima Mitsuru. Ushijima was sitting quietly by himself. Adaniya doesn't remember exactly what the Intelligence Officer was discussing but to this day he remembers very clearly what happened when he reported to Ushijima, "It's from Adm. Nimitz, Sir." At that point, Ushijima hissed furiously, "I suppose it's the same thing again, is it? What the hell is this idiot talking about!" That was the first time Adaniya had heard Ushijima talk with such anger or look so enraged. "Even now I still don't know how they used the telephone to communicate," he added, "whether they did it with the Americans directly, or whether it was via our own front line units. However, I remember that it was the first and last time I saw Ushijima in such a wild rage."

After the war, Senior Staff Officer Yahara's testimony clarifed that the U.S. force's call for the Japanese to surrender arrived on 17 June via a Japanese unit at the front line. The testimony also stated that the message was from Gen. Buckner and that it was delivered to Chief- of- Command Ushijima. I queried Adaniya as to whether that might have been incorrect and that the message hadn't come from Buckner at all. Adaniya replied confidently, "I don't remember it being from Buckner. No, it wasn't from Buckner in the Army. I'm sure that it was from Nimitz in the U.S. Navy."

By that time, nobody was feeling even remotely optimistic, and the only two possible options within the command post were surrender or suicide. Adaniya had seen countless numbers of soldiers die but he was now also witnessing the deaths of boys in the Blood and Iron Student Corps. One day, as he was sitting on a rocky outcrop and thinking about the pointless loss of so many young lives, he flew into a wild rage, saying to himself, "Who's the idiot who started this war?" But of course there was nothing he could do about it. His only option was to put his life in the hands of those issuing "military decisions." The 32nd Army was on its last legs and on 18 or 19 June when Adaniya was summoned by the staff officers, the sight that greeted him was very different: the officers were all cleaning their own pistols. Adaniya thought it strange, and when he asked what was going on they told him they had a plan to break out of Mabuni. The plan was to harass the enemy from the rear and report back to Imperial High Command. According to testimony from those involved, Senior Staff Officer Yahara had been allocated a staff member to look after Imperial Headquarters communications, officers Kimura Masaharu and Miyake Tadao were to use local connections to infiltrate various areas of the prefecture, while officers Yakumaru Kanenori and Nagano Hideo were to engage in guerrilla warfare. Adaniya's orders were to "head north and help harass the enemy from the rear."

Some of the army officers and command post staff quit the Mabuni shelter on the evening of 19 June. Adaniya and his group received their withdrawal orders the following day, the 20th, and departed that same evening. Adaniya explained, "Yahara was to make his move after confirming that Lt. Gen. Ushijima and Chief of Staff Cho were dead, but the rest of us left Mabuni around the 20th." Before setting off, however, he discussed the situation with his subordinates. "We talked about how we might die at anytime, so if anybody did manage to make it out alive, he was to contact the other men's families." It was certainly the right time for that sort of discussion. Then, all of a sudden, the shelter in which they had been hiding took a direct hit from one of the U.S. naval guns. When Adaniya looked around, he saw one of his subordinates with his foot blown off, screaming in agony. Adaniya yelled, "Get a doctor! Get a medic!" but there were so many people already wounded that there was nobody available to come to help and the man died soon after. He was from Miyazaki Prefecture and, just before he was killed, he told Adaniya that he had a house near the Ikemi Shrine and that before joining up he had been running a car repair business. "As soon as the war ended, I asked about him at the local government office but I never heard anything back from them," lamented Adaniya. "I've already forgotten his name too, but I really would like to be able to tell his family what happened." The issue obviously still weighs heavily on Adaniya's mind.

During the morning of 20 June, the day that Adaniya left Mabuni, the roar of the bombardment continued unabated. But in the afternoon, the guns mysteriously fell silent and, apart from a faint rumble in the distance toward Makabe, the quiet was something Adaniya had not experienced in a very long time. "I thought, the war was over," he explained. The end of the booming artillery was an indication that the fighting was almost over. Before setting off, Adaniya visited Matayoshi, the man from Mabuni who had earlier been treated badly by Japanese soldiers and had sought Adaniya's assistance. When Adaniya told him, "The decision's been made, we're pulling out," the man said, "Here, put this on," and handed Adaniya a kimono. The dark blue kimono came down to his knees and was obviously just what a farmer would wear, so Adaniya was pleased. Some of the soldiers were approaching civilian refugees and getting them to hand over their old, tattered clothes. Those who couldn't "acquire" a change of clothing in this manner simply discarded their uniforms, keeping only their army-issue shirts and long underpants. Many of the senior officers made off after changing into suits and the like from personal wicker trunks that they had had carried from Shuri.

Adaniya recalls that on the evening they left, the moon seemed to be brighter than he had ever seen it before. "Maybe because of the endless fighting, I'd just never had time to really look at the moon. But that night it was a full moon, as bright as day itself. It was a beautiful evening." Adaniya's men were told to assemble in the moonlight, although there were only twenty or so of them remaining. He had lost about half of his men as they withdrew from Shuri and, even after they arrived at Mabuni, their number halved again as men collapsed or died before his very eyes. Adaniya recalled, "At that stage, all formal structure had collapsed. People were going in all directions, including defeated Japanese soldiers. But there was no longer any formal distinction between officers and men." Adaniya said to his exhausted men, "It's no longer possible for us to operate as a cohesive unit. If you have family, friends or people you know nearby, go and see them. After that, get in behind the enemy, link up with the Kunigami Detachment, and take your orders from them." Those were the last orders that Adaniya issued.

But he also gave them some advice for when they moved out. "One option is to cut straight through the middle of enemy lines, but that's too dangerous. The best way to get out of here is to stay as close to the coastline as you can. Also, it's easy for the enemy to see you if you move about in groups, so make sure you travel in small numbers." His advice was based on having heard that many officers had been killed while taking the direct route through the middle, plus from scouts' reports which had identified enemy positions. But above all, it was his local knowledge from being born and raised in Okinawa and knowing the island's geography that made him suggest a course along the coast. After issuing his instructions and dismissing his men, Adaniya prepared to head off, abandoning the shelter he had been in for almost a month. By then it was already late at night.

Adaniya hid his pistol and sword at the back of a rocky outcrop. He also wrapped up his binoculars in his uniform and then in a *furoshiki*, hid them in the same place and then headed away. At that stage he felt, "I might be able to come back and get these at some point." However, several years after the war ended, he returned to the spot, but the sword and the pistol were no longer there. His uniform had rotted badly so he left it where it was. Adaniya was now dressed as a civilian, so couldn't openly carry weapons, but did hide two hand grenades in a towel inside his kimono. Of course, they were so he could take his own life. Three of his subordinates followed Adaniya, a sentry and two of his friends who had asked to join them. The bright moonlight that evening meant they ran the risk of being spotted by the enemy, but Adaniya felt it was still a better option than stumbling along in the dark looking for tracks.

Adaniya and his group left Mabuni and made their way northeast along the coastline. They were heading for the Kunigami Detachment up in the hills of the northern region of Kunigami where they would link up, and take the fight to the enemy. Making their way along the coast, they came across vast numbers of dead bodies scattered everywhere. But they didn't see a living soul, either military or civilian, either in the water or on land. The dead bodies floated in and out with each wave, while others had already been washed up on the shore where they lay silhouetted in the moonlight. But by then Adaniya felt nothing—such sights were all too common on the battlefield of Okinawa.

They were just short of Giizabanta where they spotted some American soldiers resting on a hill. The enemy soldiers saw Adaniya's group passing close by and immediately fired their machine guns wildly in their direction. Unable to move any farther ahead, they had no option but to hide behind a rocky outcrop and stay put. "I knew it was impossible to go any farther on land. Our only choice was to take to the water," Adaniya explained. After a while, one of his subordinates noticed a small *sabani* skiff bobbing about in the waves. It was damaged but Adaniya felt that they could use it to get away. The four of them held tightly on to the skiff with one hand and used their free hands to gently push their way through the water. However, they also had to abandon that idea before long. "Even though it was June, it was cold. Just when I was thinking that we could not keep paddling along like that a bullet whizzed over my head so we turned back."

So for the second time, they went back to where they started and spent the night there, unsure of what to do next. The following morning, a straightforward way to escape presented itself. A number of civilians, men women, elderly, and children had formed into a group and were filing along the shore heading for Gushikami. Adaniya and his men simply joined the group and started walking, doing their best to look as if they belonged there. Adaniya had already discarded his uniform, and his only weapons were the two hand grenades concealed inside his clothes. In his old farmer's kimono that just reached his knees, there was nothing to distinguish him from the civilians around him who had lost everything in the fighting. The group was quickly taken into custody by the Americans, so the only option left to them to get to Kunigami was to wait for the opportunity to escape from a holding camp.

The camp was located on a flat area facing what is now the Gushikami Elementary School. Before entering the camp, however, they were interrogated by American soldiers. That was when Adaniya became separated from his men. When an American asked, "Age?" Adaniya, who was really forty years old, immediately replied, "Fifty-seven." Maybe in the back of his mind he was thinking that members of the Home Guard were all under forty-five years of age. "I hadn't had a haircut for quite some time so it was pretty long, plus I'd gone quite gray as well so that was lucky," Adaniya explained. The American didn't seem to suspect that anything was strange at all so Adaniya's interrogation finished with the single question about his age. His three subordinates, however, were around twenty years old. When they said that they were civilians, the American soldiers didn't believe them and put them into a compound surrounded by a wire mesh fence.

Adaniya's life as a soldier ended the day he entered the camp, and he spent his days there passing himself off as a civilian until the war came to a close. "Soon after the war ended," he explained, "I discovered that Yahara (Senior Staff Officer Hiromichi Yahara) had been in the same camp. He wrote in his memoir that he wore an old suit and passed himself off as a civilian. But after that, I didn't hear much of him at all. There were a lot of people there from the prefectural office and the police and many of them would have known who he was because he had been in charge of military strategies. Someone must have told the Americans that he was there."

Adaniya had been inextricably pulled away from his work as a teacher and toward the army. Looking back on it all now, he recalls, "How could we have been so stupid? Once the Great East Asian War started, we did bayonet training at school and dug potatoes to increase food production. It wasn't education in the real sense of the word. Schools became schools in name only. The outcome for all those young people who cooperated with the war effort was that they got killed in the fighting, one after the other. It was just terrible," he muttered. Adaniya had known that once the people of Japan had been trapped by the war machine history had pushed them inevitably toward disaster.

In January 1946, the first repatriation ship out of Naha steamed slowly away from the harbor. On board were some of the officers and men who, the previous year, had suffered a hell such as nobody had ever experienced, leaving them utterly and totally exhausted. But, having regained their strength after many months in American POW camps, the men were much brighter knowing that they were finally going back home to their families. Every man on that ship felt the same sense of joy at leaving Okinawa, which was so scarred by the ravages of war that its very landscape had been altered. One of the men was Kazuo Tamaki and his sense of relief at being able to return to his hometown of Kagoshima was plain to see. According to American records, Tamaki was a civilian from Naha who had had some teaching experience in Korea. However, that information was just part of the lies he told the Americans when he was captured. His real name was Kiyoshi Haginouchi and of course he was not a civilian, but a lieutenant in Okinawa's *Kempeitai* [military police].

Now aged eighty-three (in 1983) and living in good health in Kagoshima, Haginouchi recalled those years. "The Americans knew I had been in the *Kempeitai* but I guess that inside the camp they just let it pass. It was probably the easiest option for them." Haginouchi actually performed an important task during the fighting on Okinawa, namely identifying the bodies of Lt. Gen. Ushijima and Chief of Staff Cho, whose deaths effectively signaled the end of the Battle of Okinawa. Moreover, he also instructed the 32nd Army's Lt. Sakaguchi Masaru, who assisted with the suicides, on the old-style ritual protocols to be used.

Haginouchi and Lt. Sakaguchi from Kumamoto Prefecture were particularly good friends. They were the same age, held the same rank, and had reached the fourth dan at kendo so they had much in common. Before the Battle of Okinawa commenced, Sakaguchi was taught by Haginouchi how to officially assist with a ritual suicide. "Sakaguchi thought that assisting with ritual suicides was something that the *Kempeitai* would do. I told him not to talk such crap so he asked me, 'What are the protocols of ritual suicide?' So I told him everything I knew. A long time before the Americans landed, I would say January or February, or even earlier than that, Sakaguchi knew that this day would come," explained Haginouchi.

In mid-June, Haginouchi was captured in a cave in Tamagusuku while waiting for the chance to escape to Chinen Peninsula. "As well as some adjutants, inside the cave were around ten men from the *Kempeitai* including W.O. Katsuren, Sgt. Maj. Taira, plus about twenty civilians. For my escape I had swapped my army uniform for a kimono made of serge." After separating from his adjutants, Haginouchi was captured as a civilian but somewhat strangely, the American Intelligence Officer frequently approached Haginouchi. "I think they knew who I was at that stage," he explained. From around 20 June, he told Haginouchi over and over again that Ushijima was not dead but had escaped in a submarine, although each time Haginouchi refuted the claim. Then around 25 June, the officer said to Haginouchi, "Well, if you know Ushijima, can you identify the body?" and they took him away to Mabuni.

"I was taken to view the 'headless corpse' at a place about thirty or forty meters below the Command Post cave where it faced the coast. The bodies had been lined up there, buried in a hollow covered with some stones," Haginouchi explained. One of the bodies had been decapitated, but was clad in full army uniform with a military decoration attached, and white gloves. Haginouchi had taught Lt. Sakaguchi the protocols of ritual suicide and it did not take him long to work out that the body was that of Lt. Gen. Ushijima, a man older than himself but from the same part of Japan. The other body was wrapped in a slip made from two white sheets sewn together. He was wearing army uniform trousers but with only a white singlet above the waist. Written in ink on the singlet were the words extolling Chief of Staff Cho Isamu's loyalty to the nation. Having actually been there himself, Haginouchi looked doubtfully at the photo that the Americans had supposedly taken of the scene where the two officers had committed suicide. In the Battle of Okinawa many officers took their own lives, and even today he is not sure whether or not the photograph represents what the Americans claim it does.

Stranded on the Senkaku Islands

The fighting on the main island of Okinawa was all but over by 30 June 1945. That evening, the wharf at Ishigaki-jima was the scene of frenetic activity as civilians crowded onto evacuation ships bound for Taiwan. The military had requisitioned two ships for the trip, the *Chihaya No. 1* (*Tomofuku Maru*), and the *Chihaya No. 5* (*Isshin Maru*). Estimates of the total number of civilians crammed on board these two ships vary widely, with suggestions of 120, 180, or 240 people, but there is no doubting the fact that they were both jam-packed with evacuees.

"They were army orders so we simply had to get on board, but it was so crowded that there was hardly enough room to sit with our legs out in front of us," is how Oto Ishido described the situation. Because her husband was working on an island in the Pacific for a company manufacturing sugar, she found himself stranded in Naha and was on Miyako-jima when the war ended. Their eldest son had already been sent to high school in Taiwan, so the other four children were being evacuated. There were two boys, including their third and youngest son who was at kindergarten and two girls, the elder of whom who had been attending a girls' high school.

Even on remote Ishigaki-jima, people were being evacuated into the hills in order to escape the American air raids, while civilians on Hateruma-jima endured a living hell of malaria and starvation as a result of their forced evacuation to Iriomote-jima. Their evacuation ship received orders from the military to evacuate them to Taiwan about a week before departure.

Although the Battle of Okinawa is usually regarded as having finished on 23 June, hostilities on Miyako-jima and the Yaeyama Islands continued until the Japanese surrender on 15 August. This situation gave rise to the tragedy of the Senkaku Islands Shipwreck Incident.

While the incident is not well known, it involved the deaths of around seventy people—mainly civilians, but also some soldiers, Taiwanese and Koreans—from American air attacks and subsequently from the rigors of life on an uninhabited island. Twenty others who made it off the island later died from mental and physical breakdowns, and most of those who survived have remained tight-lipped about their hellish experience.

The experiences of the survivors were first recorded in Volume 10 of the Prefectural Historical Records, published after their repatriation. Yoshitomo Ishigaki (then aged forty-two) of Tonoshiro in Ishigaki City, together with six others originally from Ishigaki and Miyako, collated their experiences. The comments from Ishido, another survivor, were deliberate and solemn. Needless to say, it was no easy task for an elderly person to recall something so horrific that happened such a long time ago.

She said that almost fifty days of suffering, all the while looking after four children, "Reduced me to the stage where I barely looked human." She also explained that in their struggle with starvation, "We ate albatross once, and I'd never realized how delicious they tasted." Through the testimony of those who experienced that living hell, let's now retrace their journey starting with when the boats first set sail.

According to Kinjo Chinkichi from Arakawa in Ishigaki City, the *Isshin Maru* (*Chihaya Maru No. 5)* and the *Tomofuku Maru* (*Chihaya Maru No. 1)* each weighed 150 tons and were operating in the islands south of Okinawa dredging for shellfish. In order to defend the route between Ishigaki and Taiwan, which U.S. forces controlled from the sky, in the spring of 1945 the 45th Independent Mixed Brigade established the Maritime Combat Unit under Lt. Osagawa Sho-taro. The Unit requisitioned a number of fishing boats, with the *Chihaya Maru No. 1*, *Chihaya Maru No. 3*, and *Chihaya Maru No. 5* being formed into a convoy. Their captains, engineers, and crew members were all co-opted as army civilian personnel and the boats were fitted with light machine guns. Soldiers, including those originally from the area, crewed the boats. After opening up a sea lane between Ishigaki Island and Keelung in Taiwan, by-passing the Senkaku Islands, by May the Maritime Combat Unit was able to transport food and munitions.

On 30 June 1945, the boats set off on their second voyage, although the *Chihaya Maru No. 3* stayed behind due to engine problems. They loaded the evacuees onto the empty ships headed for Taiwan and, according to Iramina Kokichi (then in his first year at elementary school) who was evacuated to what is now Taouyuan in Hsinchu County in Taiwan, even a makeshift school was set up at their destination. The distance between the two islands was not great, so a close relationship had already developed before the war as many people had made the journey there seeking employment, seasonal work and schooling. On the evening of that fateful day of 30 June, the two ships with the evacuees aboard slipped out of Ishigaki Port under cover of darkness.

The convoy left Ishigaki Harbor and headed directly for the port of Funauki on Iriomote. Apart from the *Chihaya Maru No. 1* (*Tomofuku Maru*) and the *Chihaya No. 5* (*Isshin Maru*), there was also one other smaller vessel in the convoy, carrying wounded soldiers to Taiwan via Yonaguni Island. Under the command of Lt. Osagawa of the Maritime Combat Unit, the main convoy sailed directly to its destination. The two boats carrying the evacuees steered a course for Taiwan via the Senkaku Islands, with Sgt. Yamauchi Gen in command.

Ohama Nagamitsu was working at the Yaeyama Post Office at the time. "By then," he explained, "the post office had ceased operations. My family had been evacuated to Taiwan so I also headed to Sotoyamada with my workmates."

"I boarded the *Tomofuku-maru*. People from Okawa and Ishigaki were on my boat, while on the other boat were people from Tonoshiro and Arakawa. Because I was on 'official business,' I could choose whichever boat I wished. Shortly after we left the port, we could see that the streets of Ishigaki were ablaze. We left Funauki on 2 July."

According to Kinjo Chinkichi, chief engineer on the *Isshin-maru* at the time, "we left Funauki at around 7:00 PM on 2 July and took the same route as we had on our first trip (via the Senkaku Islands), planning to arrive in Keelung around 5:00 PM the following day." The sea was calm, there was not much wind, and some of the people onboard were singing happily. However, at around 2:00 PM on the 3rd, shortly before we were due to enter the port, both evacuee boats were detected by an American plane, apparently a B-24.

Miyara Tochi from Okawa on Ishigaki-jima followed his parents and three elderly women from his family on board the *Isshin Maru*. In his personal notes (Prefectural History Vol. 10), his vivid recollection of the attack is described as follows: "We were out in the middle of the ocean with nothing to protect us from the attack; not even a blade of grass to hide behind. With barely a glimmer of a hope of surviving, everybody on board was plunged into total despair. At the moment that we heard the thunderous roar of the planes, we were caught in their machine gun fire. An elderly woman on my right collapsed, yelling. A child on my left was hit and a person in front of me was badly wounded and screaming. I raced out of the hold and, when I got out onto the deck, I remember seeing people gasping for breath, barely alive. Someone whose hand had been shot off at the wrist was groaning in agony."

The B-24s arced round in the sky and attacked again. The *Isshin Maru* was ablaze, so any survivors trapped onboard were burned alive. Those who were able to, leapt into the sea to escape the flames.

"I heard that enemy planes were attacking us and, still not really believing that it was happening, I went up on deck, only to be immediately caught up in the hail of machine-gun fire. Our own machine guns were firing back but even when we hit them, bits would just fall off with no real effect. They were so close I could see the pilots' faces," explained Kinjo.

Around seventy of the evacuees died in the attack, as were the captain of the *Isshin Maru*, Miyagi Saburo, crew member Ikehara Shinsho, and the chief engineer of the *Tomofuku Maru*, Nakama Takehide. Those who managed to escape the attack with their lives had no time to feel relieved. None of them could have ever imagined the suffering that awaited them.

After the slaughter, the American planes flew away. Fortunately, the *Tomofuku Maru* did not catch fire, so they were able to lower her lifeboats and rescue the people drifting in the water. However, because the majority of the evacuees were elderly folk, women and children, many of them drowned. While Nakama, the chief engineer on the *Tomofuku Maru*, died instantly, Kinjo Chinkichi, his counterpart on the *Isshin Maru*, which had foundered in the flames, was unharmed. He worked tirelessly to repair the *Tomofuku Maru's* engine and the following morning (the 4th) at around 7:00 AM, with the engine barely turning over, the *Tomofuku Maru* arrived at Uotsuri-jima in the Senkaku group. Ishido Moto, who had stayed inside her cabin hugging her four children during the strafing attacks waiting for the "living hell" to end, explained, "We were told to disembark but all we could see was an uninhabited island with nothing on it. I thought we were headed for Taiwan."

Among the evacuees who landed on Uotsuri-jima was the family of Miyara Sachiko from Okawa in Ishigaki. At the time, she was looking after her two sons and five daughters. Her eldest daughter was in the fifth grade at elementary school, while the youngest child was just one and a half years of age. Her husband, Kenryo, had been drafted into the Home Guard. "Because I had the children with me, we were told to evacuate ahead of the rest. So together with my husband's brothers and an aunt, we were moved out early in the piece." She had heard that Taiwan was a big place and that they'd be safe there, so she took the plunge and decided to evacuate with her family.

Their life on the uninhabited island had begun. Initially, food was distributed on a communal basis, including handing over whatever items the survivors had brought with them. They managed to scratch together a little rice, some new shoots of fan palms and other vegetables, which they boiled up in a metal container. At the start, this broth tasted so bad that it was difficult to swallow. Miyara handed over all her rice and smoked tuna, but a just week later the communal approach came to a sudden halt and it became a case of everyone looking out for themselves as far as finding food was concerned. From that day on, the terrible struggle to feed herself and her seven children began. "In the beginning, we gathered mizuna mustard greens and *sakuna* [Peucedanum japonicum], but they quickly ran out. We knew that we could eat the sweet-tasting grass, so we basically ate anything. We had good supplies of fresh water, while natural salt gleamed as white as snow down by the water's edge.

The new shoots of fan palms were a precious source of food. They would cut off the tops so they could get at the new shoots that would go on to become leaves. However, a great deal of physical energy was required to cut them down. They also ate hermit crabs that they caught beneath the screw pines. However, catching them required such agility and energy that before long the task was too much for them in their weakened condition. One day when they were out looking for things to eat, her second eldest daughter, Nobuko (then in her third grade at elementary school) caught a sparrow. Even the tiny amount of meat on that bird was like a wonderful feast that evening as all eight of them had a taste of the flesh. As one day followed another, Miyara and her children had become anxious that their husband and father back on Ishigaki-jima must be distraught that they had vanished without trace. One day, they all looked out toward the sea and yelled out:

Daddyyyyy . . . !

We're not dead . . . !

We really are alive and we will come home!

Stay alive, Daddy . . . don't die!

Ishido Oto and her children were another shipwrecked family who had the same battle with starvation. "We were so envious of those people who were able to catch fish. We didn't have the energy to cut down the fan palms, so the children and I could only eat the soft parts that the others left." Twelve years old at the time, Shimoji Hiroshi explained, "I couldn't stand feeling so hungry any longer and, even though I'd been told, 'whatever you do, don't eat these,' I snuck away from my uncle to eat some broad beans. But just as I was thinking to myself, 'These are all right to eat,' I felt really sick and vomited uncontrollably. Ever since then, even though it's been almost thirty years, I still can't bring myself to eat beans of any sort." (*Prefectural History*, Vol. 10). People died from starvation but because the island was solid rock all they could do was wrap the dead bodies in fan palms and cover them with stones. The stench of death was everywhere.

They tasted every green thing growing on the island and consumed just about everything that was edible, so their supply of food quickly started to run out. As they became weaker and weaker, many in the group died in quick succession. At first, they were hopeful that a boat would come to rescue them, but gradually those hopes faded into the endless days of their wretched existence. Having given up all hope, "All we could do was wait there until we died. Early in August, about a month after we had been shipwrecked, we agreed to dispatch a 'do or die squad.'" Using the planking and nails from an old shipwreck washed up on the other side of the island, they were going to launch their own boat so they could make contact with the outside world. There seemed to be no other way to save the survivors.

Several days after the shipwreck, the *Chihaya Maru No. 1* (*Tomofuku Maru*), mechanical repairs complete, set off for Ishigaki to let people know what had happened. On the way, however, the engine broke down so the crew abandoned ship and took to the lifeboat, only just managing to make it back to Uotsuri-jima. With that, the last means of contacting those who had been shipwrecked was lost. Yet they had a stroke of good luck when building their little boat, for not only was one of their number Yagi Yoshio, a boat builder, but he had managed to save his tools from the burning vessel.

The evacuees' spirits soared. Even those who had been lying around thinking, "I'm already done for," headed off to get boat-building materials. They ripped the planking off the old wreck, pulled out the nails and straightened them, one by one. While the men dismantled the hulk and hauled various bits and pieces back, the women pooled their spare cloth and made a sail. Yagi drove himself almost to total exhaustion so that after ten days they had completed a five-meter *sabani* fishing skiff, the boat which was going to sail the 170 kilometer journey to Ishigaki-jima.

The "do or die squad" consisted mainly of crew members. Together with the seven-man crew of Uehara Kametaro (then aged 22), Enokawa Seicho (18), Irei Ryosei (also 18), Irei Seitoku (age unknown), Misato Yukichi (17), Misato Seikichi (20) and Kinjo Chinkichi, was Sgt. Yamauchi. Then, just as they were about to set off, a warrant officer from the paymaster's section also climbed aboard. Before they cast off, they cut their nails and hair which they left with the others as remembrance tokens in case they didn't make it. Around 5:00 PM on 12 August, the surviving evacuees, by now all on the brink of death from starvation, gathered to bid farewell to the little boat which carried their last vestige of hope with it. They wore red *hachimaki* headbands made from a kimono provided by one of the evacuees who told them, "This was my grandmother's good luck kimono that she wore for her eighty-eighth birthday. I want you to make it safely and get someone to rescue us." The crew attached their sea chart and compass, on which the success or failure of their journey rested, firmly to the mast. Then, with a fair wind at their backs, the vessel sailed away. They were in constant fear of encountering enemy planes and, whenever one drew near, they would flip their boat upside down and wait underneath it for the aircraft to fly away.

The next day—the 13th—the wind died away so the only option was to use shells to paddle for all they were worth. Even as they did so, the fear that "I wonder if we will ever make it to the Yaeyamas" filled their minds. Exhaustion was closing in when suddenly they spotted two mountains through a break in the clouds. "There aren't any mountains on Miyako. That must be Omoto-dake on Ishigaki . . . surely." Kinjo explained, "Our hunger and suffering simply vanished and we suddenly felt so much better. Our eyes lit up and the strength returned to our paddling arms. We paddled for all we were worth."

On the evening of the following day—the 14th—their little boat arrived in Sokochi Bay in Kabira. Since they set off, they had kept up their energy by eating fan palm shoots each midday and evening. All they could do was hug each other's exhausted bodies and weep. They were simply too exhausted to move. Then, one of the crew picked some wild guavas growing nearby and tossed them over to the others. As they bit into the fruit, they gradually began to realize they were still alive.

The news soon reached the IJA unit stationed at Muribushi-utaki in Kabira and from there to the brigade where they were astounded to learn of the terrible circumstances of the evacuees. They then informed Taiwan by cable and on 16 August—the day after the war ended—planes dropped food supplies onto Uotsuri-jima. Kinjo explained, "It felt as if the gods of Muribushi-utaki had pulled us all the way and I am still eternally grateful." Kinjo has never been back to the Senkaku Islands. He said, "To tell you the truth, I start to shake and I don't even like talking about it."

Those who had been left behind on Uotsuri-jima had no way of knowing that the war had ended, but on 15 August, a plane was spotted overhead. Because the evacuees had already experienced one American air attack, as soon as they heard the roar of aircraft engines, they immediately dashed away and hid behind some rocks. From their hiding place, they stared up at the plane circling overhead. Clearly visible on its fuselage was the red circle from the Japanese national flag.

"It's one of ours!" somebody yelled out, at which the others came running out from behind the rocks. Tears poured down the faces of the evacuees, who by this stage really were in the depths of despair. Cries of *"Banzai! Banzai!"* rang out. "They made it! They've told them about us!" Their joy at finally making contact with the outside world was enormous. A parcel containing dried biscuits and little round sugar sweets was dropped by parachute. "As the plane flew in very low and dropped the parachute, we got a real fright as we truly through they were bombs," explained Ohama Eijo. "We were so relieved because those food parcels saved our lives." There were enough dried biscuits for the evacuees to receive about twenty-five each. The sugar sweets were for those who were ill, on the condition that each such person went out and retrieved them themselves. Miyara Sachiko left her eldest daughter—who was too sick to walk—in their little hut. She then lifted her desperately ill baby onto her back and took the hand of her eldest son and her fourth daughter. Her second daughter hoisted their fifth daughter onto her back and took the hand of the third daughter. When her children cried out, "Ahh, it hurts . . . I can't walk," the mother urged them to walk, finally managing to pick up all seven portions of sweets for her family.

Three days later, on the 18th, three rescue boats arrived at Uotsuri-jima. Hearing the call "Boats . . . boats have arrived!!" the evacuees tore down all the fan palms and grass tufts off their huts and lit a fire at the inlet mooring to guide the boat in. "From today, Uotsuri is out of my life forever!" they thought. After almost fifty days, they ripped down their tiny, damp hovels and threw the whole lot onto the fire. Aboard one of the rescue ships was Lt. Osagawa Kotaro of the Maritime Combat Unit, along with members of council. A bushel of rice—something they had only been able to dream about—was given out to each family group. Miyara Sachiko quickly cooked up a rice gruel, but as her seven children tried to eat even the smallest amount, it came straight back up as their stomachs were already unable to absorb any solid food. The effects of their starvation existence continued long after they made it safely back to Ishigaki.

Boarding the rescue boats, they were permitted to take only the absolute minimum with them, so they had to abandon everything they had gathered together for the evacuation. "We were told 'Anyone who wants to keep their belongings has to stay here.' It was really upsetting," Miyara Sachiko explained angrily, "to hear that everybody's precious belongings were to be left behind, but we left with nothing except the clothes on our backs." Miyara Tochi lost his elderly mother and an elderly female relative. His father Tosei, aged eighty-two at the time, was critically ill and unable to move. His grandson Tofusa "was very weak. Some people told us to leave him there but apparently Ohama Eijun carried him in a straw basket and put him on the boat. He saved my grandson's life." Circumstances meant that they talked of leaving the critically ill behind so the evacuees couldn't even take the remains of those who had been buried on the island's rocky shoreline. After the war, some people went back to collect them but they had been washed away by the tide and not a single remnant was found.

On the afternoon of 19 August, they arrived at Ishigaki after having been away since 30 June. Incredibly, during their rescue no one told the evacuees about the war having ended. They were all so exhausted and in such poor physical condition that their appearance had changed dramatically. "My father came to meet us," explained Miyara Sachiko, "but he didn't recognize me. We were so emaciated and looked so different that no one could tell whether we were male or female, young or old. Only when my second daughter got off the boat and ran toward him did he finally work out who I was." It was a long time before the evacuees regained their physical health. Some died because their stomachs were so weak that they simply couldn't eat, while quite a number of the very emaciated ones died without recovering at all. Miyara Sachiko, who lost her fifth daughter during the first week and her second son the following week, recorded the following comments in the Prefectural historical records. "Only seven months after our rescue was I able to start walking again, and during the first four months, I had to wear diapers all the time. When I think about it, I got to death's door but thank goodness I was turned away. I realize that I was lucky beyond measure to have escaped with my life. My eternal prayer is that I will never have to experience war again."

The Senkaku Islands Incident produced many casualties. Three rescue boats carried the survivors to Ishigaki, and it seemed that, for the time being at least, the tragedy was at an end. However, another tragedy had already been unfolding for several days, one that was to put the Senkaku Islands back into the spotlight. Six men who had gone to the neighboring Minamiko-jima in search of food found themselves left behind by the rescue vessels and were forced to experience yet another taste of hell on earth. Aged forty-seven at the time, Iramina Kokichi was one of the six men. A few years ago, he met up with Miyagawa Motoki, one of the survivors (aged thirty-one at the time of the tragedy) and was able to ask him about what happened back then. His version of events is as follows.

As well as Iramina and Miyagawa, the six men included Murayama (then aged sixty-nine), Suzuki who had been living on Ishigaki, Okamoto, and another young man also from the main islands. On the day the evacuees were rescued, the six men were actually on the neighboring Minamiko-jima. The reason for this was that after it was decided to send the "do or die" mission, the six men crossed to Minamiko to gather albatross meat for the "do or die" travelers to take. After two or three days, they were returning with albatross meat and eggs which would provide the men with the essential nutrition they needed to complete the voyage. However, the fierce current that runs between the two islands decided their fate by sweeping them away in the wrong direction. The tide between the two islands flowed in a southerly direction. The men started paddling for all they were worth but soon had no choice but to tack across the current because, if they had continued to go with the tide, they would have ended up at Kitako-jima and, if they hadn't managed that, they would have been in danger of ending up in the East China Sea.

Although the six men managed to collect the food supplies, they then struggled to get back in the face of the powerful current, and it took them ten days to eventually return to Uotsuri-jima. However, the rescue of the shipwrecked evacuees had taken place much earlier than the six men had anticipated. They were all already off the island, leaving behind nothing but a note which read, "We can't risk the lives of all of these people by waiting for you six, so we have been rescued before you. As soon as we arrive at Ishigaki we will arrange for a boat to pick you up right away, so just hang on in there for a bit longer." As soon as the elderly Iramina and Murayama read the note, their hearts sank. "We accepted all the dangers of going to Minamiko-jima to support the 'do or die' mission . . . and then they abandoned us." Their feelings of despair were extreme.

The six men gradually picked themselves back up. To increase their chances of survival, they shifted their little huts up onto higher ground, from where it would be easier to spot any passing ships. There were three huts and they slept two men to a hut. The elderly Iramina and Murayama shared one hut. Their food quickly ran out, yet the men didn't find the going too tough. Although they only ate fan palms, they cut one down each day and shared it among the six of them. Also, there were small crabs to be had, so as far as the actual amount of food went, it was sufficient. Then one day in the middle of September, Murayama remained in bed complaining of feeling ill. He died the following morning. Iramina, who was sharing the hut with him, also began calling out and crying. Two weeks later, loud yelling could be heard from inside the hut as Iramina complained of a fever and that he was feeling unwell. The following day he was unable to go out and gather the insides of a fan palm to eat so, the other four men prepared the food instead. Iramina died on the morning of 27 September, after developing a fever and becoming delirious. Like Murayama, his remains were buried near the fresh water spring. The remaining four men were not rescued until November, by a passing Taiwanese fishing boat.

As a result of the Senkaku Islands Shipwreck Incident, Takayoshi Iramina lost not only his father, but also his older sister, a nurse, during the strafing attack by the American plane. His sister ignored the warnings of those around her and with her carry-bag full of bandages and medical supplies over her shoulder, the hard-working woman disappeared without a trace. Takayoshi explained, "I don't really remember my father very well, but I still have these nagging doubts in my mind as to why no boat set sail to pick them up. The local authorities talked about sending a rescue mission, but then several months went by and in the end they were picked up by a Taiwanese fishing boat. Just because things were in such turmoil at the end of the war was no excuse to abandon six people . . ." He still cannot get these thoughts out of his mind.

Even before Okinawa reverted to Japanese sovereignty, it was widely known that there was an offshore oilfield near the Senkaku Islands, which created tension among Taiwan, China, and Japan over the sovereignty of the islands. In 1896, the Japanese government incorporated the Senkaku Islands into the Yaeyama territory and today, Uotsuri-jima is officially identified as being part of Ishigaki. The islands have been the focus of an ongoing territorial dispute with China.

Some people regarded it as unfair for compensation to be paid to residents who, because of military orders, found themselves shipwrecked as they were being evacuated to Taiwan. At the same time, there was also the matter of the *Tsushima Maru*, which the Okinawan Society for Outer Territories was pursuing in tandem with the Senkaku Islands Tragedy. In 1971 Makino Kiyoshi drew a strong reaction when he wrote in the *Okinawan Quarterly* an article called "The Senkaku Islands—aka Igunkuba Islands—a Short History." When he petitioned the prefectural governor he was told, "We are prepared to consider the case of those who died, but those who survived . . ." The sticking point was that Senkaku Islands were designated as part of Ishigaki and *not* as an outlying territory.

As a result of Makino's petitioning the council, a payment was made in May 1972. Thirty-four people who were living on Ishigaki at the time were official-ly acknowledged and each given 30,000 yen. However, the four members of Takamiyagi Shosuke's family (Takamiyagi was born in 1901 and was originally from the main island) had no family register, so they received only the official acknowledgment. Also, the family of Capt. Miyagi Saburo (killed in the attack by U.S. aircraft), plus two others, were awarded government pensions. Although it was said that payments would not be made for children under six years of age, Miyara Sachiko, explained that she received 30,000 yen for each of the two chil-dren she lost, one aged three, the other aged one, so there were also aspects of the process that were unclear.

In some cases, it seems that the confusion surrounding compensation was because of confusion over people's identities. Not only were some people from the local area, but some were from other places as well, such as the woman from Korea. Ohama Eijun explained, "She was next to me on the boat and was shot in the wrist during the attack. She made it to the uninhabited island where a soldier cut off her hand which had been connected by little more than some skin and sinew. She was later rescued from the island. I didn't ask her name but she was about thirty years old . . . she worked in the bar trade." There was also a Tai-wanese family on the boat, and Miyara Sachiko witnessed their daughter being shot in the head and killed instantly during the attack. She thinks the family was originally from Taiwan but had settled in Ishigaki around that time, but is not really sure.

In the end, unlike the full pensions awarded to the bereaved families from the *Tsushima Maru* incident, those involved in the Senkaku Islands tragedy received only a consolation payment. In its 1978 project plan, the Okinawa Association for Outer Territories Resettlement made the following request with regard to relief measures for those shipwrecked on the Senkaku Islands [abridged]:

"In January 1976, those involved in the *Tsushima Maru* incident were award-ed full pensions as requested. However, the Senkaku Islands incident was also the result of military orders and, in spite of the fact that those involved should receive the same treatment, the process has seen them handled unfairly . . . we strongly urge that this matter be resolved at the earliest possible juncture."

Forced Out by Japanese soldiers

The shelters in the southern part of the island of Okinawa ceased being a safe haven for civilians once the Japanese 32nd Army was forced to retreat southward in the face of American attacks. Whenever Japanese soldiers arrived at a cave, at least the equivalent number of civilians was forced out to make room for them. Arakaki Shin'ichi's mother, Ushi, was one of those forced out of Araree-gama (in Arakawa, Haebaru) in this manner.

The six members of his family were inside the cave, which, during the intense naval bombardment, had provided a safe refuge for them. Yet things changed dramatically when the Japanese soldiers arrived. With nothing more than "The army's using this place now so get out," as an explanation, they were no longer able to shelter in the cave. The second eldest daughter, aged twenty-two, was wounded and unable to walk, so when the family left the cave, her husband stayed behind to take care of her. Outside, shells rained down but, by keeping very low as they went, the woman and her three other children finally managed to make their way to a shelter in Ishiki.

The following morning, they were taken prisoner, so they survived. However, they never again saw the two who stayed behind in Araree-gama. They asked all over the place about them, but the only news they heard was that the daughter had been captured in Araree-gama but had died very soon after. Nobody was able to confirm whether or not her husband had made it out of the cave.

"Our eldest daughter was hit by mortar fire. If she'd been further back in the cave, she'd have been all right," Ushi explained sadly. She had urged her daughter several times to move away from the cave entrance and to go deeper into the cave. Further inside, the cave was a sea of mud, just like a paddy field, but at least it was safe. However, her daughter refused to move, complaining, "it's filthy back there."

"The cave entrance was blocked off with tatami mats but they were of no use. A piece of shrapnel went straight through, blowing off part of her foot." The bleeding wouldn't stop. The daughter was a member of the nursing corps so she actually had some medication, but she'd given it to a Japanese soldier she came across earlier saying, "Here, you use it," Ushi lamented.

"If only we'd had even some antiseptic for her, she might have survived," Shini-chi explained. She died from tetanus very soon after her capture by the Americans. "Her remains are probably still out there somewhere in Tomigusuku."

One group that remained in Araree-gama right to the end was the extend-ed family of Kiyomoto Kikue, then aged twenty-two. Four households—twen-ty-four people in all—lived there for almost two weeks until they were captured on 18 June. A year earlier, Kikue had gone to Taiton in Gushikami to get married, but toward the end of March, she revisited her parents' ancestral home at Taka-mine in Toyohara to celebrate the spring equinox. However, the bombardment and then the fighting became so intense that she had not been able to get back again. Every member of her in-law's family at Taiton, including her husband, who had been drafted from there, perished.

Up until the beginning of June, the family had been staying in a shelter in their old house, but eventually had to make their way southward. However, the move would have been too much for her grandfather and another elderly rela-tive, both almost eighty years of age, so they left them food and water and head-ed away promising, "Once we find a shelter, we'll come back and get you." What became of the two elderly men after that is unknown.

Finding a shelter was not easy because groups of Japanese soldiers were al-ready occupying every available space, even graveyard tombs. Eventually, how-ever, they managed to get into the Araree-gama. "But even after we were inside, when the naval bombardment was going on, around 100 more people heading for the center of the island jammed in behind us." Kikue described the scene around her, but when she started talking about life in the cave amid the pervad-ing stench of death, a terribly pained look came over her.

The inner extreme of the shelter was a quagmire like a paddy field. "Back there, your feet would sink straight down 20 or 30 centimeters, so everybody sat huddled together near the rocky outcrop at the entrance," Kikue explained. That morning, fourteen or fifteen Japanese soldiers arrived at the shelter. Their uniforms were in tatters and every one of their faces showed how totally exhausted they were from being constantly on the run from one place to the next. With their packs still on their backs, they went straight to sleep. Then it happened, probably 30 minutes after the soldiers arrived. "Suddenly, a shell fired from a U.S. warship scored a direct hit. I was knocked out by the blast so I don't know what happened after that. The Americans must have seen the soldiers go into the shelter."

By the time Kikue regained consciousness, the civilians had all crammed into the muddy area at the back of the shelter. In a state of panic, she also began to walk toward the rear of the shelter but realized that her *monpe* trousers had slipped right down as the tie cord was broken. When she took a closer look, she found that a fragment of shrapnel had cut across her left thigh and the left part of her belly. "I didn't feel any pain," she explained, adding that, even now, the 1-centimeter scar on her thigh and the 4-centimeter scar on her abdomen are vivid reminders that won't allow her to forget what happened.

The view from the back of the cave out to the entrance was a mountain of dead bodies. Kikue could see that Mashiki Chojun's little sister, who was also known as Tsuru, was still moving. "Tsuru just kept standing up and sitting down again," Kikue explained. "She'd been hit in the face and didn't say a word. I said to my sister-in-law that Tsuru looked so pitiable and that she should go over and give her something, so she offered her some sweet potato starch and sugared water but she didn't drink it." Kikue let out a sigh before adding quietly, "The next morning, Tsuru was dead."

Two of the twenty-four members of Kikue's extended family who had taken refuge in Araree-gama also died at that stage. One of them was married and, after ten years without children, they had finally produced a son the previous year. Hit in the stomach by a piece of shrapnel, the young mother screamed out "Masakazu [her baby's name] . . . is Masakazu OK?" as her internal organs spilled out. Then she passed away.

"I'd say that there were about thirty or forty dead bodies, but my younger brother reckons that there were at least fifty. To begin with, we carried them out in straw baskets and buried them in the fields nearby. However, after a while the sky filled up with American planes, so we just left most of them lying where they were in the shelter." As the pile of bodies started to decompose, they gave off an awful stench. The survivors gathered the bodies into one corner and covered them with dirt but that was not enough to stop the smell of death. Eventually, they got used to that smell, but they were then plagued by hordes of maggots.

The rice that they had brought with them when they fled south was enough for each person to have a single rice ball, about the size of a child's fist, per day. They cooked the rice near the shelter entrance, but keeping the invading maggots at bay as they waited for the cooker to heat up was a real problem. They laid planks on top of the mud and stayed on those, but the maggots eventually made their way there as well. The water dripping down from the shelter roof, soaking their blankets, compounded their misery.

After the naval bombardment abated, the others left the shelter and headed away, leaving only Kikue and her relatives inside. They were taken prisoner by the Americans on 18 June but Kikue had two hand grenades tucked inside her clothing. One was to throw at the American soldiers, while the other was to take her own life rather than be violated by them. She had been given the grenades and told what to do by some Japanese soldiers near her home. Arakaki Ushi explained in Okinawan dialect, "Everything about that shelter was awful. It was so wet and we were starving . . ."

Countless bodies at Giizabanta

Giizabanta—a jagged, rocky area near Cape Kyan at the southern end of the main island of Okinawa. Magnificent, sheer cliffs rise high up dozens of meters from the sea with the coastline littered with huge rocks.

By the end of May 1945, the forces defending Okinawa had been defeated in the fighting around Urasoe and Shuri and found themselves being slowly pushed into the southwest corner of the island. Large numbers of shell-shocked civilians also made their way south toward Mabuni in search of a safe haven. In all, there were over 100,000 civilians and around 30,000 soldiers. Like hordes of ants, they gathered among the sugar cane fields on Kyan Peninsula, which measures barely 7 kilometers from east to west. There, a tragic scenario began to unfold as they found themselves trapped between the relentless U.S. machine guns on land and the fire from small naval vessels out to sea.

I visited the Okinawa Prefectural Peace Memorial Museum. On display there are personal narratives of civilians who experienced the war firsthand, including some from people who have written about what happened at Giizabanta. "It was when I sheltered under some adan trees . . . There was blood and pieces of human flesh flying around, falling on me. I wondered what on earth it was. It stuck to my kimono." Beyond the rocky headland behind the Okinawa Prefectural Peace Memorial Museum there are vertical bluffs where thousands, indeed tens of thousands, of lives were lost.

Morimi Moriyasu took part in the fighting on Okinawa as a member of the Blood and Iron Student Corps. After being captured at Giizabanta, he witnessed what was effectively the end of the fighting. "My feet were sore from the jagged rocks. All around us it was pitch dark, and whenever I took a few steps, I kept bumping into things. When I had a closer look, I realized they were dead bodies. Not just one or two. There were so many bodies that it was hard to avoid them as we walked along."

Out on the water, through loud speakers on the smaller U.S. navy vessels, the Americans made repeated calls for them to surrender. The boats were so close that "We could tell the American soldiers on board were using binoculars to watch us." As soon as they spotted a Japanese soldier with a gun, they would yell out, "Drop that weapon!" If the soldier hid, the Americans would threaten him with, "If you don't drop that weapon in the next couple of minutes, we'll open fire!" Each time a soldier threw his gun away, the Americans called out, "That's it! Thank you!"

One after another, even the civilians who had been petrified at the start gradually complied with the calls to surrender. Where they were on the cliff, the pile of weapons from the surrendering soldiers grew higher and higher. "I think it was 22 June. I was also taken prisoner but part of me also felt relieved about that," explained Moromi.

Yonamine Moriaki also has bitter memories of Giizabanta that he cannot erase. In order to escape the fighting, Yonamine, his father and a group relatives, eight people in all, had fled from their home village of Ozato to Tamagusuku and Gushikami and had eventually made it south to Mabuni. "Getting down the cliff by holding onto creepers and vines was not too bad, but about halfway down we came under fire from American naval vessels. It was terrible. My uncle died instantly when he was hit by a rock fragment, and four or five women in their fifties also died. Some had their arms blown off, some were decapitated . . . the whole scene was indescribable."

There is a fresh water spring bubbling at the bottom of Giizabanta. Back then, the water from that spring saved the lives of many people. Yonamine remembers, "I didn't want to be captured by the enemy so I did all I could to get away from there. But eventually I became thirsty and, when I looked around, I saw this spring. I was so excited and drank as much as I could but only when my stomach became bloated did I realize that the water was putrid. Ayahashi also told me, "There were dead bodies lying all around that spring, but everybody still drank from it." That spring is still there today.

The 32nd Army falls apart

After the withdrawal from Shuri, the Chihaya Unit and the Kikusui Unit [infiltration unit] of the Blood and Iron Student Corps were ordered to go on secret operations, including disruption raids, behind enemy lines. Tomimura Moriteru, a member of the Chihaya Unit, explained, "So that we could get others to cooperate with us, we were issued with identification cards which Intelligence had produced. But while we were made very welcome in some places, we were chased out of other shelters altogether."

According to the 32nd Army's Postwar Demobilization Group records, armed with explosives and special communications equipment the Kikusui Unit launched a series of raids after the withdrawal from Shuri. The documents show that "some of them carried out raids in Mabuni and Itoman and some may have penetrated behind enemy lines." As for the Chihaya Unit, the records also show that "most of the men who went on raids dressed as locals were killed before they reached their objective. Only a small number survived and it is unclear what became of them."

The Battle of Okinawa was now hurtling faster and faster toward its brutal and savage conclusion. Civilians forced into the island's natural caves and behind rocky outcrops to escape the American artillery were driven away at gun- and bayonet-point by the Japanese soldiers inside. By mid-June, the 32nd Army had already lost its cohesion. The war seemed almost back to front: officers and men who should have been fighting had gone into hiding, while unarmed civilians were wandering around exposed to the ferocious bombardment.

Eventually, a number of people stepped forward from among the civilians in response to the Americans urging them to surrender. After tying dirty strips of white cloth onto branches, they began trudging along the coastline under American guard toward Gushikami. Adaniya Ken, an officer with Headquarters Unit, told us about what he witnessed during the latter part of June. "From the back, those civilians looked exhausted as they walked away with only the few household items they could carry on their heads. Then I looked again and was taken aback to see that there were a whole lot of soldiers in among the group, but without their uniforms." They might have looked like civilians to the Americans, but to Adaniya and the others, they stood out by a mile. Even though they were carrying young children and posing as civilians, they were wearing IJA issue shirts and trousers. They were obviously deserters. Until just a short time before, soldiers heading out to surrender had attracted fire from their comrades, but on this occasion not a shot was fired. Any semblance of a cohesive fighting force had disappeared and they feared that every shot they fired, the return fire would be 20 or 30 times as intense.

One day, after having witnessed the deaths of many adult soldiers and boys of the Blood and Iron Student Corps, Adaniya was overcome with feelings of wild rage at the waste of life. But with nobody to vent his anger on, he knew that his own destiny was still inherently linked to that of the army.

Adaniya remembers it as the 18th or 19th June. He had been called to the Headquarters Unit and, when he arrived there to see what it was all about, the men were all cleaning their pistols. That was the first time he'd heard about the plans to escape from Mabuni. Adaniya's orders were to "Head north and do all you can to harass the enemy from behind their own lines." But what followed was nothing as heroic as breaking through the enemy's lines at all. Rather, the soldiers visited a cave where civilians were sheltering, "procured" their ragged old clothes, and put them on. But high-ranking officers, on the other hand, had their own suits and kimonos. As the group followed the muddy tracks beneath a withering hail of artillery fire during the Shuri withdrawal, their officers' clothes had been packed in their special wicker baskets that members of the Blood and Iron Corps carried with great care. There were also officers who had lost their belongings during the retreat, and of course, with them, the lives of the young students carrying those baskets. But still, most of the boys had been convinced that the baskets contained important documents.

The Blood and Iron Student Corps received the Dissolution Order on 19 June, its instruction being "make your way north." Chihaya Unit member Nakata Shoei explained, "We were told to head for Kunigami. Even if we were taken prisoner, we were to wait for further instructions from the military. We were told that under no circumstance were we to die needlessly. In groups of three we were to break through enemy lines and await further orders." Even after he had received the Dissolution Order, Takara Yoshio of the Fortification Construction Unit had no idea what to do. While there were very few of his own unit left, there were so many enemy soldiers around that he couldn't even begin to estimate the number. Takara had put the last of his army rice rations in a sock for safekeeping. He and his buddies agreed that they should eat the rice first and then break through to Kunigami in the north. However, they didn't have any water so, in order to wash the rice, they went down to the coastline, scooped up some seawater and used that. Along the coastline at that stage, there seemed to be hundreds of dead bodies floating in the tide. They then cooked the rice in saltwater, rolled it into rice balls and ate it. The blood stained water had turned the color of the rice from white to red, so it was like traditional festive red rice.

Wherever they went, they could no longer tell who were soldiers and who were civilians. Civilians who had trusted the IJA right up to the very last minute were now witnessing firsthand the true character of their own soldiers and had as much to fear of them as of the Americans. The Japanese soldiers could do nothing against the overwhelming firepower of the Americans, but they used what little authority they had left to force their will upon the civilians. Their actions starkly demonstrated the effects of war as they stole food from civilians and chased them out of the caves in order to seek refuge there themselves. As the fighting was coming to an end around the 10 June, Uchima Takeyoshi of the Fortification Construction Unit was one of about 200 soldiers and civilians crammed into a natural shelter along the coast near Mabuni. They could hear the voices of the American soldiers up above, while out in front of them, the ocean was covered with American warships.

One day, at the shelter entrance a woman aged about fifty was comforting a baby in the Okinawan dialect. "The baby was crying its eyes out as it had no milk, no water, and nothing to eat. The people inside the shelter were really unsettled by the noise." Suddenly, an NCO inside the shelter drew his sword and yelled at the woman, 'You're an Okinawan. You're trying to let the enemy know where we are, aren't you!' Then he slashed out wildly at her left hand. The woman screamed in her local dialect "Ahhh . . . my hand!" and ran back outside. Anybody who spoke in their local dialect was assumed to be a spy," Uchima explained.

Around 21 or 22 June, Uchima and the members of the Normal School's Blood and Iron Student Corps were ordered to build a ceiling inside the shelter in preparation for the "last supper." A "last supper" to be held for Lt. Gen. Ushijima and Prefectural Governor Shimada Akira could not have been more inappropriate in the light of what was going around them. Outside the Command Post shelter in Mabuni, civilians were doing everything they could to survive one more day, as hordes of soldiers had changed from being human beings into something resembling a pack of wild animals. To build the ceiling, the Normal School contingent got tiles from the rubble at Komesu. They formed two rows and passed the tiles along the line from one person to the next. They kept working until they were interrupted by mortar fire, although by then they were already so exhausted that they were barely able to stand up. When they glanced inside the shelter the following evening, there were Lt. Gen. Ushijima and Chief of Staff Cho, dressed in uniforms covered in military decorations. It was the last time they would look that resplendent.

Members of the Blood and Iron Student Corps went out on infiltration raids against the enemy, but many of their young lives were lost. Between the middle of June and early fall, those students who were lucky enough to survive because they'd used the raids as a chance to head to the many shelters around Mabuni, had all been captured by the Americans. They very soon realized that the enemy were not the white foreign devils they had been told about. In fact, what they found was the speed with which some people adjust to new masters. When they asked the Japanese official in charge of the POW camp to care for one of their wounded buddies, the reply was, "You may be just student soldiers, but you're still soldiers. Look after him yourselves . . ." Before the fighting began, those who had been urging them to join the battle alongside the regular soldiers were already wielding their authority under American control. Less than three months had passed from the start of the fighting through to the collapse of the 32nd Army, but the painful lessons these young "soldiers" learned during that time would serve as the starting point of their lives in the postwar period.

Call for surrender

One day at the end of March 1945, a message in somewhat awkward Japanese suddenly came through a wireless radio receiver inside the Headquarters shelter. According to Araki Minoru, then adjutant to Chief of Staff Cho Isamu, it stated, "We will soon carry out our landings on the main island of Okinawa. The time has come for an honorable surrender." It was sent in the name of Lt. Gen. Simon Bolivar Buckner, Commander of the U.S. 10th Army and could be taken both as a signal of the impending hostilities and a call for surrender.

"I don't know whether or not it was sent by a Japanese-American, but I remember that the language used was a little unnatural," says Araki. He went on to explain that both Ushijima and Cho smiled as they said, "What are they talking about? Not fighting is hardly an option for us."

Araki had been stationed on Miyako-jima as a battalion commander in the 45th Independent Mixed Brigade, but at the end of 1944 he was posted to the Headquarters Staff Section. The moment that he received the order to move, he knew that the inevitable American invasion of Okinawa would require him to be prepared to make the ultimate sacrifice.

His main duties as adjutant to the chief of staff were to organize for Lt. Gen. Cho's operational orders to be conveyed by radio or messenger to the various units. His constant close proximity to Cho meant he had many opportunities to overhear the chief of staff's discussions with Lt. Gen. Ushijima or other high-ranking officers in the 32nd Army.

At the end of March, shortly before the U.S. landings, V/Adm. Minoru Ota, commander of the Naval Base Forces on Okinawa, came to the 32nd Army Command Post. In the Command Staff Room, Ota discussed with Ushijima and Cho the probable strength of the U.S. forces massing against them. "We had just fewer than 100,000 soldiers to call upon, including those who had been recruited locally in Okinawa. They forecast that the Americans would commit between 450,000 and 500,000 troops to the battle in order to take control of Okinawa. This was a figure that we would just not be able to cope with. They all agreed that we had no chance of victory," said Araki.

"The commander and his chief of staff never made that comment in front of other people, but they had definitely made up their minds that they were going to die. Even if they requested reinforcements from the main islands of Japan, such units could never get to us. In other words, Okinawa had effectively been abandoned, but they were obliged to follow orders and fight," says Araki about the military commanders on Okinawa already knowing that their fate was sealed.

At that stage, still firmly believing that victory was assured, Normal School students were working hard to dig more shelters in the Command Post underground complex. Blood and Iron Student Corps units and nurse aide units were being organized one after another, but the evacuation of non-combatants from areas where fighting was expected to occur was still far from complete.

At the 32nd Army Command Post there was one officer from Okinawa. His name was Adaniya Ken, a former teacher at the Agriculture and Forestry School who had been called up as a lieutenant to be attached to Headquarters in the second round of conscription that occurred soon after New Year in 1945. His duties after the fighting became increasingly fierce were to go out to the battlefield to ascertain the situation at the front, or to convey messages to the various units.

A witness to untold inhumane acts, Adaniya was only able to bring himself to speak about these nightmare experiences several decades after the war's end.

Adaniya remembers it as being mid-June. It was after the 32nd Army had withdrawn from Shuri to Mabuni in the very south of Okinawa's main island. He was summoned by the Staff Officers' Section and went into the Command Post, which was located in a natural cave at Mabuni Hill. The chief intelligence officer operating the telephone near the entrance to the cave relayed a message to Lt. Gen. Ushijima, who was standing behind him.

"It's a message from Adm. Nimitz." Adaniya remembers being surprised at those words that suggested communication with the American forces. But Ushijima's response was even more surprising. "The same thing again, isn't it? Don't give me this rubbish you idiot!" yelled Ushijima who flew into a rage, the first time that Adaniya can remember such a reaction.

Adaniya thinks that the message was a call for the Japanese forces to surrender and emphasizes that "It was from the U.S. Navy's Adm. Nimitz, not Lt. Gen. Buckner of the U.S. Army." At that stage when the only options left were to commit suicide or to surrender, he laments, "If only they had chosen to surrender, just think how many young lives would have been saved."

In response to this and to statements by Araki Minoru, who served as adjutant to the chief of staff, about Lt. Gen. Buckner's call to surrender, Jin Naomichi, then Air Liaison Staff Officer, flatly denies that there was any call to surrender from the American military.

"There was no way that there would be any communication with the enemy. That's the role of politicians and not the military," says Jin. He continues, denying this in terms of the nature of the military itself, "To the military there is only attack or defense. They only think about how they can use their fighting capability to deal with the enemy. While the fighting was continuing, both before and after the American landings, there were no opportunities whatsoever for either party to talk with the other."

A military that saw nothing beyond victory or defeat in battle . . . Add to this all the civilians who believed, or rather were not permitted to doubt, that anything other than victory could occur, and the extent of the tragedy is further magnified.

CHAPTER 10

MALARIA AND STARVATION

Another aspect of the civilian experience during the Battle of Okinawa was the forced evacuation to malaria-infested areas, with the most notable example being that of the residents of the Yaeyama Islands, where as many as 3,647 people died of malaria.[1]

By the end of the war, approximately 300,000 residents of the main island of Okinawa had either fled to or been relocated to the northern Yambaru area.[2] Before the cessation of hostilities, stragglers from the Kunigami Detachment of the IJA caused havoc in the Yambaru, demanding food from civilians and killing those who refused.[3] Before crossing to Iriomote-jima, the residents of Hateruma-jima were told that, because Americans were meat-eaters, all livestock was to be slaughtered for use by the IJA to avoid these animals falling into the hands of the enemy. It is even suggested that the real reason behind the forced relocation of civilians was to secure their food supplies for military use.[4]

Apart from the problem of malaria, the lack of food meant that, had the Americans not moved quickly to establish camps to provide the bare minimum of sustenance and medicine, death by starvation would have further dramatically reduced the population of Okinawa. By the time they were taken into captivity, many of the civilians in the Yambaru had barely survived by eating grass. While the camps and field hospitals set up by the U.S. military undoubtedly saved thousands of lives, the concentration of people weakened by starvation meant that malaria spread rapidly, claiming the lives of many civilians within the camps.[5]

On Miyako-jima and in the Yaeyama Islands, the presence of large numbers of IJA soldiers placed unbearable strain on the food available, so when the weakened population then had to contend with malaria, local residents died one after another. On Miyako-jima, the population of 60,000 had to share meager food supplies with a garrison of 30,000 troops, so it is not surprising that some hamlets were effectively wiped out during the months the battle was fought on Okinawa.

1. Ota Peace Research Institute. 2010:7.
2. Oshiro, M. 2007: 166.
3. Oshiro, M. 2007: 166.
4. Miyara, S. 2004: 175.
5. Oshiro, M. 2007: 166.

A total of 53.8 percent of the 30,000 people in the Yaeyama Islands contracted malaria and 21.5 percent of those died.[6] Of the 1,500 residents of Hateruma-jima who were forcibly relocated to Iriomote-jima, 1,396 contracted malaria with 488 dying. This represents one-third of the population of Hateruma-jima.[7]

The Government of Japan still does not pay any form of pension to bereaved families of people who died after contracting malaria because they were forced to relocate to infested areas.[8]

Malaria in the Yaeyama Islands in 1945

Name of island	Population	Number who contracted malaria	Number who died
Ishigaki	19,050	10,060	2,496
Taketomi	1,430	77	7
Kohama	1,079	862	124
Kuroshima	1,345	128	19
Aragusuku	255	144	24
Hateruma	1,590	1,587	477
Hatoma	560	526	59
Iriomote	1,627	327	75
Yonaguni	4,745	3,171	366
Totals	**31,681**	**16,882**	**3,647**

Mainichi Shimbun Tokubetsuhodobu-Shuzaijin, "Okinawa-senso mararia jiken," as cited in Ota Peace Research Institute, *Okinawa kanren shiryo* 2010: 7.

Taken prisoner in June 1945

The evening edition of the *Ryukyu Shimpo* dated 23 May 1984 carried a photo with the caption *Japanese soldier surrenders—"hands up" and clad only in loincloth.* Clutching a copy of that edition, Adaniya Seikichi visited the *Ryukyu Shimpo* office the very next day, believing he was the soldier in the photo. "I was taken prisoner toward the end of June 1945 in the southern part of Okinawa. But I didn't surrender, you realize. I was captured by American soldiers and I clearly

6. Oshiro, M. 2007: 167.
7. Okinawa Heiwa Network. 2008: 35.
8. Okinawa Heiwa Network. 2008: 35.

remember being forced to walk along a gravel road just like in this picture." The photo is not very clear, making it difficult to confirm whether or not it is Adaniya, but there would not be many men who were made to walk all the way to the POW camp wearing only a loincloth. Almost forty years after the war ended, he has not forgotten what happened. "I accepted that I was going to die," he said.

Adaniya recalls being taken prisoner sometime after 5:00 PM on 26 June. He was captured in a small forest northeast of what is now the Komesu Elementary School behind the settlement of Odo in Itoman. At the time, he and a former classmate, Oshiro Tsuneo, were the only two in a man-made shelter in that little forest. As soon as he left the cave to search for water he was surrounded at the entrance by four Americans. One of them pointed his rifle at Adaniya while another gestured toward him to put his hands up. "I was confused for a second but then I realized what was happening and did as I was told." Their interrogation was very rough. "While they were frisking me they found the hand grenade I had on me and immediately ripped my clothes off. They didn't even undo the buttons on my jacket."

Any Japanese soldier captured in possession of his dagger or pistol was made to strip off. That's why many of them dumped their army uniforms and changed into civilian clothes. "But for me, my capture was so sudden that I didn't have the chance to do anything like that. I had on my full uniform . . . and my steel helmet. Also, I was in signals and had a model 98 hand grenade so I could take my own life. But to be honest, I thought that I'd be killed there and then anyway." Yet looking back, Adaniya realizes he had no need to fear for his life. "I was resigned to being killed by an American bullet sometime while I was out looking for water, but I never imagined that I'd be taken prisoner like that."

Stripped down to his loincloth because of the hand grenade he was carrying, Adaniya was forced to walk about eight kilometers from the cave to the POW camp. All the while he was being prodded from behind by an American soldier's rifle, and at no point was he allowed to put his hands down. On 26 May, two days after hearing Adaniya's war experiences, he took me to the shelter at Itoman where he had been captured. We headed south along Prefectural Road No. 7 from Naha and past Tomigusuku until we came to the Makabe area of Itoman. He drove a little farther and then stopped the car just before a bend this side of Komesu Elementary School. "I'm sure that's the forest there," Adaniya explained, pointing as he got out of the car. The place where he was captured is to the north of the Odo area. We took a narrow track across a field and then through some sugar cane that was as tall as us.

The area was covered in thick vegetation, which hid the shelter. When we got to the entrance—the spot where Adanaya believed he had been taken prisoner—he raised both hands above his head. "When I was captured, I put both hands up in the air like this and, because I was carrying a grenade, I was stripped down to just my loincloth. There were some dead Japanese soldiers lying in the cave at that point, and I can still remember the terrible stench . . . it went straight up our noses. We hadn't had anything resembling a proper meal for months. When we left the shelter just looking for water, we'd go to local houses and peer down into their old wells to see if there was any water in them. Because shells were flying all around us we were risking our lives. But I use to think that if I could just have a drink of water, I wouldn't really care if I died . . ."

Oshiro who was captured with Adaniya had been a classmate at No. 2 Kokumin School at Tomigusuku. One day as Adaniya had gone all the way to Makabe looking for water, he noticed Oshiro alone in a pigsty. "His mother was lying there, having been sent flying by a shell blast and Oshiro had found her there several days later. I comforted him and led him back to the cave, but when we were taken prisoner we were separated because he was a civilian. Apparently he died from malnutrition after the war." Recalling the old friends he lost, Adaniya looked out right across the field of sugar cane as he continued to talk. During the fighting, many civilians hid in the cane fields and quenched their thirst by sucking the moisture from the sugar cane. If they actually broke a piece off, the sharp "crack" would draw the enemy's attention so they gnawed away at the plants still in the ground. However, sometimes at night an American Cessna would fly over and spray the fields with petrol. Then they'd set the whole thing on fire.

Around 7 February 1945, Adaniya joined the 24th Infantry Division where he was put into a signals unit. In May he was sent to the front line at Ichinichibashi where his role was to observe and send detailed reports to the Command Post about the types of weapons the Americans were using and how many troops they had. "We had old fashioned rifles but the enemy had automatic weapons. It was crazy trying to fight against those. Also, they obviously had high-powered transmitters because I ended up getting nothing but static on my set and I couldn't get any replies. In the end, I dumped my transmitter on a track at Ozato and came to Makabe with just my hand grenade in case I needed to take my own life." After that he was captured in the forest behind the Odo area.

With Adaniya leading the way, we decided to follow the same road he had been forced to walk on his way to the POW camp after being captured. He explained that he had things to do that evening so he didn't have much time, but possibly because he was reliving each of the harsh experiences he'd endured there forty years earlier he completely forgot about the time and became absorbed in retracing his footsteps along that road. After his capture, Adaniya was taken for a time to the southern part of Odo, now National Highway No. 331. Three captured Japanese soldiers and ten civilians were being held there but Adaniya was the only one wearing just a loincloth.

With both hands raised above his head, Adaniya said that he'd walked through Komesu, Makabe, and Kuniyoshi until he reached what is now the Itoman traffic roundabout. He had a rest before heading for Shiohira where the POW camp had been, walking 8 kilometers and not once being allowed to put his hands down. By the time he arrived at the camp the sun had already set. I asked what had gone through Adaniya's mind the day he walked that same road clad only in a loincloth. "I didn't feel in the least embarrassed," he explained. "In fact, when I look back on it now, my only thought was that I wanted to at least have a good drink of water before they killed me."

Communal graves in Nago

Oura Bay in the Nago region of Okinawa is an idyllic location. It is especially beautiful in summer, when the almost overpowering heat allows one to sense even more intensely the fragrances of the bay, while little crabs rustle about, seemingly cooled by the shade from the trees along the river.

In July 1945, civilians who had fled to the hills from about February began returning. With nothing left to eat, news that the war was going badly, plus having even heard English voices nearby, they came down from the hills depressed and despondent. They were captured by the Americans and detained as soon as they appeared. The numbers in the various camps increased each day as civilians from central and southern Okinawa arrived to join them.

The Americans eventually established garrisons at Sedake and Ourasaki, hoisting their flag in the Sedake garrison at the Kushi Kokumin School. The civilians who had come down from the hills were administered by the military. Status as a municipality was given to Higashiki, Okawa, Oura, Futami, Sedake, Teima, Mihara, Abu and Kayo, and a mayor was appointed. The population as of August 1945 was around 30,000 and, under the mayor, they worked to set up and manage departments of police, education, health, industry, labor, and rationing. The region of Kushi was also given the same status and it was there that civilians from Nakijin, Motobu, and Ie were held.

In November of the same year, residents originally from both Itoman and

Kanegusuku in the Sedake area began returning to their hometowns en masse. Thereafter, those from other areas also began to head home, leading to a decline in the populations of Kushi and Sedake. As a result, in January 1946 the two municipalities merged under the single name of Kushi-Son.

Locals say that for those who had come down from the hills, life in the U.S. internment camps was especially harsh—harsh beyond words. In *Okinawa no Dokoku*, in which Nakata Eimatsu writes about his wartime and postwar experiences, he describes the living conditions in Ourasaki.

"Large tents were erected on a site totally devoid of trees and vegetation. Each tent accommodated three or four families and, because of the searing heat of the sun, it was like a steam sauna inside them. Also, we had no access to fresh water of any kind. The food shortage was so serious that we went down to the beach and ate seaweed, as well as to the hills where we randomly grabbed any edible-looking leaves of trees and plants and ate those as well. In one dreadful incident, a whole family died after eating leaves that were too young and still poisonous."

But such appalling conditions were certainly not restricted to Ourasaki. Malaria accompanied by high fever was so widespread that barely anybody escaped. In particular, young children and the elderly, weakened by starvation, died one after another. The names of those who died in the presence of family were recorded in a register and were buried with grave markers, but many others died without even being able to tell anyone their name. While the population of Okawa today is only around 100, back then over 4,000 prisoners were held in the internment camp there, of whom more than one thousand perished. However, the interment register at the Ourasaki cemetery shows that only 613 people were buried there. Eventually, the cemetery was no longer looked after and the remains of those with family connections were removed. Yet even today, there are many unidentified human remains still lying there. Documents of the Prefectural Relief Division indicate that there are "between one and two hundred bodies" at Okawa, and "several hundred" at Sedake. Under the blazing sun, we walked around the site with its unimpeded view down the sloping terrain and out across the tranquil Oura Bay. "I think some of them are still buried right there where you're standing," explained Nishihira Kazuki, chief of the Sedake Ward.

Malaria was known as "time fever" because the symptoms appeared at the same time every day. According to Nishihira, "Just when you feel a fit of the chills coming on, you then develop a high temperature and eventually your whole body starts to really shake." The fever would subside in about 30 minutes when they took yellow tablets that they got from the American soldiers, but their entire body "right down to their eyes" turned yellow as well. Malaria was a scourge throughout the whole Oura Bay region, and it was merciless in the way it ravaged the people who had sought refuge there. Everybody—men and women, young and old—contracted it at least once, with the frail old people and malnourished children dying from it in droves.

Nishihira brought out the burial register drawn up in November 1945. The register identifies those people detained in Sedake (which then had a population of 6,669) who died from causes such as malaria and malnutrition. Meticulously compiled, it contains the names and former addresses of all 613 victims, categorized according to which burial sites in which of nine different locations within five areas they were temporarily buried. As one might expect, many of the victims were over sixty or under ten years of age, most originally from the central and southern regions of Mawashi, Yomitan, Nishihara, and Naha.

Comparing the register with the grave markers meant that recovery of the remains was a relatively straightforward process, so once their lives had begun to settle down in the postwar period, a constant stream of families arrived to collect the remains of loved ones. However, because many people also perished without being able to tell anyone their names, their bodies remained unexhumed for several decades. Holding the burial register map, they walked around following Nishihira's directions. Although they lost their way at times because the map did not distinguish between roads and rivers, and the topography of the area had changed as well, they were able to confirm the correct location.

Records held by the Prefectural Relief Division show that the number of remains at Nabegohara in Sedake is estimated to be "several hundred" while the number at Higashihara is "unknown." We walked around Nabegohara and, when we took the road along the river shaded by trees, we saw several dozen crabs of about five centimeters across crawling around making their familiar rustling sound. "We ate plants and seaweed . . . we ate anything we could get. Small crabs were a real treat," explained Nishihira, adding, "There were grave markers all over the place." Today some parts of Nabegohara are hills and fields, but other parts are used for growing vegetables.

On one side, Higashihara looks down over Oura Bay and is separate from the other burial sites. At the place indicated by the number "5" on their map, they found graves with a fresh water spring flowing beside them. "That burial site over there was full so they used the area here as well." Because of the thick vegetation and steep terrain, the general feeling is that excavation would be difficult. Moreover, there are other sites where they can't even guess the numbers of human remains.

Nishihira then showed us around the area. Only a few of the garcinia trees remain, although back then they were everywhere. A fine-looking house with red tiles was still there. Known as Nakachi, the dwelling has stood there for over 100 years, obviously surviving the ravages of war. Homes like Nakachi were used for holding internees, with any number of families living in them together. Once the houses were full, rows of tiny huts, worse than chicken coops, began to appear.

"The people were really crammed into those houses . . . as many as five or six families at a time," explained Nishihira, one of the few local men actually in Sedake back then. Because over 6,000 people had fled to the area, rows of little huts soon began to appear, extending right down to the shoreline. Those "chicken coops" gave some protection from the wind and rain so they sprang up all over the place. "At night, so many people slept with their heads facing the garcinia trees and their legs stretched out over the path that nobody could walk along the path."

In his role with the Agriculture Committee, Nishihira was involved in the distribution of food, which really got underway when the Americans eventually started trucking in rice, cornmeal, corned beef, canned peaches, asparagus, and various other foods.

"Back then, there was no sense of order or fair play," Nishihira explained. Some people received their portion of food and then took a second serving. In the worst cases, people would do things like distract the American troops and make off with a whole load of food bound for the next town.

They built a shed called the "Milk House" where five women were involved in handing out milk to civilians three times a day. Nishihira's wife Meriko was one of those five women. "They mixed the milk up in a huge pot and served it to the people waiting in the queue, one at a time. Of course, they handed out milk to everybody so it was very well received," Nishihira continued.

But if there was food and milk, the question then remains as to why 600 people died. Nishihira explained. "First of all, a lot of them died because there was absolutely no food at all around July. Second, I believe that even when they had food right in front of them, many were so weak because of their various illnesses that they couldn't eat it anyway. And there were others who wanted the food but their bodies just wouldn't accept it. That's how bad the malaria and malnutrition were. There was an American hospital nearby although, rather than a real hospital, it was more like a camp for sick people. The seriously ill people were taken away to Ginoza."

"I heard that as many as twenty people died each day," added Ikemiya Shuto-ku who managed a store in Sedake. Like Nishihira, Ikemiya was a local, interned there after the war. "There were a lot of people. Let me see now . . . as I recall, 1,100 people came from Naha, 700 from Ozato, and 700 from Yomitan. I heard that 600 people died in all."

"The huts that the displaced civilians lived in were no bigger than this," explained Ikemiya, getting to his feet and gesturing with both hands to indicate an area approximately half the size of his store. They were about 4 meters by 4 meters. There was a kitchen as well. He also explained that some shelters were far more basic, where people just poked smaller branches in among the garcinia trees and built a platform on top of that which they supported with wooden props. It couldn't have protected them from the rain, or even the wind for that matter.

"That was just the way it was; they were all like that. We ate algae . . . we ate grass from the fields. We ate every frog and crab until there were no more left," added Ikemiya.

Taking the road 2 or 3 kilometers out of Oura brought us to Okawa Ward, a small ward tucked in among the hills and with a population of about 100 people. With the help of Higa Kenken, the Ward Chairman, we requested that some of the locals who had been there at the time and who knew about what happened, to meet us in the community center. Four people came out to meet us, Mekaru Seijin, Taira Eitoku, Sakihama Hidekazu, and Higa, the Ward Chairman himself. Sakihama started the ball rolling.

"I heard that 1,017 people died here and that most of them were buried on my piece of land, and there were grave markers all over the place. I have about one hectare, and I think that over 1,000 people died here." Because grave markers had been put up, there would have been a burial register as well, just as there had been at Sedake, but it has been lost.

Taira then told us what he knew about the grave markers. "I think it was two or three years after the war ended. One day when the rain was really pelting down, an elderly woman from the area removed the grave markers from up in the hills to use as firewood." Prefectural records show that the number of unclaimed bodies in Okawa Ward is between 100 and 200. Many of the dead had no relatives, which perhaps explains why so many were never recovered. Taira then continued. "A lot of them died after contracting malaria. When somebody died, relatives or people from their village would wrap the body in a blanket and carry it back up into the hills."

Then Mekaru took up the story. "There was a medical team at the time with laborers who used to dig holes to bury the bodies in. Almost all of the refugees were from the south. They mostly traveled on ships from Baten to Oura and were then transported here." Most of them were already very weak even before they arrived, which is also why so many of them died.

Sakihama explained, "Even today, bereaved families carrying shovels still come here accompanied by a *yuta* or spiritual medium. They have come from as far away as Brazil and Hawaii, but most of them never find the remains of their loved ones. Instead, they take home a small stone as a memento. In the late 1970s, I asked the government to carry out a search because until then I can't use my own land as I wish. I want them to do something about it." Sakihama currently uses his land for growing mandarin oranges and, after talking with us at the local community center, he took us out to visit his plot of land. "Look at this," he began, pointing out an oval indentation in the dirt about 50 centimeters in size. There were several such indentations. "I think this is where someone was buried," he continued. Because his mandarin trees were only seedlings when he planted them, it is not yet a major problem. "But I still cannot make proper use of my own land," he lamented.

Name tag given by father is found four decades later

A copper plate name tag buried for four decades around the neck of its wearer who was killed during the Battle of Okinawa has been returned to the bereaved family. The words "Naha City, Tondo-cho, 3-37, Terasaka Masako" were engraved on the oval shaped name tag. Each of the children in the Terasaka family was given one of these tags by their father so that, if they were ever split up, their identity could be confirmed.

On the night of 5 to 6 June 1984, the remains of thirty people killed in the battle were discovered by men constructing a new road at a location near what had been the field hospital of the 62nd Infantry Division at Arakawa in Haebaru. The area in which the remains were found was where the military disposed of the bodies of those who died in the field hospital, plus the bodies of soldiers who had been killed in the fierce fighting around Shuri. Since the war, work has been carried out retrieving the bones of those killed in the battle, but it is clear that there are still many more buried in places that are not easily accessible.

It was confirmed that one of the bodies among the thirty found was unquestionably that of Terasaka Masako. The copper name tag that young Masako's father had given her during the chaotic days of the battle had been the key to identifying her remains.

Masako's father Masaharu, who died during the battle, was originally from Iwate Prefecture. When he was about twenty years old he came to Okinawa as a crewmember on a ship and remained on the island. He had three boys and six girls with his wife Machi. Their oldest son, Masao, joined the navy, and their second son, Kiyoshi, fought in the Battle of Okinawa as a member of the Home Guard. Masako's mother Machi had heard about her husband's last moments and that he had told someone he'd buried their daughter Masako's body near the field hospital at Shuri. She had been there to look for the copper plate name tag but had found no sign of it. Masako's remains were identified first by her younger sister, Obayashi Kazuko, who recognized the name tag right away. Struggling to get the words out as she rubbed the blackened name tag, Kazuko said, "Dad made them for us. We each had one." The image of her sister four decades earlier and the recollection of her father's love for his children must have created a wave of emotion in her. "We searched this area over and over again with our mother. I never thought that we'd ever find Masako after all these years. It's thanks to the name tags that Dad made for us." Again and again, as though she could not believe that she had it, Kazuko stared hard at the name tag she held in her hands.

When Kazuko told her mother Machi, who was sick in hospital in Itoman, about the find, the first thing her mother said was, "Was there a name tag around her neck?" Machi tearfully told the hospital nurse that she wanted to be taken to where her daughter's remains were immediately. The nurse calmed the woman down, and the next day she was accompanied by her surviving daughters to the place where the thirty sets of remains had been laid out.

On a day in June when the sun's fierce rays beat down upon them, Terasaka Machi was finally reunited with her daughter after thirty-nine years. Overcome with emotion, she embraced the skeletal remains with the copper name tag around them and wept. What must have been going through the mind of this old woman who had lost her husband and two children during the war, and then struggled to raise the remaining children by herself throughout the postwar years?

Only two out of family of thirteen survive

How can a boy who was not even ten years old remember things so clearly? Despite almost four decades having passed since the end of the war, he talked in minute detail about his experiences, adding that rather than having a good memory, he remembers because it was just too terrible to forget. Out of his family of thirteen who fled some of the fiercest fighting at Shuri, Nishihara and Haebaru, eleven were killed. Nako Yoshio was just nine years old at the time. Before the war he lived in Tera, where he attended the No. 1 Shuri Kokumin School. As he entered second grade, the war seemed to be getting ominously close and his activities at school assumed a distinctly military tone. "In front of our classroom there were two life-size straw figures that we used to stab with bamboo spears. As we did that we yelled out names like 'Roosevelt! . . . Chang Kai-shek!' and then we'd start our lessons."

There were thirteen in Yoshio's family, including his grandfather, his mother and father, younger sisters, younger brothers, uncles and aunts. As a member of the Home Guard, his father's job was to cut timber in Nago, although he returned home in the autumn of 1944 and started digging a shelter in a nearby forest. Because his family was too big to all fit into the shelter he had dug, he got access to shelters in three separate locations. At the time, Yoshio's uncle's wife was frail and had been admitted to hospital at Nishimachi in Naha.

On 9 October 1944 her doctor told her she could go home the following day. The next morning, Yoshio went to school as usual. "Everything was normal as I headed off that morning, but in the afternoon as I was on my way home after school, the adults were all going into Binjiru Forest. I was curious so I followed them." The next thing he saw was the blazing inferno of Naha, as red as a brilliant sunset, and what seemed like dozens of U.S warplanes forming up and making one low level attack after another. "There was a Japanese Army fortified position in the forest and when our soldiers saw the U.S. planes they fired their rifles at them. You've got to laugh, as there was no way they were ever going to hit them."

The hospital was burned to the ground in the air raid on Naha on 10 October 1944. Yoshio's uncle and his wife, who had been so happy about her being discharged, never made it home. From then on, the intensity of the air raids and naval bombardments increased every day. "There was a Japanese communications unit on nearby Mt. Kunjan. They had dozens of wireless masts but they were all knocked down during the raids. Even inside the shelters we could hear the deafening thud of . . . boom . . . thump . . ." Realizing it would be too dangerous to stay there, the family left Tera and shifted down the hill to Ikeda in Nishihara. Ikeda was located in the valley between Untamamui and Kukujimui. Numerous shelters had been dug on both sides of the stream that ran through the valley, and people from around Tera had also sought refuge in them. Because of the size of Yoshio's family, they occupied two shelters. Yoshio and his parents were in the shelter downstream, while all but three of the family were in the shelter upstream. That was where Yoshio was sealed in his shelter, effectively burying him alive.

Based on what he remembered when he was just nine years old, Yoshio searched for the shelter at Nishihara in Ikeda. We walked across a valley overgrown with thick vegetation and fallen trees. "Here it is," he said, but the place he was pointing at looked nothing like a shelter as the entrance had completely collapsed. "However, everything else that we saw in front of us certainly matched the rest of the description. It had a stream running through the middle of it just as there had been during the war. "This is where Gima and his family stayed," Yoshio explained. Its entrance was about one meter square and it went in about a hundred and fifty centimeters. On the wall was a small hole for the Buddhist mortuary tablet. The sight was enough to make me gasp. One day when Yoshio was living with his parents in the cave at Ikeda, he saw a U.S. reconnaissance aircraft up in the sky above them. The bombardment started not long after the plane flew away. As usual, the shells poured in like driving rain for quite some time, and when it ceased, the ground was churned upside down and strewn around like a landslide. The cave entrance was blocked.

"I was terrified. I just sat there, blocking my ears, eyes and nose with my hands." When he regained his senses, everything was pitch-black. Using the shelter's emergency shovel and small pickaxe, his father Yoshihide began digging to clear out the entrance. Yoshio joined in to help what was, without question, a job on which their very lives depended. Eventually they managed to dig a small hole that let some sunlight in. "The soil wasn't the normal hard stuff, it was the soft soil so that helped us." Having just managed to escape with their lives, they headed for the shelter upstream. The entrances there were on two levels, with the shelter being divided into a lower and upper level, joined by a path running through the middle, so it was like a two-story cave. Yoshio and some of his family entered the lower level while another family of six or seven people from Nishihara occupied the upper level.

"One day while we were under mortar attack," Yoshio explained, "both my parents and I got hit in the legs. My mother's wound was particularly serious. It didn't bleed that much but her wounds swelled up and turned green. Before long, maggots started to come out. The smell was awful and around the wound was very itchy and painful. It was terrible." He rolled up his trouser leg and showed me the scar from his own wound. "Dad mixed up some pork fat and salt and rubbed that onto our wounds . . . I guess it was instead of proper medicine."

The Americans were getting close by that point. "I don't remember the date, but what happened is still very clear in my mind." One evening, it happened in the flash of an eye. Two hand grenades were tossed into both levels of the shelter at the same time. As a loud "thump" resounded, the family in the upper level tumbled down the path and into the lower level. "I think every single person in that family from Nishihara was hit in the blast, but they weren't all killed as I could hear them groaning in agony. We too were staring death in the face and, because the others had fallen and were blocking the shelter entrance, we trod on them as we made our way outside."

After leaving Ikeda, Yoshio and his family once again headed for Shuri, using two empty tombs as shelters along the way. "There were tatami mats inside the tomb with muddy water under them." It was from that tomb that Yoshio saw his first ever American soldier. "I'd often been told by my father and grandfather that anyone caught by the Americans would be sliced up like a piece of vegetable, so I was terrified." To young Yoshio, that meant that if he got caught he'd have his arms and legs cut off and his ears ripped off.

Life in the empty tomb had begun. There was nothing to eat so young Yoshio went scavenging around the area and in an empty cave he found a discarded fish tin. It still contained a little of the liquid in one corner. Yoshio took the can back with him and used it to catch some of the rainwater dripping from the ceiling of the tomb. He stirred it around with his finger and drank it. "I'd never tasted anything so delicious in my life. I will never forget how good it was," he explained. In front of the tomb was a steep hill covered in burned trees and scorched tussock as far as the eye could see. One evening as Yoshio was hanging around in front of the tomb, he saw some people—unlike anybody he had ever seen before—climbing up the hill toward him. "I realized straight away that they were Americans. Remembering what my father had told me about being cut up like a vegetable, I scrambled back inside the tomb and told him there were enemy soldiers outside." In the tomb, they held their breath. They could hear voices outside yelling out to them but they couldn't understand the words. Immediately after that, a hand grenade was thrown into the tomb and in a split second everything was blown upside down. "Luckily, Dad and I survived. Mom was still alive but couldn't move as she was badly wounded. Dad left her where she was, grabbed my hand and headed outside." They raced down the hill.

They ran off through the darkness, surrounded by the burned remains of sugarcane fields. Then, a flare went up and everything was lit up as bright as daylight. As they ran along, Yoshio and his father were perfect targets, caught like silhouettes in the brilliant light. Young Yoshio fell as a bullet hit him in his left side and came out through his back. His entire body was wracked with a burning pain, and when he asked his father for water, the man dashed away replying, "I'll go and get some . . . I won't be long." Yoshio explained, "I can't help thinking that he went back to the tomb where my brothers and sisters were." He never saw his father again and only after the war did he hear from someone he knew that his father had died in an American POW camp at Hyakuna on 20 June. The last he saw of his younger sisters and brothers and other family members was in the tomb. Left alone in the sugarcane field, young Yoshio lost consciousness but came to because of the burning heat on his face.

He was desperate for water and looked around, but there was nothing. He was unable to move. He thought about drinking his own urine and, from where he was lying on the ground, used his heel to dig a small hollow in the earth to serve as a bowl. He passed a dribble of reddish urine and slowly propped himself up to try and drink even a few drops. However, as he lowered his face, there was nothing left as the liquid had soaked into the soil. Yoshio fainted again and then regained consciousness for the second time. The next thing he knew, an American soldier was kicking him with the toe of his boot. "I was terrified and pretended to be dead," but the American touched Yoshio's hand and must have felt his body heat. Then they placed him on stretcher.

He arrived at a nearby U.S. fortified position. "I couldn't believe it. American troops naked from the waist up were standing there shaving . . . some were drinking coffee. It was a completely different world from what I was used to. They even had toilet paper. So while I was just a child, I was amazed at the huge difference between our army and the enemy." Yoshio was then taken to a hospital where he stayed until the end of the war. Ironically, the only two to survive were Yoshio and his mother who had been left behind in the cave. They have never managed to recover the remains of the other eleven family members.

Only one survives

Sesoko Seijun's elder brother by seven years showed no signs of relenting in his efforts to change his younger brother's mind. As Seijun left his parents' evacuation point of Kin and headed for his own assembly point at Shuri, the elder brother raised his voice to try to persuade the younger Seijun not to join the Signals Unit. "Can't you see? Japan doesn't have a hope of winning this war. If they're sending students your age out there just to get killed, then it's all over." Masamune (the elder brother and Normal School teacher trainee) continued in his efforts to dissuade young Seijun, a second year student at the Prefectural Fisheries School. By the time he set off, the distant rumble of naval artillery had changed to a closer, ear-splitting roar, but young Seijun paid no heed to his brother's remonstrations. More concerned that the boys he was heading away with might hear his brother's "sissy behavior," he simply turned away and looked back a couple of times as he walked off.

Training for the Fisheries School's Signals Unit began in the New Year. The training program ran every day once the School had relocated to temporary classrooms in a training hall at Ginowan. "In the daytime we dug shelters and in the evenings we had signals training, so all we wanted to do was sleep . . . we just wanted to sleep." Their work involved building tank traps, 5 meters wide and about 3 meters deep. He remembers the depth because, "In order to sneak breaks from work, we could climb on each other's shoulders inside the observation post to see if an NCO was nearby or not." The Signals training NCO instructed us, "Now that you have signed up, we want you to start doing your duties as members of the Signals Unit as quickly as possible. We need to protect military secrets, so meeting family members is forbidden."

At the start, they did wireless training but the military soon decided that, "We were just a pack of dumb students who couldn't cope with wireless equipment," so partway through, the training changed to landline. Because they were so tired after their daytime work, many of the boys would nod off. However, a swift slap or a jab from a military sword scabbard soon woke them up. The intensive training finished on 28 March. "The order to join our unit came on 1 April, and while the Army wanted to take us away there and then, the school managed to get our departure postponed, arguing that we had to get our families' permission." He recalls that goat stew was served up at the gathering in front of the training hall before they went home.

By the time Sesoko made it back to his house in Yonabaru, the family had already fled to Kin, so he continued in that direction. The road had been teeming with refugees but, as dawn broke, there was not a soul to be seen anywhere. However, by following the road through the hills during the daytime as well, he finally caught up with his family at Kincho. The area around the shelter was overcrowded with evacuees, all of them looking absolutely terrified. After Sesoko had finished telling his parents about the school and various other things, he broached the topic of joining the Army. The look on his parents' faces changed to one of surprise. "It's already dangerous down south. Stay with us here in Kincho," they implored him.

He talked the matter over with his parents but they were unable to agree. It was actually his elder brother, Masamune, who was doing the persuading and eventually his parents began to relent, suggesting, "If you go with your older brother, I guess that'll be okay." Masamune had been given two days' leave to help his parents get ready to evacuate. Then he said to his little brother, "OK, *you* can go. But you're not to put any pressure on anyone else." He had already arranged departure details with some friends, and when he arrived at their assembly point, three of them were already waiting. As Seijun turned to bid farewell to his parents, he noticed tears pouring down his older brother's cheeks. The parents hugged the younger boy, urging him to "Please be careful." Then they bid farewell to both sons. Although it was Masamune who had talked their parents round, as soon as they edged away from their friends, he started badgering his younger brother, "Go back home to Mom and Dad."

The older brother already sensed that Japan would be defeated. "He'd snuck past the military police and talked to a captured American pilot who had been put in a cage in front of the Normal School. Of course Masamune's English wasn't very good, but he was staggered at what he could understand about the difference between America's warplane and ship-building capability and ours." But even that explanation didn't change the younger boy's mind. "Our militarist education had blinded me to the truth. It wasn't until after the war ended that I realized how right my brother was."

The sound of gunfire intensified as Sesoko reached Ishikawa and then Awase. As he approached Ginowan, he shuddered as he witnessed scenes of battle for the first time. He ran as fast as he could to Shuri, arriving at his elder brother's lodgings before dawn. Having given up trying to persuade his younger brother to say behind, Masamune suggested his grandmother's house in Ozato as a rendezvous and said, "If things get really dangerous, go there as quickly as you can." He then handed Seijun the black jacket his parents had given him when he first enrolled at the Normal School. That was the last time he saw it because the exhausted Seijun later left it behind in a shelter in Haebaru during the withdrawal. Of course, he had no way of knowing at that stage that, of the twenty-two boys who had joined the Fisheries School Signals Unit, he would be the only one to survive.

Just before dawn on 1 April, all the members of the Fisheries School Signals Unit fell in at 32nd Army Command Headquarters. While they were all supposed to have obtained their parents' permission to join, not all had done so. After the war, as part of his postwar administration duties, Oyakawa Mitsushige had visited the household of every boy. That was when he learned that some students had joined up in spite of their parents' objections and that quite a number had lied to their parents in order to get away to join the Unit. One such student was Uwamae Kanichi, who was later killed in the fighting. At the family home in Henza, Uwamae's mother was vehemently opposed to the idea of her son's joining the Unit. Her husband had been killed when the coastal vessel he was on was strafed by American aircraft as it was returning from Oshima, so the mother was never going to agree to her only son being sent away to war. She prostrated herself at the house entrance and screamed, "If you still think you're going, you'll have to walk over my body to do so." Unable to step over his own mother, he retreated toward the back of the house in silence. However, she soon discovered that her son had slipped out the back door, climbed over the stone wall and set off for Shuri.

Sesoko Seijun was amazed when he first entered the underground shelter at Shuri Castle. "When did they build this massive place?" he wondered upon seeing the size of the shelter. After being guided in from the entrance by one of the soldiers, they went deep into the cavernous area where other students were still excavating, putting up pine logs for props as they worked. An NCO arrived at the students' assembly point and addressed them as they stood lined up in ranks. "As from today," he said, "you're attached to the Army Signals Unit as privates, second class." They discarded their old Fisheries School uniforms and donned military uniforms, minus the "star" rank insignia that should have been on the collar, as brand new "army private, second class."

They were attached to the Intelligence Section and divided into two groups of eleven, rotating daytime and evening shifts. Their work involved sending intelligence gathered by the information office on the state of the fighting, plus general instructions, to command headquarters, as well as reporting on enemy movements from their observation post. Five members from each group manned the observation post while the other six worked in the information room. It was quite dark inside the shelter. Exhausted from working day and night shifts, the students used to lie down in little nooks and crannies in the corridor to recover. "We often saw General Ushijima, the overall commander, and Chief of Staff Cho. On one occasion, Ushijima patted some of us on the head and said, "Well done you students. Good effort!" But as Cho walked past us in those narrow passageways, he would bellow, 'Get out of the way!'"

They watched U.S. troop movements from a spot near the main hall of Shuri Castle. "There was a vertical internal passageway from the shelter so we'd go up a ladder to where two of us would man the observation post. We monitored the area, hiding among the stone walls, then used our field telephone to report below what we'd seen." But it wasn't just the area around Shuri. By looking further afield, they could also see as far as parts of Naha and Aja. They reported on the huge numbers of U.S. ships out on the water, information about U.S. naval batteries, numbers of incoming U.S. planes, and how the land battle was going. From time to time a shell would land near them, cutting off the phone line between the shelter and the observation post. Reconnecting the line was a dangerous job. With U.S. artillery now deployed on the Keise Islands west of Naha, the bombardment became more intense, and on many occasions their camouflage netting was hurled up into the air by the blasts from the incoming shells. "So with the situation the way it was, it really lifted our spirits when our kamikaze planes scored a direct hit on a warship one evening and sank it—we clapped our hands in delight."

Sesoko Masaka explained, "Because shells often landed so close, sometimes we could barely breathe because of the clouds of sand they kicked up. Manning that observation post was so dangerous that I often used to wonder when I was going to die. And yet, I felt better going out to the lookout than being shut inside the murky darkness of the shelter. I actually quite looked forward to it." On 17 April, about a month and a half into their work in the Intelligence Section, the Fisheries School Signals Unit suffered its first casualties, Tomon Tomohide and Omine Seiichi, both first year students. The fighting had now reached Shuri. While the two students were in a different group from Sesoko, the news of their death immediately spread to everyone in the shelter. As part of their job of carrying food, they had been making their way to the field kitchen outside the shelter but were killed when a shell landed right beside them. One of the boys had his head blown off and, when Sesoko and the others checked out the area, they found the body of the other dead student lying between two bales of rice. "We had all accepted that we were going to die so there was no great feeling of sadness. But it certainly increased our hatred of the Americans, and all we could think about was 'no matter what, we'll get our revenge.'" The remains of the two boys were buried with their peers looking on. Vowing that anyone who survived would somehow get the remains to the boys' families, they buried them using a shell-splintered tree trunk to mark the spot.

Soon after the war ended, Sesoko went back but the old tree trunk they had used as a marker was gone and the area had changed completely from when he was last there. He worked out the general area as accurately as he could and dug up a number of places, all without success. "I was feeling really tired and, when

I stopped for a break, I fell straight into a short sleep," he explained. "I saw the faces of the two boys there before me, plain as day. Then, when I started digging again, I found their remains just as we had buried them. So, I contacted their families and was able to reunite them."

Around 27 May, about ten days after the first casualties, activity at the Command Post shelter had become frantic with the staff officers working flat out. Sesoko asked one of the Kainan School students working in the decoding office, "Hey, what's happening?" but the only answer he got was, "It's secret!" Before long, an NCO arrived at the Intelligence Office with their orders. The Model 99 telephones and important documents were taken outside the shelter and burned. "Make sure you eat your fill," the NCO told them all. White rice was brought in and distributed along with tins of pineapple, tuna, shellfish, and the like. "There were even cans of food that we hadn't seen before. We were told to eat as much of the canned food in particular as we could stuff in, so we did. We couldn't believe what a great feast we were having," Sesoko said.

Once they had finished eating, they were given rifles, ammunition, hand grenades and two days supply of hardtack. "Then, a group—excluding me—was ordered to head south as an advance party." Twelve or thirteen of them assembled near the shelter entrance, the sleeves of their uniforms covering their fingertips and the cuffs of their trousers rolled up several times making it immediately obvious that they were just schoolboys. They were told that the officers' basket trunks, which they were to carry in pairs, contained "important documents." Each pair carried two trunks slung over a pole but at 30 kgs each, plus the weight of their own kit, the poles dug into their shoulders. As if that wasn't enough, the rain made the baskets even heavier.

They lost their footing and slipped over into the mud again and again. Up to their waists as they crossed flooded rivers, they only thing they managed to keep above the water were the basket trunks. When the distance from the soldiers ahead of them stretched out, an officer waved his sword at them and yelled, "If any of you slacken off the pace, I'll give a piece of this!" They were utterly exhausted by the time they arrived at the Army Hospital in Haebaru. They were at the hospital for a day but, when they were about to leave, they heard an army surgeon say to the wounded soldiers, "Those of you can walk, make your way south." Without uttering a sound, the female students darted in among the patients who were clearly unable to walk and gave them phials of liquid. The men knew that it was poison to use to take their own lives, and the sight of the wounded soldiers in the deathly quiet shelter thanking the army surgeon as they received their dose was so unsettling that Sesoko has never been able to erase it from his mind.

Along the way they spent a night in a tomb before arriving at Mabuni. The fighting had not yet reached Mabuni, which was still very much a tranquil village surrounded by lush vegetation. To recover from the grueling march, they stayed briefly in local dwellings deserted by their owners and were even able to take a bath. Once Sesoko was over his fatigue, he glanced toward the basket trunks that had been such a burden during their march in the rain. "I can't just leave all those important documents soaking there like that," he thought. "I'll have to dry them out." He opened one of the baskets and yelled out in disgust at what he saw, "What!" The only things inside the basket were wooden *geta*, underwear, and items of clothing . . . just the officers' personal effects!

Around the time the fighting spread to the areas around Mabuni, Sesoko and the others from the Fisheries School Signals Unit were moved to a combat squad. The tasks of lugging 15 kg explosive devices on their backs for blowing up tanks and, at night, infiltrating U.S. lines, were given to those young kids in their baggy army uniforms in the same way as they were given to fully fledged soldiers. Nevertheless, at first it was only the regular soldiers who went out on the infiltration raids. Each evening, infiltration squads would leave the shelter one after the other, but only a third would make it back in the hours just before dawn, their arms hanging at their sides or dragging their feet along. "Their commander met those soldiers in front of the shelter, bellowing at them things like, 'You gutless lot!' Then, the next night they'd be ordered out on another raid," Sesoko explained.

In mid-June, Sesoko also took part in his first infiltration raid and was amazed when he observed American forces up close at night. Their lights were ablaze and he could even hear party music playing. It was so different from the Japanese soldiers who had to lie low inside the murky darkness of their shelters during the day, only venturing outside once the sun had gone down. Then, suddenly, right beside them, came the rat-rat-tat of raking machine-gun fire. It only needed someone to touch the perimeter wire for the Americans to realize another night raid was upon them. Not daring to move a muscle, the raiders' only option was to wait until the firing stopped. It was around then that some of the soldiers just wounded on infiltration raids died reciting Buddhist prayers when they got back to the shelter entrance. "They said their prayers in unison with a priest from Osaka, and the plaintive sound of their chanting reverberating into the darkness of the shelter was quite eerie." Sesoko also saw an officer who had lost his mind. The man was ranting and raving on top of a hill to the right of the shelter as he looked up at the American warplanes and screamed out at them. Hanging down limply by his side, his left arm seemed to be broken, so he swung his sword around with his right hand. The naval barrage was intense, so it was a miracle that the incoming rounds missed him.

On 20 June, the attack squad carried out its final infiltration raid. The Fisheries School students—divided into two platoons of seven students each—were all there. Six boys from the Signals Unit were absent because they had departed the previous evening after receiving special orders to take a group of senior officers to Yoron Island in dugout canoes. Although Sesoko had also been given that order, he was wounded in the foot on the way and was told to stay behind. The mission that the other six boys went on was top secret so nobody knew anything about it and they were never seen again. They all lined up outside the shelter to get their instructions from the company commander, Capt. Masunaga. As the cups of "good luck" water were passed round, they felt uncomfortable about the prospect of not coming back alive. All they could say to the younger ones was, "Do your best!"

Things didn't work out quite in keeping with the gallant intention of "infiltration raid." Endless flares lit up the area and the shelling was relentless. They had barely made a few hundred meters in an hour. In order to avoid being heard, they removed their belts and wore soft *jika-tabi* on their feet, but they were soon detected and mortar shells and machine gun bullets poured in on them. As the hours passed, so did the number of boys killed, and with almost nothing to show for their efforts, they had no choice but to pull back before dawn. In Sesoko's platoon, all seven boys from the Signals Unit got back alive, but none of the seven boys who had accompanied the other platoon survived. After resting up inside the shelter during the day, the survivors were organized into another infiltration squad. After launching a repeat of the previous night's raid, all seven again made it back alive. The seven boys in the Signals Unit then shifted to the Command Headquarters shelter. After being told, "You boys are to protect the shelter entrance!" they lined up directly below the vertical tunnel shaft, but before the day was over they found themselves under attack. The machine gun at the observation post burst into life only to stop almost immediately. Then the inside of the shelter shook and smoke starting drifting their way. A few moments later, there was a strange smell. Just as Sesoko thought to himself, "It's petrol!" there was the roar of an explosion and a sheet of flame, followed by rocks falling from above.

Kinjo Masatoshi and Toma Tsuguo were killed instantly by the blast. Tonaki Moritoshi bled to death, while Tokashiki Toshihiko, who died shortly after, kept hitting himself on the head and muttering deliriously, "I wish I could stay alive and do more for my country." Pinned beneath fallen rocks and unable to move, Sesoko yelled out for someone to help him. A soldier with one arm blown off came across and, without uttering a word, used his remaining arm to move the pile of rocks, one at a time. Sesoko immediately reported to the senior officers at the back of the Command Post shelter that "All the students have been buried alive in the shaft to the tunnel." As soon as Sesoko had delivered his desperate message, Lt. Gen. Ushijima replied gratefully with, "Thank you for such a brave effort, you students." He then asked Sesoko, "What's your name?" and "What school are you from?" "I'm Sesoko Seijun, Sir, private second class from the Fisheries School Blood and Iron Unit," Sesoko replied, mustering all his strength and standing ram-rod straight.

After delivering his news, Sesoko went back down to help the NCO but was immediately ordered back to defend the shelter entrance. However, he had suffered a serious blow to the chest in the rock fall and he was still dazed. As he staggered off toward the shelter entrance, he fainted and fell to the ground. He has no idea how long he was out for but, when he came round, he was struggling to breath because his throat was full of blood. There was no sign of anyone inside the shelter so he groped his way toward the entrance, walking over dead bodies as he went. Beside one of the bodies he noticed some uneaten rice, which he shoved in his mouth but couldn't keep down. However, he did manage to drink some water from a bottle to clear his throat.

At the shelter entrance, he heard a voice and when he went over to investigate, he found a soldier searching for something or other. Surprised to see Sesoko, the man said to him, "Idiot! What the hell are you doing here? The Command Post soldiers have gone out on a banzai attack, so get out of here right now." Then he added, "There are some students at the back of the shelter." Toward the back were two students from the Fisheries School Signals Unit, Uwamae Kanichi and Toma Tsuguo, plus another student from Kainan School who had been blinded in the blast. The four of them decided how to get out, but the boy from Kainan School responded, "I'll just hold you back . . . go without me." Sesoko try to persuade him, saying, "Come with us as far as you can," but it was to no avail. The three boys had no choice but to leave him behind. As the last of them was leaving the shelter, a voice from the back called out to them, "Good luck, guys!" The sound of a hand grenade exploding immediately followed. Believing in "Eternity through death for the emperor and country," yet another young man had taken his own life.

The coastline below was teeming with people, so they were unable to find a safe shelter anywhere. They could see countless dead bodies down by the waterline. But rather than all those corpses reflected in the moonlight, what caught Sesoko's eye were things like the fruit, onions and carrots, perfectly good food thrown away by the American troops. He grabbed everything he could reach, then searched some of the dead bodies for clothing. IJA stragglers had already occupied the best rocky enclaves, so they spent the next three days wandering along the coastline looking for safe haven. Once they reached Komesu, they found a perfect place to shelter with its own fresh water spring. However, some soldiers who were already sheltering there threatened the boys with knives and screamed at them, "Go somewhere else!"

Just then, from nearby a corporal called out, "Hey, you kids, come in here." His name was Yajima Hidetoshi and he also gave the three boys something to eat. When they asked him what he was doing, he explained that he had commanded some students in the battle but had lost many of his comrades and student soldiers. "Even now, I am still so grateful to Cpl. Yajima," Sesoko explained. Back then, the competition among those IJA stragglers for food was horrendous. Two soldiers who had stored a large quantity of food inside the shelter were well known by those around them. One day, a hand grenade was thrown into the shelter and both men were killed instantly. Needless to say, the food disappeared at once.

Before long, Sesoko and the other two from the Fisheries School Signals Unit teamed up with another group comprising a married couple accompanied by three girls, a regular private soldier called Chinen and a first-year student called Gushiken from the Technical School. There was nobody left from the units fighting the Americans, but there were many groups of people along the foreshore who still couldn't believe they had been defeated. Hiding during the day and coming out at night to look for food and occasionally talking on the beach, Sesoko's existence with the others continued for over a month until the end of July. They ventured farther and farther afield because of the food they picked up mainly along the coast, plus the fact that the fighting had also come to an end by then. Their food supplies improved still further as they pilfered supplies from U.S. military camps and stole crops from the fields.

On one occasion, six of the group went out to a field of potatoes and came away with their bag stuffed full. Even today, Sesoko still remembers the whiteness of their teeth gleaming in the moonlight. Their "harvest" had been substantial, but it had a tragic ending. Because their bag was heavy, they took a short cut back to their hiding place, but it was a route seeded with land mines because of the number of IJA stragglers who hung around the area. Pvt. Chinen knew about land mines so he led the way. "I was next, followed by Toma and Uwamae, with the girls at the rear." They decided to keep about ten meters apart and had been really careful all the way when suddenly Sesoko heard a terrific explosion. He remembers nothing after that as he was knocked unconscious by the blast and hurled about 5 meters. Chinen was killed immediately, with only bits of his flesh remaining. The wife of a man behind Chinen was also killed, eviscerated by shrapnel from the landmine. One of his student friends, who himself had been wounded in the left leg, carried the unconscious Sesoko on his back to the bottom of the bluff which was 30 meters high. "Toma carried me on his back and, even now when I see it, I think how grateful I am to him for lugging me down that difficult terrain," Sesoko said.

Toma later died from the wound he sustained to his left foot when the mine exploded. Just as he was about to die, his head remained upright and he didn't utter a word. But his whole body convulsed and it was all the others could do to hold him down as he thrashed about. Sesoko promised, "If we make it out alive, we'll get your remains back to your family," and felt that the look in his eyes changed to one of inner peace. They rolled his remains up in a U.S. army blanket and buried it in a cranny inside the shelter. After the battle was over, Sesoko volunteered to become a civilian policeman and so was comparatively free to move about. He took the remains back to Toma's parents and then quit his role as a policeman.

Gushiken, the Technical School student, died early in August. Shortly after Sesoko had teamed up with the others, he came across Gushiken, his stomach wounds bandaged up and wandering around seemingly lost. So, he also ended up joining Sesoko's group. "He was good-looking, slightly built at only 140 cm and with bright eyes. I remember that he was from Shuri, spoke clearly and, by the sound of things, had a relative who was a member of parliament or in some other high-ranking position." Because of his size, he used to run and fetch water as soon as it was daylight because "The Americans would think he was just a kid and wouldn't shoot him." However, on the third day of his water duties, he was cut down by a machine gun up on top of a hill overlooking the shore, falling to the ground as soon as he was hit. The others watched as his dead body was swept further and further out to sea but none of them could leave the shelter to do anything. Sesoko has looked for Gushiken's name on the Technical School list of war dead, but it was not there.

Sesoko and the others were taken prisoner on 3 October, well after the war ended. Uwamae Kanichi, injured by falling rocks when the Command Post shelter collapsed in late June, had become very weak. Sesoko's condition had also deteriorated, having sustained thirty separate wounds—some minor, some major—when he was hurled through the air by the blast from a landmine. When they arrived at the POW camp in the south, Sesoko told the senior local police officer who was in charge of the camp, "Uwamae is very weak. I want a doctor to look at him." However, he was rebuffed with, "He may be a student soldier, but a private second class is a private second class . . . Can't help you." They were then put on a truck and taken to another camp at Yaka where Uwamae's wounds worsened and where he died two or three days later. "The same top dogs in the local police who, in cahoots with the army, threw their weight around inciting us to go to battle, were lording it over us again, only this time under the auspices of the U.S. military. That guy just wiped his hands of the last of my buddies who was still alive. Even now, I'm still furious; my hatred toward that bastard has not subsided." Because the students were so innocent and their sacrifice was so great, Sesoko has never been able to forgive the self-serving nature of those adults who changed their allegiances so quickly.

Family wiped out

It was not unusual for entire families to be killed during the Battle of Okinawa. In fact, approximately 380 households were wiped out, accounting for more than 1,500 people. The true number is likely to be far higher than this, but of course it is impossible to verify because there is no one left to comment on each of these tragedies. In many cases, the scene of the families' deaths is unknown.

The family of Azama Yoshinobu is one such example. Before the war they lived in Kami-Izumicho. At the head of the family of six was the father, Yoshinobu (born in 1893), who worked in a metalwork yard connected to the prefectural railroad and his wife Makato (born in 1892). The children were their eldest son Yoshiaki (born in 1919), second son Yoshimasa (born in 1922) daughter Kiku (born in 1924) and third son Yoshihiro (born in 1930). Yoshinobu had served as a soldier in China, so the children had a strict upbringing. Azama Yoshihei, a relative who knew the family, commented, "They were quiet, well-mannered people."

As the fighting intensified, Yoshinobu's family and Yoshihei's mother Tsuru and his younger sister Kiyo entered a dugout shelter on the property of a nearby farm. But before too long, that location became increasingly dangerous so Tsuru suggested to Yoshinobu that they evacuate to the Yambaru in the north of Okinawa. However, Yoshinobu was selling dumplings to the IJA to earn a living and said that they would stay on a little longer. From that point on, there is no record of anyone seeing any of the members of Yoshinobu Azama's family again.

Yoshihei said, "I was drafted and went to China in 1943, before the fighting started on Okinawa. I returned in 1947, so I have no idea what happened to my uncle and his family while I was away. I heard a little from my mother, but I don't know where any of the family died. If we knew that, at least we could go there and pray for the repose of their souls. I made some spirit tablets and I suppose that's as much as we can do." Very few people know of Yoshinobu's family, and Yoshihei only has vague memories of them.

Among the memorials at Mabuni, there is one called *Shizutama-no-Hi*, which is dedicated to the souls of those people whose families lost everyone in the Battle of Okinawa.

Breakdown of Deaths during the Battle of Okinawa of Children under Fourteen Years of Age[9]

Situation at time of death	Number	Age	Number
Forced out of a shelter	10,101	0	181
Engaged in cooking or other tasks for the IJA	343	1	989
Suicide	313	2	1,244
Carrying food supplies	194	3	1,027
With soldiers whose unit had been destroyed	150	4	1,009
With parents	100	5	846
Carrying ammunition	89	6	733
Constructing fortifications	85	7	767
Starvation	76	8	748
Shot by Japanese troops	14	9	697
Acting as a messenger	5	10	715
Transporting wounded soldiers	3	11	697
Other	10	12	757
		13	1074
Total	**11,483**		**11,483**

9.   Ota Peace Research Institute. 2010:8

CHAPTER 11

INTERNMENT CAMPS

From even before hostilities ended, U.S. forces had set up holding camps in the central region of Okinawa for prisoners of war and non-combatants. Interrogations were carried out in any attempt to prevent Japanese soldiers from hiding themselves among local civilians.

Most of the civilians who were held in these camps arrived there in very poor physical condition with no belongings other than the clothes they were wearing. The U.S. military authorities provided minimum requirements of food, clothing, tents and medicine, but still many people died of malnutrition or malaria.

The prisoners of war were divided into four separate types of camps: officers, regular Japanese soldiers, Okinawan recruits, and Korean laborers.[1] Large numbers of civilians were moved from one camp to another as the U.S. military's need for land changed.[2]

In June 1945, about 3,000 prisoners of war of Okinawan origin were sent to Hawaii. In October of 1946 the POWs from the main islands began to be shipped back to Japan, and by the end of 1946 almost all had been repatriated.[3]

Remains found of mother holding a baby

In the mid-1960s, the discovery of the remains of a mother holding her dead baby in Oroku in the south-western area of Naha attracted a great deal of attention among local residents. The owner of the land being developed, who was the person who found the remains, went around the neighborhood asking people if they knew who this might be, but when no one had any knowledge of the identity, he had no option but to gather up the bones in a bag and take them to the communal ossuary in Oroku. After that, it is said that the bones were interred at the ossuary in Mabuni for unknown victims of the Battle of Okinawa.

"That was definitely my mother and my younger brother. The place where they were dug out from was used as an air raid shelter during the war. We piled

---

1.   Okinawa Heiwa Network. 2008: 62
2.   Ota, M. 1988: 51
3.   Okinawa Heiwa Network. 2008: 62

up earth by the entrance inside the shelter to stop the bomb blasts affecting us inside, and I buried the two of them right beside that."

While he was just nine years old at the time, Uehara Jintaro spoke with the confidence of someone who was certain that he remembered events accurately. He remembers that the rainy season had just started in 1945 and that it was near Oroku Junction. His mother Kamado, then forty-two years old, was fatally wounded by a shell from an American warship when she left the shelter they were in to go to another shelter to borrow some rice and a pot.

Jintaro had been out with his mother, but because he was walking directly behind her he was unscathed. "My mother was hit and fell backward on top of me, so I suppose that was what saved me," said Jintaro. "She had been hit in the thigh and the flesh was hanging off the bone and her hair had all been burned off in the flash from the explosion." Kamado's sister-in-law and some others helped carry her back to the shelter where her five children were waiting.

"She survived for another four or five days. We children did what we could, spreading some lard on my baby brother's diapers and putting that on the wound, but it just started putrefying. She really wanted to drink water, so we gave her a kettle of it to drink from and before too long she seemed to lose her mind, then stopped breathing. We'd been told not to give badly wounded people water, but . . ."

Jintaro and the other children were at a loss as to what to do. Just before she died, his mother said to him that his being the eldest of the children meant that he needed to take charge and look after his younger brothers, but at nine years old he had no idea what course of action they should take.

"My youngest brother, Yasunao, was just eight months old, so still a baby. After our mother died he was so hungry that all he did was cry. We squeezed her breasts and milk came out, so we put baby Yasunao on her breasts to suckle. He managed to do this for two or three days." But when his mother's milk ran out he started crying again, and so a soldier who just happened to be going past in the shelter picked him up and took him to the shelter next door where the soldiers were. The soldier then wrapped a towel around his neck and strangled the baby. "We buried Yasunao together with our mother, whom we'd buried a day or so earlier. We wanted to put him in her arms, but because rigor mortis had set in, all four of us had to really pull hard to move her arms a little wider to slip his body in."

We spoke to Kamado's sister-in-law, Higa Masuyo, who had helped carry Jintaro's mother back to the shelter after she had been badly wounded. She recalled the scene, "When I heard what had happened, I ran to where she'd been hit and realized that she was in a really bad way. Her clothing was burned and the skin on half of her face hung down from the burns. It looked just like how the skin peels off a grilled potato. The flesh had been ripped off her thigh to such an extent that I could see the bone. I remember that for a second I thought that I was going to faint . . . I'll never forget the look of joy on her face when she saw that we had come to help."

Masuyo and her husband carried Kamado back to the shelter where the five children and Jintaro's grandmother were waiting. They did all they could for Kamado, but she died just a few days later.

Masuyo said, "When we heard that Kamado had died, my husband and I went from our shelter just near where they were, and helped bury her." She remembers that after that, she was told by Jintaro's grandmother, "You're still young and can get through this, so get away from here while you can." Saying, "If I'm going to die, I want to die in my home," the old lady also left the shelter, leaving the five children behind. Then, just a few days later . . .

There was an army shelter right next to the air raid shelter that Jintaro and the other children were in, and a soldier in his late forties suddenly appeared in front of the children. There was a narrow passageway connecting the two shelters and this soldier used to appear through there and occasionally steal food from them.

"Yasunao was crying, so once when that soldier came, he said 'I'll look after the baby for you,' and took him away. Just a short time later we heard a strange noise and I thought, 'What's going on here . . .' and rushed over to the soldiers' shelter, but there was no one there. When Jintaro had a look around the area, he found the body of baby Yasunao on the ground with a towel wrapped around his neck. When he touched his brother's body it was still warm and he remembers that the baby's face was covered in spots.

Jintaro's voice faltered as he continued his explanation, saying that, not longer after this, down by a nearby river he was shocked to find the body of the soldier who had killed his younger brother.

After the war, Jintaro moved to Tokyo before returning to Okinawa in the mid-1970s. So when his mother and younger brother's remains were found he was not in Okinawa to claim them.

Remains found in a thicket of lead trees

Another set of remains has been found, this time in some undergrowth near Cape Kyan in Itoman, the scene of some of the fiercest fighting in the Battle of Okinawa. Irabu Yoshinori found the remains when was looking for a hermit crab to use as bait on a day out fishing. The bones were collected at the end of August 1983 and would be interred in the ossuary for war dead in Mabuni in early September.

The remains were found in among a thicket of lead trees down toward the sea in an area almost totally occupied by fields of sugarcane. It is a place that it is totally quiet except for the occasional sound of birds or waves breaking on the rocks down below. The skeleton was lying there just as the soldier fell almost forty years earlier. There was a bullet hole in his skull and a pair of decayed army-issue shoes lay beside the remains. The bones having mostly been reduced to dust meant that the scene reflected the fact that almost four decades had passed since the battle. Nevertheless the stark reality of death in war was still as raw as ever.

In June 1945, in the area of Kyan in Itoman, units under the command of the 62nd Infantry Division looked to engage the American forces advancing toward the 32nd Army Command Post at Mabuni. However, by 20 June they were effectively destroyed with the remnants launching themselves at the enemy in a suicide attack.

There were approximately 100 Okinawan soldiers of the Home Guard involved in this final act of the battle, but more than half of them were killed, as were countless civilians from the central or southern region of the main island of Okinawa who were attempting to flee the fighting. Those last days of the battle are said to have involved so much carnage that the entire area was littered with corpses. People attempting to flee were so panic-stricken that they were incapable of stopping to help a loved one hit by an enemy bullet.

In this same area, Japanese soldiers are said to have sent many local civilians to their deaths. Kubotama Iko, who was a member of the Home Guard, and Kume Keikichi, a school teacher, described it as follows: "There were plenty of safe natural caves down by Cape Kyan, and civilians had fled down there and were sheltering in these caves, but Japanese soldiers appeared and ejected the civilians at gunpoint. The people driven out were in such a pitiful situation and then the Japanese soldiers, whom they had thought were there to protect them, had in fact betrayed them. They did their best to get away, but the enemy fire was so heavy that almost all of them were killed."

In October 1952, the residents of Kyan came to recover the bones of civilians and soldiers that had been left there and built a memorial near the coast that they named *Heiwa-no-To* [Peace Memorial Tower] where they interred the bones. It is said that the remains of more than a thousand people were collected. Kuniyoshi Tsugiko recalls that, "In the time immediately after the war, there were countless human bones down on the coast. There were also lots in the thickets of lead trees near the coast. In fact there were so many that it wasn't uncommon for people to just part the branches of the bushes and go a few paces in, and before they knew it they were stepping on bones. I was just a child then, but I remember collecting bones and taking them to the Peace Memorial Tower to be interred."

While the collection of bones would seem to be almost complete, those that remain are likely to be in places that make them extremely difficult to retrieve.

The sugarcane plants rustle in the breeze as the call of lovely, small birds and the sound of the waves remind us that we are now in a time of peace. I could not help but feel that somewhere amid the serenity of this scene I could hear the souls of the forgotten dead crying out to me.

Search for the location where father died

Urasoe Elementary School in Nakama, Urasoe. These days, seeing young children running around so happily and carefree in the school's playground, it is difficult to imagine that this was the scene of fierce fighting during the Battle of Okinawa. The ruins of Urasoe Castle, which was destroyed in the 1609 invasion of the Ryukyu Kingdom by the Satsuma Domain, are located on the hill behind the school, and urban development in this area has progressed at a rapid pace in recent years. Early in 1984, 39 years after the war ended, a man bearing a cherry tree seedling came from the Tohoku region in search of the place where his father died.

Almost four decades after his father's death, Oba Hiro from Yamagata Prefecture had finally found the place where his father was killed and on this occasion had come with his wife Ryoko to pay his respects. Guided by Kakazu Seisuke of Ginowan City, who knew the details of his father Oba Shotaro's death, Oba went straight from the airport to Urasoe Elementary School. He was undeterred by the heavy rain falling that day and wanted to go as quickly as possible to where his father had died.

It was just after 1:00 PM when they arrived, to be met by the principal of Urasoe Elementary School, Kadekaru Yoshitomo who been briefed by Kakazu on the reason for the visit. When they settled into their seats in the principal's office, Oba asked Kakazu to tell him about what he remembered of his father's death. Kakazu said, "It's such a long time ago that I can't recall the specific date and time, but I'll tell you what I do remember."

"Capt. Oba was killed just by that palm tree that you can see over there. I didn't actually see this myself, but I heard it from Sgt. Inoue who ran back through the shellfire and came into the shelter where I was resting after being wounded. He ran in and said 'The captain's been hit!' There was an enemy machine gun emplacement very near where we were, so it's likely that your father was killed by fire from there. I have no doubt that the location of the captain's death that I heard from Sgt. Inoue was correct."

On 27 April 1945, the American forces commenced their second offensive in the area of Nakama, Maeda, and Kochi. In the evening of 29 April, two days after the Americans launched this attack, the eleven remaining soldiers of No. 5 Company of the 2nd Battalion of the Yamagata 32nd Infantry Regiment who were still capable of fighting left their shelter behind Capt. Oba Shotaro to attack the American forces.

At that stage, Kakazu was resting in the shelter after having been hit in the arm, legs and back with pieces of shrapnel. He remembers that a Pvt. Sato was also there with him in the shelter, but died of tetanus after just a short time. By this stage, Kakazu's company had effectively been wiped out. He said, "Capt. Oba and the other men left the shelter with three days' supply of food each, but they had only small arms and swords. Sgt. Inoue, who had managed to make it back to where I was, said that the remnants of the company who had sallied forth were smashed to smithereens in what seemed like the blink of an eye." Capt. Oba died that day at the age of forty-two, much younger than his son Hiro who had come to Okinawa to find out about his father's death.

Sgt. Inoue returned to Hokkaido after the war but has since passed away, so the only person who knew anything about the death of Capt. Oba is Kakazu Seisuke. Oba Hiro said, "I had heard rumors that my father had been killed by shellfire from a tank, but I do feel better now that I know the truth. Until today, I didn't know where or how my father died, so I am happy to now have that information." Bowing several times to Kakazu, Oba left the principal's office and walked out toward the spot where it happened.

The spot where Capt. Oba was killed was beside a palm tree. Mr. and Mrs. Oba and Kakazu each placed a bouquet of flowers there as well as an offering of pickles, a delicacy from Yamagata Prefecture, before they prayed for the repose of Capt. Oba's soul. Oba Hiro had been to Okinawa thirteen years earlier in attempt to find where his father died and, having no luck in gaining any information, he had offered prayers in a location far from the real spot. His father Oba Shotaro's photograph became wet in the heavy rain that fell that day on the Urasoe Elementary School, but Hiro's wife Ryoko was not distracted as she recited the sutras. In Oba Hiro's heart the feeling that he had finally managed to be "reunited" with his dead father outweighed any amount of rain.

Oba Shotaro joined the IJA when he was twenty years old. "Yamagata was a relatively poor area, so just getting enough food to survive was an issue in those days. With that being the case, my father joined up to become a career soldier so he could get food to eat," said Oba.

After Shotaro joined the army, his unit was deployed to Manchuria, then to Hokkaido before returning to Manchuria. In August 1944 the unit made the fateful journey to Okinawa, where he was posted with his 400 men to southern Okinawa. Kakazu recalls that the headquarters of the 2nd Battalion was set up there in Yamagusuku in Itoman. As each day passed, the intensity of the American offensive increased and before too long a report came that the frontline at Urasoe was in danger of collapsing. Capt. Oba's No. 5 Company was called up from the reserves to help bolster the defensive line, but not long after it arrived at the ruins of Urasoe Castle it was the focus of a ferocious attack from a U.S. armored unit and was very soon destroyed.

Kakazu recalls the awful scene saying, "We lost all cohesion in the chaos and our own guys were even being killed by friendly fire. It was an absolutely terrible situation to be in." Oba Hiro listened intently to the older man's recollection of the events that culminated in his father's death.

Oba only has one memory of his father, from 1942, when he was just eight years old. "Dad had come back to Japan from Manchuria to be posted to Hokkaido, but before that he was able to spend just two days with his family back in Yamagata. I remember how he took his uniform off and put on a kimono to wear when he took me to watch a movie. I was in second grade at elementary school then. On the way back, we passed a soldier in the street, and when I shouted out to my father, 'He looks just like you, Dad!' he told me to be quiet. Maybe he didn't want to be saluting other soldiers when he was out of uniform." Listening to the conversation, Oba's wife Ryoko commented, "Maybe he wanted to forget that he was a military man when he was with his son for such a short time."

After paying his respects to his father, the next day, back in late January 1983, Oba and his wife were guided by Kakazu to the cave in Yamagusuku, Itoman, where the headquarters of the 2nd Battalion of the Yamagata 32nd Infantry Regiment had been located. "There were still bones down in there. When I see that kind of thing, I realize the terrible sacrifices that the people of Okinawa made for the defense of the main islands of Japan," he said apologetically.

During the three days that Oba Hiro and his wife Ryoko were in Okinawa, they traveled around visiting as many old battle sites as they could. They were lost for words when they heard from Kakazu about how people had killed themselves jumping onto the rocks in the sea off the cliffs at Cape Kyan. When they went to the Yamagata Memorial they took a candle and lit some incense inside the cave.

"I was fortunate. Kakazu-san tells me that my father's remains were collected and taken to be interred at the ossuary at *Urawa-no-To* in Urasoe, so I was able to pray there for the repose of my father's soul. But, I'm sure that there must be many families who still don't know any details about how their loved ones were killed in the battle."

He added one thing that he had observed during their stay. "While we were moving around in the car it was fine, but as soon as we stopped to visit a cave or somewhere there had been fighting, it would all of a sudden start raining."

May 1945 was a month dominated by early summer rain, and many people remember having to slog their way southward through incessant rain. Maybe Oba Shotaro and the thousands of others who died such sad deaths during that season in 1945 were trying to say something to Oba Hiro and his wife.

Compiling a list of war dead

As Irei Shinjun thumbed through a list giving the names, dates, and places of death of people killed in the Battle of Okinawa, he began to describe the final moments of friends in his unit.

"My friend Horonai Masao, who'd told me that he was Ainu, had been hit in both legs by fragments from a hand grenade and was in a lot of pain. Nakahodo Nobuyoshi was hit in the chest the moment he went to pull the trigger on his machine gun. I can still clearly remember how, when we went to get his body at night, it was completely rigid and still in the same position he'd been in when he died. Just the previous day, as we pulled out of Untamamui, he'd said, 'I wonder if I'll ever be able to go back home and see my family.'"

There were many cases in which they could not recover the bodies of their friends from where they had hurriedly buried them. Shells from the U.S. bombardment poured in, ripping up the landscape beyond recognition. Irei and four others buried Taba Masayuki from Tsuken-jima and, because Irei clearly remembered the location, he was able to go back later and dig up the remains. "We were lucky with Taba just to be able to find where he was buried. The remains of very few people were able to be identified like that." All of the other four people who helped bury Taba were subsequently killed in the course of the battle.

Irei says that they fought so close to the enemy that they could hear the voices and see the faces of the U.S. soldiers. Of the 50 men in Irei's platoon, only two survived the hand grenade combat in Kohatsu, Nishihara. Irei had a cut on his temple from a piece of shrapnel and a burn on the back of his hand from a white phosphorus grenade. In addition to that, when he went out to get some ammunition he was caught in a barrage from a U.S. warship and a piece of shrapnel hit him in the right kneecap. "In the cave in Arakaki in Itoman, we wounded soldiers were told that we were 'in the way' so we were thrown out the cave," said Irei as he gazed at the scar on the back of his hand.

On 15 October 1944, not long after he had started work in a local company, Irei joined the 89th Infantry Regiment at its headquarters at Gushikami Kokumin School, in Gushikawa. He remembers there being 298 new soldiers from the local area, of whom just thirty-two survived to be demobilized after the war.

Every year in autumn, a memorial service is held in Nishihara for those killed during the fierce fighting there. People still come forward on these occasions to ask Irei for information about how various loved ones met their fate, but because there were several different units within the 24th Infantry Division, without further details of what specific unit someone was attached to, more often than not he cannot give a response that provides any form of solace.

Thinking that the small network of survivors might be able to give some information if it were someone who joined up at the same time as him, Irei asked the 89th Infantry Regiment's Veterans Group if they had a list of the names of people who died during the battle. In response, he received such a list from Niwa Toshiaki, who had been attached to the Regimental Headquarters during the battle. However, the addresses on the list used the old, prewar system, making it difficult to contact the bereaved families. Irei asked the *Ryukyu Shimpo* to put the word out for families of soldiers who joined the 89th Infantry Regiment in Gushikawa on 15 October 1944 to contact him. As a result, Higa Masao contacted him, and Irei was able to pass on details of the death of Higa's younger brother, Tsukasaburo.

Despite decades having passed since the war, everyday Irei faces the mental scars he bears.

CHAPTER 12

KYOSEI-RENKO—FORCED MIGRATION OF KOREAN CITIZENS TO HELP JAPAN'S WAR EFFORT

As the protracted fighting in China and the Pacific resulted in a labor shortage for Japan's war effort, in October 1939 the process of *kyosei-renko* [forced migration] began by which tens of thousands of men and women from Korea, which had been annexed by Japan in 1910 and was therefore "Japanese territory," were sent to Japan. Between 1939 and 1945 a total of 670,000 young Korean men were sent to the main islands of Japan as laborers[1] and, while precise numbers are unknown, it is thought that between 600 and 800 women, plus as many as 10,000 or more men were[2] sent to Okinawa.

Some of the men were drafted into the Japanese army[3] and actually fought in battle, although most served as military laborers [*gunpu*] digging shelters and building military facilities.[4] As the fighting reached Okinawa, *gunpu* were allocated the most dangerous tasks of transporting ammunition, guarding army shelters and hunting for food, all the while exposed to enemy fire. Often banned from taking refuge in the shelters themselves, they worked long hours, suffered discrimination (including from local Okinawans), brutal beatings, and some of the highest mortality rates of the battle.[5] Weakened from malnutrition, those caught stealing food would be lynched or shot by IJA soldiers,[6] as were any who were caught trying to escape or surrender.[7] Three of the most notorious incidents involving *gunpu* occurred on the Kerama Islands of Tokashiki and Aka, where substantial deployments of Korean laborers were stationed. A number were shot for supposedly spying and stealing food, while on Aka, fifty more were accused of trying to escape. They were forced to dig a cave and were then herded into it after which thirteen were executed "as an example to the others." On Tokashiki-jima, eight *gunpu* were accused of trying to assist the enemy and were

1. Dower, J. 1986: 47.
2. Hayashi, H. 2010: 76-7.
3. Hayashi, H. 2010: 76.
4. Hayashi, H. 2010: 76-7.
5. Oshiro, M. 2008: 183.
6. Okinawa Heiwa Network. 2008: 38.
7. Hayashi, H. 2001: 317.

summarily beheaded.[8]

The plight of the *ianfu* [comfort women] was no less appalling as they were forced to provide sexual services to IJA troops as a "relief scheme' for battle-weary soldiers."[9] The women lived and worked in what were euphemistically called "comfort stations" [*ianjo*], with the first of Okinawa's *ianjo* being established on Ie-Jima off the west coast of Okinawa in June 1944.[10] About 130 stations were set up in all regions of Okinawa prefecture,[11] and private houses were frequently commandeered for this purpose, often with nothing more than a blanket as the dividing wall between women.[12] Almost all of the *ianfu* were Koreans (a small number were Okinawan women), including young girls and mothers, tricked or kidnapped directly from Korea.[13] Ordered to serve dozens of men a day in unsanitary conditions, most also suffered abuse and violence. After the battle ended, U.S. troops used several existing comfort stations, although these were closed down by the U.S. military authorities within a few weeks. However, the Americans also established new stations and drafted captured Korean comfort women to work there.[14] Often simply recorded as "military goods," many *ianfu* were killed in the fighting, while others subsequently took their own lives. At the end of the war, fewer than 3,000 Korean survivors (men and women) were in American custody,[15] meaning that as many as 8000 may have been killed in the Battle of Okinawa.

Koreans killed in the battle

On a cold, windy day in November 1983, a memorial service was held at Mabuni in Itoman for the Koreans who lost their lives during the Battle of Okinawa. A group of twenty members of bereaved families came from across South Korea for the service. After the recital of sutras and speeches from the people who organized the event, an elderly lady was invited by the master of ceremonies to speak on behalf of the bereaved families. Mrs. Lee came up to the podium, bowed carefully and then in Japanese that she still remembered after all these years, slowly said, "*Arigato gozaimasu*" [Thank you]. Her tears, then her sobbing, made any

8. Oshiro, M. 2008: 181-2.
9. Hayashi, H. 2010: 46.
10. Hayashi, H. 2001: 62.
11. Okinawa Heiwa Network. 2008: 39.
12. Okinawa Heiwa Network. 2008: 38.
13. Hayashi, H. 2010: 76.
14. Hayashi, H. 2001: 363.
15. Oshiro, M. 2008: 181.

further words unintelligible. Overwhelmed by the sight of this old lady weeping uncontrollably in front of them, many of the people in attendance lost their composure and the scene was transformed into an outpouring of emotion.

Mrs. Lee's husband, Kojinfu, was killed in October 1943 when the ship he was on board was sunk off Okinawa as it sailed southward from Japan.

"He liked the sea. He was a quiet, honest man," said Lee. Her husband started working for the Imperial Japanese Navy as a military employee in 1940. On that last voyage, he was a crewmember of a vessel carrying soldiers and supplies south from Japan.

Back in those days, Mrs. Lee always looked forward to the letters that her husband would send to her back in Korea where she lived with their five year-old son and three year-old daughter. Comments from her husband such as, "Eventually we'll be together again and live in Osaka. I know that it's tough for you at the moment, but stay strong and wait for the time when we are reunited," kept her going.

However, one day a message came from Japan stating, "October 1943, died in action at sea near Okinawa." The only details that she could get from her husband's friends were that the ship had been sunk by the enemy during daytime, so she did not know specifically when, where, or how he died. When she spoke to different people, one talked of the ship being torpedoed and another of it being attacked from the air. Not knowing the truth of the matter only served to worsen her pain.

"At that stage, all I could do was worry about what was going to become of me and the children. It was really, really tough. But they grew up safe and sound and I now have no concerns there." In the summer of 1983, a South Korean television channel carried out a campaign designed to reunite families separated during the war. When she saw thousands of people shedding tears of joy and embracing upon meeting lost family members, Lee once again lamented the loss of her husband, but then told us with a smile, "He's waiting for me in heaven." In November 1983 she came to Okinawa for the first time. Forty years of sadness welled up when she stood in front of the memorial near the sea where her husband lost his life. "I was just overwhelmed by the sadness of it all. I'm sorry."

"Korea was separated from Japan when it lost the war and my children and I were cut adrift, but I understand that tens of thousands of people died in the Battle of Okinawa, so I know that there are many, many people who feel the same sadness as me. Wars happen all over the world and bring such sadness. Peace is the most precious thing we have."

One of the group of bereaved family members said, "When a high-ranking officer in the military dies, there is always a record of how it happened. But there are so many cases of people of lower rank being killed in war without anyone knowing the details. There is something inherently wrong with this."

Tears shed on meeting after thirty-nine years

This series of articles facilitated a reunion in December 1983 between people who had not met for decades. It started with a request from a former IJA soldier living in Aichi Prefecture to the effect that, "I'd like you to help me find the Arakaki family. I've been to Okinawa three times and have tried to find them, but without success." It seems that the old soldier had been looked after by this family for just over two months and that when he met the old lady at Naha Airport for the first time in thirty-nine years they both shed tears of joy at being reunited. During the Battle of Okinawa many IJA soldiers were put up by local families. Some soldiers lived with families for a period before leaving to fight on battlefields. Very few of the Japanese soldiers survived and were fortunate enough to be reunited with their local host-family decades later.

This old soldier was Totani Keiichi, who lived in Konan City in Aichi Prefecture. He signed up in February 1942 and was posted to Manchuria. In October 1944, he was moved to Naha, which of course at that stage was still a smoldering ruin after the large-scale air raids of the 10th of that month. His first duties after arriving in Naha were to help clear away piles of burned wreckage and rubble.

Totani said, "To be honest, when I first saw Okinawan people, I was rather surprised. They were much darker than us and they were quite short. They also went about barefoot and we couldn't understand what they were saying. I thought, 'We really have come to an interesting place here!'" It is not hard to imagine a tall twenty-four-year-old soldier thinking that way.

In Okinawa he was in a unit of the 32nd Army and from the time he arrived he boarded with the family of Arakaki Uto in Nesabu, Tomigusuku. Totani said, "The first thing that got me was the toilet because there were pigs down below," "Our duties were digging shelters, nothing else," "I remember that the family had a young baby. I used to carry him on my back and play with him."

That household was that of Arakaki Uto, who was reunited with him at the airport. "I remember there being the grandmother, an aunt and a daughter," he said, but almost all of the people he remembered had passed away, so his reunion was with Higa Kamato, Arakaki Kameko and Oshiro Koto, who was living next to the Arakaki family back then. There more they spoke, the more he remembered of those times.

"They used to call me 'Tani-san' and were very kind to me. They didn't have much in those days but they served me all sorts of nice food. I remember the potatoes as being particularly delicious."

His life as a member of the Arakaki family continued for around two months until he was moved to Tsukazan near Haebaru at the end of December 1944. In early 1945 he was again moved to Awase, then to Kadena at the end of March. When the American forces landed in April he was at Shuri and took part in the fierce fighting there.

"One after another, I lost my friends in the fighting. Me too, I was hit. Have a look . . . In a mortar attack in May," he said as he took off his shirt revealing an obvious scar under his right armpit. "Of the 130 guys in my unit, as far as I know, there are only two of us still alive. Sometimes I struggle to even understand how I survived. In some ways, I'm even a little embarrassed that I did . . ."

After they met at the airport, Totani and his hosts went to the Arakaki residence in Nesabu, Tomigusuku. It was a one-story house in the same location as they had lived during the war. When Totani asked, "Is it the same building?" Arakaki Kameko replied, "No, that was burned down during the battle, so we built this one after the war. When they went for a walk around the house, Totani started to remember all sorts of things—the water tanks on top of the houses to collect rainwater, the unpaved roads, the green grass and the blue sky. These things allowed him to remember the few enjoyable aspects of the battle.

The members of his unit all stayed in private dwellings in Nesabu. Eight soldiers, including Totani, stayed with the Arakaki family.

At that stage, in addition to Kameko and Kamato (Kameko's mother's older sister), in the Arakaki house there was Uto (grandmother), Ushi (mother), Haruko Nagamine (cousin), Kinjo Fumiko (Haruko's younger sister), and Haruko's son, Yasuaki. Except for baby Yasuaki it was an all-woman household. "The soldiers from Yamato [mainland Japan] were surprised at this." "But they were all nice young men," said Kamato.

When Totani finished his duties each day, he came home and played with the family's baby son, or went next door to chat with the neighbors. "He came over to our house a lot. Our father liked having guests and loved to chat with people, so he'd serve some tea and chunks of brown sugar and chat for ages," said Oshiro Koto. No doubt they also talked about what life was like back in Totani's hometown in Aichi Prefecture.

But by this stage, the fighting was getting closer and closer to Okinawa.

Before long Totani and his unit were moved to Tsukazan, and in their place some soldiers from the 24th Infantry Division came to board at the Arakaki's house. It was about that time that they started to use the shelter dug behind the house on a much more regular basis. When the Americans landed, the fierce naval bombardment continued into the night. First of all, Arakaki Uto was killed by a naval shell that landed near the entrance to the shelter. Then their house was burned down and the area of Nesabu was reduced to scorched earth. Next, their shelter was burned out and rendered unusable. Both Haruko and Yasuaki died of malnutrition in the camp at Henoko, and Fumiko died of illness soon after the war.

The war was indiscriminate in the way it dealt out life or death. "I really wanted to meet Yasuaki," said Tonaki. He placed some incense on the family's Buddhist altar and prayed in front of the photograph of Haruko. Kamato held Totani's hand as he again said, "I wanted to meet him."

Before coming to Okinawa, Totani said, "Back then I was young, I thought that it'd be all right to die at any stage. If the enemy appeared, and if the need presented itself, I was prepared to be killed in close combat if I could kill some of the enemy. But these days, now that I have become a parent and have my children and grandchildren around me, I think that we must never make these young people go through the experiences that I did. When I became a parent myself I came to understand the feelings of all those parents who had to send their children off to war."

Meeting thirty-nine years after the 10 October 1944 air raid

"Please help me find a Col. Umezu Shin from the 32nd Army and his orderly, a soldier by the name of Tsujita from Toyama Prefecture." This request was received by the *Ryukyu Shimpo* from Yamada Hideko. When it was passed on to the *Kita Nippon Shimbun* in Toyama Prefecture, a response came in right away to the effect that Tsujita was alive and well, and that he had been to Okinawa several times and had tried to find Yamada. It was also established that Col. Umezu Shin had passed away after an illness in November 1962. Arriving in Okinawa on 9 October 1983, by curious coincidence, Tsujita was to meet Yamada Hideko again almost exactly thirty-nine years after the air raid of 10 October 1944.

Before the battle, Yamada's parents' house at Uenokura, in Naha, had been requisitioned by the military to be used by the officer in charge of the 32nd Army's weapons supplies. Also, because her father and older brother had been conscripted, the only people in the house were Hideko and her mother, Yamada

Shizuka. The first story Tsujita told was about Hideko's mother.

"She was very strict on matters of courtesy and was always telling me off for something. If I didn't eat all of a meal she'd say, 'Always finish a meal you've started!'" said Tsujita, recalling the days when he was a young twenty-three-year-old soldier. "I also used to get Shizuka's mother to write letters for me. She used to write such beautiful characters. Sometimes I'd get her to cook *udon* noodles for me and I remember how delicious they were. I still make the same sort of noodles these days. There was some vintage *awamori* in the storehouse and I was keen to try it, but I couldn't just go and take it. Then one day, Yamada snuck some out of the storehouse for me. It tasted really good." For her part, Yamada Hideko said, "I certainly don't remember that!"

The two pieced together scenes with snippets from their memories, but one set of details they were both clear on was the matter of the air raid on 10 October 1944.

The air raid involved a total of 900 aircraft and mostly targeted airfields and ports, causing widespread destruction throughout Okinawa. Naha was hit particularly hard in the afternoon with repeated attacks involving incendiaries, rockets, and strafing. Uenokura and the port area of Naha burned for two days. More than 600 people were killed and 90 percent of Naha was reduced to ashes.

Yamada says, "I think it was before 7:00 AM. Birds came flying our way from the direction of Oroku—so many that they seemed to fill the sky. Then just when I heard what sounded like fireworks going off, machine-gun bullets and balls of flames came flying at us." When he heard that sound, Tsujita immediately knew that they were under attack from the air. Col. Umezu also realized the danger and shouted out "Oh no!" He must have shouted it out loud and clear because both Yamada and Tsujita remember this moment.

As fortune would have it, from two or three days earlier a ship loaded with a large amount of ammunition was berthed in Naha Port. "That's what the colonel was shouting about. On top of that, our fighter planes had all gone to Taiwan, so he knew what was going to happen," said Tsujita.

Yamada and her mother hid in an air raid shelter in their garden and in the time between each raid they went up to put out what they could of the fires burning in the house. Bomb blasts had blown the doors off and glasses and pots had melted in the heat of the inferno. At the same time, Tsujita had to run through the flames to take important documents such as lists of weapons and ammunition to headquarters, but on the way he delivered some rice and canned food to the Yamadas in their shelter. After that, Hideko and her mother evacuated to

Shuri, but Hideko remembers being astounded by the sight of Naha burning. "People had collapsed by the side of the road and others around us were wailing in distress. I remember seeing people hit and killed right in front of me." It must have been a scene from hell.

Tsujita was wounded during the air raid and changed units as a result, which saw him transferred to Taiwan in December 1944, where he remained until the war ended.

Exactly thirty-nine years after the 10 October 1944 air raid, Tsujita and Yamada visited the memorials in southern Okinawa and strolled through the streets of Uenokura. Tsujita said, "It feels as if a huge weight pressing down on my chest has been lifted off." He left Okinawa saying to Yamada, "I look forward to seeing you in Toyama . . ."

Memorials in Komesu

The *Churei-no-To* Memorial at Komesu. It pays tribute to the 159 people of Komesu who died in families in which not even one person survived, and to the countless civilians and soldiers who passed away in caves near the memorial. Kiyoshi Kubota, who put together the list of families that were wiped out and helped recover remains after the war, took part in the battle as a member of the Home Guard, and lost his parents, his wife and a child in the fighting. He spent time in a shelter occupied by local civilians and IJA soldiers. Kubota was conscripted into the army in November 1944.

"We were all gathered together in the grounds of Kanegusuku Elementary School. I suppose there would have been about 100 of us. I was attached to a unit in Nashiro." It was effectively a human-torpedo unit equipped with pencil-shaped suicide boats about 7 to 8 meters long and 2 meters wide that carried a large amount of explosives on the stern. Controlled by one man, the idea was to ram enemy vessels and detonate the charge.

"The explosives filled a metal drum, so packing them in was one of our jobs. I think that there were ten vessels. During the day we'd bury the boats in holes dug in the sand and hide them with some grass, and at night, several dozen of us members of the Home Guard would carry them down to the water's edge when the order was given to do so."

The vessels were ordered to go out several times, but on each occasion they returned a while later. The reason for this wasn't clear, but Kubota suggests that it may have been because they "missed their chance with the enemy ships." Then one day, the sun came up before they could hide the boats, and they were spotted by an enemy plane, which attacked, destroying every single one of them.

In February 1945 Kubota was attached to a 32nd Army unit at Untamamui where he was allocated odd jobs mostly around helping the cooks.

As the fighting became more intense, members of the Home Guard were ordered to leave each unit and go their own way. Kubota returned to Komesu. He heard that his parents were in a cave near their house.

There was a large space in the cave just beyond the entrance and it had boards in it to provide a flat floor surface for the approximately 100 Japanese soldiers in there. From there, after going through a narrow passageway crouched over, there was another large open area. That is where the civilians were. Water dripped from the stalactites on the top of the cave and the space lit by just the faintest of light was jam-packed with people. "My father and my two children were in there." It was so crowded that it was not possible to even lie down. Kubota's father was curled up as though to protect the two young children.

When he heard that his mother had left the cave to get some water, but had not returned, he went out to look for her. He found his mother on the way to the well. She was sort of sitting down so he called out to her. "She didn't reply, and when I stepped forward to touch her shoulder I saw that the top of her head had been opened up. She was dead." The shells continued to come in so he could only afford a short time to grieve if he were to avoid the same fate. Kubota said, "I thought then that if I were to die then and there with my mother that would be all right." He buried his mother's body in a shallow hole, intending to come to get her when he could, and returned to the cave.

"The atmosphere inside the cave was eerie—hard to describe. Soldiers were brandishing bayonets and yelling. When one of my children started to cry, a soldier came over and said he'd kill the child if it didn't stop crying. You could tell that he really meant it. I was young and hot-blooded so I said something back to the soldier and took the two children and my father and left the cave."

After leaving the cave Kubota and his family headed toward the coastline. On the way, his father was hit in the leg by a piece of shrapnel. He said to Kubota, "I'm done for. You take the children and get out of here."

"In the end, we were taken captive down on the coast. The two children and I survived, but I lost both parents, my wife and our third child, who was with her. The person who buried my wife and child was then killed, so I was never able to find out where their remains were. The same applies to my father. It was dark and I couldn't remember exactly where we left him," said Kubota.

After the war, people who had been evacuated from Komesu started to come back, and relatives of families who were all killed started to collect the remains. "Straight after the war, there was a real shortage of all sorts of supplies, so many people went into the caves to get the planks from in there. That of course meant that the bones inside were mixed up in the process of getting the timber out and it became impossible to tell the difference between the remains of soldiers and civilians. I did my best to create lists outside the cave of people who had died after being there, trying to focus particularly on families that were all killed."

"When I was recording this there were twenty households, but after that that number increased and I think that it ultimately totaled about thirty-five families."

Based on the list that Kubota created, beside where the cave was located there is a memorial bearing the names of the 159 people of families that were wiped out. Of course, the number of people who lost their lives in the cave is far greater than this. Those who went inside to gather the remains said that the cave floor was covered with bones.

Near the *Churei-no-To* is the *Chinkon-no-To* memorial. There are also seventy names engraved on this. They belonged to people in families that were wiped out. Maybe it is because no one visits, but the approach to this memorial was rather overgrown. "The entrance to the cave was just behind here," said Kubota pointing to a spot beyond the memorial. The entrance was narrow with a rather long vertical shaft, only just big enough for one person to get down holding on to a rope. At the bottom it opens up into a larger area and because there is a spring inside, they did not lack water. When I prompted him to comment on what happened here, Kubota said, "I hear that the Americans poured petrol in and lit it. Most of the people down there would have choked to death on the fumes." Pointing at some names on the memorial. Kubota said, "The people in this family were relatives of mine."

After the battle, civilians secure food and timber supplies from the former Command Post

Reduced to piles of rubble, the tragic remains of the great wooden pillars of Shuri Castle bore no resemblance whatsoever to their resplendent former shape as part of the focal point of the Ryukyu dynasty. The entrance to the 32nd Army Command Post shelter was a gaping hole in the midst of this desolate scene. At the end of September 1945, a group sent by the Okinawa Advisory Council, based in the Ishikawa area of central Okinawa, went into the Command Post. Kinjo Hideko, then in Ishikawa, was one of that group. She recalls that a friend on the Advisory Council arranged for her to go to Shuri on a U.S. Army truck.

"It was dark inside the cave so we each carried a candle. There were bales of rice stacked up in there and I remember how the adults each carried as much out as they could. I took about 10 kgs. It was really fresh, dry brown rice. We took it home and ate it."

Until then, Kinjo hadn't even known of the existence of the Command Post. "It was very long and we were inside for quite some time. There were beds and rooms in there for individual people. I looked inside one of those rooms and remember seeing piles of documents, sheet music, and a guitar. When we came out of the cave complex I remember being impressed by the size of the corridor leading out. It was almost like a hotel, large and well lit. Really surprising."

It was not until December, three months after the war officially ended, that residents began to return to Shuri, which in those days was part of the Itoman district. An advance party of about fifty people went to Shuri to start work on the recovery process. Seeking wooden posts and beams and any remaining food supplies, the first places the returning civilians from the camps headed for were the cave shelters used by the military, and needless to say, the Command Post was also a focus of their attention.

Hamamoto Choko recalls those days. "There was no firewood anywhere, so we went into the cave shelters and gathered wood to burn so we could cook rice to eat. Then schools and houses were built and the recovery started for Shuri."

Local residents began to come back, so rows of standardized housing using two by four wooden frames were erected on what had previously been the Memorial Sports Ground of the Normal School. Civilians searched the Command Post and other IJA cave shelters in the area for anything that might be of use as they looked to survive. This was at least in part almost a symbolic act of reclaiming the area under Shuri Castle back from the military, which had transformed it into a fortress.

Letters sent to family

One old, tattered letter . . . A teacher at Yaeyama High School, Senaha Nagahiro, held a piece of coarse writing paper covered on one side with neatly written sentences. "This is very important to me," said Senaha, referring to the letter sent by his father Nagahide to his grandfather Naganobu.

His father Nagahide died in the Battle of Okinawa at the age of thirty-two, but the surviving members of the family were unable to locate any bones or relics to remember him by. This letter is the only thing they have through which to focus their feelings toward their late father. Dated 20 January 1945, it was sent by Nagahide to his family in Yaeyama when he was working as a teacher at the Kokumin School affiliated to the Okinawa Normal School.

The envelope in which it was sent was recycled from its previous use of sending out an invoice for tuition fees, so on the back it bears the name "Nagamine Kazuo 2nd Grade" and has "1943 academic year" written on it.

The letter starts by relating how in the wake of the 10 October 1944 air raids on Naha, transporting mail by ship had become difficult and that he had just managed to find a vessel that was due to sail for the Yaeyama Islands. He added that he had heard that the Yaeyamas had been bombed on 13 and 14 January, but that he was relieved to hear that everyone was safe. He added that there had been air raids on 3, 4, 20 and 21 January, but added that "No bombs have fallen on Shuri, so there is no damage here at all. Please put your minds at ease, as I will not throw my life away."

He went on to write that in such pressing times he expected to be called up soon, but assured them that he would "stay fit and well and committed to working with undiminished fervor until the last American enemy is annihilated." In the context of the people of Japan coming to realize that it looked increasingly obvious that the war would be lost, to spur them on he added a request that his family should "also pray for and strive toward absolute victory for the Empire of Japan."

He touches upon his feelings for his family, but then quickly moves to deny them, writing, "There are times when being separated from my family like this makes me think all sorts of things, but I know that this is merely idle sentiment and that such thoughts must be banished in times like this." However, the closing sentences are definitely those written by a father. "I want to send some pencils, ink, brushes and paper, but since Naha was badly damaged in the air raids it's hard to find such things. Hiroshi-chan will start school soon, so by then I will definitely find some and send them over." Everyday goods were becoming increasingly difficult to acquire and then of course there was the problem of getting them to the Yaeyamas.

Before long, Nagahide was conscripted into the army and killed in battle. Apparently he died in a field hospital near Tsukazan in Haebaru on 28 May 1945. He had his right leg blown off and died from loss of blood. In his last moments, he is said to have told a friend, "I've got no regrets. I ask you to help look after my son's education. When they bury me, put me in the ground with my head facing my homeland in the Yaeyamas."

After the war, his family searched for the spot where he was supposed to have been buried, but the lie of the land had completely changed so they were unable to find anything. The small stones they picked up near where Nagahide is supposed to have been buried are all they have to remind them of him. Those in the Yaeyamas also struggled during the war years. To avoid being caught up in the fighting, local people fled from the settlements into the hills, only to find malaria waiting for them. Many lost their lives as a result.

Naganobu said, "It is only recently that I have come to really appreciate my father and the meaning of love for one's family. War does nothing other than destroy people's lives and rip families apart. This sort of thing must never be allowed to happen again." Senaha Nagahide's children and grandchildren have gained much from this one letter.

Farewell letters recovered

Around May 1947, almost two years after the Battle of Okinawa ended, a large number of farewell letters and locks of hair were excavated from the forest at Bin in Tomigusuku. During the war, as the horrors of battle approached, students of the First Prefectural Middle School in the Blood and Iron Corps attached to the IJA left around 100 such items addressed to their families. The stained and tattered messages were each placed in an envelope with the school's name on it.

> Dear Father
>
> When I was alive I did not make as much of my education as I should have and it is unfortunate that this message will be the only thing that remains of me. As a soldier of the Empire of Japan, I too shall die a glorious death. Please take care of yourself Father and do what you can for the country after I've gone.
>
> Dear Mother
>
> How are you? I will soon die a glorious death. Please help Moronao to also become a good soldier and raise Junko so that she is proud to be a good wife who does not let her country down. I hope that my big sister will also stay well.
>
> Dear Family
>
> My greatest wish as a Japanese man is to die a glorious death protecting our homeland Okinawa from the enemy. I will do my best until the end. Please do not worry about me, but I wish I could see you all, just one more time.
>
> Nagamine Tamotsu

At the time he wrote these letters in 1945, young Nagamine was a fifth grade student. As a member of the Blood and Iron Student Corps he was attached to the Survey Unit of the 5th Artillery Command. He died in the fighting at Shuri, aged seventeen. Sadly, when his farewell letters were retrieved, nobody came forward to claim them. His comments are brave and give us a glimpse of the extent of the reach of Japan's militarism of the time, although his final words, "I wish I could see you all, just one more time," tear at the heart strings and are surely the genuine feelings of a young man assailed by much more than personal emotions. It was a time when the constant presence of IJA officers and other military people ruled out the use of words expressing sensitivity or timidity. Most of the other students wrote what would be termed "admirable" letters in that right to the very end they claimed they had nothing to regret. "Nowadays, people would find it hard to believe what we wrote, but that's just how things were in those days . . . we were educated to be like that." Yasumura Hidetoshi, the central figure in recovering the letters, smiled as he remembered how things had been during the war. Then he recalled how he'd dug them up with his own hands, going over it scene by scene as though to confirm it all in his mind.

Yasumura had been serving in China, but when the war was over he went back to civilian life on his home of Kume-jima. After a time, he shifted to Itoman on the main island of Okinawa. As well as himself, there were several others from Kume-jima also living at Itoman, including two men trying to track down the remains of their brothers who had been killed in the Battle of Okinawa. The two men were Seiko Nakamichi (Hidetoshi Yasumura's step-brother) and Shimabukuro Yoshiharu, who had been in Hidetoshi's class at elementary school on Kume-jima. The dead brothers of both men had apparently attended the First Prefectural Middle School and, after joining the Blood and Iron Student Corps, were killed in action. Only the remains of Yoshiharu's brother Yoshitoshi were returned to his parents, while nobody seemed to know where the remains of Seiko's brother Seijun were.

That was about the time Hidetoshi heard a rumor that the last messages of the First Middle School students had been buried somewhere. During the war, it seems that a clerk at the school, Nakahara Hirokazu, had gathered all the letters up and buried them for safekeeping. Yasumura was surprised at this because, "Nakahara was the same age as my own father. I knew what he looked like," he explained, adding his resolve that "I was determined to meet him and find out where the letters had been buried. For the sake of the surviving family members, I had to get those mementoes back." Around March 1947, when Yasumura was living in Itoman, he called on Nakahara in Ishikawa in central Okinawa to ask about the whereabouts of the farewell letters.

Nakahara had been a clerk at the school during the war and was indeed the person who had gathered up the letters and buried them in a safe place. Also, he was a contemporary of Yasumura's own father Hirohide and, like Hirohide, was from Nishime in Gushikawa on Kume-jima. Therefore, Hidetoshi himself remembered Nakahara from when he was just a small boy. He visited Nakahara shortly after the war finished, a time when he still needed documentation in order to leave his village. He explained his mission to the Itoman police and, after the paperwork was completed, he hurried off to Ishikawa. When he arrived at Nakahara's house, he was shown in through the main entrance to the tatami room at the back of the house. Yasumura recalled that scene.

"Nakahara was sitting facing a brazier. He was coughing hard so was sort of hunched over leaning forward when I appeared. After exchanging greetings, I quickly broached the matter of the farewell letters. Nakahara appeared to have difficulty speaking because during the war a shell blast had damaged his throat right down to his lungs." Yasumura explained that some people from Nakahara's home of Kume-jima were looking for their brother's remains and that he wanted to help. "I heard from an old classmate that you kept the farewell letters from those First Middle School students," he explained to Nakahara, "and that they are buried somewhere for safekeeping. If you don't mind, I'd like to try to find them."

"Is that right? Well in that case, yes, please go and retrieve them for me." Nakahara gladly agreed and thanked Hidetoshi. "I've been worried about those letters for a long time," he explained. "If I were in better health I'd go and get them myself and return them to the families. It's good that you live down in the southern part of Okinawa. So yes, I'd really like you to go and get them for me." Nakahara looked for a slip of paper and a pencil and started to draw a rough map of the area where he had buried the letters. He then explained how the letters came to be there.

In the spring of 1945, having accepted that their fate was to be "killed in battle," the staff and students of the First Prefectural Middle School who had been mobilized into the Blood and Iron Student Corps each wrote farewell letters to their families. The name of the previous principal was stamped on the back of each brown paper envelope while on the front, the students wrote their registered domicile, their current address, their unit name, and their own name. They then placed their letters, some strands of hair and fingernail clippings in the envelopes. In those days, the boys all had shaved heads so rather than actual "strands" of hair, all they could manage was something like a few flecks of short hair. They couldn't tie up a lock of hair the way the girls did, so they wrapped their tiny offerings in paper and simply put them in the same envelopes as their farewell letters. Nakahara the school clerk then gathered up all the envelopes containing the letters and human mementos and looked after them.

As the ferocious fighting unfolded, the Blood and Iron Student Corps withdrew from Shuri and made their way, via Haebaru, as far as Bin in Tomigusuku. During that whole time, Nakahara kept those envelopes with him. In the forest at Bin, the Blood and Iron Student Corps took up a position in a cave that had previously been used by an artillery unit, but before long they got the order to head farther south. According to the information they received, the Americans were crossing the Minami-Meiji Bridge at that very time and Nakahara decided that he could not keep moving as required if he kept all the envelopes and other things with him. So, he put them, the locks of hair, the graduation certificates, and the school's portable safety box into two separate saké containers. He then dug a hole and buried everything beneath a rock he had selected to mark the location. Early in June, he left Bin. As he drew the sketch of the area, he explained to Yasumura, "The hole I dug under the rock was quite deep. So deep that I could get the whole upper part of my body in."

As he drew his map, Nakahara explained more details of where he had buried the letters during the fighting. "Right here is a big pine tree, and over here . . . that's where the rock was. If you dig down beneath the rock, you should find two containers. The envelopes containing the boys' letters, hair and so on, plus their graduation certificates and some other important documents to do with the school are also in those containers. They should be fine as the paper was waxed and the jars were sealed shut." Listening to Nakahara's explanation, Yasumura thought to himself, "Nakahara risked his life to bury all those things so I've got to dig them out really carefully." He also knew that he couldn't do it all on his own. Once he got back to the southern part of the island, the first thing he wanted to do was to confirm the location.

Yasumura explained to Nakahara, "I'll be in touch with you as soon as I've found the spot. Then, could I get your eldest son Hirotoshi to help me with the digging?" Yasumura then left Nakahara's house in Ishikawa and headed away. A few days later, he made his way alone to the forest at Bin but was astonished at what he found. The whole area had been completely burned during the war leaving the trees as just charred remains and the hillside bare. Needless to say, Nakahara's map was of no use. The tall tree he had told him about as a landmark was nowhere to be seen and there were so many rocks that Hidetoshi had no way of knowing which was the one Nakahara had mentioned. Yasumura realized he had no choice but to dig the entire area, every last inch of it. Early one morning at the beginning of May, he asked Shimabukuro and Nakamichi, the two men who had been searching for their brother's remains, for their help and both men made their way back to the area. It was one of those days when the sun's rays were so intense that it felt like mid-summer, but they put on their long sleeved working clothes and set to with sickles, forks, machetes, and hoes.

Yasumura explained what happened that day. "There were three of us. We divided the whole area (near the sacred place or *utaki* in Bin) where the mementoes had been buried into three separate zones and started digging together, but there was no sign of the containers that Nakahara said he had buried. I remember how hot it was and how the sweat poured down our faces as the afternoon dragged on." They had started at eight that morning so by early evening the three had already been digging for more than eight hours. The sun was sinking in the west and they must have dug 40 or 50 meters. "If we dig this much and still don't find it, let's call it a day and come back some other day," suggested Yasumura to the other two as he was getting ready to leave. Then suddenly, one rock in particular caught his eye. He thought to himself, "The soil by that rock looks different from the rest of the area and there's not a single snail there either. This bit must have been dug over previously." Yasumura suddenly felt like leaping for joy."

"What a stroke of luck, just as we were about to head home. I immediately stuck my hoe into that little mound of earth beneath the rock. It was easy to dig as the soil was so different from where we had been working up till then. I was sure there was something buried there and, as I was scraping the soil away, suddenly I came across what was obviously the top of a pot of some kind. Excitedly, I called out to the other two to come over. The first thing we did was light a stick of black incense we had with us and put our hands together in prayer. Then I explained to the souls of the First Middle School students what we were doing and asked them if it was okay for me to bring the letters out." After digging more than one meter down, they recovered two saké containers and a portable security box. Just as Nakahara had said, the containers were securely sealed with waxed paper, but the seal of one container was broken and water had seeped in. When they opened the sealed container, the farewell letters in their envelopes and the graduation certificates were in almost perfect condition. Even now, that highly emotional scene is still indelibly etched in Yasumura's memory. "Among the documents was the graduation certificate of Shimabukuro Yoshitoshi who was killed in the battle.

Yoshiharu clutched his brother's certificate to his chest and, with huge tears roll-ing down his cheeks said, 'I'm going to take this home with me.'"

In the shade of a large, damp rocky outcrop of limestone in the forest at Bin in Tomigusuku, Yasumura Hidetoshi and the others had retrieved the farewell letters left by the First Prefectural Middle School students. Their letters had been placed in envelopes and put inside the two casks. The envelopes had been badly damaged and the ink with which the students had written their addresses during the war was so faint that many were undecipherable. Yasumura continued his story. "Two thirds of them had deteriorated so much that it was impossible to read them. Also, the metal fittings on the safety box had corroded and the bank notes inside were in tatters. All in all, our delight at having worked so hard and found what we were looking for was actually tinged with sadness that not all the boys' farewell letters had survived intact."

Because on the first day they had only intended to confirm the location, after digging up the items, they placed the casks back in the hole and sprinkled some light soil over the area to disguise where they had been digging. After lighting some more incense, they headed for Itoman. But that was also when Shima-bukuro Yoshitoshi began begging to be allowed to take his brother's farewell letter home with him then and there. "He wouldn't listen. He just kept saying that he wanted to show Yoshitoshi's graduation certificate to his mother. He was in tears, so in the end I agreed that he could take it home with him," recalled Yasumura. Several days later, Hidetoshi sent a message via an acquaintance to Nakahara Hirokazu in Ishikawa that "the farewell letters were exactly where Na-kahara buried them." Also, just as he had promised Nakahara during his earlier visit, Yasumura subsequently asked Nakahara's eldest son Hirotoshi to join the recovery project. He also asked his own nephew Hidetoshi Yasumura (also a former student of the First Prefectural Middle School) to join in and the three men headed off to the forest at Bin for a second dig.

They dug out the farewell letters for the second time. Not sure what to do with those that had almost rotted completely away, they finally decided that there was no point in taking back envelopes with writing that was totally illegible. From the cask still sealed with waxed paper, they removed most of the farewell letters (with the tiny ends of hair wrapped inside) and the graduation certificates, leav-ing behind only those that were difficult to read because of the mildew. From the water-damaged cask, they recovered about a third of the letters and certificates, but decided to leave the remaining documents in the container. The small safety box had also deteriorated so badly that they simply discarded it. They put all the recovered mementos and other bits and pieces in a backpack Hirotoshi had with him and set off for Ishikawa, while Hidetoshi took the cask from which they had retrieved all the contents back to Itoman. Nakamichi Seijun's mother who had traveled from Kume-jima to Itoman then took that same cask back to Kume-ji-ma. At the time of the Battle of Okinawa, Seijun was in his fourth year at the First Prefectural Middle School. He was attached to the 32nd Army's heavy field artillery unit and was killed at Makabe in Miwa (now Itoman). Seijun's remains were never returned to the family, and his mother later told Yasumura as she stood there weeping, "From now, this cask will represent my son's spirit." Even today, this still upsets Yasumura. "The real pity was that we didn't bring back *all* the farewell letters, even though some were in tatters," he explained.

So what became of the envelopes containing the farewell letters and tiny clippings of hair which Yasumura Hidetoshi and the others recovered from the forest at Bin? Nakahara Hirotoshi (eldest son of Nakahara Hirokazu, the First Prefectural Middle School clerk who originally saved the boys' letters) gathered them up, put them in his backpack and handed them over to his father. Both Hirotoshi and his father Hirokazu have already passed away, but Hirokazu's younger brother Nakahara Shigeru, who went on to become principal at Cha-tan High School, told us what happened. In 1944 when Shigeru was in the fifth grade at the First Prefectural Middle School, he was evacuated to Yatsushiro in Kumamoto Prefecture. From there, he went to China and Manchuria to work but returned to Okinawa after the war was over. "It would have been 1948 when I came back from China. By then, the letters had already been dug up and were being carefully stored in at our home in Ishikawa. My father died not long after that and, according to what my mother subsequently told me, the farewell notes had been left by boys from the First Prefectural Middle School and my brother Hirokazu had dug them up. At that time, Mr. Nozaki, who was then principal of Ishikawa High School, apparently called at our house and a member of our family just handed him the letters." That Mr. Nozaki was Nozaki Shingen who had been deputy principal at the First Prefectural Middle School before the war.

On 30 November 1949, a newspaper published the following piece entitled *Farewell Letters Recovered*. "Around 100 farewell letters and tiny clippings of hair were recently dug up inside a cave at Bin. The mementos were left behind by First Prefectural Middle School principal Fujino Norio along with members of his staff and students. The letters were dug up by the Nakahara brothers whose father alluded to their whereabouts in his own will, then, via Mr. Nozaki, the ipal of Ishikawa High School, the letters were subsequently handed over to

Hokama Seisho (principal of the Shuri School of Languages and former teacher at the First Prefectural Middle School) and remain in his care." Based on this newspaper coverage and Shigeru's recollections, we approached Nozaki's daughter Yoko in an attempt to retrace the movements of the farewell letters. Yoko explained, "My father is already dead so I asked my mother but she doesn't remember anything at all about the letters." So unfortunately, we have no idea at all as to how Nozaki came to have the letters.

At the same time, Hokama Seisho is not sure that he remembers it correctly either, explaining, "I simply don't remember receiving the letters from Nozaki. All I remember is that Nakahara and some others retrieved them and that they retained them." Memories about what happened tend to fade almost forty years on. Also, the fact that most of those involved with the farewell letters have since died makes it difficult to establish what actually happened. Out of the 100 or so letters, if the bereaved families were known they had the letters returned to them. However, the letters of unknown families, together with a number of letters that the bereaved families agreed to donate, are now in safe keeping in the Yoshu Hall behind Shuri High School in Naha.

I recently visited that Yoshu Hall and one of the teachers from Shuri High School, Kimura Tomosada, took me to the room where all the documents associated with the First Prefectural Middle School are kept. He took several boxes out of a cupboard and showed me the farewell letters they contained. Some tiny clippings of hair fell out of a tattered and decayed envelope. Kimura pointed to one of the boxes in particular, inside which was a piece of tree bark with First Middle School student Yamauchi Shoei's poem of death carved into it. Just before he left for the front, Yamauchi Shoei returned home to see his parents. However, there was nobody at the house so he carved his final words into the bark of a tree in the garden. He was killed in the fighting at Kochinda.

"Does anybody have a photo of my brother who was killed in the fighting?" This is the question one woman suddenly asked as she moved around those attending a gathering at a Naha hotel on the evening in January 1983. The gathering was the Sakura Group, the alumni's general meeting organized by former students who had entered the First Prefectural Middle School in 1944. Standing out among all the elderly men at the meeting, that one woman was Inafuku Kazuko, and she identified herself saying, "I am Nakadomari Ryoken's sister. We don't even have one photo of my brother. My mother says that he had a small scar below his nose. She is now very old and I would love to let her see a photo of her son ..." During the Battle of Okinawa, her brother Ryoken was a third grader at the First Prefectural Middle School but was killed in a bomb blast while preparing food near a cave in Shuri. Inafuku Kazuko continued, "The sad thing for us is that after all these years no memento of my brother has ever been returned to our family. I kept thinking . . . even if we had just one photo . . . and then I heard about the meeting so I decided to come along."

However, Kazuko's hopes came to nothing and her journey to Naha all the way from central Okinawa was in vain. The members of the Sakura Group were the last of the First Prefectural Middle School students and two semesters ahead of Ryoken. Because they had been in a different class, there was nobody at the meeting with any knowledge of a photo of her brother. But Ryoken, who had been a member of the Blood and Iron Student Corps, had indeed written his farewell letter along with the other students and, when Yasumura Hidetoshi and the others dug up the letters in 1947, Ryoken's was among them. In among all those letters that were so badly damaged by moisture, Ryoken's last words were still decipherable.

> Dear Father and Mother,
> The next round of fighting will be the decisive battle, one that will decide whether we win or lose the war. It is we young ones who must answer our nation's call in this time of crisis. [abridged] Father and Mother, remember that the Empire of Japan is sacred, so please treasure and protect it. Goodbye.
> Nakadomari Ryoken
> Year Three Group

CHAPTER 13

AMERICAN EXCESSES

American troops on Okinawa did not pursue a policy of torture, rape, and murder of civilians as Japanese military officials had warned. In fact, the official policy was to take prisoners where possible and to protect civilians.[1] However, while many American soldiers performed acts of humanity far beyond the Geneva Conventions' requirements and, while civilian prisoners were generally well treated,[2] American troops were not infrequently involved in rape, killing those (IJA and civilians) attempting to surrender, and mistreating prisoners.

Civilian rape was "... one of the most widely ignored crimes of the war ... most Okinawans over the age sixty-five either know or have heard of a woman who was raped."[3] Even in POW camps, the rape of civilian women was common, including in broad daylight, as Americans conducted "girl hunts" through the rows of tents.[4] Also, while numerous reports testify to the fairness by Americans inside POW camps, in direct contravention of the Hague Conventions, many were forced to donate blood, construct military facilities, and transport ammunition.[5]

Refusing to accept surrender or killing Japanese soldiers who had already surrendered was "widespread in some areas."[6] American troops frequently "... shot groups of Japanese soldiers who emerged after being promised safe capture,"[7] including enticing them from their caves with chocolates and tobacco.[8]

In a separate, but related, category to the excesses mentioned above was the often tragic contact between U.S. forces and civilians trying to relocate at night, hiding in caves or killed by U.S. military action in situations which in modern times might be euphemistically termed "collateral damage."

For example, Joe Drago of I Company, 3rd Bn, 22nd Marines, Sixth Marine

---

1. Hayashi, H. 2001: 356.
2. Hayashi, H. 2001: 356.
3. Weber, M. 2000: 25.
4. Oshiro, M. 2007: 145-173.
5. Oshiro, M. 2007: 173.
6. Feifer, G. 1992: 485-498.
7. Hayashi, H. 2001: 488 and 494.
8. Hayashi, H. 2001: 344

Division recounted his experience of seeing Okinawan civilians killed as they approached the U.S. perimeter at night, probably around 4 or 5 April as the Sixth Marines advanced north toward Motobu Peninsula. Understandably nervous about IJA nightime infiltration raids, U.S. forces had dropped leaflets telling civilians not to move at night, but such information of course did not reach every group of desperate locals. Drago recalls, "When dawn came [we] left our foxholes, observed the carnage strewed about the road . . . untold numbers . . . women, old men, children. My guesstimate, in the hundreds."[9] Particularly early on in the campaign, similar incidents on a smaller scale, would have occurred at night as the U.S. forces advanced but were yet to make contact with the IJA initial lines of defense.

Another tragic and more common occurrence was the death of civilians in caves in the area of southern Okinawa after the remnants of the Japanese 32nd Army had retreated from Shuri. As is related in this work, U.S. troops often appealed to civilians through interpreters, or in broken Japanese, to come out and surrender. However, the presence in a cave or dugout shelter of just a few IJA soldiers prepared to fight to the death, or the inability to react quickly enough to the appeal to surrender, often proved fatal. One shot fired from inside the cave by a single Japanese soldier not prepared to surrender would invite a reaction that might involve a satchel charge or white phosphorus grenades being thrown in, a blast from a flamethrower, TNT being inserted into a hole drilled above the cave and detonated to collapse the ceiling onto the people in the space inside, or even gasoline being poured in and lit. U.S. troops on the outside had no quick method of clarifying the soldier/civilian ratio in a cave, so more often than not they would simply neutralize it and move on. The tragedy of the attack on the No. 3 Surgery Cave in Ihara on 19 June 1945 is typical in this respect.[10]

The third aspect involved Okinawan civilians falling victim to what might be referred to as the U.S. pursuit of "military objectives." There are two notable examples of this, the first being the bombing and strafing of Naha City on 10 October 1944, the second being the furious bombardment targeting the roads in the southern area of Itoman in mid-June, but particularly after the death of Lt. Gen. Buckner on 18 June.

The air raids of 10 October involved five waves of attacks over a period of nine hours on targets throughout the prefecture, but the fourth and fifth raids focused on the city of Naha. Almost half of the 1,300 killed or wounded were

---

9.   Lacey, L. 2007: 73-75. (Also from email communication with Joe Drago.)
10.   Himeyuri Peace Museum. 2002: 42.

civilians, and 90 percent of the city was burned to the ground.[11] This was the first step toward the U.S. bombing of indiscriminate targets that destroyed much of urban Japan in 1945.[12]

While civilians were caught in the crossfire throughout the Battle of Okinawa, it is important to note that more than 80 percent of the civilian deaths occurred from June onward after the battered remnants of the Japanese army withdrew southward to the area where as many as 100,000 civilians had fled. After the last tenuous defensive line between Yaezu-dake and Yoza-dake collapsed on 9 June, the Americans commenced "mopping up" operations. Some commentators suggest that the slaughter of IJA soldiers and civilians that occurred in the area north of Mabuni was an act of revenge for the death of Lt. Gen. Buckner at Maezato on 18 June.[13]

Ruins of the U.S. Army Field Hospital at Ginoza

Recovering the remains of loved ones or disposing of unexploded ordnance does not heal psychological wounds, as bereaved families bear the scars of the past forever. On the anniversary of the end of WW II on 15 August 1983, many people were still frustrated and hurt that the actual place of death of their relatives was still unknown, or that they have been unable to be reunited with friends and family displaced in the conflict.

Defeat . . . foreign rule . . . the struggle to return to Japanese sovereignty . . . economic turmoil . . . surviving the tumultuous postwar years and the unwelcome effects of the presence of U.S. military bases. Such has been the lot of the Okinawan people since the battle fought for their homeland. But in the background to that, as the passage of time sees people's perception of the Battle of Okinawa fade, as we celebrate "recovery and prosperity," are we not faced with one fundamental question regarding the postwar era, namely, have we really come to terms with the vestiges of the war?

We are unable to put the war behind us as long as there are still people out there who are yet to receive the remains of family members killed or have to live their lives near unexploded ordnance, or have never heard the details of where their loved ones passed away. The large number of people still "unaccounted for" is surely testimony to the fact that some aspects of the postwar period are still unresolved.

---

11. *Okinawasen Shimbun*. 2005: Issue 3; 15.
12. Hayashi, H. 2010: 227-228.
13. Okinawa Heiwa Network. 2008: 14-15.

For the people of Okinawa, the only location within the forty-seven prefectures of Japan to experience fighting on land, a pledge for lasting peace, and a thorough approach to dealing with the legacy of the war should go hand in hand. Digging up what can be recovered becomes an even more urgent task as the remaining survivors of the war grow fewer in number. With this in mind, we hope that we can sift through the last vestiges of war before it is too late, finding the last bones of those killed, the last unexploded shell, and link as many bereaved families up once again with their loved ones. The unfortunate reality of course is that with decades having passed, rather than existing as bones, most often the remains have transformed to dust, crumbling away to nothing when they are touched.

In the period between the closing stages of the Battle of Okinawa and the end of the war itself, many wounded civilians were transported to the U.S. Army Field Hospital at Ginoza. As the fighting raged during the final weeks of the battle, the number of wounded flooding in increased, including those with skin hanging off them after suffering hideous burns, with limbs blown off, and with wounds covered in maggots. Some died before they could receive any form of treatment at all, and many passed away on the way to the Field Hospital. Those who died were buried in the woods near the hospital, and before long corpses were being disposed of as though they were garbage.

The bodies were buried in what is now Ginoza Village, near to what is today the entrance to the Okinawa Expressway. The excavation carried out on this occasion was done because the site was where a community gymnasium was to be built, so the idea was to recover whatever bones may be there before the construction of the gymnasium commenced.

The site was prepared by cutting the grass, felling the pine trees growing there and removing the top layer of soil. This immediately revealed more than 100 graves. When the exhumation of the contents of those graves began, each day between ten and twenty sets of remains were dug up. Each of the graves also contained personal belongings of those who died as well as empty Coca Cola bottles, which the American soldiers often drank. Bereaved family members are said to have used the empty bottles to mark the graves or as vases for offerings of flowers. The bottles were basically the same as those in use decades later, creating a sad contrast between the human remains that had lost all semblance of their mortal form and the immutable shape of the bottles.

By the end of the excavation, 168 graves were opened up to and 161 bodies exhumed. Some graves did not contain any remains, which people suggested was because in years gone by families had already come to claim the remains of loved ones, but at the same time, there were also graves that contained the remains of four or five people.

A member of the excavation team, China Sadanori (Ginoza Education Committee member in charge of Cultural Assets) commented, "Some couldn't really be called graves as such. They were just holes in the ground into which bodies had been thrown, but others did have belongings placed beside the body, so they could be called graves. I suppose they did what they could in the circumstances to be respectful."

China Sadanori's professional background involves the handling of cultural assets, so he ensured that the excavation was carried out with great care. He made sure that each set of bones, crumbling away to dust as they were, was carefully placed into a plastic bag, recorded with their burial number and location details so that bereaved family members could confirm the remains of loved ones.

Every day many such family members visited the exhumation site and some even came on several occasions. It is difficult to imagine how these people felt as they listened to explanations from staff and gazed down into a hole where their family member's body had lain for so many years.

"But they only buried my mother's body by herself," said one family member after seeing four bodies exhumed from a hole. There were also stoic family members who said things like, "But it must be one of these," "Maybe so," "But they only buried the one body . . ." Many could not hold back the emotion as they tried to find the remains of their loved ones.

Among the belongings of the dead were seven grave markers with names written on them, and another seven with numbers carved in them. A piece of cloth dyed yellow and black also emerged, as well as some hair tied in a knot, a comb, and a water bottle. The only thing missing was the family member.

Approximately 500 people including members of bereaved families attended the Joint Memorial Service held at 2:00 PM on 24 July 1983. The sun beat down on the lines of people, many of whom struggled to hold back tears. I still cannot forget the elderly lady whose eyes were bloodshot from hours of sobbing. Her sadness was understandable—she had lost her four-year-old son during the battle.

China Sadanori explained, "The root of the tree had grown around something, creating a curve that matched the outline of a young child's skull." The bones themselves had long since been transformed to dust.

By June 1945, almost all of the wounded in the Ginoza Area U.S. Military

Government Hospital G6-59 were civilians in a serious condition.

The hospital covered an area on both sides of what is now Route 329, and at the location where Ginoza Elementary School currently stands, there were large tents marked from A to E, with a field kitchen beside them. On one side, facing the road, there were the hospital tents in an area nestled among the barracks and other huts. The tents were all full of lines of simple wooden, fold-up beds.

The inside of the tents was like a sauna. There were flies everywhere buzzing around people with horribly burned faces, or whose wounds were covered in maggots. Others relieved themselves on the beds or simply lay there groaning.

"There were flies everywhere," said Omine Naoko, who was seventeen years old at the time. She had helped the nurses in the hospital tents.

"It was awful . . . just so hot, we were all hungry and the smell was just disgusting," she recalls. "There were people who had had the skin burned off their backs and others who would have fits, fall out of their beds, and roll around on the ground in agony. People whom I saw lying there one day were dead the next. I lost all fear of death. I remember even thinking, 'That person's maybe got one more day.' They were really scary times," she said calmly.

The sun beat down on the tents making them unbearably hot inside. Patients incapable of moving were bathed in sweat. Each patient had only the clothes they had arrived in and, despite constantly sweating, they could not get anything washed properly. They tied up the sides of the tents to let the outside air come in, but of course some patients were then exposed to the baking sun.

"I suppose it's the passage of time that allows me to remember that it was hot and smelled so bad. At the time I didn't really notice those things. But I do clearly remember how hungry we were."

Omine recalls how so many of the patients would say, "Please, can you give me something to eat? They all had terrible wounds, but the first thing they would say was, 'I'm hungry.' Maybe feelings of hunger were stronger than those of pain. It was quite strange."

Two meals were served at the hospital—morning and evening. At about 8:00 AM, for breakfast, they were given a rice ball just a little bigger than a ping-pong ball with some brackish tasting soup. At about 5:00 PM, the evening meal was a rice ball and something like boiled soybeans. Needless to say, the combined quantity of food received each day was not enough to qualify as one proper meal.

Urasaki Jun, who went on to become chief of the Demographics Division in the Okinawa Prefectural Office, and was cared for at the Ginoza Field Hospital, wrote the following in his book *Okinawa Kakuseneri*:

> When I woke in the morning the first thing I thought of was eating.
> If I woke in the middle of the night, again, my thoughts were on food . . .
> When I pressed the skin around my wounds pus would squirt out; it was
> unbearably painful. But that pain seemed to disappear for a short time after
> I ate something . . .When human beings are enduring hunger it seems that
> we concentrate every fiber of our being on that struggle.

All of the nurses, patients, and family members I met in the course of this project all spoke of the constant hunger they experienced.

Each of the hospital tents was staffed by one, or sometimes two, American medics of non-commissioned officer rank, under whom there was an Okinawan squad leader, and then several local workers. Most of them were male POWs, whose main tasks were physical work such as putting up tents and carrying the wounded patients from one point to another, while female workers assisted with the nursing duties or helped with the cooking. There were five or six doctors, specializing in internal medicine, dentistry and ophthalmology, but not one surgeon or qualified nurse.

There were between 300 and 500 people "hospitalized" at any one time. Day after day, truckloads of wounded people were brought in on two-and-a-half-ton trucks, but the numbers coming in seemed to be matched by those succumbing to their wounds. Bodies were taken to the "corpse area" beside the hospital tents and left there for two or three days, during which an attempt was made to notify the bereaved family. After that, the bodies were disposed of, sometimes more than thirty a day.

The task of digging the communal graves was carried out by groups of ten or so Okinawan POWs. They worked steadily with picks and shovels from 8:30 AM to 4:30 PM. Miyagi Kametaro, then seventeen years of age, recalls: "Every morning, we would leave where we were being held overnight and go to the "corpse area" to check on the number of bodies, before going to start digging the holes. The bodies were left outside for several days so their torsos and legs really swelled up. When we buried them we wrapped each body in a green blanket and tossed them into the hole, often more than one in each hole. I remember that there were many old women in their sixties and seventies."

He recalled how they would work in pairs to dig the holes and that on the worst days they would bury as many as thirty-two bodies. A normal day would involve five to seven burials. It was a job that everyone disliked, so as a reward for digging graves they were given an especially large rice ball. "That was the only reason we did it really," said Miyagi.

Many people died, but there were also those who were murdered, particularly among the most badly wounded. Some survivors have testified that they saw patients who had no chance of survival left out exposed to the burning sun.

Squad leader in Tent A at Ginoza Field Hospital, Shibamoto Tokeshi, an Okinawan who was the only local person treated as though he were a doctor, submitted notes entitled, *What I Saw in a US Field Hospital* to the *Naha City History*. In these, he wrote: "If patients were groaning, even just a little . . . an army surgeon would come over and start by injecting that patient with morphine. When that took effect and the patient became groggy, the surgeon injected them with about twenty cc of a white liquid. When about half of that had gone into the patient's vein from the syringe, every sinew in their body seemed to go stiff, making a noise as though they were grinding their teeth. Then the patient would go limp."

Tokeiji's notes include several other shocking references. He wrote: "All of the patients who died in this field hospital, be they male or female, young or old, had their livers cut out." "The MPs working at the hospital were known to rape women patients in broad daylight." And, "They shot two IJA soldiers without a word of warning."

What on earth would they have done with the livers cut from the bodies of patients? No one I spoke to in the course of this project could remember instances of rape or murder in the field hospital but, at the same time, no one said that it was totally out of the question.

It is said that between 300 and 500 wounded came to the U.S. Army Field Hospital at Ginoza. The remains of 161 people were exhumed in the course of the project that I covered and people say that another 100 or 200 bodies were buried in the area that is now a small pine forest. Many bodies were also exhumed in the late sixties, and following the war some families will have collected the remains of family members, so it is difficult to put a figure on how many people died at the field hospital.

Of course, not all the patients died. But while many people recovered from their physical wounds, the psychological scars from their horrific experiences during the war will never disappear.

Back in 1945, people held at the camp at Goya used to say that those who were sent to Ginoza Field Hospital would never come out alive, testimony to the fact that people with the severest of wounds were sent to Ginoza.

One fifteen-year-old girl caught up in the fighting at Itoman suffered serious burns to the left side of her body from a flamethrower. She was taken to Ginoza after having been to camps at Nakagusuku and Goya and recalled that years after the war when she happened to meet people who had been at Goya with her, they all said, "So, you survived?"

Luckily for this young lady, she recovered from her burns in two or three months and was moved to the Okubo Camp, which was relatively close. "There were many people whose wounds were covered in maggots. We didn't really concern ourselves about that too much, but I suppose that was because almost everyone was like that. Rather than that, I remember feeling sorry for the people who had inhaled gas in the caves. They really struggled to breathe." But even more than this, she clearly remembers her reunion with her mother in the hospital.

When she was at the camp at Kochiya (now Matsuda), she heard that her mother, from whom she had become separated during the fighting, was in Tent B at Ginoza Field Hospital. From then on, she went to check each of the beds in Tent B every day.

This tent had four wings, all attached in the middle where the medical orderlies station was located. From there, four lines of beds stretched out in four directions. She went around to all of the beds many times, checking the faces of each person, but could not find her mother. After a week of searching, just when she was about to give up and return, one of the patients called out to her. It was a woman whom she knew. As it happens, when she sat down on the bed facing the woman she immediately saw her mother.

She was shocked to find her mother by sheer chance after having looked so hard for her the previous few days. But rather than looking back at her daughter, the mother was sitting there staring blankly off into the distance. When the woman said, "Tomorrow she's going to be put in the bath," the girl picked up her mother and carried her on her back to the camp at Kochiya. Patients in a critical condition were put into the bath to purify themselves before they died (i.e., were euthanized). In that sense, at Ginoza Field Hospital "being put into the bath" meant imminent death.

In 1983, her mother was ninety-one years old and still fit and well. The fortuitous reunion with her daughter had been the difference between life and death. The daughter comments, "Back in those days we did our best for the emperor and for the nation, but I wonder what on earth the emperor actually meant. A war that claims people's lives as easily as it did . . . it was all just a murderous game . . . Even now I get really angry when I hear the word 'emperor' used. I don't mean that the emperor as a person is bad, but that I hate what was done in the name of the 'emperor.'"

Nagatohara communal grave

"There was smoke rising into the sky from cooking fires around the triangular huts in the busy village of Kochiya." This is what the teacher read to his pupils in an open-air classroom in Kochiya (now Matsuda Ward of Ginoza) straight after the war ended, but there was a hellish side to what appeared at first to be a pleasant setting.

There is an old reddish-colored notebook at the Ginoza Municipal Office. The characters written in it are difficult to read, but it is a record of the names of the people who died at the evacuee camp at Kochiya during the seven months from June 1945.

During that period, many people who had fled northward from the fighting in the southern and central regions of Okinawa were being held in camps set up in the various settlements of Ginoza. For that purpose, the American occupying forces set up six separate local bodies within the municipality of Ginoza—Kanna, Fukuyama, Sokei, Ginoza, Kochiya and Takamatsu, and held those evacuees there.

At that stage there were more than 100,000 people in these six locations. The current population of Ginoza is just over 5,000 so the huge influx of people was far beyond what they had ever seen there previously. There were more than 34,000 people in Kochiya and the adjacent area of Takamatsu, with a great deal of movement between the two. "There were so many people that it was hard to imagine that it was actually Kochiya. But among every ten people I would meet, I would only know one," recalled a local resident. The food supply could not keep pace with the increase in population, resulting in many deaths from starvation and malaria.

The man who created the notebook that served as a register of deaths was a farmer by the name of Higa Heisuke. In those days, there was no functioning local authority, and the camp at Kochiya was located on the land he owned. He and his cousin Oshiro Gensuke recorded the name, age, address of each person who died, then made a grave-marker and carried out the burial. The number of names written in the notebook climbed to 600 for Graveyard No. 1 and 800 for Graveyard No. 2, a total of 1,400 people. Once things settled down in the first one or two years after the war, when people came to Kochiya to claim the remains of loved ones, Higa would use the notebook to help them find the location of the grave and stand by to witness the handing over of the remains. This was without doubt the most any individual could do in these circumstances.

After that the notebook did the rounds at the local Community Health Center and municipal office, becoming tattered and worn with even one section being lost. The notebook as it exists now includes the names of approximately 400 people. When we look at the new list, copied by municipal office staff while the writing in the original notebook was still legible, we see that the first entry on the list is for "Toma Tadayuki, two years old, from Tomigusuku, died 30 June 1945." From there on, the names are those of children three years old, two years old, and five years old.

Higa Heisuke's daughter Yoneko says "I was fourteen years old at the time and went with my father to the burials. I still clearly remember the first baby that we buried. It was really sad." But that was merely the start in that a total of 1400 people died and were buried there.

Burial at Nakaoji in Nago

Nakaoji in Nago overlooks the Haneji Inland Sea. During the Battle for Okinawa, there was a place similar to a retirement home in Nakaoji where the especially weak and elderly refugees were interned. It is said that elderly people died there almost on a daily basis. They were buried on the other side of the Nakaoji Bridge, about one kilometer along the coast toward Nakaoji. The graves were in a partially cleared field between two stands of trees. It was the middle of the summer of 1945; the rainy season was over, and every day the searing heat of the sun bore down. The people sent out to dig the pits were barely conscious at times because of the heat and the hunger they had to endure. One of them was a sixteen-year-old girl, and for her, working there all day from eight in the morning until sunset was extremely tough.

It was just before midday and the body of an elderly woman who had died from malnutrition had been brought to a deep pit. As usual, the body was carried on a stretcher by two men and placed near the edge of the hole. Just as they were lowering the body into the grave, the girl instinctively looked away in shock. The elderly woman whom she had assumed was dead, suddenly looked up and stared straight at the girl. Although she was accustomed to dealing with corpses, every muscle in the girl's back froze. Seeing the girl paralyzed with fear, the men pulled some clothing up over the elderly woman's face. Then they placed the body straight into the grave and shoveled dirt on top.

Decades had passed but Kuba Hideko has never been able to get what happened that day out of her mind. "It was just so tragic. I wonder where that old lady was from. They just thought that because her family hadn't come for her, she had no relatives left. She was about seventy. No . . . she just looked seventy because she was so haggard. I think she was really only in her fifties. The Americans had apparently given orders to quickly bury anyone who had no chance of survival." Although Kuba had already said she didn't want to talk about such a ghastly incident, she then added, albeit very deliberately, "But, it was tragic; being buried while she was still alive . . . and her remains still not retrieved because they didn't leave anything to mark the spot. Although I could feel the old lady staring at me, she was so frail that she just couldn't open her mouth. But she was still alive . . . her eyes were imploring me. That old woman was buried before she was actually dead. I still remember it . . . but there were three of us there . . ." It was a time when people had lost their appreciation of the sanctity of life.

There were always dead bodies lying near where Kuba was digging. One day she found a body lying face down by a river, still in the same position as when he had tried to drink the water. The man had been bringing logs down out of the hills for the construction of huts. On another occasion, Kuba noticed a potato plant whose vines had grown far longer than normal. As she reached out and touched the leaves, she noticed a decomposed body lying next to the plant. The corners of her eyes moistened as she murmured, "The body must have provided nutrition for vines for them to grow that long."

So what became of the bodies that had been buried there? We asked Miyazato Fukuei, who was chief of the Nakaoji Ward after the fighting ended. His answer pleased Kuba: "I know that several years after the war was over, the area was put under cultivation. If I remember rightly, all the bodies were recovered at that stage. The local youth association played a leading role in the project and the remains would have been enshrined as 'unclaimed dead' in the monument for war victims near Haneji." But in reality, the remains exhumed during the postwar confusion were merely given a group burial there and then. Certainly nobody ever came to claim them, and any clues indicating their whereabouts have probably been lost forever. "I see. So the area is now used for growing sugar-cane," Kuba mused. "In that case I'll certainly go to pay my respects at the monument."

Okinawa Shimpo newspaper

During the Battle of Okinawa, the *Okinawa Shimpo* newspaper was one of the few sources of information available to local residents. Established in December 1940 and published until the end of May 1945, which was after the Battle of Okinawa had commenced, it was printed in a cave for the last two months and in total operated for just five and a half years. It was caught up in the war just as its readers were and finally disappeared from the scene along with the tens of thousands of Okinawans who died in the course of the battle.

The newspaper began to be printed in a shelter at the end of March. They got the Normal School to let them use the left side of the Ryukon Shelter, which had been dug out by the Normal School Blood and Iron Student Corps.

A giant akagi tree and rocks that seemed to protect the entrance made reporter Makiminato Tokuzo think "The shelter looked as though it would be able to withstand whatever shells the U.S. Navy could throw its way."

The type cases and printing presses were lined up inside the narrow confines of the shelter, which also served as home to the newspaper's staff and their family members, thirty people in total. The printing machines were not of the rotary type capable of producing large quantities of newspapers, but old-style foot pedal plate presses. The staff would do the typesetting for the printing press by the dim light of an electric bulb or a candle.

Occasionally the rush of air from a blast near the entrance would blow out the candles and knock the typeset characters onto the ground.

The reporters risked their lives running from one shelter or cave to the next through a hail of shells. One of the newspaper staff, Oyama Kazuo, was in charge of covering news out of the Naha Police shelter in Hantagawa as well as the Prefectural Office cave in Shikina. The police were an important source of information in terms of following the developments among the civilian population.

"I'd scamper down the cobblestones of Kinjo south of Shuri, running as fast as I could as the shells came in thick and fast. I knew that as soon as I left that shelter I could be killed any moment," said Oyama.

Makiminato was in charge of news from the 32nd Army Command Post and was also a member of the military media section. He would always head from the Ryukon Shelter to Headquarters at about 6:00 AM when the American gunnery crews took a break for breakfast. He recalled, "The rock walls had all been knocked over in the bombardment and it was difficult to move quickly because the rocks had spilled all over the road. It was a real struggle to get to the Command Post Shelter, but I eventually got there."

Shells from the U.S. Navy relentlessly pummeled the area around the Ryukon Shelter. One night the giant akagi tree hiding the entrance to the shelter was completely obliterated and the entrance itself also collapsed when hit in a bombing raid. Makiminato remembers, "When a shell from the bombardment struck the rock near the entrance a strange smell drifted around the area." In later years, Makiminato wrote a poem in which he referred to this as the "rock of death."

The *Okinawa Shimpo* was the product of a merger on 20 December 1940, ordered by the Prefectural Police, of the three newspapers the *Okinawa Nippo*, the *Okinawa Asahi Shimbun* and the *Ryukyu Shimpo*. The aim of merging the newspapers like this was to regulate the power of speech, and this move was the second of its type after one carried out in Miyazaki Prefecture. When the Pacific War broke out about one year after that, newspapers were entrusted with the task of boosting support for the war on the home front.

War hero Lt. Omasu Matsuichi from Yonaguni Island southwest of Okinawa, who was revered for his acts of heroism before losing his life in the Battle of Guadalcanal, provided the ideal material for whipping up fervor for the war effort. The *Okinawa Shimpo*, and the Okinawa editions of the national newspapers the *Asahi* or the *Mainichi* newspapers vied for top honors in covering the Omasu story.

With regard to newspapers assuming the role of boosting support for the war, Masatsugu Uema, who worked for the Okinawa office of the *Asahi Shimbun* at that time, said, "We did not have any doubts whatsoever about writing articles that encouraged the public to support the war," and reflects that "When people get caught up in a war, they lose the ability to see things for what they really are."

The *Okinawa Shimpo* was the same. "There were reporters who were totally devoted to carrying out their duties even once the war had started. We did our best to unite the people of Okinawa in their support for the war. I still feel guilty about the role we played," said Oyama Kazuo with more than a tinge of regret in his voice.

Makiminato Tokuzo insists that newspapers should not have headed down that track. "They may have been able to just stop publishing. But I suppose that we were caught like a rabbit in the headlights and were unable to do that."

The rotary presses in Jikkanji in Naha were destroyed in the air raid of 10 October 1944, but the staff were able to continue printing with presses that had been stored in Matsuo, also in Naha. Uema remembers the strange sunset viewed through the smoke rising from the ruins of Naha the day of the air raid - "It was as though the world was about to come to an end."

In mid-February 1945, Uema was told by Intelligence Staff Officer Maj. Yakumaru Kanenori of the Command Post staff that American forces had landed on Iwo-jima and that their intention was to attack Okinawa, not Taiwan. "I think he was telling me this to get me, and maybe him too, ready for what was to come. But the way he said it certainly did not suggest a sense of despair that Okinawa would be obliterated in the process."

At that stage, construction of the Command Post shelter under Shuri Castle was progressing at a furious pace.

The *Okinawa Shimpo* newspapers printed in the shelter were delivered by the police, soldiers, the Okinawa branch of the Imperial Rule Assistance Association [Taisei Yokusankai], and the Chihaya Unit of the Normal School Blood and Iron Student Corps.

The only existing edition of the paper from those printed after the American landing is that published on 19 April. Its headline reads, "More than 18,000 killed." Oyama Kazuo has this copy of the newspaper.

"All we wrote were stories about how well the war was supposed to be going. If we went to the Prefectural Office shelter or the police, all we could get was glorious stories about the war, and comments from the governor or chief of police were just designed to keep the civilians' spirits up." The newspaper was full of nothing but impassioned rhetoric and propaganda.

Makiminato Tokuzo said of the newspaper back then, "It was no longer really functioning as a newspaper in the true sense. To survive during the war years it had no choice but to transform itself like that."

The clear deterioration in the situation at the front had an impact on the behavior of those in the shelter. Among the soldiers whose morale was clearly deteriorating, there were some who manifested this in the form of hostility toward the local civilians. Lt. Masunaga Tadasu of the Intelligence Section was an example of this.

Uema says, "He was fine at the start but after a while he started saying things like 'The civilians in Okinawa are spying on us. We can't rule out that the police and newspaper reporters are as well.'"

On 23 May, Oyama happened to be in the Command Post Shelter at Shuri, which was a scene of frenzied activity. A soldier who recognized Oyama told him that they were going to withdraw southward. Just a few steps away, Lt. Masunaga and another journalist were arguing in the information section of the shelter. "Why don't you tell us what's happening?" . . . "Because it's classified military information" . . . "So after getting us do what you want, you're leaving us behind?"

On 25 May it was decided to discontinue the *Okinawa Shimpo*. Staff buried the compositor's table and left the shelter by moonlight. With this, the *Okinawa Shimpo*, which came into being under police orders during the war years, ceased operation during the confusion of the 32nd Army's retreat. About two months later, this time under instructions from the American military, the *Uruma Shimpo* (today the *Ryukyu Shimpo*) was set up. It was published using the compositor's table that had been buried in the *Okinawa Shimpo* shelter. After the war, the Monument to Journalists Who Lost their Lives in the War was erected at Naminoue in Naha. Inscribed on the monument are the names of twelve staff from the *Okinawa Shimpo*, together with the names of Munesada Toshihide from the *Asahi Shimbun* and Shimose Yutaka from the *Mainichi Shimbun*.

Survivors from the 89th Infantry Regiment come to collect bones

As happens every year with the approach of spring, a group has again arrived from Hokkaido to retrieve human remains from Yoza in Gushikami. Minami Yoshio and several others down from Ashoro in Hokkaido are survivors of the 89th Infantry Regiment. They began to recover human remains in 1954 and, although their visit coincides with the busy time of the sugarcane harvest, every year the team—including a number of women—makes the journey south. Asato Toyo and Haru, both married women, are also part of the group. In the year prior to the Battle of Okinawa, Minami was among those transferred south to Yoza from Nakagami. The two ladies' association with the 24th Infantry Division was re-established through the human remains recovery project.

"There are still many human remains in the woods near here. If you really set your mind to it, you'd soon find a hundred, or even two hundred, sets of bones," said the ladies. During the battle, civilians and soldiers were all mixed in together here trying to escape from the shelling. They both saw countless numbers of people die before their very eyes. The human remains picked up here over time have left them both with many vivid memories of how things were back then.

"When I say that we've recovered the human remains, it's only in areas where they were easy to find. At the end of the war, the stench from the dead bodies was terrible, so they were covered under piles of rocks. There were so many, there was barely room to walk in between them. As far as collecting the rest is concerned, it needs more than just the locals. We have to get help from the prefectural or even the national level . . . "

Some skeletons were completely bound up by the roots of trees, and there were skulls with sago palm trees growing out through the nasal cavity. After being left there for several decades, those things just made the remains look all the more pitiful. Since 1954, 189 skeletons have been recovered, but it is a task that seems endless, however many years they search.

For Asato Toyo and Haru, the war in Okinawa began when the 24th Infantry Division arrived. The war began gradually for them both, but by the end they had been reduced to pitiful, wretched human beings. Here is their story about the battle.

The 24th Infantry Division was transferred to Yoza following the Naha air raid on 10 October 1944. Several rows of barracks stood near Maeyama in a field to the east of the village, made out of pine trees from the nearby hills. The Division's move to Yoza changed the lives of the locals. They now needed permission to move around their own farms because it meant passing through the area where the soldiers were based. They were also ordered to provide vegetables to the camp. The two women explained, "In the beginning, we didn't grow much in the way of vegetables at Yoza, so all we could do was take them *kandaba* [potato leaves]. But they just yelled at us saying that it was only fit for goats. The officers had the luxury of fish and sticky rice, while the unfortunate enlisted men only got rice with potato mixed in."

Every day men and women were put into groups and sent out to dig entrenchments, and locals also helped make tank barriers. "We piled up rocks about 2 meters high. It was tough work but when the American tanks finally appeared, they were no use at all," explained Haru with a wry smile.

Once the air raids became more intense, they had to remain inside the shelter every day. There were two or three families in each shelter or tomb, and anyone who tried to get back to their own home was stopped by the soldiers. The reason they were not allowed to return home was that their houses had been burned after the Americans landed in April. From Maeyama, Toyo watched as the homes burned. "It took only one or two hours," she explained. "Just as I was thinking that just the eastern side of the village was ablaze, the flames actually engulfed the entire village." She then added, "For all that, I kept thinking that war wasn't as tough as I thought it would be. We didn't have to move away anywhere. We just rounded up stray horses and cows and we had enough to eat." However, somebody who had returned from Hawaii took her to task saying, "Sure, some people can survive a war, but remember that a lot are going to get killed." It did not take her long to learn the truth of those words.

After they moved to a shelter in a place known as Uwaburi to the south of Yoza, Toyo and Haru came across some students from the Normal School setting off on an infiltration raid. The two women were on their way back from collecting water at the Giza River when they met the students who called out to them and asked for some of the water. They were carrying ammunition. "Their faces were gaunt, and they said they were from Sachihija [Toizaki River] at Ameku in Naha. They'd been sent out on a raid but had walked straight into the enemy at Maekawa. I was going to tell them to dump their ammunition and flee with us but I couldn't bring myself to say it. I knew they wouldn't survive."

A total of ten people were living in the shelter, including Toyo and her three children, Haru and her child and four elderly people. The civilians also "shared" the shelter at Uwaburi with a signals unit. "The soldiers said to us, 'We'll be using just part of the shelter, so we won't cause you any problems.' We'd heard a lot of stories about civilians being kicked out of shelters by soldiers, but the way they treated us was just the opposite. They were very thoughtful," explained Haru.

Something the women have never forgotten is hearing members of the signals unit scream out "Enemy fire! Enemy fire!" Then, a merciless volley of American shells cut the wires. Toyo explained, "Every time that happened some of the soldiers would go outside the shelter and reconnect the telephone lines. I don't know how far they went, but what a terrible job that must have been." They had to abandon that shelter in the middle of June. When they looked toward Uejo, the place was surrounded by flames from flamethrowers. They knew the enemy would soon be upon their shelter. They fled to the coastline below their position at a spring in the south of the island. Staying behind some large rocks enabled them to hide from the American ships on the sea directly in front of them. Also, water poured down in front of them like a waterfall.

Haru explained, "Then a boat pulled right in close and a voice called out 'Come on out!' But I thought that if I did that, I'd be killed. I got a real surprise the first time I saw an American soldier. They were wearing singlets as they were pounding us with their guns on the boats offshore." Both women clearly recall 20 June when a Japanese soldier scrambled down the cliff. His face showing no sign of compassion for Toyo, Haru, and their families, he called out viciously, "Hey, if you lot are going to die anyway, arrange it so those kids up there die with you!" The following evening when they went back up the cliff, they found three children huddled beneath a rocky outcrop, sobbing. It was a difficult place to get to, so nobody had taken them under their care. Everybody was struggling just to look after themselves.

Haru and Toyo asked the young girl wearing a school uniform who said they were from Shuri. She was about ten years old and a third grader. Their mother had gone to fetch their belongings but had not returned. Her brother aged seven kept calling out to his mother, and her four year old sister kept sobbing, "I want to go to sleep." Haru and Toyo went searching nearby and found a dead women lying face up. "She was quite well dressed, so we could tell that she was from the city." The two of them then went into a nearby field and gathered up as much sugar cane as they could carry, which they gave to the three children. "Here, this will keep you going for ten days, so stay here," they told the children. The women were still looking after their own families so that was the best they could do. "I felt no feelings of sadness for their mother who was already dead," explained Haru. "But I felt really sorry for the three children she'd left behind."

The two women saw all manner of dead bodies lying around the Giza River area. Some were burned and lying beneath sago palms and rocky outcrops, but both women said they still talk more about the pitiful sight of those three children. Then, two or three days later on 23 June, just when they had used up all their food, they were captured. On their way to the internment camp, there was no sign of the children under the rocky outcrop. Toyo said with a sad look on her face, "Even now, I still worry about whether or not they survived."

CHAPTER 14

PSYCHOLOGICAL IMPACT

Narratives on the civilian experience of the Battle of Okinawa invariably include mention of people who were no longer mentally capable of functioning normally. More often than not, this is referred to as "brain fever" and may have been either encephalitis or, more likely, a form of acute stress disorder. Civilians becoming desensitized to death everywhere around them were also common, and several of the chapters in this book refer to people who had effectively entered a state of emotional paralysis.

The Battle of Okinawa featured the highest rate of combat fatigue (acute stress disorder) among American troops out of all the campaigns in the Pacific War. U.S. forces suffered over 26,000 non-combat casualties, twice the number of men killed in action.[1] If we consider that the U.S. forces were affected to this extent, despite having the psychological advantage of knowing that they would win both the battle and the war and had enough firepower to leave areas of southern Okinawa looking like a lunar landscape, we start to get an idea of the terrible psychological pressure on the local civilians.

Decades after the Battle of Okinawa was fought, many civilian survivors have also suffered from the effects of late-onset post-traumatic stress disorder [PTSD]. The experiences described in this book are examples of the horrors of war that many people tried to, and in many cases succeeded in, bottling up for years until the *Ryukyu Shimpo* project encouraged them to speak up.

It goes without saying that in the early postwar years, before modern aspects of mental healthcare were developed, no particular connection was made in Okinawa between wartime experiences and cases of psychological disorders, alcoholism, domestic violence, and suicides. There was no formal system of counseling to help traumatized or psychologically scarred Okinawans; they simply tried to get on with their lives as best they could in the knowledge that everyone had been affected in some way.

Between one quarter and one third of the prefecture's 1945 population were killed in the battle, so we can safely state that the vast majority of Okinawans lost

---

1. Appleman, R. 1948: 490.

family members and experienced unimaginable horrors in early to mid-1945.[2] Many had their homes destroyed and were forced to wander southward ahead of the U.S. advance, sleeping in over-crowded caves [*gama*] for weeks on end. By mid-June, when corpses littered the ground in the southern region of the main island, apart from the regular horrors of war inflicted directly by the enemy, locals had witnessed Japanese soldiers ejecting helpless civilians into the U.S, bombardment, urging civilians to take their own lives rather than be captured, stealing food from locals, raping local women, summarily executing civilians as "spies," and shooting comrades who attempted to surrender. Needless to say, in addition to the trauma of being caught up in the battle, seeing such acts committed by people who were ostensibly there to protect Okinawa was a psychological shock of the highest order for the locals. In the last few weeks of the battle, the moral fabric that holds a normal society together in peacetime had come apart at the seams. That the prevalence of schizophrenia in Okinawa in 1966 was 3.4 times that of the main islands of Japan is surely no coincidence.[3]

Symptoms such as nightmares, sleeplessness, panic attacks, imagining the smell of death in the air, physical pain, and diminished physical function can often be traced back to experiences during the battle.[4] Often in cases of late-onset PTSD, the "distractions" of a busy working career have kept such symptoms at bay until after retirement. The legacy of the battle lives on with the many cases in Okinawa of elderly people in their seventies reporting the advent of symptoms of PTSD.

---

2.   McCormack, G., & Norimatsu, S. 2012: 17.
3.   Nakagawa, S. 1966.
4.   Arizuka, R. 2011

Timeline for the Battle of Okinawa

24 January 1942	Imperial Rule Assistance Young Men's Corps established in Okinawa
September 1942	Construction of naval airfield at Hirae on Ishigaki-jima commences, with civilians drafted to carry out the work
25 June 1943	Japanese government ratifies Guidelines for the Mobilization of Students during Wartime
21 July 1943	National Service Draft Ordinance amended to increase draftee numbers and hours of work
30 July 1943	Promulgation of national mobilization for female students
	Izumi Shuki appointed governor of Okinawa
30 September 1943	Imperial Headquarters ratifies total war of attrition for Okinawa and strengthens forces defending the Ryukyu Islands and Taiwan.
2 October 1943	Cancellation of deferment of military training option for students
1 December 1943	First intake of student military draftees departs for the front
24 December 1943	Conscription age lowered by one year
4 February 1944	Announcement of strategies to increase military education at universities and secondary and technical schools
25 February 1944	Government ratifies Outline of Decisive War Emergency Measures
22 March 1944	32nd Army formed on Ryukyu Islands as defense garrison for Okinawa, under the direct control of Imperial HQ
29 March 1944	Government ratifies Outline of middle school emergency measures
3 May 1944	44th Independent Mixed Brigade and 45th Independent Mixed Brigade join the 32nd Army. Construction begins on airfields on southern, eastern and central Okinawa, plus on Ie-jima and western Miyako-jima. All males and females, elementary school pupils through to the elderly, without exception, were conscripted for this work
29 June 1944	Toyama Maru heading for Okinawa with 44th Independent Mixed Brigade and 45th Brigade on board sunk by U.S. submarine with the loss of over 5,000 officers and men
1 July 1944	Lt. Gen. Isamu Cho arrives on Okinawa to provide strategic support for the 32nd Army
7 July 1944	Emergency War Cabinet ratifies mass evacuation of elderly women, young girls, and students from the Ryukyu Islands
	Japanese forces on Saipan wiped out

Timeline for the Battle of Okinawa

8 July 1944	Lt. Gen. Cho Isamu appointed as chief of staff of 32nd Army
11 July 1944	32nd Army incorporated into 10th Area Army
17 July 1944	24th Infantry Division joins 32nd Army
20 July 1944	64th Independent Mixed Brigade joins 32nd Army
24 July 1944	62nd Infantry Division, 59th Independent Mixed Brigade and 60th Independent Mixed Brigade ordered to join 32nd Army
4 August 1944	24th Infantry Division arrives on Okinawa
10 August 1944	Lt. Gen. Ushijima appointed as 32nd Army's commander in chief
19 August 1944	62nd Infantry Division arrives on Okinawa
22 August 1944	Student evacuation ship Tsushima Maru sunk by U.S. submarine with loss of 1,484 lives.
23 August 1944	Order of Female Labor and the Order of Student Labor promulgated
16 September 1944	32nd Army concentrates on airfield facilities for all-out ground war
10 October 1944	U.S. carrier-based planes carry out massive air raid on Okinawa
18 October 1944	All Okinawan males over the age of 17 drafted into military service
29 October 1944	All Okinawan males between the ages of 21 and 45 drafted into Home Guard
13 November 1944	Imperial GHQ informs 32nd Army of withdrawal of 9th Infantry Division
26 November 1944	9th Infantry Division leaves for Taiwan
1 December 1944	Special Emergency Volunteer units formed throughout Okinawa
3 January 1945	U.S. carrier-based aircraft bomb Taiwan, Yaeyama, Amami, Miyako, and the main island of Okinawa
10 January 1945	32nd Army HQ moves from Asato to Shuri
12 January 1945	Almost 700 U.S. carrier-based aircraft attack Amami, Miyako, the Yaeyamas, and Okinawa.Okinawa Governor Shuki Izumi transfers to Kagawa Prefecture
20 January 1945	Second Home Guard Draft conscripting most males aged 17 to 45
25 January 1945	Outline of decisive war emergency measures ratified by Supreme Council for War Guidance
26 January 1945	32nd Army announces changes in its deployment on the main island of Okinawa
31 January 1945	Akira Shimada arrives in Okinawa to take up post as governor. 32nd Army announces Okinawa's second Home Guard Draft for healthy Okinawan males aged 17 to 45
3 February 1945	Student mobilization throughout Okinawa Prefecture increases, with special training in signals, observation and nursing implemented.

TIMELINE FOR THE BATTLE OF OKINAWA

7 February 1945	32nd Army Chief of Staff Isamu Cho instructs Governor Shimada to secure six months' emergency food supplies for Okinawan civilians.
	Okinawa prefectural administration moves to war footing
10 February 1945	Governor Shimada orders 100,000 citizens from the central and southern parts of Okinawa to evacuate to northern regions
15 February 1945	32nd Army announces battle plan to troops and civilians throughout Okinawa under the slogan: "One Plane for One Warship, One Boat for One Ship, One Man for Ten of the Enemy or One Tank"
	Formation of national defense volunteer units throughout Okinawa begins
19 February 1945	American forces land on Iwo-jima
	Formation of volunteer unit organizations begins in boys' and girls' schools throughout Okinawa
1 March 1945	U.S. carrier-based planes attack Miyako-jima
	Students from 2nd Prefectural Middle School assigned to 2nd Infantry Regiment of 44th Independent Mixed Brigade (also known as the Kunigami Support Unit)
6 March 1945	Promulgation of National Labor Service Mobilization Law: all Okinawan men and women aged 15 to 45 conscripted
10 March 1945	32nd Army orders the destruction of Ie-jima Airfield
17 March 1945	IJA forces on Iwo-jima annihilated
23 March 1945	U.S. Navy Task Force commences air attacks on pre-invasion targets on the main island of Okinawa
	Girls from Second Prefectural Girls' School attached to 24th Infantry Division's 1st Field Hospital
24 March 1945	U.S. Navy commences bombardment of main island of Okinawa
25 March 1945	Girls from the First Prefectural Girls' School attached to the Haebaru Army Hospital
	Prefectural administration offices move from Naha to underground shelter at Shuri Castle
	Americans launch naval bombardment of Okinawa and the Kerama Islands
26 March 1945	U.S. 77th Infantry land on Aka, Geruma, and Zamami in the Kerama Islands. 234 civilians commit suicide on Zamami, 53 on Geruma
	British naval bombardment of Sakishima Islands region
	Students from Third Prefectural Middle School, Kainan Middle School, and the Prefectural Agricultural School form Blood and Iron Units and are attached to military units across Okinawa. Girls from Third Prefectural Girls' School attached as student nurses to all military units in the north

TIMELINE FOR THE BATTLE OF OKINAWA

27 March 1945	U.S. forces invade and take Tokashiki-jima and the islands of Kuba, Amuro, and Aharen
	Girls from Shuri Girls' School (*Zuisen* Corps) and from Showa Girls' School (*Deigo* Corps) allocated to the 62nd Infantry Division's field hospital as student nurses
	Students from First Prefectural Middle School attached to 32nd Army's Signals Corps
28 March 1945	Incident of compulsory mass suicide on Tokashiki-jima (329 people)
29 March 1945	U.S. Navy bombards Amami Oshima and Sakishima
	Students from First Prefectural Middle School and Prefectural Technical School form Blood and Iron Student Corps and are attached to the 32nd Army
31 March 1945	America announces control of Kerama Islands
	32nd Army Headquarters cancels evacuation of elderly and young girls to the northern areas
	Girls from Sekitoku Girls' School attached as nurse aides to the 24th Infantry Division
	Students from Naha Commercial School form Blood and Iron Student Corps and join the 22nd Independent Infantry Regiment.
	Boys from the Okinawa Normal School form Blood and Iron Student Corps under direct control of Command Headquarters
1 April 1945	American forces land on central west coast of Okinawa at Chatan and Yomitan. On the same day they capture the Northern and Central Airfields
	U.S. military proclaims the Establishment of United States Civil Administration of the Ryukyu Islands, establishes naval control in Yomitan and guarantees safety of civilians
	Students from Prefectural Fisheries School join the Intelligence Section of the 32nd Army Headquarters Signals Unit as messengers
2 April 1945	Mass suicide in Chibichiri-gama (83 people)
4 April 1945	US forces advance as far as Chatan, Shimabukuro, Oyama, and Ginowan
	Americans divide Okinawa into north and south across a line from Nakadomari to Ishikawa and begin their advance toward the Kunigami region
5 April 1945	Students from the Prefectural Fisheries School form Blood and Iron Corps
6 April 1945	Americans capture Katsuren Peninsula
7 April 1945	Americans attack Nago
	Japanese battleship *Yamato* sunk in Japan Sea
8 April 1945	U.S. forces advance to a line connecting Uchidomari and Makiminato on the west coast and Tsuha on the east coast.

TIMELINE FOR THE BATTLE OF OKINAWA

9 April 1945	Major offensive begins on the Kakazu Ridge and continues through to April 14
	32nd Army Headquarters issues order stating that anyone heard using the Okinawan dialect is to be executed as a spy
10 April 1945	Americans land on Tsuken-jima
11 April 1945	Americans attack toward Naha
15 April 1945	Japanese Naval Security Unit executes three American POWs on Ishigaki-jima
16 April 1945	Americans land on Ie-jima
18 April 1945	U.S. forces take control of Motobu Peninsula
	American war correspondent Ernie Pyle killed on Ie-jima
19 April 1945	U.S. forces launch first major offensive against 62nd Division's outer perimeter forces at Shuri
	U.S. forces use napalm to completely destroy Yonabaru
20 April 1945	IJA positions at Makiminato and Iso destroyed. Defending units outside Shuri begin to collapse.
21 April 1945	Japanese forces withdraw from the Kakazu area
	U.S. declares control of Ie Island
	U.S. ships bombard Minami and Kita Daito Islands
24 April 1945	32nd Army forced to pull back to line joining Nakama, Maeda, and Kochi
	Order given to noncombatants around Shuri to move south
25 April 1945	Okinawa Prefectural Administration moves from Sobe in Mawashi to the police shelter at Hantagawa
	Americans launch their second major offensive, concentrating on Nakanishi and Jitchaku in the west; Nakama, Maeda and Kochi in the central region; and Kohatsu and Gaja in the east.
27 April 1945	Emergency Meeting for all city, town, and village leaders in Okinawa's southern region held in police shelter at Hantagawa
3-4 May 1945	32nd Army launches general offensive
5 May 1945	32nd Army attacks routed and offensive canceled
6 May 1945	Okinawa Rear Echelon Advisory Volunteers set up under Governor Shimada to promote fighting spirit among the populace, increase night-time production and give advice on life in shelters
9 May 1945	32nd Army assumes a defensive stance around Shuri (until 23 May)
10 May 1945	U.S. forces establish forward attack base on Ie-jima
12 May 1945	Stragglers from the IJA Kunigami Detachment massacre 30 civilians at Tonokiya in Ogimi

Timeline for the Battle of Okinawa

14 May 1945	IJA withdraws to positions at Kyozuka and Takushi
	U.S. forces attack Asato in Naha
17 May 1945	IJA fiercely defends Ishimine (until 21 May)
	U.S. forces take Ahacha Highland
19 May 1945	U.S. forces take the Amekudai area in the west and Yonabaru in the east.
21 May 1945	American Marines take Hill 52 otherwise known as Sugar Loaf, (located in what is now Omoromachi)
22 May 1945	American troops enter Naha. 32nd Army decides that it will withdraw from the Shuri Line as far as Mabuni in the south
	Wartime Education Order issued by which all schools were required to organize their students into military units
	Heavy rain starts to fall
24 May 1945	Approximately 120 airborne commandoes of the *Giretsu* Special Forces Unit launch a surprise attack on airfields in northern and central Okinawa. The entire unit is wiped out except for one survivor who manages to join the 32nd Army Headquarters Unit in mid-June
	Publication of Okinawa's only newspaper *Okinawa Shimpo* canceled.
	Prefectural administration shifts from a shelter at Hantagawa to a field artillery shelter at Shitahaku in Kochinda
27 May 1945	32nd Army Headquarters Unit withdraws from Shuri and moves to Mabuni via Tsukazan
29 May 1945	U.S. forces take Naha
31 May 1945	Shuri comes under intense U.S. pressure
4 June 1945	32nd Army completes the withdrawal of its main force to the Kyan and Mabuni area
	U.S. forces move into Oroku
	Americans take Iheya-jima
9 June 1945	Americans take Aguni-jima
	Governor Shimada orders the dispersal of the Police Garrison
10 June 1945	Commander of U.S. 10th Army Lieutenant General Buckner sends Lieutenant General Ushijima a request for Japanese surrender
11 June 1945	Americans advance to a line connecting Itoman, Yoza, Yaezu-dake, and Gushikami
13 June 1945	Remaining personnel of the Japanese Imperial Japanese Naval Base Force on Oroku commit themselves to a suicidal attack
17 June 1945	32nd Army refuses to negotiate a surrender U.S. forces secure a line including Kuniyoshi, Yoza, Maehira and Nakaza

TIMELINE FOR THE BATTLE OF OKINAWA

18 June 1945	32nd Army Commander-in-Chief Ushijima sends farewell telegram to the deputy chief of the Imperial General Staff and the 10th Area Army
	Commander of U.S. 10th Army Lt. Gen. Buckner killed at Maezato
	Contact lost with Governor Shimada and Chief of Police Arai at Mabuni
	32nd Army orders dissolution of the Blood and Iron Student Corps and the student nurse units
19 June 1945	Himeyuri nurse aides attached to No. 3 Field Hospital take their own lives in a cave at Ihara
	Organized resistance by Japanese forces on Okinawa ceases
21 June 1945	American forces take Makabe and Mabuni
	U.S. forces declare Okinawa secured
22 June 1945	Promulgation of Wartime Emergency Measures Law (implemented 23 June)
	Commander-in-Chief Ushijima and Chief-of-Staff Cho commit ritual suicide at Mabuni
26 June 1945	U.S. forces land on Kume-jima and secure it by 30 June
29 June 1945	Civilians on Kume-jima murdered by Japanese soldiers
30 June 1945	U.S. forces complete mopping up operations in southern Okinawa
2 July 1945	American military announces that the Battle for Okinawa is over
3 July 1945	Two evacuee vessels attacked on route from Ishigaki-jima to Taiwan. Beginning of Senkaku Island Shipwreck Incident
15 August 1945	Unconditional surrender of Japan
7 September 1945	Ryukyu Islands garrison formally surrenders to U.S. 10th Army HQ at Kadena (Battle for Okinawa officially ends)
	Japanese forces on Okinawa sign surrender documents
29 January 1946	Japan loses governance of Okinawa, Miyako, Yaeyama, and Amami
17 August 1946	First repatriation ship from Japanese main islands arrives in Okinawa
28 April 1952	Under terms of San Francisco Peace Treaty, Okinawa officially placed under American governance
15 May 1972	Okinawa returned to Japanese sovereignty

References

Aniya, Masaaki. Okinawasen no shudan-jiketsu (Kyosei shudan-shi) (Mass suicide in the Battle of Okinawa (Compulsory group suicides) Tokyo: Gunshuku mondai shiryo (Disarmament Review), December 2007.

Appleman, Roy E., et al. *Okinawa: The Last Battle*. Washington, DC: OCMH, Department of the Army, 1948.

Arasaki, Moriteru, et al. *Kanko Kosu de wa nai Okinawa* (The Okinawa that is not in the Sightseeing Map). Tokyo: Kobunken, 2002.

Arizuka, Ryouji. *Okinawa-sen to seishin-hoken, Dai Ippo* (The Battle of Okinawa and Mental Health) (*Nihon Seishin Hoken Yobo Gakkai Shouroku)*, 2011.

Cook, H,T., and T.F. Cook. *Japan at War: An Oral History*. London: Phoenix Press. 1992.

Dower, John. *War without Mercy: Race and Power in the Pacific*. New York: Pantheon, 1986.

—. *Embracing Defeat*. London: Penguin Press, 1999.

Feifer, George. *Tennozan*. New York: Ticknor & Fields, 1992.

Foster, Simon. *Okinawa 1945*. London: Cassell, 1994.

Gama—Okinawa no senseki Bukku (Caves—Okinawa battle sites guidebook), Naha: Okinawa Jiji Shuppan, 2009.

Hallas, James H. *Killing Ground on Okinawa: The Battle for Sugar Loaf Hill*. Annapolis, MD: Naval Institute Press. 2007.

Hanson, Victor Davis. *Ripples of Battle: How Wars Fought Long Ago Still Determine How We Fight, How We Live, and How We Think*. New York: Anchor Books, 2003.

Hastings, Max. *Nemesis*. London: Harper Perennial, 2008.

Hayashi, Hirofumi. *Okinawasen to Minshu* (The Battle of Okinawa and Okinawans). Tokyo: Otsuki shoten, 2001.

—. *Okinawasen ga tou mono*. (What the Battle of Okinawa tells us). Tokyo: Otsuki shoten, 2010.

Himeyuri Peace Museum, *Peace*. Naha, Okinawa: Himeyuri Peace Museum, 2002. (1st published 1990).

—. *Himeyuri Heiwa Kinen: Shiryokan Gaido Bukku*. Naha, Okinawa: Himeyuri Peace Museum, 2004.

Huber, Thomas M. *Japan's Battle of Okinawa* (Leavenworth Papers series No.18). U.S. Army Combat Studies Institute, 1990.

Ienaga, Saburo. The Pacific War, 1931-1945. Trans. Frank Baldwin. New York: Pantheon Books, 1978.

Inagaki, T. *Okinawa: Higu no sakusen*. Tokyo: Shinchosha, 1984.

Kunimori, Yasuhiro. *Okinawasen no Nihonhei* (The Japanese Soldiers in the Battle of Okinawa). Tokyo: Iwanami Shoten, 2010.

Lacey, Laura. *Stay Off the Skyline, the Sixth Marine Division in Okinawa*. Washington, DC: Potomac Books, 2007.

McCormack, Gavan, and Norimatsu Satoko. *Resistant Islands—Okinawa Confronts Japan and the United States*. Plymouth, MA: Rowman & Littlefield, 2012.

Martin, Jo Nobuko. *A Princess Lily of the Ryukyus*. Tokyo: Shin Nippon Kyoiku Tosho 1984.

Miyara, Saku. *Nihongun to Senso Mararia* (The Japanese Army and Malaria during the Pacific War). Tokyo: Shin-Nippon Shuppansha, 2004.

Nakagawa, Shiro. *Okinawa-ken Seishin-eisei chousa* (Mental health survey of Okinawa). 1966.

Okinawa Heiwa Network. *Aruku, Miru, Kangaeru Okinawa* (Walk, See, Think Okinawa). Naha, Okinawa: Okinawa Jiji Shuppan, 2008.

Okinawa no senso iseki (Battle sites in Okinawa), Naha, Okinawa: Okinawa Jiji Shuppan, 2008.

Okinawasen Shimbun (*Ryukyu Shimpo Battle of Okinawa Newspaper*), 2005.

Oshiro, Masayasu. *Okinawasen no shinjitsu to waikyoku* (The Battle of Okinawa—Truth and Distortion). Tokyo: Kobunken, 2007.

—. *Okinawasen—Minshu no me de toraeru senso* (The Battle of Okinawa as seen by the people) Tokyo: Kobunken, 2008.

Ota, Masahide. *Chi de aganatta mono* (Those who paid the price in blood). Haebaru: Naha Shuppansha, 2000.

Ota, Masahide. *The Battle of Okinawa*. Kume Publishing, 1988.

Ota Peace Research Institute, *Okinawa kanren shiryo—Okinawa sen oyobi kichi mondai* (Naha, Okinawa: Ota Peace Research Institute, 2010).

Rubringer, R. "Education in Wartime Japan, 1937–1947." In Lowe, R. (ed) *Education and the Second World War: Studies and Schooling in Social Change.* London: The Falmer Press, 1992. 59-72.

Saki, Ryuzo. *Okinawa Jumin Gyakusatsu* (Excesses Committed Against the People of Okinawa). Tokyo: Tokuma Shoten, 1982.

Senkaku-shoto senji-sonan-shibotsusha Irei-no-hi Kensetsu-jigyo Kiseikai. *Chinmoku no Sakebi*, (Scream into Silence) Ishigaki, Okinawa: Nanzansha, 2006.

Sloan, Bill. *The Ultimate Battle*. New York: Simon & Schuster, 2007.

Tobe, Ryoichi, Teramoto Yoshiya, Kamata Shin'ichi, Suginoo Yoshio, Murai Tomohide, Nonaka Ikujiro. *Shippai no Honshitsu* (The Essence of Failure) Tokyo: Chuko Bunko, 1984.

Tsushima-maru Memorial Museum Official Guidebook, 2010.

Urasaki, Jun. *Kieta Okinawa-ken*, (The Okinawa that Disappeared) Naha: Okinawa Jiji Shuppan, 1965.

Weber, M. (2000). A Dark Secret of World War II Comes to Light. *Institute for Historical Review* 19:50.

Yahara, Hiromichi. *The Battle for Okinawa*, New York: John Wiley and Sons, 1995.

Yomiuri Shimbun War Responsibility Reexamination Committee. *Carnage in Okinawa. Japan Echo*, Volume 36, Number 5, 2009.

Yoshihama, Shinobu, Oshiro Kazuki, Ikeda Yoshifumi, Uechi Katsuya, Koga Noriko. *Okinawa Rikugun Byoin Haebaru-Go* (Okinawa Haebaru Army Hospital Shelter) Tokyo: Kobunken, 2010.

About the Translators

Mark Ealey is a freelance translator who specializes in modern Japanese history and has focused on Okinawan issues in recent years. Previous translations of non-fiction are *Phoney Alliance—Anglo-Soviet Diplomacy in 1941* by Akino Yutaka, *Japan of the East, Japan of the West* by Ogura Kazuo, *The Kurillian Knot—A History of Russo-Japanese Border Negotiations*, by Kimura Hiroshi and of historical fiction are *Shipwrecks*, *One Man's Justice* and *Typhoon of Steel*, all by Yoshimura Akira.

Alastair McLauchlan was a French/Japanese translator and has published over twenty peer-reviewed academic papers in a wide range of international journals. He published two major English translations, namely *Where Are the Sunflowers* by Kurihara Miwako and *The Buraku Issue: Questions and Answers* by Kitaguchi Suehiro. He also published two original books based on his own research, *The Negative L2 Climate: Understanding Attrition among Second Language Students* and *Prejudice and Discrimination in Japan: The Buraku Issue*.